Instructional Leadership

A Research-Based Guide to Learning in Schools

FOURTH EDITION

Instructional Leadership

A Research-Based Guide to Learning in Schools

Anita Woolfolk Hoy
The Ohio State University

Wayne Kolter Hoy
The Ohio State University

PEARSON

Boston   Columbus   Indianapolis   New York   San Francisco   Upper Saddle River
Amsterdam   Cape Town   Dubai   London   Madrid   Milan   Munich   Paris   Montréal   Toronto
Delhi   Mexico City   São Paulo   Sydney   Hong Kong   Seoul   Singapore   Taipei   Tokyo

Vice President and Editorial Director: *Jeffery W. Johnston*
Senior Acquisitions Editor: *Meredith D. Fossel*
Editorial Assistant: *Krista Slavicek*
Vice President, Director of Marketing: *Margaret Waples*
Senior Marketing Manager: *Chris Barry*
Senior Managing Editor: *Pamela D. Bennett*
Senior Project Manager: *Mary Irvin*
Senior Operations Supervisor: *Matt Ottenweller*
Senior Art Director: *Diane Lorenzo*
Cover Designer: *Karen Salzbach*
Cover Art: *Fotolia*
Project Coordination and Composition: *Element LLC*
Printer/Binder: *Courier Westford*
Cover Printer: *Courier Westford*
Text Font: *Janson Text*

Credits and acknowledgments for materials borrowed from other sources and reproduced, with permission, in this textbook appear on the appropriate page within the text.

Every effort has been made to provide accurate and current Internet information in this book. However, the Internet and information posted on it are constantly changing, so it is inevitable that some of the Internet addresses listed in this textbook will change.

Library of Congress Cataloging-in-Publication Data

Hoy, Anita Woolfolk
  Instructional leadership : a research-based guide to learning in schools / Anita Woolfolk
Hoy, Wayne Kolter Hoy. — 4th ed.
     p. cm.
  Includes bibliographical references and index.
  ISBN 978-0-13-267807-0
 1. Educational leadership—Handbooks, manuals, etc. 2. Teaching—Handbooks, manuals,
etc. 3. Learning—Handbooks, manuals, etc. I. Hoy, Wayne K. II. Title.
  LB2805.H713 2013
  371.2—dc23
                              2012023120

10 9 8 7 6 5 4 3 2 1

ISBN 10:   0-13-267807-1
ISBN 13: 978-0-13-267807-0

Dedicated to Our Students

ABOUT THE AUTHORS

So you will know your authors a bit better, here is some information.

Anita Woolfolk Hoy was born in Fort Worth, Texas. She is a Texas Longhorn—all of her degrees are from the University of Texas, Austin, the last one a Ph.D. in Educational Psychology. After graduating, she worked as a school psychologist with students and teachers in elementary and secondary schools in fifteen counties of central Texas. She began her career in higher education as a professor of educational psychology at Rutgers University, and then moved to The Ohio State University in 1994.

Wayne Kolter Hoy was born in Lock Haven, Pennsylvania. He is a Nittany Lion—his Master's and Doctorate in educational administration were earned at The Pennsylvania State University. He has served on the faculties of Oklahoma State University and Rutgers University, where he was a Distinguished Professor and Associate Dean for Academic Affairs. In 1994, Wayne was appointed the Novice Fawcett Chair of Educational Administration, an endowed professorship at The Ohio State University. Anita joined the faculty as well. Their three children, now grown and living in San Francisco and Columbus, continue to keep them informed about technology and the modern world.

As to their professional lives, Anita's research focuses on teachers' thinking and beliefs, particularly teachers' sense of efficacy, and the role of educational psychology in the preparation of teachers. For many years she was the editor of the journal *Theory Into Practice*, which brings the best ideas from research to practicing educators. With students and colleagues, she has published over 80 book chapters and research articles in journals such as *Teaching and Teacher Education, Contemporary Educational Psychology, The Journal of Educational Psychology, Educational Psychologist, American Educational Research Journal, Review of Educational Research, Educational Researcher, Journal of Consulting and Clinical Psychology, The Journal of Experimental Education, The Journal of School Psychology,* and *The Elementary School Journal,* among others. She received the Alumni Award for Professional Research from the Rutgers University Graduate School of Education. Anita has served as Vice-President for Division K (Teaching & Teacher Education) of the American Educational Research Association and President of Division 15 (Educational Psychology) of the American Psychological Association. Her textbook, *Educational Psychology* (Allyn & Bacon), is in its 12th edition and has been translated into over a dozen different languages.

Wayne's primary professional interests are theory and research in administration and leadership, the sociology of organizations, and the social psychology of administration. He is the author or co-author of twelve books in the areas of educational administration, supervision of instruction, instructional leadership, organizational climate, school trust, and quantitative analysis. With students and colleagues, he has published over 140 book chapters and research articles in journals such as *Educational Administration Quarterly*, *The Journal of Educational Administration*, *Journal of School Leadership*, *Sociology of Education*, *Journal of Educational Psychology*, *American Educational Research Journal*, *Review of Educational Research*, *Teaching and Teacher Education*, *Educational Researcher*, *The Journal of Experimental Education*, and *The Elementary School Journal*, among others. He also has served as President of the University Council for Educational Administration (UCEA) and Secretary-Treasurer of the National Conference for Educational Administration. He has received the Lindback Foundation Award for Distinguished Teaching from Rutgers University; the Alumni Award for Professional Research from the Rutgers University Graduate School of Education; the Excellence in Education Award from The Pennsylvania State University; and in 1996, he became an Alumni Fellow of The Pennsylvania State University. In 2003, he was awarded the Roald Campbell Lifetime Achievement Award in Educational Administration. His textbook with Cecil Miskel, *Educational Administration: Theory, Research, and Practice*, is in its 9th edition.

PREFACE

Instructional Leadership is predicated on the assumption that teachers and principals need to work together as colleagues to improve teaching and learning in schools. Traditional supervision in which the principal rates the effectiveness of teachers is an outmoded concept, one that was always more ritual than reality. We believe that this is the first text of its kind, one written for principals to help them understand current theories of teaching and learning as well as the practical applications of these perspectives. The text uses a learning-centered approach that emphasizes making decisions based on what supports student learning.

We don't believe that instructional supervision can be effective unless the parties involved have a good understanding of how students learn. Although principals may take the lead in cooperative and professional endeavors, in the end it is the teachers who determine their success. Perhaps just as important as taking the lead in instructional matters is developing a school climate where instructional leadership flourishes and emerges spontaneously from teachers themselves.

The text addresses the critical aspects of the teaching–learning process: student differences, learning, motivation, teaching, classroom management, assessing student learning, and assessing and changing school climate and culture. Each chapter is grounded in the latest research and theory in that area and provides specific suggestions for applying that knowledge to practice. After the Introduction, each chapter begins with a **Preview of Key Points** and a **Leadership Challenge**, an actual teaching problem, and ends with suggestions for projects to relate theory to practice in the form of professional **Portfolio** exercises. Moreover, throughout the chapters, **Theory into Action Guidelines** and **A Principal's Perspective** provide concrete suggestions. We are again grateful to Thomas Reed, a successful former principal, superintendent, and Fawcett Scholar at The Ohio State University, for sharing his knowledge for the **Principal's Perspectives**. Also, each chapter includes an **Instructional Leader's Toolbox**, a collection of contemporary readings, useful websites, and helpful organizations. Finally, the text concludes with **Appendices**, which include instruments for assessing your school learning environment.

New to This Edition

New to this edition is a section on *Technology Leadership*, written by Dr. Anika Ball Anthony of The Ohio State University. In addition, *over 300* new studies and analyses enriched our examination of the crucial topics in this text. Following are specific changes to this edition:

CHAPTER 1: Introduction to Teaching and Learning
- Expanded coverage of the future of the No Child Left Behind Act
- New discussion of recent research on teaching

- New section on instructional leadership in the 21st century
- New section on technology leadership

CHAPTER 2: Student Diversity
- New section on today's diverse classroom
- New material on constructing a resilient classroom
- New material on the effects of poverty on learning
- Revised discussion on dialects
- Revised discussion of second language learning and bilingual education
- New *Theory into Action Guidelines* on Promoting Language Learning
- New section on immigrant students and Generation 1.5
- New material on gender differences in the classroom
- New and revised suggested readings

CHAPTER 3: Student Abilities and Challenges
- Revised discussion of intelligence including multiple intelligences
- Revised discussion of Sternberg's concept of "wisdom"
- New material on tracking and flexible grouping
- New material on teaching gifted students and students with ADHD
- Updated section on students with learning disabilities
- Updated section on individual education programs
- New and revised suggested readings

CHAPTER 4: Learning
- New material on functional behavioral analysis
- Revised discussion of working memory and flashbulb memories
- New *Point/Counterpoint* on the value of homework
- Updated discussion of cognitive views of learning and cognitive science
- New section on metacognition and learning strategies
- Expanded discussion of constructivism, scaffolding, and problem-based learning
- Expanded discussion of cooperative learning including new *Theory into Action Guidelines*
- New and revised suggested readings

CHAPTER 5: Motivation
- New description of classroom goal structures
- New discussion of catching and holding student interests
- New section on *How Can Teachers Avoid Boring Their Students?*
- New and revised suggested readings

CHAPTER 6: Teaching
- New section on the importance of teacher-student relationships
- New description of expertise in teaching

- New section on enthusiasm in teaching and the dimension of classroom climate
- New section on recent research on teaching
- Revised section on standards and objectives, including examples of technology standards for teachers
- New sections on *Differentiated Instruction* and *Adaptive Teaching*
- New and revised suggested readings

CHAPTER 7: Classroom Management
- Revised section on student self-regulation
- Updated material on class routines and rules
- New section on *Caring Relationships: Connections with School*
- New section on *Bullying and Cyber-Bullying*
- New *Theory into Action Guidelines* on *Handling Potentially Explosive Situations*
- New and revised suggested readings

CHAPTER 8: Assessing Student Learning
- New discussion of formative and summative assessment
- Revised section on interpreting information from achievement tests
- Updated discussion on using high-stakes tests to hold teachers accountable
- New *Point/Counterpoint* on retaining students in their grade and "academic red-shirting"
- Updated information about performance assessment
- New and revised suggested readings

CHAPTER 9: Assessing and Changing School Culture and Climate
- Revised and expanded section on academic optimism
- New section on *A Culture of Control*
- New section on organizational citizenship
- New and revised suggested readings

Acknowledgments

Our colleagues and students are important sources of ideas and criticism. We would like to thank and acknowledge them for their suggestions and encouragement in this project:

Jana Alig-Mielcarek, The Ohio State University
Anika Ball Anthony, The Ohio State University
Lauren Bailes, The Ohio State University
Michael DiPaola, College of William & Mary
Harry Galinsky, Superintendent, Paramus, NJ
Pamela J. Gaskill, The Ohio State University
Roger D. Goddard, University of Michigan
Eileen McMahon, The Ohio State University

Thomas Reed, The Ohio State University
Amy Schrepfer-Tarter, The Ohio State University
Page A. Smith, The University of Texas, San Antonio
Scott R. Sweetland, The Ohio State University
C. John Tarter, University of Alabama
Megan Tschannen-Moran, College of William & Mary

In addition, we thank the following reviewers for their helpful suggestions: Floyd D. Beachum, Lehigh University; Mindy Kay Salmans, Fort Hays State University; and George W. Semich, Robert Morris University.

CONTENTS

Introduction to Teaching and Learning

Schools are about teaching and learning; all other activities are secondary to these basic goals. Teaching and learning are elaborate and complex processes; this book is about understanding those processes. It is not a book about administration, but it is a book for administrators because the fundamental purpose of schooling is student learning. School leaders are responsible for creating learning organizations. Even though we focus on principals, this text is for all school leaders who are interested in improving teaching and learning, whether they are teachers, curriculum and instructional specialists, or administrators; in the end, instructional leadership is a shared responsibility.

The centrality of student learning in the school is irrefutable; in fact, preparation standards for school leaders embrace this fundamental truth in their second standard (Council of Chief State School Officers, 2008). This standard describes an effective school administrator as a leader in the field of education who supports and encourages the success of every student. Such a leader advocates for a program of instruction that advances student learning and also develops and sustains a school culture that fosters the growth and development of everyone involved, students and staff.

We argue that school leaders cannot achieve this purpose without a clear and deep understanding of students, teaching, learning, motivation, assessment, and technology, along with a nurturing school culture. Our book deals with issues pertaining to all six Interstate School Leaders Licensure Consortium (ISLLC) Standards.

The Role of the Instructional Leader

A critical role for all principals is that of instructional leader. We are not suggesting that principals alone are responsible for leadership in instruction. Clearly that is not the case. Leadership in instructional matters should emerge freely from both principals and teachers. After all, teachers deliver the instruction in the classroom; they have expertise in curriculum and teaching, and they have mastered a substantive body of knowledge. Principals, however, are responsible for developing school climates and cultures that support the very best instructional practices. Thus, it is principals who should forge a partnership with teachers, with the primary goal of improving teaching and learning.

There is no one way to engage in such cooperation, but instructional leaders need to spend time in classrooms as colleagues and engage teachers in conversations about learning and teaching. Improvement is a continuous process, and is not fostered by a ritual observation that principals make once or twice a year. Professional conversations and professional development should revolve around improving instruction, increasing teachers' understanding of how students learn, and applying appropriate teaching strategies for different situations. Cooperation, colleagueship, expertise, and teamwork are hallmarks of successful improvement and are substitutes for traditional supervision (DiPaola & Hoy, 2008).

Although principals may take the lead in cooperative and professional endeavors, in the end teachers are the ones who determine their success. Perhaps just as important as taking the lead in instructional matters is developing school climates and school cultures where instructional leadership flourishes and emerges spontaneously from teachers. Above all, principals must communicate clear visions of instructional excellence and continuous professional development consistent with the goal of improving teaching and learning. What does this mean? How does it get translated into action?

1. Academic excellence should be a strong motivating force in the school. Increasingly, the research is affirming that a school's academic emphasis is critical to student achievement (Goddard, Sweetland, & Hoy, 2000; Hoy & Sabo, 1998;

Hoy, Tarter, & Woolfolk Hoy, 2006a). The instructional leader should ensure a learning environment that is orderly, serious, and focused on high but achievable academic goals. The principal must demonstrate in both words and actions an optimistic belief that all students can achieve, while developing a school culture in which teachers and students alike respect hard work and academic success.

2. The pursuit of instructional excellence and continuous improvement are ongoing and cooperative activities by instructional leaders and teachers. Areas such as student growth and achievement, school climate, teacher and student motivation, and faculty morale should be monitored and assessed regularly with the aim of improvement.

3. Teachers are at the center of instructional improvement; in the end, only the teachers can change and improve their instructional practice in the classroom; hence, teacher motivation and self-regulation are critical to improvement. Teachers must decide that they want to progress.

4. Principals must provide constructive support and obtain the resources and materials necessary for teachers to be successful in the classroom; indeed, resource support is a basic principal role.

5. Principals should be intellectual leaders who keep abreast of the latest developments in teaching, learning, motivation, classroom management, and assessment, as well as share best practices in each area with teachers.

6. Principals should take the lead in recognizing and celebrating educational achievement among students and teachers because such activities reinforce a vision and culture of academic excellence.

7. Finally, principals are pivotal in developing a culture of optimism. Such a culture is one in which the faculty has a collective sense of efficacy (a belief that the faculty can do the job), trusts parents and students to work cooperatively, and focuses on academic emphasis and high performance. Optimism about the successful accomplishment of student learning in spite of obstacles is an important key to effective student performance (Hoy & Smith, 2007; Hoy, Tarter, & Woolfolk Hoy, 2006; McGuigan & Hoy, 2006).

Wang, Haertal, and Walberg (1993, 1997) did a meta-analysis of more than 10,000 statistical findings on the most significant influences on learning and found a reasonable consensus; in general, direct influences have a greater impact on student learning than indirect ones. Fifty years of research contradicts the current reliance on school restructuring as the key to school reform. Classroom management, student metacognitive and cognitive processes (e.g., study skills, background knowledge, work habits), instruction, motivation, and assessment have a greater impact on learning than indirect influences such as restructuring, district policy, and school policy. One exception to the general finding was school culture. School culture does seem to make an important difference by providing a school context that reinforces important teaching and learning practices. Increasingly, the research suggests that the *key to improving student learning lies in what happens in the classroom:* The teacher is critical. Instructional leadership calls for principals to work with teacher colleagues to improve instruction by providing a school culture and climate where change is linked to the best available knowledge about student learning.

A Principal's Perspective

C. R. prided himself on being a visionary leader. An optimist who saw the good in every person in every situation, he was an inspiring, energetic, and creative principal who thrived on facing the seemingly impossible. Late in his career he was recruited by a failing school district to deliver its once proud high school from a malaise of underachievement and apathy by students and faculty alike. Driven by the personal improvement writing of Steven Covey (2004)*, C. R. set out to change the climate of the school one teacher at a time. He invigorated professional growth of the staff by focusing on their personal goals, ambitions, and needs. Personal mission statements and action plans dominated faculty meetings in the first semester. Predictably confronted with skepticism early on, C. R. persisted, modeling his trust of his teachers by frequently seeking authentic feedback from them through nonthreatening methods. He openly shared his personal goals and demonstrated self-regulation as he genuinely assessed his own progress. To foster cooperation and instill ownership of the school's achievement record, he enlisted committees of teachers to review all facets of the educational program, from budget allocations to curricular programming. Open to all suggestions, he harbored no sacred cows and honored the committees' work by adopting their recommendations as his own. In a short time, a talented but once divisive and uncommitted collection of teachers transformed into a trusting, efficacious faculty that systematically propelled the school toward excellence. Reflecting the newly enhanced culture and climate of the school, student achievement rose steadily while community perception and confidence in the district returned to its previously high levels.

*Covey, S. R. (2004). *The 7 habits of highly effective people: Powerful lessons in personal change.* New York: Free Press. Based on a true story.

Instructional Leadership After No Child Left Behind

On January 8, 2002, President George W. Bush signed into law the No Child Left Behind (NCLB) Act. Actually, NCLB was the most recent authorization of the Elementary and Secondary Education Act (ESEA), which was first passed in 1965. The 2002 reauthorization had a new name to reflect the sweeping changes that came with it. In a nutshell, NCLB requires that all students in grades 3 through 8 and once more in high school must take standardized achievement tests in reading and mathematics every year. In addition, they must be tested in science—one test a year in each of three grade spans (3–5, 6–9, 10–12). Based on these test scores, schools are judged to determine if their students are making adequate yearly progress (AYP) toward becoming proficient in the subjects tested. States have some say in defining proficiency and in setting AYP standards. But no matter how states define these standards, NCLB requires that all students in the schools must reach proficiency by the end of the 2013–2014 school year. In addition, schools must develop AYP goals and report scores separately for several groups, including racial and ethnic minority students, students with disabilities, students whose first language is not English, and students from low-income homes. See Figure 1.1 for the NCLB timeline from 1965 to 2014.

FIGURE 1.1   NCLB Timeline

April 11, 1965:	President Lyndon B. Johnson signed into law the *Elementary and Secondary Education Act (ESEA)* as part of his War on Poverty. This was the United States's first general aid program for education. One part of the law, the Title I section, was targeted to improve the education of the nation's poorest students.
October 20, 1994:	ESEA was reauthorized in the *Improving American Schools Act*, signed by President Bill Clinton. This law required states to identify schools not making adequate yearly progress based on assessments of at least mathematics and language arts.
	"Each State plan shall demonstrate that the State has developed or adopted a set of high-quality, yearly student assessments, including assessments in at least mathematics and reading or language arts . . . ." (*Improving American Schools Act*, H.R. 6, pp. 7-8).
January 8, 2002:	President George W. Bush signed the *No Child Left Behind Act* (NCLB; P.L 107-110; 115 Stat. 1425).
	"The purpose of this title is to ensure that all children have a fair, equal, and significant opportunity to obtain a high-quality education and reach, at a minimum, proficiency on challenging State academic achievement standards and state academic assessments" (SEC. 1001).
2005–2006:	Reading and mathematics tests must be administered every year in 3rd–8th grade, once in 10th–12th grade.
June 30, 2006:	All teachers must be highly qualified. A state plan:
	. . . shall include an annual increase in the percentage of highly qualified teachers at each local educational agency, and school, to ensure that all teachers teaching in core academic subjects in each public elementary school and secondary school are highly qualified not later than the end of the 2005–2006 school year (Public Law 107–110. p. 80–81).
2007:	Science test added, one a year in each of these grade spans, 3–5, 6–9, 10–12.
2007:	ESEA was supposed to be reauthorized.
2010:	The Obama Administration releases *A Blueprint for Reform: The Reauthorization of the Elementary and Secondary Education Act.*
2011:	The Department of Education waived the requirement to reach 100% proficiency for states that could demonstrate they had adopted their own testing and accountability programs and were making progress toward the goal of college or career readiness for all their high school graduates.
2013–2014:	The original NCLB Act requires all students must be proficient by the end of this school year.

Sources: Adapted from: http://www.isbe.net/nclb/htmls/timeline.htm http://federaleducationpolicy.wordpress.com/2011/02/20/the-improving-americas-schools-act-of-1994/ http://federaleducationpolicy.wordpress.com/2011/02/19/2002-no-child-left-behind-act-of-2001/

The effects of NCLB on you as a principal, teacher, or parent have been profound. James Popham (2005), an assessment expert, puts it this way: "Today's public school teachers are now obligated to take part in an educational game whose rules have been dramatically altered because of a significant federal law. The NCLB Act, almost literally, seems likely to trump almost everything it touches" (p. 4).*

We start the first chapter of this text describing NCLB because, as Popham notes, it will affect teaching life every day. What does NCLB mean for schools? Words that come to mind are *accountability*, *student achievement*, *closing achievement gaps*, *raising expectations*—but the first word that comes to mind for most principals and teachers is *testing*. To fully comply with NCLB in the 2007–2008 academic year, states gave about 68 million tests (Guilfoyle, 2006). Has NCLB helped schools, teachers, and students succeed? You can see in the *Point/Counterpoint* that this is a hotly debated question.

*Source: Classroom assessment: What teachers need to know by W. James Popham. Allyn & Bacon, 2005.

POINT/COUNTERPOINT

Has NCLB Been a Positive Force in Schools?

POINT

Yes, scores are up; students are learning.
In many ways, No Child Left Behind was the product of frustration with administrators and teachers. Educators have known for years about achievement gaps and the poor test performance of students in poverty, yet, according to policymakers in Washington, no one was taking responsibility to make things better—government officials seemed to believe that educators made excuses rather than taking actions. "In a real sense, NCLB was a mighty yawp of frustration uttered by Washington policy makers tired of nicely asking educators to cooperate— and ready to ruffle some feathers" (Hess & Petrilli, 2004, p. 14).

Margaret Spellings, U.S. Secretary of Education under President George Bush, often noted, "what gets measured gets done." Even educators who criticized NCLB conceded that the law made it more difficult to ignore the learning needs of students who all too often were overlooked—racial minorities, students in poverty, students with special needs, and English language learners. So the successes and failures of schools, especially the failures with particular groups of students, had become much more transparent. Concern with achievement gaps grew. Low-achieving schools received greater attention, and there was more accountability in every school. And schools worked harder to align state and national content standards with their curricula. The idea of getting better qualified teachers into all classrooms, especially classrooms for the poorest students, was important, too. More schools started creating data systems to follow students over several years (Jennings & Rentner, 2006; Lewis, 2007).

Did students learn more? The answer seems to be yes; at least some students learned more of the basics that are tested. The scores of the lowest-achieving students were improving (Lewis, 2007). Scores are up in reading and math for about 75% of states and districts—achievement gaps were generally narrowing (Jennings & Rentner, 2006).

COUNTERPOINT

No, NCLB has hurt schools, teachers, and students.
Few educators question that what gets measured gets done. But that, say many, is the problem. More and more, the tests determine the curriculum—if it is not on the test, then there is no time or money for teaching it. That means social studies, art, music, physical education, languages, drama, and literature are not high priorities. As the educational sociologist David Labaree said more than fifteen years ago,

"Whatever is not on the test is not worth knowing, whatever is on the test need be learned only in the superficial manner that is required to achieve a passing grade" (1997, p. 46). Sarah Butzim, director of the Institute for Innovation, says, "NCLB has been stifling innovation, rather than encouraging it, as the law had intended. And it needs to be fixed" (Butzim, 2007, p. 768).

Another problem is that rather than getting better at helping students learn, some schools have gotten better at getting around the rules by lowering standards, excluding students who do not test well, teaching directly to the test, or encouraging low-scoring students to be absent on testing day. This temptation to "get around the rules" should not be surprising to anyone who knows the unintended consequences of systems that rely on punishment to control children or adults—humans are clever and often find ways to avoid the punishment, including cheating and manipulating the system. Any undergraduate psychology major knows that punishment is a bad way to change behaviors.

In some schools, administrators and teachers are targeting the "bubble kids," students who are almost at mastery level, and just ignoring the lower-achieving students who are far from mastery. This makes the school's numbers look better as more "bubble" students pass, but leaves the lowest-achieving students even further behind. In addition, there is evidence that the higher-achieving students of all income levels and racial groups are regressing back to the mean as attention and resources are directed to lower-performing students (Lewis, 2007).

Other critics of NCLB have complained that the required focus on basic skills for everyone has taken money and attention away from the advanced STEM subjects (Science, Technology, Engineering, Mathematics) that are the foundation for innovation. The ability of any country to compete in the global economy rests on knowledge and skills in these subjects (Hess & Rotherham, 2007).

Finally, there are critics who claim that students spend only part of their time in schools and much more time in homes, in neighborhoods, and in front of televisions. Schools cannot overcome all these other influences without massive changes in social policies such as health care and employment opportunities (Hess & Rotherham, 2007).

A press release from the Obama administration about their blueprint for the reauthorization of NCLB sums up the situation, "NCLB highlighted the achievement gap and created a national conversation about student achievement. But it also created incentives for states to lower their standards; emphasized punishing failure over rewarding success; focused on absolute scores, rather than recognizing growth and progress; and prescribed a pass-fail, one-size-fits-all series of interventions for schools that miss their goals" (Abrevaya, 2010).

NCLB was supposed to be reauthorized in 2007 or 2008. On March 13, 2010, The Obama Administration released *A Blueprint for Reform: The Reauthorization of the Elementary and Secondary Education Act* to describe a vision for the reauthorization of NCLB (see http://www2.ed.gov/policy/elsec/leg/blueprint/publicationtoc.html for a copy). One of the major changes suggested was to move from a punishment-based system to one that rewards excellent teaching and student growth. In a March 15 press release, Secretary of Education Arnie Duncan said:

> "A rigorous and fair accountability system measures student growth, rewards schools that accelerate student achievement, and identifies and rewards outstanding teachers and leaders. NCLB says that a fifth-grade teacher who helps a student reading at a second-grade level reach a fourth-grade level, within one year, has thus missed [his or her] goal. In fact, that teacher is an excellent teacher and should be applauded." (Abrevaya, 2010)

The Blueprint described five priorities (USDE, 2010):

1. **College- and Career-Ready Students:** Regardless of their income, race, ethnic or language background, or disability status, every student should graduate from high school ready for college and a career. To accomplish this goal, the blueprint recommends *improved assessments* and *turnaround grants* to transform schools. In 2011, the Secretary of Education waived the requirement to reach 100% proficiency for states that could demonstrate they had adopted their own testing and accountability programs and were making progress toward the goal of college or career readiness for all of their high school graduates (Dillion, 2011).

2. **Great Teachers and Leaders in Every School:** "A great teacher can make the difference between a student who achieves at high levels and a student who slips through the cracks, and a great principal can help teachers succeed as part of a strong, well-supported instructional team" (p. 13). To support this goal, the blueprint proposes a Teacher and Leader Improvement Fund of competitive grants and new pathways for preparing educators. The focus of this book is to create great leaders in every school.

3. **Equity and Opportunity for All Students:** All students will be included in an accountability system that builds on college- and career-ready standards, rewards progress and success, and requires rigorous interventions in the lowest-performing schools.

4. **Raise the Bar and Reward Excellence:** *Race to the Top*, a series of competitive grants for schools, has provided incentives for excellence by encouraging state and local leaders to work together on ambitious reforms, make tough choices, and develop comprehensive plans that change policies and practices to improve outcomes for students.

5. **Promote Innovation and Continuous Improvement:** In addition to the Race to the Top grants, an Investing in Innovation Fund will support local and non-profit leaders as they develop and scale up programs that have demonstrated success, and discover the next generation of innovative solutions.

Time will tell how these proposals unfold. Let's turn now to those people we are trying not to leave behind—the students.

Student Differences

We begin our analysis of teaching and learning with the students. Chapters 2 and 3 discuss the broad range of differences students bring to schools and classrooms. Students differ in culture, learning styles, gender, and intelligence. Each of these differences has implications for teaching and learning.

In Chapter 2, "Student Diversity," we note that in 2003, 12% of the people living in the United States were born in another country, and 18% spoke a language other than English at home—half of these families spoke Spanish. By 2050, Latinos will comprise about one quarter of the U.S. population (U.S. Census Bureau, 2010b). Teachers and administrators will have to work together to create classrooms that are good for all students. The challenge will be creating tolerance, respect, and understanding among a diverse student and teacher school community.

The number of children in poverty in the United States is almost 50% higher than in *any other developed Western nation* and five to eight times higher than in many prominent industrialized nations. Compared to children from affluent families, children growing up in poverty have lower average scores on achievement tests, are at least twice as likely to be kept back in school, and drop out more often. We examine some ways to foster resilience in students faced with these challenges.

Cultural differences often are associated with diversity in learning styles. Although students may have different learning styles or preferences, the consequences for teaching and learning are not clear; in fact, popular programs have far outrun what we know about how to deal with such differences. Indeed, the research gives one pause.

Gender differences and sex stereotyping are two other problems that face most teachers and administrators. Gender discrimination in the classroom, as well as students' concerns about sexual orientation, are just a few of the challenges facing school leaders. To act wisely is to first understand the facts and consequences; however, the issues are complex and often there are two sides. Consider the *Point/Counterpoint* on the differences in learning styles between boys and girls.

POINT/COUNTERPOINT

Do Boys and Girls Learn Differently?

According to the National Association for Single Sex Public Education, in 2007 nationwide, at least 253 public schools offered single-sex classes, and 51 schools were entirely single sex. In 1995, only 3 public schools offered single-sex classes (Bauer, 2007). Is this a good idea? There are a few documented sex differences in mental abilities. Do these translate into different ways of learning and, thus, different needs in the classroom?

POINT

Yes, boys and girls learn differently.
Since at least the 1960s, there have been questions about whether schools serve boys well. Accusations that schools were trying to destroy "boys' culture" and forcing "feminine, frilly content" on boys caused some public concern (Connell, 1996). More recently, according to Connell:

Discrimination against girls has ended, the argument runs. Indeed, thanks to feminism, girls have special treatment and special programs. Now, what about the boys? It is boys who are slower to learn to read, more likely to drop out of school, more likely to be disciplined, more likely to be in programs for children with special needs. In school it is girls who are doing better, boys who are in trouble—and special programs for boys that are needed. (p. 207)

In their book, *Boys and Girls Learn Differently*, Michael Gurian and Patricia Henley (2001) make a similar argument that boys and girls need different teaching approaches. Since publishing this book, Michael Gurian claims that research increasingly has supported the existence of differences in the brains of boys and girls. He suggests that these brain-based gender differences should serve as the basis for developing strategies to help boys and girls succeed in school. In addition he founded the

(Continued)

POINT/COUNTERPOINT   Continued

Gurian Institute to apply gender science on a large scale to education. This institute has trained more than 50,000 teachers (Gurian & Stevens, 2011).

Other books by Gurian that expand upon the initial theory of gender differences in learning are: *The minds of boys: Saving our sons from falling behind in school and life* (Gurian & Stevens, 2005), *The wonder of boys: What parents, mentors, and educators can do to shape boys into exceptional men* (Gurian, 2006) *Strategies for teaching boys and girls: Elementary and secondary level* (Gurian, Stevens, & King, 2008), and *Successful single-sex classrooms: A practical guide to teaching boys and girls separately* (Gurian, Stevens, & Daniels, 2009).

Gurian and Henley (2001) recommend developing girls' leadership abilities, encouraging them to enjoy healthy competition, providing them with extra access to technology, and helping them understand the impact of the media on their self-images.

COUNTERPOINT

No, differences are too small or inconsistent to have educational implications.

Many of Gurian and Henley's (2001) claims about sex differences in learning are based on sex differences in the brain. But John Bruer (1999) cautions that

> although males are superior to females at mentally rotating objects, this seems to be the only spatial task for which psychologists have found such a difference. Moreover, when they do find gender differences, these differences tend to be very small . . . . The scientific consensus among psychologists and neuroscientists who conduct these studies is that whatever gender differences exist may have interesting consequences for the scientific study of the brain, but they have no practical or instructional consequences. (p. 655)

In fact, there are boys who thrive in schools and boys who do not; girls who are strong in mathematics and girls who have difficulties; boys who excel in languages and those who do not. There is some evidence that the activities used to teach math may make a difference for girls. Elementary-age girls may do better in math if they learn in cooperative as opposed to competitive activities. Certainly it makes sense to balance both cooperative and competitive approaches so that students who learn better each way have equal opportunities (Fennema & Peterson, 1988).

Source: Connell excerpt from "Teaching the boys: New research on masculinity, and gender strategies for schools" by R. W. Connell, from *Teachers College Record*, Winter 1996, 98(2). Teachers College Record. Bruer excerpt from "In Search of . . . Brain-Based Education" by John Bruer, from *Phi Delta Kappan*, May 1999, Volume 80(9). Copyright © 1999 by John Bruer. Reprinted with permission of the author.

In Chapter 3, "Student Abilities and Challenges," we explore the meaning of intelligence, dealing with differences in student academic abilities and the learning challenges that many students face. Intelligence is one dimension of student difference that clearly has implications for schools. There are many different conceptions about intelligence, as well as some misconceptions. We examine both. We also look at how intelligence has been measured and the best ways of using the information from those assessments. Beliefs about intelligence influence the structure and design of the curriculum. Administrators invariably confront practical issues such as ability grouping and programs for the gifted when they try to organize their schools for effective learning.

There are continuing concerns about the requirements of legislation that mandate the inclusion of students with learning and behavior problems in the classroom. We discuss three of the most common challenges—students with attention deficit hyperactive disorder (ADHD), learning disabilities, and autism spectrum disorders—and then look at effective assessment and teaching for these students.

Learning

Because learning is a complex cognitive process, there is no single best explanation of learning. Different theories of learning offer more or less useful explanations depending on what is to be explained. We examine three general theories of learning—behavioral, cognitive, and constructivist—each with a different focus, as you will see in Chapter 4.

Behavioral theories of learning stress observable changes in behaviors, skills, and habits. Attention is clearly on behavior. Learning is viewed as a change in behavior brought about by experience, with virtually no concern for the mental or internal processes of thinking. Behavior is what people do. The intellectual underpinnings of behavioral theory rest with Skinner's (1950) work with operant conditioning; functional behavioral assessment and positive behavior supports are applications of this theory of learning. When specific skills and behaviors need to be learned, teaching approaches consistent with behavioral learning theory are quite effective.

Cognitive theories of learning deal with thinking, remembering, creating, and problem solving. The way information is remembered and processed as well as how individuals use their knowledge to regulate their thinking are critical in this perspective. New views of working memory and cognitive load play prominent roles in current cognitive theories. Some of the most important applications of cognitive theories are teaching students how to learn and remember by using learning tactics such as note taking, mnemonics, and visual organizers. Teaching strategies based on cognitive views of learning, particularly on information processing, highlight the importance of attention, organization, practice, and elaboration in learning. They also provide ways to give students more control over their own learning by developing and improving their self-regulated learning strategies. The emphasis of the cognitive approach is on what is happening "inside the head" of the learner.

Constructivist theories of learning are concerned with how individuals make meaning of events and activities; hence, learning is viewed as the construction of knowledge. In general, constructivism assumes that people create and construct knowledge rather than internalize it from the external environment, but there are different approaches to constructivism. Some constructivist views emphasize the shared and social construction of knowledge while others see social forces as less important. Constructivist perspectives on learning and teaching, which are increasingly influential today, are grounded in the research of Piaget, Bruner, Dewey, and Vygotsky. Inquiry and problem-based learning, cognitive apprenticeships, and cooperative learning are typical teaching strategies that are consistent with constructivist approaches. The essence of the constructivist approach is that it places the students' own efforts at the center of the educational process—thus the notion of student-centered teaching.

Each of these approaches to learning (Chapter 4) has much to offer; in fact, each brings with it advantages and disadvantages. We think of these main learning theories as three pillars for teaching. Students must first understand and make sense of the material (constructivist); then they must remember what they have understood (cognitive–information processing); and then they must practice and apply (behavioral) their new skills and understanding to make them more fluid and automatic, a permanent part of their repertoire. Failure to attend to any part of the process means lower-quality learning. It is not sufficient to know one perspective; indeed, knowledgeable teachers and administrators should understand, remember, and apply all of these perspectives appropriately.

Motivation

Effective teaching and learning depend on motivated students; hence, teachers must know how to stimulate, direct, and maintain high levels of interest among students, discussed in Chapter 5. Teachers can create intrinsic motivation by stimulating students' curiosity and making them feel more competent as they learn, but that is easier said than done because some tasks simply are not inherently interesting. Teachers cannot count on intrinsic motivation to energize all of their students all of the time. There are times when teachers must use extrinsic means to motivate students without undermining intrinsic aspects of learning. To do this, teachers need to know the factors that influence motivation. Five approaches to motivation are important in this regard.

Behaviorists explain motivation with concepts such as rewards (attractive consequences) and incentives (promise of a reward). Thus, according to the behavioral view, understanding student motivation begins with a careful analysis of the incentives and rewards present in the classroom. Providing grades, stars, and so on for learning—or demerits for misbehavior—are attempts to motivate students by extrinsic means of incentives, rewards, and punishments, but there is much more to motivating students than manipulating rewards and incentives.

In fact, proponents of humanistic psychology such as Carl Rogers argue that such behavioral explanations do not adequately explain why people act as they do. These humanistic explanations are based on the belief that people are continually motivated by the inborn need to fulfill their potential. Thus, from the humanistic perspective, to motivate means to encourage people's inner resources: their sense of competence, self-esteem, autonomy, and self-actualization. When we examine the role of needs in motivation, we will see two examples of the humanistic approach: Maslow's theory of the hierarchy of needs and Deci's self-determination theory.

Cognitive explanations of motivation also developed as a reaction to behavioral views. These perspectives argue that our behavior is determined by our thinking, not simply by whether we have been rewarded or punished for the behavior in the past. Behavior is initiated and regulated by an individual's plans, goals, schemas, expectations, and attributions. People are viewed as active and curious, searching for information to solve personally relevant problems; the focus of motivation is internal and personal.

Social cognitive theories of motivation are integrations of behavioral and cognitive approaches. They take into account both the behaviorists' concern with the effects or outcomes of behavior and the cognitivists' interest in the impact of individual beliefs and expectations. In other words, the important questions are, "If I try hard, can I succeed?" and "If I succeed, will the outcome be valuable or rewarding to me?"

Finally, sociocultural theories of motivation stress engaged participation in learning communities. Such theories focus on developing and maintaining group identities through authentic participation in the activities of the group.

Teachers and administrators must understand all these perspectives if they are to be effective in improving student learning. For example, goals that are specific, challenging, and realistic are effective in motivating students. Motivation is affected by such individual needs as self-esteem and achievement, but students have different needs at different times. Motivation is also affected by students' beliefs about the causes of successes and failures; for example, when students believe effort can improve their capabilities, they persist longer and reach higher levels of achievement. In fact, simply believing that they have the ability to be successful is a strong motivator.

In sum, student motivation to learn is enhanced when teachers use strategies that help students develop confidence in their ability to learn, see the value of the learning, and stay focused on learning without resorting to self-protective and self-defeating beliefs and actions. We will explore both the current explanations of motivation as well as the development of strategies to enhance motivation and performance, including strategies that capitalize on students' funds of cultural knowledge.

Teaching

Good teaching matters. It is the sine qua non of schooling. In fact, good teaching is what instructional leadership is about: finding ways to improve teaching and learning, so we have devoted Chapter 6 to teaching. There are no simple answers to what good teaching is, but we know it is anchored in expertise. Expert teachers work from integrated sets of principles instead of dealing with each new event as a discrete and novel problem. They have broad professional knowledge in academic subjects as well as that unique form of knowledge, pedagogical content knowledge, which combines mastery of *academic content* with knowing *how to teach* the content and how to match instruction to *student differences*. We will look at successful teachers from a variety of settings and examine their similarities and differences.

Effective teachers are also warm and enthusiastic in their teaching. Warmth, friendliness, and understanding seem to be the teacher traits most strongly related to student attitudes. In other words, teachers who are warm and friendly tend to have students who like them and the class in general; however, being warm, friendly, and enthusiastic is not enough to guarantee student achievement. Research has identified teacher clarity and organization as important characteristics of effective teachers. Recent large-scale longitudinal research has identified three aspects of class climate that are related to positive student outcomes in preschool and elementary school students: teacher *emotional support*, similar to teacher warmth and enthusiasm; a *cognitive* dimension, instructional support, which includes concept development (activities and discussions that promote student higher-order thinking) and quality feedback that is specific and focused on the learning process; and *behavioral* concerns such as classroom and lesson management, with clear activities and routines that make more time for student learning and are really engaging—similar to the teacher characteristics of clarity and organization (Jerome, Hamre, & Pianta, 2009; Luckner & Pianta, 2011). We will examine the practical implications of these findings for the classroom.

Effective teachers are creative and organized, and the basis for their organization is planning. Planning influences what students will learn because planning transforms the available time and curriculum materials into activities, assignments, and tasks for students. There is, however, no one model for effective planning. For experienced teachers, planning is a creative problem-solving process of determining how to accomplish many lessons and segments of lessons. Experienced teachers know what to expect and how to proceed, so they don't necessarily follow the detailed lesson-planning models that are so useful for beginning teachers. For all teachers, regardless of experience, clear objectives—both cognitive and affective—are a key to successful planning.

In the end, students have to do the learning, but teachers can create situations that guide, support, stimulate, and encourage learning, just as administrators can do for teachers. In spite of the debates and different viewpoints, it remains clear that there is no one best way to teach. Different goals require different methods. Teacher-centered instruction leads to better performance on achievement tests, whereas the open, informal methods like discovery learning or inquiry approaches are associated with better performance on tests of creativity, abstract thinking, and problem solving. In addition, open methods are better for improving attitudes toward school and for stimulating curiosity, cooperation among students, and lower absence rates.

Our goal is to help teachers and administrators understand the complexities of teaching and learning so that they can make better, more reasoned decisions in these areas.

Classroom Management

Chapter 7 focuses on management. Classrooms are distinctive environments that affect participants regardless of how students are organized for learning or what educational philosophy the teacher espouses (Doyle, 1986, 2006). Classrooms are crowded with people, tasks, and time pressures. There are many students—all with differing goals, preferences, and abilities—who must share resources, accomplish various tasks, and use and reuse materials. In addition, actions typically have multiple effects. Calling on low-ability students may encourage their participation and thinking, but it also may slow the discussion and lead to management problems if the students cannot answer. Moreover, everything happens at once and the pace is fast. Teachers have literally hundreds of exchanges with students during a single day. In this rapid-fire existence, events are unpredictable and public. Finally, classrooms have histories. The meaning of a particular action depends in part on what has happened before. To manage these complex places is a challenge for all, but an especially major one for beginning teachers.

No productive activity can take place in a group without the cooperation of members; hence, a fundamental task of teaching is to enlist students' support in activities that will lead to learning, and the first step in achieving cooperation is to organize the learning environment in a productive way. But order for its own sake is a hollow ritual. There are at least three reasons why classroom management is important: to make more time for learning, to include everyone in learning, and to develop systems that help students better manage their own learning.

Research on effective elementary and secondary classroom managers shows that these teachers have carefully planned rules and procedures (including consequences) for their classes; they teach these rules and procedures early in the school year using explanations, examples, practice, correction, and student involvement. In fact, getting started with a careful system of rules and procedures the first week of school sets the tone for the rest of the year. One area that requires good rules and procedures today involves managing technology. In Chapter 7 we also will give some useful guidelines and considerations.

Rules and procedures are a start, but not enough. Teachers need to establish a climate of trust and respect to create a positive community for learning. Once a good classroom environment is established, it must be maintained by encouraging student engagement and by preventing management problems. "With-it-ness," overlapping, group focus, and movement management are the skills of teachers who prevent problems. For special or more difficult situations, positive behavior supports often are helpful in preventing disruptive classroom episodes. Another way to prevent discipline problems is to create caring relationships and classroom communities for students and teachers.

Even with the best prevention practices, there will be discipline problems in the classroom. Conflicts between students, though potentially dangerous, can become occasions for learning conflict negotiation and peer-mediation strategies. One possible source of conflict is management that is unresponsive to students' cultural background and perceptions of schools. Establishing a positive learning context includes understanding teachers' and students' beliefs about respect as well as focusing attention on the factors that support motivation to learn. Our goal is to give teachers and principals the tools to succeed in that endeavor.

Assessing Student Learning

The teaching-learning cycle is not complete without evaluation and assessment—the topic of Chapter 8. In fact, all teaching involves assessing and evaluating learning. Increasingly, evaluation and measurement specialists are using the term *assessment* to describe the process of gathering information about student learning. Assessment is broader than testing and measurement. Assessments can be formative or summative and may be designed by classroom teachers or by local, state, or national agencies such as school districts or the Educational Testing Service. Today's assessments can go well beyond paper-and-pencil exercises to observations of performances and the development of portfolios and artifacts.

Teachers and administrators are increasingly being called on to make assessments of student learning and to interpret the results of tests. Hence, they need to know the difference between norm-referenced and criterion-referenced tests. They must understand the concepts and language of test makers—*sample, mean, mode, median, standard deviation, reliability, validity, normal distribution, percentile scores, standard scores, grade-equivalent scores*—because they will be called on to interpret test results to parents and policymakers.

Several kinds of standardized tests are used in schools today. There are three broad categories of standardized tests: achievement, diagnostic, and aptitude (including interest). Principals and teachers will probably encounter achievement and aptitude tests most frequently because they are important tools for diagnosing learning problems and measuring the success of schooling. Today, many important decisions about students, teachers, and schools are based in part on the results of standardized tests. Because the decisions affected by test scores are so critical, many educators call this process *high-stakes testing;* in fact, all states have statewide mandated testing for public school students under NCLB.

We will consider a number of critical questions about standardized tests. For example, what role should testing play in making decisions about people? What effects do high-stakes tests have on the curriculum? Do some students have an unfair advantage in taking tests? How can we help students with disabilities prepare for testing?

Although standardized tests are important and will likely increase in their significance, most tests given to students to evaluate their performance are teacher-made tests. In the end, teachers are the ones who give grades and decide who will be promoted and who will repeat, in addition to what and how to teach. Teachers are concerned with *formative* assessment, diagnosing the strengths and weaknesses of students so they can build an instructional program that will be effective. Teachers also must make *summative* assessments at the end of instruction to determine the level of accomplishment.

One of the main criticisms of standardized tests—that they control the curriculum, emphasizing recall of facts instead of thinking and problem solving—is a major criticism of classroom tests as well. What can be done? One proposed solution is authentic assessment. Authentic tests require students to apply skills and abilities as they would in real life. For example, they might use fractions to design a floor plan for a student lounge. If our instructional goals for students include the abilities to write, speak, listen, create, think critically, solve problems, or apply knowledge, then our tests should ask students to write, speak, listen, create, think, solve, and apply. The concern with authentic assessment has led to the development of several new approaches based on the goal of *performance in context*. Facts are used in a context where they apply; for example, the student uses grammar facts to write a persuasive letter to a software company requesting donations for the class computer center.

Portfolios and exhibitions are two approaches to assessment that require performance in context. With these approaches, it is difficult to tell where instruction stops and assessment starts because the two processes are interwoven. A portfolio is a purposeful collection of student work that demonstrates the student's efforts, progress, and achievements. An exhibition is a performance test that has two additional features. First, it is public, so students preparing exhibitions must take the audience into account; communication and understanding are essential. Second, an exhibition often requires many hours of preparation, because it is the culminating experience of a whole program of study. Another alternative is informal assessments such as journals that gather information from multiple sources to help teachers make decisions.

Finally, it is important to consider the effects of grades and grading on students. Teachers and administrators need to learn how to take advantage of the positive functions of grading and feedback while avoiding their negative consequences. That is no mean feat, but it is possible. Which do you think are better, traditional tests or authentic assessments? Take a look at the *Point/Counterpoint* arguments. Chapter 8 deals with the issues of assessment and grading in more detail.

POINT/COUNTERPOINT

Which Are Better: Traditional Tests or Authentic Assessments?

We have seen the advantages and disadvantages of standardized tests, but what about classroom testing? Are traditional multiple-choice and essay tests useful in classroom assessment?

POINT

Traditional tests are a poor basis for classroom assessment. In his article "Standards, Not Standardization: Evoking Quality Student Work," Grant Wiggins (1991) makes a strong case for giving students standards of excellence against which they can judge their accomplishments. But these standards should not be higher scores on multiple-choice tests. When scores on traditional tests become the standard, the message to students is that only right answers matter and the thinking behind the answers is unimportant. Wiggins notes that we don't judge major companies like Apple or Procter & Gamble by giving their employees multiple-choice tests. We don't judge the San Francisco Giants by giving their players and managers an essay test. For companies and sports teams, banks, singers, actors, hair stylists—you get the idea—we look at the quality of their work. How does their performance compare to standards of excellence in their field?

In a second article, Wiggins (1993) continues to argue for assessment that makes sense, that tests knowledge as it is applied in real-world situations. Understanding cannot be measured by tests that ask students to use skills and knowledge out of context. They must apply those skills in diverse contexts to solve authentic problems.

COUNTERPOINT

Traditional tests can play an important role.
Most psychologists and educators would agree with Wiggins that setting clear, high, authentic standards is important, but many also believe that traditional tests are useful in this process. Learning may be more than knowing the right answers, but right answers are important. While schooling is about learning to think and solve problems, it is also about knowledge. Students must have something to think about—facts, ideas, concepts, principles, theories, explanations, arguments, images, opinions. Well-designed traditional tests can evaluate students' knowledge effectively and efficiently (Airasian, 2005; Kirst, 1991b). Some educators believe that traditional testing should play an even greater role than it currently does. Educational policy analysts suggest that American students, compared to students in many other developed countries, lack essential knowledge because American schools emphasize process—critical thinking, self-esteem, problem solving—more than content. In order to teach more about a content area, teachers will need to determine how well their students are learning that content, and traditional testing provides useful information about content learning.

Tests are also valuable in motivating and guiding students' learning. There is research evidence that frequent testing encourages learning and retention (Nungester & Duchastel, 1982). In fact, students generally learn more in classes with more rather than fewer tests (Dempster, 1991).

Assessing and Changing School Culture and Climate

The school is a complex social system. Teachers teach in classrooms, but classrooms are only a part of the broader social system of the school. Just as a positive classroom climate is critical for effective teaching and learning, so too are the culture and climate of the school. The concepts of culture and climate are two ways to capture the feel or atmosphere of the school workplace. These two approaches to examining the collective identity of the workplace, its culture and climate, come from different intellectual traditions, but both perspectives are attempts to understand the influence of social context on school life. Thus, both should be useful to teachers and principals as they grapple with the way social conditions in the school affect teaching and learning.

Organizational culture is a pattern of shared orientations that binds the unit together and gives it a distinctive identity. To understand the culture of a school, one must comprehend the meanings and the shared orientations of the school at four levels: its artifacts, norms, values, and tacit assumptions. Although there is no one culture that is best for every school, there are some tacit assumptions that facilitate the process of supervision as improvement of instruction. Consider the following set of basic assumptions that Schein (1992) labels the heart of a learning culture.

1. Teachers and students are proactive problem solvers and learners.
2. Solutions to problems derive from a pragmatic search; knowledge is found in many forms: scientific research, experience, trial and error, and clinical research in which teachers and supervisors work things out together.
3. Teachers are basically good and are amenable to change and improvement.
4. Creativity and innovation are central to learning.
5. Both individualism and teamwork are important aspects of human interaction.
6. Diversity is a resource that has the potential to enhance learning.

Schools anchored with such assumptions have created learning cultures that encourage learning and improvement among all participants—students, teachers, and administrators. A culture of academic optimism is one important school property that links shared beliefs of the faculty with student achievement. The current conception of academic optimism, however, includes cognitive (efficacy), affective (trust), and behavioral components (academic emphasis). Academic optimism is a collective set of beliefs about strengths and capabilities in schools that paints a rich picture of human agency in which optimism is the overarching idea that unites efficacy and trust with academic emphasis. A school culture permeated with such beliefs has a sense of the possible.

Another way to view and measure school culture is in terms of control, especially the shared values and beliefs of the school for controlling students. The model of the **humanistic culture** views a school as an educational community in which students learn through cooperation, experience, and self-control. The faculty believes that students should be self-regulated learners who take responsibility for their actions. Misbehavior is viewed in sociological and psychological terms; causes for deviant behavior are sought. The goal is for each student to be a responsible citizen of a learning community. Optimism, understanding, self-direction, and close friendly relations are hallmarks of the humanistic school. The model for the **custodial culture** is a traditional school, with a focus on control, status, and power. Teachers believe that control is critical, teacher status is important, communication is one-way downward, and student misbehavior is a personal affront against teachers. Cynicism, strict teacher direction, mistrust, impersonality, and strong teacher control imbue the custodial school.

Another aspect of the school context that sets the scene for effective teaching and learning is organizational climate. Teachers' performance in schools is determined in part by the climate in which they work. Climate is a general concept that refers to teachers' perceptions of the school's work environment; it is affected by the formal organization, informal organization, and politics, all of which, including climate, affect the motivations and behavior of teachers. School climate is a relatively enduring quality of the school environment that is experienced by teachers, influences their behavior, and is based on their collective perceptions. Climate is to a school what personality is to an individual.

We examine organizational climate from several perspectives: *openness*, that is, the extent to which behaviors in the school are authentic and real; the *health* of the interpersonal dynamics among the students, teachers, and principal; and the *collective efficacy* of the school, that is, the extent to which the teachers as a group believe their ability to organize and teach will enable them to overcome extant student difficulties and help students achieve academically. Each of these climate perspectives brings with it a set of reliable and valid measures that teachers and principals can use to assess the functionality of the climate of their school.

Organizations are in a constant state of flux. Their change can be progressive, regressive, or aimless. Schools can develop their own learning procedures to solve their problems. They can become places where teachers and principals can continually expand their capacity to create the results they desire, where emergent patterns of thinking are nurtured, where collective aspiration is liberated, and where people are constantly learning how to learn (Senge, 1990). We will illustrate how teachers and administrators can use the climate framework and its measures as bases for organizational change. Using an organizational development approach, we will demonstrate how one school identified a climate problem, established a problem-solving team, diagnosed potential causes of the problem, developed an action plan, and set the stage for improving teaching and learning (see Chapter 9).

Instructional Leadership for 21st Century Learning

In 2008, the Association for Supervision and Curriculum Development issued a position statement about the type of education students need today (ASCD, 2008).

Educating Students in a Changing World

As educators in the 21st century, we are charged with teaching students to be successful in a complex, interconnected world. This responsibility requires schools to prepare students for technological, cultural, economic, informational, and demographic changes.

To accomplish these goals, the Partnership for 21st Century Learning—a national organization with representatives from the National Education Association, educational publishers, technology companies, the American Association of School Librarians, the Educational Testing Service, the National Academy Foundation, toy companies, private foundations, the Walt Disney Company, and others—has developed a framework that describes what is needed for 21st century learning (see Figure 1.2). The emphasis is on a blending of core subject knowledge and expertise with specific *learning and innovation skills* (creativity, innovation, critical thinking, problem solving, communication, and collaboration); *information, media, and technology skills* (information literacy, media, and information and communications technology literacy); and *life and career skills* (adaptability, self-direction and initiative, social and

FIGURE 1.2   A Framework for 21st Century Learning
The rainbow arch sections represent critical 21st century student outcomes, and the pools at the base of the rainbow represent support systems.

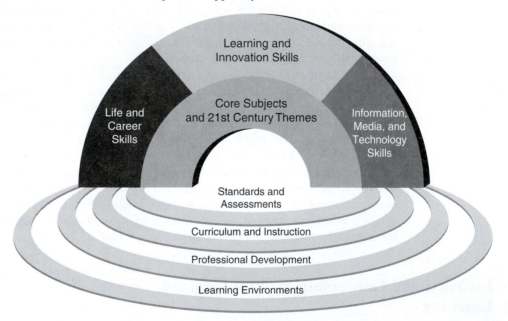

Source: "21st Century Student Outcomes and Support Systems" from Partnership for 21st Century Skills website. Copyright © by Partnership for 21st Century Skills. Reprinted with permission.

cross-cultural skills, productivity and accountability, leadership and responsibility). Tools for instructional leaders are available from the Partnership for 21st Century Skills (http://www.p21.org/).

Technology and Instructional Leadership[1]

Some researchers believe that by 2015, emerging technologies such as cloud computing for data storage and analysis, collaborative learning environments (e.g., wikis, group blogging systems, social networks), game-based learning, and mobile learning will be widely adopted in K–12 education, further enabling opportunities for authentic, inquiry-based, ubiquitous, and collaborative learning experiences (Johnson, Smith, Levine, & Haywood, 2010). Technology is likely to provide the next great revolution in education, initially as textbooks become digitized, electronic tablets substitute for traditional texts, delivery of instruction migrates to computers, and social media facilitate the exchange of knowledge networks and ideas. In fact, some estimates are that by 2019 about 50% of courses will be delivered online (Christensen & Horn, 2008).

Current and Future Uses of Technology. Technology can and has been used across a variety of school settings in pursuit of goals such as increasing student achievement as measured by standardized test scores, making school more engaging for students, and supporting reform-oriented instruction aimed at developing higher-order thinking skills such as critical thinking and problem solving. Another goal for technology use in schools has been to help students learn how to use and communicate with modern-day tools. Just as books, paper, and pencils are essential tools for helping students learn how to read and produce written text, some would argue that students must also become technologically literate, given that the world beyond school extensively uses electronic media as a means for communication. Table 1.1 offers examples of a variety of ways technology can be used to support teaching and learning (Borwein, 2005; Means, 1994; Partnership for 21st Century Skills, 2004; Pea, 1987; Zucker, 2008).

No one can predict exactly the shape of technology's impact on education, yet most agree that the classroom teacher will remain a key element of teaching and learning in public education, even if the teacher's role changes to take advantage of expanding technological options. We view the technological revolution in schools as an opportunity to improve teaching and learning, but freely admit that researchers are still in the early stages of understanding how schools should adapt to effectively implement technology in pursuit of educational goals (Anthony, 2011; Christensen, Horn, & Johnson, 2008; Collins & Halverson, 2009; Cuban, Kirkpatrick, & Peck, 2001). Table 1.1 summarized the current uses of technology in schools, but we predict that as software and hardware become more user friendly and less expensive, the integration of technology in schools will increase dramatically. For example, platforms of learner tools will become available,

[1]This section written by Anika Ball Anthony, the Ohio State University.

TABLE 1.1   Uses of Technology to Achieve Teaching and Learning Goals

Teaching and Learning Goals	Technological Tools
Improve students' mastery of subject area knowledge and skills	Tutorial or drill-and-practice programs Personalized learning systems Digital textbooks
Increase student motivation	Educational games Design and creativity software Videos and images that display authentic examples
Support reform-oriented instruction for critical thinking, problem solving, and identity development	Simulation applications Internet and information databases Knowledge-organization applications Electronic probes and sensors for data collection Spreadsheets, databases, and graphing calculators for data analysis Social media for collaborative learning
Prepare students for the 21st century workplace	Multi-media data visualization Mobile devices for ubiquitous access and learner control Software and equipment for creating graphics, movies, and music Productivity and scheduling software
Provide resources to support teachers' preferred instructional approaches	Lectures: Visual support with presentation software Inquiry: Data collection, analysis, communication applications Deduction and inference: Web searches to locate information for evaluation and argumentation
Improve system-wide efficiency and effectiveness	Resources for professional development, customizing instructional materials, student assessments, and communication Resources for data collection, storage, and analysis to support supervision and shared decision making

Source: A. B. Anthony (2012), created for this book.

much like the ubiquitous apps that make smart phones and tablets appealing, which will enable learners with vastly different learning needs and styles to master materials they would have struggled to learn using traditional methods. In this quickly evolving environment, principals will need to become technology leaders.

Technology Leadership.   In the modern information explosion environment, educational technology becomes increasingly vital day by day, and principals with efficient technology leadership skills are the key to creating and implementing successful policies and technology education plans (Anderson & Dexter, 2005; Chang, Chin, & Hsu, 2008; Flanagan & Jacobsen, 2003). **Technology leadership** is an emerging role focused on fostering school conditions that support technology integration. Associated roles and responsibilities often include providing visionary leadership; promoting a school culture for digital learning (International Society for Technology in Education, 2009); modeling technology use; leading schools and districts in developing plans for school-based technology initiatives; budgeting, selecting, and working with vendors (McNabb, Valdez, et al., 1999); organizing technology professional development; and collecting data on how technology supports school restructuring efforts (Anderson & Dexter, 2000; J. Davidson, 2003; Dexter, 2008; Hawkins, Spielvogel, & Panush, 1996; McNabb, Hawkes, & Rouk, 1999; Picciano, 2006). Technology leaders also attend to legal issues surrounding the use of technology in schools (Quinn, 2003).

One Example of Technology Leadership: Supervision. Instructional leaders should and can be on the cutting edge of technological innovations to improve teaching and learning. Michael DiPaola (mfdipa@wm.edu) and his associates have developed a toolbox composed of data collection systems and digitized forms to improve the supervision process. Supervisors use the digitized form on a tablet or laptop to collect classroom data focused on specific research-based, high-yield instructional strategies (Hattie, 2008; Hattie & Timperley, 2007). At the conclusion of the observation period, the completed form can be emailed to the teacher as a PDF file to provide immediate and authentic feedback about their instruction.

Teachers and supervisors select from a variety of electronic forms targeting specific instructional strategies to focus the observation. These tools are unique because they are linked to a computer server so that feedback is not only quick and focused on a particular instructional strategy, but also the data from every observation are accumulated in a searchable database. Principals and supervisors have the ability to analyze a cumulative record of observations to review data collected by different observers and track teacher progress over time.

The teacher and supervisor, for example, might want to observe and analyze the cognitive level of questions that are being asked in a particular class by a teacher in terms of Bloom's taxonomy: remembering, understanding, applying, analyzing, evaluating, and creating (see Chapter 7). The supervisor using either a laptop or electronic tablet records on the digitized form (see Figure 1.3) the number and type of each question as it is raised as well as the wait time for the question. These data are recorded electronically and before classes are over for the day and, as noted above, the teacher is supplied a PDF summarizing the number and kinds of questions asked that day in that class. The feedback can then be used to develop strategies to improve questioning skills.

The point is that increasingly, teachers and principals are going to be using computer technology to study and improve teaching in the classroom. The data will be collected electronically, stored "in the cloud," and be available immediately for analysis. Teaching and learning will become more student centered and eventually everyone, including students, will use computer apps to create, understand, improve, design, and customize entire courses.

Over the short term, most students and teachers will continue to use conventional textbooks, but little by little, textbooks will give way to electronic formats augmented by student-centric learning tools, which will create learning tool modules to generate entire courses designed for a variety of learners (Christensen, Horn, & Johnson, 2008). Instructional leaders of the future face not only a myriad of everyday problems but also the technological challenges of the future.

FIGURE 1.3 Sample Form for Teacher Evaluation.

Cognitive Levels of Questions and Wait Time

Teacher: _____

Date: _____

Class Observed: _____

Follow up Dialogue Date: _____

Administrator: _____

Observation: *Start Time:* _____ *End Time:* _____

Number of Students in the Class: _____

Directions: The purpose of this form is to record the cognitive level of each question the teacher poses during a lesson or lesson segment. For each question, identify the level of the question and count the number of seconds the teacher waits until letting a student respond. Record the number of seconds in the corresponding row in each question's column.

	Wait Time in Seconds											
Cognitive Level	Q1	Q2	Q3	Q4	Q5	Q6	Q7	Q8	Q9	Q10	Q11	**Total Questions Asked**
Remembering												
Understanding												
Applying												
Analyzing												
Evaluating												
Creating												

Sample Stems

Remembering
What is the definition for...
What happened after...
How many...
Who did...
When was...
Define the word...
Which is true or false?

Understanding
Explain what happened after...
Provide a definition of...
What is the purpose of...
Explain why ___ caused ___
What are some examples?
Who was the key character?
How are these ideas different?
What do you think could happen?

Applying
What is another instance of...
Demonstrate the way to...
Which one is most like...
Could this have happened in...
How would you organize these ideas?
Which factors would you change?

Analyzing
What steps are important in the process of...
The solution would be to...
What's the relationship between...
What other conclusions can you reach about...
If ___, then, ___
What do you see as other possible outcomes?

Evaluating
How would you have handled...
How would you feel if...
Defend your position about...
What do you think should be the outcome?
What changes would you recommend?

Creating
Devise your own way to...
Develop a proposal for...
How would you deal with...
Can you see a solution to...
What would happen if...
How many ways can you...
Design a ___ to ___

© *DCD*

Summary

This is a book about understanding and improving teaching and learning. We have provided an overview of our strategy for accomplishing that goal in this chapter. We began with a discussion of the role of instructional leadership and then examined the likely impact of the No Child Left Behind Act on instructional leadership. Then we turned to the students: how they differ in intelligence, emotion, learning styles, gender, and race. Each of these differences has implications for teaching and learning that are explored in some detail (Chapters 2 and 3). Most experts agree that learning occurs when there is a stable change in an individual's skill, knowledge, or behavior, but some emphasize behavior and skills while others emphasize cognition and knowledge. Because learning is a complex cognitive process, there is no single best explanation of learning. Different perspectives are more or less useful depending on what kind of learning is to be explained. We examine three general explanations of learning—behavioral, cognitive, and constructivist—each with a different focus and each with different consequences (Chapter 4).

Effective teaching and learning depend on motivated students; hence, teachers must know how to stimulate, direct, and maintain high levels of student engagement. Motivation to learn is enhanced when teachers use strategies that help students develop confidence in their ability to learn, see the value of the learning, and stay focused on learning without resorting to self-protective and self-defeating beliefs and actions. Five approaches to motivation are important in this regard: behavioral, humanistic, cognitive, social cognitive, and sociocultural theories. Each perspective has something to offer to improve teaching and learning (Chapter 5). In the end, students have to do the learning, but teachers must create situations that guide, support, stimulate, and encourage learning. Good teaching is critical to student learning, but there is no one best way to teach. Different goals require different methods. Teacher-centered, student-centered, discovery, and inquiry methods are all more or less effective depending on the task and goal (Chapter 6).

Teachers not only have to motivate and teach, but also must be able to manage the classroom. Inevitably there will be discipline problems in the classroom. When conflicts arise, teachers can deal more effectively with the situation if they first determine who "owns" the problem and then respond appropriately with empathetic listening and problem solving. Establishing a positive learning context also includes giving attention to the factors that support motivation to learn, such as tasks, autonomy, recognition, grouping, evaluation, and time (Chapter 7). All teaching involves assessing and evaluating learning. Assessment involves standardized and teacher-made tests, objective and essay tests, local and national tests, reliability and validity, traditional and innovative tests, and portfolios and exhibitions. Appropriate assessment is becoming increasingly more important for teachers and administrators as pressure mounts for school accountability (Chapter 8).

Teaching and learning are affected by the organizational context: the culture and climate of the school. Open, healthy, optimistic, and efficacious school environments are pivotal in improving teaching and learning. Administrators and teachers need to assess their school environment and then work together to develop and improve the learning environment (Chapter 9).

Finally, administrators today must exercise technology leadership to take advantage of the educational possibilities in cloud computing for data storage and analysis, collaborative learning environments (e.g., wikis, group blogging systems, social networks), game-based learning, and mobile learning. Technology leadership is an emerging role focused on fostering school conditions that support technology integration. Associated roles and responsibilities often include providing visionary leadership, promoting a school culture for digital learning, modeling technology use, leading schools and districts in developing plans for school-based technology initiatives, budgeting, selecting and working with vendors, organizing technology professional development, and collecting data on how technology supports school restructuring efforts.

In sum, we will address the critical aspects of the teaching–learning process: student differences, learning, student and teacher motivation, teaching, classroom management, assessing student learning, and assessing and changing school climate and culture. Each chapter is grounded in the latest research and theory in that area and provides specific ideas for applying that knowledge to practice, including many *Theory into Action* guidelines with concrete suggestions and *A Principal's Perspective*, a true story of how one principal solved a problem of practice related to the ideas in the chapter. The following chapters begin with a *Preview of Key Points* and a *Leadership Challenge*, an actual school problem. They conclude with suggestions of projects to relate theory to practice in the form of professional *Portfolio* exercises and an *Instructional Leader's Toolbox*, a collection of contemporary readings, useful websites, and helpful organizations.

KEY TERMS

custodial culture (19)   humanistic culture (18)   technology leadership (22)

DEVELOPING YOUR PORTFOLIO

Portfolios are increasingly being used for the licensure, hiring, and evaluation of principals; thus portfolios serve many purposes. There are two major uses for portfolios. The first is for the professional growth and reflection of the individual who is developing the portfolio. The second is as an assessment for external audiences—college and university programs, state licensure boards, and districts that are hiring principals.

At the end of every chapter in this book you will read suggestions for possible entries into your professional portfolio. Each idea asks you to create a product that incorporates the knowledge from the chapter into a plan, newsletter, presentation, or policy statement. A portfolio is not a scrapbook of clippings, notes, transcripts, and awards. Rather, it is a planned collection that reveals your philosophy, skills, and accomplishments. Often portfolios are developed to demonstrate competence in the Interstate School Leaders Licensure Consortium (ISLLC) Standards: development and implementation of a vision of learning; creation of a school culture that supports student learning; management of a safe, efficient, and effective learning environment; appropriate collaboration with families and the community; ethical practice; and understanding of the larger context of schooling. The exercises in this book will help you, especially with the first two standards.

For your first exercise, decide how you will organize your portfolio. Examine other principals' portfolios and develop ideas for your own.

INSTRUCTIONAL LEADER'S TOOLBOX

Readings

Anthony, A. B. (2011). Innovation in educational organizations: Implications for research and administrative practice. In M. DiPaola & P. Forsyth (Eds.), *Leading research in educational administration: A festschrift for Wayne K. Hoy* (pp. 163–182). Greenwich, CT: Information Age.

Darling-Hammond, L., & Bransford, J. (2005). *Preparing teachers for a changing world: What teachers should learn and be able to do.* San Francisco, CA: Jossey-Bass.

Dietz, M. E. (2001). *Designing the school leader's portfolio.* Arlington Heights, IL: Skylight Professional Development.

Educational Leadership. (November, 2006). Special issue on "NCLB: Taking stock, looking forward" (vol. 64, No. 3).

Good, T. L., & Brophy, J. E. (2008). *Looking in classrooms* (10th ed.). Boston, MA: Allyn & Bacon/Longman.

Kilbane, C. R., & Milman, N. B. (2003). *What every teacher should know about creating a digital portfolio.* Boston, MA: Allyn & Bacon.

Kimball, M. (2003). *The web portfolio guide: Creating electronic portfolios for the web.* Boston, MA: Allyn & Bacon.

Slavin, R. E., & Olatokunbo, S. F. (1998). *Show me the evidence: Proven and promising programs for America's schools.* Thousand Oaks, CA: Corwin.

Woolfolk Hoy, A. E., & Perry, N. (2012). *Child and adolescent development.* Columbus, OH: Pearson/Merrill.

Websites

www.bestevidence.org/
  Best Evidence Encyclopedia, Johns Hopkins University

http://electronicportfolios.com/portfolios.html
  Using Technology to Support Alternative Assessment and Electronic Portfolios

www.proteacher.com
  The Vent—a discussion group for new teachers

Organizations

http://ascd.org
  Association for Supervision and Curriculum Development (ASCD)

www.ccsso.org
  Council of Chief State School Officers

www.iel.org
  Institute for Educational Leadership

www.naesp.org
  National Association of Elementary School Principals

www.nassp.org
  National Association of Secondary School Principals

CHAPTER
2

Student Diversity

PREVIEW: KEY POINTS

1. By 2050, Latinos will comprise about one quarter of the U.S. population (U.S. Bureau of the Census, 2010b).

2. One in five American children lives in poverty; one in twelve lives in extreme poverty. A child is born into poverty in the United States every 33 seconds.

3. A key to overcoming the educational problems resulting from poverty is fostering resilience in students, in teachers, and in classrooms.

4. Academic self-efficacy is a belief in your own ability to learn, and it is one of the consistent predictors of academic achievement.

5. A dialect is a variety of language spoken by a particular group; it is important that teachers remember that differences in dialect are not errors.

6. Bilingualism is an asset, not a liability, provided there is balance—equal fluency in both languages.

7. To create a culturally inclusive classroom, teachers must know, respect, and effectively teach all their students.

8. Learning styles are preferred ways of learning and processing information. Teachers need to be aware of cultural differences in learning styles so they can be sure their teaching approaches are consistent with their students' learning styles.

9. There appear to be some gender differences in spatial and mathematical abilities, but these do not hold across all cultures and situations.

10. Teachers are in a position to reinforce or challenge gender stereotypes through their choice of materials and interactions with students.

Leadership Challenge

You are the principal of a fairly homogeneous elementary school. In fact, most of your students are middle- or upper-middle class and white. In January, a new student enters your school, the daughter of an African American professor who recently moved to the nearby college. After a few weeks, one of your third-grade teachers comes to you with a potential problem. She has noticed that the new student is not being included in many activities. She sits alone in the library and plays alone at recess. All these things are troubling to your teacher, but most disturbing of all is that yesterday the teacher overheard two of her higher-achieving girls talking about their "White Girls Club." Your teacher is shocked and has turned to you for advice.

1. Would you investigate to learn more about this "club"? How?
2. What advice do you give this teacher?
3. Should you formulate a plan of action? What should you do? What should the teacher do?
4. If you find that the students have created a club that excludes nonwhite students, what would you do?
5. Do you need a school policy on this matter? If so, what should the policy be? If not, why not?

Schools and instructional leaders today must deal with a wealth of student differences. These differences pose challenges (as evident in the situation above) but provide opportunities as well. This chapter examines student differences in culture and gender. We begin with the differences the principal faces in dealing with the "White Girls Club."

Today's Diverse Classrooms

Who are the students in American classrooms today? Here are a few statistics about the United States and Canada (taken from Children's Defense Fund, 2008; Dewan, 2010; Freisen, 2010; Meece & Kurtz-Costes, 2001; U.S. Bureau of the Census, 2010a).

- In 2003, 12% of the people living in the United States were born in another country, and 18% spoke a language other than English at home—half of these families spoke Spanish.
- Today, 22% of children under the age of 18 are Latino. By 2050, Latinos will comprise about one quarter of the U.S. population (U.S. Bureau of the Census, 2010b).
- In Canada, projections are that by 2031, one in three Canadians will belong to a visible minority, with South Asians being the largest group represented. About 17% of the population report that their first language is not French or English, but instead one of over 100 other languages.
- One in five American children lives in poverty and one in twelve lives in extreme poverty, defined in 2011 by the United States Department of Health and Human Services as an annual income of $22,350 for a family of four ($27,940 in Alaska and $25,710 in Hawaii). The numbers are very similar for Canada.
- More than half of all children in poverty live in eight states: California, Texas, New York, Florida, Illinois, Ohio, Georgia, and Michigan. In contrast, because of the effects of mass media, these diverse students share many similarities today, particularly the fact that most are far more technologically literate than their teachers. For example: According to a recent survey, 29% of students in grades 3–5 and 56% of students in grades 9–12 had access to cell phones; 42% and 67% respectively had access to laptop computers; and the numbers were 55% and 85% for MP3 music players (Project Tomorrow, 2010).
- The students in the Project Tomorrow survey reported that the two greatest obstacles to their using technology in school were filters that stopped them from accessing the websites they needed for homework and bans on using their own mobile devices (namely cell phones) at school.

Poverty and School Achievement

One in five Americans under the age of 18 lives in poverty. That means about 16.4 million children. And almost half of these children can be classified as living in deep poverty—in families with incomes 50% below the poverty threshold. But the rate of poverty is higher for African American, Native American, and Latino children—35% of African American, 34% of Native American, and 31% of Latino children lived in poverty in 2008, whereas 13% of Asian and 11% of non-Hispanic White children were poor (National Poverty Center, 2011). African American and Latino families headed by single women have the highest poverty rate—about 50% (Moore, Redd, Burkhauser, Mbwana, & Collins, 2009). Contrary to many stereotypes, more poor children live in suburban and rural areas than in central cities (Children's Defense Fund, 2010).

Compared to students in poverty, students of all ethnic groups from wealthier homes show higher average levels of achievement on test scores, and they stay in school longer (Berliner, 2005; Gutman, Sameroff, & Cole, 2003). The average correlation between SES and school achievement is moderate, about .30, based on research articles published between 1990 and 2000 (Sirin, 2005). Poor children are at least twice as likely as nonpoor children to be kept back in school. And the longer the child is in poverty, the stronger the impact is on achievement. For example, even when we take into account parents' education, the chance that children will be retained in grades or placed in special education increases by 2% to 3% for every year the children live in poverty (Ackerman, Brown, & Izard, 2004; Bronfenbrenner, McClelland, Wethington, Moen, & Ceci, 1996).

What are the effects of poverty that might explain the lower school achievement of these students? It is not low income itself, but the material hardships that come with poverty, that lead to greater parental stress and fewer resources for children's achievement (Gershoff, Aber, Raver, & Lennon, 2007). The negative effects of poverty begin even before a child is born. Families in poverty have less access to good prenatal and infant health care and nutrition. Over half of all adolescent mothers receive no prenatal care at all. Poor mothers and adolescent mothers are more likely to have premature babies, and prematurity is associated with many cognitive and learning problems. Children in poverty are more likely to be exposed to both legal drugs (nicotine, alcohol) and illegal drugs (cocaine, heroin) before birth. Children whose mothers take drugs during pregnancy can have problems with organization, attention, and language skills.

In the early years, compared to children in middle-class and wealthy families, poor children are four times as likely to experience stress due to evictions, lack of food, overcrowding, or utility disconnections. High levels of stress increase the production of hormones that can interfere with the flow of blood in the brain and impair the development of synaptic connections (Shonkoff, 2006). In addition, stress hormones can deplete tryptophan (Richell, Deakin, & Anderson, 2005), an amino acid that calms impulsive and violent behaviors (Hudley & Novack, 2007). Increased stress and stress hormones are related to more frequent school absences, decreased attention and concentration, problems with memory and thinking, reduced motivation and effort, greater risk for depression, and reduced neurogenesis (growth of new brain cells) (Jensen, 2009). As they grow, poor children breathe more polluted air and drink more contaminated water (Evans, 2004). Poor children are at least twice as likely as non-poor children to suffer lead poisoning, which is associated with lower school achievement and long-term neurological impairment (McLoyd, 1998).

Poor children have less access to books, computers, high-quality day care, libraries, trips, and museums (Evans, 2004). Home and neighborhood resources seem to have the greatest impact on children's achievement when school is not in session—during the summer or before children enter school. For example, one study suggested that the four summer vacations between 2nd and 6th grade accounted for 80% of the achievement differences between poor and advantaged students (Allington & McGill-Frazen, 2003). This truly is a case of the rich getting richer. In addition, low-income students are more likely to attend schools with inadequate resources and less-effective teachers (Evans, 2004). When low-SES students receive an inferior education, their academic skills are inferior and their life chances are limited, beginning with not being prepared for higher education (Anyon, 1980; Knapp & Woolverton, 2003).

Of course, not all low-income families lack resources. Many of these families provide rich learning environments for their children. In fact, "most disadvantaged children grow up in relatively stable and secure environments" (Ackerman & Brown, 2006, p. 92). As instructional leaders, you and your teachers can learn from these families to focus on and foster the strengths of your students, rather than dwelling on deficit thinking.

Teaching to Overcome Poverty and Foster Resilience

Many children at risk for academic failure not only survive, they thrive. They are resilient students. What can we learn from these students? What can teachers and schools do to encourage **resilience?**

Resilient Students.   People vary in their capacity to be resilient. Students who seem able to thrive in spite of serious challenges are actively engaged in school. They have good interpersonal skills, confidence in their own ability to learn, positive attitudes toward school, pride in their ethnicity, and high expectations (Borman & Overman, 2004; Lee, 2005). Also, students who have high intelligence or valued talents are more protected from risks. Being easygoing and optimistic is associated with resilience as well. Factors outside the student—interpersonal relationships and social support—matter too. It helps to have a warm relationship with a parent who has high expectations and supports learning by organizing space and time at home for study. But even without such a parent, a strong bond with someone competent—grandparent, aunt, uncle, teacher, administrator, mentor, or other caring adult—can serve the same supportive function. Involvement in school, community, or religious activities can provide more connections to concerned adults and also teach lessons in social skills and leadership (Berk, 2005).

Resilient Classrooms.   You can't choose personalities or parents for your students. Even if you were able to, stresses could still build up for very resilient students. Beth Doll and her colleagues (2005) suggest that we have to change classrooms instead of kids because "alternative strategies will be more enduring and most successful when they are integrated into naturally occurring systems of support [like schools] that surround children" (p. 3). In addition, there is some evidence that changes in classrooms—like reducing class size and fostering supportive relationships with teachers—have a greater impact on the academic achievement of African American students compared to Latino and white students (Borman & Overman, 2004). So how can you create a classroom that supports resilience?

Borman and Overman (2004) identify two characteristics of schools associated with academic resilience: a *safe, orderly environment* and *positive teacher–student relationships*. In their book on resilient classrooms, Doll and her colleagues (2005) draw on research in education and psychology on best practices for children in poverty and children with disabilities to describe the characteristics of resilient classrooms. There are two strands of elements that bind students to their classroom communities. One strand emphasizes the self-agency of students—their capacity to set and pursue goals. The second strand emphasizes caring and connected relationships in the classroom and the school.

The *Self-Agency Strand* fosters three key beliefs:

- *Academic self-efficacy*, a belief in your own ability to learn, is one of the most consistent predictors of academic achievement. As you will see in Chapter 5, self-efficacy emerges when students tackle challenging, meaningful tasks with the support needed to be successful and they see other students do the same. Accurate and encouraging feedback from teachers also helps.
- *Behavioral self-control* or student self-regulation is essential for a safe and orderly learning environment. Chapters 5 and 7 will give you ideas for helping students develop self-regulation knowledge and skills.
- *Academic self-determination,* making choices, setting goals, and following through comprise the third element in the Self-Agency Strand. As you will see in Chapter 5, students who are self-determined are more motivated and committed to learning.

The *Relationship Strand* includes three important relationships:

- *Caring teacher–student relationships* are consistently associated with better school performance, especially for students who face serious challenges. We will examine the power of caring teachers in Chapters 6 and 7.
- *Effective peer relations* also are critical in connecting students to school.
- *Effective home–school relationships* are the final element in building a caring, connected network for students. James Comer has found that when parents stay involved, their children's grades and test scores improve (Comer, Haynes, & Joyner, 1996). The *Theory into Action Guidelines* on the next page give some ideas for connecting with families.

Constructing a Resilient Classroom.   To build student self-agency and relationships, the two strands of resilience, use Doll et al.'s (2005) student questionnaires for gathering data about classrooms. One questionnaire asks students to respond "Yes," "Sometimes," or "Never" to six statements*:

1. My teacher listens carefully when I talk.
2. My teacher helps me when I need help.
3. My teacher respects me.
4. My teacher believes that I am an important member of this class.
5. My teacher makes it fun to be in class.
6. My teacher is fair to me.

*Excerpts from *Resilient Classrooms: Creating Healthy Environments for Learning*, by Beth Doll, Katherine Brehm and Steven Zucker. Copyright © 2005 by Guilford Publications, Inc. Reprinted with permission.

THEORY INTO ACTION GUIDELINES

Partnerships with Families

Joyce Epstein (1995) describes six types of family/school/community partnerships. The following guidelines are based on her six categories:

Parenting partnerships: Help all families establish home environments to support children as students.

Examples
1. Offer workshops, videos, courses, family literacy fairs, and other informational programs to help parents cope with parenting situations that they identify as important.
2. Establish family support programs to assist with nutrition, health, and social services.
3. Find ways to help families share information with the school about the child's cultural background, talents, and needs—learn from the families.

Communication: Design effective forms for school-to-home and home-to-school communication.

Examples
1. Make sure communications fit the needs of families. Provide translations, visual support, large print—whatever is needed to make communication effective.
2. Visit families in their territory after gaining their permission. Don't expect family members to come to school until a trusting relationship is established.
3. Balance messages about problems with communications of accomplishments and positive information.

Volunteering: Recruit and organize parent help and support.

Examples
1. Do an annual postcard survey to identify family talents, interests, times available, and suggestions for improvements.
2. Establish a structure (telephone tree, etc.) to keep all families informed. Make sure families without telephones are included.
3. If possible, set aside a room for volunteer meetings and projects.

Learning at home: Provide information and ideas for families about how to help children with schoolwork and learning activities.

Examples
1. Provide assignment schedules, homework policies, and tips on how to help with schoolwork without doing the work.
2. Get family input into curriculum planning—have idea and activity exchanges.
3. Send home learning packets and enjoyable learning activities, especially over holidays and summers.

Decision-making partnerships: Include families in school decisions, developing family and community leaders and representatives.

Examples
1. Create family advisory committees for the school with parent representatives.
2. Make sure all families are in a network with their representative.

Community partnerships: Identify and integrate resources and services from the community to strengthen school programs, family practices, and student learning and development.

Examples
1. Have students and parents research existing resources—build a database.
2. Identify service projects for students—explore service learning.
3. Identify community members who are school alumni and get them involved in school programs.

Source: Excerpt from "School/Family/Community Partnerships: Caring for Children We Share" by Joyce L. Epstein, from *Phi Delta Kappan*, May 1995, Volume 76(9). Copyright © 1995 by Phi Delta Kappa International. Reprinted with permission of Phi Delta Kappa International, www.pdkintl.org.

Doll et al. describe one teacher who used this questionnaire and found that almost half of her students did not have any fun in class. They said the teacher was not fair and did not listen carefully to them, help or respect them, or believe in them. Based on these findings, the teacher revised her plans to become more supportive and make class more engaging.

Focusing on Strengths.   Rather than focusing on achievement gaps, many educators have called for more research on the successes of students placed at risk. Berry (2005) studied two middle-school-aged African American boys who were successful in mathematics. In the lives of those students, Berry found support and high expectations from family and teachers, positive math experiences in preschool and elementary school, connections to church and athletic extracurricular activities, and positive identities as math students. Berry encouraged educators and researchers "to focus on the success stories of those African American men and boys who are successful to identify the strengths, skills, and other significant factors it takes to foster success" (p. 61). One final theme characterized the successful African American boys—their families had prepared them to understand and deal with discrimination.

Next we turn to another kind of diversity, one based on language.

Language Differences in the Classroom

In the classroom, quite a bit happens through language. In this section, we will examine two kinds of language differences—dialect differences and bilingualism.

A **dialect** is a variation of a language spoken by particular group. The dialect differences could be based on region of a country, social class, age ("teen talk"), or even gender. The dialect is part of the group's collective identity. Actually, every person reading this book speaks at least one dialect, maybe more, because there is no one absolute standard English. The English language has several dialects, including Australian, Canadian, British, and American. Within each of these dialects are variations. A few examples for American English are Southern, Bostonian, Cajun, and African American Vernacular (Garcia, 2002).

Dialects differ in their rules about pronunciation, grammar, and vocabulary, but it is important to remember that these differences are not errors. Each dialect is logical, complex, and rule-governed. An example of this is the use of the double negative (Brice & Brice, 2009). In many versions of American English, the double negative construction, such as "I don't have no more," is incorrect. But in many dialects such as some varieties of African American English and in other languages (for instance, Russian, French, Spanish, and Hungarian), the double negative is part of the grammatical rules. To say "I don't want anything" in Spanish, you must literally say, "I don't want nothing," or "No quiero nada." Table 2.1 on the next page gives some other examples of dialect differences.

Dialects and Teaching.   Although the various dialects of a language may be equally logical, complex, and rule-governed, should teachers show respect for the dialect and make learning easier for children by teaching in their dialect? To do this would rob children of the opportunity to learn the speech needed to take advantage of many

TABLE 2.1   A Few Examples of Dialect Differences in African American English and Spanish-Influenced English

Area of Language	Standard English	African American English
Sounds: Final consonants dropped	hand, picked	han, pick
Noun plurals	Two puppies	Two puppy
Noun possessives	Mama's house	Mama house
Past tense	John came.	John come.
Use of *being* verb	John is sick.	John sick.
Use of *bin* for remote past	She has been running for a long time.	She bin running.
Multiple negation	I don't ever have any problems.	I don't never have no problems.
Area of Language	**Standard English**	**Spanish Influenced English**
Sounds: Alternate *ch* and *sh* sounds	Chair, snow	Share, chow
Sounds: Final consonants dropped	Start, least	Star, leas
Reflexive pronouns	Himself, themselves	Hisself, theirselves
Borrow for *lend*	Lend me a pencil.	Borrow me a pencil.
Barely for *recently*	They recently graduated from high school.	They barely graduated from high school.
Multiple negation	I don't have any pain.	I don't have no pain.
Using words from Spanish	15-year-old girl's coming out party	quinceañera

Source: Adapted from *Language development: Monolingual and bilingual acquisitions* by Alejandro E. Brice and Roanne G. Brice. Copyright © 2009 by Pearson Education, Inc. Printed and Electronically reproduced by permission of Pearson Education, Inc., Upper Saddle River, New Jersey.

social and occupational opportunities as adults. Moving between two speech forms is called **code switching,** something we all have learned to do. Sometimes the code is formal speech for educational or professional communication. Sometimes the code is informal for talk among friends and family. Sometimes the codes are different dialects. Even young children recognize variations in codes. Lisa Delpit (1995) describes the reaction of one of her 1st-grade students to her very first reading lesson. After she carefully recited the memorized introduction from the teacher's manual, a student raised his hand and asked, "Teacher, how come you talkin' like a white person? You talkin' just like my momma talk when she get on the phone."

The best teaching approach seems to be to focus on understanding the children and accepting their dialects as valid and correct language systems, but to teach formal English (or whatever the dominant language is in your country) as an alternative. Learning formal speech is easy for most children whose original language is a dialect, as long as they have good models. How can teachers cope with linguistic diversity in the classroom? First, they can be sensitive to their own possible negative stereotypes about children who speak a different dialect. Second, principals and teachers can ensure comprehension by repeating instructions using different words and by asking students to paraphrase instructions or give examples. The *Theory into Action Guidelines* give more ideas.

THEORY INTO ACTION GUIDELINES

Dialects

1. Become familiar with features of the students' dialect. This will allow you to understand students better and to distinguish a reading miscue (a noncomprehension feature) from a comprehension error. Students should not be interrupted during the oral reading process. Correction of comprehension features is best done after the reading segment.

2. Allow students to listen to a passage or story first. This can be done in two ways: (a) finish the story and then ask comprehension questions, or (b) interrupt the story at key comprehension segments and ask students to predict the outcome.

3. Use predictable stories, which can be familiar episodes in literature, music, or history. They can be original works or experiential readings.

4. Use visual aids to enhance comprehension. Visual images, whether pictures or words, will aid word recognition and comprehension.

5. Use "cloze procedure" deletions to focus on vocabulary and meaning. Cloze procedures are selected deletions of words from a passage in order to focus on a specific text feature. *Examples:* (a) The little red hen found an ear of corn. The little red _____ said, "Who will dry the ear of _____?" (vocabulary focus) (b) Today I feel like a (*noun*). (grammar focus) (c) There was a (*pain*) in the pit of his stomach. (semantic focus)

6. Allow students to retell the story or passage in various speech styles. Have students select different people to whom they would like to retell the story (family member, principal, friend), and assist them in selecting synonyms most appropriate to each audience. This allows both teacher and student to become language authorities.

7. Integrate reading, speaking, and writing skills whenever possible.

8. Use the computer (if available) as a time-on-task exercise. The microcomputer can effectively assist in teaching the reading techniques of skimming (general idea), scanning (focused reference), reading for comprehension (mastery of total message), and critical reading (inference and evaluation).

9. Teach students directly how to switch between home and school dialects.

10. Give practice with feedback and correction in using school dialect. All learning takes practice.

Source: Adapted from Comprehensive multicultural education: Theory and practice, 6th Edition, by Christine I. Bennett. Copyright © 1990 by Pearson Education, Inc. Printed and Electronically reproduced by permission of Pearson Education, Inc., Upper Saddle River, New Jersey.

Bilingualism.   As we are writing these words, we have just returned from an international conference on learning and instruction. We listened to researchers from Finland, France, Spain, Italy, Cyprus, Turkey, Belgium, the Netherlands, and Germany describe their work in near perfect English and then speak to others in their native language. We felt lucky that English was the conference language and also a bit limited that we speak *only* English. Many people are truly **bilingual;** they learn two languages simultaneously while they are growing up. In fact, the United States is "one of the few countries in the world that takes pride in the fact that we speak only one language" (Noguera, 2005, p. 13).

Benefits of Bilingualism.   There is no cognitive penalty for children who learn and speak two languages. In fact, there are benefits. Higher degrees of bilingualism are correlated with increased cognitive abilities in such areas as concept formation, creativity, and cognitive flexibility. In addition, these children have more advanced awareness about language; for example, they are more likely to notice grammar errors. These findings seem to hold as long as there is no stigma attached to being bilingual and children are not expected to abandon their first language to learn the second (Bialystok, 2001; Bialystok, Majumder, & Martin, 2003; Galambos & Goldin-Meadow, 1990; Hamers & Blanc, 2000; Ricciardelli, 1992). In addition, speaking two languages is an asset for those graduates entering the business world (Mears, 1998).

If you mastered your own first language, then added a second or third language, you are an example of *additive bilingualism*—you kept your first language and added another. But if you lost your first language when you added a second one, you experienced *subtractive bilingualism* (Norbert, 2005). Even though the advantages of bilingualism seem clear, many children and adults are losing their **heritage language** (Montrul, 2010)—the language spoken in a student's home or by older relatives when the larger society outside the home speaks a different language. In many countries, there are schools that focus on retaining heritage languages and cultures. Students attend these schools afternoons, weekends, or summers in addition to their regular public school (Creese, 2009).

The topic of bilingualism sparks heated debates and touches many emotions. One reason is the changing demographics mentioned earlier in this chapter. In the United States, from 1995 to 2005, there was an almost 100% increase in the number of students who speak Asian languages and a 65% increase in the number of Spanish-speaking students. In fact, the United States has the fifth largest Spanish-speaking population in the world (Lessow-Hurley, 2005). The states with the largest number of English learners are Texas, California, Florida, New York, and Illinois, but numbers are surging in the Midwest, South, Nevada, and Oregon (Peregoy & Boyle, 2009). As a principal, you should be aware that there are a number of misconceptions about becoming bilingual; see Table 2.2 for a few.

Second Language Learning.   Proficiency in a second language has two separate aspects: face-to-face communication (known as *basic* or *contextualized language skills*) and academic uses of language such as reading and doing grammar exercises (known as *academic English*) (Fillmore & Snow, 2000; Garcia, 2002). **Academic language** is the entire range of language used in elementary, secondary, and university level schools. Academic language includes the general words and concepts used in many subjects such as *analyze, evaluate,* or *summarize,* as well as words and strategies specific to disciplines such as *angle, factor the equation,* or *derivative* in math, a *factor* in statistics, or a *derivative* in finance (you see how complicated this gets when the same word has two very different meanings in different fields). Academic language is associated with abstract, higher-order, complex concepts (Vogt, Echevarria, & Short, 2010).

Two other terms that you will see associated with bilingualism are **English language learners (ELLs),** describing students whose primary or heritage language

TABLE 2.2   Myths about Bilingual Students

In the following table, L1 means the original language and L2 means the second language.

Myth	Truth
Learning a second language (L2) takes little time and effort.	Learning English as a second language takes 2–3 years for oral and 5–7 years for academic language use.
All language skills (listening, speaking, reading, writing) transfer from L1 to L2.	Reading is the skill that transfers most readily.
Code switching is an indication of a language disorder.	Code switching indicates high-level language skills in both L1 and L2.
All bilinguals easily maintain both languages.	It takes great effort and attention to maintain high-level skills in both languages.
Children do not lose their first language.	Loss of L1 and underdevelopment of L2 are problems for second language learners (semilingual in L1 and L2).
Exposure to English is sufficient for L2 learning.	To learn L2, students need to have a reason to communicate, access to English speakers, interaction, support, feedback, and time.
To learn English, students' parents need to speak only English at home.	Children need to use both languages in many contexts.
Reading in L1 is detrimental to learning English.	Literacy-rich environments in either L1 or L2 support development of necessary prereading skills.
Language disorders must be identified by tests in English.	Children must be tested in both L1 and L2 to determine language disorders.

Source: Table From *The Hispanic child: Speech, language, culture and education,* 1st edition, by Alejandro E. Brice. Copyright © 2002 by Pearson Education, Inc. Printed and Electronically reproduced by permission of Pearson Education, Inc., Upper Saddle River, New Jersey.

is not English, and **English as a second language (ESL)** classrooms where these students learn English. The *Principal's Perspective* tells how a real principal improved reading instruction in her school for ELL students.

A Principal's Perspective

D. R. served approximately 720 students in preschool through 4th grades, including 65 students with special needs and a widely diverse population of ESL students. Even before the No Child Left Behind mandates, there had been an ongoing district-wide goal to increase reading achievement scores at all grade levels and among all students. D. R. dedicated much of her first year as principal to carefully observing and evaluating her school's reading program. She was perplexed to find that while the students in general were making significant gains in reading achievement, subgroups of students, specifically those in ESL and special education programs, were lagging in their performance scores.

After meeting with teachers, she discovered an incompatibility in reading instruction for these students, referred to by Jim Shipley and associates (2000) as "random acts of improvement." Regular classroom teachers were trained in and used one particular research-based reading program while teachers of children with special needs used something different. The result was inconsistent and unsupported reading instruction for these children as they moved between their classroom and the resource room.

Without declaring one program superior to the other, the principal emphasized the need for consistency in reading instruction and clarified that all teachers in the school must teach the same reading strategies. Rather than retraining 45 classroom teachers already using an identical program, the most cost-effective and efficient decision was to train and support all special needs teachers in the predominant reading framework. Even though it is widely accepted that no one set of teaching techniques will be effective for every student, maintaining alignment in instruction and assessment is critical to the success of emergent readers, especially those moving between regular and resource classrooms.

For more ideas, see the following resources:

Shipley, J., & Wescott, M. C. (2000). *Systems check: School improvement resource guide.* Seminole, FL: Jim Shipley & Associates.

Literacy Collaborative at the Ohio State University. www.lcosu.org/

Research on Bilingual Programs.   It is difficult to separate politics from practice in the debate about bilingual education. It is clear that high-quality bilingual education programs can have positive results. Students improve in the subjects taught in their native languages, in their mastery of English, and in self-esteem as well (Francis, Lesaux, & August, 2006; Gersten, 2006). ESL programs seem to have positive effects on reading comprehension (Proctor, August, Carlo, & Snow, 2006; Vaughn et al., 2006). But attention today is shifting from a debate about general approaches to a focus on effective teaching strategies. As you will see many times in this book, the combination of clarity of learning goals, direct instruction in needed skills (including phonics, vocabulary, comprehension and story retelling, learning strategies and tactics), teacher- or peer-guided practice leading to independent practice, authentic and engaging tasks, interactions and conversations that are academically focused, and warm encouragement from the teacher seems to be effective. If both languages can be integrated into the classroom, ELL students may participate more actively, learn English faster, and be less frustrated (Crawford, 1996; Gersten, 1996b; Vaughn et al., 2006). See the *Theory into Action Guidelines* for ideas to improve your teaching of English language learners.

Cultural Diversity

There are many definitions of *culture*. Most include some or all of the following: the knowledge, skills, rules, norms, practices, traditions, self-definitions, institutions (educational, legal, communal, religious, political, etc.), language, and values that shape and guide beliefs and behavior in a particular group of people as well as the art, literature,

THEORY INTO ACTION GUIDELINES

Promoting Learning and Language Acquisition

Provide structures, frameworks, scaffolds, and strategies.

Examples
1. "Think aloud" as you solve a problem by building on and clarifying the input of students.
2. Use visual organizers, story maps, or other aids to help students organize and relate information.

Teach relevant background knowledge and key vocabulary concepts.

Examples
1. Informally assess students' current background knowledge. Directly teach needed information, if missing.
2. Focus on key vocabulary words and use those words consistently.

Give focused and useful feedback.

Examples
1. Focus feedback on meaning, not grammar, syntax, or pronunciation.
2. Give frequent, brief, clear feedback—use words from the student's first language when you can.
3. Make sure to let students know when they are successful.

4. Break assignments and activities into smaller, "bite-sized pieces" with feedback after each "bite."

Keeps students involved and engaged.

Examples
1. Use small group and pairs work.
2. Create situations where students talk at length.
3. Challenge students with clear higher-order questions—allow time to think and write out answers, maybe in pairs.

Show authentic respect for students' culture and language.

Examples
1. Learn about your students' personal and language background: What languages are spoken at home? When did the family arrive? How long have they lived in the United States? What schooling did they receive in other countries?
2. Learn about the students' religious background, food preferences and restrictions, and family customs; then incorporate students' experiences into writing and language arts activities.
3. Learn some key words in the students' languages.
4. View diversity as an asset; reject cultural deficit notions.

Sources: Based on *Reading, writing, and learning in ESL: A resource book for teaching K-12 English learners,* 5th Edition, by S. F. Peregoy and O. F. Boyle. Allyn & Bacon, 2009; *Sheltered content instruction: Teaching English learners with diverse abilities,* 4th Edition, by J. Echevarria and A. Graves. Pearson, 2011; and "Literacy instruction for language-minority students: The transition years" by R. Gersten, from *The Elementary School Journal,* January 1996, Volume 96(3). University of Chicago Press.

---

folklore, and artifacts produced and passed down to the next generation (Cohen, 2009, 2010; Pai & Alder, 2001). The group creates a culture—a program for living—and communicates the culture to members. Even symptoms of psychological disorders are affected by culture. In industrialized cultures where cleanliness is emphasized, people with obsessive-compulsive disorders often become obsessed with cleaning their hands, whereas in Bali, where social networks are emphasized, people with obsessive-compulsive disorders often become obsessed with knowing all the details about the lives of their friends and family—their social network (Lemelson, 2003).

Cultural groups can be defined along regional, ethnic, religious, racial, gender, social class, or other lines. Each of us is a member of many groups, so we all are influenced by many different cultures. Sometimes the influences are incompatible or even contradictory. For example, if you are a feminist but also a Roman Catholic, you might have trouble reconciling the two different cultures' beliefs about the ordination of women as priests. Your personal belief on the issue will be based, in part, on how strongly you identify with each group (Banks, 1997, 2002). Each person is a unique product of many influences, a member of a variety of groups.

The United States truly is a diverse society. By the year 2020, almost two-thirds of the school-age population will be from African American, Asian, Latina/Latino, or other ethnic groups (Meece & Kurtz-Costes, 2001). Many of these children will be immigrants. *Immigrants* voluntarily leave their country to become permanent residents in a new place. People from Mexico are the largest U.S. immigrant group (Okagaki, 2006). *Refugees* are a special group of immigrants who also relocate voluntarily, but they are fleeing their home country because it is not safe. The United States requires that individuals seeking refugee status have "a well-founded fear of persecution on account of race, religion, nationality, membership in a particular social group, or political opinion" (U.S. Citizenship and Immigration Services, 2011). Since 1975, more than 3,000,000 refugees have permanently resettled in the United States, half of them children (Refugee Council USA, 2011).

Today some researchers include another kind of immigrant, sometimes called **Generation 1.5** because their characteristics, educational experiences, and language fluencies are somewhere in between those of students born in the United States and students who are recent immigrants (Gonzalez, 2010). They were not born in the United States, but have lived here most of their lives because they came with their families when they were young. The language spoken in their homes may not be English, but they often speak fluent conversational English, even if their academic English is not as well developed. Actually, there are several kinds of Generation 1.5 students:

- Students from United States territories such as Puerto Rico, Guam, or American Samoa.
- Children who were brought to the United States before they were adolescents.
- Children who are sent by their often-wealthy parents to live in the United States in order to receive an education. These so called "parachute children" are often from South Korea, Taiwan, Singapore, or Hong Kong and some have been targets for kidnapping and ransom attempts (Lelyverld, 1999).
- Children of families who move back and forth between different countries.
- Immigrants from Jamaica, Nigeria, India, or Singapore who speak other "Englishes."

These students may share several characteristics and challenges. They may not have developed strong literacy skills in the language used at home because their schooling was not in that language. They may have acquired much of their English through listening to and speaking with friends or older siblings, watching television, or listening to music. They have been called *"ear learners"* because they have built their knowledge of English on the language they have heard in their environment. But what they hear is often colloquial language or slang, so they may have trouble learning how to read and write accurately in English. Many of us know whether the grammar is correct in what we hear or read because we have heard (mostly) accurate grammar all our lives—our ears have taught us well.

But for many Generation 1.5 students, ear learning has given them an imperfect, even inaccurate conception of English grammar. Because they are "ear learners," they may use incorrect verb or noun forms, mispronounce plurals, or mix up words that sound very similar, for example, *confident* and *confidence*. They rely on context, gestures, facial cues, and intonations to make sense of language, so reading is more difficult and proofreading is hard because they cannot "hear" mistakes. Complex academic reading and writing assignments are very challenging (Harklau, Losey, & Siegal, 1999; Reid & Byrd 1998; Roberge, 2002).

In contrast, many of our international graduate students who learned English mostly as *"eye learners"* through reading, writing, and vocabulary and grammar exercises can write well, but they have more difficulty with oral interactions. Knowing what kind of students are in your school and how they first learned English should help you and your teachers understand the mistakes they make and the challenges they face.

We have touched on a wide range of differences in this chapter. How can schools provide an appropriate education for all their students? One response is to make classrooms compatible with students' cultural heritage. Such a classroom is described as being *culturally compatible* or *culturally inclusive*.

Creating Culturally Inclusive Classrooms

Rosa Hernandez Sheets (2005) uses the term *culturally inclusive* to describe classrooms that provide culturally diverse students equitable access to the teaching–learning process. The goal of creating **culturally inclusive classrooms** is to eliminate racism, classism, and prejudice while adapting the content and methods of instruction to meet the needs of all students. Almost 25 years ago, Roland Tharp (1989) outlined three dimensions of classrooms—social organization, learning styles, and participation structures—that can be tailored to adapt the classroom to the needs of students.

Social Organization

Tharp (1989) states that "a central task of educational design is to make the organization of teaching, learning, and performance compatible with the social structures in which students are most productive, engaged, and likely to learn" (p. 350). Social structure or social organization in this context means the ways people interact to accomplish a particular goal. For example, the social organization of Hawaiian society depends heavily on collaboration and cooperation. Children play together in groups of friends and siblings, with older children often caring for the younger ones. When cooperative work groups of four or five boys and girls were established in Hawaiian classrooms, student learning and participation improved (Okagaki, 2001; 2006). The teacher worked intensively with one group while the children in the remaining groups helped each other. But when the same structure was tried in a Navajo classroom, students would not work together. These students are socialized to be more solitary and not to play with the opposite sex. By setting up same-sex working groups of only two or three Navajo students, teachers encouraged them to help each other. If you have students from several cultures, you may need choices and variety in grouping structures.

Tharp's (1989) second classroom dimension that can be tailored to students is learning style—a topic that requires critical analysis.

Learning Styles

To look at **learning styles,** let's consider what Sheets (2005) has to say about teachers who design culturally inclusive classrooms. These teachers (1) recognize the various ways all their students display their capabilities—their cultural *practices* and *values;* (2) respond to students' *preferred styles of learning;* and (3) understand that a particular group's cultural practices, values, and learning preferences *may not apply* to everyone in that group.

Cultural Practices and Values.   Results of some research suggest that Hispanic American students are more oriented toward family and group loyalty. This may mean that these students prefer cooperative activities and dislike being made to compete with fellow students (Garcia, 1992; Vasquez, 1990). Four values shared by many Hispanic students (not all—remember Sheets' third characteristic above) are:

> **Familismo**—tightly knit families. Discussing family problems or business outside the family may be seen as disloyal.
>
> **Simpatia**—value of interpersonal harmony. Assertively voicing personal opinions or arguing may be seen as inappropriate.
>
> **Respecto**—respect for people in authority.
>
> **Personalismo**—valuing of close interpersonal relationships; discomfort with distant, cold, professional relationships. (Dingfelder, 2005)

Cultural Differences in Learning Styles.   Learning styles are preferred ways of learning and processing information. The learning styles of many African Americans may be inconsistent with teaching approaches in most schools. Some of the characteristics of this learning style are a visual/global rather than a verbal/analytic approach; a preference for reasoning by inference rather than formal logic; a focus on people and relationships; a preference for energetic involvement in several activities simultaneously rather than routine, step-by-step learning; a tendency to approximate numbers, space, and time; and a greater dependence on nonverbal communication. Students of color who identify with their traditional cultures tend to respond to open-ended questions with more than one answer, as opposed to single, "right" answer questions. Questions that focus on meaning or the "big picture" may be more productive than questions that focus on details (Bennett, 1999; Gay, 2000; Sheets, 2005).

Native Americans also appear to have a more global, visual style of learning. For example, Navajo students prefer hearing a story all the way through to the end before discussing parts of the story. Teachers who stop to ask questions seem odd to these students and interrupt their learning process (Tharp, 1989). Also, these students sometimes show strong preferences for learning privately, through trial and error, rather than having their mistakes made public (Vasquez, 1990).

There has been little research on the learning styles of Asian Americans, perhaps because they are seen as "successful minorities." Some educators suggest that Asian children tend to value teacher approval and to work well in structured, quiet learning environments where there are clear goals and social support (Manning & Baruth, 1996). Other research suggests that there are clear and deep differences in Asian and Western styles of learning. Students from Asian cultures tend be more interdependent and to value learning with others, which might explain some of their success in school. Western values emphasize independence and individual learning, which might explain some of the United States' successes in science, technology, and innovation (Chang et al., 2011). But there are dangers in stereotyping Asian and Asian American students as quiet, hardworking, and passive.

Individual Learning Styles and Preferences.   Since the late 1970s, a great deal has been written about differences in students' **learning preferences** (Dunn & Dunn, 1978, 1987; Dunn & Griggs, 2003; Gregorc, 1982; Keefe, 1982). Learning preferences are often called *learning styles* in these writings, but we believe *preferences* is a more accurate label because it describes preferences for particular learning environments— for example, where, when, with whom, or with what lighting, food, or music you like to study. There are a number of instruments for assessing students' learning preferences: *Learning Style Inventory* (Dunn, Dunn, & Price, 1989), *Learning Styles Inventory* (Kolb, 1985), and the *Learning Style Profile* (Keefe & Monk, 1986). Are these useful tools? The answer is not simple, as you can see in the *Point/Counterpoint* on the next page.

Misuses and Uses of Learning Styles Research.   In considering this research on learning styles, particularly in relation to cultural groups, you should keep two points in mind. First, the validity of some of the learning styles research has been strongly questioned, as we saw in the *Point/Counterpoint*. Second, there is a heated debate today about whether identifying ethnic group differences in learning styles and preferences is a dangerous racist, sexist exercise. In our society we are quick to move from the notion of "difference" to the idea of "deficits" and stereotypes. If used with caution and common sense, these general guidelines can help teachers be more sensitive to individual and group differences. It is dangerous and incorrect, however, to assume that every individual in a group shares the same learning style. Get to know your students as individuals.

Tharp's (1989) third classroom dimension that can be tailored to students is participation structures.

| POINT/COUNTERPOINT | Should Teachers Focus on Students' Learning Styles? |

POINT

Teaching to different learning styles has no strong research basis.

Tests of learning style have been strongly criticized for lacking evidence of reliability and validity (Krätzig & Arbuthnott, 2006; Pashler, McDaniel, Rohrer, & Bjork, 2009; Wintergerst, DeCapua, & Itzen, 2001). In fact, in an extensive examination of learning styles instruments, researchers at the Learning Skills Research Centre in England concluded, "With regard to Dunn and Dunn (Section 3.2), Gregorc (Section 3.1) and Riding (Section 4.1), our examination of the reliability and validity of their learning style instruments strongly suggests that they should not be used in education or business" (Coffield et al., 2004, p. 127).* In addition, in two experimental studies that assessed college students' visual, auditory, and kinesthetic learning styles and then matched teaching to style, the results were clear. The students used general beliefs and memories—not specific, accurate experiences—to diagnose their learning style. Second, their self-assessed style did not correlate with their performance (Krätzig & Arbuthnott, 2006). If college students have trouble identifying their own learning style, think about 4th or 9th graders!

In summary, the most recent review of learning styles research ends with these words: "The contrast between the enormous popularity of the learning-styles approach within education and the lack of credible evidence for its utility is, in our opinion, striking and disturbing. If classification of students' learning styles has practical utility, it remains to be demonstrated" (Pashler et al., 2009, p. 117). So why are these ideas so popular? Part of the answer is that many thriving commercial companies are making large profits by providing advice to teachers, tutors, and managers about learning styles based on "inflated claims and sweeping conclusions which go beyond the current knowledge base" (Coffield et al., 2004, p. 127).* Money talks.

COUNTERPOINT

Some differences in learning styles do matter.

There is one learning styles distinction that has research support. Richard Mayer (e.g., Mayer & Massa, 2003) has been studying the distinction between visual and verbal learners, with a focus on learning from computer-based multimedia. He is finding that there is a visualizer–verbalizer dimension and that it has three facets: *cognitive spatial ability* (low or high), *cognitive style* (visualizer vs. verbalizer), and *learning preference* (verbal learner vs. visual learner), as shown in Table 2.3.

Source: Learning styles and pedagogy in post-16 learning by Frank Coffield, et al. Learning and Skills Research Centre, 2004.

TABLE 2.3   Three Facets of the Visualizer–Verbalizer Dimension

Facet	Types of learners	Definition
Cognitive ability	High spatial ability	High proficiency in creating, holding, and manipulating spatial representations.
	Low spatial ability	Low proficiency in creating, holding, and manipulating spatial representations.
Cognitive style	Visualizer	Uses visual modes of thinking.
	Verbalizer	Uses verbal modes of thinking.
Learning preference	Visual learner	Prefers instruction involving pictures.
	Verbal learner	Prefers instruction involving words.

Source: "Three facets of visual and verbal learners: Cognitive ability, cognitive style, and learning preference" by Richard E. Mayer and Laura J. Massa, from *Journal of Educational Psychology*, December 2003, Volume 95(4): pp. 833–846. American Psychological Association. Reprinted with permission.

So the issue is more complex than a person simply being a visual or a verbal learner. A student might have a preference for learning with pictures, but low spatial ability could make using pictures to learn less effective. These differences can be reliably measured, but research has not identified the effects of teaching to these styles; certainly, presenting information in multiple modalities might be useful.

Schools can make learning options available. Having quiet, private corners as well as large tables for working; comfortable cushions as well as straight chairs; brightly lighted desks along with darker areas; headphones for listening to music as well as earplugs; structured as well as open-ended assignments; information available on films and CDs as well as in books. All these options will allow students to work and learn in their preferred mode at least some of the time. Will making these alterations lead to greater learning? Here the answer is not clear. Very bright students appear to need less structure and to prefer quiet, solitary learning (Torrance, 1986) and the visual–verbal distinction seems to be valid, so be flexible and experiment to understand what works best for your students.

Participation Structures

The classroom is a special setting for communicating; it has its own set of rules for when, how, to whom, about what subject, and in what manner to use language. To be successful, students must know these communication rules. This is not such an easy task. As class activities change, rules change. Sometimes you have to raise your hand (during the teacher's presentation), but sometimes you don't (during storytime on the rug). Sometimes it is good to ask a question (during discussion), but other times it isn't so good (when the teacher is scolding you). The differing activity rules are called **participation structures.**

Some students are simply better than others at reading the classroom situation because the participation structures of school match the structures they have learned in their middle-class homes. These students often appear to be more competent because they know the unwritten rules. Students from different cultural backgrounds may have learned participation structures that conflict with the behaviors expected in school. For example, one study found that the home conversation style of Hawaiian children is to chime in with contributions to a story. In school, however, this overlapping style is viewed as "interrupting." When the teachers in one school learned about these differences and made their reading groups more like their students' home conversation groups, the young Hawaiian children in their classes improved in reading (Au, 1980; Tharp, 1989). In another example, researchers found that Pueblo Indian students participated twice as much in classes where teachers waited longer to react. Waiting longer also helps girls to participate more freely in math and science classes (Grossman & Grossman, 1994).

Sources of misunderstanding can be very subtle. The families of racial and ethnic minority students often have to be vigilant about discrimination to protect their children. Teachers may unintentionally offend these families if they are not sensitive to possible messages of discrimination. Carol Orange (2005) described a teacher who sent home a holiday worksheet that featured an alphabetical list of all the students in the class. Three students' names were not in the typed list, but were handwritten, out of order, and on the side of the sheet. Two of these students were Latino and one was African American. The mother of the African American student was very upset that her son was truly "marginalized" (written in the margins) on the list. The reason was that those three students were added to the class later in the year, after the list was set up. But the teacher could have avoided this insult (unintended on her part) by redoing the list to give every student a place—a small but important symbol indicating that she valued each one of them.

What should principals and teachers do? Especially in the early grades, you and your teachers should make communication rules for activities clear and explicit. Do not assume students know what to do. Use cues to signal students when changes occur. Explain and demonstrate appropriate behavior. We have seen teachers show young children how to "talk in your inside voice" or "whisper so you won't disturb others." One teacher said and then demonstrated, "If you have to interrupt me while I'm working with other children, stand quietly beside me until I can help you."

Culturally Relevant Pedagogy

Over the last 25 years, several researchers have focused on teachers who are especially successful with students of color and students in poverty (Bennett, 1999; Delpit, 1995; Ladson-Billings, 1994, 1995; Moll, Amanti, Neff, & Gonzalez, 1992). For example, for three years Gloria Ladson-Billings (1990, 1992, 1995) studied excellent teachers in a California school district that served an African American community. Ladson-Billings (1995) was able to examine in depth eight of the nine teachers who were nominated by *both parents and principals*. Based on her research, she developed a **culturally relevant pedagogy** that encompasses but goes beyond considerations of sociolinguistics or social organizations to include three elements. Students must:

1. *Experience academic success*. No matter how limited the school resources are or how much bias they face in the larger society, students must develop skills in literacy, mathematics, social sciences, and technology. In addition, they must learn the social and political skills needed to be active, effective participants in our democratic society.
2. *Develop/maintain their cultural competence*. Even while learning to succeed in the larger society, students must not sacrifice their cultural capabilities and connections. For example, one teacher brought in a community expert known for her sweet potato pies to work with students. Follow-up lessons included investigations of George Washington Carver's sweet potato research, numerical analyses of taste tests, marketing plans for selling pies, and research on the educational preparation needed to become a chef.
3. *Develop a critical consciousness to challenge the status quo*. Excellent teachers help students recognize and effectively challenge inequities. For example, in one school students mobilized to investigate the funding formulas that allowed middle-class

students to have newer books, wrote letters to the newspaper editor to challenge these inequities, and updated their texts with current information from other sources.

Lisa Delpit (2003) describes three steps for teaching students of color that are consistent with culturally relevant pedagogy: (1) Teachers must be convinced of the "inherent intellectual capability, humanity, and spiritual character" (p. 20) of their students—they must believe in the children. There are many examples around the country of schools where low-income African American students are reading well above grade level and doing advanced math. When scores are low, the fault is not in the students but in their education. (2) Teachers must fight the foolish idea that test scores or scripted lessons make for good learning. Delpit says that successful instruction is "constant, rigorous, integrated across disciplines, connected to students' lived cultures, connected to their intellectual legacies, engaging, and designed for critical thinking and problem solving that is useful beyond the classroom" (p. 18). (3) Teachers must learn who their children are and understand the legacies they bring. Then students can explore their own intellectual legacies and understand the important reasons for academic, social, physical, and moral excellence—not just to get good grades or good jobs but also "for our community, for your ancestors, for your descendants" (p. 19).* In the past, discussions of teaching students from racial, ethnic, or language minority groups have focused on remediating problems or overcoming perceived deficits. But thinking today emphasizes teaching to the strengths and the resilience of these students. See the *Theory into Action Guidelines* on the next page for more ideas about creating culturally inclusive classrooms.

Gender Differences in the Classroom

The word *gender* usually refers to traits and behaviors that a particular culture judges to be appropriate for males and for females. Through their interactions with family, peers, teachers, and the environment in general, children begin to form **gender schemas,** or organized networks of knowledge about what it means to be male or female. These schemas help the children make sense of the world and guide their behavior. So a young girl whose schema for "girls" includes "girls play with dolls and not with trucks" or "girls can't be scientists" will pay attention to, remember, and interact more with dolls than trucks, and she may avoid science activities (Liben & Signorella, 1993; Martin & Little, 1990). In contrast to gender, *sex* refers to biological differences (Brannon, 2002; Deaux, 1993). Are there biological differences in mental abilities? Is gender discrimination a problem in schools? We will consider each question.

Differences in Mental Abilities

Only 23% of the scientists and engineers and just 10% of the physicists in the United States are women, even though women earn about half of the bachelor's degrees in chemistry, biology, and mathematics and about 20% of the bachelor's degrees in

*Sources: "Educators as 'seed people' growing a new future" by Lisa Delpit, from *Educational Researcher*, October 2003, Volume 7(32). Sage Publications, Inc.; and *SBA: The reawakening of the African mind* by Asa Hilliard. Makare Publishing Company, 1997.

THEORY INTO ACTION GUIDELINES

Culturally Inclusive Classrooms

Experiment with different grouping arrangements to encourage cooperation.

Examples

1. Try "study buddies" and pairs.
2. Organize heterogeneous groups of four or five.
3. Establish larger teams for older students.

Provide a variety of ways to learn material to accommodate a range of learning styles.

Examples

1. Give students verbal materials at different reading levels.
2. Offer visual materials—charts, diagrams, models.
3. Provide tapes for listening and viewing.
4. Set up activities and projects.

Teach classroom procedures directly, even ways of doing things that you think everyone will know.

Examples

1. Tell students how to get the teacher's attention.
2. Explain when and how to interrupt the teacher if students need help.
3. Show which materials students can take and which require permission.
4. Demonstrate acceptable ways to disagree with or challenge another student.

Learn the meaning of different behaviors for your students.

Examples

1. Ask students how they feel when you correct or praise them. What gives them this message?

2. Talk to family and community members and other teachers to discover the meaning of expressions, gestures, or other responses that are unfamiliar to you.

Emphasize meaning in teaching.

Examples

1. Make sure students understand what they read.
2. Try storytelling and other modes that don't require written materials.
3. Use examples that relate abstract concepts to everyday experiences; for instance, relate negative numbers to being overdrawn in your checkbook.

Get to know the customs, traditions, and values of your students.

Examples

1. Use holidays as a chance to discuss the origins and meaning of traditions.
2. Analyze different traditions for common themes.
3. Attend community fairs and festivals.

Help students detect racist messages.

Examples

1. Analyze curriculum materials for biases.
2. Make students "bias detectives," reporting comments from the media.
3. Discuss the ways that students communicate biased messages about each other and what should be done when this happens.
4. Discuss expressions of prejudice such as anti-Semitism.

For more ideas, see the Education Alliance at Brown University: www.alliance.brown.edu/tdl/tl-strategies/crt-principles.shtml

physics, computer science, and engineering (Hill, Corbett, & St. Rose, 2010). In contrast, several recent international *meta-analyses* (analyses that combine data from many different studies on the same topic) have found few differences in mathematics achievement for boys and girls. For example, Sara Lindberg and her colleagues analyzed data from 242 studies that included 1.3 million elementary through high school students. Overall, they found that in the United States and some other nations, girls' and boys' performance in mathematics is comparable, but there are some differences by nations—girls scored higher than boys in several countries such as Russia, Bahrain, and Mexico, and boys' scores were higher in other countries such as Switzerland, the Netherlands, and African nations (Else-Quest, Hyde, & Linn, 2010; Lindberg et al., 2010). Also, the International Comparisons in Fourth-Grade Reading Literacy (Mullis, Martin, Gonzalez, & Kennedy, 2003) revealed that in 34 countries, 4th grade boys scored below girls in reading literacy. Finally, girls in general tend to get higher grades than boys in mathematics classes. Are all these differences between males and females due to ability, interest, culture, social pressure, discrimination, or some other factor? Let's see if we can make sense of this issue.

From infancy through the preschool years, most studies find few differences between boys and girls in overall mental and motor development or in specific abilities. However, during the school years, scores on some tests of specific abilities show sex differences. For example, from elementary through high school, girls score higher than boys on tests of reading and writing, and fewer girls require remediation in reading (Halpern, 2000; Hyde, 2005; Lindberg, Hyde, Peterson, & Linn, 2010). But academically gifted boys in the United States perform better than girls on advanced mathematics tests. In 2001, twice as many boys as girls scored over 700 on the math SATs, but boys also were more likely than girls to get all the answers wrong (Angier & Chang, 2005). In fact, the scores of males tend to be more variable in general, so there are more males than females with very high *and* very low scores on tests (Berk, 2005; Willingham & Cole, 1997). There also are more boys than girls diagnosed with learning disabilities, attention deficit hyperactive disorder (ADHD), and autism. When Alfredo Ardila and his colleagues (2011) tested 788 children, age 5 to 16 from Mexico and Colombia, they found only a few small differences between boys and girls in the abilities tested. They concluded: ". . . gender differences during cognitive development are minimal, appear only on a small number of tests, and account for only a low percentage of the score variance" (p. 984).*

What is the basis for the differences? The answers are complex. For example, males on average are better on tests that require mental rotation of a figure in space, prediction of the trajectories of moving objects, and navigating. Some researchers argue that evolution has favored these skills in males (Buss, 1995; Geary, 1995, 1999), but others relate these skills to males' more active play styles, their greater experience with video games, and their participation in athletics (Else-Quest et al., 2010; Stumpf, 1995). Some educational psychologists believe that spatial skills are neglected in school curriculums and that even a small amount of instruction can make a big difference for students (Uttal, Hand, & Newcombe, 2009). The cross-cultural comparisons suggest that much of the difference in mathematics scores comes from learning, not biology. And studies showing that adults rated a math paper attributed to "John T. McKay" a full point higher on a 5-point scale than the same paper attributed to "Joan T. McKay" suggests that discrimination and stereotyped expectations play a role as well (Angier & Chang, 2005).

This brings us to our next question: Is gender discrimination a problem in schools?

*Source: "Gender differences in cognitive development" by Alfredo Ardila, et al., from *Developmental Psychology*, July 2011, Volume 47(4): pp. 984–990. American Psychological Association. Reprinted with permission.

Gender Discrimination in Classrooms

There has been quite a bit of research on teachers' treatment of male and female students. One of the best-documented findings of the past 30 years is that teachers interact more with boys than with girls. This is true from preschool to college. Teachers ask more questions of males, give males more feedback (praise, criticism, and correction), and provide more specific and valuable comments to boys. As girls move through the grades, they have less and less to say. By the time students reach college, men are twice as likely to initiate comments as women (Bailey, 1993; Sadker & Sadker, 2000; Wingate, 1986). The effect of these differences is that from preschool through college, girls on the average receive 1,800 fewer hours of attention and instruction than boys (Sadker, Sadker, & Klein, 1991). These differences are not evenly distributed. Some boys, generally high-achieving white students, receive more than their share. Minority-group boys, like girls, tend to receive much less attention from teachers.

Stereotypes are perpetuated in many ways, some obvious, some subtle. Guidance counselors, parents, and teachers often do not protest at all when a bright girl says she doesn't want to take any more math or science courses, but when a boy of the same ability wants to forget about math or science, they will object (Sadker & Sadker, 2000). However, there are some aspects of school that may be biased against boys. For example, following rules and being neat are rewarded, and these behaviors are more often associated with girls. In addition, a majority of elementary teachers are women (DeZolt & Hull, 2001). It is a challenge to make schools responsive to both males and females. The *Theory into Action Guidelines* provide ideas for your school about how to avoid sexism.

Sexual Identity

Sexual identity includes gender identity, gender-role behaviors, and sexual orientation (Ruble, Martin, & Berenbaum, 2006). *Gender identity* is a person's self-identification as male or female. *Gender-role behaviors* are those behaviors and characteristics that the culture associates with each gender, and *sexual orientation* involves the person's choice of a sexual partner. Relations among these three elements are complex. For example, a woman may identify herself as a female (gender identity), but behave in ways that are not consistent with the gender role (play football), and may be heterosexual, bisexual, or homosexual in her orientation. So sexual identity is a complicated construction of beliefs, attitudes, and behaviors.

Sexual Orientation.   During adolescence, about 8% of boys and 6% of girls report engaging in some same-sex activity or feeling strong attractions to individuals of their own sex. Males are more likely than females to experiment with same-sex partners as adolescents, but females are more likely to experiment later, often in college. Fewer adolescents actually have a homosexual or bisexual orientation—about 4% of adolescents identify themselves as gay (males who choose male partners), lesbian (females who choose female partners), or bisexual (people who have partners of both sexes). This number increases to between 5% and 13% for adults (Savin-Williams, 2006).

THEORY INTO ACTION GUIDELINES

Avoiding Sexism

Check to see if textbooks and other materials you are using present an honest view of the options open to both males and females.

Examples

1. Are both males and females portrayed in traditional and nontraditional roles at work, at leisure, and at home?
2. Discuss your analyses with teachers, and ask "Do you find sex role biases in other materials—magazine advertising, TV programs, news reporting?" for example.

Watch for any unintended biases in your teachers' classroom practices.

Examples

1. Do teachers group students by sex for certain activities? Is the grouping appropriate?

2. Do teachers call on one sex or the other for certain answers—boys for math and girls for poetry, for example?

Look for ways in which your school may be limiting the options open to male or female students.

Examples

1. What advice is given by guidance counselors to students in course and career decisions?
2. Is there a good sports program for both girls and boys?

For lessons that identify sexism in schools, see www.tolerance.org/teach/activities/activity.jsp?ar=299

Scientists debate the origins of homosexuality. Most of the research has been with men, so less is known about women. Evidence so far suggests that both biological and social factors are involved. For example, sexual orientation is more similar for identical twins than for fraternal twins, but not all identical twins have the same sexual orientation (Ruble et al., 2006).

There are quite a few models describing the development of sexual orientation as part of identity. Generally, the models include the following or similar stages (Yarhouse, 2001):*

- *Feeling different*—Beginning around age 6, the child may be less interested in the activities of other children who are the same sex. Some children may find this difference troubling and fear being "found out." Others do not experience these anxieties.
- *Feeling confused*—In adolescence, as they feel attractions to peers of the same sex, students may be confused, upset, lonely, and unsure of what to do. They may lack role models and may try to change themselves by becoming involved in activities and dating patterns that fit heterosexual stereotypes.

Sources: Based on *Development through the lifespan*, 4th Edition, by Laura E. Berk. Allyn & Bacon, 2007; and "Sexual identity development: The influence of valuative frameworks on identity synthesis" by Mark A. Yarhouse, from *Psychotherapy*, 2001, Volume 38(3). American Psychological Association.

■ *Acceptance*—As young adults, many individuals sort through sexual orientation issues and identify themselves as gay, lesbian, or bisexual. They may or may not make their sexual orientation public, but might share the information with a few friends.

The problem with phase models of identity development is that the identity achieved is assumed to be final. Actually, newer models emphasize that sexual orientation can be flexible, complex, and multifaceted; it can change over the lifetime. For example, individuals may have dated or married opposite-sex partners at one point in their lives, but have same-sex attractions or partners later in their lives, or vice versa (Garnets, 2002).

Teachers and administrators are seldom the first people to hear about the adolescent's sexual identity concerns. But if a student does seek you out, Table 2.4 has some ideas for reaching out.

TABLE 2.4   Reaching Out to Help Students with Questions on Sexual Orientation and Gender Identity

These ideas derive from The Attic Youth Center's training and education program, The James H. Bryson Institute, that provides educational workshops to youth and youth-service providers on creating safe, affirming, and respectful spaces for lesbian, gay, bisexual, transgender and questioning (LGBTQ) individuals.

Reaching Out

If a lesbian, gay, bisexual, or transgender youth or a youth questioning his or her own sexual orientation should come to you directly for assistance, remember the following simple, 5-point plan:

LISTEN It seems obvious, but the best thing that you can do in the beginning is allow that individual to vent and express what is going on in his or her life.

AFFIRM Tell them, "You are not alone."—this is crucial. A lot of LGBTQ youth feel isolated and lack peers with whom they can discuss issues around sexual orientation and gender identity. Letting them know that there are others dealing with the same questions is invaluable. This statement is also important because it does not involve a judgment call on your part.

REFER You do not have to be the expert. A referral to someone who is trained to deal with these issues can be a gift you are giving to that student, not a dismissal of responsibility.

ADDRESS Deal with harassers—do not overlook issues of verbal or physical harassment around sexual orientation and gender identity. It is important to create and maintain an environment where all youth feel safe, supported, and respected.

FOLLOW-UP Be sure to check in with the individual to see if the situation has improved and if there is anything further you may be able to do.

There are also some things that you as an individual can do to better serve LGBTQ youth and youth dealing with issues around sexual orientation and gender identity:

■ Work on your own comfortability around issues of sexual orientation and gender identity.

■ Get training on how to present information on sexual orientation and gender identity effectively.

■ Speak up—not just when you see an instance of harassment or violence, but also when you see a lack of services.

■ Dispel myths around sexual orientation and gender identity by researching updated information and sharing what you learn.

■ Challenge yourself to set aside your own personal biases to better serve students dealing with issues around sexual orientation and gender identity.

Source: Excerpt from a training handout created by The Attic Youth Center's Bryson Institute. Copyright © 2012 by The Attic Youth Center, Carrie E. Jacobs, and Kelly Kroehle. Reprinted with permission.

The most important individual differences for schools are the differences in students' academic abilities. These also are complex and often misunderstood. We turn to these differences in the next chapter.

Summary

Statistics point to increasing cultural diversity in American society. Everyone is a member of many cultural groups, defined in terms of geographic region, nationality, ethnicity, race, gender, social class, and religion. Membership in a particular group does not determine behavior or values but makes certain values and kinds of behavior more likely. Wide variations exist within each group. Compared to students in poverty, however, students of all ethnic groups from wealthier homes show higher average levels of achievement on test scores and stay in school longer. Nevertheless, many students at risk for academic failure survive and thrive when teachers and schools support resilience and self-efficacy.

Language differences among students include dialects, bilingualism, and culture-based communication styles. Dialects are not inferior languages and should be respected, but formal English should be taught for academic contexts. Bilingual students may have some degree of limitation in English proficiency, and also must often struggle with social adjustment problems relating to biculturalism. While there is much debate over how to help bilingual students master English, studies show it is best if they are not forced to abandon their first language. The more proficient students are in their first language, the faster they will learn the second. Mastering academic language skills in any new language takes five to seven years.

Culturally inclusive classrooms are free of racism, sexism, and ethnic prejudice and provide equal educational opportunities for all students. Dimensions of classroom life that can be modified to that end are social organization, learning-style formats, and participation structures. Teachers, however, should avoid stereotypes of culture-based learning styles and must not assume that every individual in a group shares the same style. Communication may break down in classrooms because of differences in sociolinguistic styles and skills. Teachers can directly teach appropriate participation structures and be sensitive to culture-based communication rules. To help create compatible multicultural classrooms, teachers must know and respect all their students, have high expectations of them, and teach them what they need to know to succeed. Culturally relevant pedagogy ensures that students experience academic challenge and success, maintain their cultural competence, and develop a critical consciousness to challenge the status quo.

Learning preferences are individual preferences for particular learning modes and environments. Some of the most promising research is on verbalizer versus visualizer learning approaches. Even though cognitive styles and learning preferences are not related to intelligence or effort, they may affect school performance; however, not all measures of learning styles and preferences are valid or reliable. Beware.

Educational equity for females and males is also an issue. Research shows that gender-role stereotyping begins in the preschool years and continues through gender bias in the school curriculum and sex discrimination in the classroom. Teachers often unintentionally perpetuate these problems. Research on the causes of these differences has been inconclusive, except to indicate that academic socialization and teachers' treatment of male and female students in mathematics classes do play a role. Principals and teachers can use many strategies for reducing gender bias as well as providing support for students who are dealing with questions of sexual orientation.

KEY TERMS

academic language (38)
bilingual (37)
code switching (36)
culturally inclusive classroom (43)
culturally relevant pedagogy (48)
dialect (38)

English as a second language (ESL) (39)
English language learners (ELLs) (38)
gender schemas (49)
Generation 1.5 (42)

heritage language (38)
learning preferences (45)
learning styles (44)
participation structures (47)
resilience (32)
sexual identity (52)

DEVELOPING YOUR PORTFOLIO

1. Develop a plan for communicating with families of students who do not speak English at home. What kinds of information would you need to communicate to them? What information could they provide that would help you teach their children? What form would the communications take?

2. Develop a position statement and action plan on culturally relevant teaching. How could you support your teachers in examining and improving their practices? What are your expectations? What resources would you provide?

3. Devise a plan to determine if your school's STEM subjects (Science, Technology, Engineering, Mathematics) are attracting a representative number of girls and minority group students. If the numbers are lower than you want, develop an action plan addressing the problem.

INSTRUCTIONAL LEADER'S TOOLBOX

Readings

Educational Leadership. (2010, November). Special issue on "Closing opportunity gaps."
Educational Leadership. (2009, April). Special issue on "Supporting English language learners."
Educational Leadership. (2008, April). Special issue on "Poverty and learning."
Educational Leadership. (2006, September). Special section on teaching "With boys in mind," pp. 8–78.
Ladson-Billings, G. (1995). But that is just good teaching! The case for culturally relevant pedagogy. *Theory into Practice, 34,* 161–165.
Pashler, H., McDaniel, M., Rohrer, D., & Bjork, R. (2009). Learning styles: Concepts and evidence. *Psychological Science in the Public Interest, 9,* 105–119.

Phi Delta Kappan. (2011, March). Special section on "Educating rural and remote students."
Pogrow, S. (2006). Restructuring high-poverty schools for success: A description of the Hi-Perform school design. *Phi Delta Kappan, 88,* 223–229.

Websites

www.cln.org/
    Community Learning Network: a Canadian site with information on multiculturalism
www.edchange.org
    EdChange: Professional Development, Scholarship & Activism for Diversity, Social Justice & Community Growth

www.woodrow.org/teachers/math/gender/
   Modified Fennema-Sherman Attitude: assessment of attitudes toward mathematics

www.cln.org/subjects/mc.html
   Multicultural curriculum and instructional resources

http://mathforum.org/social/math.women.html
   Resources on Women and Mathematics

Organizations

www.al-anon.org
   Al-Anon/Alateen: This organization provides support for the family members of alcoholics.

www.csos.jhu.edu/crespar/index.htm
   Center for Research on the Education of Students Placed at Risk

www.nabe.org
   National Association for Bilingual Education

http://nlchp.org/
   National Law Center on Homelessness and Poverty

www.nmci.org/index.htm
   National Multicultural Institute: The mission of this institute is to increase knowledge, awareness, and respect among people of different racial, ethnic, and cultural backgrounds.

www.nn4youth.org/
   National Network for Youth

www.newhorizons.org
   New Horizons: Johns Hopkins University site that identifies and communicates successful strategies as a leading-edge web resource for educational practice.

www.researchtopractice.info/
   Research and Training Center on Early Childhood Development

http://spice.stanford.edu/
   Stanford Program on International and Cross-Cultural Education

CHAPTER

3

Student Abilities and Challenges

PREVIEW: KEY POINTS

1. Over the years there have been many theories about intelligence, but most current views emphasize abstract thinking, reasoning, and problem solving; some interpretations of intelligence emphasize multiple abilities, including emotional intelligence, whereas others stress the processes of analytical, creative, and practical thinking.

2. The Flynn effect is the observation that in industrialized countries, in a generation the average IQ scores go up about 18 points as measured by standardized IQ tests.

3. Grouping students by ability seems to be advantageous for high achievers, but approaches such as heterogeneous and cross-age grouping work better for other students.

4. Teachers are not always successful at identifying gifted students, but once they are identified, both acceleration and enrichment may be necessary to give highly gifted students an appropriate education.

5. Students may have different cognitive styles (preferred ways of processing information) and different learning preferences; the research on learning preferences is weak, but the visualizer–verbalizer style shows promise.

6. Approximately 3% to 5% of elementary school students have attention deficit hyperactive disorder (ADHD): boys are three to four times more likely than girls to be identified as hyperactive.

7. Legal changes since the mid-1970s have required regular teachers to be responsible for more students with learning and behavior problems; the largest group represented is students with learning disabilities.

8. To provide students with disabilities with the least restrictive placement and an individual educational program, the students may be taught in inclusive classrooms using collaborative or cooperative teaching models.

Leadership Challenge

Several of your teachers have asked to speak to you. They believe they are seeing a trend developing in the school. More than ever this year, or so it seems, parents are requesting that their children be tested for learning disabilities or assessed for 504 plans. In fact, the school psychologist is backlogged and behind by many months in completing scheduled tests. One of the teachers ventures an explanation for the sharp increase in testing requests. A group of parents has found out that children identified as having learning disabilities or eligible for Section 504 plans are allowed more time to complete standardized tests and have other accommodations, even for tests like the PSAT and SAT, that could open admission doors for them. But another teacher suggests that the flood of requests is more likely due to new policies that have resulted in better communications with families about the options available for their children. Whatever the reason, you are beginning to get calls from parents wondering what's with the delay on their testing requests.

- How would you proceed? Would you investigate to learn why there are so many new testing requests? How would you obtain this information?
- If you find out that some parents seem to want testing to give their children more time, what would you do?
- If the requests seem to be a result of better communications with families, how would you proceed?

The most important individual differences for schools are the differences in students' academic abilities and the challenges the students face. Intelligence is one of the most complex and misunderstood of the academic abilities.

Individual Differences in Intelligence

Because the concept of intelligence is so important in education, so controversial, and so often misunderstood, we will spend quite a few pages discussing it. Let us begin with a basic question: What is intelligence?

What Is Intelligence? Single, Multiple, Triarchic

The idea that people vary in what we call **intelligence** has been with us for a long time. Plato discussed similar variations over 2,000 years ago. Most early theories about the nature of intelligence involved one or more of the following three themes: (1) the capacity to learn; (2) the total knowledge a person has acquired; and (3) the ability to adapt successfully to new situations and to the environment in general. A recent definition captures these elements and stresses higher-order thinking: "the ability to reason deductively or inductively, think abstractly, use analogies, synthesize information, and apply it to new domains" (Kanazawa, 2010, p. 281).

Intelligence: One Ability or Many?   There are moderate to high correlations among all mental tests. In fact, this positive intercorrelation among scores for all cognitive tasks "is arguably both the best established and the most striking phenomenon in the psychological study of intelligence" (van der Mass et al., 2006, p. 855). What could explain these results? Charles Spearman (1927) suggested mental energy, which he called *g* or **general intelligence,** was used to perform any mental test, but each test also requires some specific abilities in addition to *g*. Today, psychologists generally agree that we can mathematically compute a common factor (*g*) across cognitive tests, but this computed factor is simply an indication or measure of general intelligence—it is not general intelligence itself (Kanazawa, 2010). But just having a mathematical indicator of intelligence isn't much help in understanding human abilities; the notion of *g* does not have much explanatory power (Blair, 2006).

Raymond Cattell and John Horn proposed a theory of fluid and crystallized intelligence that is more helpful in providing explanations (Cattell, 1987; Horn, 1998; Kanazawa, 2010). Sometimes people assume that fluid intelligence is process—the ability to learn—and crystallized intelligence is content—what you have learned. But it isn't quite that simple. **Fluid intelligence** is the mental efficiency and reasoning ability included in Kanazawa's definition of intelligence, quoted above. The neurophysiological underpinnings of fluid intelligence may be related to changes in brain volume, myelinization (coating of neural fibers that makes processing faster), the density of dopamine receptors, or processing abilities in the prefrontal lobe of the brain such as selective attention and especially *working memory* (Waterhouse, 2006), an aspect of brain functioning we will explore in Chapter 4. This aspect of intelligence increases until late adolescence (about age 22) because it is grounded in brain development, and then declines gradually with age. Fluid intelligence is sensitive to injuries and diseases.

In contrast, **crystallized intelligence** is the ability to apply the problem-solving methods appropriate in your cultural context—the "application to new domains" part of Kanazawa's definition of intelligence. Crystallized intelligence can increase throughout the life span because it includes learned skills and knowledge such as reading, facts, and how to hail a cab, make a quilt, or design a unit on symbolism in poetry. By investing fluid intelligence in solving problems, we develop our crystallized intelligence, but many tasks in life such as mathematical reasoning draw on both fluid and crystallized intelligence (Ferrer & McArdle, 2004; Finkel, Reynolds, McArdle, Gatz, & Pederson, 2003; Hunt, 2000).

In spite of the correlations among the various tests of different abilities, some psychologists insist that there are several separate mental abilities (Gardner, 1983; Guilford, 1988).

Multiple Intelligences.   While Howard Gardner was a developmental psychologist doing research with two very different groups—artistically gifted students at Harvard's Project Zero and patients with brain injuries at Boston's Veterans Administration Medical Center—he started thinking about a new theory of intelligence. Time and time again at the VA Medical Center, Gardner observed brain-injured patients who were lost spatially, but could do all kinds of verbal tasks, and other patients who had the opposite set of abilities and problems. He also worked with young children at Project Zero who could draw expertly but not craft a good sentence, and vice versa. Gardner concluded that there are several separate mental abilities, and developed his now-famous **theory of multiple intelligences** that describes at least eight separate intelligences (1983, 2003, 2009).

According to Gardner's (1983, 2003) theory of multiple intelligences (see Figure 3.1 on the next page), there are at least eight separate intelligences: linguistic (verbal), musical, spatial, logical-mathematical, bodily-kinesthetic (movement), interpersonal (understanding others), intrapersonal (understanding self), and naturalist (observing and understanding natural and human-made patterns and systems). Gardner stresses that there may be more kinds of intelligence—eight is not a magic number. He has speculated that there may be a spiritual intelligence or an existential intelligence or the ability to contemplate big questions about the meaning of life (Gardner, 2003). As Gardner witnessed firsthand in his early research with veterans and students, individuals may excel in one of these eight areas but have no remarkable abilities in the other seven.

What are these intelligences? Gardner believes that intelligence has a biological base. An intelligence is a "biopsychological potential to process information in certain ways in order to solve problems or create products that are valued in at least one culture or community" (Gardner, 2009, p. 5). Varying cultures and eras of history place different values on the eight intelligences. A naturalist intelligence is critical in farming cultures, whereas verbal and mathematical intelligences are important in technological cultures. In fact, Gardner suggests what industrialized cultures usually label as *intelligence* is just a combination of linguistic and logical mathematical skills, especially those taught in modern, secular schools (2009).

Multiple Intelligences Go to School.   An advantage of the multiple intelligences perspective is that it expands our thinking about abilities and avenues for teaching, but the theory has been misused. Some teachers embrace a simplistic version of Gardner's

FIGURE 3.1   Eight Intelligences
Howard Gardner's theory of multiple intelligences suggests that there are eight kinds of human abilities.
An individual might have strengths or weaknesses in one or several areas.

Logical-Mathematical	Linguistic
Skills: • Sensitivity to, and capacity to discern logical or numerical patterns. • Ability to handle long chains of reasoning. *Example/Career Paths:* Scientist Mathematician Engineer	*Skills:* • Sensitivity to sounds, rhythms, and word meanings. • Sensitivity to different functions of language. *Example/Career Paths:* Poet Journalist Novelist
Musical	**Spatial**
Skills: • Ability to appreciate and produce rhythm, tone, pitch, and timbre. • Appreciation of forms of musical expression. *Example/Career Paths:* Composer Pianist Drummer	*Skills:* • Ability to perceive the visual and spatial world accurately. • Ability to perform transformations on those perceptions. *Example/Career Paths:* Sculptor Navigator Architect
Interpersonal	**Intrapersonal**
Skills: • Ability to read the moods and motivations of others. • Ability to understand desires and needs of others and respond appropriately. *Example/Career Paths:* Therapist Salesperson Mediator	*Skills:* • Knowledge of your own strengths, weaknesses, capabilities, and needs and ability to use these to guide your behavior. • Access to your own feelings. *Example:* Anyone with detailed accurate knowledge of self
Naturalist	**Bodily-Kinesthetic**
Skills: • Ability to recognize plants and animals. • Ability use categories and systems to understand the natural world. *Example/Career Paths:* Farmer Gardener Animal tracker	*Skills:* • Ability to control body movements and know where your body is in space. • Ability to handle objects skillfully. *Example/Career Paths:* Dancer Gymnast Juggler

Sources: Based on "Multiple intelligences go to school," by H. Gardner and T. Hatch, *Educational Researcher*, *18*(8), 1989 and "Are there additional intelligences? The case for the naturalist, spiritual, and existential intelligences," by H. Gardner (1999) from *Educational information and transformation*. Edited by Jeffrey Kane. Prentice Hall, 1999.

theory. They include every "intelligence" in every lesson, no matter how inappropriate. A better way to use the theory is to focus on six Entry Points—narrative, logical-quantitative, aesthetic, experiential, interpersonal, and existential/foundational—in designing a curriculum (Gardner, 1991). For example, to teach about evolution, teachers might use the Entry Points as follows (Kornhaber, Fierros, & Veenema, 2004):

Narrative: Provide rich stories about Darwin's voyage to the Galapagos Islands or traditional folktales about the different plants and animals.

Logical-quantitative: Examine Darwin's attempts to map the distributions of the species or pose logical problems about what would happen to the ecosystem if one species disappeared.

Aesthetic: Examine Darwin's drawings of the species he studied on the Galapagos Islands.

Experiential: Do laboratory activities such as breeding fruit flies or completing virtual simulations of evolutionary processes.

Interpersonal: Form research teams or hold debates.

Existential/foundational: Consider questions about why species die out or the purpose for variation in species.*

Table 3.1 lists some other positive applications of Gardner's (1998) work, as well as some misuses.

*Adapted from "Entry points: A tool for developing curriculum," from *Multiple intelligences: Best ideas from research and practice*, 1st Edition, by Mindy Kornhaber, Edward Fierros and Shirley Veenema. Copyright © 2004 by Pearson Education, Inc. Printed and Electronically reproduced by permission of Pearson Education, Inc., Upper Saddle River, New Jersey.

TABLE 3.1   Misuses and Applications of Multiple Intelligence Theory

Howard Gardner has addressed some of the negative and positive applications of his theory.

Misuses:

1. **Trying to teach all concepts or subjects using all intelligences:** Gardner believes there is no point in trying to use every intelligence in teaching every lesson because it is a waste of time to develop all those approaches—apply those pathways that make sense.
2. **Assuming that it is enough just to apply a certain intelligence, no matter how you use it:** Just moving while you read will not guaranteed better understanding.
3. **Using an intelligence as a background for other activities**, such as playing music while students solve math problems. For many students, the sounds will distract or divide attention.
4. **Mixing intelligences with other desirable qualities:** There are many good reasons to use cooperative learning—saying that this approach develops interpersonal intelligence is not enough. Is cooperative learning a good way to reach your learning objectives?
5. **Direct evaluation or even grading of intelligences without regard to context:** Grade on learning—intelligence development should not be graded.

Good uses:

1. **The cultivation of desired capabilities:** Use the intelligences to think about and develop the skills and capabilities that are important and valuable in the students' culture and community.
2. **Approaching a concept, subject matter, discipline in a variety of ways:** Schools try to cover too much. Focus on key ideas, concepts, and skills and use an appropriate variety of approaches so every student can learn.
3. **The personalization of education:** The multiple intelligence perspective challenges all educators to take individual differences seriously and honor them in teaching.

Criticisms and Lessons

Gardner's multiple intelligences theory has not received wide acceptance in the scientific community. However, many educators and schools have embraced Gardner's ideas and believe that multiple intelligences practices increase student achievement, improve discipline, and encourage parent participation (Kornhaber, Fierros, & Veenema, 2004). But there is not yet strong research evidence that adopting a multiple intelligences approach will enhance learning. In one of the few carefully designed evaluations, Callahan, Tomlinson, and Plucker (1997) found no significant gains in either achievement or self-concept for students who participated in START, a multiple intelligences approach to identifying and promoting talent in students who were at risk of failing.

After 20 years of work on his multiple intelligences theory, Gardner (2009) believes two lessons are most important for teachers. First, teachers should take the individual differences among students seriously and differentiate their instruction to connect with each student. Much of this book will help you do just that. Second, any discipline, skill, or concept should be taught in several appropriate ways (but not eight ways every time). Anything worth knowing has different representations and multiple connections to various ways of thinking. And understandings can be expressed in words, images, movements, tables, charts, numbers, equations, poetry, and on and on. These two big ideas should *guide* educational interventions, but Gardner stresses that his theory is not itself an educational intervention. The MI theory expands our thinking about abilities and avenues for teaching, but learning is still hard work, even if there are multiple paths to knowledge.

Intelligence as a Process.   As you can see, the theories of Spearman and Gardner tend to describe how individuals differ in the content of intelligence—the different abilities. More recent work in cognitive psychology has emphasized instead the information processing that is common to all people. How do humans gather and use information to solve problems and behave intelligently? New views of intelligence are growing out of this work. For example, the debates in the 2006 issue of *Behavioral and Brain Sciences* emphasized working memory capacity and executive control processes such as the abilities to focus attention and inhibit impulses as aspects of fluid cognitive abilities.

Robert Sternberg's (1985, 2004, Stemler, Sternberg, Grigorenko, Jarvin, & Sharpes, 2009) **triarchic theory of successful intelligence** is a cognitive process approach to understanding intelligence. *Successful intelligence* includes "the skills and knowledge needed for success in life, according to one's own definition of success, within one's own sociocultural context" (Sternberg, 2004, p. 326). Sternberg prefers the term *successful intelligence* to stress that intelligence is more than what is tested by mental abilities measures: intelligence is about success in life. As you might guess from the name, this theory has three parts: analytic, creative, and practical. Analytic intelligence involves the mental processes of the individual that lead to more or less intelligent behavior. Some processes are specific; that is, they are necessary for only one kind of task, such as solving analogies. Other processes such as monitoring progress are very general and may be necessary in almost every cognitive task.

The second part of Sternberg's theory, creativity, involves coping with new experiences. Intelligent behavior is marked by two characteristics: (1) *insight*, or the ability to deal effectively with novel situations, and (2) *automaticity*, the ability to become efficient and automatic in thinking and problem solving. The third part, practical intelligence, highlights the importance of choosing an environment in which you can succeed, adapting to that environment, and reshaping it if necessary. People who are successful often seek situations in which their abilities will be valuable and then work hard to capitalize on those abilities and compensate for any weaknesses. Thus, intelligence in this third sense involves practical matters such as career choice or social skills (Grigorenko & Sternberg, 2001).

In recent years, Sternberg has added the concept of "wisdom" to his explanation of successful intelligence to create the *WICS theory* (Wisdom, Intelligence, Creativity Synthesized). According to WICS theory, the goal of education is to help citizens use: "(a) creativity to generate new ideas and problems as well as possible solutions to the problems, (b) analytical intelligence to evaluate the quality of these solutions, (c) practical intelligence to implement decisions and persuade others of their value, and (d) wisdom to ensure that these decisions help achieve a common good over the long and short terms" (Grigorenko et al., 2009, p. 965).*

Principals, teachers, and parents are most familiar with intelligence as a number or score on an IQ test. Let's next consider an important question.

What Does an IQ Score Mean?

Most intelligence tests are designed so that they have certain statistical characteristics. For example, the average score is 100. Fifty percent of the people from the general population who take the tests will score 100 or above, and 50% will score below 100. About 68% of the general population will earn IQ scores between 85 and 115. Only about 16% of the population will receive scores below 85, and only 16% will score above 115. Note, however, that these figures hold true for white, native-born Americans whose first language is standard English. Whether IQ tests should even be used with ethnic minority group students is hotly debated.

Group versus Individual IQ Tests. Individual intelligence tests (such as the Stanford-Binet or Wechsler Scales) have to be administered to one student at a time by a trained psychologist and take about two hours. Most of the questions are asked orally and do not require reading or writing. A student usually pays closer attention and is more motivated to do well when working directly with an adult. Psychologists also have developed group tests that can be given to whole classes or schools. Compared to an individual test, a group test is much less likely to yield an accurate picture of any one person's abilities. When students take tests in a group, they may do poorly because they do not understand the instructions, because their pencils break, because they are distracted by other students, or because they do not shine on paper-and-pencil tests. As an instructional leader, you should be very wary of IQ scores based on group tests. The *Theory into Action Guidelines* give ideas for helping teachers and parents interpret scores from intelligence tests.

Source: "Are SSATS and GPA enough? A theory-based approach to predicting academic success in secondary school" by Elena L. Grigorenko, et al., from *Journal of Educational Psychology,* November 2009, Volume 101(4): pp. 964–981. American Psychological Association. Reprinted with permission.

THEORY INTO ACTION GUIDELINES

Interpreting Intelligence Test Scores

Check to see if the score is based on an individual or a group test. Be wary of group test scores.

Examples

1. Individual tests include the Wechsler Scales (WPPSI-III, WISC-IV, WAIS-III), the Stanford-Binet, the McCarthy Scales of Children's Abilities, the Woodcock-Johnson Psycho-Educational Battery, the Naglieri Nonverbal Ability Test—Individual, and the Kaufman Assessment Battery for Children.

2. Group tests include the Otis-Lennon School Abilities Tests, Slosson Intelligence Test, Raven Progressive Matrices, Naglieri Nonverbal Ability Test—Multiform, Differential Abilities Scales, and Wide Range Intelligence Test.

Remember that IQ tests are only estimates of general aptitude for learning.

Examples

1. Ignore small differences in scores among students.

2. Bear in mind that even an individual student's scores may change over time for many reasons, including measurement error.

3. Be aware that a total score is usually an average of scores on several kinds of questions. A score in the middle or average range may mean that the student performed at the average on every kind of question or that the student did quite well in some areas (for example, on verbal tasks) and rather poorly in other areas (for example, on visual–spatial tasks).

Remember that IQ scores reflect a student's past experiences and learning.

Examples

1. Consider these scores as predictors of school abilities, not measures of innate intellectual abilities.

2. If a student is doing well in your school, do not change your opinion or lower your expectations just because one score seems low.

3. Be wary of IQ scores for minority students and for students whose first language was not English. Even scores on "culture-free" tests are lower for disadvantaged students.

The Flynn Effect: Are We Getting Smarter?   Ever since IQ tests were introduced in the early 1900s, scores in twenty different industrialized countries and some more traditional cultures have been rising (Daley, Whaley, Sigman, Espinosa, & Neumann, 2003). In fact, in a generation, the average score goes up about 18 points on standardized IQ tests—maybe you really are smarter than your parents! This is called the **Flynn effect** after James Flynn, a political scientist who documented the phenomenon. Some explanations include better nutrition and medical care for children and parents, increasing complexity in the environment that stimulates thinking, smaller families who give more attention to their children, increased literacy of parents, more and better schooling, and better preparation for taking tests. One result of the Flynn effect is the norms used to determine scores (more about norms in Chapter 8) have to be continually revised. In other words, to keep a score of 100 as the average, the test questions have to be made more difficult. This increasing difficulty has implications for any program that uses IQ scores as part of the entrance requirements. For example, students who were not identified as having intellectual disabilities a generation ago might be identified as disabled now because the test questions are harder (Kanaya, Scullin, & Ceci, 2003).

Intelligence and Achievement. Scoring higher on IQ tests is related to school achievement for children in all ethnic groups. But what about life after school? Do people who score high on IQ tests achieve more in life? Here the answer is less clear because life success and education are intertwined. High school graduates earn over $200,000 more than non-graduates in their lifetime; college graduates earn over $1,100,000 more; grads with doctoral degrees earn $2,400,000 more; and graduates with professional degrees (physicians, lawyers, etc.) earn over $3,400,000 more in their lifetime (Cheeseman Day & Newburger, 2002). People with higher intelligence test scores tend to complete more years of school and to have higher-status jobs. However, when the number of years of education is held constant, the correlation decreases between IQ scores, income, and success in later life.

For all adults caring for children—parents, teachers, administrators, counselors, medical workers—it is especially important to realize that cognitive skills, like any other skills, are always improvable. *Intelligence is a current state of affairs,* affected by past experiences and open to future changes, as the Flynn effect demonstrates. Even if intelligence is a limited potential, the potential is still quite large. For example, Japanese and Chinese children know much more mathematics than American children, but their intelligence test scores are quite similar. This superiority in math probably is related to differences in the way mathematics is taught and studied in the three countries and to the self-motivation skills of many Asian students (Baron, 1998; Stevenson & Stigler, 1992).

A Principal's Perspective

"What's best for kids?" is a question that guides decision-making processes of many educators, principals and teachers alike, and also serves as an exhibition of their student-centered orientation. However, answering this rhetorical question with actions is not so straightforward as it may seem. T. R., a principal and superintendent for many years, shares his thoughts.

Obviously, educators make innumerable decisions daily that impact students. What is less obvious is how each decision a principal or a teacher makes regarding students in general impacts students individually. In fact, academic accountability prescribed in No Child Left Behind (NCLB, 2002; reauthorized 2007) states that solutions and strategies that might be best for most students *are not good enough* for all students. Rather, NCLB and its focus on ensuring the academic progress of every child has shifted the question to "What's best for this child in this subject in this specific situation at this point in time?" This is no easy task when a single principal is charged with monitoring as many as 40 classroom teachers, each of whom serves 20 to 30 students who are from different ethnic backgrounds, read at five or more distinct levels, demonstrate varying degrees of independence and cognitive ability, and have widely varying nonschool experiences and family support structures.

However, the enormity of this task has not dissuaded student-focused leaders from implementing effective practices that attempt to address all of these needs. One example of how a principal can support meeting individual student needs is by bringing together teachers at the end of a school year to carefully consider individual characteristics when assigning students to class lists for the following school year. In most cases, teachers and principals strive to craft heterogeneous groupings of students that will allow teachers to efficiently and effectively meet students' needs based on cognitive ability, behavior, and the ability to work independently, to name just a few criteria. In another example, principals may assemble classroom teachers and support staff regularly each week or each month to serve on intervention teams that review multiple data points of individual student progress, especially for students with identified cognitive deficits or challenges. Typically, these teams then identify the areas where each student has made insufficient progress, develop specific intervention strategies, determine action steps for implementing the strategies, and establish timelines for measuring and assessing the success of newly defined interventions.

Clearly, the principal's role as instructional leader has never been more important than when considered in the context of meeting the needs of every child. As a result, reviewing, understanding, and effectively applying research regarding the emotional, social, academic, and physical development of individual students is an essential component of decision making when considering the question, "What's best for kids—what's best for this particular child right now?"

For ideas about individualizing instruction, see: Tomlinson, C. (2005, Summer). Differentiated instruction. *Theory Into Practice, 44*(3) (special issue).

Teaching Students with Ability Differences

Ability grouping has moved in and out of favor since the early 1900s. Today, teachers are encouraged to use forms of cooperative learning and heterogeneous grouping to deal with ability differences in their classes. In this section we consider how to handle differences in academic ability. Is ability grouping a solution to the challenge of ability differences? If so, when should it be used, and for whom?

Between-Class Ability Grouping

When whole classes are formed based on ability, the process is called **between-class ability grouping** or **tracking,** a common practice in secondary schools and some elementary schools as well. Most high schools have "college prep" courses and "general" courses or, for example, high-, middle-, and low-ability classes in particular subjects.

Recently there has been a press for **detracking,** or teaching all students in mixed ability groups, and then providing extra help for those who struggle and enrichment for those who learn quickly (Rubin, 2006). Jeannie Oakes and A. S. Wells (2002) describe several different ways to teach effectively in secondary schools without using tracking:

- Eliminate remedial courses and have one regular and one advanced track.
- Offer honors assignment options or challenge pull-out activities within each course.

- Require all students to take a common core of classes; then allow self-selection into advanced classes after the core.
- Encourage minority group students to enroll in advanced placement courses.
- Provide additional times during intercessions when struggling students can get extra help.
- Provide tutoring before and after school.
- Staff a homework help center with teachers, parents, and community volunteers.
- Instead of "dumbing down" content, teach students learning strategies for dealing with difficult material.

There are criticisms of both tracking and detracking. The *Point/Counterpoint* looks at both sides.

POINT/COUNTERPOINT

Is Tracking an Effective Strategy?

Tracking students into different classes or strands (college prep, vocational, remedial, gifted, and so on) has been standard procedure in many schools for a long time, but does it work? Critics say tracking is harmful while supporters claim it is useful, even though it presents challenges.

POINT

Tracking is harmful and should be eliminated.
Although on the surface this seems to be an efficient way to teach, research has consistently shown that segregation by ability causes problems for low-achieving students (Castle, Deniz, & Tortora, 2005; Garmon, Nystrand, Berends, & LePore, 1995; National Research Council, Institute of Medicine, 2004).

Low-ability classes seem to receive lower-quality instruction in general. Teachers tend to emphasize lower-level objectives and routine procedures, with less academic focus. Often there are more management problems and, with these problems, increased stress and decreased enthusiasm. These differences in instruction and the teachers' negative attitudes may mean that low expectations are communicated to the students. Attendance may drop. The lower tracks often have a disproportionate number of minority group and economically disadvantaged students, so ability grouping, in effect, resegregates schools. Possibilities for friendships become limited to students in the same ability range. Class assignments are often made on the basis of group IQ tests instead of tests in the subject area itself. Yet the results of group IQ tests are not reliable guides for what individual students are ready to learn in a particular subject area (Good & Brophy, 2003; Lucas & Berends, 2002).

COUNTERPOINT

Eliminating tracking will hurt many students.
Researchers who have looked closely at tracking believe that it may be harmful for some students some of the time, but not for all students and not all of the time. First, as most people agree, tracking seems to have positive effects for the high-track students. Gifted programs, honors classes, and advanced placement classes seem to work. High-ability students tend to perform better in honors or gifted classes than in regular classes (Fuchs, Fuchs, Hamlett, & Karns, 1998; Robinson & Clinkenbeard, 1998). No one, especially parents, wants to eliminate the positive effects of these programs. And the chance of being assigned to a high track is 10% greater for African American students (Gamoran & Mare, 1989), so detracking could be a special disservice to these students.

(Continued)

The second exception is the nongraded elementary school. In this arrangement, students are grouped by ability in particular subjects, regardless of their age or grade. A reading class might therefore have students from several grades, all working on the same level on reading. This *cross-grade grouping* seems to increase achievement and self-esteem for students of all abilities as long as the grouping allows teachers to give more direct instruction to the groups (Ong, Allison, & Haladyna, 2000).

So what is the answer? As usual, it is more complicated than simply detracking versus tracking. Careful attention to every student's achievement may mean different answers at different times.

Within-Class and Flexible Ability Grouping

Today it is not unusual to have 3- to 5-year ability differences in any given classroom (Castle, Deniz, & Tortora, 2005); thus many elementary school classes are grouped for reading, and some are grouped for math. But there is no clear evidence that this **within-class ability grouping** is superior to other approaches. In fact, students in lower-ability groups are less likely to be asked critical comprehension questions and are given fewer opportunities to make choices about what to read (Chorzempa & Graham, 2006). For schools with lower-SES students, grouping often means that these students are segregated into lower-ability tracks.

Thoughtfully constructed and well-taught ability groups in math and reading can be effective, but other approaches such as cooperative learning are available too. The point of any grouping strategy should be to provide appropriate challenge and support—that is, to reach children within their "zone of proximal development" (Vygotsky, 1997). Flexible grouping is one possible answer.

Flexible Grouping.   In **flexible grouping,** students are grouped and regrouped based on their learning needs. Assessment is continuous so that students are always working within their zone of proximal development. Arrangements might include small groups, partners, individuals, and even the whole class—depending on which grouping best supports each student's learning of the particular academic content. Flexible grouping approaches include high-level instruction and high expectations for all students, regardless of their group placement (Corno, 2008). One 5-year longitudinal study of flexible grouping in a high-needs urban elementary school found 10% to 57% increases in students who reached mastery level, depending on the subject area and grade level. Teachers received training and support in the assessment, grouping, and teaching strategies needed, and by the end of the study, 95% of the teachers were using flexible grouping. The teachers in the study believed that some of the gains came because students were more focused on learning and more confident (Castle et al., 2005).

If you use ability groups in your school, the *Theory into Action Guidelines* should help your teachers make the approach more effective (Good & Brophy, 2008; Slavin, 1987).

THEORY INTO ACTION GUIDELINES

Ability Grouping

Form and reform groups on the basis of students' current performance in the subject being taught.

Examples

1. Use scores on the most recent reading assessments to establish reading groups, and rely on current math performance to form math groups.
2. Change group placement frequently when students' achievement changes.

Discourage comparisons between groups and encourage students to develop a whole-class spirit.

Examples

1. Don't seat groups together outside the context of their reading or math group.
2. Avoid naming ability groups—save names for mixed-ability or whole-class teams.

Group by ability for one or, at the most, two subjects.

Examples

1. Make sure there are many lessons and projects that mix members from the groups.

2. Experiment with learning strategies in which cooperation is stressed (described in Chapter 4).
3. Keep the number of groups small (two or three at most) so that you can provide as much direct teaching as possible—leaving students alone for too long leads to less learning.

Make sure teachers, methods, and pace are adjusted to fit the needs of the group.

Examples

1. Organize and teach groups so that low-achieving students get appropriate extra instruction—not just the same material again.
2. Experiment with alternatives to grouping. There are alternatives to within-class grouping that appear more effective for some subjects. Mason and Good (1993) found that supplementing whole-class instruction in math with remediation and enrichment for students when they needed it worked better than dividing the class into two ability groups and teaching these groups separately.

What should instructional leaders do when they face more extreme differences in student ability? We turn to this question next.

Students Who Are Gifted and Talented

Sally Reis and her colleagues (2002) tell a true story about Latoya, a little girl who entered 1st grade in a large urban district already reading with great skill and interest. Her observant teacher administered a reading test and confirmed that Latoya read at the 5th-grade level! Her parents noted that Latoya had started reading when she was three and had been devouring books ever since. This seems to be a very happy story, but the sad truth is that in her struggling urban school, Latoya received no particular accommodations, and by 5th grade she was still reading at just above the 5th-grade level. Her 5th-grade teacher had no idea that Latoya had ever been an advanced reader.

Latoya is not alone. She is part of a group with special needs that is often overlooked by the schools: **gifted and talented students.** There is growing recognition that gifted students are being poorly served by most public schools. A national study found that more than one-half of all gifted students do not achieve in school at a level equal to their ability

(Tomlinson-Keasey, 1990). Yet a survey of the states in 2008 by the National Association for Gifted Children (NAGC) found that at least a dozen states would not allow students to start kindergarten early, even if they were reading at a high level. At least 30 states allow only 11th and 12th graders to take college courses (Kronholz, 2011).

Who Are the Gifted?   There are many definitions of gifted because individuals can have many different gifts. Remember that Gardner (2003) identified eight separate "intelligences," and Sternberg (1997) suggests a triarchic model. Renzulli and Reis (2003) have a different three-part conception of giftedness: above-average general ability, a high level of creativity, and a high level of task commitment or motivation to achieve. Truly gifted children are not the students who simply learn quickly with little effort. The work of gifted students is original, extremely advanced for their age, and potentially of lasting importance. These children may read fluently with little instruction by age three or four. They may play a musical instrument like a skillful adult, turn a visit to the grocery store into a mathematical puzzle, and become fascinated with algebra when their friends are having trouble with simple addition (Winner, 2000). Recent conceptions widen the view of giftedness to include attention to the children's culture, language, and exceptionalities (Association for the Gifted, 2001).

Identifying a gifted child is not always easy. Many parents provide early educational experiences for their children. Some students with intellectual gifts and talents also have learning problems such as difficulties hearing, learning disabilities, or attention deficit disorders, and their talents will be missed if the abilities as well as the problems are not properly assessed. And older students may actually try to hide their abilities from their friends and teachers.

The best single predictor of academic giftedness is still the individual IQ test, but these tests are costly and time consuming, and far from perfect. Group achievement and intelligence tests tend to underestimate the IQs of very bright children. Group tests may be appropriate for screening, but they are not appropriate for making placement decisions. One answer is a case study approach—many kinds of information are gathered: test scores, grades, examples of work, projects and portfolios, letters or ratings from teachers, self-ratings, and so on (Renzulli & Reis, 1991, 2003). Especially for recognizing artistic talent, experts in the field can be called in to judge the merits of a child's creations. Creativity tests and tests of self-regulation skills may identify some children who were not picked up by other measures, particularly minority students who may be at a disadvantage on the other types of tests (Grigorenko et al., 2009).

Teaching Gifted Students.   One researcher asked 13,000 gifted students in seven states to name one word for their experiences. The most commonly used word was "waiting." "Waiting for teachers to move ahead, waiting for classmates to catch up, waiting to learn something new—always waiting" (Kronholz, 2011, p. 3). Instead of waiting, some educators believe that gifted students should be *accelerated*—moved quickly through the grades or through particular subjects. Other educators prefer *enrichment*—giving the students additional, more sophisticated, and more thought-provoking work, but keeping them with their age-mates in school. Actually, both may be appropriate (Torrance, 1986). One way of doing this is through *curriculum compacting*—assessing a student over the goals of the instructional unit, then teaching only for those goals not yet reached. The time saved can be used for learning goals that include enrichment, sophistication, and novelty (Reis & Renzulli, 2004).

Many people object to acceleration, but most careful studies indicate that truly gifted students who begin primary, elementary, junior high, high school, college, or even graduate school early do as well as, and usually better than, nongifted students who are progressing at the normal pace. Social and emotional adjustment does not appear to be impaired. Skipping grades may not be the best solution for a particular student, but it does not deserve the bad name it has been given (Jones & Southern, 1991; Richardson & Benbow, 1990). In fact, Colangelo, Assouline, and Gross (2004) collected the research on the many benefits of acceleration and published two volumes called *A Nation Deceived: How Schools Hold Back America's Brightest Children.* These publications from the University of Iowa make a powerful case for acceleration.

An alternative to skipping grades is to accelerate students in one or two particular subjects, but keep them with peers for most classes. For students who are extremely advanced intellectually (for example, those scoring 160 or higher on an intelligence test), the only practical solution may be to accelerate their education (Davis, Rimm, & Siegle, 2011; Kronholz, 2011).

Teaching methods for gifted students should encourage abstract thinking, creativity, and independence, not just the learning of greater quantities of facts. In working with gifted and talented students, a teacher must be imaginative, flexible, and unthreatened by their capabilities. Instructional leaders must ask: What does this student need most? What does the student already know, and what is she or he ready to learn? Who can help me to teach them? Answers might come from faculty members at nearby colleges, retired professionals, books, museums, or older students. Strategies might be as simple as letting the child do math with the next grade. Increasingly, more flexible programs are being devised for gifted students: summer institutes or camps; courses at nearby colleges; classes with local artists, musicians, or dancers; independent research projects; selected classes in high school for younger students; honors classes; and special-interest clubs (Rosenberg, Westling, & McLeskey, 2011).

Reaching Every Student: Giftedness and Diversity.   There are three groups of students who are underrepresented in gifted education programs: women, students with learning disabilities, and students living in poverty (Stormont, Stebbins, & Holliday, 2001).

Girls and Giftedness.   "Gifted adolescent females are particularly at risk for underachievement, social and emotional problems, and feelings of isolation" (Stormont et al., 2001, p. 415). As young girls develop their identities in adolescence, they often reject being labeled as gifted; being accepted and popular, "fitting in," may become more important than achievement (Basow & Rubin, 1999). As they grow older, girls may even deliberately score lower on standardized tests and take fewer challenging courses. How can teachers reach girls who are gifted? Here are some ideas:

- Notice when girls' test scores in middle or high school seem to decline.
- Encourage assertiveness, achievement, high goals, and demanding work from all students.
- Provide models of achievement through speakers, internships, or readings.
- Look for and support gifts in arenas other than academic achievement.

Gifted Students with Learning Disabilities: Twice-Exceptional.   These twice-exceptional students may be more angry and frustrated by the problems they encounter than their peers are (Stormont et al., 2001). Learning problems may be subtle, and the student is fine through elementary school but begins to have difficulties as academic work gets harder in the later grades. Learning problems may be severe and may mask the gifts, so these students are seldom identified for gifted programs. Or the student's gifts may be used to compensate for learning disabilities, so the student seems just average to teachers (McCoach, Kehle, Bray, & Siegle, 2001). Here are some ideas for supporting twice-exceptional students:

- Identify these students by looking longitudinally at achievement: who was a high achiever in elementary school but began having trouble as more and more reading was required in later grades?
- Remediate skill deficits but also identify and develop talents and strengths.
- Promote emotional support, especially for this group.
- Help students learn to compensate directly for their learning problems and teach them to "tune in" to their own strengths and difficulties.
- Find help for career planning that takes advantage of their gifts and talents.

Gifted Students Who Live in Poverty.   Health problems, lack of resources, homelessness, fears about safety and survival, frequent moves, responsibilities for the care of other family members—all make achievement in school more difficult. To identify students with gifts, do the following:

- Use alternative assessment, teacher nomination, creativity tests. Look for students who are expressive, good storytellers, and able to improvise when they have limited materials. Try dynamic assessments that give students clues and observe how they solve problems using the clues.
- Be sensitive to cultural differences in values about cooperative or solitary achievement (Ford, 2000).
- Use multicultural strategies to encourage both achievement and the development of racial identities.

Students with Learning Challenges

Thus far we have focused mostly on schools' responses to the varying abilities and styles of students. For the rest of the chapter, we will consider problems that can interfere with learning. It is beyond this book to discuss all the exceptionalities, but there are three that are the source of much confusion in teaching: attention deficit disorder, learning disabilities, and autism spectrum disorders.

Hyperactivity and Attention Disorders

Today, attention-deficit hyperactive disorder (ADHD) is common. A few years ago, we opened the newspaper and saw the headline, "ADHD diagnoses soar in 4 years."

The Centers for Disease Control now puts the number of children in the United States who are diagnosed with ADHD as 1 in 10 (Wechsler, 2010). But the United States is not alone. A report from the 2nd International Congress on ADHD (Thome & Reddy, 2009) noted evidence is increasing that ADHD is a worldwide problem and that people with ADHD have striking and consistent characteristics in every culture. The rates in different countries vary from 4% to 10% worldwide (Fabiano et al., 2009; Gerwe et al., 2009).

Actually, hyperactivity is not one particular condition, but two kinds of problems that may or may not occur together: difficulty paying attention and impulsive-hyperactivity problems (problems controlling impulses and slowing down constant activity). About half the children diagnosed in the United States have both conditions. Today, most psychologists agree that the main problem for children labeled hyperactive is directing and maintaining attention, not simply controlling their physical activity. The American Psychiatric Association (APA) has established a diagnostic category called **attention-deficit hyperactivity disorder (ADHD)** to identify children with this problem. The APA defines ADHD as "a pervasive pattern of inattention, impulsivity and/or hyperactivity that is more frequent and severe than is typically observed in individuals at a comparable level of development" (American Psychiatric Association, DSM-IV-TR, 2000, p. 78). Some of the indicators listed in the DSM-IV-TR are:

- **Inattention:** Doesn't pay close attention to class activities, details of work, teacher directions, class discussions; can't organize work, notebooks, desk, assignments; easily distracted and forgetful.
- **Hyperactivity:** Fidgets and squirms; can't stay in assigned seat; can't move slowly, seems driven by a motor to go fast; talks excessively.
- **Impulsivity:** Blurts out answers; has trouble waiting for a turn; interrupts.

All children show some of these behaviors some of the time, but children with ADHD are likely to have some of these symptoms before age 7, the symptoms occur across many settings (not just school), and the symptoms lead to problems learning and getting along with others. ADHD usually is diagnosed in elementary school, but research suggests that problems with attention and hyperactivity may begin to show up as early as 3 years old (Friedman-Weieneth, Harvey, Youngswirth, & Goldstein, 2007). Even though about 2 to 3 times more boys than girls are identified as hyperactive, the gap appears to be narrowing. Girls have the same symptoms as boys, but tend to show the symptoms in less obvious ways, so they may not be identified as often and thus may miss getting appropriate support (Friend, 2011).

Just a few years ago, most psychologists thought that ADHD diminished as children entered adolescence, but now there is evidence that the problems can persist into adulthood for at least half of those with ADHD (Hirvikoski et al., 2011). Adolescence—with the increased stresses of puberty, transition to middle or high school, more demanding academic work, and more engrossing social relationships—can be an especially difficult time for students with ADHD (Taylor, 1998). When children diagnosed with ADHD become adults, about 30% have no more symptoms, 25% have persistent behavioral problems such as drug use or criminal behaviors, and around 25% develop major depression (Rosenberg et al., 2011).

Ritalin and other prescribed drugs such as Adderall, Focalin, Dexadrine, Vyvanse, and Cylert are stimulants, but in particular dosages, they tend to have paradoxical effects on many children with ADHD. Short-term effects include possible improvements in social behaviors such as cooperation, attention, and compliance. Research suggests that about 70% to 80% of children with ADHD are more manageable and better able to benefit from educational and social interventions when on medication (Hutchinson, 2009). In fact, both stimulants such as Adderall and Ritalin and non-stimulant treatments such as Strattera appear to have some helpful effects for many children and adolescents with ADHD (Kratchovil, 2009). Positive results also have been reported with Buspar, usually used to treat anxiety, and even some supplements such as pycnogenol (Trebaticka et al., 2009). There is also some evidence that Strattera might have positive effects on working memory, planning, and inhibition—at least for the Chinese children studied (Yang et al., 2009). German researchers studying the effects of longer-acting, once-a-day Concerta concluded that the transition from short-acting stimulants to Concerta was "associated with significant improvements in daily functioning in several areas of life, severity of disease, and in quality of life" (Gerwe et al., 2009, p. 185).

But many children experience negative side effects when taking these drugs, such as increased heart rate and higher blood pressure, interference with growth rate, insomnia, weight loss, and nausea (Smith & Tyler, 2010). For most children, these side effects are mild and can be controlled by adjusting the dosage. However, little is known about the long-term effects of drug therapy. For example, use of Strattera may lead to increased thoughts of suicide. As an educator, you need to keep up with the research on treatments for ADHD.

The bottom line is that even if students in your school are on medication, it is critical that they also learn the academic and social skills they will need to succeed. They need to learn how and when to apply learning strategies and study skills. Also, they need to be encouraged to persist when challenged by difficult tasks and to see themselves as having control over their learning and behavior. Medication alone will not make this happen, but it may help. For learning to occur, medication must be paired with other effective interventions.

David Nylund (2000) describes a therapy for ADHD called SMART that has important implications for educators. Rather than treating the problem child, Nylund's idea is to enlist the child's strengths to conquer his or her problems: in other words, put the child in control. New metaphors for the situation are developed. Rather than seeing the problems as inside the child, Nylund helps everyone see ADHD, "Trouble," "Boredom," and other enemies of learning as outside the child—demons to be conquered or unruly spirits to be enlisted in the service of what *the child* wants to accomplish. The focus is on solutions.

Ask your teachers to look for times when the student is engaged, even short times, and to note what is different about them. Discover the student's strengths and allow yourself to be amazed by them. Make changes in teaching that support the changes the student is trying to make, such as using more pictures and visual supports, providing a variety of activities (especially activities that allow movement), recognizing successes, breaking long activities or lectures into shorter segments, and protecting the privacy of students by not letting everyone know they are taking medications.

Learning Disabilities

How do you explain what is wrong with a student who has no developmental disabilities; who has normal vision, hearing, and language capabilities; and who still cannot learn to read, write, or compute? One explanation is that the student has a **learning disability.** This is a relatively new and controversial category. There is no fully agreed-upon definition. One text on learning disabilities gives eight definitions (Hallahan et al., 2005), including the definition used in IDEA (Individuals with Disabilities Education Act): "a disorder in one or more of the basic psychological processes involved in understanding or using language, spoken or written" (p. 15). Most definitions agree that students with learning disabilities perform significantly below what would be expected, given their other abilities.

Students with Learning Disabilities. Students with learning disabilities are not all alike. The most common characteristics are specific difficulties in one or more academic areas; poor fine motor coordination; problems paying attention; hyperactivity and impulsivity; problems organizing and interpreting visual and auditory information; disorders of thinking, memory, speech, and hearing; and difficulties making and keeping friends (Hallahan & Kauffman, 2006; Rosenberg et al., 2011). As you can see, many students with other disabilities (such as attention deficit disorder) and many students without disabilities may have some of the same characteristics. To complicate the situation even more, not all students with learning disabilities will have these problems, and few will have all of the problems. These students may be well below average in some academic areas, but average or strong in others.

Most students with learning disabilities have difficulties reading and writing. Table 3.2 on the next page lists some of the most common problems and signs, although these problems are not always indicators of learning disabilities. For English-speaking students, these difficulties appear to be *phonemic awareness*—problems with relating sounds to letters that make up words, making spelling challenging as well (Lyon, Shaywitz, & Shaywitz, 2003; Willcutt et al., 2001). Math, both computation and problem solving, is the second most common problem for students with learning disabilities. The writing of some students with learning disabilities is virtually unreadable, and their spoken language can be halting and disorganized. Many researchers trace some of these problems to the students' inability to use effective learning strategies, which we discuss in Chapter 4. Students with learning disabilities often lack effective ways to approach academic tasks. They don't know how to focus on the relevant information, get organized, apply learning strategies and study skills, change strategies when one isn't working, or evaluate their learning. They tend to be passive learners, in part because they don't know how to learn. Working independently is especially trying, so homework and seatwork are often left incomplete (Hallahan et al., 2005).

TABLE 3.2   Potential Signs of Learning Disabilities

Do any of your students show these signs? They could be indications of learning disabilities.

Anxiety around reading

- Is reluctant to read
- Cries or acts out to avoid reading
- Seems tense when reading

Has difficulty recognizing words or letters

- Inserts an incorrect word; substitutes or skips words
- Reverses letters or numbers—42 for 24, for example
- Mispronounces words—"cape" for "cope"
- Mixes up order of words in sentences "I can bikes ride" for "I can ride bikes."
- Reads very slowly and with little fluency—starts and stops often

Poor vocabulary skills

- Can't read new vocabulary words
- Has limited vocabulary

Has difficulty with understanding or remembering what was read

- Can't recall basic facts from the reading
- Can't make inferences or identify the main idea

Based on information from Smith, D. D., & Tyler, N. C. (2010). *Introduction to special education: Making a difference* (7th ed.). Columbus, OH: Merrill and Helpguide.org. http://www.helpguide.org/mental/learning_disabilities.htm

Early diagnosis is important so that students with learning disabilities do not become terribly frustrated and discouraged or develop bad habits in an attempt to compensate. The students themselves do not understand why they are having such trouble, and they may become victims of **learned helplessness.** This condition was first identified in learning experiments with animals. The animals were put in situations where they received punishment (electric shocks) that they could not control. Later, when the situation was changed and they could have escaped the shocks or turned them off, the animals didn't even bother trying (Seligman, 1975). They had learned to be helpless victims. Students with learning disabilities may also come to believe that they cannot control or improve their own learning. This is a powerful belief. The students never exert the effort to discover that they can make a difference in their own learning, so they remain passive and helpless.

Teaching Students with Learning Disabilities.   Two general approaches, preferably used together, are highly effective for students with learning disabilities (Friend, 2011). The first is *direct instruction*, described in Chapter 6. The basics of this approach are clear explanations and demonstrations of new material, instruction in small steps with practice after each step, immediate feedback, and teacher guidance and support. The second general approach is *strategy instruction*, described in Chapter 4. Strategies are specific rules for focusing attention and accomplishing tasks, such as **TREE** for supporting elementary students' persuasive writing:

> **T**opic sentence: Tell what you believe.
>
> **R**easons: Tell 3 or more reasons why you believe this. Will your readers believe this?
>
> **E**nding: Wrap it up!
>
> **E**xamine: Check for all 3 parts.*

These strategies have to be taught using good direct instruction—explanation, examples, and practice with feedback. Direct teaching of skills and strategies is especially important for students with reading disabilities. And the teaching does not have to focus on low-level skills. Here are some general strategies taken from Hardman, Drew, and Egan (2005):

Preschool Years

- Keep verbal instructions short and simple.
- Match level of content carefully to the child's developmental level.
- Give multiple examples to clarify meaning.
- Allow more practice than usual, especially when material is new.

Elementary School Years

- Keep verbal instructions short and simple; have students repeat directions back to you to be sure they understand.
- Use mnemonics (memory strategies) in instruction to teach students how to remember.
- Repeat main points several times.
- Provide additional time for learning and practice—reteach when necessary.

Secondary School and Transition Years

- Directly teach self-monitoring strategies, such as cueing students to ask, "Was I paying attention?"
- Connect new material to knowledge the student already has.
- Teach students to use external memory strategies and devices (tape-recording, note-taking, to-do lists, and so on).

You may be thinking that these are good ideas for many students who need more support and direct teaching of study skills. You are right.

*Excerpt from *Special education: Contemporary perspectives for school professionals*, 3rd Edition, by Marilyn D. Friend. Copyright © 2011 by Pearson Education, Inc. Printed and Electronically reproduced by permission of Pearson Education, Inc., Upper Saddle River, New Jersey.

Autism Spectrum Disorders and Asperger Syndrome

You may be familiar with the term *autism*. In 1990, autism was added to the IDEA list of disabilities qualifying for special services. It is defined as "a developmental disability significantly affecting verbal and nonverbal communication and social interaction, generally evident before age three, that adversely affects the child's educational performance" (34 Federal Code of Regulations § 300.7). We have used the term preferred by professionals in the field, **autism spectrum disorders,** to emphasize that autism includes a range of disorders from mild to major. Estimates of the number of children with autism vary greatly, but are increasing dramatically. IDEA places the number on the autism spectrum at about 1 in 88 of all children. The most recent report from the Centers for Disease Control is 1 in every 252 girls and 1 in every 54 boys (CDC, 2012). Other estimates range as high a 1% of all children, ages 3 to 17 (Friend, 2011).

From early on, children with autism spectrum disorders may have difficulties in social relations. Children with autism do not form connections with others; they avoid eye contact; or they don't share feelings such as enjoyment or interest with others. Communication is impaired. About half of these students are nonverbal; they have no or very few language skills. Others make up their own languages. They may obsessively insist on regularity and sameness in their environments—change is very disturbing. They may repeat behaviors and have restricted interests, watching the same DVD over and over, for example. They may be very sensitive to light, sound, touch, or other sensory information. Sounds may be painful, for example, or the slight flickering of fluorescent lights may seem like constant bursts of light, causing severe headaches (Franklin, 2007). They may be able to memorize words or steps in problem solving, but not use them appropriately or be very confused when the situation changes or questions are asked in a different way (Friend, 2008).

Asperger syndrome is one of the disabilities included in the autism spectrum. These children have many characteristics described above, but have the greatest trouble with social relations. Language is less affected. Their speech may be fluent but unusual, mixing up pronouns of "I" and "you," for example (Friend, 2008). Many students with autism also have moderate to severe intellectual disabilities, but those with Asperger syndrome usually have average to above average intelligence.

Theory of Mind.   One current explanation for autism and Asperger syndrome is that children with these disorders lack a theory of mind—an understanding that they and other people have minds, thoughts, and emotions. They have difficulty explaining their own behaviors, appreciating that other people might have different feelings, and predicting how behaviors might affect emotions. So, for example, a student may not understand why classmates are bored by his constant repetition of stories or obscure facts about topics he finds fascinating. Or the student may stand too close or too far away when interacting, not realizing that she is making other people uncomfortable (Friend, 2008; Harris, 2006).

Interventions.   Early and intense interventions that focus on communication and social relations are particularly important for children with autism spectrum disorders.

As they move into elementary school, some of these students will be in inclusive settings, others in specialized classes, and many in some combination of these two. Collaboration among teachers and the family is particularly important. Supports such as smaller classes, structured environments, a class "buddy" to give support, a safe "home base" for times of stress, consistency in instruction and transition routines, assistive technologies, and the use of visual supports may be part of a collaborative plan (Friend, 2008). Through adolescence and the transition to adulthood, the acquisition of life, work, and social skills are important educational goals.

Inclusion

No matter what grade or subject you supervise, your teachers will work with students with learning challenges in their classrooms. In the United States, beginning in 1975 with PL 94-142 (the Education of the Handicapped Act), a series of laws has led to revolutionary changes in the education of children with disabilities. The legislation, now called the **Individuals with Disabilities Education Improvement Act (IDEA or sometimes IDEIA),** was revised in 1990, 1997, and 2004. At the most general level, the law now requires states to provide a free, appropriate public education (FAPE) for all students with disabilities who participate in special education. There are no exceptions—the law requires **zero reject.** This policy also applies to students with communicable diseases such as AIDS. The expenses of meeting the special needs of these students are considered a public responsibility. Let's examine the requirements in these laws. There are three major points of interest to principals and teachers: the concept of "least restrictive placement," the protection of the rights of students with disabilities and of their parents, and the individualized education program (IEP).

Least Restrictive Placement. The laws require states to develop procedures for educating each child in the **least restrictive placement.** This means a setting that is as close to the general education class setting as possible. Over the years, recommended approaches to achieve this have moved from **mainstreaming** (including children with special needs in a few regular education classes as convenient), to integration (fitting the child with special needs into existing class structures), to **inclusion** (restructuring educational settings to promote belonging for all students) (Avramidis, Bayliss, & Burden, 2000). Even though the IDEA legislation does not use the word *inclusion*, today, the least restrictive environment is assumed to be inclusion as much as possible. In the end, successful inclusion probably depends on teachers being knowledgeable and well prepared, getting the support they need to teach, and being committed to inclusion. However, an emphasis on standardized testing may interfere with good teaching for included students (Friend, 2011; Idol, 2006; Kemp & Carter, 2006).

The Rights of Students and Parents. Several stipulations in these laws protect the rights of parents and students. Schools must have procedures for maintaining the confidentiality of school records. Testing practices must not discriminate against students from different cultural backgrounds. Parents have the right to see all records relating to the testing, placement, and teaching of their child. If they wish, parents may obtain

THEORY INTO ACTION GUIDELINES

Productive Family Conferences

Plan and prepare for a productive conference.

Examples

1. Have a clear purpose and gather the needed information. If you want to discuss student progress, have work samples.
2. Send home a list of questions and ask families to bring the information to the conference. Sample questions from Friend and Bursuck (2006) are:
   - What is your child's favorite class activity?
   - Does your child have worries about any class activities? If so, what are they?
   - What are your priorities for your child's education this year?
   - What questions do you have about your child's education in my class this year?
   - How could we at school help make this the most successful year ever for your child?
   - Are there any topics you want to discuss at the conference that I might need to prepare for? If so, please let me know.
   - Would you like other individuals to participate in the conference? If so, please give me a list of their names.
   - Is there particular school information you would like me to have available? If so, please let me know. (p. 100)

During the conference, create and maintain an atmosphere of collaboration and respect.

Examples

1. Arrange the room for private conversation. Put a "Do Not Disturb" sign on your door to avoid interruptions. Meet around a conference table for better collaboration. Have tissues available.
2. Address families as "Mr." and "Ms.," not "Mom" and "Dad" or "Grandma." Use students' names.
3. Listen to families' concerns and build on their ideas for their children.

After the conference, keep good records and follow up on decisions.

Examples

1. Make notes to yourself and keep them organized.
2. Summarize any actions or decisions in writing and send a copy to the family and any other teachers or professionals involved.
3. Communicate with families on other occasions, especially when there is good news to share.

Source: Excerpt from *Including students with special needs: A practical guide for classroom teachers*, 4th Edition, by Marilyn Friend and William D. Bursuck. Copyright © 2006 by Pearson Education, Inc. Printed and Electronically reproduced by permission of Pearson Education, Inc., Upper Saddle River, New Jersey.

an independent evaluation of their child. Parents may bring an advocate or representative to the meeting at which the IEP is developed. Students whose parents are unavailable must be assigned a surrogate parent to participate in the planning. Parents must receive written notice (in their native language) before any evaluation or change in placement is made. Finally, parents have the right to challenge the program developed for their child, and are protected by due process of law. Because principals and teachers often have conferences with these families, we have provided some *Theory into Action Guidelines* to make the meetings more effective, but be aware that these guidelines are more general and apply to all students and their parents.

Individual Education Program. The drafters of the laws recognized that each student is unique and may need a specially tailored program to make progress. The **individualized education program (IEP)** is an agreement between parents and the school about the services that will be provided. The IEP is written by a team that includes the student's parents or guardians, a general education teacher who works with the student, a special education teacher, a representative of the school district (often the principal), a qualified person who can interpret the student's evaluation results (often a school psychologist), and (if appropriate) the student. For students 16 and older, the team may include representatives from outside agencies who are providing services to help the student make transitions to life and support services after school. If the school and parents agree, the team could add other people who have special knowledge of the child (for example, a therapist). The program usually is updated each year. The IEP must state in writing:

1. The student's *present level of academic achievement and functional performance* (sometimes referred to as *PLAAFP*).
2. Annual goals—measurable performance goals for the year. Students with significant needs or multiple disabilities may also have *short-term objectives* or *benchmarks* to make sure progress is continuous. The plan must tell how progress toward these goals and objectives will be measured. Parents must get progress reports at least as often as report cards are sent home for all students.
3. A statement of specific special education and related services to be provided to the student and details of when and where those services will be initiated. This statement can include descriptions of supplementary aids and assistive technologies (for example, using speech recognition software such as *Dragon®* to dictate answers or compose essays, or writing using a computer).
4. An explanation of how much of the student's program WILL NOT be in regular classroom and school settings.
5. A statement about how the student will participate in state and district-wide assessments, particularly those required by the No Child Left Behind accountability procedures.
6. Beginning at age 14 and by age 16, a statement of needed transitional services to move the student toward further education or work in adult life. (Friend, 2011; Rosenberg, Westling, & McLeskey, 2011)

Section 504 Protections for Students   As a consequence of the civil rights movement in the 1960s and 1970s, the federal government passed the Vocational Rehabilitation Act of 1973. Section 504 of that law prevents discrimination against people with disabilities in any programs, such as public schools, that receive federal money.

Through **Section 504,** all school-age children are ensured an equal opportunity to participate in school activities. The definition of *disability* is broad in Section 504. If a student has a condition that substantially limits participation in school, then the school must develop a plan for giving that student access to education, even though the school gets no extra funds. To get assistance through Section 504, students must be assessed, often by a team, and a plan developed. Unlike IDEA, however, there are fewer rules about how this must happen, so individual schools design their own procedures (Friend, 2011). Look at Table 3.3 on the next page to see an example of the kinds of accommodations that might be made for a student. Many of these ideas seem to be "just good teaching." But we have been surprised to see how many teachers won't let students use calculators or tape recorders because "they should learn to do it like everyone else!"

TABLE 3.3   Examples of Accommodations under Section 504

The types of accommodations that can be written into a Section 504 plan are almost without limit. Some accommodations may relate to physical changes in the learning environment (for example, air filters are installed to remove allergens). However, many students who have Section 504 plans have functional impairments related to their learning or behavior, and their needs are somewhat similar to those of students with disabilities. The following is a sample of instructional accommodations that could be incorporated into a Section 504 plan:

- Seat the student nearest to where the teacher does most of his/her instruction.
- Have the student sit next to a peer who can help as needed.
- Seat the student away from the distractions of doorways or windows.
- Fold assignments in half so that the student is less overwhelmed by the quantity of work.
- Make directions telegraphic, that is, concise and clear.
- Allow use of a calculator or tape recorder.
- Use voice recognition software on the computer for written assignments.
- Mark right answers instead of wrong answers.
- Send a set of textbooks to be left at home so the student does not have to remember to bring books from school.
- Provide books on tape so the student can listen to assignments instead of reading them.

Source: Adapted from *Including students with special needs: A practice guide for classroom teachers*, 6th Edition, by Marilyn Friend and William D. Bursuck. Copyright © 2012 by Pearson Education, Inc. Printed and Electronically reproduced by permission of Pearson Education, Inc., Upper Saddle River, New Jersey.

Two major groups are considered for Section 504 accommodations: students with medical or health needs such as diabetes, drug addictions, severe allergies, communicable diseases, temporary disabilities resulting from accidents, or alcoholism; and students with ADHD. We have already spent some time with the second group because teachers must spend quite a bit of time with them. Students with ADHD now also qualify for services under the "Other Health Impaired" category of IDEA, so your school district may serve these students under either IDEA or Section 504.

Effective Teaching in Inclusive Classrooms

Effective teaching for students with learning challenges does not require a unique set of skills. It is a combination of good teaching practices and sensitivity to students. Students with disabilities need to learn the academic material, and they need to be full participants in the day-to-day life of the classroom. To accomplish the first goal of academic learning, Larrivee (1985) concludes that effective teachers do the following: Use time efficiently by having smooth management routines, avoiding discipline problems, and planning carefully. Ask questions at the right level of difficulty. Give supportive, positive feedback to students, helping them figure out the right answer if they are on the right track but have an incorrect answer.

To accomplish the second goal of integrating students with disabilities into the day-to-day life of the classroom, Ferguson, Ferguson, and Bogdan (1987) give the following guidelines:

1. Mix students with disabilities into groups with students who do not have disabilities. Avoid resegregating students into separate groups.
2. Instead of sending students out for special services like speech therapy, remedial reading, or individualized instruction, try to integrate the special help into the class setting, perhaps during a time when the other students are working independently too.
3. Make sure your language and behavior is a good model for everyone.
4. Give students with disabilities extended practice that is distributed over days and weeks, use *advance organizers* to help students focus on what they already know, and be sure to state objectives clearly (Swanson, 2001).
5. Teach about differences among people as part of the curriculum. Let students become familiar with aids for people with disabilities, such as hearing aids, sign language, communication boards, and so on.
6. Have students work together in cooperative groups or on special projects such as role playing, biographical interviews, or lab assignments.
7. Try to keep the schedules and activity patterns of all students similar.

Decision Making. Making decisions in the best interest of students is a complex job. Figure 3.2 on the next page guides you and your teachers through the process of identifying, assessing, and planning for students in your school.

Even though there are many good tests and careful procedures for making special education placement decisions, racial and ethnic minority students are overrepresented in the disability categories and underrepresented in gifted programs. For example, almost 20% of all students defined as having disabilities under IDEA are African American, but only 15% of all students attending school are African American. The overrepresentation is worse when we look at specific categories: 34% of all students identified as having intellectual disabilities/mental retardation and 27% of students identified as having emotional disturbance are African American—twice as high as we would expect based on the percentage of African American students in the United States. And these students are more likely than white or Asian students to be placed outside of the general education system for most of their school day. In contrast, African American and Hispanic students comprise only about 8% each of the students served in gifted and talented programs (Friend, 2008).

For almost four decades, educators have struggled to understand the causes of these over- and underrepresentations. Explanations include the higher poverty rates among African American and Hispanic families leading to poorer prenatal care, nutrition, and health care; systematic biases in teachers' attitudes, curriculum, instruction, and the referral process itself; and lack of preparation for teachers to work effectively with ethnic minority students (Friend, 2008). To deal with the referral problem, educators have recommended gathering more information about a student before a formal referral is made. How long has the student been in the United States? What about

FIGURE 3.2 The Decision-Making Process for Special Education
When a response to intervention (RTI) model is used, the data collected during that phase may be central to the assessment and decision-making process. MDT refers to a Multidisciplinary Team.

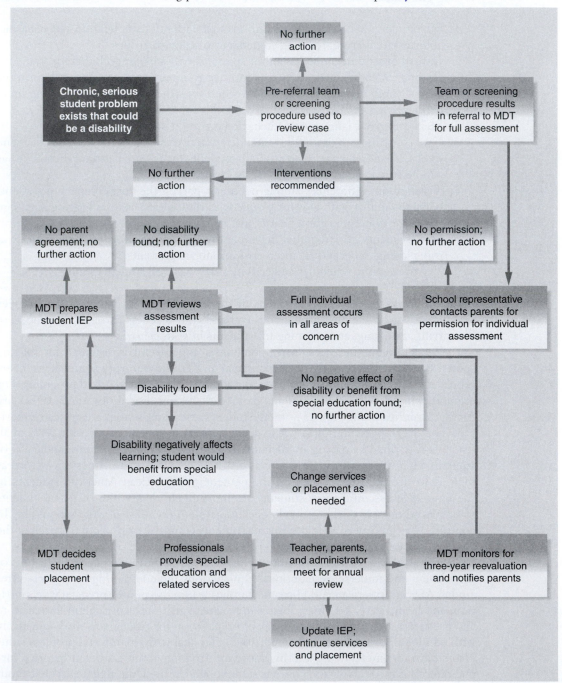

proficiency with English? Are there unusual stressors such as being homeless? Is the teacher knowledgeable about and respectful of the student's culture? Is the classroom culturally compatible and engaging (Chapter 2)? Can the student's abilities be assessed through alternative approaches such as creativity tests and portfolios or performances (Chapter 8)? Having more knowledge about the student and his or her circumstances outside of school should help teachers make better decisions about what programs are appropriate (Friend, 2008; Gonzales, Brusca-Vega, & Yawkey, 1997; National Alliance of Black School Educators, 2002). In fact, instruction should be differentiated to better match the needs of all students.

Summary

Spearman suggests there is one mental attribute, which he called *g*, or general intelligence, that is used to perform on any mental test, but that each test also requires some specific abilities in addition to *g*. Gardner contends that an intelligence is a biological and psychological potential to solve problems and create products or outcomes that are valued by a culture. He identifies at least eight separate intelligences: linguistic, musical, spatial, logical-mathematical, bodily-kinesthetic, interpersonal, intrapersonal (these last two are similar to the idea of emotional intelligence), and naturalist; he now suggests perhaps existential as well. Gardner does not deny the existence of a general ability, but questions how useful *g* is as an explanation for human achievements.

Sternberg's triarchic theory of intelligence is a cognitive process approach to understanding intelligence with three parts: analytic, creative, and practical. Analytic intelligence involves the mental processes that lead to more or less intelligent behavior. Creative intelligence involves coping with new experiences through insight, or the ability to deal effectively with novel situations, and automaticity, or the ability to become efficient and automatic in thinking and problem solving. The third part is practical intelligence—choosing to live and work in a context where success is likely, adapting to that context, and reshaping it if necessary.

Intelligence is measured through individual tests (such as Stanford-Binet, Wechsler, Woodcock-Johnston, and Kauffman Assessment Battery) and group tests (such as Otis-Lennon School Abilities Tests, Slosson Intelligence Test, Raven Progressive Matrices, and Wide Range Intelligence Test). Compared to an individual test, a group test is much less likely to yield an accurate picture of any one person's abilities. The average score is 100; 50% of the people from the general population who take the tests will score 100 or above, and 50% will score below 100. About 68% of the general population will earn IQ scores between 85 and 115. Only about 16% of the population will receive scores below 85, and only 16% will score above 115. These figures hold true for white, native-born Americans whose first language is standard English. Intelligence predicts success in school, but is less predictive of success in life when level of education is taken into account.

Between-class ability grouping is a common practice in secondary schools and some elementary schools as well. Most high schools have "college prep" courses and "general" courses or, for example, high-, middle-, and low-ability classes in particular subjects. Academic ability groupings can have both disadvantages and advantages for students and teachers. Low-ability classes seem to receive lower-quality instruction in general. Teachers tend to emphasize lower-level objectives and routine procedures, with less academic focus. Often there are more student behavior problems and, along with these problems, increased teacher stress and decreased enthusiasm. The lower tracks often have a disproportionate number of minority group and economically disadvantaged students, so ability grouping becomes segregation in school. Cross-age grouping by subject can be an effective way to deal with ability differences in nongraded elementary schools. Within-class ability grouping, if handled sensitively and flexibly, can have positive effects, but alternatives such as cooperative learning are also possible.

Ability grouping has benefits for gifted students, as does acceleration. Many people object to acceleration, but most careful studies indicate that truly gifted students who are accelerated do as well as, and usually better than, nongifted students who are progressing at the normal pace. Gifted students tend to prefer the company of older playmates and may be bored if kept with children of their own age. Skipping grades may not be the best solution for a particular student, but for students who are extremely advanced intellectually (160 or higher on an individual intelligence test), the only practical solution may be to accelerate their education.

Three common learning problems in the schools are attention deficit disorders, autism spectrum disorders, and specific learning disabilities. *Attention-deficit hyperactivity disorder* (ADHD) is the term used to describe the behavior of individuals of any age with hyperactivity and attention difficulties. Use of medication to address ADHD is controversial, but currently on the rise. About 70% of children with ADHD are more manageable when on medication. But for many there are negative side effects, and little is known about the long-term effects of drug therapy. There also is no evidence that the drugs lead to improvement in academic learning or peer relationships. *Autism* is a developmental disability that affects communication and social interaction. Autism spectrum disorders range along a continuum from mild to major disorders. Early interventions are particularly important for children with such disorders.

Specific learning disabilities involve significant difficulties in the acquisition and use of listening, speaking, reading, writing, reasoning, or mathematical skills. These disorders are intrinsic to the individual and may occur across the life span. Students with learning disabilities may become victims of learned helplessness when they come to believe that they cannot control or improve their own learning and therefore cannot succeed. A focus on learning strategies often helps students with learning disabilities.

At the most general level, IDEA, the Individuals with Disabilities Education Act, requires states to provide a free, appropriate public education (FAPE) for all students with disabilities who participate in special education. There are no exceptions—the law requires zero reject. Provisions of the law require that each student with special needs be educated in the least restrictive environment according to an individualized education program. The law also protects the rights of these students and their parents. Recent legislation extends services to include transition programming for students with special needs who are 16 years old and older.

KEY TERMS

attention-deficit hyperactivity
disorder (ADHD) (75)
autism spectrum disorders (80)
between-class ability
grouping (68)
crystallized intelligence (60)
detracking (68)
flexible grouping (70)
fluid intelligence (60)
Flynn effect (66)
g (general intelligence) (60)
gifted and talented students (71)

inclusion (81)
individualized education program
(IEP) (82)
Individuals with Disabilities
Education Act (IDEA, also
called Individuals with
Disabilities Education
Improvement Act or
IDEIA) (81)
intelligence (60)
learned helplessness (78)
learning disability (77)

least restrictive placement (81)
mainstreaming (81)
Section 504 (83)
theory of multiple
intelligences (61)
tracking (68)
triarchic theory of successful
intelligence (64)
within-class ability grouping (70)
zero reject (81)

DEVELOPING YOUR PORTFOLIO

1. Develop a position statement and action plan
on the appropriate use of school-level student
groupings.

   What is your philosophy about ability grouping
and tracking? Be sure to support your perspective
with the available research.

   What will you do? Develop a plan for implementing this philosophy in your school.

   How will you do it? Develop a realistic implementation strategy.

2. Develop a position statement and action plan on
inclusion that complies with PL 94-142 and the
subsequent modifications and extensions of the law.

   What is your philosophy about inclusion? Be sure
to support your perspective with the available research and the law.

Develop a plan for implementing this philosophy in your school. Be sure to include how you
will comply with the "least restrictive placement"
and other provisions of PL 94-142 as well as your
district's policies on inclusion. Does the district
policy facilitate or hinder your philosophy about
inclusion? How?

Develop a framework and checklist to ensure that
your school is in compliance with the relevant
laws.

3. Develop a school policy on the use of results from
intelligence tests. What sort of testing should
be done? Who should have access? How should
scores be used to support students' learning? But-
tress your positions with current research and
theory on intelligence.

INSTRUCTIONAL LEADER'S TOOLBOX

Readings

Benson, E. (2003). Intelligent intelligence testing. *Monitor
on Psychology, 34*(2), 48.

Campbell, L., Campbell, B., & Dickinson, D. (2004).
Teaching and learning through multiple intelligences
(3rd ed.). Boston, MA: Allyn & Bacon.

Gardner, H. (2009). Birth and the spreading of a meme. In
J-Q Chen, S. Moran, & H. Gardner (eds.), *Multiple*

intelligences around the world (pp. 3–16). San Francisco, CA: Wiley.

Neisser, U., et al. (1996). Intelligence: Knowns and un-
knowns. *American Psychologist, 51,* 77–101.

Nylund, D. (2000). *Treating Huckleberry Finn: A new narrative approach to working with kids diagnosed ADD/
ADHD.* San Francisco, CA: Jossey-Bass.

Websites

www.umaine.edu/edhd/
> A collection of child development websites

www.cln.org/
> Community Learning Network: a Canadian site with information on multiculturalism

www.thearc.org
> Resources on the Web for individuals with disabilities

http://idea.ed.gov/
> IDEA (Individuals with Disabilities Education Act)

www.edwebproject.org/
> Introduction to multiple intelligences

http://pzweb.harvard.edu/
> Project Zero

Organizations

www.aacap.org/
> American Academy of Child and Adolescent Psychiatry: This organization helps families understand the developmental, emotional, and behavioral disorders affecting children and adolescents.

www.aagc.org/
> American Association for Gifted Children

www.cec.sped.org/
> Council for Exceptional Children

www.ldanatl.org/
> Learning Disabilities Association

www.nacd.org /
> The National Academy of Child Development: An international organization of parents and professionals dedicated to helping children and adults reach their full potential. The site includes resources for parents and links to research articles.

www.add.org/
> Attention Deficit Disorder Association

www.ocecd.org/
> Ohio Coalition for the Education of Children with Disabilities

www.researchtopractice.info/
> Research and Training Center on Early Childhood Development

www.equipforequality.org/
> Equip for Equality: Advancing civil and human rights for people with disabilities

CHAPTER

4

Learning

PREVIEW: KEY POINTS

1. Learning occurs when experience leads to a relatively permanent change in an individual's knowledge or behavior.

2. There are many explanations for learning, but the most useful are the behavioral, cognitive, and constructivist perspectives.

3. Behavioral explanations of learning emphasize the importance of antecedents (cues and prompts) and consequences (reinforcement and punishment) in shaping behavior.

4. Functional behavioral assessments with positive behavior supports and homework are applications of the behavioral approach.

5. Cognitive explanations of learning highlight the importance of prior knowledge in focusing attention, making sense of new information, and supporting memory.

6. Information processing is a cognitive theory of memory that describes how information is taken in; processed (combined with prior knowledge); stored in long-term memory in the forms of episodes, productions, images and schemas, and retrieved.

7. Learning strategies such as underlining, highlighting, and graphing are applications of the cognitive approach.

8. Constructivist views of learning explain learning in terms of the individual and social construction of knowledge; knowledge is judged not so much by its accuracy as by its usefulness.

9. Features of constructivist applications include complex real-life tasks, social interaction and shared responsibility, multiple representations of content, and student-centered teaching.

10. Three promising applications of the constructivist approach are inquiry or problem-based learning, cognitive apprenticeships, and cooperative learning.

Leadership Challenge

Your school's social studies department is highly regarded for its innovative approach to teaching. The program is oriented toward inquiry as a process, rather than the retention of historical facts. Typically, curriculum is developed by the department. The teachers are enthusiastic about their program, and it is well received by the students. You do not always agree with the direction of the curriculum, but there is little question that this is a highly skilled and professional group of teachers whom you respect.

Recent state educational reforms have argued for back to basics and the use of curricular materials that stress recall of specific persons, places, and events in state and national history. The reform is supported by a battery of state tests. Although the state maintained that no personally damaging or insulting comparisons would be made, your community has made them. The superintendent has her feet to the fire on this issue, and now you, too, are feeling the heat. Recent test scores show that your students are not doing nearly as well in history as they are in science and mathematics. The superintendent has "requested" that you integrate the state curricular materials into the history program to correct the current deficiencies. Your history faculty, on the other hand, claim that this is exactly the wrong tack to take to develop inquiring minds. They are not overly concerned with the students' performance on the state tests because they claim the tests measure the wrong thing. Parents, however, cannot understand why their children are not doing as well in history as they are in math and science; in fact, at the last board meeting the superintendent promised that the history scores would rise.

> What do students need to "know" about history?
>
> What is the role of rote memory in learning?
>
> What do the behavioral, cognitive, and constructivist perspectives on learning have to offer?
>
> How does one achieve the right balance of teaching facts and teaching for discovery and understanding?

Source: The above situation has been adapted from Hoy, W. K., & Tarter, C. J. (1995). *Administrators solving the problems of practice: Decision making, concepts, cases, and consequences*: Boston: Allyn & Bacon.

What Is Learning?

Learning is at the center of schooling. Learning is a goal and a process—a noun and a verb. As a goal, learning (new knowledge and skills) is the outcome instructional leaders work toward as they interact with teachers. Learning is the teachers' goal with their students. But learning is also a process. In order to design useful learning environments in schools and classrooms, we must understand how people learn. The purpose of this chapter is to examine briefly what is known about learning so that your work with teachers and their work with students can be informed by and compatible with the ways that people learn. We will examine the contemporary contributions to education of three major perspectives on learning: behavioral, cognitive, and constructivist, noting specific strategies for teaching that are consistent with each perspective. Our goal is not to pick the "best" or most popular explanation of learning, but instead to use the best from each explanation, because each tells us something different and useful about the complex phenomenon that is human learning.

When we hear the word *learning*, most of us think of studying and school. We think about subjects or skills we intend to master, such as algebra, history, chemistry, or karate. But learning is not limited to school. We learn every day of our lives. Babies learn to kick their legs to make the mobile above their cribs move, teens learn the lyrics to all their favorite songs, and every few years we all learn to find a new style of dress attractive when the old styles go out of fashion. This last example shows that learning is not always intentional. We don't try to like new styles and dislike old ones; it just seems to happen that way. So what is this powerful phenomenon called learning?

In the broadest sense, **learning** occurs when practice or experience causes a relatively permanent change in an individual's knowledge, behaviors, or attitudes. The change may be deliberate or unintentional, for better or for worse (Hill, 2002). To qualify as learning, this change must be brought about by the interaction of a person with his or her physical or social environment. Changes due simply to maturation, such as growing taller or turning gray, do not qualify as learning. Temporary changes due to illness, fatigue, or hunger are also excluded from a general definition of learning. A person who has gone without food for two days does not learn to be hungry, and a person who is ill does not learn to run more slowly. Of course, learning plays a part in how we respond to hunger or illness (Mayer, 2011).

Our definition specifies that the changes resulting from learning are in the individual's knowledge, attitudes, or behavior. Although most learning theorists would agree with this statement, some tend to emphasize changes in knowledge and attitudes, others the changes in behavior (Gredler, 2005; Swartz, Wasserman, & Robbins, 2002). Behavioral psychologists emphasize observable changes in behaviors, skills, and habits. Cognitive psychologists, who focus on changes in knowledge, believe learning is an internal mental activity that cannot be observed directly. Cognitive psychologists studying learning are interested in unobservable mental processes such as thinking, remembering, and solving problems. Psychologists who favor constructivist views are interested in how people make meaning; learning is seen as the construction of knowledge.

Different theories of learning have had different impacts on education and have supported different practices. In the 1960s and early 1970s, behavioral views of learning dominated education. But beginning in the 1980s, cognitive and constructivist explanations became more prevalent. Even though there are differences in these explanations, each provides insights about some aspect of learning, in part because they focus on different kinds of outcomes. Each perspective provides instructional leaders with tools for improving instruction. We begin our explorations of learning with the behavioral perspective.

Behavioral Views of Learning

The behavioral approach to learning developed out of work by Skinner and others who defined learning as a change in behavior brought about by experience, with little concern for the mental or internal aspects of learning. Behavior, like response or action, is simply a word for what a person does in a particular situation. Conceptually, we may think of a behavior as sandwiched between two sets of environmental influences: those that precede it (its *antecedents*) and those that follow it (its *consequences*) (Skinner, 1950). This relationship can be shown very simply as antecedent–behavior–consequence, or A–B–C. As behavior is ongoing, a given consequence becomes an antecedent for the next ABC sequence. Research shows that behavior can be altered by changes in the antecedents, the consequences, or both. Early work focused on consequences.

Types of Consequences

According to the behavioral view, consequences determine to a great extent whether a person will repeat the behavior that led to the consequences. The type and timing of consequences can strengthen or weaken behaviors. Consequences that strengthen behaviors are called *reinforcers*.

Reinforcement.   Although *reinforcement* is commonly understood to mean "reward," this term has a particular meaning in learning theory. A **reinforcer** is any consequence that strengthens the behavior it follows. So, by definition, reinforced behaviors increase in frequency or duration. The **reinforcement process** can be diagrammed as follows:

CONSEQUENCE   EFFECT

Behavior $\longrightarrow$ reinforcer $\longrightarrow$ strengthened or repeated behavior

We can be fairly certain that food will be a reinforcer for a hungry animal, but what about people? It is not clear why an event acts as a reinforcer for an individual, but there are many theories about why reinforcement works. For example, some psychologists suggest that reinforcers satisfy needs, whereas other psychologists believe that reinforcers reduce tension or stimulate a part of the brain (Rachlin, 1991). Whether the consequences of any action are reinforcing probably depends on the individual's perception of the event and the meaning it holds for her or him (Landrum & Kauffman, 2006). For example, students who repeatedly are sent to the principal's office for misbehaving may be indicating that *something* about this consequence is reinforcing for them, even if it doesn't seem desirable to their teachers.

There are two types of reinforcement. The first, called **positive reinforcement,** occurs when the behavior produces (adds) a new stimulus. Examples include wearing a new outfit producing many compliments, or, for a student, falling out of a chair producing cheers and laughter from classmates. When teachers claim that a student misbehaves "just to get attention," they are applying a behavioral explanation based on positive reinforcement, assuming that attention is a positive reinforcer for the student.

Notice that positive reinforcement can occur even when the behavior being reinforced (falling out of a chair or disrupting math class) is not "positive" from the teacher's point of view. In fact, positive reinforcement of inappropriate behaviors occurs unintentionally in many classrooms. Teachers and principals help maintain problem behaviors by inadvertently reinforcing them. We once worked with a principal in a middle school who was concerned about a student. The boy had lost his father a few years earlier and was having trouble in a number of subjects, especially math. The student was sent to the office from math at least twice a week. When he arrived, the boy got the principal's undivided attention for at least ten minutes. After a scolding, they talked sports because the principal liked the student and was concerned that he had no male role models. It is easy to spot the reinforcers in this situation, even though the principal did not mean to be part of the problem.

When the consequence that strengthens a behavior is the appearance (addition) of a new stimulus, the situation is defined as *positive* (+) reinforcement. In contrast, when the consequence that strengthens a behavior is the disappearance (subtraction) of a stimulus, the process is called **negative (−) reinforcement.** If a particular action leads to stopping, avoiding, or escaping an aversive situation, that action is likely to be repeated in a similar situation. A common example is the car seat belt buzzer. As soon as you attach your seat belt, the irritating buzzer stops. You are likely to *repeat* this "buckling up" action in the future (so the process is *reinforcement*) because the behavior made an aversive buzzing stimulus *disappear* (so the kind of reinforcement is *negative*).

The student who was repeatedly sent to the principal's office from math class not only spent time with the principal talking sports (positive reinforcement), he also escaped math class (negative reinforcement). Whatever the student did to get kicked out of math class is likely to continue (and it did) because the behavior led to both positive and negative reinforcers. The "negative" in negative reinforcement does not imply that the behavior being reinforced is necessarily bad. The meaning is closer to that of "negative" numbers—something is subtracted. Associate positive and negative reinforcement with adding or subtracting something following a behavior, leading to an increase in that behavior.

Punishment.   Negative reinforcement is often confused with punishment. In fact, when you understand the difference between negative reinforcement and punishment, you will know more than most of your colleagues. The process of reinforcement (positive or negative) always involves strengthening behavior. **Punishment,** on the other hand, involves decreasing or suppressing behavior. A behavior followed by a "punisher" is *less* likely to be repeated in similar situations in the future. Again, it is the effect that defines a consequence as punishment, and different people have different perceptions of what is punishing. One student may find suspension from school punishing, while another student wouldn't mind at all. The process of punishment is diagrammed as follows:

CONSEQUENCE   EFFECT
Behavior $\longrightarrow$ punisher $\longrightarrow$ weakened or decreased behavior

Like reinforcement, punishment may take one of two forms. The first type has been called Type I punishment, but this name isn't very informative, so we use the term **presentation punishment.** It occurs when the presentation of a stimulus following the behavior suppresses or decreases the behavior. When teachers assign demerits, extra work, running laps, and so on, they are using presentation punishment. The other type of punishment (Type II punishment) we call **removal punishment** because it involves removing a stimulus. When teachers or parents take away privileges after a young person has behaved inappropriately, they are applying removal punishment. With both types, the effect is to decrease or slow down the behavior that led to the punishment. Figure 4.1 on the next page summarizes the processes of reinforcement and punishment we have just discussed.

Antecedents and Behavior Change

Antecedents.   The events preceding behaviors, the **antecedents,** provide information about which behaviors will lead to positive consequences and which to negative. We all learn to discriminate—to read situations. When should a principal ask the board for additional resources, after a budget cut or when a good story about the school has appeared in the local paper? The antecedent cue of a school principal standing in the hall helps students discriminate the probable consequences of running or attempting to break into a locker. We often respond to such antecedent cues without fully realizing that they are influencing our behavior. But we can use cues deliberately.

FIGURE 4.1 Kinds of Reinforcement and Punishment
Negative reinforcements and punishment are often confused. It may help you to remember that reinforcement is always associated with increases in behaviors, and punishment always involves decreasing or suppressing behavior.

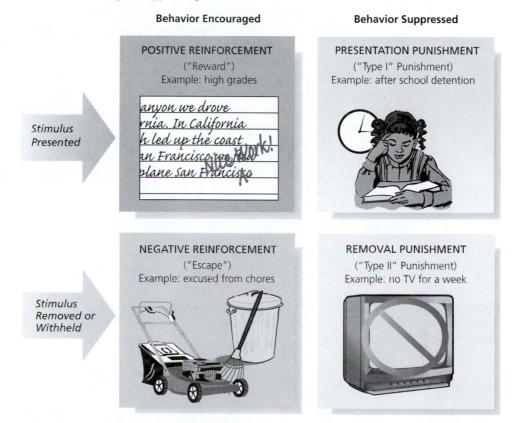

Source: Figure from *Educational psychology*, 12th Edition, by Anita E. Woolfolk. Copyright © 2013 by Pearson Education, Inc. Printed and Electronically reproduced by permission of Pearson Education, Inc., Upper Saddle River, New Jersey.

Cueing.   By definition, **cueing** is the act of providing an antecedent stimulus just before a particular behavior is to take place. Cueing is particularly useful in setting the stage for behaviors that must occur at a specific time but are easily forgotten. In working with young people, teachers often find themselves correcting behaviors after the fact. For example, they may ask students, "When are you going to start remembering to . . . ?" But the mistake is already made, and the young person is left with only two choices, to promise to try harder or to say, "Why don't you leave me alone?" Neither response is very satisfying. Presenting a nonjudgmental cue, such as a checklist, can help prevent these negative confrontations. When a student performs appropriately after a cue, the teacher can reinforce his or her accomplishment instead of punishing a failure.

Prompting.   Sometimes students need help in learning to respond to a cue. One approach is to provide an additional cue, called a *prompt*, following the first cue. There are two principles for using a cue and a prompt to teach a new behavior. First, make sure the environmental stimulus that you want to become a cue occurs immediately before the prompt you are using, so students will learn to respond to the cue and not rely only on the prompt. Second, fade the prompt as soon as possible so students do not become dependent on it (Alberto & Troutman, 2009).

An example of cueing and **prompting** is providing students with a checklist or reminder sheet. Figure 4.2 is a checklist for the steps in peer tutoring. Working in pairs is the cue; the checklist is the prompt. As students learn the procedures, the teacher may stop using the checklist, but may remind the students of the steps. When no written or oral prompts are necessary, the students have learned to respond appropriately to the environmental cue of working in pairs; they have learned how to behave in tutoring situations. But the teacher should continue to monitor the process, recognize good work, and correct mistakes. Before a tutoring session, the teacher might ask students to close their eyes and "see" the checklist, focusing on each step. As students work, the teacher could listen to their interactions and continue to coach students as they improve their tutoring skills.

Principals and teachers can make good use of behavioral principles, particularly in their wise and caring applications of reinforcement and punishment. The *Theory into Action Guidelines* on the next page give examples that will help your teachers apply the behavioral theory described above. Instructional leaders not only need to know the theory; they also must be able to demonstrate and apply it as they work with their teachers.

FIGURE 4.2   Written Prompts: A Peer-Tutoring Checklist
By using this checklist, students are reminded how to be effective tutors. As they become more proficient, the checklist may be less necessary.

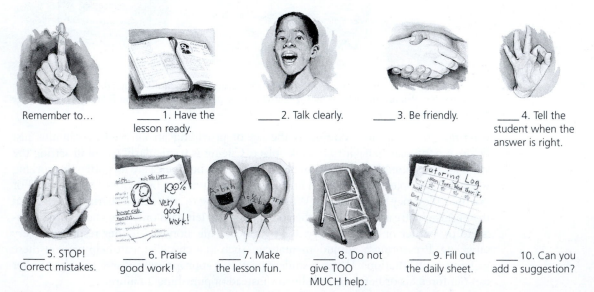

Remember to…

_____ 1. Have the lesson ready.

_____ 2. Talk clearly.

_____ 3. Be friendly.

_____ 4. Tell the student when the answer is right.

_____ 5. STOP! Correct mistakes.

_____ 6. Praise good work!

_____ 7. Make the lesson fun.

_____ 8. Do not give TOO MUCH help.

_____ 9. Fill out the daily sheet.

_____ 10. Can you add a suggestion?

Source: Excerpt from *Achieving educational excellence: Behavior analysis for school personnel* by Beth Sulzer-Azaroff and G. Roy Mayer. Copyright © 1994 by Beth Sulzer-Azaroff and G. Roy Mayer, Reprinted with permission of the authors.

THEORY INTO ACTION GUIDELINES

Using Reinforcement and Punishment

Associate positive, pleasant events with learning tasks.

Examples

1. Emphasize group competition and cooperation over individual competition. Many students have negative emotional responses to individual competition that may generalize to other learning.
2. Make division drills fun by having students decide how to divide refreshments equally, then letting them eat the results.
3. Make voluntary reading appealing by creating a comfortable reading corner with pillows, colorful displays of books, and reading props such as puppets (see Weinstein, Romano, and Mignano, 2011, for more ideas).

Help students to risk anxiety-producing situations voluntarily and successfully.

Examples

1. Assign a shy student the responsibility of teaching two other students how to distribute materials for map study.
2. Devise small steps toward a larger goal. For example, give ungraded practice tests daily, and then weekly, to students who tend to "freeze" in test situations.
3. Allow a student who is afraid of speaking in front of the class to read a report to a small group while seated, then read it while standing, then give the report from notes instead of reading it verbatim. Next, move in stages toward having the student give a report to the whole class.

Be clear, systematic, and genuine in giving praise.

Examples

1. Make sure praise is tied directly to appropriate behavior.
2. Make sure the student understands the specific action or accomplishment that is being praised. Say, "You returned this poster on time and in good condition," not, "You were very responsible."
3. Tie praise to students' improving competence or to the value of their accomplishment. Say, "I noticed that you double-checked all your problems. Your score reflects your careful work."

Attribute the student's success to effort and ability so the student will gain confidence that success is possible again.

Examples

1. Don't imply that the success may be based on luck, extra help, or easy material.
2. Ask students to describe the problems they encountered and how they solved them.

When students are tackling new material or trying new skills, give plenty of reinforcement.

Examples

1. Find and comment on something right in every student's first life drawing.
2. Reinforce students for encouraging each other. "French pronunciation is difficult and awkward at first. Let's help each other by eliminating all giggles when someone is brave enough to attempt a new word."

After new behaviors are established, give reinforcement on an unpredictable schedule to encourage persistence.

Examples

1. Offer surprise rewards for good participation in class.
2. Start classes with a short, written extra-credit question. Students don't have to answer, but a good answer will add points to their total grade for the semester.
3. Make sure the good students get compliments for their work from time to time. Don't take them for granted.

(Continued)

THEORY INTO ACTION GUIDELINES Continued

Make sure all students, even those who often cause problems, receive some praise, privileges, or other rewards when they do something well.

Examples

1. Review your class list occasionally to make sure all students are receiving some reinforcement.
2. Set standards for reinforcement so that all students will have a chance to be rewarded.
3. Let students suggest their own reinforcers or choose from a "menu" of reinforcers with "weekly specials."

Be consistent in your application of punishment.

Examples

1. Avoid inadvertently reinforcing the behavior you are trying to punish. Keep confrontations private, so that students don't become heroes for standing up to the teacher in a public showdown.
2. Let students know in advance the consequences of breaking the rules by posting major class rules for younger students or outlining rules and consequences in a course syllabus for older students.
3. Tell students they will receive only one warning before punishment is given. Give the warning in a calm way, then follow through.
4. Make punishment as unavoidable and immediate as is reasonably possible.

Focus on the students' actions, not on the students' personal qualities.

Examples

1. Reprimand in a calm but firm voice.
2. Avoid vindictive or sarcastic words or tones of voice. You might hear your own angry words later when students imitate your sarcasm.
3. Stress the need to end the problem behavior instead of expressing any dislike you might feel for the student.

Adapt the punishment to the infraction.

Examples

1. Ignore minor misbehaviors that do not disrupt the class, or stop these misbehaviors with a disapproving glance or a move toward the student.
2. Don't use homework as a punishment for misbehaviors like talking in class.
3. When a student misbehaves to gain peer acceptance, removal from the group of friends can be effective, since this is really time out from a reinforcing situation.
4. If the problem behaviors continue, analyze the situation and try a new approach. Your punishment may not be very punishing, or you may be inadvertently reinforcing the misbehavior.

Teaching Applications of Behavioral Theories

The behavioral approach to learning has made several important contributions to instruction, including systems for specifying learning objectives (we will look at this topic in Chapter 6 when we discuss planning and teaching) and class management systems such as group consequences, token economies, and contingency contracts. These approaches are especially useful when the goal is to learn explicit information or change behaviors and when the material is sequential and factual (Alberto & Troutman, 2009; Kazdin, 2001). As an example of a teaching approach, let's consider a system that supports students' positive behaviors rather than punishing mistakes.

Functional Behavioral Assessment and Positive Behavior Support

Teachers in both regular and special education classes have had success with a new approach that begins by asking, "What are students getting out of their problem behaviors—what functions do these behaviors serve?" The focus is on the *why* of the behavior, not on the *what* (Lane, Falk, & Wehby, 2006; Stage et al., 2008). The reasons for problem behaviors generally fall into four categories (Barnhill, 2005; Maag & Kemp, 2003). Students act out to:

1. receive attention from others—teachers, parent, or peers.
2. escape from some unpleasant situation—an academic or social demand.
3. get a desired item or activity.
4. meet sensory needs (such as stimulation from rocking or flapping arms for some children with autism).

If the reason for the behavior is known, then the teacher can devise ways of supporting positive behaviors that will serve the same "why" function. For example, in the situation we described earlier, the student who was repeatedly sent out of math class to the principal's office, it is easy to spot the function of the classroom disruptions—they always led to (1) escape from math class (negative reinforcement) and (2) one-on-one time with the principal (positive reinforcement after a little bit of reprimanding). Working with the principal and math teacher, we developed a way to support the student's positive behaviors in math by getting him some extra tutoring and by giving him time with the principal when he completed math problems instead of when he acted up in class. The new positive behaviors served many of the same functions as the old problem behaviors.

Discovering the "Why": Functional Behavioral Assessments. The process of understanding a problem behavior is known as **functional behavioral assessment (FBA)**—"a collection of methods or procedures used to obtain information about antecedents, behaviors, and consequences to determine the reason or function of the behavior" (Barnhill, 2005, p. 132). Many different procedures might help you determine the functions of a behavior. You can simply interview students about their behaviors. In one study, students were asked to describe what they did that got them in trouble in school, what happened just before, and what happened right after they acted out. Even though the students were not always sure why they acted out, they seemed to benefit from talking to a concerned adult who was trying to understand their situation, not just reprimand them (Murdock, O'Neill, & Cunningham, 2005). You also can observe students with these questions in mind: When and where does the problem behavior occur? What people or activities are involved? What happens right before—what do others do or say and what did the target student do or say? What happens right after the behavior—what did you, other students, or the target student do or say? What does the target student gain or escape from—what changes after the student acts out? A more structured approach is shown in Figure 4.3—an observation guide for functional behavioral

FIGURE 4.3   A Simple Structured Observation Guide for Functional Behavioral Analysis Using the ABC Frame

Student Name: Denton R.   Date: 2/25/2012
Location: Math—Mrs. B   Observer: Mr. B.
Start time: 1:02   Stop time: 1:15

A. Antecedents	B. Behaviors	C. Consequences
1:03 Students get out books and open to begin class.	D. pulls out his cap and puts it on.	Students around D. start laughing and saying "Hey."
1:05 Teacher notices D. and tells him to remove his cap.	D. stands, slowly removes his cap, and bows.	Students applaud.
1:14 Teacher asks D. a question.	D. says, "Man, I don't know."	Another student says, "Yeah, you're stupid." Others laugh.

Source: Figure from *Including students with special needs: A practice guide for classroom teachers*, 6th Edition, by Marilyn Friend and William D. Bursuck. Copyright © 2012 by Pearson Education, Inc. Printed and Electronically reproduced by permission of Pearson Education, Inc., Upper Saddle River, New Jersey.

assessment based on a simple ABC analysis. Using this information, the teacher found out that the student acted out whenever the class was transitioning to another activity. The sources of reinforcement for the student are clear too.

With information from a functional behavioral assessment, administrators and teachers can develop an intervention package of positive behavior supports, as we did with the math student.

Positive Behavior Supports.   The Individuals with Disabilities Education Act (IDEA, 1997) discussed in Chapter 2 requires positive behavior supports (PBS) for students with disabilities and those at risk for special education placement. **Positive behavior supports** are interventions designed to replace problem behaviors with new actions that serve the same purpose for the student.

Positive behavior supports based on functional behavioral assessments can help students with disabilities succeed in inclusion classrooms. For example, the disruptive behavior of a five-year-old boy with an intellectual disability was nearly eliminated in a relatively short time through a PBS intervention that was based on a functional assessment conducted by the regular teaching staff and the special education teacher. The intervention included making sure tasks assigned were at the right difficulty level, providing assistance with these tasks, teaching the student how to request assistance, and teaching the student how to request a break from assigned work (Soodak & McCarthy, 2006; Umbreit, 1995). But these approaches are not only for students with special needs. Research shows that disciplinary referrals decrease when the whole school uses these interventions for all students. Because about 5% of students account for half of the discipline referrals, it makes sense to develop interventions for those students. Positive behavior interventions based on functional assessments can reduce these behavior problems by 80% (Crone & Horner, 2003).

POINT/COUNTERPOINT

Is Homework a Valuable Use of Time?

Like so many methods in education, homework has moved in and out of favor. In the early 1900s, homework was seen as an important path to mental discipline, but by the 1940s, homework was criticized as too much drill and low-level learning. Then, in the 1950s, homework was rediscovered as a way to catch up with the Soviet Union in science and mathematics, only to be seen as putting too much pressure on students during the more laid-back 1960s. By the 1980s, homework was in again as a way to improve the standing of American children compared to students around the world (Cooper & Valentine, 2001). Today, homework is increasing in early elementary schools (Hofferth & Sandberg, 2000). Everyone has done homework—were those hours well spent?

POINT

Homework does not help students learn.
No matter how interesting an activity is, students will eventually get bored with it—so why give them work both in and out of school? They will simply grow weary of learning. And important opportunities are lost for community involvement or leisure activities that would create well-rounded citizens. When parents help with homework, they can do more harm than good—sometimes confusing their children or teaching them incorrectly. And students from poorer families often must work, so they miss doing their homework; then the learning discrepancy between the rich and the poor grows even greater. Besides, the research is inconsistent about the effects of homework. For example, one study found that in-class work was better than homework in helping elementary students learn (Cooper & Valentine, 2001). In his book, *The Homework Myth: Why Our Kids Get Too Much of a Bad Thing*, Alfie Kohn (2006) suggests that schools adopt no homework as the default policy. "Changing the default to no homework would likely have two practical consequences: The number of assignments would decline and the quality of those assignments would rise. Both of these, I

believe, represent significant improvements in our children's education" (p. 168).

COUNTERPOINT

Well-planned homework can work for many students.
Harris Cooper and his colleagues reviewed many studies of homework and concluded that there is little relationship between homework and learning for young students, but the relationship between homework and achievement grows progressively stronger for older students. Most of the studies involved math and reading or English homework, however, and not social studies, science, or other subjects. There is recent evidence that students in high school who do more homework (and watch less television after school) have higher grades, even when other factors such as gender, grade level, ethnicity, SES, and amount of adult supervision are taken into consideration (Cooper, Robinson, & Patall, 2006; Cooper & Valentine, 2001; Cooper, Valentine, Nye, & Kindsay, 1999). Consistent with all these findings, the National PTA makes these recommendations:

> [F]or children in grades K–2, homework is most effective when it does not exceed 10–20 minutes each day; older students, in grades 3–6, can handle 30–60 minutes a day; in junior and senior high school, the amount of homework will vary by subject. (Henderson, 1996, p. 1)

Most research examines the relationship between amount of time spent on homework (as reported by students or parents) and achievement in terms of grades or achievement tests. Another approach is to focus on effort instead of time. Students' self-reported effort on homework is consistently and positively related to student achievement (Trautwein, 2007). "High homework effort means that a student does his or her best to solve the tasks assigned. There need not be a close relationship between effort and time on homework: A student putting as much effort as possible into a homework assignment might finish in 5 min or still

(Continued)

be working after an hour" (Trautwein & Lüdtke, 2007, p. 432). Students are more likely to put in effort if they see the homework as interesting, valuable, reasonably challenging, and not anxiety provoking—this could require some differentiated

homework assignments (Dettmers, Trautwein, Ludtke, Kunter, & Baumert, 2010). So the challenge is to get students to put their best efforts into appropriate homework and not assign homework that is low quality.

Sources: Kohn excerpt from *The homework myth: Why our kids get too much of a bad thing* by Alfie Kohn. Da Capo Press, 2006. National Parent Teacher Association excerpt from "Help your student get the most out of homework." Copyright © 1996 by National Parent Teacher Association. Reprinted with permission. Trautwein & Lüdtke excerpt from "Students' self-reported effort and time on homework in six school subjects: Between-students differences and within-student variation" by Ulrich Trauwein and Oliver Lüdtke, from *Journal of Educational Psychology*, May 2007, Volume 99(2): pp. 432–444. American Psychological Association. Reprinted with permission.

Homework

One of the implications of the behavioral view is that learning requires the practice of correct responses—practice makes permanent. Educators have been studying the effects of homework for over 80 years (Cooper, 2004; Cooper & Valentine, 2001; Corno, 2000; Trautwein & Koller, 2003). Homework is one form of practice, but the value of homework has been debated, as you can see in the *Point/Counterpoint*.

Cognitive Views of Learning

The cognitive view is both the oldest and one of the youngest perspectives in psychology. It is old because discussions of the nature of knowledge, the value of reason, and the contents of the mind date back at least to the ancient Greek philosophers (Gluck, Mercado, & Myers, 2008). From the late 1800s until several decades ago, however, cognitive studies fell from favor and behaviorism thrived. Today, there is renewed interest in learning, thinking, and problem solving. The focus is the scientific study of memory and cognition—broadly defined as "the mental events and knowledge we use when we recognize an object, remember a name, have an idea, understand a sentence, or solve a problem" (Ashcraft & Radvansky, 2010, p. 2). The emphasis is on everyday thinking, even though the study of abnormal thinking (as in schizophrenia) can help us understand cognition better at times. The **cognitive view of learning** can be described as a generally agreed-upon philosophical orientation. Most importantly, cognitive psychologists assume that mental processes exist, that they can be studied scientifically, and that humans are active information processors.

In the past few years, the study of memory and cognition has become interdisciplinary and often is called **cognitive science**—the study of thinking, language, and, increasingly, the brain. Cognitive science views cognition as the operation of a very complex but coordinated system of multiple memory components interacting rapidly and simultaneously (Ashcraft & Radvansky, 2010).

Knowledge and Learning

Current cognitive approaches suggest that one of the most important elements in the learning process is what the individual brings to the learning situation. What we already know determines to a great extent what we will pay attention to, perceive, learn, remember, and forget (Bransford, Brown, & Cocking, 2002; Bransford, Derry, Berliner, & Hammerness, 2005). For example, compared to 4th graders with little knowledge of soccer, 4th graders who were soccer experts learned and remembered far more new soccer terms, even though the abilities of the two groups to learn and remember nonsoccer terms were the same. The difference was the soccer experts used their soccer knowledge to organize and cluster the soccer terms, which helped them remember (Schneider & Bjorklund, 1992).

There are different kinds of knowledge. Some is general—it applies to many different situations. For example, general knowledge about how to read or write or use a computer is useful in and out of school. **Domain-specific knowledge,** on the other hand, pertains to a particular task or subject. For example, knowing that the shortstop plays between second and third base is specific to the domain of baseball. Another way to categorize knowledge is as *declarative, procedural,* or *self-regulatory* (Schraw, 2006).

Declarative knowledge can be articulated through words and symbol systems of all kinds—Braille, sign language, dance or musical notation, mathematical symbols, and so on. Declarative knowledge is "knowing that" something is the case. The range of declarative knowledge is tremendous. You can know very specific facts (the atomic weight of gold is 196.967), or generalities (leaves of some trees change color in autumn), or personal preferences (we don't like cold weather), or rules (to divide fractions, invert the divisor and multiply). Small units of declarative knowledge can be organized into larger units; for example, principles of reinforcement and punishment can be organized in your thinking into a theory of behavioral learning.

Procedural knowledge is "knowing how" to do something such as divide fractions or design a website—it is knowledge in action. Procedural knowledge must be demonstrated. Notice that repeating the rule "to divide fractions, invert the divisor and multiply" shows declarative knowledge—the student can state the rule. But to show procedural knowledge, the student must act. When faced with a fraction to divide, the student must divide correctly. Students demonstrate procedural knowledge when they translate a passage into Spanish, correctly categorize a geometric shape, or craft a coherent paragraph.

Self-regulatory knowledge is the ability to manage your learning—knowing how and when to use your declarative and procedural knowledge (Schraw, 2006). It takes self-regulatory knowledge to know when to read every word in a text and when to skim or when to apply a strategy for overcoming procrastination. Self-regulatory knowledge has also been called *conditional knowledge* (Paris & Cunningham, 1996). For many students, this kind of knowledge is a stumbling block. They have the facts and can do the procedures, but they don't seem to understand how to apply what they know at the appropriate time. Self-regulatory knowledge can be specific to a subject area (when to use the formula for calculating area, not perimeter, in geometry) or more general (how to summarize key points or use diagrams to organize information).

TABLE 4.1   Kinds of Knowledge

	General Knowledge	Domain-Specific Knowledge
Declarative	Hours the library is open	The definition of *hypotenuse*
	Rules of grammar	The lines of the poem "The Raven"
Procedural	How to use your computer	How to solve an oxidation-reduction equation
	How to drive	How to throw a pot on a potter's wheel
Self-Regulatory	When to give up and try another approach	When to use the formula for calculating volume
	When to skim and when to read carefully	When to rush the net in tennis

Source: Table from *Educational psychology*, 12th Edition, by Anita E. Woolfolk. Copyright © 2013 by Pearson Education, Inc. Printed and Electronically reproduced by permission of Pearson Education, Inc., Upper Saddle River, New Jersey.

In fact, all three kinds of knowledge—declarative, procedural, and self-regulatory—can be either general or domain-specific, as you can see in Table 4.1 (Schraw, 2006).

To be used, knowledge must be remembered. What do we know about memory?

An Information Processing Model

There are a number of theories of memory, but the most common are the information processing explanations (Ashcraft & Radvansky, 2010; Bruning et al., 2011; Sternberg & Sternberg, 2012). We will use this well-researched framework for examining learning and memory.

Early information processing views of memory used the computer as a model. Like the computer, the human mind takes in information, performs operations on it to change its form and content, stores the information, retrieves it when needed, and generates responses to it. According to this model, stimuli from the environment (input) flow into the sensory registers, one for each sensing modality (seeing, hearing, tasting, etc.). From there, some information is encoded and moves to short-term memory. Short-term memory holds information very briefly, combines it with information from long-term memory, and with enough effort, moves some information into long-term memory storage. Short-term memory is also responsible for generating responses or output.

This model proved helpful, but also incomplete. For example, in the model, information moved through the system mostly in one way, from sensory registers to long-term memory, but research indicated many more interactions and connections among the processes. The model could not explain how several cognitive processes could happen simultaneously—like many small computers operating in parallel. A more recent cognitive science information processing model retains some of the features of the old approach, but emphasizes the role of working memory, attention, and the interactions among the elements of the system, as shown in Figure 4.4 on the next page, which is based on several sources (Ashcraft & Radvansky, 2010; Bruning et al., 2011; Sternberg & Sternberg, 2012).

In order to understand this model, let's examine each element more carefully.

FIGURE 4.4 A Recent Version of the Information Processing Model
Information is encoded in sensory memory, where perception and attention determine what will be held in working memory for further use. In working memory, executive processes manage the flow of information and integrate new information with knowledge from long-term memory. Thoroughly processed and connected information becomes part of long-term memory, and when activated again, becomes part of working memory (which might simply be the activated portion of long-term memory). Implicit memories are formed without conscious effort. All three elements of the system interact with each other to guide perception; represent, organize, and interpret information; apply and modify propositions, concepts, images, schemas, and strategies; construct knowledge; and solve problems. Attention has a role in all three memory processes and in the interactions among them.

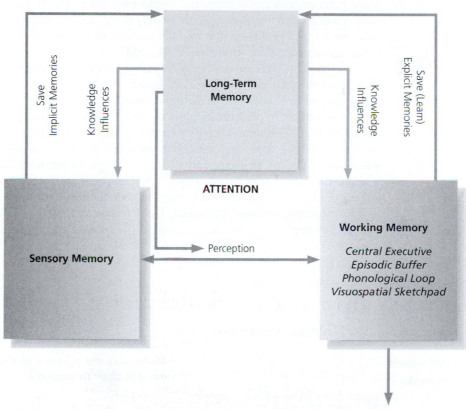

Source: Figure from *Educational psychology,* 12th Edition, by Anita E. Woolfolk. Copyright © 2013 by Pearson Education, Inc. Printed and Electronically reproduced by permission of Pearson Education, Inc., Upper Saddle River, New Jersey.

Sensory Memory

As you can see, **sensory memory** is the initial processing that transforms incoming stimuli (sights, sounds, smells, and so on) into information so we can make sense of them. We hold information, in the form of images or sounds or other codes, for only a very few seconds. **Attention** (maintaining cognitive focus on something and resisting distractions) is critical at this stage. What is not attended to is lost. This is actually useful because if every variation in color, movement, sound, smell, temperature, and so on ended up in memory, life would be impossible. But attention is *selective*. What we pay attention to is guided to a certain extent by what we already know and what we need to know, so attention is involved in and influenced by all three memory processes—sensory, working, and long-term.

Attention also is a very limited resource. We can pay attention to only one demanding task at time. For example, if you learned to drive a stick shift, there probably was a time when you couldn't listen to the radio and drive at the same time. After some practice, you could listen, but might turn the radio off when traffic was heavy. After years of practice, some people plan lessons or presentations as they drive. This is because many processes that initially require attention and concentration become automatic with practice (Bransford et al., 2005).

So the first step in learning is to pay attention. Students cannot process something that they do not recognize or perceive (Lachter, Forster, & Ruthruff, 2004). Many factors in the classroom influence student attention. A teacher might begin a science lesson on air pressure by blowing up a balloon until it pops. Bright colors, underlining, highlighting of written or spoken words, calling students by name, surprise events, intriguing questions, variety in tasks and teaching methods, and changes in voice level, lighting, or pacing can all be used to gain attention. And students have to maintain attention; they have to stay focused on the important features of the learning situation. How can instructional leaders help teachers develop strategies for capturing and maintaining students' attention? The *Theory into Action Guidelines* provide some concrete examples.

THEORY INTO ACTION GUIDELINES

Capturing and Holding Attention

Use signals.

Examples
1. Develop a signal that tells students to stop what they are doing and focus on you. Some teachers move to a particular spot in the room, flick the lights, or play a chord on the class piano.
2. Avoid distracting behaviors, such as tapping a pencil, that interfere with both signals and attention to learning.
3. Give short, clear directions before, not during, transitions.

Make sure the purpose of the lesson or assignment is clear to students.

Examples
1. Write the goals or objectives on the board and discuss them with students before starting. Ask students to summarize or restate the goals.
2. Explain the reasons for learning, and ask students for examples of how they will apply their understanding of the material.
3. Tie the new material to previous lessons—show an outline or map of how the new topic fits with previous and upcoming material.

(Continued)

THEORY INTO ACTION GUIDELINES **Continued**

Emphasize variety, curiosity, and surprise.

Examples

1. Arouse curiosity with questions such as "What would happen if . . . ?"
2. Create shock by staging an unexpected event such as a loud argument just before a lesson on communication.
3. Alter the physical environment by changing the arrangement of the room or moving to a different setting.
4. Shift sensory channels by giving a lesson that requires students to touch, smell, or taste.
5. Use movements, gestures, and voice inflection—walk around the room, point, and speak softly

and then more emphatically. (The second author has been known to jump up on his desk to make an important point in his college classes!)

Ask questions and provide frames for answering.

Examples

1. Ask students why the material is important, how they intend to study, and what strategies they will use.
2. Give students self-checking or self-editing guides that focus on common mistakes, or have them work in pairs to improve each other's work—sometimes it is difficult to pay attention to your own errors.

Working Memory

Once noticed and transformed into patterns, the information in sensory memory is available for further processing. The working space of the memory system is called (surprise) **working memory.** It is the interface where new information is held temporarily (no more than 20 seconds or so) and combined with knowledge from long-term memory, to solve problems or understand a talk on leadership, for example. Working memory "contains" what you are thinking about at the moment. You may have heard the term *short-term memory.* This is similar to working memory but refers only to the storage space available. Working memory includes both temporary storage and active processing; it is the process or stage where active mental effort is applied to new and old information.

A current view of working memory is that it is composed of at least four elements: the *central executive* that controls attention and other mental resources (the "worker" of working memory), the *phonological loop* that briefly holds verbal and acoustical (sound) information, and the *visuospatial sketchpad* for visual and spatial information. Information from the phonological loop and the visuospatial sketchpad is integrated with information from long-term memory in an *episodic buffer.* This episodic buffer is the true workbench of working memory—the point where information from many sources is pulled together and processed (Baddeley, 2007; Baddeley, Hitch, & Allen, 2009; Jarrold, Tam, Baddeley, & Harvey, 2011).

Capacity and Contents. Working memory capacity is limited. In experimental situations it appears that the capacity of working memory is only about five to nine separate new items at once (Miller, 1956). For example, if someone tells you a phone number, you can remember it long enough to dial the number, but would you try to remember two phone numbers? Two new phone numbers (fourteen digits) probably cannot be stored simultaneously. We are discussing the recall of *new* information. In daily life we certainly can hold more than five to nine bits of information at once. You don't have to pay attention to why you are calling or how to dial because these do not entail new knowledge. However, because of the working memory's limitations, if you were in a foreign country and were attempting to use an unfamiliar telephone system, you might very well have trouble remembering the phone number because you were trying to figure out the phone system at the same time.

It is clear that the duration of information in working memory is short, about 5 to 20 seconds. This is why working memory has been called *short-term memory*. It may seem to you that a memory system with a 20-second time limit is not very useful. But without this system, you would have already forgotten what you read in the first part of this sentence before you came to these last few words. This would clearly make understanding sentences difficult.

Cognitive Load.   One of the most important concepts related to working memory is **cognitive load,** the amount of mental resources, mostly working memory, required to perform a particular task. The extent of cognitive load in a given situation depends on many things, including what the person already knows about the task and what supports are available. There are three kinds of cognitive load. One is unavoidable, one gets in the way, and one is valuable.

Intrinsic cognitive load is unavoidable—it is the amount of cognitive processing required to figure out the material. That amount depends on how many elements you have to take into account, how complicated the interactions among the elements are, and your level of expertise in the problem area (Antonenko, Paas, Grabner, & van Gog, 2010). Intrinsic cognitive load is essential to the task—it cannot be eliminated. But good instruction can help manage intrinsic load.

Extraneous cognitive load is the cognitive capacity you use to deal with problems not related to the learning task, such as struggling with a disorganized lecture or a poorly written textbook (not this one, of course!). Instruction can help manage extraneous load by providing supports and focusing attention on the main ideas.

The good cognitive load is called *germane* because it is directly related to (germane to) high quality learning. *Germane cognitive load* comes from deep processing of relevant information—organizing and integrating the material with what you already know and forming new understandings. Instruction can support this process by asking students to explain the material to each other or to themselves, draw or chart their understandings, take useful notes, and use other good learning strategies that encourage deep processing (Berthold & Renkl, 2009; Mayer, 2011, van Gog, Pass, & Sweller, 2010).

Retaining Information in Working Memory.   Because information in working memory is fragile and easily lost, especially when cognitive load is high, the information must be kept activated to be retained. When activation fades, forgetting follows. To keep information activated in working memory for longer than 20 seconds, most people keep rehearsing the information mentally (Anderson, 1995, 2010).

There are two types of rehearsal. **Maintenance rehearsal** involves repeating the information in your mind. As long as you repeat the information, it can be maintained

in working memory indefinitely. Maintenance rehearsal is useful for retaining something you plan to use and then forget, like a phone number. **Elaborative rehearsal**
involves connecting the information you are trying to remember with something you
already know, that is, with information from long-term memory. For example, if you
meet someone at a party whose name is the same as yours, you don't have to repeat
the name to keep it in memory, you just have to make the connection. This kind of rehearsal not only retains information in working memory but also helps move information from working memory to long-term memory. Rehearsal is thus an *executive control
process* that affects the flow of information through the information processing system.

The limited capacity of working memory can also be somewhat circumvented by
the control process of **chunking.** Because the *number* of bits of information, not the
size of each bit, is the limitation for working memory, you can retain more information
if you can group individual bits of information. For example, if you have to remember
the six digits 3, 5, 4, 8, 7, and 0, it is easier to put them together into three chunks of
two digits each (35, 48, 70) or two chunks of three digits each (354, 870). With these
changes, there are only two or three bits of information rather than six to hold at one
time. Chunking helps you remember a telephone number or a Social Security number.

Long-Term Memory

Working memory holds the information that is currently activated, such as a telephone
number you have just found and are about to dial. Long-term memory holds the information that is well learned, such as all the other telephone numbers you know. Recently,
however, some psychologists have suggested that there are not two separate memory
stores (working and long term). Rather, working memory is the part of long-term memory that works on (processes) *currently activated* information. The difference between
working memory and long-term memory just may be in how activated or inactive a particular memory is (Anderson, 2010; Wilson, 2001). This model sees memory as a set of
nested systems with very short-term storage (phonological loop, visuospatial sketchpad)
nested in working memory, which is just the active part of long-term memory that does
the integrating of old and new information (Sternberg & Sternberg, 2012).

Capacity and Duration of Long-Term Memory.   Information enters working
memory very quickly. To move information into long-term storage requires more time
and a bit of effort. Whereas the capacity of working memory is limited, the capacity of
long-term memory appears to be, for all practical purposes, unlimited. In addition, once
information is securely stored in long-term memory, it can remain there permanently.
Theoretically, we should be able to remember as much as we want for as long as we
want. Of course, the problem is finding the right information when it is needed.

Contents of Long-Term Memory.   Most cognitive psychologists distinguish three
categories of long-term memory: episodic, procedural, and semantic. Memory for information tied to a particular place and time, especially information about the events
of your own life, is called *episodic memory*. **Episodic memory** keeps track of the order
of things, so it is also a good place to store jokes, gossip, or plots from films. Memories

for dramatic or emotional episodes in your life are called **flashbulb memories.** This kind of episodic memory is vivid and complete, as if your brain demanded that you "record this moment." Under stress, more glucose energy goes to fuel brain activity while stress-induced hormones signal the brain that something important is happening (Myers, 2005). So when we have strong emotional reactions, memories are stronger and more lasting. Many people have vivid memories of very positive or very negative events in school—winning a prize or being humiliated, for example. You probably know just where you were and what you were doing on 9/11.

Memory for how to do things is called **procedural memory.** It may take a while to learn a procedure—such as how to ski, serve a tennis ball, or factor an equation—but once learned, this knowledge tends to be remembered for a long time. Procedural memories are represented as condition–action rules, sometimes called *productions.* Productions specify what to do under certain conditions: if A occurs, then do B. A production might be something like, "If you want to snow ski faster, lean back slightly," or "If your goal is to increase student attention, and a student has been paying attention a bit longer than usual, then praise the student." People can't necessarily state all their condition–action rules, but they act on them nevertheless. The more practiced the procedure, the more automatic the action (Anderson, 1995). **Semantic memory** is memory for meaning. Two important ways that these memories are stored are by images and schemas.

Images are representations based on perceptions, on the structure or appearance of the information (Anderson, 1995). As we form images, we try to remember or recreate the physical attributes and spatial structure of information. For example, when asked how many windowpanes are in their living room, most people call up an image of the windows "in their mind's eye" and count the panes—the more panes, the longer it takes to respond (Mendell, 1971). Images are useful in making many practical decisions such as how a sofa might look in your living room or how to line up a golf shot. Images may also be helpful in abstract reasoning. Physicists such as Faraday and Einstein have reported creating images to reason about complex new problems (Gagné, Yekovich, & Yekovich, 1993).

Schemas (sometimes called *schemata*) are abstract knowledge structures that organize vast amounts of information. A schema (the singular form) is a pattern or guide for understanding an event, a concept, or a skill. The schema tells you what features are typical of a category—what to expect. The schema is like a pattern, specifying the "standard" relationships in an object or situation. And schemas are individual. For example, a museum curator and a salesperson may have very different schemas about antiques.

Storing and Retrieving Information in Long-Term Memory

How can we make the most effective use of our practically unlimited capacity to learn and remember? The way you learn information in the first place—the way you process it at the outset—seems to affect its recall later. One important requirement is that you integrate new material with information already stored in long-term memory as you construct an understanding. Here *elaboration*, *organization*, and *context* play a role.

Elaboration is the addition of meaning to new information through its connection with already existing knowledge. In other words, we apply our schemas and draw on already existing knowledge to construct an understanding; this frequently changes our existing knowledge in the process. We often elaborate automatically. For example, a paragraph about a historic figure in the seventeenth century tends to activate our existing knowledge about that period; we use the old knowledge to understand the new. Material that is elaborated when first learned will be easier to recall later. First, as we saw earlier, elaboration is a form of rehearsal. It keeps the information activated in working memory long enough to have a chance for permanent storage in long-term memory.

Second, elaboration builds extra links to existing knowledge. The more one bit of information or knowledge is associated with other bits, the more routes there are to follow to get to the original bit. To put it another way, you have several "handles," or retrieval cues, by which you can recognize or "pick up" the information you might be seeking (Schunk, 2012). The more people elaborate new ideas, the more they "make them their own," the deeper their understanding becomes and the better their memory will be for the knowledge. We help students to elaborate when we ask them to translate information into their own words, create examples, explain to a peer, draw the relationships, or apply the information to solve new problems. Of course, if students elaborate new information by making incorrect connections or developing misguided explanations, these misconceptions will be stored and remembered too.

Organization is a second element of processing that improves learning. Material that is well organized is easier to learn and to remember than bits and pieces of information, especially if the information is complex or extensive. Placing a concept in a structure will help you learn and remember either general definitions or specific examples. The structure serves as a guide back to the information when you need it. For example, Table 4.1 (on page 106) organizes information about kinds of knowledge.

Context is a third element of processing that influences learning. Aspects of physical and emotional context—places, rooms, moods, who is with us—are learned along with other information. Later, if you try to remember the information, it will be easier if the current context is similar to the original one (Ashcraft & Radvansky, 2010). For example, in a classic study, scuba divers who learned a list of words underwater and then were tested underwater remembered more than scuba divers who learned underwater but were tested on dry land (Godden & Baddeley, 1975). In another study, students who learned material in one type of room performed better on tests taken in a similar room than they did on comparable tests taken in a very different-looking room (Smith, Glenberg, & Bjork, 1978). So, studying for a test under "test-like" conditions (not at McDonald's, for example) may result in improved performance.

Craik and Lockhart (1972) suggested that what determines how long information is remembered is how thoroughly the information is analyzed and connected with other information. The more completely information is processed, the better our chances are of remembering it. For example, according to the levels of processing theory, if you were asked to sort pictures of dogs based on the color of their coats, you might not remember many of the pictures later. But if asked to rate each dog on how likely it is to chase you as you jog, you probably would remember more of the pictures. To rate the dogs as dangerous, you must pay attention to details in the pictures, relate features of the dogs to characteristics associated with danger, and so on. This rating procedure requires "deeper" processing and more focus on the meaning of the features in the photos.

Retrieving Information from Long-Term Memory.   When we need to use information from long-term memory, we search for it. Sometimes the search is conscious, as when you see a friend approaching and try to recall her name. At other times locating and using information from long-term memory is automatic, as when you call your home or solve a math problem without having to search for each step. Think of long-term memory as a huge shelf full of tools and supplies ready to be brought to the workbench of working memory to accomplish a task. The shelf (long-term memory) stores an incredible amount, but it may be hard to quickly find what you are looking for. The workbench (working memory) is small, but anything on it is immediately available. Because it is small, however, supplies (bits of information) sometimes are lost when the workbench overflows or when one bit of information covers (interferes with) another (Gagné, 1985).

The size of the long-term memory network is huge, but only one small area is activated at any one time. Only the information we are currently thinking about is in working memory. Information is retrieved in this network through the spread of activation. When particular information is active—when we are thinking about it— other closely associated knowledge can be activated as well, and activation can spread through the network (Anderson, 2010). Thus, as you focus on the thought, "I'd like to go for a drive to see the fall leaves today," related ideas such as "I should rake leaves" and "The car needs an oil change" come to mind. As activation spreads from the "car trip" to the "oil change," the original thought, or active memory, disappears from working memory because of the limited space.

In long-term memory the information is still available, even when it is not activated, even when you are not thinking about it at the moment. If spreading activation does not "find" the information we seek, then we might still come up with the answer through *reconstruction*, a problem-solving process that makes use of logic, cues, and other knowledge to construct a reasonable answer by filling in any missing parts. Sometimes reconstructed recollections are incorrect—we think, "It's not like me to say something like that," even if we did!

Forgetting

Information lost from working memory truly disappears. No amount of effort will bring it back. But information stored in long-term memory may be available, given the right cues. Information appears to be lost from long-term memory through time decay and interference. For example, memory for Spanish–English vocabulary decreases for about three years after a person's last course in Spanish, then stays level for about 25 years, then drops again for the next 25 years. One explanation for this decline is that neural connections, like muscles, grow weak without use. Also, the physiological deterioration that comes with age could account for the later declines because some neurons simply die (Anderson, 2010). Finally, newer memories may interfere with or obscure older memories, and older memories may interfere with memory for new material.

It appears that teaching strategies that encourage student engagement and lead to higher levels of initial learning (such as frequent reviews and tests, elaborated feedback, high standards, mastery learning, and active involvement in learning projects) are associated with longer retention. But initial learning is not enough; students have to practice their understanding. In fact, many cognitive psychologists believe that the failures of education, such as the inability of many Harvard graduates to explain why it is colder in winter than in summer, are really failures to retain what was once understood (Pashler, 2006). What can instructional leaders do to use the principles of information processing to improve instruction? See the *Theory into Action Guidelines*.

THEORY INTO ACTION GUIDELINES

Applying Information Processing

Make sure you have the students' attention.

Examples

1. Develop a signal that tells students to stop what they are doing and focus on you. Make sure students respond to the signal—don't let them ignore it. Practice using the signal.
2. Move around the room, use gestures, and avoid speaking in a monotone.
3. Begin a lesson by asking a question that stimulates interest in the topic.
4. Regain the attention of individual students by walking closer to them, using their names, or asking them a question.

Help students separate essential from nonessential details and focus on the most important information.

Examples

1. Summarize instructional objectives to indicate what students should be learning. Relate the material you are presenting to the objectives as you teach: "Now I'm going to explain exactly how you can find the information you need to meet Objective One on the board—determining the tone of the story."

2. When you make an important point, pause, repeat, ask a student to paraphrase, note the information on the board in colored chalk, or tell students to highlight the point in their notes or readings.

Help students make connections between new information and what they already know.

Examples

1. Review prerequisites to help students bring to mind the information they will need to understand new material: "Who can tell us the definition of a quadrilateral? Now, what is a rhombus? Is a square a quadrilateral? Is a square a rhombus? What did we say yesterday about how you can tell? Today we are going to look at some other quadrilaterals."
2. Use an outline or diagram to show how new information fits with the framework you have been developing. For example, "Now that you know the duties of the FBI, where would you expect to find it in this diagram of the branches of the U.S. government?"
3. Give an assignment that specifically calls for the use of new information along with information already learned.

(Continued)

THEORY INTO ACTION GUIDELINES **Continued**

Provide for repetition and review of information.

Examples

1. Begin the class with a quick review of the homework assignment.
2. Give frequent, short tests.
3. Build practice and repetition into games, or have students work with partners to quiz each other.

Present material in a clear, organized way.

Examples

1. Make the purpose of the lesson very clear.
2. Give students a brief outline to follow. Put the same outline on an overhead so you can keep yourself on track. When students ask questions

or make comments, relate these to the appropriate section of the outline.

3. Use summaries in the middle and at the end of the lesson.

Focus on meaning, not memorization.

Examples

1. In teaching new words, help students associate the new word to a related word they already understand: "*Enmity* is from the same base as *enemy.*"
2. In teaching about remainders, have students group twelve objects into sets of 2, 3, 4, 5, 6, and ask them to count the "leftovers" in each case.

Metacognition, Regulation, and Individual Differences

One question that intrigues many educators and cognitive psychologists is why some people learn and remember more than others. For those who hold an information processing view, part of the answer lies in the **executive control processes** that guide the flow of information through the system. We have already discussed a number of control processes, including selective attention, maintenance rehearsal, elaborative rehearsal, organization, and elaboration. These executive control processes are sometimes called *metacognition*. Emily Fox and Michelle Riconscente (2008, p. 373) define **metacognition** simply as "knowledge or awareness of self as knower." Metacognition literally means cognition about cognition—or thinking about thinking—something William James wrote about over 100 years ago (although he did not give it that name).

Metacognition regulates thinking and learning (Bruning et al., 2011; Nelson, 1996). There are three essential skills: *planning*, *monitoring*, and *evaluating*. *Planning* involves deciding how much time to give to a task, which resources to gather, which strategies to use, how to start, what order to follow, what to skim and what to give intense attention to, and so on. *Monitoring* is the real-time awareness of "how I'm doing." Monitoring is asking, "Is this making sense? Am I trying to go too fast? Have I studied enough?" *Evaluating* involves making judgments about the processes and outcomes of thinking and learning. "Should I change strategies? Get help? Give up for now? Is this memo (painting, model, poem, plan, etc.) finished?" The notion of *reflection* in teaching—thinking back on what happened in class and why, and thinking forward to what you might do next time—is really about metacognition in teaching (Sawyer, 2006).

Some differences in metacognitive abilities are the result of development. Younger children, for example, may not be aware of the purpose of a lesson—they may think the point is simply to finish. They also may not be good at gauging the difficulty of a task—they may think that reading for fun and reading a science book are the same (Gredler, 2009). As children grow older, they are more able to exercise executive control over strategies. For example, they are more able to determine if they have understood instructions or if they have studied enough to remember a set of items. Metacognitive abilities begin to develop around ages 5 to 7 and improve throughout school (Flavell, Green, & Flavell, 1995; Woolfolk & Perry, 2012).

Not all differences in metacognitive abilities have to do with age or maturation. Some individual differences probably are caused by biological differences or by variations in learning experiences. In fact, many students diagnosed as having learning disabilities actually have attention disorders (Hallahan & Kauffman, 2006), particularly with long tasks. Thus, there is great variability even among students of the same developmental level, but these differences do not appear to be related to intellectual abilities. In fact, superior metacognitive skills can compensate for lower levels of ability, so these metacognitive skills can be especially important for students who often have trouble in school (Schunk, 2012; Swanson, 1990).

Cognitive Contributions: Learning Strategies

Most teachers will tell you that they want their students to "learn how to learn." Years of research indicate that using good learning strategies helps students learn and that these strategies can be taught (Hamman, Berthelot, Saia, & Crowley, 2000). But were you taught "how to learn"? Powerful and sophisticated learning strategies and study skills are seldom taught directly until high school or even college, so most students have little practice with them. In contrast, early on, students usually discover repetition and rote learning on their own, so they have extensive practice with these strategies. And, unfortunately, some teachers think that memorizing is learning (Beghetto, 2008; Woolfolk Hoy & Murphy, 2001). This may explain why many students cling to flash cards and memorizing; they don't know what else to do to learn (Willoughby, Porter, Belsito, & Yearsley, 1999).

As we saw earlier, the way something is learned in the first place greatly influences how readily we remember the information and how appropriately we can apply the knowledge later. First, students must be *cognitively engaged* in order to learn—they have to *focus attention* on the relevant or important aspects of the material. Second, they have to *invest effort*, make connections, elaborate, translate, invent, organize, and reorganize in order to think and *process deeply*—the greater the practice and processing, the stronger the learning. Finally, students must *regulate and monitor* their own learning—keep track of what is making sense and notice when a new approach is needed; that is, they must be *metacognitive*. The emphasis today is on helping students develop effective learning strategies that focus attention and effort, process information deeply, and monitor understanding.

Being Strategic about Learning

Learning strategies are a special kind of procedural knowledge—*knowing how* to do something. There are thousands of strategies. Some are general and taught in school, such as summarizing or outlining. Others are specific to a subject, such as using a mnemonic to remember the order of the planets: "My Very Educated Mother Just Served Us Nachos" for Mercury, Venus, Earth, Mars, Jupiter, Saturn, Uranus, and Neptune. Other strategies may be unique, invented by an individual to learn Chinese characters, for example. Learning strategies can be cognitive (summarizing, identifying the main idea), metacognitive (monitoring comprehension—do I understand?), or behavioral (using an Internet dictionary, setting a timer to work till time's up) (Cantrell, Almasi, Carter, Rintamaa, & Madden, 2010). All are ways of accomplishing a learning task that are intentionally applied when usual methods have not worked and strategic effort is needed (Harris, Alexander, & Graham, 2008). Over time, as you become more expert at using the strategies, less intentional effort is needed. Ultimately you may become more automatic in applying the strategies; in other words, the strategies will become your usual way of accomplishing that kind of task, until they don't work and new strategies are needed. Table 4.2 summarizes several learning strategies.

TABLE 4.2   Examples of Learning Strategies

	Examples
Planning and Focusing Attention	Setting goals and timetables
	Underlining and highlighting
	Skimming, looking for headings and topic sentences
Organizing and Remembering	Making organizational charts
	Creating flowcharts, Venn diagrams
	Using mnemonics, imagery
Comprehension	Concept mapping, webs
	Summarizing, outlining and note-taking
	Creating examples
	Explaining to a peer
Cognitive Monitoring	Making predictions
	Self-questioning and self-testing
	Identifying what doesn't make sense
Practice	Using part practice (practicing selected parts such as just the ball toss in serving a tennis ball or summarizing just the meaning of new vocabulary)
	Using whole practice (practicing all the moves together to serve a tennis ball or summarizing the whole paragraph)

Skilled learners have a wide range of learning strategies that they can apply fairly automatically. Using learning strategies and study skills is related to higher GPAs in high school and persistence in college (Robbins et al., 2004). Researchers have identified several important principles:

1. Students must be exposed to a number of different strategies, not only general learning strategies but also very specific strategies for particular subjects, such as the graphic strategies described later in this section.
2. Students should be taught self-regulatory (conditional) knowledge about when, where, and why to use various strategies. Although this may seem obvious, teachers often neglect this step. A strategy is more likely to be maintained and employed if students know when, where, and why to use it.
3. Students may know when and how to use a strategy, but unless they also develop the desire to employ these skills, general learning ability will not improve. Several learning strategy programs include a motivational training component.
4. Students need to believe that they can learn new strategies, that the effort will pay off, and that they can "get smarter" by applying these strategies.
5. Students need some background knowledge and useful schemas in the area being studied to make sense of learning materials. It will be difficult to find the main idea in a paragraph about *ichthyology*, for example, if you don't know much about fish. So students may need direct instruction in schematic (content) knowledge along with strategy training.

There are literally hundreds of strategies that can be taught. The point for teachers is to teach subject-appropriate learning strategies directly and to support strategic learning through coaching and guided practice. Teaching strategies based on cognitive views of learning, particularly information processing, highlight the importance of attention, organization, rehearsal (practice), and elaboration in learning and provide ways to give students more control over their own learning by developing and improving their own metacognitive skills. The focus is on what is happening "inside the head" of the learner. Using the cognitive theory just explicated, principals can give their teachers hands-on examples to develop more effective ways to teach learning strategies. The *Theory into Action Guidelines* illustrate both the principles and practices of such strategies for students.

THEORY INTO ACTION GUIDELINES

Learning Strategies

Make sure you have the necessary declarative knowledge (facts, concepts, ideas) to understand new information.

Examples

1. Keep definitions of key vocabulary available as you study.
2. Review required facts and concepts before attempting new material.

Find out what type of test the teacher will give (essay, short answer), and study the material with that in mind.

Examples

1. For a test with detailed questions, practice writing answers to possible questions.
2. For a multiple-choice test, use associations and images to remember definitions of key terms.

(Continued)

THEORY INTO ACTION GUIDELINES **Continued**

Make sure you are familiar with the organization of the materials to be learned.

Examples

1. Preview the headings, introductions, topic sentences, and summaries of the text.
2. Be alert for words and phrases that signal relationships, such as *on the other hand, because, first, second, however, since.*

Know your own cognitive skills and use them deliberately.

Examples

1. Use examples and analogies to relate new material to something you care about and understand well, such as sports, hobbies, or films.
2. If one study technique is not working, try another—the goal is to stay involved, not to use any particular strategy.

Study the right information in the right way.

Examples

1. Be sure you know exactly what topics and readings the test will cover.

2. Spend your time on the important, difficult, and unfamiliar material that will be required for the test or assignment.
3. Keep a list of the parts of the text that give you trouble and spend more time on those pages.
4. Process the important information thoroughly by using mnemonics, forming images, creating examples, answering questions, making notes in your own words, and elaborating on the text. Do not try to memorize the author's words—use your own.

Monitor your own comprehension.

Examples

1. Use questioning to check your understanding.
2. When reading speed slows down, decide if the information in the passage is important. If it is, note the problem so you can reread or get help to understand. If it is not important, ignore it.
3. Check your understanding by working with a friend and quizzing one another.

Constructivist Theories of Learning

In this section we look beyond the individual to expand our understanding of learning and teaching. Consider this situation:

> A young child who has never been to the hospital is in her bed in the pediatric wing. The nurse at the station down the hall calls over the intercom above the bed, "Hi Chelsea, how are you doing? Do you need anything?" The girl looks puzzled and does not answer. The nurse repeats the question with the same result. Finally, the nurse says emphatically, "Chelsea, are you there? Say something!" The little girl responds tentatively, "Hello, Wall—I'm here."

Chelsea encountered a new situation—a talking wall. The wall is persistent. It sounds like a grown-up wall. She shouldn't talk to strangers, but she is not sure about walls. She uses what she knows and what the situation provides to *construct* meaning and to act.

Here is another example of constructing meaning. This time, Kate and her 9-year-old son Ethan co-construct understandings as they buy groceries:

ETHAN: (running to get a shopping cart) Do we need the big one?

KATE: We might—better too big than not big enough. Here is our list—where do we go first?

ETHAN: We need ice cream for the party! (Ethan heads toward frozen foods.)

KATE: Whoa! What happened to the ice cream carton you left out on the kitchen counter?

ETHAN: It melted and it wasn't out that long. I promise!

Kate: Right and we may be in this store a while, so let's start with things that won't melt while we are shopping—I usually buy produce first.

ETHAN: What's "produce"?

KATE: Things that grow—fruits and vegetables "produced" by farmers.

ETHAN: OK, the list says cucumbers. Here they are. Wait, there are two kinds. Which do you want? The little ones say "local." What's local?

KATE: Local means from around here—close to us, close to our "location." Hmmm.—the big ones are 75 cents *each* and these smaller ones are $1.15 *a pound*. How would you decide which is a better deal?

ETHAN: I guess bigger is better, right? Or is local better?

KATE: Well, I wonder if they cost the same for the amount you get—per pound. How could you figure that out?

ETHAN: I don't know—the price for a pound isn't on the big ones, just the price each.

KATE: When the doctor wants to know how many pounds you weigh, she puts you on a scale. What if you weighed a big cucumber over there on that food scale?

ETHAN: OK—it weighs ½ a pound.

KATE: So half a pound costs 75 cents—what would a whole pound cost—that's 2 halves make a whole?

ETHAN: 75 cents plus 75 cents–$1.50—Gee, the bigger ones are more expensive. So the smaller ones are better and they are "local"—that's good too, right?

KATE: Maybe. I like to support our local farmers. Where are the small cucumbers from—look at the tiny print on the label.

ETHAN: Virginia—is that close to us?

KATE: Not really—it is about a 6-hour drive from here . . .

Look at the knowledge being co-constructed about planning ahead, vocabulary, math, problem solving, and even geography. Constructivist theories of learning focus on how people make meaning, both on their own like Chelsea and in interaction with others like Ethan.

Different Versions of Constructivism

Constructivism is a broad term used by philosophers, curriculum designers, psychologists, educators, and others. Ernst von Glasersfeld (1997, p. 204) calls it "a vast and woolly area in contemporary psychology, epistemology, and education." Constructivist perspectives are grounded in the research of Piaget, Vygotsky, Bruner, and Rogoff; as well as the philosophy of John Dewey and the work in anthropology of Jean Lave, to mention just a few intellectual roots.

There is no one constructivist theory of learning, but most constructivist theories agree on two central ideas:

Central Idea 1: Learners are active in constructing their own knowledge.

Central Idea 2: Social interactions are important in this knowledge construction process (Bruning, Schraw, & Norby, 2011).

Constructivist approaches in science and mathematics education, in educational psychology and anthropology, and in computer-based education all embrace these two ideas. But even though many psychologists and educators use the term *constructivism*, they often mean very different things (Martin, 2006; McCaslin & Hickey, 2001; Phillips, 1997).

One way to organize constructivist views is to talk about two forms of constructivism: psychological and social construction (Palincsar, 1998; Phillips, 1997). We could oversimplify a bit and say that psychological constructivists focus on how individuals use information, resources, and even help from others to build and improve their mental models and problem-solving strategies. In contrast, social constructivists view learning as increasing our abilities to participate with others in activities that are meaningful in the culture (Windschitl, 2002). Let's look a bit closer at each type of constructivism.

Psychological/Individual Constructivism. The **psychological constructivists** "are concerned with how *individuals* build up certain elements of their cognitive or emotional apparatus" (Phillips, 1997, p. 153). These constructivists might be interested in individual knowledge, beliefs, self-concept, or identity, so they are sometimes called *individual* constructivists; they all focus on the inner psychological life of people. Chelsea talking to the wall in the previous section was making meaning using her own individual knowledge and beliefs about how to respond when someone (or something) talks to you. She was using what she knew to impose intellectual structure on her world (Piaget, 1971; Windschitl, 2002). Some educational and developmental psychologists have referred to Piaget's kind of constructivism as **"first wave constructivism"** or "solo" constructivism, with its emphasis on individual meaning making (DeCorte, Greer, & Verschaffel, 1996; Paris, Byrnes, & Paris, 2001).

Vygotsky's Social Constructivism.   Vygotsky believed that social interaction, activity, and cultural tools shape individual development and learning, just as Ethan's interactions at the grocery store with his mother shaped his learning about planning ahead, vocabulary, math, problem solving, measurement, food sources, and geography. By participating in a broad range of activities and using tools with others (both actual tools such as calculators and psychological signs and symbols such as language and number systems), learners *appropriate* (take for themselves) the outcomes produced by working together (Gredler, 2005; Palincsar, 1998). Putting learning in social and cultural context is **"second wave constructivism"** (Paris, Byrnes, & Paris, 2001).

Because his theory relies heavily on social interactions and the cultural context to explain learning, most psychologists classify Vygotsky as a **social constructivist** (Palincsar, 1998; Prawat, 1996), but some theorists categorize Vygotsky as a psychological constructivist because he was primarily interested in development within the individual (Moshman, 1997; Phillips, 1997). In a sense, he is both. One advantage of his theory of learning is that it gives us a way to consider both the psychological and the social; he bridges both camps. For example, Vygotsky's concept of the *zone of proximal development*—the area where a child can solve a problem with the help (scaffolding) of an adult or more able peer—has been called a place where culture and cognition create each other (Cole, 1985). Culture creates cognition when the adult uses tools and practices from the culture (language, maps, computers, looms, music, etc.) to steer the child toward goals the culture values (reading, writing, weaving, dance). Cognition creates culture as the adult and child together generate new practices and problem solutions to add to the cultural group's repertoire (Serpell, 1993). One way of integrating individual and social constructivism is to think of knowledge as individually constructed and socially mediated (Windschitl, 2002).

The term *constructivism* is sometimes used to talk about how public knowledge is created. Although this is not our main concern, it is worth a quick look.

Sociological Constructivism.   Sociological constructivists (sometimes called *constructionists*) do not focus on individual learning. Their concern is how public knowledge in disciplines such as science, math, economics, or history is constructed. Beyond this kind of academic knowledge, sociological constructivists also are interested in how commonsense ideas, everyday beliefs, and commonly held understandings about the world are communicated to new members of a sociocultural group (Gergen, 1997; Phillips, 1997). Questions raised might include who determines what constitutes history or the proper way to behave in public or how to get elected class president. There is no true knowledge, according to these theorists. All of knowledge is socially constructed, and, more important, some people have more power than others do in defining what constitutes such knowledge. Relationships between and among teachers, students, families, and the community are the central issues. Collaboration to understand diverse viewpoints is encouraged, and traditional bodies of knowledge often are challenged (Gergen, 1997). The philosophies of Jacques Dierrida and Michel Foucault are important sources for constructionists. Vygotsky's theory, with its attention to how cognition creates culture, has some elements in common with constructionism.

Teaching Applications of Constructivist Perspectives

We have looked at some areas of disagreement among the constructivist perspectives, but what about areas of agreement? All constructivist theories assume that knowing develops as learners, like Chelsea and Ethan, try to make sense of their experiences. "Learners, therefore, are not empty vessels waiting to be filled, but rather active organisms seeking meaning" (Driscoll, 2005, p. 487). These learners construct mental models or schemata and continue to revise them to make better sense of their experiences. Their constructions do not necessarily resemble external reality; rather they are the unique interpretations of the learner, like Chelsea's friendly persistent wall. This doesn't mean that all constructions are equally useful or viable. Learners test their understandings against experience and the understandings of other people—they negotiate and co-construct meanings like Ethan did with his mother.

Constructivists share similar goals for learning. They emphasize knowledge in use rather than the storing of inert facts, concepts, and skills. Learning goals include developing abilities to find and solve ill-structured problems, critical thinking, inquiry, self-determination, and openness to multiple perspectives (Driscoll, 2005).

Elements of Constructivist Teaching

Even though there is no single constructivist theory, many constructivist teaching approaches recommend

1. authentic tasks and complex, challenging learning environments
2. social negotiation and shared responsibility as a part of learning
3. multiple representations of content and support of learning through scaffolding
4. understanding that knowledge is constructed
5. student-centered instruction (Driscoll, 2005; Marshall, 1992)

Let's look more closely at these dimensions of constructivist teaching.

Authentic Tasks.   Constructivists believe that students should not be given stripped-down, simplified problems and basic skills drills, but instead should deal with complex situations and "fuzzy," ill-structured problems. The world beyond school presents few simplified problems or step-by-step directions, so schools should be sure that every student has experience solving complex problems. These problems should be embedded in authentic tasks and activities, the kinds of situations that students will face as they apply what they are learning to real-world problems (Needles & Knapp, 1994).

Social Negotiation.   Many constructivists share Vygotsky's belief that higher mental processes develop through social interaction, so collaboration in learning is valued. The Language Development and Hypermedia Group (1992) suggests that a major goal of teaching is to develop students' abilities to establish and defend their own positions while respecting the positions of others. To accomplish this exchange, students must talk and listen to each other.

Multiple Representations.   When students encounter only one representation of content—one model, analogy, or way of understanding complex content—they often oversimplify as they try to apply that single approach to every situation. Rand Spiro and his colleagues (1991) suggest that "revisiting the same material, at different times, in rearranged contexts, for different purposes, and from different conceptual perspectives is essential for attaining the goals of advanced knowledge acquisition" (p. 28). This idea is not entirely new. Years ago Jerome Bruner (1966) described the advantages of a *spiral curriculum*, which is a way of teaching that introduces the fundamental structure of all subjects—the "big ideas"—early in the school years, then revisits the subjects in more and more complex forms over time.

In addition, constructivist approaches include **scaffolding** to support students' developing expertise. One implication of Vygotsky's theory of cognitive development is that deep understanding requires that students grapple with problems in their zone of proximal development; and they need scaffolding in order to work in that zone. Here is a good definition of scaffolding that emphasizes its dynamic interactive nature as well as the knowledge that both teacher and student bring—both are experts on something: "Scaffolding is a powerful conception of teaching and learning in which teachers and students create meaningful connections between teachers' cultural knowledge and the everyday experience and knowledge of the student" (McCaslin & Hickey, 2001, p. 137). Look back at the grocery store conversation between Ethan and his mother at the beginning of the previous section. Notice how the mother used the melted ice cream on the kitchen counter and the scale in the doctor's office—connections to Ethan's experience and knowledge—to scaffold Ethan's understanding.

Even though there are different views of scaffolding, most educational psychologists agree on three characteristics (van de Pol, Volman, & Beishuizen, 2010):

1. **Contingency Support:** The teacher is constantly adjusting, differentiating, and tailoring responses to the student.
2. **Fading:** The teacher gradually withdraws support as the student's understanding and skills deepen.
3. **Transferring Responsibility:** Students assume more and more responsibility for their own learning.

Understanding Knowledge Construction.   The assumptions we make, our beliefs, and our experiences shape what each of us comes to "know" about the world. Different assumptions and different experiences lead to different knowledge. Constructivists stress the importance of understanding the knowledge construction process so that students will be aware of the influences that shape their thinking; thus they will be able to choose, develop, and defend positions in a self-critical way while respecting the positions of others.

Student-Centered Instruction.   The last characteristic of constructivist teaching listed by Driscoll (2005) is student-centered instruction. Following are four examples of student-centered instruction that are consistent with the other dimensions of constructivist teaching as well—inquiry learning, problem-based learning, cognitive apprenticeships, and cooperative learning.

Inquiry Learning

John Dewey described the basic **inquiry learning** format in 1910. There have been many adaptations of this strategy, but the form usually includes the following elements (Echevarria, 2003; Lashley, Matczynski, & Rowley, 2002): The teacher presents a puzzling event, question, or problem. The students

1. formulate hypotheses to explain the event or solve the problem.
2. collect data to test the hypotheses.
3. draw conclusions.
4. reflect on the original problem and on the thinking processes needed to solve it.

Shirley Magnusson and Annemarie Palincsar have developed a teachers' guide for planning, implementing, and assessing different phases of inquiry science units. The model is called Guided Inquiry Supporting Multiple Literacies (or GIsML). Figure 4.5 shows the GIsML cycle.

The teacher first identifies a curriculum area and some general guiding questions, puzzles, or problems. For example, an elementary teacher chooses communication as the area and asks this general question: "How and why do humans and animals communicate?" Next, several specific focus questions are posed. "How do whales communicate? How do gorillas communicate?" The focus questions have to be carefully chosen to guide students toward important understandings. One key idea in understanding animal communication is the relationship between the animal's structures, survival functions, and habitat. Animals have specific *structures*, such as large ears or echo-locators, that *function* to find food or attract mates or identify predators, and these structures and functions are related to the animals' *habitats*. So focus questions must ask about animals with different structures for communication, different functional needs for survival, and different habitats. Questions about animals with the same kinds of structures or the same habitats would not be good focus points for inquiry (Magnusson & Palincsar, 1995).

The next phase is to engage students in the inquiry, perhaps by playing different animal sounds, having students make guesses and claims about communication, and asking the students questions about their guesses and claims. Then the students conduct both first-hand and second-hand investigations. *First-hand investigations* are direct experiences and experiments, for example, measuring the size of bats' eyes and ears in relation to their bodies (using pictures or videos, not real bats!). In *second-hand investigations*, students consult books, the Internet, interviews with experts, and so on to find specific information or get new ideas. As part of investigating, the students begin to identify patterns. The curved line in Figure 4.5 shows that cycles can be repeated. In fact, students might go through several cycles of investigation, pattern identification, and reporting results before moving on to constructing explanations and making final reports. Another possible cycle is to evaluate explanations before reporting by making and then checking predictions, applying the explanation to new situations.

Inquiry teaching allows students to learn content and process at the same time. In the examples above, students learned about animal communication and habitats. In addition, they learned the inquiry process itself: how to solve problems, evaluate solutions, and think critically. Inquiry has much in common with guided discovery learning

FIGURE 4.5   A Model to Guide Teacher Thinking About Inquiry-Based Science Instruction
The straight lines show the sequence of phases in instruction and the curved lines show cycles that might be repeated during instruction.

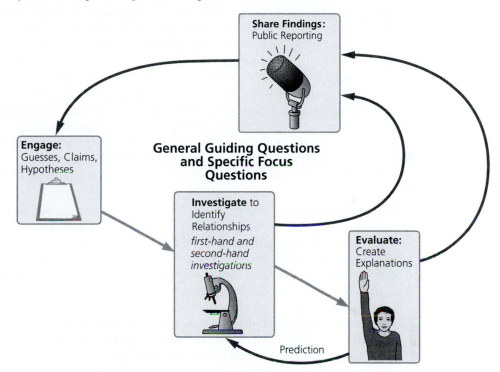

Source: Figure from *Educational psychology*, 12th Edition, by Anita E. Woolfolk. Copyright © 2013 by Pearson Education, Inc. Based on "Designing a community of practice: Principles and practice of the GIsML community" by A. Palincsar, et al., from *Teaching and teacher education*, January 1998, Volume 14(1). Printed and Electronically reproduced by permission of Pearson Education, Inc., Upper Saddle River, New Jersey.

in that inquiry methods require great preparation, organization, and monitoring to be sure everyone is engaged and challenged (Kindsvatter, Wilen, & Ishler, 1988).

Problem-Based Learning

In **problem-based learning,** students are confronted with a real problem that has meaning for them. This problem launches their inquiry as they collaborate to find solutions. In true problem-based learning, the problem is real and the students' actions matter. "Problem-based learning turns instruction topsy-turvy. Students meet an ill-structured problem before they receive any instruction. In place of covering the curriculum, learners probe deeply into issues searching for connections, grappling with complexity, and using knowledge to fashion solutions" (Stepien & Gallagher, 1993, p. 26).*

Source: "Problem-based learning: As authentic as it gets" by William Stepien and Shelagh Gallagher, from *Educational Leadership*, April 1993, Volume 50(7). Association for Supervision and Curriculum Development.

In true problem-based learning, the problem is real and the students' actions matter. For example, during the 2010 Deepwater oil spill, many teachers used the problem as a springboard for learning. Their students researched how this spill compared to others in size, location, costliness, causes, and attempted solutions. What could be done? How do currents and tides play a role? What locations, businesses, and wildlife are in the greatest danger? What will the short-term and long-term financial and environmental impacts be? What actions can students take to play a positive role? A number of teachers blogged about using the oil spill in problem-based learning and collected resources for other teachers (see http://www.edutopia.org/blog/oil-spill-project-based-learning-resources).

The teacher's role in problem-based learning is to identify engaging problems and appropriate resources; orient students to the problem by describing objectives and rationales; organize the students by helping them set goals and define tasks; support, coach, and mentor students as they gather information, craft solutions, and prepare artifacts (models, reports, videos, PowerPoints, portfolios, etc.); and support students' reflections on their own learning outcomes and processes (Arends & Kilcher, 2010).

Research on Inquiry and Problem-Based Learning.   Inquiry methods are similar to discovery and share some of the same problems, so inquiry must be carefully planned and organized, especially for less prepared students who may lack the background knowledge and problem-solving skills needed to benefit. Some research has shown that discovery methods are ineffective and even detrimental for lower-ability students (Corno & Snow, 1986; Slavin, Karweit, & Madden, 1989). A distinction is usually made between pure discovery learning, in which the students work on their own to a very great extent, and **guided discovery,** in which the teacher provides some direction.

We know that working memory is severely limited when it is dealing with novel information from the outside, but almost unlimited when it is dealing with familiar, well-practiced, and organized information from long-term memory. Because most inquiry and problem-based lessons require students to deal with the former—novel information and fuzzy problems—many educational psychology researchers believe that unguided discovery methods do not fit our information processing capabilities and often put a strain on working memory (Kirschner, Sweller, & Clark, 2006, 2007). Reviewing thirty years of research on pure discovery learning, Richard Mayer (2004) concludes:

> Like some zombie that keeps returning from its grave, pure discovery continues to have its advocates. However, anyone who takes an evidence-based approach to educational practice must ask the same question: Where is the evidence that it works? In spite of calls for free discovery in every decade, the supporting evidence is hard to find. (p. 17)*

Activity-based teaching in science appears to be better than traditional methods in terms of students' understanding of the scientific method and creativity, but about the same for learning science content (Bredderman, 1983).

In terms of problem-based learning, Cindy Hmelo-Silver (2004) reviewed the research and found good evidence that problem-based learning supports the

*Source: "Should there be a three-strike rule against pure discovery learning? A case for guided methods of instruction" by Richard E. Mayer, from *American Psychologist,* January 2004, Volume 59(1): pp. 14–19. American Psychological Association. Reprinted with permission.

construction of flexible knowledge and the development of problem solving and self-directed learning skills, but there is less evidence that participating in problem-based learning is intrinsically motivating or that it teaches students to collaborate. In addition, most of the research has been done in higher education, especially medical schools.

In medical school, students learning with problem-based methods as opposed to traditional approaches appear to be better at clinical skills such as problem formation and reasoning, but worse in their basic knowledge of science and less prepared in science (Albanese & Mitchell, 1993). And some students, those who are better at self-regulation, benefit more from problem-based methods (Evensen, Salisbury-Glennon, & Glenn, 2001). The best approach may be a balance of content-focused and inquiry or problem-based methods (Arends, 2004). For example, Eva Toth, David Klahr, and Zhe Chen (2000) tested a balanced approach for teaching 4th graders how to use the controlled variable strategy in science to design good experiments. The method had three phases: (1) in small groups, students conducted exploratory experiments to identify variables that made a ball roll farther down a ramp; (2) the teacher led a discussion, explained the controlled variable strategy, and modeled good thinking about experiment design; and (3) the students designed and conducted application experiments to isolate which variables caused the ball to roll farther. The combination of inquiry, discussion, explanation, and modeling was successful in helping the students understand the concepts.

Cognitive Apprenticeships

Over the centuries, apprenticeships have proved to be an effective form of education. By working alongside a master and perhaps other apprentices, young people have learned many skills, trades, and crafts. Why are they so effective? Apprenticeships are rich in information because the master knows a great deal about the subject. Working with more knowledgeable guides provides models, demonstrations, and corrections, as well as a personal bond that is motivating. The performances required of the learner are real and important and grow more complex as the learner becomes more competent (Collins, Brown, & Holum, 1991; Collins, Brown, & Newman, 1989; Hung, 1999).

Collins and his colleagues (1989) suggest that knowledge and skills learned in school have become too separated from their use in the world beyond school. To correct this imbalance, some educators recommend that schools adopt many of the features of apprenticeships. But rather than learning to sculpt or dance or build a cabinet, apprenticeships in school would focus on cognitive objectives such as reading comprehension or writing or mathematical problem solving. There are many **cognitive apprenticeship** models, but most share six features:

1. Students observe an expert (usually the teacher) model the performance.
2. Students get external support through coaching or tutoring (including hints, feedback, models, reminders).
3. Conceptual scaffolding (in the form of outlines, explanations, notes, definitions, formulas, procedures, etc.) is provided and then gradually faded as the student becomes more competent and proficient.
4. Students continually articulate their knowledge, putting into words their understanding of the processes and content being learned.

5. Students reflect on their progress, comparing their problem solving to an expert's performance and to their own earlier performances.

6. Students are required to explore new ways to apply what they are learning—ways that they have not practiced at the master's side.

One way to connect learning to the outside world is to include parents in students' learning. The *Principal's Perspective* tells how an actual elementary principal accomplished this goal.

A Principal's Perspective

Mindful of the research on the impact of home environment on student achievement (Marzano, 2003; Reeves, 2000), D. W. knew that to make the academic gains in reading she envisioned for her elementary school, she would have to somehow enhance parental involvement at home. Combining the resources of a statewide reading grant and an established school–business partnership with a local hospital, D. W. purchased an assortment of books, games, and information cards to include in 150 book bags that students could take home for a couple of days at a time to read together with their parents, grandparents, babysitters, and even siblings. The bags also included a journal in which parents could share feedback and general comments with the school.

But D. W. also knew that making quality reading materials more accessible to families was not enough. If parents were to be true partners in their children's education, they also would need strategies and techniques to most effectively use the reading materials at home. So she enlisted the expertise of her teaching staff and organized a series of family reading nights throughout the school year. At these events, teachers taught parents how to use decoding and questioning techniques familiar to the students from school and gave them the confidence and the strategies to be genuine partners in their children's reading development.

Marzano, R. J. (2003). *What works in schools: Translating research into action.* Alexandria, VA: Association of Supervision and Curriculum Development.

Reeves, D. B. (2000). *Accountability in action: A blueprint for learning organizations.* Denver, CO: Advanced Learning Press.

Group Work and Cooperation in Learning

Clearly, collaboration and cooperation are important in many visions of innovation and school reform. Teachers are expected to collaborate with parents, administrators, and each other. Today, evolving constructivist perspectives on learning fuel interest in collaboration and cooperative learning. Two characteristics of constructivist teaching—complex, real-life learning environments and social interaction (Driscoll, 2005)—are consistent with the use of cooperative learning structures. As educators focus on learning in real contexts, "there is a heightened interest in situations where elaboration, interpretation, explanation, and argumentation are integral to the activity of the group and where learning is supported by other individuals" (Webb & Palincsar, 1996, p. 844).

The History of Cooperative Learning.   Cooperative learning has a long history in American education, moving in and out of favor over the years. For the past four decades, researchers have examined collaboration and cooperation in schools. David and Roger Johnson (2009a) note

> From being discounted and ignored, cooperative learning has steadily progressed to being one of the dominant instructional practices throughout the world. Cooperative learning is now utilized in schools and universities throughout most of the world in every subject area and from preschool through graduate school and adult training programs. (p. 365)*

Although there are some inconsistencies, the majority of the studies indicate that truly cooperative groups have positive effects—from preschool to college—on students' empathy, tolerance for differences, feelings of acceptance, friendships, self-confidence, awareness of the perspectives of others, higher-level reasoning, problem solving, and even school attendance (Galton, Hargreaves, & Pell, 2009; Gillies & Boyle, 2011; Solomon, Watson, & Battistich, 2001). It is even argued that cooperative learning experiences are crucial in preventing many of the social problems that plague children and adolescents (Gillies, 2003, 2004).

Theoretical Underpinnings of Cooperative Learning.   Advocates of different theories of learning find value in cooperative learning, but not for the same reasons.

In terms of *academic/cognitive goals*, information processing theorists suggest that group discussion can help participants rehearse, elaborate, and expand their knowledge. As group members question and explain, they have to organize their knowledge, make connections, and review—all processes that support information processing and memory. Advocates of a Piagetian perspective assert that the interactions in groups can create the cognitive conflict and disequilibrium that lead an individual to question his or her understanding and try out new ideas or, as Piaget (1985) said, "to go beyond his current state and strike out in new directions" (p. 10). Educators who favor Vygotsky's theory suggest that social interaction is important for learning because higher mental functions such as reasoning, comprehension, and critical thinking originate in social interactions and are then internalized by individuals. Thus, cooperative learning provides the social support and scaffolding that students need to move learning forward.

In terms of *interpersonal/social goals*, research indicates that cooperative learning has a positive impact on interracial friendships, prejudice reduction, acceptance of disabled students, self-esteem, peer support for academic goals, altruism, empathy, social perspective taking, liking fellow classmates and feeling liked, sense of responsibility and control over learning, and time on task. Positive effects often are attributed to the process of working toward common goals as equals, which was shown in laboratory studies years ago to increase liking and respect among individuals from different racial or social groups (Allport, 1954). The motivation growing from the praise and encouragement of peers working toward a common goal also brings positive effects (Arends & Kilcher, 2010). Thus, cooperative strategies have been touted as particularly useful in combating the detrimental social effects of cliques in middle school and high schools, the negative effects of competition on student self-esteem, and the alienation of students who are not members of popular social groups (Aronson, 2000a; Aronson & Patnoe, 1997).

Source: "An educational psychology success story: Social interdependence theory and cooperative learning" by David W. Johnson and Roger T. Johnson, from *Educational Researcher*, June 2009, Volume 38(5). Sage Publications, Inc.

Elements of Cooperative Learning.   David and Roger Johnson (2009a) list five elements that define true **cooperative learning** groups. (1) Students *interact face-to-face* and close together, not across the room. (2) Group members experience *positive interdependence:* They need each other for support, explanations, and guidance. (3) Even though they work together and help each other, members of the group must ultimately demonstrate learning on their own; they are held *individually accountable* for learning, often through individual tests or other assessments. (4) *Collaborative skills* are necessary for effective group functioning. Often these skills, such as giving constructive feedback, reaching consensus, and involving every member, must be taught and practiced before the groups tackle a learning task. (5) Finally, members monitor *group processes* and relationships to make sure the group is working effectively and to learn about the dynamics of groups. They take time to ask, "How are we doing as a group? Is everyone working together?"

What Can Go Wrong: Misuses of Group Learning.   Without careful planning and monitoring by the teacher, group interactions can hinder learning and reduce rather than improve social relations in classes (Gillies & Boyle, 2011). For example, if there is pressure in a group for conformity—perhaps because rewards are being misused or one student dominates the others—interactions can be unproductive and unreflective. Misconceptions might be reinforced or the worst, not the best, ideas may be combined to construct a superficial understanding (Battistich, Solomon, & Delucci, 1993). Students who work in groups but arrive at wrong answers may be more confident that they are right—a case of "two heads are worse than one" (Puncochar & Fox, 2004). Also, the ideas of low-status students may be ignored or even ridiculed while the contributions of high-status students are accepted and reinforced, regardless of the merit of either set of ideas (Anderson, Holland, & Palincsar, 1997; Cohen, 1986). The next sections examine how teachers can avoid these problems and encourage true cooperation.

Setting Up Cooperative Groups.   O'Donnell & O'Kelly (1994) note that determining the size of a group depends in part on the purpose of the group activity. If the purpose is for the group members to review, rehearse information, or practice, larger groups (between four and six students) are useful. But if the goal is to encourage each student to participate in discussions, problem solving, or computer learning, then groups of two to four members work best. Also, some research indicates that when there are just a few girls in a group, they tend to be left out of the discussions unless they are the most able or assertive members. By contrast, when there are only one or two boys in the group, they tend to dominate and be "interviewed" by the girls unless these boys are less able than the girls or are very shy. In general, for very shy and introverted students, individual learning may be a better approach (Webb, 1985; Webb & Palincsar, 1996).

   In practice, the effects of learning in a group vary, depending on what actually happens in the group and who is in it. If only a few people take responsibility for the work, these people will learn, but the nonparticipating members probably will not. Students who ask questions, get answers, and attempt explanations are more likely to learn than students whose questions go unasked or unanswered. In fact, there is evidence that the more a student provides elaborated, thoughtful explanations to other students in a group, the more the *explainer* learns. Giving good explanations appears to be even more important for learning than receiving explanations (Webb, Farivar, & Mastergeorge, 2002; Webb & Palincsar, 1996). In order to explain, you have to organize the information, put it into your own words, think of examples and analogies (which connect the information to things you already know), and test your understanding by answering questions. These are excellent learning strategies (King, 1990, 2002; O'Donnell & O'Kelly, 1994).

Some teachers assign roles such as reporter or discussion manager to students to encourage cooperation and full participation. Such roles should be assigned with engagement and learning in mind. In groups that focus on practice, review, or mastery of basic skills, roles should support persistence, encouragement, and participation. In groups that focus on higher-order problem solving or complex learning, roles should encourage thoughtful discussion, sharing of explanations and insights, probing, brainstorming, and creativity. Teachers must be careful, however, not to communicate to students that the major purpose of the groups is simply to do the roles; otherwise the roles become ends in themselves (Woolfolk Hoy & Tschannen-Moran, 1999).

Jigsaw.   An early format for cooperative learning, **Jigsaw** emphasized high interdependence. This structure was invented by Elliot Aronson and his graduate students in 1971 in Austin, Texas, "as a matter of absolute necessity to help defuse a highly explosive situation" (Aronson, 2000a, p. 216). The Austin schools had just been desegregated by court order. White, African American, and Hispanic students were together in classrooms for the first time. Hostility and turmoil ensued, with fistfights in corridors and classrooms. Aronson's answer was the Jigsaw classroom.

In Jigsaw, each group member was given part of the material to be learned by the whole group and became an "expert" on his or her piece. Students had to teach each other, so everyone's contribution was important. A more recent version, Jigsaw II, adds expert groups in which the students who have the same material from each learning group confer to make sure they understand their assigned part and then plan ways to teach the information to their learning group members. Next, students return to their learning groups, bringing their expertise to the sessions. In the end, students take an individual test covering all the material and earn points for their learning team score. Teams can work for rewards or simply for recognition (Aronson & Patnoe, 1997; Slavin, 1995).

In his first test of Jigsaw, Aronson reports that teachers "spontaneously told us of their great satisfaction with the way the atmosphere of their classrooms had been transformed. Adjunct visitors (such as music teachers and the like) were little short of amazed at the dramatically changed atmosphere in the classroom" (Aronson, 2000).* Students expressed less prejudice, were more confident, liked school better, and had higher scores on objective examinations. The overall improvements in test scores came mostly from increases in minority group children; Anglo students maintained their previous levels of performance. These findings are consistent with recent research on cooperative learning, as reviewed by Slavin (1995).

*Source: "Building empathy, compassion, and achievement in the Jigsaw classroom" by Eliot Aronson, from *Improving academic achievement: Impact of psychological factors on education*, edited by Joshua Aronson. Academic Press, 2002.

There are many other forms of cooperative learning used in schools today. It would be difficult to complete a teacher preparation program without encountering encouragement to use these methods. Kagan (1994) and Slavin (1995) have written extensively on the subject and developed many formats. No matter what the format, however, the key to learning in groups appears to be the *quality of the discussions* among the students. Talk that is interpretive—that analyzes and discusses explanations, evidence, reasons, and alternatives—is more valuable than talk that is merely descriptive. And teachers play an important role; they cannot leave the students unguided, but rather have to seed the discussion with ideas and alternatives that push and prod student thinking. The *Theory into Action Guidelines* should help your teachers use cooperative learning wisely (Palincsar, 1998; Woolfolk Hoy & Tschannen-Moran, 1999).

THEORY INTO ACTION GUIDELINES

Using Cooperative Learning

Fit group size and composition to your learning goals.

Examples
1. For social skills and team-building goals, use groups of 2–5, common interest groups, mixed groups, or random groups.
2. For structured fact and skill-based practice and review tasks, use groups of 2–4, mixed ability such as high-middle and middle-low or high-low and middle-middle group compositions.
3. For higher-level conceptual and thinking tasks, use groups of 2–4; select members to encourage interaction.

Assign appropriate roles.

Examples
1. For social skills and team-building goals, assign roles to monitor participation and conflict; rotate leadership of the group.
2. For structured fact and skill-based practice and review tasks, assign roles to monitor engagement and insure low-status students have resources to offer, as in Jigsaw.
3. For higher-level conceptual and thinking tasks, assign roles only to encourage interaction, divergent thinking, and extended, connected discourse, as in debate teams, or group facilitator. Don't let roles get in the way of learning.

Make sure you assume a supporting role as the teacher.

Examples
1. For social skills and team-building goals, be a model and encourager.
2. For structured fact and skill-based practice and review tasks, be a model, director, or coach.
3. For higher-level conceptual and thinking tasks, be a model and facilitator.

Move around the room and monitor the groups.

Examples
1. For social skills and team-building goals, watch for listening, turn-taking, encouraging, and managing conflict.
2. For structured fact and skill-based practice and review tasks, watch for questioning, giving multiple elaborated explanations, attention, and practice.
3. For higher-level conceptual and thinking tasks, watch for questioning, explaining, elaborating, probing, divergent thinking, providing rationales, synthesizing, using and connecting knowledge sources.

(Continued)

THEORY INTO ACTION GUIDELINES **Continued**

Start small and simple until you and the students know how to use cooperative methods.

Examples

1. For social skills and team-building goals, try one or two skills, such as listening and paraphrasing.

2. For structured fact and skill-based practice and review tasks, try pairs of students quizzing each other.

3. For higher-level conceptual and thinking tasks, try reciprocal questioning using pairs and just a few question stems.

For more information on cooperative learning, see: http://www.co-operation.org/ http://edtech.kennesaw.edu/intech/cooperativelearning.htm

Dilemmas of Constructivist Practice

Years ago, Larry Cremin (1961) observed that progressive, innovative pedagogies require infinitely skilled teachers. Today, the same could be said about constructivist teaching. We have already seen that there are many varieties of constructivism and many practices that flow from these different conceptions. We also know that all teaching today happens in a context of high-stakes testing and accountability. In these situations, constructivist teachers face many challenges. Mark Windschitl (2002) identified four teacher dilemmas of constructivism in practice. The first is conceptual: How do I make sense of cognitive versus social conceptions of constructivism and reconcile these different perspectives with my practice? For example, are the classrooms in my school supposed to be collections of individuals working to challenge and change their personal conceptual understandings or communities of learners whose development is measured by participation in authentic disciplinary practices? The second dilemma is pedagogical. How do I teach in truly constructivist ways that honor my students' attempts to think for themselves but still ensure that they learn the academic material? Will my teachers need to place limits on students' construction of their own ideas? What types of assessments will capture the learning we are striving for in this school? The third are cultural dilemmas about what activities, cultural knowledge, and ways of talking will build a community in a diverse classroom. How do I build on students' cultural funds of knowledge while acknowledging but seeing beyond my own past experiences? Finally, there are political dilemmas. Will constructivist approaches adequately prepare students in my school for high-stakes testing for college admissions?

We think of the three main learning theories as three pillars for teaching. Students must first understand and make sense of the material (constructivist); then they must remember what they have understood (cognitive—information processing); and then they must practice and apply (behavioral) their new skills and understanding to make them more fluid and automatic, a permanent part of their repertoire. Failure to attend to any part of the process means lower-quality learning. All three approaches to learning provide principals and teachers with ways of thinking about and solving the problems of practice. Table 4.3 presents the behavioral and selected constructivist perspectives on learning.

TABLE 4.3 Four Views of Learning

There are variations within each of these views of learning that differ in emphasis.
There is also an overlap in constructivist views.

	Cognitive		Constructivist	
	Behavioral	*Information Processing*	*Psychological/Individual*	*Social/Situated*
	Skinner	**J. Anderson**	**Piaget**	**Vygotsky**
Knowledge	Fixed body of knowledge to acquire	Fixed body of knowledge to acquire	Changing body of knowledge, individually constructed in social world	Socially constructed knowledge
	Stimulated from outside	Stimulated from outside Prior knowledge influences how information is processed	Built on what learner brings	Built on what participants contribute, construct together
Learning	Acquisition of facts, skills, concepts	Acquisition of facts, skills, concepts, and strategies	Active construction, restructuring prior knowledge	Collaborative construction of socially defined knowledge and values
	Occurs through drill, guided practice	Occurs through the effective application of strategies	Occurs through multiple opportunities and diverse processes to connect to what is already known	Occurs through socially constructed opportunities
				Co-construct knowledge with students
Teaching	Transmission Presentation (Telling)	Transmission Guide students toward more "accurate" and complete knowledge	Challenge, guide thinking toward more complete understanding	Facilitator, guide, co-participant
Role of Teacher	Manager, supervisor	Teach and model effective strategies	Facilitator, guide	Co-construct different interpretations of knowledge; listen to socially constructed conceptions
	Correct wrong answers	Correct misconceptions	Listen for student's current conceptions, ideas, thinking	
Role of Peers	Not usually considered	Not necessary but can influence information processing	Not necessary but can stimulate thinking, raise questions	Ordinary part of process of knowledge construction
Role of Student	Passive reception of information	Active processor of information, strategy user	Active construction (within mind)	Active co-construction with others and self
	Active listener, direction-follower	Organizer and reorganizer of information	Active thinker, explainer, interpreter, questioner	Active thinker, explainer, interpreter, questioner
		Rememberer		Active social participant

Source: Adapted from "Reconceptualizing learning for restructured schools" by Hermine Marshall, Paper presented at the Annual Meeting of the American Educational Research Association, April 1992. Copyright © 1992 by Hermine Marshall. Adapted with permission of the author.

Summary

Although theorists disagree about the definitions of *learning*, most would agree that learning occurs when experience causes a change in a person's knowledge or behavior.

Behavioral views of learning focus on the role of external events—antecedents and consequences—in changing observable behaviors. Consequences that increase behaviors are called reinforcers, and consequences that decrease behaviors are called punishers. A behavioral perspective is most useful in understanding and dealing with classroom management issues. For example, functional behavioral assessments with positive behavior supports are applications of behavioral learning. Another example you may have used is homework with its emphasis on practicing skills. Cognitive views of learning focus on the human mind's active attempts to make sense of the world. Knowledge is a central force in cognitive perspectives. The individual's prior knowledge affects what he or she will pay attention to, recognize, understand, remember, and forget. Knowledge can be general or domain specific and declarative, procedural, or conditional, but to be useful, knowledge must be remembered. One influential model of memory is information processing, which describes how information moves from sensory memory (which holds a wealth of sensations and images very briefly) to working memory (where the information is elaborated and connected to existing knowledge) to long-term memory (where the information can be held for a long time, depending on how well it was learned in the first place and how interconnected it is to other information). People vary in how well they learn and remember based in part on their metacognitive knowledge, their abilities to plan, monitor, and regulate their own thinking. There are many teaching applications of cognitive views including learning strategies to help organize and elaborate material.

Constructivist views of learning emphasize the importance of students' construction of knowledge; however, there are many different constructivist explanations of learning. Psychological constructivists are concerned with how *individuals* make sense of their worlds. These constructivists might be interested in individual knowledge, beliefs, self-concept, or identity, so they are sometimes called *individual* constructivists; they all focus on the inner psychological life of people. Social constructivists believe that social interaction, cultural tools, and activity shape individual development and learning. By participating in a broad range of activities with others, learners appropriate (take for themselves) the outcomes produced by working together; they acquire new strategies and knowledge of their world. Finally, sociological constructivists are interested in how public knowledge in disciplines such as science, math, economics, or history is constructed as well as how everyday beliefs and commonly held understandings about the world are communicated to new members of a sociocultural group.

Constructivist approaches to teaching recommend complex, challenging learning environments; social negotiation and collaboration; multiple representations of content; understanding that knowledge is a human construction; and student-centered methods such as inquiry learning, problem-based learning, cognitive apprenticeships, and cooperative learning.

Each of these three perspectives provides valuable insights into learning; hence, the issue is not which perspective is best but rather what each perspective brings to the table in understanding a variety of teaching and learning problems. Just as there is no one best way to teach (Chapter 6), this is no one best way to learn. Behavioral, cognitive, and constructivist viewpoints of learning complement each other and enhance our understanding of learning.

KEY TERMS

antecedents (96)
attention (108)
chunking (111)
cognitive apprenticeship (129)
cognitive load (110)
cognitive science (104)
cognitive view of learning (104)
constructivism (122)
cooperative learning (132)
cueing (97)
declarative knowledge (105)
domain-specific knowledge (105)
elaboration (113)
elaborative rehearsal (111)
episodic memory (111)
executive control processes (116)
first wave constructivism (122)

flashbulb memory (112)
functional behavioral assessment
    (FBA) (101)
guided discovery (128)
information processing (106)
inquiry learning (126)
Jigsaw (133)
learning (93)
learning strategies (117)
maintenance rehearsal (110)
metacognition (116)
negative reinforcement (95)
positive behavior supports (102)
positive reinforcement (95)
presentation punishment (96)
problem-based learning (127)
procedural knowledge (105)

procedural memory (112)
prompting (98)
psychological constructivists (122)
punishment (96)
reinforcement process (95)
reinforcer (95)
removal punishment (96)
scaffolding (125)
schemas (112)
second wave constructivism (123)
Self-regulatory knowledge (105)
semantic memory (112)
sensory memory (107)
social constructivist (123)
working memory (109)

DEVELOPING YOUR PORTFOLIO

1. As principal, you have decided that your elementary school needs a writing program that is a good balance of skills and composition. Prepare a short position paper on the advantages and disadvantages of each approach. Then prepare a plan that incorporates the best of both approaches. Support your argument with current research and theory on learning.

2. Prepare a PowerPoint presentation on the strengths and weaknesses of each of the learning perspectives discussed in this chapter: behavioral,

cognitive, and constructivist. Be sure to discuss the situations for which each perspective is most appropriate. For example, list the tasks or situations for which the behavioral approach is best. Give at least one example for each approach.

3. Reread the Leadership Challenge at the beginning of this chapter and assume you are the principal in that school. Develop a plan for working with the history department to resolve the issue such that both extremes (the traditionalists and the constructivists) are satisfied.

INSTRUCTIONAL LEADER'S TOOLBOX

Readings

Bransford, J., Derry, S., Berliner, D., Hammerness, K., with Beckett, K. L. (2005). Theories of learning and their roles in teaching. In L. Darling-Hammond & J. Bransford (Eds.), *Preparing teachers for a changing world: What teachers should learn and be able to do* (pp. 40–87). San Francisco, CA: Jossey-Bass.

Pashler, H. (2006). How we learn. *APS Observer, 19*(3), 24–34.

Paul, A. M. (2011, September 10). The trouble with homework. *New York Times*, Sunday Review Section, p. 6.

Phillips, D. (1995). The good, the bad, and the ugly: The many faces of constructivism. *Educational Researcher, 24*(7), 5–12.

Schunk, D. (2012). *Learning theories: An educational perspective* (6th ed.). Boston, MA: Allyn & Bacon/Pearson.

Tobias, S. (2010). Generative learning theory, paradigm shifts, and constructivism in educational psychology: A tribute to Merl Wittrock. *Educational Psychologist, 45*, 51–54.

Wiggins, G., & McTighe, J. (2005). *Understanding by design: Expanded 2nd edition.* Alexandria, VA: Association for Supervision and Curriculum Development.

Websites

www.ericdigests.org/pre-924/critical.htm
    Critical Thinking in the Social Studies
www.ericdigests.org/1993/early.htm
    Problem Solving in Early Childhood Classrooms
www.ericdigests.org/pre-9212/problem.htm
    Teaching Problem Solving—Secondary School Science
www.gwu.edu/~tip/
    Theories of Learning
http://forum.swarthmore.edu/mathed/constructivism.html
    Constructivism in mathematics teaching

Organizations

www.wolftrap.org/institute/
    Wolf Trap Institute for Early Learning through the Arts: Organization to help early childhood professionals use the arts as part of their care and instruction of young children. The Institute is accessible on the Web by going to the main site for Wolf Trap and then selecting "education."
www.ascd.org/
    Association for Supervision and Curriculum Development
www.ciera.org/
    Center for the Improvement of Early Reading Achievement

CHAPTER

5 Motivation

PREVIEW: KEY POINTS

1. Motivation is the spring of action, an internal state that arouses, directs, and maintains behavior.

2. Whether motivation is intrinsic or extrinsic is determined by the individual's perception of causality for the action: internal causality → intrinsic motivation; external causality → extrinsic motivation.

3. Five major approaches to motivation are behavioral (rewards and incentives); humanistic (self-actualization); cognitive (beliefs, attributions, and expectations); social cognitive (outcomes combined with beliefs, goals, expectations, and self-efficacy); and sociocultural (engaged participation in learning communities).

4. Goals that are specific and moderately challenging, and that can be reached in the near future with reasonable effort are the most motivating goals; in schools, goals that focus on learning (not performance) are the most powerful.

5. If goals are to be strong motivators, they must be accepted by the individual and feedback concerning progress must be continuous.

6. Motivation is affected by the individual's need for safety, self-esteem, connections to others, self-determination, achievement, and self-actualization; people have different needs at different times.

7. Motivation also is affected by the individual's beliefs about the causes of successes and failures and whether ability can improve; believing that effort can improve ability leads to greater persistence and achievement in school.

8. Self-efficacy, the belief that you have the ability to orchestrate the actions to manage a particular situation, is a significant source of motivation.

9. Anxiety can interfere with motivation and learning by affecting attention, information processing, and performance.

10. Motivation to learn is enhanced when teachers employ strategies that help students have confidence in their abilities to learn, see the value of the learning task, and stay focused on learning without resorting to self-protective and self-defeating beliefs and actions.

Leadership Challenge

For some reason this year, many of the students in your middle school classes seem defeated about learning. At a recent faculty meeting, teachers started to complain about their students: "They look at an assignment and protest: 'This is too long (too hard, too much)!' and 'We can't do this by tomorrow (Monday, next week)!' Because they don't exert much effort, of course, they prove themselves right every time; they can't do the work." Your teachers claim that neither pep talks nor punishments for incomplete work are making a dent in the students' defeatist attitudes. And the "I can't" attitude seems contagious. Even the better students are starting to drag their feet, protest longer assignments, and invest minimal effort in class. Teachers also maintain that more students have started to cheat on tests to save their sinking grades. A few teachers blame the negative attitudes on students from the "projects" who are new to the school this year because the other middle school in the district was closed and they had to be redistributed. A cloud of despair seems to be hovering over the whole school. You are starting to dread Mondays. You need to show some leadership, and you begin by asking yourself these questions:

- Are these students "unmotivated"?
- Why might they be so pessimistic about learning?
- How can you help your teachers get a handle on this problem?
- What can you and your teachers do to change student attitudes toward school work?
- How can teachers get students to believe in themselves?
- What perspectives on motivation seem most useful?

Motivation: A Definition

Motivation is usually defined as *an internal state that arouses, directs, and maintains behavior.* Psychologists studying motivation have focused on five basic questions. First, what choices do people make about their behavior? Why do some students, for example, focus on their homework while others watch television? Second, having made a decision, how long is it before the person actually gets started? Why do some students start their homework right away, while others procrastinate? Third, what is the intensity or level of involvement in the chosen activity? Once the book bag is opened, is the student engaged and focused or just going through the motions? Fourth, what causes a person to persist or to give up? Will a student read the entire Shakespeare assignment or just a few pages? Finally, what is the individual thinking and feeling while engaged in the activity? Is the student enjoying Shakespeare, worrying about an upcoming test, or daydreaming (Graham & Weiner, 1996; Pintrich, Marx, & Boyle, 1993)?

Intrinsic and Extrinsic Motivation

We all know how it feels to be motivated, to move energetically toward a goal. We also know what it is like to work hard, even if we are not fascinated by the task. What energizes and directs our behavior? The explanation could be drives, needs, incentives, fears, goals, social pressure, self-confidence, interests, curiosity, beliefs, values, expectations, and more. Some psychologists have explained motivation in terms of personal *traits* or individual characteristics. Certain people, so the theory goes, have a strong need to achieve, a fear of tests, or an enduring interest in art, so they behave accordingly. They work hard to achieve, avoid tests, or spend hours in art galleries. Other psychologists see motivation more as a *state*, a temporary situation. If, for example, you are reading this paragraph because you have an examination tomorrow, you are motivated (at least for now) by the situation. Of course, the motivation we experience at any given time usually is a combination of trait and state.

As you can see, some explanations of motivation rely on internal, personal factors such as needs, interests, curiosity, and enjoyment. Other explanations point to external, environmental factors: rewards, social pressure, punishment, and so on. Motivation that stems from factors such as interest or curiosity is called **intrinsic motivation.** Intrinsic motivation is the natural tendency to seek out and conquer challenges as we pursue personal interests and exercise capabilities (Deci & Ryan, 1985; Reeve, 1996). When we are intrinsically motivated, we do not need incentives or punishments because the activity itself is rewarding. James Raffini (1996) states simply that intrinsic motivation is "what motivates us to do something when we don't have to do anything" (p. 3). Intrinsic motivation is associated with many positive outcomes in school such as academic achievement, creativity, reading comprehension and enjoyment, and using deep learning strategies (Corpus, McClintic-Gilbert, & Hayenga, 2009).

In contrast, when we do something to earn a merit increase, to avoid criticism from parents, to please the superintendent, or for some other reason that has very little to do with the task itself, we experience **extrinsic motivation.** We are not really interested in the activity for its own sake; we care only about what it will gain us. Extrinsic motivation is associated with negative emotions, poor academic achievement, and maladaptive learning strategies (Corpus et al., 2009).

It is impossible to tell just by looking if a behavior is intrinsically or extrinsically motivated. The essential difference between the two types of motivation is the person's reason for acting, that is, whether the **locus of causality** for the action (the location of the cause) is internal or external. Students who read or practice their backstrokes or paint may be reading, stroking, or painting because they freely chose the activity based on personal interests (internal locus of causality/intrinsic motivation), or because someone or something else outside is influencing them (external locus of causality/extrinsic motivation).

Is your motivation for reading this page intrinsic or extrinsic? Is your locus of causality internal or external? As you try to answer this question, you probably realize that the dichotomy between intrinsic and extrinsic motivation is too simple, too all-or-nothing. Human activities fall along a continuum from fully self-determined (internal causality/intrinsic motivation) to fully determined by others (external causality/extrinsic motivation). For example, teachers may freely choose to work hard on activities that they don't find particularly enjoyable because they know the activities are important in reaching a valued goal, like spending hours studying or preparing a portfolio in order to earn National Board Certification. Is this intrinsic or extrinsic motivation? Actually it is in between: the person is freely choosing to respond to outside causes such as certification requirements. The person has *internalized* an external cause.

Recently, the notion of intrinsic and extrinsic motivation as two ends of a continuum has been challenged. An alternative explanation is that motivation can include both intrinsic and extrinsic factors. Intrinsic and extrinsic tendencies are two independent possibilities; at any given time, we can be motivated by some aspects of each (Covington & Mueller, 2001). This makes sense because in school, both intrinsic and extrinsic motivation are useful. Teaching can create intrinsic motivation by connecting to students' interests and supporting growing competence, but you know this won't work all the time. Did you find long division inherently interesting? Was your curiosity piqued by irregular verbs? If teachers count on intrinsic motivation to energize all of their students all of the time, they will be disappointed. There are situations when incentives and external supports are necessary. Principals and teachers must encourage and nurture intrinsic motivation while making sure that extrinsic motivation supports learning (Brophy, 1988; Deci, Koestner, & Ryan, 1999; Ryan & Deci, 1996). To do this, they need to know about the factors that influence motivation.

Five General Approaches to Motivation

Motivation is a vast and complicated subject with many theories developed in laboratories, through games and simulations, and in clinical or industrial settings. Our examination of the field will be selective; otherwise we would never finish the topic. As with learning, there are several general explanations for motivation. Each has something to offer principals and teachers.

Behavioral Approaches to Motivation. Behaviorists explain motivation with concepts such as "reward" and "incentive." A **reward** is an attractive object or event supplied as a consequence of a particular behavior. An **incentive** is an expected object or event that encourages or discourages behavior—the promise of a reward. Thus, according to the behavioral view, understanding motivation begins with a careful analysis of the incentives and rewards present in the school and classroom. Providing grades, stickers, certificates, and so on for learning—or demerits for misbehavior—are attempts to motivate students by extrinsic means of incentives, rewards, and punishments. Of course, in any individual case, many other factors will affect how a person behaves.

Humanistic Approaches to Motivation. In the 1940s, proponents of humanistic psychology such as Carl Rogers argued that neither of the dominant schools of psychology, behavioral or Freudian, adequately explained why people act as they do. Humanistic interpretations of motivation emphasize such intrinsic sources of motivation as a person's needs for "self-actualization" (Maslow, 1968, 1970), the inborn "actualizing tendency" (Rogers & Freiberg, 1994), or the need for "self-determination" (Deci, Vallerand, Pelletier, & Ryan, 1991). From the humanistic perspective, to motivate means to encourage peoples' inner resources, their sense of competence, self-esteem, autonomy, and self-actualization. When we examine the role of needs in motivation, we will see two examples of the humanistic approach: Maslow's theory of the hierarchy of needs and Deci's self-determination theory.

Cognitive Approaches to Motivation. In many ways, cognitive theories of motivation also developed as a reaction to the behavioral views. Cognitive theorists believe that behavior is determined by our thinking, not simply by whether we have been rewarded or punished for the behavior in the past (Stipek, 2002). Behavior is initiated and regulated by plans (Miller, Galanter, & Pribram, 1960), goals (Locke & Latham, 1990), schemas (Ortony, Clore, & Collins, 1988), expectations (Vroom, 1964), and attributions (Weiner, 1992, 2000, 2010). One of the central assumptions in cognitive approaches is that people respond not to external events or physical conditions like hunger, but rather to their interpretations of these events. In cognitive theories, people are seen as active and curious, searching for information to solve personally relevant problems. Thus, cognitive theorists emphasize intrinsic motivation. We will see examples of cognitive theories of motivation when we examine Bernard Weiner's attribution theory.

Social Cognitive Approaches to Motivation.   Social cognitive theories of motivation are integrations of behavioral and cognitive approaches: They take into account both the behaviorists' concern with the consequences of behavior and the cognitivists' interest in the impact of individual beliefs and expectations. Many influential social cognitive explanations of motivation can be characterized as **expectancy-value theories.** This means that motivation is seen as the product of two main forces: the individual's expectation of reaching a goal and the value of that goal to him or her. In other words, the important questions are, "If I try hard, can I succeed?" and "If I succeed, will the outcome be valuable or rewarding to me?" If there is no motivation for either question, then there will be no motivation to work toward a goal. Bandura's self-efficacy theory, discussed later in this chapter, is an example of a social cognitive motivation (Pintrich & Schunk, 2002).

Sociocultural Approaches to Motivation.   Sociocultural theories of motivation emphasize participation in communities of practice. People engage in activities to maintain their identities and their interpersonal relations within the community. Thus, students are motivated to learn if they are members of a classroom or school community that values learning. Just as we learn to speak and dress and conduct ourselves in restaurants or shopping malls by being socialized—watching and learning from more capable members of the culture—we also learn to be students by watching and learning from members of our community. In other words, we learn by the company we keep (Eccles, 2009; Hickey, 2003; Rogoff, Turkanis, & Bartlett, 2001).

The concept of identity is central in sociocultural views of motivation. When we perceive ourselves as soccer players, or football fans, or engineers, or teachers, or principals, we have an identity within a group. Part of our socialization is moving from peripheral to central participation in that group, much like going from an internship to the actual role with increased responsibility. We are motivated to learn the values and practices of the community to keep our identity as community members (Lave & Wenger, 1991; Wenger, 1998). The challenge in schools is to be sure that all students and teachers are fully participating members of the community because motivation comes from identity, and identity comes from participation.

Some classrooms are intentionally structured as learning communities. For example, Brown and Campione (1996) developed learning communities for middle school students around research projects in science, as we saw in Chapter 4. Scardamalia and Bereiter (1996) designed a learning community using a computer system called CSILE—Computer-Supported Intentional Learning Environment—that encourages collaboration among students about questions, hypotheses, and findings.

TABLE 5.1   Five Views of Motivation

	Behavioral	**Humanistic**	**Cognitive**	**Social Cognitive**	**Sociocultural**
Source of Motivation	Extrinsic	Intrinsic	Intrinsic	Intrinsic and Extrinsic	Intrinsic
Important Influences	Reinforcers, rewards, incentives, and punishers	Need for self-esteem, self-fulfillment, and self-determination	Beliefs, attributions for success and failure, expectations	Goals, expectations, intentions, self-efficacy	Engaged participation in learning communities: maintaining identity through participation in activities of group
Key Theorists	Skinner	Maslow Deci	Weiner Graham	Locke & Latham Bandura	Lave Wenger

Source: Table from *Educational psychology*, 12th Edition, by Anita E. Woolfolk. Copyright © 2013 by Pearson Education, Inc. Printed and Electronically reproduced by permission of Pearson Education, Inc., Upper Saddle River, New Jersey.

The behavioral, humanistic, cognitive, social cognitive, and sociocultural approaches to motivation are summarized in Table 5.1. These general theoretical perspectives differ in their answers to the question "What is motivation?" but each contributes in its own way to a comprehensive understanding of human motivation.

Motivation to Learn in School

Instructional leaders are concerned about developing a particular kind of motivation in their schools, the motivation to learn. Jere Brophy (1988) describes student **motivation to learn** as "a student tendency to find academic activities meaningful and worthwhile and to try to derive the intended academic benefits from them" (p. 205). Motivation to learn can be construed as both a general trait (some students or teachers have more than others) and a situation-specific state (some situations encourage motivation to learn more than others). What makes student motivation a challenge in classrooms? In an interview, Jere Brophy (2003) listed four obstacles:

1. Because students have to go to school where the curriculum is set for them, students cannot choose to study what interests them.
2. In a class of 20 to 30 students, it is difficult to teach for each student's needs so some students are always bored while others are lost.
3. Classrooms are public, so failures are embarrassing for teachers and students alike. Grading adds to the problem by including parents in this public display of failure.
4. Teachers and students get into the rut of "covering" content and doing "busy work" assignments.

It would be wonderful if all students came to school filled with the motivation to learn, but they don't. And even if they did, schoolwork might still seem boring or unimportant to some students some of the time. Instructional leaders have three major goals. The first is to get students productively involved with the work of the class: in other words, to create a *state* of motivation to learn. Second, teachers want students to move beyond simple participation to cognitive engagement, to think deeply about what they study. Finally, the long-term goal is to develop in students the *trait* of being motivated to learn so they will be able to educate themselves for their entire lives (Blumenfeld, Puro, & Mergendoller, 1992).

As you can already see, motivation is a complex subject. But principals and teachers need working knowledge. What can they do to support motivation to learn in their schools and classrooms? We will draw from a number of theories to examine four key elements that "build" motivation to learn: *goals*, *needs*, *beliefs*, and *emotions*. By keeping in mind these four important aspects of motivation, you can greatly enhance learning in your school.

Goals and Motivation

A **goal** is the achievement an individual is striving to accomplish. Goals motivate people to act in order to reduce the discrepancy between "where they are" and "where they want to be." There are four main reasons why goal setting improves performance. First, goals direct our attention to the task at hand. Second, goals mobilize effort. (The harder the goal, to a point, the greater the effort.) Third, goals increase persistence. (When we have a clear goal, we are less likely to be distracted or to give up until we reach the goal.) Finally, goals promote the development of new strategies when old strategies fall short (Locke & Latham, 2002).

Types of Goals and Goal Orientations

The types of goals we set influence the amount of motivation we have to reach them. Goals that are specific, moderately difficult, and likely to be reached in the near future tend to enhance motivation and persistence (Pintrich & Schunk, 2002; Stipek, 1996). Specific goals provide clear standards for judging performance. For example, Ralph Ferretti and his colleagues (2009) gave 4th and 6th grade students either a general goal for writing a persuasive essay ("write a letter to a teacher about whether or not students should be given more out-of-class assignments...") or the general goal elaborated with specific subgoals such as:

- You need to say very clearly what your opinion or viewpoint is;
- You need to think of two or more reasons to back up your opinion;
- You need to explain why those reasons are good reasons for your opinion. (p. 580)*

Source: "Do goals affect the structure of students' argumentative writing strategies?" by Ralph P. Ferretti, William E. Lewis and Scott Andrews-Weckerly, from *Journal of Educational Psychology*, August 2009, Volume 101(3): pp. 577–589. American Psychological Association. Reprinted with permission.

Both students with and without learning disabilities wrote more persuasive essays when they were given specific subgoals.

Moderate difficulty provides a challenge, but not an unreasonable one. Finally, goals that can be reached fairly soon are not likely to be pushed aside by more immediate concerns. Groups like Alcoholics Anonymous show they are aware of the motivating value of short-term goals when they encourage their members to stop drinking "one day at a time."

Goals are specific targets. **Goal orientations** are patterns of beliefs about goals related to achievement in school. Goal orientations include the reasons why we pursue goals and the standards we use to evaluate progress toward goals. For example, your target might be to make an A in this course. Are you doing so in order to master the content—to learn all about it—or to perform—to look good in the eyes of your friends and family? In classrooms, there are four main goal orientations: mastery (learning), performance (looking good), work-avoidance, and social (Murphy & Alexander, 2000; Pintrich & Schunk, 2002).

The most common distinction in research on students' goals is between learning goals (also referred to as *task goals* or *mastery goals*) and performance goals (also called *ability goals* or *ego goals*). The point of a **learning goal** is to improve, to learn, no matter how many mistakes you make or how awkward you appear. Students who set learning goals tend to seek challenges and persist when they encounter difficulties. Nicholls and Miller (1984) call these students **task-involved learners** because they are concerned with mastering the task and they are not worried about how their performance "measures up" compared to others in the class. We often say that these people "get lost in their work." In addition, task-involved learners are more likely to seek appropriate help, use deeper cognitive processing strategies, and apply better study strategies (Anderman & Patrick, 2012; Butler & Neuman, 1995; Kaplan & Maehr, 2007).

The second kind of goal is a **performance goal.** Students with performance goals care about demonstrating their ability to others. They may be focused on getting good test scores and grades or they may be more concerned with winning and beating other students (Wolters, Yu, & Pintrich, 1996). Students whose goal is outperforming others may do things to look smart, such as choosing easy books in order to "read the most books" (Young, 1997). If winning is impossible, they may adopt defensive, failure-avoiding strategies: they pretend not to care, make a show of "not really trying," or cheat (Jagacinski & Nicholls, 1987; Pintrich & Schunk, 2002). The evaluation of their performance by others, not what they learn or how hard they try, is what matters. Nicholls and Miller (1984) refer to these students as **ego-involved learners** because they are preoccupied with themselves. Deborah Stipek (2002) lists the following behaviors as indicative of a student who is ego-involved with classwork—and Anderman and Patrick (2012) agree:

1. Cheats/copies from classmates' papers
2. Seeks attention for good performance
3. Works hard only on graded assignments
4. Is upset by and hides papers with low grades

5. Compares grades with classmates
6. Chooses tasks that are most likely to result in positive evaluations
7. Is uncomfortable with assignments that have unclear evaluation criteria and repeatedly checks with the teacher

Are performance goals always bad? There is a similarity between intrinsic versus extrinsic motivation and mastery versus performance goal orientations. Mastery-oriented students tend to be motivated by intrinsic factors, whereas performance-oriented students tend to respond to extrinsic motivation. Earlier research indicated that performance goals generally were detrimental to learning, but, like extrinsic motivation, a performance goal orientation may not be all bad all of the time. In fact, some recent research indicates that both mastery and performance goals are associated with using active learning strategies and high self-efficacy (Stipek, 2002). And, like intrinsic and extrinsic motivation, students can pursue mastery and performance goals at the same time, and often do.

Some students, however, don't want to learn or to look smart; they have **work-avoidant goals** and just want to do as little work as possible. These students try to complete assignments and activities as quickly as possible without exerting much effort (Pintrich & Schunk, 2002). They feel successful when they don't have to try hard, when the work is easy, or when they can "goof off." A final category of goals becomes more important as students get older—**social goals.** As students move into adolescence, their social networks change to include more peers. Nonacademic activities such as athletics, dating, and "hanging out" compete with schoolwork (Urdan & Maehr, 1995). Social goals include a wide variety of needs and motives with different relationships to learning; some help but some hinder learning. For example, adolescents' goal of maintaining friendly relations in a cooperative learning group can get in the way of learning when group members don't challenge wrong answers or misconceptions because they are afraid to hurt other members' feelings (Anderson, Holland, & Palincsar, 1997). Certainly, pursuing goals such as having fun with friends or avoiding being labeled a "nerd" can get in the way of learning. On the other hand, goals of bringing honor to your family or team by working hard can support learning (Urdan & Maehr, 1995).

We have been discussing goals in separate categories, but in reality, teachers and students have to pursue several goals at once and coordinate them so they can make decisions about what to do and how to act (Bong, 2009; Darnon, Dompnier, Gillieron, & Butera, 2010). As noted above, sometimes social and academic goals are incompatible. For example, if students do not see a connection between achievement in school and success in life, particularly because discrimination prevents them from succeeding, then those students are not likely to set academic achievement as a goal. Such anti-academic students and groups of students probably exist in every high school (Committee on Increasing High School Students' Engagement and Motivation to Learn, 2004; Wentzel, 1999). Sometimes, succeeding in the peer group means not succeeding in school—and succeeding in the peer group is important. The need for social relationships is basic and strong for most people.

Feedback and Goal Acceptance

Besides having specific goals and creating supportive social relationships, there are two additional factors that make goal setting in the classroom effective. The first is *feedback*. In order to be motivated by a discrepancy between "where you are" and "where you want to be," you must have an accurate sense of both your current status and how far you have to go. There is evidence that feedback emphasizing progress is the most effective. In one study, feedback to adults emphasized either that they had accomplished 75% of the standards set or that they had fallen short of the standards by 25%. When the feedback highlighted accomplishment, the subjects' self-confidence, analytic thinking, and performance were all enhanced (Bandura, 1997).

The second factor affecting motivation to pursue a goal is *goal acceptance*. If students reject goals set by others or refuse to set their own goals, then motivation will suffer. Generally, students are more willing to commit to the goals of others if the goals seem realistic, reasonably difficult, and meaningful—and if good reasons are given for the value of the goals (Grolnick, Gurland, Jacob, & Decourcey, 2002). Commitment matters—the relationship between higher goals and better performance is strongest when people are committed to the goals (Locke & Latham, 2002).

Goals: Lessons for Teachers and Principals

Students and teachers are more likely to work toward goals that are clear, specific, reasonable, moderately challenging, and attainable within a relatively short period of time. If teachers focus on student performance, high grades, competition, and achievement, they may encourage students to set performance goals. This will undermine the students' ability to learn and could encourage cheating or self-defeating actions (Anderman & Maehr, 1994). If any reward or incentive systems are used, make sure participants (teachers or students) understand that the goal is to learn and improve in some area, not just to perform well or look smart. And be sure the goal is not too difficult. Individual students or teachers may not yet be expert at setting their own goals or keeping the goal in mind, so encouragement and accurate feedback are necessary.

Finally, the way students perceive their class defines the *classroom goal structure*—the goals that students think are emphasized in the class (Murayama & Elliot, 2009). Lisa Fast and her colleagues (2010) found that 4th through 6th grade students had significantly higher levels of self-efficacy and mathematics achievement when they perceived their math teachers as caring, and the classes as challenging and mastery oriented. So challenge, support, and a focus on learning, not looking good, seem to create a positive classroom environment. The *Theory into Action Guidelines* give principals and teachers ideas for involving families in goal setting in schools.

Needs and Motivation

A **need** can be defined as "a biological or psychological requirement; a state of deprivation that motivates a person to take action toward a goal" (Darley, Glucksberg, & Kinchla, 1991, p. 743). Our needs are seldom satisfied completely and perfectly;

THEORY INTO ACTION GUIDELINES

Family and Community Partnerships

Understand family goals for children.

Examples

1. In an informal setting, around a coffee pot or snacks, meet with families individually or in small groups to listen to what they want for their children.
2. Mail out questionnaires or send response cards home with students, asking what skills the families believe their children most need to work on. Pick one goal for each child and develop a plan for working toward the goal both inside and outside school. Share the plan with the families and ask for feedback.

Identify student and family interests that can be related to goals.

Examples

1. Ask a member of the family to share a skill or hobby with the class.
2. Identify "family favorites"—favorite foods, music, vacations, sports, colors, activities, hymns, movies, games, snacks, recipes, memories. Tie class lessons to interests.

Give families a way to track progress toward goals.

Examples

1. Provide simple "progress charts" or goal cards that can be posted on the refrigerator.
2. Ask for feedback (and mean it) about parents' perceptions of your effectiveness in helping students reach goals.

---

improvement is always possible. People are thus motivated by the tensions the needs create to move toward goals that could satisfy the needs. Let's look at one very influential humanistic theory of motivation that deals with this central concept.

Maslow's Hierarchy

Abraham Maslow has had a great impact on the psychology of motivation. Maslow (1970) suggested that humans have a **hierarchy of needs** ranging from lower-level needs for survival and safety to higher-level needs for intellectual achievement and finally self-actualization. **Self-actualization** is Maslow's term for self-fulfillment, the realization of personal potential.

Maslow (1968) called the four lower-level needs—survival, safety, belonging, and self-esteem—**deficiency needs.** When these needs are satisfied, the motivation for fulfilling them decreases. He labeled the three higher-level needs—intellectual achievement, aesthetic appreciation, and self-actualization—**being needs.** When they are met, a person's motivation does not cease; instead, it increases to seek further fulfillment. For example, the more successful you are in your efforts to develop professionally, the harder you are likely to strive for even greater improvement. Unlike the deficiency needs, these being needs can never be completely filled. The motivation to achieve them is endlessly renewed.

Maslow's theory has been criticized for the very obvious reason that people do not always appear to behave as the theory would predict. Most of us move back and forth among different types of needs and may even be motivated by many different needs at the same time. Some people deny themselves safety or friendship in order to achieve knowledge, understanding, or greater self-esteem.

Criticisms aside, Maslow's theory does give us a way of looking at the whole person, whose physical, emotional, and intellectual needs are all interrelated. This has important implications for education. A child whose feelings of safety and sense of belonging are threatened by divorce may have little interest in learning to divide fractions. If a school is a fearful, unpredictable place where neither teachers nor students know where they stand, they are likely to be more concerned with security and less with teaching or learning. Students' desires to fill lower-level needs may at times conflict with a teacher's desire to have them achieve higher-level goals. Belonging to a social group and maintaining self-esteem within that group, for example, are important to students. If doing what the teacher says conflicts with group rules, students may choose to ignore the teacher's wishes or even defy the teacher.

A great deal has been written about needs and motivation. For teaching, the most fully developed and relevant work involves the need to achieve.

Achievement Motivation

David McClelland and John Atkinson were among the first to concentrate on the study of achievement motivation (McClelland, Atkinson, Clark, & Lowell, 1953). People who strive for excellence in a field for the sake of achieving, not for some reward, are considered to have a high need for achievement. There are two general explanations for the source of achievement motivation (Stipek, 2002). Some psychologists see achievement motivation as a stable and unconscious trait, something the individual has more or less of. The origins of high achievement motivation are assumed to be in the family and cultural group of the child. If achievement, initiative, and competitiveness are encouraged and reinforced in the home, and if parents let children solve problems on their own without becoming irritated by the children's initial failures, children are more likely to develop a high need for achievement (McClelland & Pilon, 1983). Children who see that their actions can have an impact and who are taught how to recognize a good performance are more likely to grow up with the desire to excel (Schunk, 2000).

Other theorists see achievement motivation as a set of conscious beliefs and values shaped mainly by recent experiences with success and failure and by factors in the immediate situation such as the difficulty of the task or the incentives available. Thus, you might have high achievement motivation when working with teachers in one subject because you know it well and value it, but low achievement motivation when working in another area because you are less familiar with that subject and you question the real value of the material (Stipek, 2002).

Atkinson (1964) added a new consideration to the theory of achievement need when he noted that all people have a need to avoid failure as well as a need to achieve. If the need to avoid failure is greater than the need to achieve in a particular situation, the risk will be threatening rather than challenging, and the resultant motivation will be to avoid the situation. If students' motivation to achieve is greater than their motivation to avoid failure, a moderate amount of failure can often enhance their desire to pursue a problem. They are determined to achieve, so they try again. On the other hand, success gained too easily can actually decrease motivation for those with high achievement needs. In contrast, students motivated by the need to avoid failure are usually discouraged by failure and encouraged by success.

A Principal's Perspective

T. G. was a service-oriented principal who constantly sought input from his faculty, staff, students, and parents regarding ways to improve his middle school and his leadership. Using a variety of nonthreatening methods to gather feedback, he heard this recurring concern from the classified staff: Cooks, custodians, bus drivers, secretaries, and teacher aides were growing increasingly disconnected from the school's mission. T. G. realized that the intense focus on academic achievement was crowding out the contributions of the support staff. These employees were beginning to feel uncelebrated, unwelcome, and undervalued. He also knew that if he didn't act to reverse the deteriorating morale, ultimately they would feel unmotivated. Mindful of the importance of the support staff to the overall educational climate of the school, T. G. decided to dedicate the first five minutes of every monthly staff meeting to the recognition of classified workers. He called it "The Curtain Call" and invited *all* employees to stay for the brief recognition. Selecting two or three names in advance, he asked them to stand, identified their positions and years of service to the school, and added some interesting facts about the work they do, such as "These cooks served over 12,000 hot lunches to our students last month" or "Every night these custodians sweep around 400 desks and carry out one thousand pounds of trash." In the end, teachers applauded, the workers smiled, and everyone was reminded that while academic achievement was the most important thing, it wasn't the only thing.

A more recent approach to motivation that focuses on human needs is self-determination theory (Deci & Ryan, 2002).

The Need for Self-Determination

Self-determination is the need to experience choices to have our own wishes, rather than external rewards or pressures, determine what we do and how we do it. People constantly struggle against pressure from external controls such as the rules, schedules, deadlines, orders, and limits imposed by others. Sometimes help is even rejected so that the individual can remain in command, a possible problem for principals striving to be instructional leaders (Deci & Ryan, 2002; Reeve, Deci, & Ryan, 2004; Ryan & Deci, 2000).

Classroom environments that support student self-determination and autonomy are associated with greater student interest, sense of competence, creativity, conceptual learning, and preference for challenge. These relationships appear to hold from 1st grade through graduate school (Deci & Ryan, 2002; Jang, Reeve, & Deci, 2010; Moller, Deci, & Ryan, 2006; Reeve, 2009; Shih, 2008). When students can make choices, they are more likely to believe that the work is important, even if it is not "fun." Thus, they tend to internalize educational goals and take them as their own. In contrast to autonomy-supporting classrooms, controlling environments tend to improve performance only on rote recall tasks. When students are pressured to perform, however, they often seek the quickest, easiest solution. But even though controlling styles of teaching are less effective, teachers are under pressure from administrators, accountability requirements, and parents to be in charge and to have their classrooms under control. Students often are passive and unengaged or even defiant in reaction to the controlling behavior of teachers. Finally, some teachers equate control with useful structure and feel more comfortable with a controlling style (Reeve, 2009).

The Need for Social Support

The need for relatedness is the desire to establish close emotional bonds and attachments with others. When adults are responsive and demonstrate that they care about the students' interests and well-being, students show high intrinsic motivation. But, when students are denied the interpersonal involvement they seek from adults—when adults, for example, are unresponsive to their needs—the students lose intrinsic motivation (Solomon, Battistich, Watson, Schaps, & Lewis, 2000). Students who feel a sense of relatedness to administrators, teachers, parents, and peers are more emotionally engaged in school (Furrer & Skinner, 2003). In addition, emotional and physical problems—ranging from eating disorders to suicide—are more common among people who lack social relationships (Baumeister & Leary, 1995).

Relatedness has two components, *involvement* and *autonomy support*. Involvement is the degree to which teachers and parents are interested in and knowledgeable about their children's activities and experiences and devote time to them. When students feel a sense of belonging and personal support from their teachers, they are more interested in class work and find it more valuable (Goodenow, 1993; Stipek, 1996). All students need caring teachers, but students placed at risk have an even greater need for this kind of teacher. Positive relationships with teachers increase the likelihood that students will succeed in high school and go on to college (Stipek, 2006; Thompson, 2008; Woolfolk Hoy & Weinstein, 2006). Autonomy support is the degree to which teachers and parents encourage children to make their own choices rather than applying pressure to control the children's behavior. The *Theory into Action Guidelines* give principals and teachers ideas about how to support students' self-determination and autonomy.

Needs and Motivation: Lessons for Teachers and Principals

All people need to feel safe, secure, accepted, competent, effective, connected, and in charge of their own behavior. Some may have developed a particularly strong need to achieve. Most individuals are more motivated when they are involved with tasks that give them a sense of achievement and a chance to form positive relationships with others. No one enjoys failure, and for some people it is crushing. Students, like adults, are unlikely to stick with tasks or respond well to teachers who

THEORY INTO ACTION GUIDELINES

Supporting Self-Determination

Allow and encourage students to make choices.

Examples

1. Design several different ways to meet a learning objective (e.g., a paper, a compilation of interviews, a test, a news broadcast) and let students choose one. Encourage them to explain the reasons for their choice.
2. Appoint student committees to make suggestions about streamlining procedures such as caring for class pets or distributing equipment.
3. Provide time for independent and extended projects.

Help students plan actions to accomplish self-selected goals.

Examples

1. Experiment with goal cards. Students list their short- and long-term goals and then record three or four specific actions that will move them toward the goals. Goal cards are personal—like credit cards.
2. Encourage middle school and high school students to set goals in each subject area, record them in a goal book or on the computer, and check progress toward the goals on a regular basis.

Hold students accountable for the consequences of their choices.

Examples

1. If students choose to work with friends and do not finish a project because too much time was spent socializing, grade the project as it deserves and help the students see the connection between lost time and poor performance.
2. When students choose a topic that captures their imagination, discuss the connections between their investment in the work and the quality products that follow.

Provide rationales for limits, rules, and constraints.

Examples

1. Explain reasons for rules.
2. Respect rules and constraints in your own behavior.

Acknowledge that negative emotions are valid reactions to teacher control.

Examples

1. Communicate that it is OK (and normal) to feel bored waiting for a turn, for example.
2. Communicate that sometimes important learning involves frustration, confusion, and weariness.

Use noncontrolling, positive feedback.

Examples

1. See poor performance or behavior as a problem to be solved, not a target of criticism.
2. Avoid controlling language—*should, must, have to.*

Sources: Adapted from J. P. Raffini (1996). *150 ways to increase intrinsic motivation in the classroom.* Boston: Allyn & Bacon; and J. Reeve (1996). *Motivating others: Nurturing inner motivational resources.* Boston: Allyn & Bacon, pp. 29–31.

make them feel insecure or incompetent. They are less likely to take responsibility for learning if they believe that the teacher doesn't really care about them. The same can be said for teachers: If they feel like faceless workers or if they believe that the principal doesn't really care about them or their problems, they are not likely to respond well to help.

Attributions, Beliefs, and Motivation

Thus far, we have talked about goals and needs, but there is another factor that must be considered in explaining motivation to learn. Success will not encourage motivation if you believe it was "just lucky" and probably won't happen again. Failure is not threatening unless you believe that it implies something is "wrong" with you. In other words, our beliefs and attributions about what is happening and why—about why we succeed and why we fail—affect motivation.

Attribution Theory

Cognitive explanations of motivation, called **attribution theories,** begin with the assumption that we all ask "Why?" in our attempts to understand our successes and failures. Attribution theories of motivation describe how the individual's explanations, justifications, and excuses influence motivation (Anderman & Anderman, 2010).

Dimensions: Locus, Stability, Responsibility.   Bernard Weiner is one of the main educational psychologists responsible for relating attribution theory to school learning (Weiner, 1986, 1992, 1994; 2010; Weiner & Graham, 1989). According to Weiner, most of the causes to which students attribute their successes or failures can be characterized in terms of three dimensions:

- **Locus**—location of the cause as being either internal or external to the person. For example, attributing a great piano performance to your musical talent or hard work is an internal attribution. Explaining that the performance is based on coaching from a great teacher is an external attribution.
- **Stability**—whether the cause stays the same or can change. For example, talent is stable, but effort can change.
- **Controllability**—whether the person can control the cause. For example, effort and finding a great teacher are controllable, but innate musical talent is not.

Table 5.2 shows the eight possible combinations of these dimensions and gives examples of how teachers might explain low scores for their classes on the math portion of the annual standardized tests.

Weiner believes that these three dimensions have important implications for motivation. The internal/external locus, for example, seems to be closely related to feelings of self-esteem (Weiner, 2000). If success or failure is attributed to internal factors, success will lead to pride and increased motivation, whereas failure will diminish self-esteem. The stability dimension seems to be closely related to expectations about the future. If, for example, students attribute their success (or failure) to stable factors such as the difficulty of the subject, they will expect to succeed (or fail) in that subject in the future. But if they attribute the outcome to unstable factors such as mood or luck, they will expect (or hope for) changes in the future when confronted with similar tasks. The responsibility dimension is related to emotions such as anger, pity, gratitude, or shame. If we fail at something that we believe is controllable, we may feel guilt; if we succeed, we may feel proud. Failing at an uncontrollable task may lead to

TABLE 5.2   Weiner's Theory of Causal Attribution

There are many explanations people give for their successes and failures. Below are eight reasons teachers might give for their classes low math standardized test scores representing the eight combinations of locus, stability, and responsibility.

	Internal		External	
	Stable	**Unstable**	**Stable**	**Unstable**
Controllable	Typical Effort	Preparation	Bias	Help
Uncontrollable	Personality/Ability	Mood/Health	Test Difficulty	Luck

Dimension Classification	**Reason for Failure**
Internal-stable-controllable	I usually spend less effort on math
Internal-stable-uncontrollable	Just not a math person/can't teach math
Internal-unstable-controllable	I didn't practice giving the instructions for the test
Internal-unstable-uncontrollable	I was sick the day of the test
External-stable-controllable	Administration chose a biased test
External-stable-uncontrollable	Math section of the test is too hard
External-unstable-controllable	Didn't ask mentor for help
External-unstable-uncontrollable	Bad luck about students present on test day

shame or to anger toward the person or institution in control, while succeeding leads to feeling lucky or grateful. Also, feeling in control of your own learning seems to be related to choosing more difficult academic tasks, putting out more effort, and persisting longer in schoolwork (Schunk, 2000; Weiner, 1994).

Weiner (1994) summarizes the sequence of motivation when failure is attributed to lack of ability and ability is considered uncontrollable:

Failure → lack of ability → uncontrollable → not responsible → shame and embarrassment → performance declines in future

When failure is attributed to lack of effort, the sequence is:

Failure → lack of effort → controllable → responsible → guilt → performance improves in future

Weiner's locus and responsibility dimensions are closely related to locus of causality.

Learned Helplessness. Whatever the label, most theorists agree that a sense of choice, control, and self-determination is critical if people are to feel intrinsically motivated. When people come to believe that the events and outcomes in their lives are mostly uncontrollable, they have developed **learned helplessness** (Seligman, 1975). To understand the power of learned helplessness, consider this experiment (Hiroto

& Seligman, 1975). Subjects receive either solvable or unsolvable puzzles. In the next phase of the experiment, all subjects are given a series of solvable puzzles. The subjects who struggled with unsolvable problems in the first phase of the experiment usually solve significantly fewer puzzles in the second phase. They have learned that they cannot control the outcome, so why should they even try?

Learned helplessness appears to cause three types of deficits: motivational, cognitive, and affective. Students who feel hopeless will be unmotivated and reluctant to attempt work. They expect to fail, so they wonder why they should even try; thus motivation suffers. Because they are pessimistic about learning, these students miss opportunities to practice and improve skills and abilities, so they develop cognitive deficits. Finally, they often suffer from affective problems such as depression, anxiety, and listlessness (Alloy & Seligman, 1979). Once learned helplessness is established, it is very difficult to reverse its effects. Learned helplessness is a particular danger for students with learning disabilities and students who are the victims of discrimination.

Attributions and Student Motivation. Most students try to explain their failures to themselves. When usually successful students fail, they often make internal, controllable attributions: They misunderstood the directions, lacked the necessary knowledge, or simply did not study hard enough, for example. When students see themselves as capable and attribute occasional failure to lack of effort or insufficient knowledge—controllable causes—they usually focus on strategies for succeeding next time. This is an adaptive, mastery-oriented response, one that often leads to achievement, pride, a greater feeling of control, and a sense of self-determination (Ames, 1992).

The greatest motivational problems arise when students attribute failures to stable, uncontrollable causes. Such students may seem resigned to failure, depressed, and helpless, what we generally call "unmotivated" (Weiner, 1994; Weiner, Russell, & Lerman, 1978). These students respond to failure by focusing even more on their own inadequacy; their attitudes toward schoolwork may deteriorate even further (Ames, 1992). Apathy is a logical reaction to failure if students believe the causes are stable, unlikely to change, and beyond their control. In addition, students who view their failures in this light are less likely to seek help; they believe nothing and no one can help (Ames & Lau, 1982).

Cues about Causes. How do students determine the causes of their successes and failures? The behavior of their teachers is one cue. When teachers assume that student failure is attributable to forces beyond the students' control, they tend to respond with sympathy and to avoid giving punishments. If, however, the failures are attributed to a controllable factor such as lack of effort, the teacher's response is more likely to be anger, and punishments may follow. These tendencies seem to be consistent across time and cultures (Weiner, 1986).

What do students make of these reactions from their teachers? Graham (1991, 1996) gives some surprising answers. There is evidence that when teachers respond to students' mistakes with pity, praise for a "good try," or unsolicited help, the students are more likely to attribute their failure to an uncontrollable cause, usually lack of ability. Does this mean that teachers should be critical and withhold help? Of course not! But it is a reminder that "praise as a consolation prize" for failing (Brophy, 1985) or oversolicitous help can give unintended messages. Graham (1991) suggests that many minority group students could be the victims of well-meaning pity from teachers. See-ing the very real problems that the students face, teachers may "ease up" on require-ments so the students will "experience success" and "feel good about themselves." But a subtle communication may accompany the pity, praise, and extra help: "You don't have the ability to do this, so I will overlook your failure." Graham says, "The... pertinent question for blacks is whether their own history of academic failure makes them more likely to be the targets of sympathetic feedback from teachers and thus the recipients of low-ability cues" (1991, p. 28).* This kind of sympathetic feedback, even if well intended, can be a subtle form of racism.

Beliefs about Ability

Rate the following statements taken from Dweck (2000) on a scale from 1 (Strongly Agree) to 6 (Strongly Disagree).

____ You have a certain amount of intelligence and you really can't do much to change it.

____ You can learn new things, but you can't really change your basic intelligence.

____ No matter who you are, you can change your intelligence a lot.

____ No matter how much intelligence you have, you can always change it quite a bit.**

Some of the most powerful beliefs affecting motivation in school are about *ability*. By examining these beliefs and learning how they affect motivation, we will understand why some people set inappropriate, unmotivating goals; why some students adopt self-defeating strategies; and why some students seem to give up altogether. Adults use two basic concepts of ability (Dweck, 1999, 2002). An **entity view of ability** assumes that ability is a *stable, uncontrollable* trait—a characteristic of the individual that cannot be changed. According to this view, some people have more ability than others, but the amount each person has is set. An **incremental view of ability,** on the other hand, suggests that ability is unstable and controllable—"an ever-expanding repertoire of skills and knowledge" (Dweck & Bempechat, 1983, p. 244). By hard work, study, or practice, knowledge can be increased and thus ability can be improved. What is your view of ability? Look back at your answers to the questions above—you can tell.

Young children tend to hold an exclusively incremental view of ability. Through the early elementary grades, most students believe that effort is the same as intelli-gence. Smart people try hard and trying hard makes you smart. If you fail, you aren't smart and you didn't try hard; if you succeed, you must be a smart, hard worker (Stipek, 2002). Children are age 11 or 12 before they can differentiate among effort, ability, and performance. About this time, they come to believe that someone who succeeds

*Source: "A review of attribution theory in achievement contexts" by Sandra Graham, from *Educational Psychology Review*, 1991, Volume 3(1). Springer.

**Source: *Self theories: Their role in motivation, personality, and development* by Carol S. Dweck. Psychology Press, 2000.

without working at all must be really smart. This is when beliefs about ability begin to influence motivation (Anderman & Anderman, 2010).

Students who hold an entity view of intelligence tend to set performance goals. They seek situations where they can look smart and protect their self-esteem. They keep doing what they can do well without expending too much effort or risking failure, because either one—working hard or failing—indicates (to them) low ability. And to work hard but still fail would be a devastating blow to their sense of competence. Another strategy is to make a point of not trying at all. If you don't try and then fail, no one can accuse you of being dumb. Just before a test, a student might say, "I didn't study at all!" or "All I want to do is pass." Then, any grade above passing is a success. Procrastination is another self-protective strategy. Low grades do not imply low ability if the student can claim, "I did okay considering I didn't start the term paper until last night." Of course, even though these strategies may help students avoid the negative implications of failure, very little learning is going on. Students with learning disabilities are more likely to hold an entity view. Teachers who hold entity views are quicker to form judgments about students and slower to modify their opinions when confronted with contradictory evidence (Stipek, 2002).

Students who have an incremental notion of ability, in contrast, tend to set learning goals and seek situations in which they can improve their skills because improvement means getting smarter. Failure is not devastating; it simply indicates more work is needed, as the best athletic coaches know well. Ability is not threatened when failure signals simply that more effort is needed. Incremental theorists tend to set moderately difficult goals, the kind we have seen are the most motivating. Moreover, when students believe they can improve their ability (an incremental view), they tend to focus on the *processes* of problem solving and applying good strategies, instead of on the *products* of test scores and grades (Chen & Pajares, 2010).

One of the most powerful influences on motivation to achieve is another kind of belief, self-efficacy.

Beliefs about Self-Efficacy

Albert Bandura (1986, 1997) suggests that critical sources of motivation are predictions about possible outcomes of behavior. "Will I succeed or fail? Will I be liked or laughed at?" We imagine future consequences based on past experiences and our observations of others. These predictions are affected by **self-efficacy,** our beliefs about our personal competence or effectiveness *in a given area*. Bandura (1997) defines self-efficacy as "beliefs in one's capabilities to organize and execute the courses of action required to produce given attainments" (p. 3).

Self-Efficacy, Self-Concept, and Self-Esteem.   Most people assume self-efficacy is the same as self-concept or self-esteem, but it isn't. Self-efficacy is distinct from other conceptions of self, in that it involves judgments of capabilities *specific to a particular task*. Self-efficacy is "a context-specific assessment of competence to perform a specific task" (Pajares, 1997, p. 15). Self-concept is a more global construct that contains many perceptions about the self, including self-efficacy. Self-concept is developed as a result of external and internal comparisons, using other people or other aspects of the self as frames of reference. But self-efficacy focuses on your ability to successfully accomplish a particular task with no need for comparisons; the question is can *you* do it, not would others be successful (Marsh, Walker, & Debus, 1991). Also, efficacy beliefs are strong predictors of behavior, but self-concept has weaker predictive power (Bandura, 1997).

Compared to self-esteem, self-efficacy is concerned with judgments of personal capabilities; self-esteem is concerned with judgments of self-worth. There is no direct relationship between self-esteem and self-efficacy. It is possible to feel highly efficacious in one area and still not have a high level of self-esteem, or vice versa (Valentine, DuBois, & Cooper, 2004). For example, if you have very low self-efficacy for singing, your self-esteem as an instructional leader probably won't be affected unless you believe that singing is a critical skill for educational administrators.

Sources of Efficacy.   Bandura identified four sources of efficacy expectations: mastery experiences, physiological and emotional arousal, vicarious experiences, and social persuasion. **Mastery experiences** are our own direct experiences, the most powerful source of efficacy information. Successes raise efficacy beliefs, while failures lower efficacy. **Level of arousal** affects efficacy, depending on how the arousal is interpreted. As you face the task, are you anxious and worried (lowers efficacy) or excited and "psyched" (raises efficacy) (Bandura, 1997; Schunk, Pintrich, & Meece, 2008; Usher & Pajares, 2009)?

In **vicarious experiences,** accomplishments are modeled by someone else. The more closely the observer identifies with the model, the greater the impact on efficacy. When the model performs well, the observer's efficacy is enhanced, but when the model performs poorly, efficacy expectations decrease. Although mastery experiences generally are acknowledged as the most influential source of efficacy beliefs in adults, Keyser and Barling (1981) found that children (6th graders in this study) rely more on modeling as a source of self-efficacy information.

Social persuasion may be a "pep talk" or specific performance feedback. Social persuasion alone can't create enduring increases in self-efficacy, but a persuasive boost in self-efficacy can lead a student or teacher to make an effort, attempt new strategies, or try hard enough to succeed (Bandura, 1982). Social persuasion can counter occasional setbacks that might have instilled self-doubt and interrupted persistence. The potency of persuasion depends on the credibility, trustworthiness, and expertise of the persuader (Bandura, 1986).

Efficacy and Motivation.   Greater efficacy leads to greater effort and persistence in the face of setbacks. Efficacy also influences motivation through goal setting. If we have a high sense of efficacy in a given area, we will set higher goals, be less afraid of failure, and find new strategies when old ones fail. If our sense of efficacy is low, however, we may avoid a task altogether or give up easily when problems arise (Bandura, 1993, 1997; Zimmerman, 1995).

Self-efficacy and attributions affect each other. If success is attributed to internal or controllable causes such as ability or effort, then self-efficacy is enhanced. But if success is attributed to luck or the intervention of others, then self-efficacy may not be strengthened. And efficacy affects attributions too. People with a strong sense of self-efficacy for a given task ("I'm good at math") tend to attribute their failures to lack of effort ("I should have double-checked my work"). But people with a low sense of efficacy ("I'm terrible at math") tend to attribute their failures to lack of ability ("I'm just dumb"). So having a strong sense of efficacy for a certain task encourages controllable attributions and controllable attributions increase efficacy. You can see that if a student held an *entity view* (ability cannot be changed) and a *low sense of self-efficacy*, motivation would be destroyed when failures were attributed to lack of ability ("I just can't do this and I'll never be able to learn") (Bandura, 1997; Pintrich & Schunk, 2002).

What is the most motivating level of efficacy? Should students be accurate, optimistic, or pessimistic in their predictions? There is evidence that a higher sense of self-efficacy supports motivation, even when the efficacy is an overestimation. Children and adults who are optimistic about the future are more mentally and physically healthy, less depressed, and more motivated to achieve (Flammer, 1995). After examining almost 140 studies of motivation, Sandra Graham concluded that these qualities characterize many African Americans. She found that the African Americans studied had strong self-concepts and high expectations, even in the face of difficulties (Graham, 1994, 1995).

Of course there are dangers in underestimating abilities because then students are more likely to put out a weak effort and give up easily. But there are dangers in continually overestimating performance as well. Students who think they are better readers than they actually are may not be motivated to go back and repair misunderstandings as they read. They don't discover until it is too late that they did not really understand the material (Pintrich & Zusho, 2002). So slightly optimistic, but not unrealistic, is probably best.

Research on self-efficacy and achievement suggests that performance in school is improved and self-efficacy is increased when students (1) adopt short-term goals so it is easier to judge progress; (2) are taught to use specific learning strategies such as outlining or summarizing that help them focus attention; and (3) receive rewards based on quality of performance, not just engagement, because the former signal increasing competence (Graham & Weiner, 1996). Table 5.3 shows how the different elements we have been discussing combine to support motivation to learn.

Teacher Efficacy.   Much of our own research has focused on a particular kind of self-efficacy, sense of efficacy in teaching (Hoy & Woolfolk, 1990, 1993; Tschannen-Moran, Woolfolk Hoy, & Hoy, 1998; Woolfolk & Hoy, 1990: Woolfolk Hoy, Hoy, & Davis, 2009). **Teaching efficacy,** a teacher's belief that he or she can reach even difficult students to help them learn, appears to be one of the few personal characteristics of teachers that is correlated with student achievement. Self-efficacy theory predicts that teachers with a high sense of efficacy work harder and persist longer even when students are difficult to teach, in part because these teachers believe in themselves and in their students. Also, they are less likely to experience burnout (Fives, Hamman, & Olivarez, 2005).

We have found that prospective teachers tend to increase in their personal sense of efficacy as a consequence of completing student teaching. But sense of efficacy may

TABLE 5.3   Building a Concept of Motivation to Learn

Motivation to learn is encouraged when the sources of motivation are intrinsic, the goals are personally challenging, and the individual is focused on the task, has a mastery orientation, attributes successes and failures to
controllable causes, and believes ability can be improved.

	Optimum Characteristics of Motivation to Learn	**Characteristics That Diminish Motivation to Learn**
Source of Motivation	INTRINSIC: Personal factors such as needs, interests, curiosity, enjoyment	EXTRINSIC: Environmental factors such as rewards, social pressure, punishment
Type of Goal Set	LEARNING GOAL: Personal satisfaction in meeting challenges and improving; tendency to choose moderately difficult and challenging goals	PERFORMANCE GOAL: Desire for approval for performance in others' eyes; tendency to choose very easy or very difficult goals
Type of Involvement	TASK-INVOLVED: Concerned with mastering the task	EGO-INVOLVED: Concerned with self in others' eyes
Achievement Motivation	Motivation to ACHIEVE: mastery orientation	Motivation to AVOID FAILURE: prone to anxiety
Likely Attributions	Successes and failures attributed to CONTROLLABLE effort and ability	Success and failures attributed to UNCONTROLLABLE causes
Beliefs about Ability	INCREMENTAL VIEW: Belief that ability can be improved through hard work and added knowledge and skills	ENTITY VIEW: Belief that ability is a stable, uncontrollable trait

Source: Table from *Educational psychology*, 12th Edition, by Anita E. Woolfolk. Copyright © 2013 by Pearson Education,
Inc. Printed and Electronically reproduced by permission of Pearson Education, Inc., Upper Saddle River, New Jersey.

go down after the first year of teaching, perhaps because the support that was there
for you in student teaching is gone (Woolfolk Hoy & Burke-Spero, 2005). Teachers'
sense of efficacy is higher in schools where the other teachers and administrators have
high expectations for students and where teachers receive help from their principals in
solving instructional and management problems (Capa, 2005; Hoy & Woolfolk, 1993;
Tschannen-Moran & Woolfolk Hoy, 2007). Another important conclusion from our
research is that efficacy grows from real success with students, not just from the moral
support or cheerleading of administrators and colleagues. Any experience or training
that helps your teachers succeed in the day-to-day tasks of teaching will give them a
foundation for developing a sense of efficacy.

Teachers' Sense of Efficacy and Student Achievement.   How does a strong sense
of teacher efficacy work to increase student achievement? Teacher efficacy is context
specific; teachers do not feel equally efficacious for all teaching situations. Teachers

can feel efficacious in one situation but not in others. Even from one class to another, teachers' level of efficacy can change (Raudenbush, Rowen, & Cheong, 1992; Ross, Cousins, & Gadalla, 1996). Efficacy judgments involve both the teaching task and the context.

In analyzing the *teaching task and its context,* the relative importance of factors that make teaching difficult are weighed against an assessment of the resources available that facilitate learning. In assessing *self-perceptions of teaching competence,* the teacher assesses personal capabilities such as skills, knowledge, and strategies balanced against personal weaknesses in a particular teaching situation. The key efficacy questions are:

Teaching Task Question: How difficult is the task at hand and what resources are available?

Teaching Competence Question: Given the situation, do I have the skills and knowledge?

The interaction of these two components leads to judgments of self-efficacy for the task at hand. The consequences of these efficacy judgments may be effort, persistence, and active teaching (higher efficacy) or minimal effort, helplessness, and weak teaching (low efficacy). With Megan Tschannen-Moran, we (Tschannen-Moran, Woolfolk Hoy, & Hoy, 1998) developed a model explaining these relationships that has received research support (Ebmeier, 2003). Our model is summarized in Figure 5.1.

FIGURE 5.1   A Model of Teacher's Perceived Efficacy

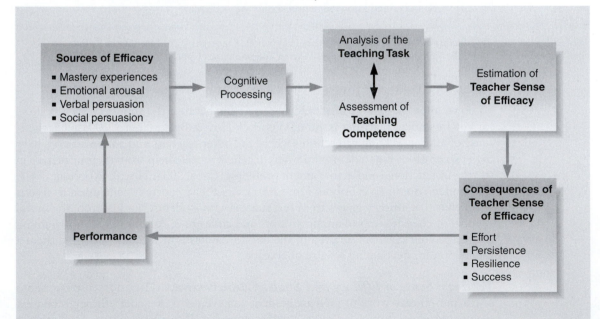

One of the things that makes teacher efficacy so powerful is its cyclical nature. As noted in Figure 5.1, a successful performance creates a new mastery experience, which provides new information (feedback) that will be processed to shape future efficacy beliefs. Greater efficacy leads to greater effort and persistence, which leads to better performance, which in turn leads to greater efficacy. The reverse is also true. Lower efficacy leads to less effort, which leads to poor teaching outcomes, which then decreases efficacy. Over time, this process stabilizes into a relatively enduring set of efficacy beliefs.

Teachers' efficacy beliefs influence their investment in their work and their level of aspiration, resilience, and persistence (Tschannen-Moran & Woolfolk Hoy, 2001). Teachers' efficacy is also related to commitment to teaching (Coladarci, 1992) and job satisfaction (Caprara, Barbaranelli, Borgogni, & Steca, 2003). Once established, efficacy beliefs seem resistant to change. A strong sense of efficacy can support higher motivation, greater effort, persistence, and resilience. Consequently, helping teachers develop strong efficacy beliefs early in their career will pay lasting dividends.

Attributions, Achievement Motivation, and Self-Worth

What are the connections among need for achievement, attributions for success and failure, beliefs about ability, self-efficacy, and self-worth? Covington and his colleagues suggest that these factors come together in three kinds of motivational sets: mastery-oriented, failure-avoiding, and failure-accepting, as shown in Table 5.4 (Covington, 1992; Covington & Mueller, 2001; Covington & Omelich, 1987).

TABLE 5.4   Mastery-Oriented, Failure-Avoiding, and Failure-Accepting Students

	Attitude toward Failure	Goals Set	Attributions	View of Ability	Strategies
Mastery-Oriented	Low fear of failure	Learning goals: moderately difficult and challenging	Effort, use of right strategy, sufficient knowledge is cause of success	Incremental; improvable	Adaptive strategies; e.g., try another way, seek help, practice/study more
Failure-Avoiding	High fear of failure	Performance goals: very hard or very easy	Lack of ability is cause of failure	Entity; set	Self-defeating strategies; e.g., make a feeble effort, pretend not to care
Failure-Accepting	Expectation of failure; depression	Performance goals or no goals	Lack of ability is cause of failure	Entity; set	Learned helplessness; likely to give up

Source: Table from *Educational psychology*, 12th Edition, by Anita E. Woolfolk. Copyright © 2013 by Pearson Education, Inc. Printed and Electronically reproduced by permission of Pearson Education, Inc., Upper Saddle River, New Jersey.

Mastery-oriented people tend to value achievement and perceive ability as improvable, so they focus on learning goals in order to increase their skills and abilities. They are not fearful of failure because failing does not threaten their sense of competence and self-worth. This allows them to set moderately difficult goals, take risks, and cope with failure constructively. They generally attribute success to their own effort, and so they assume responsibility for learning and have a strong sense of self-efficacy. They perform best in competitive situations, learn fast, have more self-confidence and energy, are more aroused, welcome concrete feedback (it does not threaten them), and are eager to learn "the rules of the game" so that they can succeed. All of these factors make for persistent, successful learning for teachers or students (Alderman, 2004; McClelland, 1985).

Failure-avoiding people tend to hold an entity view of ability, so they set performance goals. They lack a strong sense of their own competence and self-worth separate from their performance. In other words, they feel only as smart as their last test grade or performance evaluation, so they never develop a solid sense of self-efficacy. In order to feel competent, they must protect themselves (and their self-images) from failure. If they have been generally successful, they may avoid failure simply by taking few risks and "sticking with what they know." If, on the other hand, they have experienced some successes but also a good bit of failure, they may adopt the strategies we discussed earlier: procrastination, feeble efforts, setting very low or ridiculously high goals, or claiming not to care.

Unfortunately, as we have seen, failure-avoiding strategies are self-defeating, generally leading to the very failure the person was trying to avoid. If failures continue and excuses wear thin, the students or teachers may finally decide that they are incompetent. This is what they feared in the first place, but they come to accept it. Their sense of self-worth and self-efficacy deteriorate. They give up and thus become **failure-accepting people.** They are convinced that their problems are due to low ability, and they can no longer protect themselves from this conclusion. As we saw earlier, those who attribute failure to low ability and believe ability is set are likely to become depressed, apathetic, and helpless.

Teachers may be able to prevent some failure-avoiding students from becoming failure accepting by helping them to find new and more realistic goals. Also, some students may need support in aspiring to higher levels in the face of sexual or ethnic stereotypes about what they "should" want or what they "should not" be able to do well. This kind of support could make all the difference. Instead of pitying or excusing these students, teachers and schools can teach them how to learn and then hold them accountable.

Attributions and Beliefs: Lessons for Teachers and Principals

At the heart of attribution theory is the notion of individual perception. If students believe they lack the ability to deal with higher mathematics, they will probably act on this belief even if their actual abilities are well above average. These students are likely to have little motivation to tackle calculus because they expect to

THEORY INTO ACTION GUIDELINES

Encouraging Self-Worth and Self-Efficacy

Emphasize students' progress in a particular area.

Examples
1. Return to earlier material in reviews and show how "easy" it is now.
2. Encourage students to improve projects when they have learned more.
3. Keep examples of particularly good work in portfolios.

Make specific suggestions for improvement, and revise grades when improvements are made.

Examples
1. Return work with comments noting what the students did right, what they did wrong, and why they might have made the mistakes.
2. Experiment with peer editing.
3. Show students how their revised, higher grade reflects greater competence and raises their class average.

Stress connections between past efforts and past accomplishments.

Examples
1. Have individual goal-setting and goal-review conferences with students, in which you ask students to reflect on how they solved difficult problems.
2. Confront self-defeating, failure-avoiding strategies directly.

Set learning goals for your students, and model a mastery orientation for them.

Examples
1. Recognize progress and improvement.
2. Share examples of how you have developed your abilities in a given area and provide other models of achievement who are similar to your students—not supermen or women whose accomplishments seem unattainable.
3. Read stories about students who overcame physical, mental, or economic challenges.
4. Don't excuse failure because a student has problems outside school. Help the student succeed inside school.

do poorly. If students believe that failing means they are stupid, they are likely to adopt many self-protective, but also self-defeating, strategies. Just telling students to "try harder" is not particularly effective. Students need real evidence that effort will pay off, that setting a higher goal will not lead to failure, that they can improve, and that abilities can be changed. The *Theory into Action Guidelines* should help instructional leaders suggest ideas for teachers to encourage student self-worth and self-efficacy.

Interests and Emotions

How do you feel about learning? Excited, bored, curious, fearful? Today, researchers emphasize that learning is not just about the *cold cognition* of reasoning and problem solving. Learning and information processing also are influenced by emotion, so *hot cognition* plays a role in learning as well (Miller, 2002; Pintrich, 2003). Students are more likely to pay attention to, learn, and remember events, images, and readings that provoke emotional responses (Alexander & Murphy, 1998; Cowley & Underwood, 1998; Reisberg & Heuer, 1992) or that are related to their personal interests (Renninger, Hidi, & Krapp, 1992). Sometimes, emotions interfere with learning by taking up attention or working memory space that could be used for learning (Pekrun, Goetz, Titz, & Perry, 2002). How can we use these findings to support learning in school?

Tapping Interests

Unfortunately, interest in school decreases over time from elementary to high school, with boys showing greater declines than girls. The transition to middle school is particularly linked to a decline in interest. These declines are troubling because results of research on learning in school show that interest is related to students' attention, goals, grades, and depth of learning (Dotterer, McHale, & Vrouter, 2009; Hidi & Renninger, 2006).

There are two kinds of interests, personal and situational. *Personal interests* are more enduring aspects of the person, like an interest in sports, music, or ancient history. *Situational interests* are more short-lived aspects of the activity, text, or materials that catch and keep the student's attention. Both personal and situational interests are related to learning from texts—greater interest leads to more positive emotional responses to the material, then to greater persistence, deeper processing, better remembering of the material, and higher achievement (Ainley, Hidi, & Berndorf, 2002; Pintrich, 2003; Schraw & Lehman, 2001). And interests increase when students feel competent, so even if students are not initially interested in a subject or activity, they may develop interests as they experience success (Stipek, 2002).

Catching and Holding Interests.   Whenever possible, it helps to connect academic content to students' enduring personal interests. But given that the content you will teach is determined by standards in most classrooms today, it will be difficult to tailor lessons to each student's personal interests. You will have to rely more on situational interest. Here, the challenge is to not only *catch* but also *hold* students' interest (Pintrich, 2003). For example, Mathew Mitchell (1993) found that using computers, groups, and puzzles caught students' interest in secondary mathematics classes, but the interests did not hold. Lessons that held interests over time included math activities that were related to real-life problems and active participation in laboratory activities and projects (Anderman, 2004).

One source of interest is fantasy. For example, Cordova and Lepper (1996) found that students learned more math facts during a computer exercise when they were challenged, as captains of star ships, to navigate through space by solving math problems. The students got to name their ships, stock the (imaginary) galley with their favorite snacks, and name all the crew members after their friends. Principals can use the *Theory into Action Guidelines* to give teachers other ideas.

THEORY INTO ACTION GUIDELINES

Building on Students' Interests

Relate content objectives to student experiences.

Examples

1. With a teacher in another school, establish pen pals across the classes. Through writing letters, students exchange personal experiences, photos, drawings, written work, and ask and answer questions ("Have you learned cursive writing yet?" "What are you doing in math now?" "What are you reading?"). Letters can be mailed in one large mailer to save on postage.
2. Identify classroom experts for different assignments or tasks. Who knows how to use the computer for graphics? How to search the Net? How to cook? How to use an index?
3. Have a "Switch Day" when students exchange roles with a school staff or support person. Students must research the role by interviewing their staff member, prepare for the job, dress the part for the day they take over, and then evaluate their success after the switch.

Identify student interests, hobbies, and extra-curricular activities that can be incorporated into class lessons and discussions.

Examples

1. Have students design and conduct interviews and surveys to learn about each other's interests.
2. Keep the class library stocked with books that connect to students' interests and hobbies.

Support instruction with humor, personal experiences, and anecdotes that show the human side of the content.

Examples

1. Share your own hobbies, interests, and favorites.
2. Tell students there will be a surprise visitor, then dress up as the author of a story and tell about "yourself" and your writing.

Source: Adapted from *150 Ways to increase intrinsic motivation in the classroom*, 1st Edition, by James P. Raffini. Copyright © 1996 by Pearson Education, Inc. Printed and Electronically reproduced by permission of Pearson Education, Inc., Upper Saddle River, New Jersey.

However, there are cautions in responding to students' interests, as you can see in *Point/Counterpoint*.

POINT/COUNTERPOINT

Does Making Learning Fun Make for Good Learning?

When many beginning teachers are asked about how to motivate students, they often mention making learning fun. It is true that connecting to students' interests, stimulating curiosity, and using fantasy all encourage motivation and engagement. But is it necessary for learning to be fun?

POINT

Teachers should make learning fun.
When we searched "making learning fun" on Google.com, we found 10 pages of resources and references. Clearly there is interest in making learning fun. In 1987, Thomas Malone and Mark Lepper wrote a

(Continued)

POINT/COUNTERPOINT   Continued

chapter on "Making Learning Fun: A Taxonomy of Intrinsic Motivations for Learning." Research shows that passages in texts that are more interesting are remembered better (Pintrich & Schunk, 2002). For example, students who read books that interested them spent more time reading, read more words in the books, and felt more positively about reading (Guthrie & Alao, 1997). Games and simulations can make learning more fun, too. For example, when one of our daughters was in the eighth grade, all the students in her grade spent three days playing a game her teachers had designed called ULTRA. Students were divided into groups and formed their own "countries." Each country had to choose a name, symbol, national flower, and bird. They wrote and sang a national anthem and elected government officials. The teachers allocated different resources to the countries. To get all the materials needed for the completion of assigned projects, the countries had to establish trade with one another. There was a monetary system and a stock market. Students had to work with their fellow citizens to complete cooperative learning assignments. Some countries "cheated" in their trades with other nations, and this allowed debate about international relations, trust, and war. Liz says she had fun—but she also learned how to work in a group without the teacher's supervision and gained a deeper understanding of world economics and international conflicts.

COUNTERPOINT

Fun can get in the way of learning.
As far back as the early 1900s, educators warned about the dangers of focusing on fun in learning. None other than John Dewey, who wrote extensively about the role of interest in learning, cautioned that you can't make boring lessons interesting by mixing in fun like you can make bad chili good by adding some spicy hot sauce. Dewey wrote, "When things have to be made interesting, it is because interest itself is wanting. Moreover, the phrase itself is a misnomer. The thing, the object, is no more interesting than it was before" (Dewey, 1913, pp. 11–12). There is a good deal of research now indicating that adding interest by adding fascinating but irrelevant details actually gets in the way of learning the important information. These "seductive details," as they have been called, divert the readers' attention from the less interesting main ideas (Harp & Mayer, 1998). For example, students who read biographies of historical figures remembered more very interesting but unimportant information compared to interesting main ideas (Wade, Schraw, Buxton, & Hayes, 1993). Shannon Harp and Richard Mayer (1998) found similar results with high school science texts. These texts added emotional interest and seductive details about swimmers and golfers who are injured by lightning to a lesson on the process of lightning. They concluded that, "in the case of emotional interest versus cognitive interest, the verdict is clear. Adjuncts aimed at increasing emotional interest failed to improve understanding of scientific explanations" (p. 100). The seductive details may have disrupted students' attempts to follow the logic of the explanations and thus interfered with comprehending the text. Harp and Mayer conclude that "the best way to help students enjoy a passage is to help them understand it" (p. 100).*

Source: Harp & Mayer excerpts from "How seductive details do their damage: A theory of cognitive interest in science learning" by Shannon F. Harp and Richard E. Mayer, from *Journal of Educational Psychology*, September 1998, Volume 90(3): pp. 414–434. American Psychological Association. Reprinted with permission.

Arousal: Excitement and Anxiety in Learning

Just as we all know how it feels to be motivated, we all know what it is like to be aroused. **Arousal** involves both psychological and physical reactions—changes in brain wave patterns, blood pressure, heart rate, and breathing rate. We feel alert, wide awake, even excited. To understand the effects of arousal on motivation, think of two extremes. The first is late at night. You are trying for the third time to finish reading materials for a meeting tomorrow, but you are so sleepy. Your attention drifts as your eyes droop, even though you have not finished your preparation. At the other extreme, imagine that you have a television interview tomorrow, one that is sure to be watched by many parents in your district. You feel tremendous pressure from everyone to do well. You know that you need a good night's sleep, but you are wide awake. In the first case, arousal is too low, and in the second, too high.

There appears to be an optimum level of arousal for most activities. Generally speaking, a higher level of arousal is helpful on simple tasks like organizing files, but lower levels of arousal are better for complex tasks such as taking the GRE. Let's look for a moment at how to increase arousal by arousing curiosity.

Curiosity: Novelty and Complexity.   Interest and curiosity are related. Curiosity can be defined as a tendency to be interested in a wide range of areas (Pintrich, 2003). Almost 50 years ago, psychologists suggested that individuals are naturally motivated to seek novelty, surprise, and complexity (Berlyne, 1966). Research on teaching has found that variety in teaching approaches and tasks can support learning (Brophy & Good, 1986; Stipek, 2002). For younger students, the chance to manipulate and explore objects relevant to what is being studied may be the most effective way to keep curiosity stimulated. For older students, well-constructed questions, logical puzzles, and paradoxes can have the same effect. But remember that you have to do more than catch students' interest. You have to hold it, so the questions and puzzles should be related to meaningful learning.

George Lowenstein (1994) suggests that curiosity arises when attention is focused on a gap in knowledge. "Such information gaps produce the feeling of deprivation labeled *curiosity*. The curious person is motivated to obtain the missing information to reduce or eliminate the feeling of deprivation" (p. 87). This idea, similar to Piaget's (1985) concept of disequilibrium, has a number of implications for teaching. First, students need some base of knowledge before they can experience gaps in knowledge that will lead them to be curious. Second, students must be aware of the gaps in order for curiosity to result. Asking students to make guesses, then providing feedback can be helpful. Also, mistakes, properly handled, can stimulate curiosity by pointing to missing knowledge. Finally, the more we learn about a topic, the more curious we may become about that subject. As Maslow (1970) predicted, fulfilling the need to know and understand increases, not decreases, the need to know more.

Sometimes arousal is too high, not too low. Because schools are places where students are tested and graded, anxiety can become a factor in classroom motivation.

Anxiety in the Classroom.   At one time or another, everyone has experienced **anxiety,** or "general uneasiness, a sense of foreboding, a feeling of tension" (Hansen, 1977, p. 91). The effects of anxiety on school achievement are clear. "From the time of the earliest work on this problem, starting with the pioneering work of Yerkes and Dodson (1908), to the present day, researchers have consistently reported a negative correlation between virtually every aspect of school achievement and a wide range of anxiety measures" (Covington & Omelich, 1987, p. 393).* Anxiety can be both a cause

*****Source:*** "'I knew it cold before the exam': A test of the anxiety-blockage hypothesis" by Martin V. Covington and Carol L. Omelich, from *Journal of Educational Psychology*, December 1987, Volume 79(4): pp. 393–400. American Psychological Association. Reprinted with permission.

and an effect of school failure: Students do poorly because they are anxious, and their poor performance increases their anxiety. Anxiety probably is both a trait and a state. Some students tend to be anxious in many situations (*trait anxiety*), but some situations are especially anxiety provoking (*state anxiety*) (Covington, 1992).

Anxiety seems to have both cognitive and affective components. The cognitive side includes worry and negative thoughts—thinking about how bad it would be to fail and worrying that you will, for example. The affective side involves physiological and emotional reactions such as sweaty palms, upset stomach, racing heartbeat, or fear (Schunk, 2000; Zeidner, 1995). Whenever there are pressures to perform, severe consequences for failure, and competitive comparisons, anxiety may be encouraged (Wigfield & Eccles, 1989). Also, research with school-age children shows a relationship between the quality of sleep (how quickly you fall asleep and how well you sleep) and anxiety. Better-quality sleep is associated with positive arousal or an "eagerness" to learn (Meijer & van den Wittenboer, 2004). Poor-quality sleep, on the other hand, was related to debilitating anxiety and decreased school performance. You may have discovered these relationships for yourself in your own career.

How Does Anxiety Interfere with Achievement?   Sigmund Tobias (1985) suggests a model to explain how anxiety interferes with learning and test performance at three points in the learning and performance cycle. When students are learning new material, they must pay attention to it. Highly anxious students evidently divide their attention between the new material and their preoccupation with how nervous they are feeling. Much of their attention is taken up with negative thoughts about performing poorly, being criticized, and feeling embarrassed. From the beginning, anxious students may miss much of the information they are supposed to learn because their thoughts are focused on their own worries (Hill & Wigfield, 1984; Paulman & Kennelly, 1984).

But the problems do not end here. Even if they are paying attention, many anxious students have trouble learning material that is somewhat disorganized and difficult, and that requires them to rely on their memory. Unfortunately, much material in school could be described this way. Anxious students may be more easily distracted by irrelevant or incidental aspects of the task at hand. They seem to have trouble focusing on the significant details (Hill & Wigfield, 1984). In addition, many highly anxious students have poor study habits. Simply learning to be more relaxed will not automatically improve these students' performance; their learning strategies and study skills must be improved as well (Naveh-Benjamin, 1991).

Finally, anxious students often know more than they can demonstrate on a test. They may lack critical test-taking skills, or they may have learned the materials but "freeze and forget" on tests. So anxiety can interfere at one or all three points: attention, learning, and testing (Naveh-Benjamin, McKeachie, & Lin, 1987).

Coping with Anxiety.   When students face stressful situations such as tests, they can use three kinds of coping strategies: *problem solving, emotional management*, and *avoidance*. Problem-focused strategies might include planning a study schedule, borrowing good notes, or finding a protected place to study. Emotion-focused strategies are attempts to reduce the anxious feelings, for example, by using relaxation exercises or describing the feelings to a friend. Of course, the latter might become an avoidance strategy, along with going out for pizza or suddenly launching an all-out desk-cleaning attack (can't study until you get organized). Different strategies are helpful at particular points—for example, problem solving before and emotion management during an exam. In addition, different strategies fit a variety of people and situations (Zeidner, 1995).

Teachers should help highly anxious students to set realistic goals because these individuals often have difficulty making wise choices. They tend to select either extremely difficult or extremely easy tasks. In the first case, they are likely to fail, which will increase their sense of hopelessness and anxiety about school. In the second case, they will probably succeed on the easy tasks, but they will miss the sense of satisfaction that could encourage greater effort and ease their fears about schoolwork. Anxious students may need a good deal of guidance in choosing both short- and long-term goals. Goal cards, progress charts, or goal-planning journals may help here. The *Theory into Action Guidelines* present suggestions for principals to help teachers deal with anxious students.

THEORY INTO ACTION GUIDELINES

Dealing with Anxiety

Use competition carefully.

Examples

1. Monitor activities to make sure no students are being put under undue pressure.
2. During competitive games, make sure all students involved have a reasonable chance of succeeding.
3. Experiment with cooperative learning activities.

Avoid situations in which highly anxious students will have to perform in front of large groups.

Examples

1. Ask anxious students questions that can be answered yes or no, or some other brief reply.
2. Give anxious students practice in speaking before smaller groups.

Make sure all instructions are clear. Uncertainty can lead to anxiety.

Examples

1. Write test instructions on the board or on the test itself instead of giving them orally.
2. Check with students to make sure they understand. Ask several students how they would do the first question of an exercise or the sample question on a test. Correct any misconceptions.

3. Give students examples or models when using a new format or starting a new type of task, to demonstrate how it is done.

Avoid unnecessary time pressures.

Examples

1. Give occasional take-home tests.
2. Make sure all students can complete classroom tests within the period given.

Remove some of the pressures from major tests and exams.

Examples

1. Teach test-taking skills; give practice tests; provide study guides.
2. Avoid basing most of a report card grade on one test.
3. Make extra-credit work available to add points to course grades.
4. Use different types of items in testing because some students have difficulty with certain types.

Develop alternatives to written tests.

Examples

1. Try oral, open-book, or group tests.
2. Have students do projects, organize portfolios of their work, make oral presentations, or create a finished product.

How Can Teachers Avoid Boring Their Students?

Boredom is a big problem in classrooms because it is associated with difficulties in paying attention, lack of intrinsic motivation, weak effort, shallow processing of information, and poor self-regulated learning (Pekrun et al., 2010). How can you increase positive achievement emotions and decrease boredom in the subject you teach? Students are more likely to feel bored if they believe they have little control over the learning activities presented and they don't find them meaningful. Matching challenge to the students' skill levels and giving choices can increase the students' sense of control. In addition, efforts to build student interest and show the value of the activities also help to fight boredom. Remember, achievement emotions are domain specific. The fact that students enjoy and feel proud of their work in math does not mean they will enjoy English or history (Goetz, Frenzel, Hall, & Pekrun, 2008; Pekrun et al., 2010). In addition, teachers who enjoy their subjects tend to be more enthusiastic and to work harder to encourage student enjoyment, so make sure, as much as possible, that you are teaching from your own interests and passions (Brophy, 2008; Frenzel, Goetz, Lüdtke, Pekrun, & Sutton, 2009).

Now that we have a picture of some important building blocks of motivation, let's consider how to put this knowledge to work in classrooms. How will you help teachers deal with one of their greatest challenges, motivating their students?

Strategies to Encourage Motivation and Thoughtful Learning

Until four basic conditions are met, no motivational strategies will succeed. So your first step as an instructional leader working with teachers to improve their students' motivation is to determine if these basic conditions are met in your school. Once these requirements are in place, there are many strategies to help students gain confidence, value learning, and stay involved with the task (Brophy, 1988; Lepper, 1988).

Necessary Conditions in Classrooms

First, the classroom must be relatively organized and free from constant interruptions and disruptions. (Chapter 7 will give you the information you need to make sure this requirement is met.) Second, the teacher must be a patient, supportive person who never embarrasses students for making mistakes. Everyone in the class should see mistakes as opportunities for learning (Clifford, 1990, 1991). Third, the work must be challenging but reasonable. If work is too easy or too difficult, students will have little motivation to learn. They will focus on finishing, not on learning. Finally, the learning tasks must be authentic and not just busywork (Brophy, 1983; Brophy & Kher, 1986; Stipek, 2002).

Once these four basic conditions are met, the influences on students' motivation to learn in a particular situation can be summarized in three basic questions: Can I succeed at this task? Do I want to succeed? What do I need to do to succeed? (Eccles & Wigfield, 1985). As reflected in these questions, we want students to have confidence in their ability so they will approach learning with energy and enthusiasm. We want them to see the value of the tasks involved and work to learn, not just try to get the grade or get finished. We want students to believe that success will come when they apply good learning strategies instead of believing that their only option is to use self-defeating, failure-avoiding, face-saving strategies. When things get difficult, we want students to try to solve the problem and stay focused on the task, not get so worried about failure that they "freeze" with anxiety.

Can I Do It? Building Confidence and Positive Expectations

Let's assume the four basic conditions are met in your school. What's next? One of the most important factors in building expectations for success is past success. No amount of encouragement or cheerleading will substitute for real accomplishment. To ensure genuine progress, teachers in your school should be encouraged to:

1. *Begin work at the students' level and move in small steps.* The pace should be brisk, but not so fast that students have to move to the next step before they understand the previous one. This may require assigning different tasks to different students. One possibility is to have very easy and very difficult questions on every test and assignment, so all students are sure to pass some questions and fail others. This provides both success and challenge for everyone. When grades are required, make sure all the students in class have a chance to make at least a C if they work hard.

2. *Make sure learning goals are clear, specific, and possible to reach in the near future.* When long-term projects are planned, break the work into subgoals and help students feel a sense of progress toward the long-term goal. For example, a big research paper could be broken down into identifying a topic and a few basic references, doing an outline, taking notes, finding additional references and learning the form for a bibliography, writing an introduction, doing a first draft, and finally writing the polished paper. If possible, give students a range of goals at different levels of difficulty and let them choose.

3. *Stress self-comparison, not comparison with others.* Help students see the progress they are making by showing them how to use self-management strategies. Give specific feedback and corrections. Tell students what they are doing right as well as what is wrong and *why* it is wrong. Periodically, give students a question or problem that was once hard for them but now seems easy. Point out how much they have improved. Show the connections between their efforts and their accomplishments.

4. *Communicate to students that academic ability is improvable and specific to the task at hand.* In other words, the fact that a student has trouble in algebra doesn't necessarily mean that geometry will be difficult or that he or she is a bad English student. Even when a task is hard, students can improve if they stick with it. Don't undermine efforts to stress improvement by displaying only the A+ papers on the bulletin board.

5. *Model good problem solving.* Students need to see that learning is not smooth and error-free, even for the teacher. Think aloud as you work through a difficult problem and show students how you handle the situation when you reach a dead end and have to try again.

Do I Want to Do It? Seeing the Value of Learning

We can think of a task as having three kinds of value to the students (Eccles & Wigfield, 1985). *Attainment value* is the importance of doing well on the task. This aspect of value is closely tied to the needs of the individual (for example, the need to be competent, well liked, masculine, etc.) and the meaning of success to that person. A second kind of value is intrinsic or *interest value*. This is simply the enjoyment one gets from the activity itself. Some people like the experience of learning. Others enjoy the feeling of hard physical effort or the challenge of solving puzzles. Finally, tasks have *utility value;* that is, they help us achieve a short-term or long-term goal.

Principals and teachers can use intrinsic and extrinsic motivation strategies to help students see the value of the learning task. In this process the age of the student must be considered. For young children, interest value is a greater determinant of motivation than attainment or utility value. Because younger students have a more immediate, concrete focus, they have trouble perceiving the value of an activity that is linked to distant goals such as getting a good job or even preparing for the next grade. Older students, on the other hand, have the cognitive ability to think more abstractly and to connect what they are learning now with goals and future possibilities, so utility value becomes important to these students (Eccles & Wigfield, 1985).

Attainment and Intrinsic Value.   To establish attainment value, we must connect the learning task with the needs of the students. First, it must be possible for students to meet their needs for safety, belonging, and achievement in our schools. The classroom should not be a frightening or lonely place. Second, we must be sure that sexual or ethnic stereotypes do not interfere with motivation. For example, if students subscribe to rigid notions of masculinity and femininity, we must make it clear that both women and men can be high achievers in all subjects and that no subjects are the territory of only one sex. It is not "unfeminine" to be strong in mathematics, science, automobile repair, or sports. It is not "unmasculine" to be good in literature, art, music, or French. Students' beliefs about the value of a task seem to predict the choices they make, such as whether to enroll in advanced science classes or join a sports team. Efficacy expectations predict achievement in doing the task—how well the students actually perform in the advanced science class or on the team (Wigfield & Eccles, 2002). There are many strategies for encouraging intrinsic (interest) motivation. Several of the following are taken from Brophy (1988).

1. *Tie class activities to student interests* in sports, music, current events, pets, common problems or conflicts with family and friends, fads, television and cinema personalities, or other significant features of their lives (Schiefele, 1991). When possible, give students choices of research papers or reading topics so they can follow their own interests.

2. *Arouse curiosity.* Point out puzzling discrepancies between students' beliefs and the facts. For example, Stipek (2002) describes a teacher who asked her 5th grade class if there were "people" on some of the other planets. When the students said yes, the teacher asked if people needed oxygen to breathe. Since the students had just learned this fact, they responded yes to this question also. Then the teacher told them that there is no oxygen in the atmosphere of the other planets. This surprising discrepancy between what the children knew about oxygen and what they believed about life on other planets led to a rousing discussion of the atmospheres of other planets, the kinds of beings that could survive in these atmospheres, and so on. A straight lecture on the atmosphere of the planets might have put the students to sleep, but this discussion led to real interest in the subject.

3. *Make the learning task fun.* Many lessons can be taught through simulations or games. Computers, problem-based learning, cable TV, and Web connections are just a few possibilities. Students can create newspapers, videotaped debates, or learning materials for younger students.

4. *Make use of novelty and familiarity.* Don't overuse a few teaching approaches or motivational strategies. We all need some variety. Varying the goal structures of tasks (cooperative, competitive, individualistic) can help, as can using different teaching media. When the material being covered in class is abstract or unfamiliar to students, try to connect it to something they know and understand. For example, talk about the size of a large area, such as the Acropolis in Athens, in terms of football fields. Brophy (1988) describes one teacher who read a brief passage from *Spartacus* to personalize the unit on slavery in the ancient world.

Instrumental Value. Sometimes it is difficult to encourage intrinsic motivation, and so teachers must rely on the utility or "instrumental" value of tasks. That is, it is important to learn many skills because they will be needed in more advanced classes or because they are necessary for life outside school.

1. When they are not obvious, you should *explain the connections* to your students or ask them to explain how the material will be important in their lives (Hulleman, Godes, Hendricks, & Harackiewicz, 2010).

2. In some situations, teachers can *provide incentives and rewards* for learning (see Chapter 4). Remember, though, that giving rewards when students are already interested in the activity may undermine intrinsic motivation.

3. *Use ill-structured problems and authentic tasks* in teaching. Connect problems in school to real problems outside, such as buying your first car, weighing claims and making decisions about mobile phone plans, or writing a persuasive letter to a potential employer.

4. Finally, Jere Brophy (2008, p. 140) reminds us that there is more to value than interest or utility—there is the power of knowing: "Powerful ideas expand and enrich the quality of students' subjective lives." These ideas give us lenses for viewing the world, tools for making decisions, and frames for appreciating the beauty in words and images.

What Do I Need to Do to Succeed? Staying Focused on the Task

When students encounter difficulties, as they must if they are working at a challenging level, they need to keep their attention on the task. If the focus shifts to worries about performance, fear of failure, or concern with looking smart, then motivation to learn is lost. Here are some ideas principals can suggest to teachers for keeping the focus on learning.

1. *Give students frequent opportunities to respond* through questions and answers, short assignments, or demonstrations of skills. Make sure you check the students' answers so you can correct problems quickly. You don't want students to practice errors too long. Computer learning programs give students the immediate feedback they need to correct errors before they become habits.
2. When possible, *have students create a finished product.* They will be more persistent and focused on the task when the end is in sight. We all have experienced the power of the need for closure.
3. *Avoid heavy emphasis on grades and competition.* Competition will force students to be ego involved rather than task involved. Anxious students are especially hard hit by highly competitive evaluation.
4. *Reduce task risk without oversimplifying the task.* When tasks are risky (failure is likely and the consequences of failing are grave), student motivation suffers. For difficult, complex, or ambiguous tasks, provide students with plenty of time, support, resources, help, and the chance to revise or improve work.
5. *Model motivation to learn for students.* Teachers can talk about their interest in the subject and how they deal with difficult learning problems.
6. *Teach the particular learning tactics* that students will need to master the material being studied. Show students how to learn and remember so they won't be forced to fall back on self-defeating strategies or rote memorization.

Diversity in Motivation to Learn

Because students differ in terms of language, culture, economic privilege, personality, knowledge, and experience, they will also differ in their needs, goals, interests, and beliefs. For example, self-efficacy is a central concept in motivation because it is a strong predictor of academic performance. But there are cultural differences as well. Males and African American students are more likely to be overconfident in their academic abilities, so their predictions of future achievement are less accurate than those of Asian American and female students, who are much less likely to express overconfidence in their abilities. Gifted male students are less likely to be overconfident, and gifted female students are likely to underestimate their abilities, whereas students in special education classes tend to be overconfident in their sense of efficacy (Pajares, 2000).

Taking this diversity into account when designing tasks, supporting autonomy, recognizing accomplishments, grouping, making evaluations, and managing time can encourage motivation to learn. For example, embedding student writing tasks in cultural contexts is one way to catch and hold situational interest (Alderman, 2004; Bergin, 1999). When Hispanic immigrant students in junior high classes moved from writing using worksheets and standard assignments to writing about such topics as immigration, bilingualism, and gang life—factors that were important to them and to their families—their papers got longer and the writing quality was better (Rueda & Moll, 1994).

Language is a central factor in students' connections with the school. When bilingual students are encouraged to draw on both English and their heritage language, motivation and participation can increase. In his study of bilingual Hispanic students Robert Jimenez (2000) found that successful readers viewed reading as a process of making sense; they used both of their languages to understand the material. For instance, they might look for Spanish word parts in English words to help them translate. Less-successful students had a different goal. They believed that reading just meant saying the words correctly in English. It is likely their interest and sense of efficacy for reading in English would be lower, too.

Encouraging students to capitalize on their cultural knowledge can increase motivation and meaning in school. But this doesn't happen often enough. "The lack of congruence between students' life experiences and instruction in most schools has been well documented, especially for low income students, students of color, and English language learners" (Committee on Increasing High School Students' Engagement and Motivation to Learn, 2004, p. 66).

Putting It All Together

We can see how these motivational elements come together in real classrooms. Sara Dolezal and her colleagues observed and interviewed 3rd grade teachers in eight Catholic schools and determined if their students were low, moderate, or high in their level of motivation (Dolezal, Welsh, Pressley, & Vincent, 2003).

Students in the low-engagement classes were restless and chatty as they faced their easy, undemanding seatwork. The classrooms were bare, unattractive, and filled with management problems. Instruction was disorganized. The class atmosphere was generally negative. The moderately engaged classrooms were organized to be "student friendly," with reading areas, group work areas, posters, and student artwork. The teachers were warm and caring, and they connected lessons to students' background knowledge. Management routines were smooth and organized, and the class atmosphere was positive. The teachers were good at catching student attention and encouraging students to become more self-regulating, but they had trouble holding students' attention, probably because the tasks were too easy. Highly engaging teachers had all the positive qualities of student-friendly classrooms—positive atmosphere, smooth management routines, support for student self-regulation, and effective instruction—but they added more challenging tasks along with the support necessary to succeed at these tasks. Table 5.5 gives even more ideas for your teachers.

TABLE 5.5   Strategies That Encourage and Discourage Motivation in the Classroom

A Few Strategies That ENCOURAGE Motivation	
Strategy	**Example**
High academic expectations and responsibility	The teacher occasionally asks parents to review and help with some assignments with their child and asks parents for feedback.
Communication of a serious work environment and importance of good performance.	"We need to double check the work on each problem so you don't make careless mistakes."
Clear directions to achievable goals.	The teacher explains exactly how students are to solve their math problems and how to circle their answers after they are checked for accuracy.
Relating concepts and procedures across multiple subjects.	The teacher relates the concept of percentages in math to understanding election returns in social studies.
Good performance is celebrated and rewarded.	"The class did such a good job on this history unit that we will take a field trip to the museum next month."
Students work harder when the task is challenging and they have confidence in their ability to succeed.	Students are given increasingly more challenging problems only as they develop the ability to succeed at less difficult levels.
Attributions to effort rather than ability	After a correct answer, the teacher remarks, "See this is easy as we prepare and practice."
Encouraging creativity	"I need a another student to tackle something new. Someone I haven't called on yet. I need someone with imagination."
Using games to reinforce learning	Students invent questions for a quiz bowl game they have developed and like to play.
Involving parents in student projects	As part of a science and math unit, students keep a record and graph the kinds and number of "green" activities that they and their families engage in for a week.
Alternate paths to problem solutions	The teacher uses 3 ways to teach division: "estimations using multiplication ('fuzzy math')," "ratios" and "flash-card review."
Modeling effective classroom management	The teacher explains and models procedures for collecting homework, then students practice.
Stimulating student autonomy	Students are encouraged to pick their own topics for a short essay.
Positive outcomes	Ask students to set aside 10 minutes once a week to reflect on 3 things that went well that week. Write down those things and answer the question, "Why did this happen?" Be prepared to share with the class.
Optimistic encouragement	"I know this is hard stuff, but you people are doing so well; in fact, I know *teachers* who would have trouble with this problem."
Supportive communication from students about other students	Have students identify others that have been most helpful to them and describe why and how.

TABLE 5.5   Continued

<table>
<tr><th colspan="2">A Few Strategies That DISCOURAGE Motivation</th></tr>
<tr><th>Strategy</th><th>Example</th></tr>
<tr><td>Attributions to intelligence rather than effort</td><td>When students say during a lesson, "I'm just dumb" or "I can't do it," or "it's just too hard," and the teacher responds by moving on to another student, saying, "Who's smart and knows how to do this?"</td></tr>
<tr><td>The teacher emphasizes destructive competition rather than cooperation</td><td>Students are required to read an original essay to the class. In response, a student panel of five evaluators gives either a "thumbs up" or "thumbs down" sign. Laughter erupts as students get the thumb down.</td></tr>
<tr><td>Sarcastic comments on student performance</td><td>Teacher comments on an obviously poor performance, "That is a brilliant answer if I ever heard one."</td></tr>
<tr><td>Mocking behavior</td><td>The teacher mocks a student: "You are just indolent; look the word up if you don't know what I mean."</td></tr>
<tr><td>No trust</td><td>The teacher proclaims, "I can't trust you to do anything. What is wrong with you? Don't you know right from wrong?"</td></tr>
<tr><td>Pessimism</td><td>The teacher admonishes, "Although many of you will have difficulty with this assignment, I don't really care. Just do it: I want no excuses."</td></tr>
<tr><td>Busy work</td><td>The teacher provides "fun tasks" that have little to do with understanding, but keep students occupied.</td></tr>
<tr><td>Custodial messages to students</td><td>"Excuse me, just sit down, close your mouth, stay in your seat, and follow directions or I will see you after school for an hour today."</td></tr>
<tr><td>Custodial classroom management</td><td>The teacher maintains order at the expense of learning; what is important is following directions with no questions asked.</td></tr>
<tr><td>Overly challenging assignments</td><td>The teacher gives homework that only a few students will be able to do.</td></tr>
<tr><td>Just getting it done</td><td>The teacher focuses on "covering material" at the expense of understanding. "We must complete this chapter today."</td></tr>
<tr><td>Cold, stark classroom</td><td>The classroom is cold—no pictures, no bulletin board, no visual aids, and no examples of student work. Clean chalk boards are the focal point of the room.</td></tr>
<tr><td>Disorganization</td><td>There are not enough teacher handouts for each student, handouts are mixed up, and teacher is inconsistent in what is required—saying one thing one time and another a few minutes later.</td></tr>
<tr><td>Public humiliation</td><td>The teacher reads a list of all students who have performed poorly on a recent exam, has them stand, and then publicly ridicules their failed attempts with a lecture on the importance of hard work.</td></tr>
</table>

Source: See S. E. Dolezal, L. M. Welsh, M. Pressley, & M. Vincent. (2003) *Elementary School Journal*, 103, for an additional list of good and bad motivation examples for third graders.

Summary

Motivation is an internal state that arouses, directs, and maintains behavior. The study of motivation focuses on how and why people initiate actions directed toward specific goals, how intensively they are involved in the activity, how persistent they are in their attempts to reach these goals, and what they are thinking and feeling along the way. Explanations of motivation include both personal and environmental factors as well as intrinsic and extrinsic sources of motivation.

Intrinsic motivation is the natural tendency to seek out and conquer challenges as we pursue personal interests and exercise capabilities; it is motivation to do something when we don't have to. Extrinsic motivation is based on factors not related to the activity itself. We are not really interested in the activity for its own sake; we care only about what it will gain us. The essential difference between intrinsic and extrinsic motivation is the person's reason for acting, that is, whether the locus of causality for the action (the location of the cause) is internal or external, inside or outside the person. If the locus is internal, the motivation is intrinsic, and if the locus is external, the motivation is extrinsic. Most motivation has elements of both.

Behaviorists tend to emphasize extrinsic motivation caused by incentives, rewards, and punishment. Humanistic views stress the intrinsic motivation created by the need for personal growth, fulfillment, and self-determination. Cognitive psychologists stress a person's active search for meaning, understanding, and competence, and the power of the individual's beliefs and interpretations. Social cognitive views are integrations of behavioral and cognitive approaches: They take into account both the behaviorists' concern with the consequences of behavior and the cognitivists' interest in the impact of individual beliefs and expectations. Sociocultural theories of motivation emphasize participation in communities of practice. People are motivated to learn the values and practices of the community to keep their identity as community members.

Teachers are interested in a particular kind of motivation—student motivation to learn. Student motivation to learn is both a trait and a state. It involves taking academic work seriously, trying to get the most from it, and applying appropriate learning strategies in the process. In order to encourage motivation to learn, instructional leaders can create environments that give students *goals* for learning, meet students' basic and higher-level *needs*, help students and teachers have *beliefs* that support learning, and arouse *interest* while avoiding *anxiety* in learning.

Many theories of motivation feature a prominent role for goals. *Goals* increase motivation if they are specific, moderately difficult, and able to be reached in the near future. Four kinds of goals influence classroom activities. A *learning goal* is the intention to gain knowledge and master skills. Students who set learning goals are not too concerned with setbacks because they are focused on the task. A *performance goal* is the intention to get good grades or to appear smarter or more capable than others. When students adopt a *work-avoidant goal* they simply want to find the easiest way to handle the situation. Students with *social goals* can be supported or hindered in their learning, depending on the specific goal (i.e., have fun with friends or bring honor to the family). In order for goal setting to be effective in the classroom, students need accurate feedback about their progress toward goals, and they must accept the goals rather than reject them.

Needs are also an important component of many theories of motivation. Maslow has suggested that people are motivated by a hierarchy of needs, beginning with basic physiological requirements and moving up to the need for self-fulfillment. Lower-level needs must be met before higher-level needs can influence motivation. The need for achievement has been viewed as a personal characteristic nurtured by early experiences in the family and as a reaction to recent experiences with success or failure. The need to achieve is balanced by the need to avoid failure. Together, these are strong motivating forces. Several theorists emphasize the role of choice and self-determination in motivation and the need for positive relations with others. When students experience self-determination, they are intrinsically motivated: They are more interested in their work, have a greater sense of self-esteem, and learn more. In addition, teachers must acknowledge the students' perspective, offer choices, provide rationales for limits, and treat poor performance as a problem to be solved rather than a target for criticism.

The attribution theory of motivation suggests that the explanations people give for behavior, particularly their own successes and failures, have strong influences on future plans and performance. One of the important features of an attribution is whether it is internal and within a person's control or external and beyond his or her control. Teachers may cue attributions by the way they respond to students' work. Surprisingly, praise, sympathy, and unsolicited help can communicate to students that they lack the ability to do the work. When individuals believe that ability is fixed, they tend to set performance goals and strive to protect themselves from failure. When they believe ability is improvable, however, they tend to set appropriate learning goals and handle failure constructively.

Bandura suggests that sense of self-efficacy, the belief that you will be effective in a given situation, is a powerful influence on motivation. If an individual has a strong sense of self-efficacy, he or she tends to set more challenging goals and to persist even when obstacles are encountered. Self-efficacy is distinct from other conceptions of self, in that it involves judgments of capabilities *specific to a particular task*. Self-concept is a more global construct that contains many perceptions about the self, including self-efficacy. Self-concept is developed as a result of external and internal comparisons, using other people or other aspects of the self as frames of reference. Compared to self-esteem, self-efficacy is concerned with judgments of personal capabilities; self-esteem is concerned with judgments of self-worth.

Attributions and beliefs about self come together in three possible student orientations. Mastery-oriented students tend to value achievement and see ability as improvable, so they focus on learning goals in order to increase their skills and abilities. They are not fearful of failure because failing does not threaten their sense of competence and self-worth. They attribute failure to controllable causes. This allows them to take risks and cope with failure constructively. A low sense of self-worth seems to be linked with the failure-avoiding and failure-accepting strategies intended to protect the individual from the consequences of failure. These strategies may seem to help in the short term, but are damaging to motivation and self-esteem in the long run.

Learning and information processing are influenced by emotion. Students are more likely to pay attention to, learn, and remember events, images, and readings that provoke emotional responses or that are related to their personal interests. However, there are cautions in responding to students' interests. "Seductive details"—interesting bits of information that are not central to the learning but actually distract from it—can hinder learning.

There appears to be an optimum level of arousal for most activities. Generally speaking, a higher level of arousal is helpful on simple tasks, but lower levels of arousal are better for complex tasks. When arousal is too low, teachers can stimulate curiosity by pointing out gaps in knowledge or use variety in activities. Severe anxiety is an example of arousal that is too high for optimal learning. Anxiety can be the cause or the result of poor performance; it can interfere with attention to, learning of, and retrieval of information. Many anxious students need help in developing effective test-taking and study skills.

What can teachers do to motivate students? Before any strategies to encourage motivation can be effective, four conditions must exist in the classroom. The classroom must be organized and free from constant disruption, the teacher must be a supportive person who never embarrasses students for making mistakes, the work must be neither too easy nor too difficult, and, finally, the tasks set for students must be authentic, not busywork.

Once these conditions are met, teachers can use strategies that help students feel confident in their abilities to improve (e.g., set challenging but reachable goals, stress self—not other—comparisons, communicate the belief that ability is improvable), strategies that highlight the value of the learning tasks (e.g., tie tasks to student interests, arouse curiosity, show connections to the future and to real-world problems, provide incentives), and strategies that help students stay involved in the learning process without being threatened by fear of failure (e.g., provide opportunities to create a finished product, teach learning tactics, model motivation to learn for students, avoid emphasizing grades, reduce risk without oversimplifying the task).

KEY TERMS

anxiety (171)
arousal (170)
attribution theories (156)
being needs (151)
deficiency needs (151)
ego-involved learners (148)
entity view of ability (159)
expectancy-value theories (145)
extrinsic motivation (143)

failure-accepting people (166)
failure-avoiding people (166)
goal (147)
goal orientations (148)
hierarchy of needs (151)
incentive (144)
incremental view of ability (159)
intrinsic motivation (143)
learned helplessness (157)

learning goal (148)
level of arousal (161)
locus of causality (143)
mastery experience (161)
mastery-oriented people (166)
motivation (142)
motivation to learn (146)
need (150)
performance goal (148)

reward (144)   social goals (149)   vicarious experience (161)
self-actualization (151)   social persuasion (161)   work-avoidant goal (149)
self-determination (153)   task-involved learners (148)
self-efficacy (160)   teaching efficacy (162)

DEVELOPING YOUR PORTFOLIO

1. As principal of your school, outline a one-day in-service program to help your teachers understand student motivation so they can apply it in the classroom.
   a. What motivational theories will be discussed? Why? How?
   b. What hands-on approaches to motivation will be demonstrated and discussed? Why? How?
   c. How will you and your teachers decide on a motivational program to be implemented in your school? Consider the pros and cons of various approaches; then develop a rationale for your choice(s).

2. Describe how you and your teachers will develop and design a comprehensive plan for working with parents and families to improve motivation and instruction in your school.
   a. Of what utility are the various motivation theories? Which theories seem most promising given the makeup of your student body?
   b. How can parents and teachers work cooperatively to set goals?
   c. Consider plans that have both intrinsic and extrinsic rewards.

3. Develop a 45-minute PowerPoint presentation to explain your three favorite motivation theories.
   a. What theories would you select? Why?
   b. What are the strengths and weaknesses of each theory?
   c. What are the practical applications of each perspective? Give some hands-on examples of each.
   d. Develop a series of questions for your teachers to discuss about student motivation. What end products do you expect from your teachers?

INSTRUCTIONAL LEADER'S TOOLBOX

Readings

Anderman, E. M., & Anderman, L. H. (2010). *Motivating children and adolescents in schools*. Columbus, OH: Merrill/Prentice Hall.

Brophy, J. E. (2008). Developing students' appreciation for what is taught in school. *Educational Psychologist, 43*, 132–141.

Butterworth, B., & Weinstein, R. S. (1997). Enhancing motivational opportunity in elementary schooling: A case study of the ecology of principal leadership. *The Elementary School Journal, 97*, 57–80.

Childress, H. (1998). Seventeen reasons why football is better than high school. *Phi Delta Kappan, 79*, 616–619.

Committee on Increasing High School Students' Engagement and Motivation to Learn. (2004). *Engaging schools: Fostering high school students' motivation to learn*. Washington, DC: The National Academies Press.

Eccles, J. (2009). Who am I and what am I going to do with my life? Personal and collective identities as motivators of action. *Educational Psychologist, 44*, 78–89.

Raffini, J. P. (1996). *150 ways to increase intrinsic motivation in the classroom*. Boston, MA: Allyn & Bacon.

Reeve, J. (2009). Why teachers adopt a controlling motivating style toward students and how they can become more autonomy supportive. *Educational Psychologist, 44*, 159–175.

Turner, J., Patrick, H., & Meyer, D. (2011). Engaging students in learning: A Special Issue dedicated to Jere Brophy. *Theory Into Practice, 50*.

Usher, E. L., & Pajares, F. (2009). Sources of self-efficacy in mathematics: A validation study. *Contemporary Educational Psychology, 34*, 89–101.

Weiner, B. (2010). The development of an attribution-based theory of motivation: A history of ideas. *Educational Psychologist, 45*, 28–36.

Videos

What I learned from not learning, 12 minutes. An insightful examination of what really goes on in a classroom. Teachers present accurate information in unintelligible ways to uninterested students or irrelevant answers to appropriate questions. Teachers may be so intent on what they are teaching that they are unable to distinguish between students who already know what they are being taught and those who are only pretending to understand. To purchase: #CC-1915. Order from Films for the Humanities & Sciences, Inc., P.O. Box 2053, Princeton, NJ 08543, or 800-257-5126.

Head of the class, 14 minutes. This story aroused tremendous interest when it was broadcast on *60 Minutes*. It reveals the high pressure of the Japanese educational system, where the goal is to gain admission to the university. American educators must decide which elements of the Japanese educational system they should draw upon to improve their own. Order from Films for the Humanities & Sciences, Inc., P.O. Box 2053, Princeton, NJ 08543, or 800-257-5126.

Websites

www.bookitprogram.com/
  Reading Incentive Program from Pizza Hut to encourage K–6 students to read

The following websites have interesting content that can be used for a variety of purposes related to motivation and instruction.

www.historyhouse.com
  History: The History House
www.particleadventure.org
  Science: The Particle Adventure
http://whyfiles.org/
  Science: The Why Files

Organizations

http://www.iasce.net/
  International Association for the Study of Cooperation in Education

CHAPTER

6

Teaching

PREVIEW: KEY POINTS

1. Teachers make a difference, but good teaching is only one of the key elements of successful student learning.

2. Successful student learning requires a mix of engagement, support, and opportunity, as well as good teaching.

3. Expert teachers work from integrated sets of principles instead of dealing with each event as a new problem.

4. Expert teachers have a unique kind of knowledge called *pedagogical content knowledge* that combines mastery of *academic content* with knowledge about *how to teach* that content and match instruction to *student differences*.

5. There is no one model for effective planning, but having clear objectives is important.

6. Using taxonomies of objectives improves planning; a revised taxonomy in the cognitive domain has just been developed. Constructivist planning often involves themes and integrated units.

7. Characteristics of effective teaching include organization, clarity, warmth, and enthusiasm.

8. There is no one best way to teach; different goals and students require different approaches. Both teacher-centered and constructivist approaches can support student understanding.

Leadership Challenge

Your school district has adopted a highly touted, integrated curriculum approach for grades K–6. Quite a bit of time and money was spent on presenting workshops for teachers; buying big books and multiple copies of good children's literature; developing manipulatives for mathematics; building comfortable reading corners; making costumes, puppets, and other reading props; designing science projects; and generally supporting the innovations. Students and teachers are mostly pleased with the program. There seems to be more reading and more enjoyment of reading, at least for many children, but some students seem lost. The students' written work is longer and more creative. However, standardized tests indicate a drop in scores. As principal you are getting worried; after all, it was your big project and you had worked hard to sell it to members of the PTA and school board. But now some parents of students in your school are complaining that they have had to hire tutors or buy commercial programs to teach their children to read.

1. What would you do about the parents' complaints?
2. What would you advise your teachers to do about such complaints?
3. Are changes necessary? How can you find out?
4. What information do you need to make good decisions?
5. Who should be involved in these decisions?
6. Would differentiated instruction be an option? Why or why not?

Do Teachers Make a Difference?

Before we examine theory and practice about teaching, let's consider a basic question: Do teachers make a difference? We ask the question because, for a while, some researchers reported findings suggesting that wealth and social status, not teaching, were the major factors determining who learned in schools (e.g., Coleman, 1966). In fact, much of the early research on teaching was conducted by educational psychologists who refused to accept these claims that teachers were powerless in the face of poverty and societal problems (Wittrock, 1986).

Gary Fenstermacher and Virginia Richardson (2005) state that successful student learning requires four elements: student engagement, social support, opportunities to learn and teach, and good teaching. They note that

> good teaching is but one of four ingredients in this mix. The others are that the learner desires to learn and expends the necessary effort to do so; that the social surround of family, community, and peer culture support and assist in learning; and that there are sufficient facilities, time and resources (opportunities) to accomplish the learning that is sought. The point of introducing this list is to clarify that learning, if it is to be both good and successful, calls on a cluster of conditions, only one of which pertains to the nature of the teaching received by the learner. (p. 190)*

We include this reminder because sometimes it seems that answers to the question, "Do teachers make a difference?" often fall at the extremes—no difference or all the difference. Both answers are wrong. Learning rests on at least the four foundations described above (Kennedy, 2011). In this chapter we look at good teaching, an element that instructional leaders can influence and improve. Our examination of the importance of teaching will cover social, affective, and cognitive dimensions. First, we look at the social and relationship side of teaching.

Teacher–Student Relationships

Bridgett Hamre and Robert Pianta (2001) followed all the children who entered kindergarten one year in a small school district and continued in that district through the 8th grade. The researchers concluded that the quality of the teacher–student relationship in kindergarten (defined in terms of level of conflict with the child, the child's dependency on the teacher, and the teacher's affection for the child) predicted a number of academic and behavioral outcomes through the 8th grade, particularly for students with high levels of behavior problems. Even when the gender, ethnicity, cognitive ability, and behavior ratings of the student were accounted for, the relationship with the teacher still predicted aspects of school success.

In a recent study that followed children from 3rd through 5th grade, Pianta and his colleagues found that two factors helped children with lower skills in mathematics begin to close the achievement gap. The factors were higher-level (not just basic skills) instruction and positive relationships with teachers (Crosnoe, Morrison, Burchinal, Pianta, Keating, Friedman, & Clarke-Stewart, 2010). Evidence is mounting for a strong association between the quality of teacher–child relationships and school performance. In addition, students with significant behavior problems in the early years are less likely to have problems later on in school if their first teachers are sensitive to their needs and provide frequent, consistent feedback.

Source: "On making determinations of quality in teaching" by Gary D. Fenstermacher and Virginia Richardson, from *Teachers College Record*, January 2005, Volume 107(1). Teachers College Record.

Teacher Preparation and Qualifications

It has been difficult to relate student achievement to traditional teacher qualifications such as scores on college entrance examinations or licensure tests, years of experience, type of preparation, certification, or advanced degrees. There seem to be a few consistent findings, however. Students learn more mathematics from teachers who have certifications or advanced training in mathematics, as opposed to teachers who are not certified to teach math. Also, the ratings of the colleges that the teachers attended seem to have some relationship to their students' learning (Ma, 2012).

William Sanders and June Rivers (1996) studied how students are affected by having several effective or ineffective teachers in a row. They looked at 5th graders in two large metropolitan school systems in Tennessee. Students who had highly effective teachers for 3rd, 4th, and 5th grades scored an average of 83rd percentile on a standardized mathematics achievement test in one district and 96th percentile in the other. In contrast, students who had the least effective teachers three years in a row averaged 29th percentile in math achievement in one district and 44th percentile in the other, a difference of over 50 percentile points in both cases! Students with average teachers or with a mixture of low, average, and high effectiveness teachers for the three years had math scores between these extremes. Sanders and Rivers concluded that the best teachers encouraged good to excellent gains in achievement for all students, but lower-achieving students were the first to benefit from good teaching. The effects of teaching were cumulative and residual; that is, better teaching in a later grade could make up *in part* for less effective teaching in earlier grades, but could not erase all the deficits. In fact, one study found that at least 7% of the differences in test score gains for students could be traced to their teachers (Rivkin, Hanushek, & Kain, 2001).

What Is a Good Teacher?

This question has been examined by educators, psychologists, philosophers, novelists, journalists, mathematicians, scientists, historians, policymakers, and parents, to name only a few groups, so there are hundreds of possible answers.

Inside Five Classrooms

To begin our examination of good teachers, let's step inside the classrooms of several outstanding teachers. All the situations that follow are real. The first two are elementary teachers described by Weinstein, Romano, and Mignano (2011). The next three are secondary school teachers who have been studied by other researchers.

A Bilingual First Grade.   There are 25 students in Viviana's class. Most have recently emigrated from the Dominican Republic; the rest come from Nicaragua, Mexico, Puerto Rico, and Honduras. Even though the children speak little or no English when they begin school, by the time they leave in June, Viviana has helped them master the normal 1st grade curriculum for their district. She accomplishes this by teaching in Spanish early in the year to aid understanding, then gradually introducing English as the students are ready. Viviana does not want her students segregated or labeled as disadvantaged. She encourages them to take pride in their Spanish-speaking heritage while using every available opportunity to support their developing English proficiency.

Viviana's expectations for her students are high, and she makes sure the students have the resources they need. She provides materials—pencils, scissors, colors—so no child lacks the means to learn. And she supplies constant encouragement. "Viviana's commitment to her students is evident in her first-grade bilingual classroom. With an energy level that is rare, she motivates, prods, instructs, models, praises, and captivates her students…. The pace is brisk and Viviana clearly has a flair for the dramatic; she uses music, props, gestures, facial expressions, and shifts in voice tone to communicate the material" (Weinstein, Romano, & Mignano, 2011, p. 12).* Viviana's expectations for herself are high as well. She continually expands her knowledge of teaching through graduate work and participation in special training programs. To know more about her students each year, she spends hours in their homes. For Viviana, teaching is a not just a job; it is a way of life.

A Suburban Middle School. Ken teaches 5th/6th grade in a suburban middle school in central New Jersey. Ken emphasizes "process writing." His students complete first drafts, discuss them with others in the class, revise, edit, and "publish" their work. The students also keep daily journals and often use these to share personal concerns with Ken. They tell him about problems at home, fights, and fears; he always takes the time to respond in writing. The study of science is also placed in the context of the real world. Students learn about ocean ecosystems by using a special interactive software program. For social studies, the class plays two simulation games that focus on history. One is on coming of age in Native American cultures and the other is on the colonization of America.

Throughout the year Ken is very interested in the social and emotional development of his students. He wants them to learn about responsibility and fairness as well as science and social studies. This concern is evident in the way he develops his class rules at the beginning of the year. Rather than specifying do's and don'ts, Ken and his students devise a "Bill of Rights" for the class, describing the rights of the students. These rights cover most of the situations that might need a "rule." On occasion, when classes are a real challenge, he has established some "laws."

An Inner City Middle School. Another excellent teacher is described in the *Harvard Education Letter.*

> Robert Moses, founder of the Algebra Project at the Martin Luther King School in Cambridge, Massachusetts, teaches students the concept of number and sign through a physical event: they go for a ride on a subway. Choosing one subway stop as a starting point, students relate inbound and outbound to positive and negative numbers. They translate their subway ride into mathematical language by considering both the number of stops and their direction.
>
> By giving students such experiences before introducing the formal language of algebra, Moses . . . has made math more enjoyable and accessible. (Driscoll & Ruopp, 1990, p. 5)**

---

*Source: Excerpt from *Elementary classroom management: Lessons from research and practice*, 5th Edition, by Carol Simon Weinstein, Molly Romano and Andrew Mignano, Jr. Copyright © 2011 by The McGraw-Hill Companies, Inc. Reprinted with permission.

**Source: "Access to algebra" by M. Driscoll and F. Ruopp, from *Harvard Education Letter*, January/February 1990, Volume 16(1). Harvard Education Publishing Group.

An Inclusive Class.   Elliot was bright and articulate. He easily memorized stories as a child, but he could not read by himself. His problems stemmed from severe learning difficulties with auditory and visual integration and long-term visual memory. When he tried to write, everything got jumbled. Dr. Nancy White worked with Elliot's teacher, Mia Russell, to tailor intensive tutoring that specifically focused on Elliot's individual patterns and his errors. With his teachers' help over the next years, Elliot became an expert on his own learning and was transformed into an independent learner; he knew which strategies he had to use and when to use them. According to Elliot, "Learning that stuff is not fun, but it works!" (Hallahan & Kauffman, 2006, pp. 184–185).

An Advanced Math Class.   Hilda Borko and Carol Livingston (1989) describe Randy, an expert secondary school mathematics teacher. Randy's students were having trouble understanding integrals. Randy worked with his students' confusion to construct a review lesson about strategies for doing integrals. When one student said that a particular section in the book seemed "haphazard," Randy led the class through a process of organizing the material. He asked the class for general statements about useful strategies for doing integrals. He clarified their suggestions, elaborated on some, and helped students improve others. He asked the students to tie their ideas to passages in the text. Even though he accepted all reasonable suggestions, he listed only the key strategies on the board. By the end of the period, the students had transformed the disorganized material from the book into an ordered and useful outline to guide their learning. They also had a better idea about how to read and understand difficult material.

What do you see in these classrooms? The teachers are committed to their students. They must deal with a wide range of student abilities and challenges: different languages, different home lives, different learning needs. These teachers must understand their subjects and their students' thinking so well that they can spontaneously create new examples and explanations when students are confused. They must make the most abstract concepts, such as negative numbers, real and understandable for their particular students. And then there is the challenge of new technologies and techniques. The teachers must use them appropriately to accomplish important goals and not just to entertain the students. The whole time that these experts are navigating through the academic material, they also are taking care of the emotional needs of their students, propping up sagging self-esteem and encouraging responsibility. If we followed these individuals from the first day of class, we would see that they carefully plan and teach the basic procedures for living and learning in their classes. They can efficiently collect and correct homework, regroup students, give directions, distribute materials, collect lunch money, and deal with disruptions, while also making a mental note to check why one of their students is so tired.

Viviana, Ken, Robert, Mia, and Randy are examples of expert teachers, the focus of much recent research in education and psychology. For another perspective on the question "What is a good teacher?" let's examine this research on expertise in teaching.

Expert Teachers

What do expert teachers know that allows them to be so successful? How do they differ from beginners?

Pedagogical Content Knowledge. Expert teachers have elaborate systems of knowledge for understanding problems in teaching. For example, when a beginning teacher is faced with students' wrong answers on math or history tests, all of these answers may seem about the same—wrong. But for an expert teacher, wrong answers are part of a rich system of knowledge that could include how to recognize several types of wrong answers, how to identify the misunderstanding or lack of information behind each kind of mistake, what is the best way to reteach and correct the misunderstanding, which materials and activities have worked in the past, and how to test to find out whether the reteaching was successful. This unique kind of teacher knowledge that combines mastery of *academic content* with knowledge about *how to teach* that content and match instruction to *student differences* is called **pedagogical content knowledge** (Gess-Newsome, 2012; Shulman, 1987). Studies in German high schools have found that math teachers with more pedagogical content knowledge have students who are more cognitively engaged and more supported in learning, and this higher quality instruction predicts higher student math achievement (Baumert et al., 2010).

In addition, expert teachers have clear goals and take individual differences into account when planning for their students. These teachers are **reflective** practitioners, constantly trying to understand and improve their work with students (Hogan, Rabinowitz, & Craven, 2003).

Content Knowledge. Do teachers who know more about their *subject* have a more positive impact on their students? It depends on the subject. When Hill, Rowan, and Ball (2005) tested U.S. 1st and 3rd grade teachers' specific knowledge of the math concepts that they actually had to teach, along with their understanding of how to teach those concepts, they found that teachers with greater *content* and *pedagogical content knowledge* had students who learned more mathematics. High school students appear to learn more mathematics from teachers with degrees or significant coursework in mathematics (Wayne & Youngs, 2003).

When we look at teachers' knowledge of facts and concepts in other subjects, as measured by test scores and college grades, the relationship to student learning is unclear and may be indirect (Aloe & Becker, 2009). We know from Darling-Hammond and Youngs' (2002) work that the quality of teachers—as measured by whether the teachers were fully certified and had a major in their teaching field—is related to student performance. When we look at scores on teacher certification tests, there is a modest positive relationship between teachers' scores and students' achievement—the strongest evidence for this relationship is again in mathematics (Boyd, Goldhaber, Lankford, & Wyckoff, 2008).

The indirect effects of content knowledge on student achievement are that teachers who know more may make clearer presentations and recognize student difficulties more easily. They are ready for any student questions and do not have to be evasive or vague in their answers. Thus, knowledge is necessary for effective teaching because being more knowledgeable helps teachers be *clearer*, more *organized*, and more *responsive* to student questions—characteristics that have been associated with successful teaching for a long time.

Characteristics of Effective Teachers

Some of the earliest studies on effective teaching focused on the personal qualities of the teachers. Researchers thought that the key to success in teaching must lie in the characteristics of teachers (Medley, 1979). Although this assumption proved incorrect—or at least incomplete—it did teach us some lessons about three teacher characteristics: clarity, enthusiasm, and warmth.

Clarity.   Students discussing a teacher are likely to say things like, "Oh, she can really explain," or "He's so confusing!" When Barak Rosenshine and Norma Furst (1973) reviewed about 50 studies of teaching, they concluded that *clarity* was the most promising teacher behavior for future research on effective teaching. Other studies confirm the importance of clarity. Teachers who provide clear presentations and explanations tend to have students who learn more and who rate their teachers more positively. Teachers with more knowledge of the subject tend to be less vague in their explanations to the class. The less vague the teacher, the more the students learn (Evertson & Emmer, 2009, 2013).

Planning for Clarity.   Research offers guidelines for greater clarity in teaching (Comadna, Hunt, & Simonds, 2007; Evertson & Emmer, 2013). When planning a lesson, your teachers should try to anticipate the problems students will have with the material. Teachers' manuals and experienced teachers can help new teachers with this. You might also encourage your teachers to do the written parts of the lesson themselves to identify potential problems. Have definitions ready for new terms and prepare several relevant examples for concepts. Think of analogies that will make ideas easier to understand. Organize the lesson in a logical sequence; include checkpoints that incorporate oral or written questions or problems to make sure the students are following the explanations.

Plan a clear introduction to the lesson. Tell students what they will be learning and how they could approach it. Often teachers are vague about both the "what" and the "how." One study found that teachers seldom, if ever, explain the cognitive processes they want their students to practice in a seatwork activity. Bright students figure out the right process, but slower students often guess or give up. For example, an *ineffective* teacher might introduce a seatwork activity on words with prefixes by saying, "Here are some words with prefixes. Write the meaning of each in the blanks." An *effective* teacher, on the other hand, would demonstrate how to divide the words into a prefix and a root; how to determine the meaning of the root and the prefix; and how to put the two meanings together to make sense of the whole word (Berliner, 1987).

Clarity During the Lesson.   As you observe teachers, do they make clear connections between facts or concepts by using **explanatory links** such as *because, if… then,* or *therefore?* For example, when a teacher says, "The Northern economy was based on manufacturing and the North had an advantage in the Civil War," students are given two facts, but no connection between them. If there is a relationship between the two ideas, it should be indicated with an explanatory link as in, "The North had an advantage in the Civil War *because* its economy was based on manufacturing." Explanatory links tie ideas together and make them easier to learn (Berliner, 1987). Explanatory links are also helpful in labeling visual material such as graphs, concept maps, or illustrations.

Teachers also should signal transitions from one major topic to another with phrases such as "The next area…," "Now we will turn to…," or "The second step is…" Teachers might help students follow the lesson by outlining topics, listing key points, or drawing concept maps. They should continually monitor the group to see if everyone is following the lesson. Look for confident nods or puzzled stares. Throughout the lesson, teachers should choose words that are familiar to the students and also define new terms by relating them to what the students already know.

Vagueness is the enemy of understanding. Encourage teachers and students to be precise. Avoid vague words and ambiguous phrases: steer clear of "the somes": *something, someone, sometime, somehow;* "the not verys": *not very much, not very well, not very hard, not very often;* and other unspecific fillers, such as *most, not all, sort of, and so on, of course, as you know, I guess, in fact, or whatever,* and *more or less.* Use specific (and, if possible, colorful) names instead of *it, them,* and *thing.* Also, refrain from using pet phrases such as *you know, like,* and *Okay?* Another idea is to have teachers record a lesson on tape to check themselves for clarity.

Warmth and Enthusiasm.   As you are well aware, some teachers are much more enthusiastic than others. Several studies have found that ratings of teachers' enthusiasm for their subject are correlated with student achievement gains (Keller, Neumann, & Fischer, 2012), whereas warmth, friendliness, and understanding seem to be the teacher traits most strongly associated with students' liking the teacher and the class in general (Hamann, Baker, McAllister, & Bauer, 2000; Madsen, 2003; Soar & Soar, 1979). But notice: These are correlational studies. The results do not tell us that teacher enthusiasm causes student learning or that warmth causes positive attitudes, only that the two variables tend to occur together. Two possible connections are that when teachers are enthusiastic, they capture and hold student attention, and attention leads to learning. Second, enthusiastic teachers may model engagement and interest in learning and thus show students that learning is valuable. Student attention, interest, and engagement lead to learning. Of course, it is easier to be an enthusiastic teacher when your students are learning (Keller et al., 2012).

The research we have looked at has identified teacher, clarity, warmth, and enthusiasm as important characteristics of effective teachers. One caveat: Importance can be in the eye of the beholder. In one study, administrators and students agreed that teacher clarity was very important, but differed in their views of teacher knowledge.

Students rated knowledge third in importance, whereas administrators rated it nineteenth (Polk, 2006). The *Theory into Action Guidelines* summarize the practical implications that principals and teachers can use to improve learning and teaching.

THEORY INTO ACTION GUIDELINES

Characteristics of Good Teachers

Organize your lessons carefully.

Examples

1. Provide objectives that help students focus on the purpose of the lesson.
2. Begin lessons by writing a brief outline on the board, or work on an outline with the class as part of the lesson.
3. If possible, break the presentation into clear steps or stages.
4. Review periodically.

Strive for clear explanations.

Examples

1. Use concrete examples or analogies that relate to the students' own lives. Have several examples for particularly difficult points.
2. Give explanations at several levels so all students, not just the brightest, will understand.
3. Focus on one idea at a time and avoid digressions.

Communicate an enthusiasm for your subject and the day's lesson.

Examples

1. Tell students why the lesson is important. Have a better reason than "This will be on the test" or "You will need to know it next year." Emphasize the value of the learning itself.
2. Make eye contact with the students.
3. Vary your pace and volume in speaking. Use silence for emphasis.

Recent Research on Teaching

A program of large-scale, longitudinal research by Robert Pianta and his colleagues (2005, 2008; Crosnoe et al., 2010; Jerome, Hamre, & Pianta, 2009; Luckner & Pinata, 2011) has identified three aspects of classroom climate that are related to the development and learning of preschool and elementary school students. These three dimensions are consistent with the characteristics of teachers identified in earlier research on teaching, and they cover affective, behavioral, and cognitive dimensions, as you can see in Table 6.1 on the next page. The *affective* dimension in Pianta's model is teacher *emotional support*, similar to teacher warmth and enthusiasm identified in early research. The *cognitive* dimension is instructional support, which includes concept development (activities and discussions that promote student higher-order thinking) and quality feedback that is specific and focused on the learning process. Concept development and quality feedback may be easier for teachers with greater knowledge for teaching. Pianta's third dimension is classroom organization, which includes *behavioral* concerns such as classroom and lesson management, with clear activities and routines that make more time for student learning and are really engaging—similar to the teacher characteristics of clarity and organization.

Now let's get to the specifics of teaching—the first step is planning.

TABLE 6.1   Dimensions of Classroom Climate

Area of Teaching	Classroom Climate Dimension	Components	Definitions and Examples
Affective	Emotional Support	*Positive Climate*	Warmth, mutual respect, positive emotional connections between teacher and students
		Negative Climate	Disrespect, anger, hostility
		Teacher Sensitivity	Consistency and effectiveness in responding to students' academic and emotional needs
		Regard for Students' Perspectives	Activities encourage student autonomy and emphasize students' interests, motivations, and points of view
Cognitive	Instructional Support	*Concept Development*	Activities and discussion promote higher-order thinking skills and cognition
		Quality of Feedback	Consistency in providing specific, process-oriented feedback and back-and-forth exchanges to extend students' learning
Behavioral	Classroom Organization	*Behavior Management*	Teachers' effectiveness in monitoring, preventing, and redirecting misbehavior
		Productivity	How consistently learning is maximized with clear activities and routines, teacher preparation, efficient transitions, and minimal disruptions
		Instructional Learning Formats	How well materials, modalities, and activities are used to engage students in learning

Source: Table from *Educational psychology*, 12th Edition, by Anita E. Woolfolk. Copyright © 2013 by Pearson Education, Inc. Printed and Electronically reproduced by permission of Pearson Education, Inc., Upper Saddle River, New Jersey.

The First Step: Planning

In the past few years, educational researchers interviewed teachers about how they plan, asked teachers to "think out loud" while planning or to keep journals describing their plans, and even studied teachers intensively for months at a time. What have they found?

First, planning influences what students will learn because planning transforms the available time and curriculum materials into activities, assignments, and tasks for students. When a teacher decides to devote 7 hours to language arts and 15 minutes to science in a given week, the students in that class will learn more language than science. In fact, differences as dramatic as this do occur. In one school, the time allocated to mathematics ranged from 3 hours a week in one class to 6 hours a week in a class down the hall (Clark & Yinger, 1988; Karweit, 1989).

Second, teachers engage in several levels of planning—by the year, term, unit, week, and day. All the levels must be coordinated. Planning done at the beginning of the year is particularly important, because many routines and patterns are established early. For experienced teachers, unit planning seemed to be the most important level, followed by weekly and then daily planning. For beginning teachers, the focus is more likely to be on isolated day-to-day lesson planning; often these inexperienced teachers have difficulty integrating discrete lessons into more comprehensive units (Koeppen, 1998; McCutcheon & Milner, 2002; Morine-Dershimer, 2006).

Third, plans reduce—but do not eliminate—uncertainty in teaching. Even the best plans cannot (and should not) control everything that happens in class; planning must allow flexibility (Calderhead, 1996). There is some evidence that when teachers "overplan"—fill every minute and stick to the plan no matter what—their students do not learn as much as students whose teachers are flexible (Shavelson, 1987). Beginning teachers may need to be reminded that they should not proceed with a scheduled new unit if their in-class review shows that many students still don't understand the material in the unit they are currently studying.

In order to plan creatively and flexibly, teachers need to have wide-ranging knowledge about students, their interests, and abilities; the subjects being taught; alternative ways to teach and assess understanding; working with groups; the expectations and limitations of the school and community; how to apply and adapt materials and texts; and how to pull all this knowledge together into meaningful activities. The plans of beginning teachers sometimes don't work because they lack knowledge about the students or the subject: They can't estimate how long it will take students to complete an activity, for example, or they stumble when asked for an explanation or a different example (Calderhead, 1996).

In planning, collaboration can be helpful. Some educators think that a collaborative approach to planning used in Japan called *kenshu* or "mastery through study" is one reason why Japanese students do so well on international tests. A basic part of the process involves a small group of teachers developing a lesson, then videotaping one of the group members teaching the lesson. Next, all members review the tape, analyze student responses, and improve the lesson further. Other teachers try the revised lesson and more improvements follow. At the end of the school year, all the study groups may publish the results of their work. In the United States, this process is called **lesson study** (Morine-Dershimer, 2006). To learn about this approach, search the Internet using the keywords *lesson study*.

But even great lesson plan ideas taken from a terrific science website have to be adapted to your situation. Some of the adaptation comes before teaching and some comes after. In fact, much of what experienced teachers know about planning comes from looking back—reflecting—on what worked and what didn't, so encourage your teachers to look back on their plans. Collaborative reflection and revising lessons are major components of the *lesson study* approach to planning.

Finally, there is no one model for effective planning. For experienced teachers, planning is a creative problem-solving process. Experienced teachers know how to accomplish many lessons and segments of lessons. They know what to expect and how to proceed, so they don't necessarily continue to follow the detailed lesson-planning models they learned during their teacher-preparation programs. Planning is more informal, "in their heads."

The *Principal's Perspective* tells how a real principal helped a new teacher plan and teach more effectively by providing the resources she needed and giving some personal attention.

A Principal's Perspective

P. M. didn't need formal evaluations of one young teacher to realize she was in trouble. Periodic walks past her classroom early in the school year revealed a frustrated teacher floundering before uncharacteristically disinterested senior honor students. The situation deteriorated so quickly that students began seeking the principal out to complain. Oh, he had heard students complain about teachers before, but never complaints that the teacher wasn't *rigorous* enough. Parents echoed their children's concerns that they were not receiving proper preparation for postsecondary pursuits. P. M. was an outstanding classroom teacher, but he understood it was not his role to model effective instruction for this teacher. After all, as is the case with most high school principals, he lacked the depth of content knowledge necessary to effectively teach such a specialized subject. However, he did understand it was his responsibility as an instructional leader to help her in any way possible.

Acting quickly, P. M. arranged nonthreatening, weekly meetings with the teacher, during which they reviewed her lesson plans for the upcoming week, reflected on her classes from the previous week, discussed her assessment and evaluation strategies, and generally identified potential problems. Even though the teacher had been assigned a mentor at the school to assist her with the daily duties of teaching, P. M. also hired an external mentor, a content specialist, who could share specific strategies regarding the courses she was assigned to teach. This broad personal support, combined with a personalized professional development plan of workshops and readings, resulted in dramatic improvements in the teacher's knowledge, confidence, and sense of efficacy.

Source: Glickman, C. D. (2002). *Leadership for learning: How to help teachers succeed.* Alexandria, VA: Association for Supervision and Curriculum Development.

No matter how your teachers plan, they must have a learning goal in mind. In the next section we consider the range of goals possible.

Standards and Objectives for Learning

We hear quite a bit today about visions, goals, outcomes, and standards. At a very general, abstract level are the grand goals society may have for graduates of public schools such as preparing them "to succeed in college and the workplace and to compete in the global economy" (USDE, Race to The Top, 2009, p. 2). But very general goals are meaningless as potential guidelines for instruction. States may turn these grand goals into *standards* and *indicators*, such as the Colorado standard that students will "Use comprehension skills such as previewing, predicting, inferring, comparing and contrasting, rereading and self-monitoring, summarizing, etc." At this level, the indicators are close to being instructional objectives (Airasian, 2005). You probably know that you can find your state's standards at http://www.educationworld.com/standards/state/index.shtml.

An Example of Standards: Technology.   Here is an example of standards that relate to your teachers and what they should know about technology. Two widely adopted technology standards are from the International Society for Technology in Education (ISTE) and the Partnership for 21st Century Skills. The ISTE produced the National Education Technology Standards for teachers shown below (NETS•T; http://www.iste.org/standards/nets-for-teachers/nets-for-teachers-2008.aspx):

1. **Facilitate and Inspire Student Learning and Creativity***
   Teachers use their knowledge of subject matter, teaching and learning, and technology to facilitate experiences that advance student learning, creativity, and innovation in both face-to-face and virtual environments.

2. **Design and Develop Digital-Age Learning Experiences and Assessments**
   Teachers design, develop, and evaluate authentic learning experiences and assessment incorporating contemporary tools and resources to maximize content learning in context and to develop the knowledge, skills, and attitudes identified in the NETS•S.

3. **Model Digital-Age Work and Learning**
   Teachers exhibit knowledge, skills, and work processes representative of an innovative professional in a global and digital society.

4. **Promote and Model Digital Citizenship and Responsibility**
   Teachers understand local and global societal issues and responsibilities in an evolving digital culture and exhibit legal and ethical behavior in their professional practices.

5. **Engage in Professional Growth and Leadership**
   Teachers continuously improve their professional practice, model lifelong learning, and exhibit leadership in their school and professional community by promoting and demonstrating the effective use of digital tools and resources.

But what about objectives for the classroom, or instructional objectives? An **instructional objective** is a clear and unambiguous description of educational intentions for students. These specific statements describe what the students should know and be able to do at the end of the lesson or unit. Although there are many different approaches to writing objectives, each assumes that the first step in teaching is to decide what changes should take place in the learner: What are the goals of teaching?

TABLE 6.2   A Combined Method for Creating Objectives

General Objective

Comprehends scientific concepts.

Specific Examples

1. Describes the concept in his or her own words.
2. Gives an example of the concept [that is new].
3. States hypotheses based on the concept.
4. Describes how the process functions in a given situation.
5. Describes an experiment that illustrates the process.

Source: List adapted from *Gronlund's writing instructional objectives,* 8th Edition by Norman E. Gronlund and Susan M. Brookhart. Copyright © 2009 by Pearson Education, Inc. Printed and Electronically reproduced by permission of Pearson Education, Inc., Upper Saddle River, New Jersey.

Objectives written by people with behavioral views focus on observable and measurable changes in the learner. **Behavioral objectives** use terms such as *list, define, add,* or *calculate.* **Cognitive objectives,** on the other hand, emphasize thinking and comprehension, so they are more likely to include words such as *understand, recognize, create,* or *apply.* Let's look at one well-developed method of writing instructional objectives that combines specific (behavioral) and general (cognitive) ideas.

Gronlund: A Combined Approach.   Norman Gronlund (2006) believes that an objective should be stated first in general terms (*understand, solve, appreciate,* and so on). Then the teacher should clarify by listing a few sample behaviors that would provide evidence that the student has attained the objective. Look at the example in Table 6.2. The goal here is comprehension of a scientific concept. A teacher could never list all the behaviors that might be involved in "comprehension," but stating an initial, general objective along with specific examples makes the purpose clear.

The most recent research on instructional objectives tends to favor approaches similar to Gronlund's. In addition, Terry TenBrink (2006, p. 57) suggests these criteria. Objectives should be:

1. Student-oriented (emphasis on what the student is expected to do).
2. Descriptive of an appropriate learning *outcome* (both developmentally appropriate and appropriately sequenced, with more complex objectives following prerequisite objectives).
3. Clear and understandable (not too general or too specific).
4. Observable (avoid outcomes you can't see, such as "appreciating" or "realizing").*

In thinking about objectives, both teachers and students must consider what is important, what is worth learning. Teachers who have clear, appropriate goals for every student often are successful in helping the students learn. The *Theory into Action Guidelines* should help your teachers whether they decide to make thorough use of objectives or just to prepare them for certain assignments.

* *Source:* List adapted from *Evaluation: A practical guide for teachers* by Terry TenBrink. Copyright © 1974 by The McGraw-Hill Companies, Inc. Adapted with permission.

THEORY INTO ACTION GUIDELINES
Developing Objectives

Avoid "word magic"—phrases that sound noble and important but say very little, such as "Students will become deep thinkers."

Examples
1. Keep the focus on specific changes that will take place in the students' knowledge of skills.
2. Ask students to explain the meaning of the objectives. If they can't give specific examples of what you mean, the objectives are not communicating your intentions to your students.

Suit the activities to the objectives.

Examples
1. If the goal is the memorization of vocabulary, give the students memory aids and practice exercises.

2. If the goal is the ability to develop well-thought-out positions, consider position papers, debates, projects, or mock trials.
3. If you want students to become better writers, give many opportunities for writing and rewriting.

Make sure your tests are related to your objectives.

Examples
1. Write objectives and rough drafts for tests at the same time; revise these drafts of tests as the units unfold and objectives change.
2. Weight the tests according to the importance of the various objectives and the time spent on each.

Flexible and Creative Plans: Using Taxonomies

Almost 60 years ago, a group of experts in educational evaluation led by Benjamin Bloom set out to improve college and university examinations. The impact of their work has touched education at all levels around the world (Anderson & Sosniak, 1994). Bloom and his colleagues developed a **taxonomy,** or classification system, of educational objectives. Objectives were divided into three domains: *cognitive, affective,* and *psychomotor.* A handbook describing the objectives in each area was eventually published. In real life, of course, behaviors from these three domains occur simultaneously. While students are writing (psychomotor), they are also remembering or reasoning (cognitive), and they are likely to have some emotional response to the task as well (affective).

The Cognitive Domain.   The most well-known and widely used taxonomy is in the **cognitive domain**. Six basic objectives are listed in this thinking or cognitive domain (Bloom, Engelhart, Frost, Hill, & Krathwohl, 1956):

1. *Knowledge:* Remembering or recognizing something without necessarily understanding, using, or changing it.
2. *Comprehension:* Understanding the material being communicated without necessarily relating it to anything else.
3. *Application:* Using a general concept to solve a particular problem.
4. *Analysis:* Breaking something down into its parts.
5. *Synthesis:* Creating something new by combining different ideas.
6. *Evaluation:* Judging the value of materials or methods as they might be applied in a particular situation.

Updating Bloom.   Bloom's taxonomy guided educators for over 40 years. It is considered one of the most significant educational writings of the twentieth century (Anderson & Sosniak, 1994). In 1995, a group of educational researchers met to discuss revising the taxonomy (Anderson & Krathwohl, 2001), and that revision is now available. The taxonomy revisers have retained the six basic levels, but they have changed the names of three to indicate the cognitive processes involved and altered the order slightly. The six cognitive processes of the revised taxonomy are *remembering* (knowledge), *understanding* (comprehension), *applying, analyzing, evaluating,* and *creating* (synthesizing). In addition, the revisers have added a new dimension to the taxonomy to recognize that cognitive processes must process something: You have to remember or understand or apply some form of knowledge. If you look at Table 6.3, you will see the result. We now have six processes or verbs: the cognitive acts of remembering, understanding, applying, analyzing, evaluating, and creating. These processes act on four kinds of knowledge: factual, conceptual, procedural, and metacognitive.

Consider how this revised taxonomy might suggest objectives for a social studies/language arts class. An objective that targets *analysis of conceptual knowledge* is:

> After reading historical account of the battle of the Alamo, the student will be able to explain the author's point of view or bias.

An objective for *evaluating metacognitive knowledge* might be:

> Students will reflect on their strategies for identifying the biases of the author.

TABLE 6.3   A Revised Taxonomy in the Cognitive Domain

The revised taxonomy includes cognitive processes operating on different kinds of knowledge. The verbs in the chart are examples of what might be used to create objectives.

The Knowledge Dimension	The Cognitive Process Dimension					
	1. Remember	**2. Understand**	**3. Apply**	**4. Analyze**	**5. Evaluate**	**6. Create**
A. Factual Knowledge	list	summarize	classify	order	rank	combine
B. Conceptual Knowledge	describe	interpret	experiment	explain	assess	plan
C. Procedural Knowledge	tabulate	predict	calculate	differentiate	conclude	compose
D. Metacognitive Knowledge	appropriate use	execute	select strategy	change strategy	reflect	invent

Source: Table adapted from "Instruction design—The taxonomy table" by Dianna Fisher, from Oregon State University—Extended Campus website. Copyright © 2011 by Oregon State University. Reprinted with permission. Originally adapted from *A taxonomy for learning, teaching, and assessing* by Lorin W. Anderson, David R. Krathwohl, Peter W. Airasian, Kathleen A. Cruikshank, Richard E. Mayer, Paul R. Pintrich, James Raths and Merlin C. Wittrock. Copyright © 2001 by Pearson Education, Inc. Printed and Electronically reproduced by permission of Pearson Education, Inc., Upper Saddle River, New Jersey.

Certain processes are more likely to be paired with particular kinds of knowledge. For example, remembering is most often used with factual and conceptual knowledge, and metacognitive knowledge is more likely to be applied and analyzed than remembered. In two books, a complete and an abridged version, Anderson and Krathwohl (2001) describe the new taxonomy and give many examples of using this revised version to design lessons and assessments.

Applying the Taxonomy.   It is common in education to consider these six kinds of objectives as a hierarchy, with each skill building on the previous ones, but this is not entirely accurate. Some subjects, such as mathematics, do not fit this structure very well (Kreitzer & Madaus, 1994). Still, you will hear many references to *lower-level* and *higher-level objectives*, with remembering, understanding, and applying considered lower level and the other categories considered higher level. As a rough way of thinking about objectives, this can be helpful (Gronlund, 2004, 2006).

The taxonomy of objectives can also be helpful in planning *assessments* because different procedures are appropriate for objectives at the various levels. Gronlund (2006) suggests that the remembering of factual knowledge objectives can best be measured by true-false, short-answer, matching, or multiple-choice tests. Such tests will also work with the understanding, applying, and analyzing levels of the taxonomy. For measuring, evaluating, and creating objectives, however, essays, reports, projects, and portfolios are more appropriate. Essay tests will also work at the middle levels of the taxonomy.

The Affective Domain.   The objectives in the taxonomy of the **affective domain,** or domain of emotional response, run from least committed to most committed (Krathwohl, Bloom, & Masia, 1964). At the lowest level, a student would simply pay attention to a certain idea. At the highest level, the student would adopt an idea or a value and act consistently with that idea. There are five basic objectives in the affective domain.

1. *Receiving:* Being aware of or attending to something in the environment. This is the "I'll-listen-to-the-concert-but-I-won't-promise-to-like-it" level.
2. *Responding:* Showing some new behavior as a result of experience. At this level a person might applaud after the concert or hum some of the music the next day.
3. *Valuing:* Showing some definite involvement or commitment. At this point a person might choose to go to a concert instead of a film.
4. *Organization:* Integrating a new value into one's general set of values, giving it some ranking among one's general priorities. This is the level at which a person would begin to make long-range commitments to concert attendance.
5. *Characterization by value:* Acting consistently with the new value. At this highest level, a person would be firmly committed to a love of music and demonstrate it openly and consistently.

Like the basic objectives in the cognitive domain, these five objectives are very general. To write specific learning objectives, you must state what students will actually be doing when they are receiving, responding, valuing, and so on. For example, an objective for a nutrition class at the valuing level (showing involvement or commitment) might be stated:

> After completing the unit on food contents and labeling, at least 50 percent of the class will commit to the junk-food boycott project by giving up snack foods for a month.

The Psychomotor Domain.   James Cangelosi (1990) provides a useful way to think about objectives in the psychomotor domain as either voluntary muscle capabilities that require endurance, strength, flexibility, agility, or speed; or the ability to perform a specific skill. Objectives in the **psychomotor domain** should be of interest to a wide range of educators, including those in fine arts, vocational-technical education, and special education. Many other subjects, such as chemistry, physics, and biology, also require specialized movements and well-developed hand and eye coordination. Using lab equipment, the mouse on a computer, or art materials means learning new physical skills. Here are two psychomotor objectives:

> Four minutes after completing a one-mile run in eight minutes or under, your heart rate will be below 120.
>
> Use a computer track pad effectively to "drag and drop" files.

Another View: Planning from a Constructivist Perspective

Traditionally, it has been the teacher's responsibility to do most of the planning for instruction, but other ways of planning are possible. In **constructivist approaches**, planning is shared and negotiated. The teacher and students together make decisions about content, activities, and approaches. Rather than having specific student behaviors and skills as objectives, the teacher has overarching goals—"big ideas" or themes—that guide planning (Borich, 2011). These goals are understandings or abilities that the teacher returns to again and again. For the last decade, teaching with themes and integrated content have been major elements in planning and designing lessons and units, from kindergarten (Roskos & Neuman, 1998) through high school (Clarke & Agne, 1997). For example, Elaine Homestead and Karen McGinnis (middle school teachers) and Elizabeth Pate (a college professor) designed a unit on "Human Interactions" that included studying racism, world hunger, pollution, and air and water quality. Students researched issues by reading textbooks and outside sources, learning to use databases, interviewing local officials, and inviting guest speakers into class. Students had to develop knowledge in science, mathematics, and social studies. They learned to write and speak persuasively, and, in the process, raised money for hunger relief in Africa (Pate, McGinnis, & Homestead, 1995).

Elementary-age students can benefit from integrated planning, too. There is no reason to work on spelling skills, then listening skills, then writing skills, and then social studies or science. All these abilities can be developed together if students work to solve authentic problems. Some topics for integrating themes with younger children

TABLE 6.4   Some Themes for Integrated Planning for Middle and High School

Courage	Time and Space
Mystery	Groups and Institutions
Survival	Work
Human Interaction	Motion
Communities of the Future	Cause and Effect
Communication/Language	Probability and Prediction
Human Rights and Responsibilities	Change and Conservation
Identity/Coming of Age	Diversity and Variation
Interdependence	Autobiography

Sources: Adapted from *Interdisciplinary high school teaching: Strategies for integrated learning* by J. H. Clarke and R. M. Agne. Allyn & Bacon, 1997; and *Teaching through themes* by Gare Thompson. Scholastic, 1991.

are people, friendship, communications, habitats, communities, and patterns. Possibilities for older students are given in Table 6.4.

Let's assume you have an idea of what you want students to understand; now how do you teach to encourage understanding? Your teachers still need to decide what's happening on Monday. They need to design teaching that is appropriate for the objectives.

Successful Teaching: Focus on the Teacher

How would you go about identifying the keys to effective teaching? You might ask students, other principals, college professors of education, or experienced teachers to list the characteristics of good teachers. Or you could do intensive case studies of a few classrooms over a long period. You might observe classrooms, rate different teachers on certain characteristics, and then see which characteristics were associated with teachers whose students either achieved the most or were the most motivated to learn. (To do this, of course, you would have to decide how to assess achievement and motivation.) You could identify teachers whose students, year after year, learned more than students working with other teachers; then you could watch the more successful teachers and note what they do. You might also train teachers to apply several different strategies to teach the same lesson and then determine which strategy led to the greatest student learning. You could videotape teachers and then ask them to view the tapes and report what they were thinking about as they taught and what influenced their decisions while teaching. You might study transcripts of classroom dialogue to learn what helped students understand.

All these approaches and more have been used to investigate teaching. Often, researchers conduct a series of studies by making careful observations and identifying relationships between teaching and learning. The researchers then use these relationships as the basis for developing teaching approaches and testing these approaches in design experiments (Brown, 1992; Greeno, Collins, & Resnick, 1996). One successful approach identified in these studies is called *direct instruction* or *active teaching*.

Direct Instruction

Weinert and Helmke (1995) describe **direct instruction** as having the following features:

> (a) the teachers' classroom management is especially effective and the rate of student interruptive behaviors is very low; (b) the teacher maintains a strong academic focus and uses available instructional time intensively to initiate and facilitate students' learning activities; (c) the teacher insures that as many students as possible achieve good learning progress by carefully choosing appropriate tasks, clearly presenting subject-matter information and solution strategies, continuously diagnosing each student's learning progress and learning difficulties, and providing effective help through remedial instruction. (p. 138)

To this list, Xin Ma (2012) adds moving at a brisk pace and having a warm and accepting classroom climate. You can see that direct instruction applies best to the teaching of basic skills—clearly structured knowledge and essential skills—such as science facts, mathematics computations, reading vocabulary, and grammar rules (Rosenshine & Stevens, 1986). These skills involve tasks that are relatively unambiguous; they can be taught step by step and tested by standardized tests. Direct instruction is not necessarily appropriate for objectives such as helping students to write creatively, solve complex problems, or mature emotionally. How would a teacher turn these features of direct instruction into actions?

Rosenshine's Six Teaching Functions

Rosenshine and his colleagues (Rosenshine, 1988; Rosenshine & Stevens, 1986) have identified six teaching functions based on the research on effective instruction. These could serve as a checklist or framework for teaching basic skills.

1. *Review and check the previous day's work.* Reteach if students misunderstood or made errors.
2. *Present new material.* Make the purpose clear, teach in small steps, provide many examples and nonexamples.
3. *Provide guided practice.* Question students, give practice problems, and listen for misconceptions and misunderstandings. Reteach if necessary. Continue guided practice until students answer about 80 percent of the questions correctly.
4. *Give feedback and correctives based on student answers.* Reteach if necessary. (Remember, Pianta and colleagues' [2005, 2008] class climate component of instructional support included quality feedback.)

5. *Provide independent practice.* Let students apply the new learning on their own, in seatwork, cooperative groups, or homework. The success rate during independent practice should be about 95 percent. This means that students must be well prepared for the work by the presentation and guided practice and that assignments must not be too difficult. The point is for the students to practice until the skills become overlearned and automatic, until they are confident. Hold students accountable for the work they do; check it.

6. *Review weekly and monthly to consolidate learning.* Include some review items as homework. Test often, and reteach material missed on these tests.

These six functions are not steps to be followed in a particular order, but all of them are elements of effective instruction. For example, feedback, review, or reteaching should occur whenever necessary and should match the abilities of the students. There are several other models of direct instruction, but most share these elements.

Why Does Direct Instruction Work?   What aspects of direct instruction might explain its success? Linda Anderson (1989b) suggests that lessons that help students perceive links among main ideas will help them construct accurate understandings. Well-organized presentations, clear explanations, the use of explanatory links, and reviews can all help students perceive connections among ideas. If done well, a direct instruction lesson could be a resource that students use to construct understanding. For example, reviews activate prior knowledge so the student is ready to understand. Brief, clear presentations and guided practice avoid overloading the students' information processing systems and taxing their working memories. Numerous examples and explanations give many pathways and associations for building networks of concepts. Guided practice can also give the teacher a snapshot of the students' thinking and of their misconceptions, so these can be addressed directly as misconceptions rather than simply as "wrong answers."

Criticisms of Direct Instruction.   Critics say that direct instruction is limited to lower-level objectives and that it is based on traditional teaching methods, ignores innovative models, and discourages students' independent thinking. Some researchers claim that the direct instruction model is based on the *wrong* theory of learning. Teachers break material into small segments, present each segment clearly, and reinforce or correct, thus *transmitting* accurate understandings from teacher to student. By doing much of the cognitive work for students in their presentations, teachers can put students in a passive position and may prevent them from asking or even thinking of questions (Freiberg & Driscoll, 2005). These criticisms of direct instruction echo the criticisms of behavioral learning theories.

But there is ample evidence that direct instruction and explanation can help students learn actively, not passively. For younger and less-prepared learners, student-controlled learning without teacher direction and instruction can lead to systematic deficits in the students' knowledge. Without guidance, the understandings that students construct can be incomplete and misleading (Leinhardt, 2001; Sweller, Kirschner, & Clark, 2007). Deep understanding and fluid performance—whether in dance or mathematical problem solving or reading—require models of expert performance and extensive practice with feedback (Anderson, Reder, & Simon, 1995). Guided and independent practice with feedback are at the heart of the direct instruction model.

What direct instruction cannot do is *ensure* that students understand. If badly done, it may encourage students to memorize and mimic, but never to "own" the knowledge. To help students reach this goal, in the next two sections we will look at teaching for understanding. The first section focuses on the subject and the second on the learning.

Teaching for Understanding: Focus on the Subject

In middle and high schools, academic subjects become more complex and more important than basic skills in teaching. It is clear that a teacher's knowledge of the subject is critical for teaching (Ball, Lubienski, & Mewborn, 2001; Borko & Putnam, 1996). But the emphasis is on the role of the students in constructing useful understandings as they assume more and more responsibility for learning.

Keys to Good Subject Matter Teaching

Brophy* identified ten keys to successful teaching for understanding:

1. The curriculum emphasizes knowledge, skills, and values that will be useful outside as well as inside school.
2. Students become more expert by actually using knowledge in practical applications so that conceptual understanding and self-regulation develop simultaneously.
3. A few important topics are addressed in depth instead of "covering" the curriculum. Supporters of the constructivist approach believe (with Howard Gardner) that coverage is the enemy of understanding.
4. The content to be learned is organized around a small set of powerful or "big" ideas.
5. The teacher presents information but also scaffolds students' efforts to learn.
6. The students' role is to actively work to make sense of the information and make it their own.
7. Teaching begins with the students' prior knowledge—even if that understanding includes some misunderstanding—and conceptual change must be the goal.
8. Class activities include authentic tasks that call for critical thinking and problem solving, not just memorizing.
9. Higher-order thinking skills are taught and applied as students learn subject matter, not during separate, stand-alone "thinking" activities.
10. The teacher's goal is to create a learning community where dialogue and cooperation promote student understanding of content.

Source: "Effective teaching" by Jere Brophy, from *Psychology and educational practice,* edited by Herbert J. Walberg and Geneva D. Haertel. McCutchan Publishing Corporation.

The **Community of Learners** model developed by Ann Brown and Joe Campione (1996) is an example of a teaching model that includes these ten elements. In this model, which was first used in the schools of Oakland, California, students are organized into small collaborative groups to research an important topic in depth. They receive direct instruction, modeling, and coaching in the learning and research strategies they will need and practice the strategies in the context of doing the actual research. Jigsaw cooperative learning groups divide the material to be learned, and each student becomes an expert resource on one aspect of the topic. Students demonstrate their growing understandings in learning performances for real audiences. Evaluations of this model are very promising.

Criticisms of Constructivist Approaches to Subject Teaching

Constructivist approaches have done much to correct the excesses of tell-and-drill teaching. Some positive outcomes from constructivist teaching are better understanding of the material, greater enjoyment of literature, more positive attitudes toward school, better problem solving, and greater motivation (Hmelo-Silver, Ravit, & Chin, 2007; Palincsar, 1998). But a total reliance on constructivist approaches that ignores direct teaching of skills can be detrimental for some children. Constructivist approaches alone may not work for *all* children (Airasian & Walsh, 1997; Harris & Graham, 1996) or all kinds of learning (Sweller et al., 2007; Weinert & Helmke, 1995). If students fall behind because they lack specific skills, it would be unethical to withhold teaching and wait for those skills to "develop naturally," simply to be true to a particular philosophy. We agree with Jere Brophy (1997) that some constructivists "are being unrealistic, even romantic, in suggesting that teachers should routinely avoid transmitting knowledge and instead function only as discussion facilitators and scaffolders of learning" (p. 231).

Ernst von Glasersfeld (1995), a strong advocate of constructivist teaching in mathematics, believes that it is a misunderstanding of constructivism to say that memorization and rote learning always are useless. "There are, indeed, matters that can and perhaps must be learned in a purely mechanical way" (p. 5). Classrooms that integrate constructivist teaching with needed direct teaching of skills are especially good learning environments for students with special needs. Careful ongoing assessment of each student's abilities, knowledge, and motivations, followed by appropriate support, should ensure that no students are lost or left behind.

Cautions: Where's the Learning?

As an instructional leader, you will be bombarded with claims and counterclaims about teaching innovations. Many of these programs and techniques will look promising, but it makes sense to ask, "Where's the evidence for learning? Have these innovations been tested in situations similar to your own? Do the strategies improve the bottom line: student learning and motivation? What's the evidence? How large are the gains, and do they last? If the teaching approaches have not been tested, are they at least consistent with what we know about student learning and motivation? Will the teaching methods encourage student attention, cognitive investment, and long-term memory? Do they support understanding (constructivist), remembering (cognitive-information processing), and applying/practicing (behavioral) new knowledge?"

The research support for teacher effects and direct instruction is strong and based on large-scale, carefully conducted studies. As we have seen, this work is not without its critics, but if we focus on the learning of explicit information, the research on direct instruction offers good guidance.

Turning to higher-level objectives, we would expect that the newer models of teaching for subject understanding would be best. But be aware that the research base for these approaches is thin so far. As Brophy (1997) notes, many of the instructional models advocated by intellectual leaders and position statements published by professional organizations "have yet to be tested empirically, let alone enjoy a rich accumulation of systematic evidence of effects on student outcomes" (p. 226). In other words, there is no clear evidence (beyond testimonials of advocates) that these models have worked once, much less in many different schools and settings. Slavin and Fashola (1998) are even more blunt:

> Educational innovation lacks the respect for scientific evidence and independent replication that has characterized the most productive and progressive aspects of our society and economy, from medicine, technology, and engineering to agriculture. We know far more about the safety and effectiveness of our children's shampoo than we do about the reading or math programs their teachers use. Our children, our teachers, and our society deserve much better. (p. ix)*

Advocates for many widely marketed practices such as using integrated curriculum models, accommodating learning styles, developing multiple intelligences, and eliminating ability grouping base their arguments on their strong commitments to theories, but do not have evidence that these approaches lead to learning. There is probably value in all these ideas, but be aware that clear evidence of strong connections to student learning is not readily available.

Beyond Models to Outstanding Teaching

Is good teaching science or art, teacher-centered lecture or student-centered discovery, the application of general theories or the invention of situation-specific practices? Is a good teacher a good explainer or a good questioner, a "sage on the stage" or a "guide by the side" of the students? These questions have and will continue to confound educational researchers for years to come. However, one thing we do know is this: When considering the impact of all of the factors in determining student achievement, the quality of classroom teaching is critical (Lee & Shute, 2010; Reeves, 2000). That, in turn, elevates the question, "What is good teaching?" to one most vital to educational leadership. What do you think? Before you answer, read the *Point/Counterpoint* on good teaching.

*Source: *Show me the evidence!: Proven and promising programs for America's schools* by Robert E. Slavin and Olatokunbo S. Fashola. Corwin Press, 1998.

POINT/COUNTERPOINT What Is Good Teaching?

In your former education classes, you probably encountered criticisms of the scientific, teacher-centered, theory-based, lecturing *sages* on the stage. Perhaps you were even encouraged to be artistic, inventive, student-centered, questioning *guides* by the side. Now it is your responsibility as an instructional leader to supervise teachers and differentiate between good and bad instruction. So, what is it? What does it look like? What does it sound like? Let's see what the research says.

POINT

Teaching is a theory-based science.
Psychologists have spent decades studying how children think and feel, how learning occurs, what influences motivation, and how teaching affects learning. These general and abstract conceptions apply to a wide range of situations. Why should teachers have to reinvent all this knowledge? A large body of work studying real teachers in regular classrooms has identified one set of teacher characteristics and behaviors that are related to student learning: knowledge, clarity, enthusiasm, and direct or active teaching (Shuell, 1996). An effective teacher reviews, explains, checks for understanding, and reteaches if necessary, always keeping the level or difficulty and the pace just right to keep students learning. Advocates note that ignoring the direct teaching of skills can be detrimental for some children. For example, Harris and Graham (1996) describe the experiences of their daughter Leah in a progressive education school, where the teachers successfully developed their daughter's creativity, thinking, and understanding. Unfortunately, Leah's skills in reading were developing more slowly. The teachers recommended testing for learning disabilities, but when the test report arrived, results indicated no learning disability, strong comprehension abilities, and poor word attack skills. Luckily, Leah's parents knew how to teach word attack skills. Direct teaching of these skills helped Leah become an avid and able reader in about six weeks.

COUNTERPOINT

Teaching is an art, a creative reflective process.
Other educators believe that the mark of an excellent teacher is not the ability to apply techniques but the artistry of being reflective—thoughtful and inventive—about teaching (Schon, 1983). Educators who adopt this view tend to be more concerned with how teachers plan, solve problems, create instruction, and make decisions than they are with the specific techniques teachers apply. They believe teaching "is specific with respect to task, time, place, participants, and content, and that different subjects vary in those specifics" (Leinhardt, 2001, p. 334). Thus, teaching is so complex that it must be invented anew with every new subject and class. Critics of direct, teacher-centered teaching claim that breaking material into small segments, presenting each segment clearly, and reinforcing or correcting, is *transmitting* accurate understandings from teacher to student. The student is viewed as an "empty vessel" waiting to be filled with knowledge, rather than an active constructor of knowledge (Anderson, 1989a; Berg & Clough, 1991; Davis, Maher, & Noddings, 1990).

Beware of either/or choices: In spite of the criticisms and debates, there is no one best way to teach. Different goals require different methods. Direct instruction leads to better performance on achievement tests, whereas the open, informal methods such as discovery learning or inquiry approaches are associated with better performance on tests of creativity, abstract thinking, and problem solving. In addition, the open methods are better for improving attitudes toward school and for stimulating curiosity, cooperation among students, and lower absence rates (Walberg, 1990).

Of course, every subject can require some direct instruction. Noddings (1990) reminds teachers that students may need some direct instruction in how to use various manipulative materials to get the possible learning benefits from them. Students working in cooperative groups may need guidance, modeling, and practice in how to ask questions and give explanations. And to solve difficult problems, students may need some direct instruction in possible problem-solving strategies.

Source: Reeves, D. B. (2000). *Accountability in action: A blueprint for learning organizations.* Denver, CO: Advanced Learning Press. Reeves cites Education Trust, 1998. www.edtrust.org.

Our message for teachers is to match instructional methods to learning goals. In the early stages of learning, when students have little prior knowledge or even relevant personal experiences to provide a basis for discussion and analysis, it makes little sense to spend class time discussing and analyzing. Reading, researching, even memorizing may be needed to develop a common base of information to support discussion (Brophy, 1997). Personally, we hope your teachers are all "sages" by the "sides" of their students.

Differentiated Instruction

Think about the following situation. One of your teachers prepared a unit on habitats and decided to give an alternate form of the final unit test as a pretest to find out what the students already knew about the subject. Looking over the papers that night, he was dismayed. A quarter of the students made over 90% on the "final." Quite a few got around half of the questions right, but the rest of the class was clueless. The next day, when the teacher asked Shanequa why she did so well on the test, she explained that in science class last year her group (and several others) chose habitats as the focus of their special project work. The teacher stared at his lesson plans and realized that they fit practically no one in this class. What should he do? What would expert teachers such as Viviana, Ken, Mia, or Randy do? One answer is differentiated instruction.

The idea of **differentiated instruction**—adapting teaching to the abilities and needs of the learners—is an ancient one. To prove it, Lyn Corno (2008, p. 161) quotes these words of Quintilian from the 5th century BC:

> Some students are slack and need to be encouraged; others work better when given a freer rein. Some respond best when there is some threat or fear; others are paralyzed by it. Some apply themselves to the task over time, and learn best; others learn best by concentration and focus in a single burst of energy. (Quintilian, trans. 1921)

Obviously Quintilian appreciated the need for fitting instruction to the student.

Why Do We Need Differentiated Instruction? As you well know, today's classrooms are diverse. Students differ in knowledge of the subjects being taught, language, socioeconomic status (SES), culture, race, and ethnicity. They bring different strengths, abilities, and challenges to the task of learning. Many educators believe that "classes should include students of diverse needs, achievement levels, interests, and learning styles, and instruction should be differentiated to take advantage of the diversity, not ignore it" (Jackson & Davis, 2000, p. 23). Differentiated instruction (Tomlinson, 2005b) is one way of going beyond accommodating these learner differences to seeing diversity as an array of strengths on which to build. The basic idea of differentiated instruction is that teachers must take into account not only the subjects they are teaching but also the students. In differentiated classrooms, students work at different paces, sometimes exercising varied learning options, and they are assessed using indicators that fit their interests and needs (George, 2005).

Elements of Differentiation.   Differentiated instruction conceives of all students as seeking purpose, challenge, affirmation, power, and the chance to contribute. The confident teacher views these different student needs as possibilities and not problems, and responds with invitation, investment, persistence, opportunity, and reflection. The teacher works to create curriculum and instruction for each student that is focused, engaging, demanding, important, and scaffolded. Carol Ann Tomlinson (2003) describes these characteristics as the *Cogs of Differentiation.* They are called *cogs* because they are interdependent and interlocking, like the inner workings of a clock. Each student's needs interact and connect with the differentiated curriculum and instruction created by the teacher for that student.

What are some examples of differentiation in curriculum and instruction? Let's assume students in a pre-algebra class have varied interests and often have difficulty understanding the value of what they are learning in math. The teacher can modify the content and product based on student interests by using examples from sports, business, medicine, technology, and other fields to illustrate how formulas are used. She also might guide students in interviewing people engaged in a range of jobs and hobbies to find out how they use formulas in their work and then have them share those examples with others in the class. Another example is some students who are taking their first high-level course—Advanced Placement U.S. History—and who occasionally feel lost and discouraged by the course's demands. In response, the teacher might modify the learning environment and process based on student readiness and emotions by establishing study groups to help students prepare for both oral and written tests. Although much of the study group work takes place outside of class, the teacher conducts whole-class and small-group discussions about how the various groups approach studying, how the different approaches seem to work, and how students feel about their progress. The teacher also provides study guides to ensure the groups focus on critical facets of the content (Tomlinson, 2003).

Adaptive Teaching

Lyn Corno (2008) has developed a model of **adaptive teaching** that also addresses learner differences. In this approach, teachers see "learner variation as an opportunity for learning from teaching rather than as obstacles to be overcome" (p. 171). Adaptive

FIGURE 6.1   Adaptive Teaching

By matching support to current student abilities and needs, teachers build on strengths to move all students toward self-regulated learning.

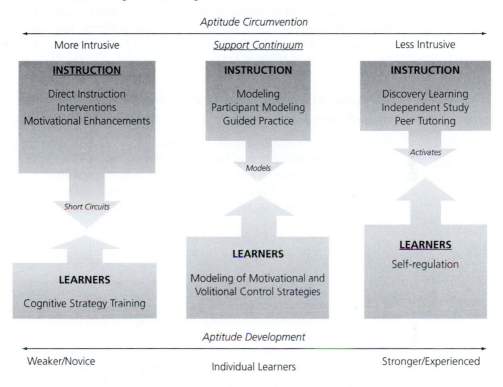

Source: Figure from *Educational psychology*, 12th Edition, by Anita E. Woolfolk. Copyright © 2013 by Pearson Education, Inc. Printed and Electronically reproduced by permission of Pearson Education, Inc., Upper Saddle River, New Jersey.

teaching provides all students with challenging instruction and uses supports when needed, but removes those supports as students become able to handle more on their own. Figure 6.1 shows the continuum of support and type of instruction that matches students' needs. As shown on the far left of the figure, when students are novices in an area or have little prior knowledge and skills, the teaching is more direct and includes well-designed motivational strategies to keep them engaged. At the same time, students are taught how to apply appropriate cognitive strategies, to give them the "skills" to learn. There are short cycles of teaching, checking for understanding, and reteaching. As students develop aptitudes in the subject, teaching moves to modeling, guided practice, and coaching. By this time, students should have improved their cognitive "skills" strategies, so teaching can also focus on motivational and volitional strategies—the "will" to learn. Finally, as students gain more knowledge and skills, teaching can move to guided discovery, independent study, and peer tutoring, with an emphasis on self-regulated learning—the kind of learning the students will need for the rest of their lives.

Adaptive teaching ensures that everyone is challenged. For example, one teacher at a magnet school described how he "iced" his curriculum with some content "just beyond the reach" of even his most advanced students. He wanted to be sure all his students found some assignments difficult. He believed "everyone needs to stretch in my class" (Corno, 2008, p. 165).

Adapting and Differentiating Instruction in Inclusive Classrooms

Your teachers probably have many concerns when they think about teaching in an inclusive classroom. Do they have enough training? Will they get the support needed from school administrators or specialists? Will working with the students with disabilities take time away from their other responsibilities? These questions are common ones, and sometimes such concerns are justified. But effective teaching for students with disabilities does not require a unique set of skills. It is a combination of good teaching practices and sensitivity to all students. Students with disabilities need to learn the academic material, and they need to be full participants in the day-to-day life of the classroom.

To accomplish the first goal of academic learning, students with learning disabilities appear to benefit from using *extended practice* distributed over days and weeks and from *advanced organizers*, such as focusing students on what they already know or stating clear objectives (Swanson, 2001).

To accomplish the second goal of integrating students with disabilities into the day-to-day life of the classroom, Marilyn Friend and William Bursuck (2012) recommend the INCLUDE strategy:

Identify the environmental, curricular, and instructional demands of your classroom.

Note students' learning strengths and needs.

Check for potential areas of student success.

Look for potential problem areas.

Use information gathered to brainstorm instructional adaptations.

Decide which adaptations to try.

Evaluate student progress.*

Table 6.5 on the next page shows how the INCLUDE strategy might be applied to students with learning and behavioral disabilities.

*Source: Including students with special needs, 3rd Edition, by Marilyn Friend and William Bursuck. Allyn & Bacon, 2002.

TABLE 6.5   Making Adaptations for Students with Learning and Behavior Disabilities Using Steps in the INCLUDE Strategy

Identify Classroom Demands	Note Student Strengths and Needs	Check for Potential Successes/Look for Potential Problems	Decide on Adaptations
Student desks in clusters of four	*Strengths* Good vocabulary skills *Needs* Difficulty attending to task	*Success* Student understands instruction if on task *Problem* Student off task—does not face instructor as she teaches	Change seating so student faces instructor
Small-group work with peers	*Strengths* Good handwriting *Needs* Oral expressive language—problem with word finding	*Success* Student acts as secretary for cooperative group *Problem* Student has difficulty expressing self in peer learning groups	Assign as secretary of group Place into compatible small group Develop social skills instruction for all students
Expect students to attend class and be on time	*Strengths* Good drawing skills *Needs* Poor time management	*Success* Student uses artistic talent in class *Problem* Student is late for class and frequently does not attend at all	Use individualized student contract for attendance and punctuality—if goals met, give student artistic responsibility in class
Textbook difficult to read	*Strengths* Good oral communication skills *Needs* Poor reading accuracy Lacks systematic strategy for reading text	*Success* Student participates well in class Good candidate for class dramatizations *Problem* Student is unable to read text for information	Provide taped textbooks Highlight student text
Lecture on women's suffrage movement to whole class	*Strengths* Very motivated and interested in class *Needs* Lack of background knowledge	*Success* Student earns points for class attendance and effort *Problem* Student lacks background knowledge to understand important information in lecture	Give student video to view before lecture Build points for attendance and working hard into grading system
Whole-class instruction on telling time to the quarter hour	*Strengths* Good coloring skills *Needs* Cannot identify numbers 7–12 Cannot count by fives	*Success* Student is able to color clock faces used in instruction *Problem* Student is unable to acquire telling time skills	Provide extra instruction on number identification and counting by fives

Summary

Teaching makes a difference, both for students' personal and social development and for their understanding of academic subjects. For mathematics, it appears that teachers who are certified to teach math or who have better mathematics preparation have students who achieve more in mathematics. This connection is not clear for other subjects. However, research has shown that if a student has an ineffective teacher for three years in a row, it is difficult for him or her to catch up. Good teaching is just one element, albeit a crucial one, in a combination that produces successful student learning. Student engagement, social support (especially from teachers), and opportunities to learn are also an important part of the mix.

It takes time and experience to become an expert teacher. These teachers have a rich store of well-organized knowledge about the many specific situations of teaching. They also have a unique kind of knowledge called *pedagogical content knowledge*, which combines mastery of *academic content* with knowledge about *how to teach* that content and match instruction to *student differences*.

For years, researchers have tried to unravel the mystery of effective teaching. They have used a variety of methods, including classroom observation, case studies, interviews, experimentation with different methods, and other approaches to study teaching in real classrooms. Results of research on teacher characteristics indicate that organization and clarity in presentation, warmth, and enthusiasm all play important parts in effective teaching. But no single way of teaching has been found to be right for each class, lesson, or day.

Teacher knowledge of the subject is necessary—because being more knowledgeable helps teachers be clearer and more organized—but it is not sufficient for effective teaching; organization and clarity also are important characteristics of good teaching. Teachers who provide clear presentations and explanations tend to have students who learn more and who rate their teachers more positively. Clarity begins with planning. Teachers must tell students what they will be learning and how they could approach it. During the lesson, teachers should avoid vague language, make clear connections between facts or concepts by using explanatory links, and check often for understanding. Finally, teacher warmth, friendliness, and understanding seem to be the traits most strongly related to positive student attitudes.

The first step in teaching is planning. Teachers engage in several levels of planning: by the year, term, unit, week, and day. All the levels must be coordinated. Accomplishing the year's plan requires breaking the work into terms, the terms into units, and the units into weeks and days. The plan determines how time and materials will be turned into activities for students. There is no single model of planning, but all plans should allow for flexibility. Most plans include instructional objectives.

An instructional objective is a clear and unambiguous description of your educational intentions for your students. Gronlund's approach suggests that an objective should be stated first in general terms and then clarified by listing sample behaviors that would provide evidence the student has attained the objective.

Bloom and others have developed taxonomies categorizing basic objectives in the cognitive, affective, and psychomotor domains. In real life, of course, behaviors from these three domains occur simultaneously. A taxonomy encourages systematic thinking about relevant objectives and ways to evaluate them. Six basic objectives are listed in the cognitive domain: remembering, understanding, applying, analyzing, evaluating, and creating. These processes can act on four kinds of knowledge: factual, conceptual, procedural, and metacognitive.

In teacher-centered approaches, teachers select learning objectives and plan how to get students to meet those objectives. Teachers control the "what" and "how" of learning. In contrast, planning is shared and negotiated in student-centered, or constructivist, approaches. The teacher and students together make decisions about content, activities, and approaches. Rather than having specific student behaviors as objectives, the teacher has overarching goals or "big ideas" that guide planning. Integrated content and teaching with themes are often part of the planning. Assessment of learning is ongoing and mutually shared by teacher and students.

After planning is the teaching itself. In teacher-centered direct instruction, the teacher gives well-organized presentations, clear explanations, carefully delivered prompts, and feedback. These actions can be resources for students as they construct understanding. In student-centered constructivist approaches, the teacher designs authentic tasks, monitors student thinking, asks questions, and prods inquiry. Constructivist approaches emphasize deep understanding of concepts (as opposed to memorization), discussion and explanation, and exploration of students' implicit understandings. Both teacher-centered and student-centered kinds of teaching may be appropriate at different times, as long as the emphasis is on student understanding.

Many educators feel that the careful use of direct instruction methods—well-organized presentations, clear explanations, carefully delivered prompts, and guided discovery—can be a resource for students as they construct understanding. In all cases, teaching methods should match learning. There is more research evidence for the value of direct instruction than for constructivist approaches, but the ideas from student-centered, constructivist models of teaching can be useful. To evaluate new approaches, ask if they match the principles of learning and motivation described in Chapters 4 and 5.

KEY TERMS

adaptive teaching (214)
affective domain (204)
behavioral objectives (201)
cognitive domain (202)
cognitive objectives (201)
Community of Learners (210)

constructivist approach (205)
differentiated instruction
  (213)
direct instruction (207)
explanatory links (195)
instructional objective (200)

lesson study (198)
pedagogical content knowledge
  (193)
psychomotor domain (205)
reflective (193)
taxonomy (202)

DEVELOPING YOUR PORTFOLIO

1. Develop a classroom observation form to provide feedback to teachers about the teaching and learning in their classroom. Consider each of the following:
   a. Teacher behavior
   b. Student behavior
   c. Classroom climate
   d. Teacher and principal attitudes
   e. Innovations
   f. Other important aspects of teaching and learning in the classroom

   Then plan a discussion of your observations with the teacher. Be sure to describe the discussion in terms of its:
   a. Place—where will you talk with the teacher?
   b. Structure—what will be the format and structure of your conversation?
   c. Goals—what are the objectives and expected outcomes?

2. Prepare a 45-minute Parent–Teacher Organization talk about direct instruction.
   a. Start by describing direct instruction.
   b. Consider the pros and cons of direct instruction.
   c. Contrast direct instruction with a constructivist approach to teaching.
   d. Consider under what situations each approach is appropriate.
   e. Propose and defend a balanced approach to teaching.

   Remember you are speaking to parents as well as your teachers.

3. As principal, develop an induction plan for beginning teachers. Describe the elements of the plan, for example:
   a. Mentors
   b. In-service orientation
   c. Recognition awards and activities
   d. Rookie roundtables
   e. Social activities
   f. Relations with experienced teachers
   g. Social and resource support

INSTRUCTIONAL LEADER'S TOOLBOX

Readings

Airasian, P. W., & Walsh, M. E. (1997). Constructivist cautions. *Phi Delta Kappan, 78,* 444–449.

Allington, R. L., & McGill-Franzen, A. (2003). The impact of the summer setback on the reading achievement gap. *Phi Delta Kappan, 85*(1), 68–75.

Anderson, L. W., & Krathwohl, D. R. (Eds.). (2001). *A taxonomy of teaching and learning: A revision of Bloom's taxonomy of educational objectives.* New York: Addison, Wesley, Longman.

Jerome, E. M., Hamre, B. K., & Pianta, R. C. (2009). Teacher–child relationships from kindergarten to sixth grade: Early childhood predictors of teacher-perceived conflict and closeness. *Social Development, 18*(4), 915–945.

LeTendre, G. (2009). Teacher quality: National trends in teacher policy. *Child Research Net.* Retrieved from www.childresearch.net

Magnusson, S. J., & Palincsar, A. S. (1995). The learning environment as a site of science reform. *Theory into Practice, 34,* 43–50.

Sweller, J., Kirschner, P. A., & Clark, R. E. (2007). Why minimally guided teaching techniques do not work: A reply to commentaries. *Educational Psychologist, 42,* 115–121.

Videos

How to make homework more meaningful by involving parents, 15 minutes. Educational Consultant: Joyce Epstein. Use homework to strengthen students' skills and make learning more meaningful. This video shows
1. Assignments that help students establish regular schedules, and demonstrate and discuss what they've learned.
2. Strategies for initiating and encouraging family participation.
3. Ways to follow up assignments with class discussion and demonstration.

Order from: Association for Supervision and Curriculum Development (ASCD), 125 N. West St., Alexandria, VA 22314-2798. Telephone: (703) 549-9110; FAX: (703) 549-3891. http://shop.ascd.org/category.cfm?categoryid=video

Websites

www.achieve.org/
    Achieve, Inc.
www.free.ed.gov/
    Federal Resources for Educational Excellence (FREE)
www.learningcommons.org/educators/library/gem.php
    The Gateway to Educational Materials
www.nbpts.org/
    National Board for Professional Teaching Standards

Organizations

www.aera.net
    American Educational Research Association
www.cec.sped.org
    Council for Exceptional Children (CEC)
www.reading.org
    International Reading Association (IRA)
www.nabe.org
    National Association for Bilingual Education
www.natcenscied.org/
    National Center for Science Education
www.ncss.org
    National Council for the Social Studies
www.ncte.org
    National Council of Teachers of English
www.nctm.org
    National Council of Teachers of Mathematics
www.iste.org/standards
    National Educational Technology Standards for Teachers
www.nsta.org
    National Science Teachers Association

CHAPTER

7

Classroom Management

PREVIEW: KEY POINTS

1. A main task of teaching is to enlist students' cooperation in activities that will lead to learning, and a first step in accomplishing this task is to organize the learning environment.

2. The goals of good classroom management are to make more time for learning, give all students access to learning, and support the development of self-management in students.

3. Research on effective elementary and secondary classroom managers shows that these teachers have carefully planned rules and procedures (including consequences) for their classes; they teach these rules and procedures early, using explanations, examples, practice, correction, and student involvement.

4. For many rule infractions, the logical consequence is "go back and do it right"; separate the deed from the doer—the problem is the behavior, not the student.

5. Once a good class environment is established, it must be maintained by encouraging student engagement and preventing management problems; "with-it-ness," overlapping, group focus, and movement management are the skills of good preventers.

6. There are several special procedures that may be helpful in maintaining positive management, including group consequences and functional assessment with behavior supports.

7. Research on discipline shows that African Americans and Latino Americans, especially males, are punished more often and more harshly than other students; consequently, these students lose time from learning as they spend time in detention or suspension. Culturally responsive classroom management might improve this situation.

8. Up to one-third of students around the world are involved in bullying as a victim, a bully, or both, but schoolwide anti-bullying programs have a mixed record of success. Cyber-bullying affects many students outside schools, so students need to be taught how to be safe online.

9. Conflicts between students, though potentially dangerous, can be the occasions for learning conflict negotiation and peer mediation strategies.

10. Communication between teacher and student is essential when problems arise; all interactions between people, even silence or neglect, communicate some meaning. At times, positive communications with families is necessary too.

Leadership Challenge

You were hired in July as principal of Samuel Proctor Elementary School. This is your first job as principal after having been a teacher for six years. It is only the second week of school and you hear screaming when you are still halfway down the hall. "Give it back, it's MINE!" "No way—come and get it!" "I hate you!" A crashing sound follows as a table full of books hits the floor. You are surprised to hear one of your first-year teachers desperately trying to get control of the situation. You subsequently learn that the teacher has no management system—no order. Students walk around the room while the teacher is talking to the class, students interrupt when the teacher is working with a group, other students torment the class goldfish, and still others open their lunches (or those of other students) for a self-determined, mid-morning snack. Some students listen, but ask a million questions off the topic. Simply taking roll and introducing the first activity is a major project. Your new teacher is trying hard, but seems completely overwhelmed.

1. How would you approach the situation?
2. Which problem behaviors should the teacher tackle first?
3. Would giving rewards or administering punishments be useful in this situation? Why or why not? What specific suggestions would you give to this teacher?
4. What action would you take?

Organizing the Learning Environment

In study after study of the factors related to student achievement, classroom management stands out as the variable with the largest impact (Marzano & Marzano, 2003). Excellence in classroom management is a mark of expertise in teaching; stress and exhaustion from managerial difficulties are precursors of burnout in teaching (Emmer & Stough, 2001). What is it about classrooms that makes management so critical?

Classrooms are particular kinds of environments. They have distinctive features that influence their inhabitants no matter how the students are organized, how the desks are arranged for learning, or what the teacher believes about education (Doyle, 1986, 2006). Classrooms are *multidimensional*. They are crowded with people, tasks, and time pressures. Many individuals—all with differing goals, preferences, and abilities—must share resources, accomplish various tasks, use and reuse materials without losing them, move in and out of the room—the list goes on. And events occur *simultaneously*—everything happens at once. Teachers have literally hundreds of *fast-paced* exchanges with students every day. In this rapid-fire existence, events are *unpredictable*. Even when plans are carefully made and the demonstration is ready, the lesson can still be interrupted by a technology crash or a loud, angry discussion right outside the classroom. Because classrooms are *public*, the way the teacher handles these unexpected intrusions is seen and judged by all. Students are always noticing if the teacher is being "fair." What happens when a rule is broken? Finally, classrooms have *histories*. The meaning of a particular teacher's or student's actions depends in part on what has happened before. The fifteenth time a student arrives late requires a different response from the teacher than the first late arrival. In addition, the history of the first few weeks of school affects life in the class for the rest of the year.

The Basic Task: Gain Their Cooperation

No productive activity can take place in a group without the cooperation of all members. This obviously applies to classrooms. Even if some students don't participate, they must allow others to do so. (We all have seen one or two students bring an entire class to a halt.) So the basic management task for teachers is to achieve order and harmony by gaining and maintaining student cooperation in class activities (Doyle, 2006). Given the multidimensional, simultaneous, fast-paced, unpredictable, public, and historical nature of classrooms, this is quite a challenge.

Gaining student cooperation means much more than dealing effectively with misbehavior. It means planning activities, having materials ready, making appropriate behavioral and academic demands on students, giving clear signals to students, accomplishing transitions smoothly, foreseeing problems and stopping them before they start, selecting and sequencing activities so that flow and interest are maintained, and much more. Also, different activities require particular managerial skills. For example, loud student comments during a hip-hop reading of *Green Eggs and Ham* in an urban classroom may be indications of engagement and cooperation, not disorderly callouts (Doyle, 2006).

Obviously, gaining the cooperation of kindergartners is not the same task as gaining the cooperation of high school seniors. During kindergarten and the first few years of elementary school, direct teaching of classroom rules and procedures is important. For children in the middle elementary years, many classroom routines have become relatively automatic, but new procedures for a particular activity may have to be taught directly, and the entire system still needs monitoring and maintenance. Toward the end of elementary school, some students begin to test and defy authority. The management challenges at this stage are to deal productively with these disruptions and to motivate students who are becoming less concerned about teachers' opinions and more interested in their social lives. By the end of high school, the challenges are to manage the curriculum, fit academic material to students' interests and abilities, and help students become more self-managing (Emmer & Evertson, 2013; Evertson & Emmer, 2013).

Managing the Learning Environment

The aim of **classroom management** is to maintain a positive, productive learning environment, relatively free of behavior problems. But order for its own sake is an empty goal. There are at least three reasons why classroom management is important.

More Time for Learning. Researchers have known for years that there is a significant relationship between time spent on content and student learning (Berliner, 1988). If you time all the different activities throughout the school day, you might be surprised by how little actual teaching takes place. Many minutes each day are lost through interruptions, disruptions, late starts, and rough transitions (Weinstein, Romano, & Mignano, 2011). So one important goal of classroom management is to expand the sheer number of minutes available for learning. This is sometimes called *allocated time*.

But simply making more time for learning will not automatically lead to achievement. To be valuable, time must be used effectively. Think back to Chapter 4. To learn, students must pay attention, process information, and practice their understanding. Time spent actively involved in specific learning tasks is often called *engaged*

FIGURE 7.1   Who Knows Where the Time Goes?
The over 1,000 hours per year of instruction mandated by most states can represent only 300 or 400 hours of quality academic learning time.

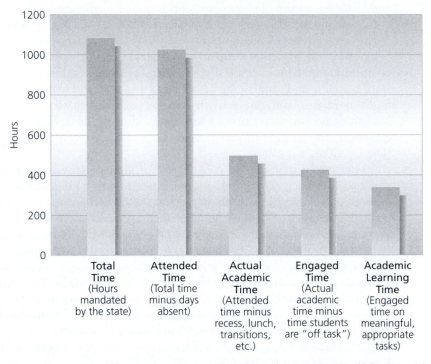

Source: Figure from *Educational psychology*, 12th Edition, by Anita E. Woolfolk. Copyright © 2013 by Pearson Education, Inc. Adapted from *Elementary classroom management: Lessons from research and practice, 4th Edition,* by Carol Simon Weinstein and Andrew Mignano, Jr. Copyright © 2007 by The McGraw-Hill Companies, Inc. Adapted with permission of The McGraw-Hill Companies, Inc. Printed and Electronically reproduced by permission of Pearson Education, Inc., Upper Saddle River, New Jersey.

time, or sometimes **time on-task.** Again, however, engaged time doesn't guarantee learning. Students may be struggling with material that is too difficult, or they may be using the wrong learning strategies. When students are working with a high rate of success—really learning and understanding—we call the time spent **academic learning time.** Figure 7.1 shows how the 1,000+ hours of time mandated for school in most states can become only about 333 hours of quality academic learning time for a typical student. *Good classroom management increases academic learning time by keeping students actively engaged in worthwhile, appropriate learning activities.*

Getting students engaged in learning early in their school careers can make a big difference. Several studies have shown that teachers' rating of students' on-task, persistent engagement in 1st grade predicts achievement test score gains and grades through 4th grade, as well as the decision to drop out of high school (Fredricks, Blumenfeld, & Paris, 2004).

Access to Learning. Each classroom activity has its own rules for participation. Sometimes these rules are clearly stated by the teacher, but often they are implicit and unstated. And the differences may be quite subtle. For example, in a reading group, students may have to raise their hands to make a comment, but in a show-and-tell circle in the same class, they may simply have to catch the teacher's eye. As we saw in Chapter 2, the rules defining who can talk; what they can talk about; and when, to whom, and how long they can talk are often called *participation structures.* In order to participate successfully in a given activity, students must understand its participation structure. The participation structures some students learn at home in interactions with family members do not match the participation structures of school activities (Cazden, 2001). But teachers are not necessarily aware of this conflict. Instead, the teachers see that a child doesn't quite fit in, always seems to say the wrong thing at the wrong time, or is very reluctant to participate, and the teachers are not sure why. Often they blame the students for being disruptive or uncooperative, and the students conclude that the teacher or the school is simply against them.

What does this mean for management? To reach the second goal of good classroom management—giving all students access to learning—*you must make sure everyone knows how to participate in class activities.* The key is awareness. What are your rules and expectations? Are they understandable, given your students' cultural backgrounds and home experiences? What unspoken rules or values may be operating? Are your teachers clearly signaling appropriate ways to participate? For some students, particularly those with behavioral and emotional challenges, direct teaching and practicing of the important behaviors may be required (Emmer & Stough, 2001).

Management for Self-Management. The third goal of any management system is to *help students become better able to manage themselves.* If teachers focus on student compliance, they will spend much of the teaching/learning time monitoring and correcting. Students come to see school as following rules, not constructing deep understanding of academic knowledge. And complex learning structures such as cooperative or problem-based learning require student **self-management.** Compliance with rules is not enough to make these learning structures work (McCaslin & Good, 1998).

The movement from demanding obedience to teaching self-regulation and self-control is a fundamental shift in discussions of classroom management today (Weinstein, 1999). Tom Savage (1999) says simply, "the most fundamental purpose of discipline is the development of self-control. Academic knowledge and technological skill will be of little consequence if those who possess them lack self-control" (p. 11). Through self-control, students demonstrate *responsibility*—the ability to fulfill their own needs without interfering with the rights and needs of others (Glasser, 1990). Students learn self-control by making choices and dealing with the consequences, setting goals and priorities, managing time, collaborating to learn, mediating disputes and making peace, and developing trusting relations with trustworthy teachers and classmates (Bear, 2005; Rogers & Freiberg, 1994).

Encouraging student self-management requires extra time, but teaching students how to take responsibility is an investment well worth the effort. There is good evidence for this claim. Nancy Perry and Rebecca Collie (2011) found that student teachers who learned how to coach their own students to be more self-regulated were more confident, less stressed, and more engaged during their student teaching compared to other prospective teachers who did not learn how to help their students to become self-regulated. This makes sense—if your teachers help students manage their own behavior and learning, they should have fewer management problems, less stress, and more time to teach, which would support a growing sense of teacher efficacy. When elementary and secondary teachers have very effective class management systems but neglect to set student self-management as a goal, their students often have trouble working independently after they graduate from these "well-managed" classes.

Creating a Positive Learning Environment: Some Research Results

What can teachers do to be good managers? For several years, researchers at the University of Texas at Austin examined classroom management quite thoroughly (Emmer & Stough, 2001; Emmer, Evertson, & Anderson, 1980; Emmer & Gerwels, 2006). Their general approach was to study a large number of classrooms, making frequent observations the first weeks of school and less frequent visits later in the year. After several months, there were dramatic differences among the classes. Some had very few management problems, whereas others had many. The most and least effective teachers were identified based on the quality of classroom management and student achievement in their classrooms later in the year.

Next, the researchers looked at their observation records of the first weeks of class to see how the effective teachers got started. Other comparisons were made between the teachers who ultimately had harmonious, high-achieving classes and those whose classes were fraught with problems. On the basis of these comparisons, management principles were developed. The researchers then taught these principles to a new group of teachers, and the results were quite positive. Teachers who applied the principles had fewer problems; their students spent more time learning and less time disrupting; and achievement was higher. The findings of these studies are detailed in two books on classroom management (Emmer & Evertson, 2009, 2013; Evertson & Emmer, 2009, 2013). Many of the ideas in the following pages are from these books.

Rules and Routines

At the elementary school level, teachers must lead 20 to 30 students of varying abilities through many different activities each day. Without efficient rules and procedures, a great deal of time is wasted answering the same question over and over. "My pencil broke. How can I do my math?" "I'm finished with my story. What should I do now?" "Jason hit me!" At the secondary school level, teachers must deal daily with over 100 students who use dozens of materials and often change rooms for each class. Secondary school students are also more likely to challenge teachers' authority. The effective managers studied by Emmer and Evertson and their respective colleagues (2006) had planned procedures and rules for coping with these situations.

Routines and Procedures. How will materials and assignments be distributed and collected? Under what conditions can students leave the room? How will grades be determined? What are the special routines for handling equipment and supplies in science, art, or vocational classes? **Routines** (sometimes called **procedures**) describe how activities are accomplished in classrooms, but they are seldom written down; they are simply the ways of getting things done in class. Carol Weinstein and her colleagues (Weinstein & Novodvorsky, 2011; Weinstein, Romano, & Mignano, 2011) suggest that teachers establish routines to cover the following areas:

1. *Administrative routines,* such as taking attendance
2. *Student movement,* such as entering and leaving or going to the bathroom
3. *Housekeeping,* such as watering plants or storing personal items
4. *Lesson-running routines,* such as how to collect assignments or return homework
5. *Interactions between teacher and student,* such as how to get the teacher's attention when help is needed
6. *Talk among students,* such as giving help or socializing

If teachers, particularly beginning teachers, are having trouble with class management, check these six areas. You might use these six areas as a framework for helping teachers think through their procedures and routines. The *Theory into Action Guidelines* on the next page should help principals coach their teachers.

Rules. Statements specifying the expected and forbidden actions in class are called **rules.** They are the dos and don'ts of classroom life. Unlike routines/procedures, rules are often written down and posted. The rules teachers set should be consistent with school rules, and also in keeping with principles of learning. For example, we know from the research on small-group learning that students benefit when they explain work to peers. They learn as they talk and teach. A rule that forbids students to help each other may be inconsistent with good learning principles. Or a rule that says, "No erasures when writing" may make students focus more on preventing mistakes than on communicating clearly in their writing (Burden, 1995; Weinstein, Romano, & Mignano, 2011). Having a few general rules that cover many specifics is better than listing all the dos and don'ts. But, if specific actions are forbidden, such as chewing gum in class or smoking in the bathrooms, then a rule should make this clear (Emmer & Gerwels, 2006).

Rules for Elementary School. Evertson and Emmer (2009) give four examples of general rules for elementary school classes:

1. *Respect and be polite to all people.* Give clear explanations of what you mean by "polite," including not hitting, fighting, or teasing. Examples of polite behavior include waiting your turn, saying "please" and "thank you," and not calling names. This applies to behavior toward adults (including substitute teachers) and peers.

T H E O R Y   I N T O   A C T I O N   G U I D E L I N E S

Developing Classroom Routines

Determine procedures for student upkeep of desks, classroom equipment, and other facilities.

Examples

1. Set aside a cleanup time each day or once a week in self-contained classes.
2. Demonstrate and have students practice how to push chairs under the desk, take and return materials stored on shelves, sharpen pencils, use the sink or water fountain, assemble lab equipment, and so on.
3. Put a rotating monitor in charge of equipment or materials.

Decide how students will be expected to enter and leave the room.

Examples

1. Have a procedure to follow as soon as students enter the room. Some teachers have a standard assignment ("Have your homework out and be checking it over" or "Do the problem of the day").
2. Inform students under what conditions they can leave the room, and make sure they understand when they need to ask permission to do so.
3. Tell students how they should gain permission to the room if they are late.
4. Set up a policy about class dismissal. Many teachers require students to be in their seats and quiet before they can leave at the end of class. The teacher, not the bell, dismisses class.

Establish a signal and teach it to your students.

Examples

1. In the classroom, flick the lights on and off, sound a chord on a piano or recorder, move to the podium and stare silently at the class, use a phrase like "Eyes, please," take out your grade book, or move to the front of the class.
2. In the halls, raise a hand, clap once, or use some other signal to indicate "Stop."

3. On the playground, raise a hand or whistle to indicate "Line up."

Set procedures for student participation in class.

Examples

1. Decide whether you will have students raise their hands for permission to speak or simply require that they wait until the speaker has finished.
2. Determine a signal to indicate that you want everyone to respond at once. Some teachers raise a cupped hand to their ear. Others preface the question with "Everyone. . . ."
3. Make sure you are clear about differences in procedures for different activities: reading group, learning center, discussion, teacher presentation, seatwork, film, peer learning group, library, and so forth.
4. Establish how many students at a time can be at the pencil sharpener, teacher's desk, learning center, sink, bookshelves, reading corner, or bathroom.

Determine how you will communicate, collect, and return assignments.

Examples

1. Establish a place for listing assignments. Some teachers reserve a particular corner of the board for listing assignments. Others write assignments in colored chalk. For younger students, it may be better to prepare assignment sheets or folders, color-coding them for math workbook, reading packet, and science kit.
2. Be clear about how and where assignments should be collected. Some teachers collect assignments in a box or bin; others have a student collect work while they introduce the next activity.

For ideas about involving students in developing rules and procedures, see www.educationworld.com/a_lesson/lesson/lesson274.shtml

2. *Be prompt and prepared.* This rule highlights the importance of the academic work in the class. Being prompt includes the beginning of the day as well as transitions between activities.
3. *Listen quietly while others are speaking.* This applies to the teacher and other students, in both large-class lessons and small-group discussions.
4. *Obey all school rules.* This reminds students that all school rules apply in your classroom. Then students cannot claim, for example, that they thought it was okay to chew gum or listen to an iPod in your class, even though these are against school rules, "because you never made a rule against it for us."

Whatever the rule, students need to be taught the behaviors that the rule includes and excludes. Examples, practice, and discussion will be needed before learning is complete. Many teachers you work with may think that their jobs are done when the rule is made or posted, and then they wonder why there are so many problems. Chances are that these teachers have not taught and practiced the rules. And, as you've seen, different activities often require different rules. This can be confusing for elementary students until they have thoroughly learned all the rules. To prevent confusion, some teachers have signs that list the rules for each activity. Then, before the activity, they post the appropriate sign (and early in the year, review the rules) as a reminder. This provides clear and consistent cues about participation structures so all students know what is expected. Of course, these rules must be explained, discussed, and practiced before the signs can have their full effect.

Rules for Secondary School.   Emmer and Evertson (2009) suggest six examples of rules for secondary students:

1. *Bring all needed materials to class.* The teacher must specify the type of pen, pencil, paper, notebook, texts, and so on.
2. *Be in your seat and ready to work when the bell rings.* Many teachers combine this rule with a standard beginning procedure for the class, such as a warm-up exercise on the board or a requirement that students have paper with a proper heading ready when the bell rings.
3. *Respect and be polite to everyone.* This covers fighting, verbal abuse, and general troublemaking.
4. *Respect other people's property.* This means property belonging to the school, the teacher, or other students.
5. *Listen and stay seated while someone else is speaking.* This applies when the teacher or other students are talking.
6. *Obey all school rules.* As with the elementary class rules, this covers many behaviors and situations, so teachers do not have to repeat every school rule for their class. It also reminds the students that their teachers will be monitoring them both inside and outside class.

These rules are more than ways to maintain order. In their study of 34 middle school classrooms, Lindsay Matsumura and her colleagues (2008) found that having explicit rules about respecting others in the classroom predicted the number of students who participated in class discussion, so it seems clear that respect is a gateway to student engagement with the academic material and class dialogue that supports learning.

Consequences.   As soon as your teachers decide on rules and procedures, they must consider what they will do when a student breaks a rule or does not follow a procedure. It is too late to make this decision after the rule has been broken. For many infractions, the logical consequence is "go back and do it right." Students who run in the hall may have to return to where they started and walk properly. Incomplete papers can be redone. Materials left out should be put back (Charles, 2002b). Teachers can use natural or logical consequences to help students take responsibility by doing the following (Elias & Schwab, 2006):

- Separate the deed from the doer—the problem is the behavior, not the student.
- Emphasize to students that they have the power to choose their actions and avoid losing control.
- Encourage student reflection, self-evaluation, and problem solving—avoid teacher lecturing.
- Help students identify and give a rationale for what they could do differently next time in a similar situation.

Sometimes consequences are more complicated. In their case studies of four expert elementary school teachers, Carol Weinstein and her colleagues (2011) found that the teachers' negative consequences fell into seven categories, as shown in Table 7.1. The main point here is that decisions about penalties (and rewards) must be made early on, so students know before they break a rule or use the wrong procedure what this will mean for them.

But there is a strong caution. Consequences, no matter how thoughtfully determined, will not prevent problems or guarantee learning. A consequence will work only when the students care about their relationship with the teacher or administrator who is asking them to follow the rules, or when the students see some value in what they are asked to do (Bodine & Crawford, 1999; Vitto, 2003). You can judge the value of the consequences used in your school by asking whether the consequences (a) have the effects intended, (b) give students choices to redirect their behavior or learn from instruction, (c) bring teachers and students closer together or push them apart, (d) model and teach appropriate prosocial behaviors, (e) interfere with instruction, and (f) would be effective with you (Vitto, 2003).

Who Sets the Rules and Consequences?   Not all rules have to be stated as rules. For example, Ken, the 5th/6th-grade teacher described in Chapter 6, works with his students to develop his class rules at the beginning of the year. Rather than specifying dos and don'ts, Ken and his students devise a "Bill of Rights" for the class, describing the rights of both the students and the teacher. These rights cover most

TABLE 7.1 Seven Categories of Penalties for Students

1. *Expressions of disappointment.* If students like and respect their teacher, then a serious, sorrowful expression of disappointment may cause students to stop and think about their behavior.
2. *Loss of privileges.* Students can lose free time. If they have not completed homework, for example, they can be required to do it during a free period or recess.
3. *Time-out: Exclusion from the group.* Students who distract their peers or fail to cooperate can be separated from the group until they are ready to cooperate. Some teachers give a student a pass for 10 to 15 minutes. The student must go to another class or study hall, where the other students and teachers ignore the offending student for that time.
4. *Written reflections on the problem.* Students can write in journals, write essays about what they did and how it affected others, or write letters of apology—if this is appropriate. Another possibility is to ask students to describe objectively what they did; then the teacher and the student can sign and date this statement. These records are available if parents or administrators need evidence of the students' behavior.
5. *Visits to the principal's office.* Expert teachers tend to use this penalty rarely, but they do use it when the situation warrants. Some schools require students to be sent to the office for certain offenses, such as fighting. If a student is told to go to the office and refuses, the teacher might call the office saying the student has been sent. Then the student has the choice of either going to the office or facing the principal's penalty for "disappearing" on the way.
6. *Detentions.* Detentions can be very brief meetings after school, during a free period, or at lunch. The main purpose is to talk about what has happened. (In high school, detentions are often used as punishments; suspensions and expulsions are available as more extreme measures.)
7. *Contacting parents.* If problems become a repeated pattern, most teachers contact the student's family. This is done to seek support for helping the student, not to blame the parents or punish the student.

Source: List excerpted from *Elementary classroom management: Lessons from research and practice,* 4th Edition, by Carol Simon Weinstein and Andrew Mignano, Jr. Copyright © 2007 by The McGraw-Hill Companies, Inc. Reprinted with permission.

of the situations that might need a "rule." The rights for one recent year's class included, for example:

- The right to whisper when the teacher isn't talking.
- The right to a two-minute break between work periods.
- The right to have choices about the day's schedule.
- The right to work and learn without being bothered.
- The right to talk to the class without anyone else talking.
- The right to choose a table.*

In recent years, when Ken has had some very difficult classes, he and his students have had to establish some "laws" that protect students' rights, such as "transitions and

*Source: Excerpts from *Elementary classroom management: Lessons from research and practice,* 4th Edition, by Carol Simon Weinstein and Andrew Mignano, Jr. Copyright © 2007 by The McGraw-Hill Companies, Inc. Reprinted with permission.

movements are calm, quiet, careful and elegant" and "follow all classroom and school procedures, like: bathroom; pencil; lunch and recess; morning; dismissal; and. . . ."

Developing rights and responsibilities rather than rules makes a very important point to students. "Teaching children that something is wrong *because there is a rule against it* is not the same as teaching them that there is a rule against it *because it is wrong*, and helping them to understand why this is so" (Weinstein, 1999, p. 154).* Students should understand that the rules are developed so that everyone can live and learn together.

If your teachers are going to involve students in setting rules or creating a constitution, they may need to wait until they have established a sense of community in their classrooms, described in a later section of this chapter. Before students can contribute meaningfully to the class rules, they need to trust the teacher and the situation (Elias & Schwab, 2006).

Planning for Computer Uses

Many classrooms today have computers. Some classes have only one, others have several, and some classes are labs with a computer for every student. Using computers productively brings with it management challenges. Computers can be used to connect to powerful knowledge bases around the world; as tools for writing, drawing, calculating, and designing; to simulate scientific experiments or life in other times and places; to collaborate and communicate with people across the hall or across the ocean; to publish work or make presentations; and to keep track of appointments, assignments, or grades. To get the greatest benefits from computers in their classrooms, teachers must have good management systems.

Most classrooms will not have a computer for every student. In fact, many have only one computer or none at all. The *Theory into Action Guidelines* for using computers in regular classrooms give some ideas.

Source: "Reflections on best practices and promising programs: Beyond assertive classroom discipline" by Carol Simon Weinstein, from *Beyond behaviorism: Changing the classroom management paradigm*, edited by H. Jerome Freiberg. Pearson Education, Inc., 1999.

THEORY INTO ACTION GUIDELINES

Using Computers: Management Issues

If you have only one computer in your classroom: Provide convenient access.

Examples
1. Find a central location if the computer is used to display material for the class.
2. Find a spot on the side of the room that allows seating and view of the screen, but does not crowd or disturb other students if the computer is used as a workstation for individuals or small groups.

Be prepared.

Examples
1. Check to be sure software needed for a lesson or an assignment is installed and working.
2. Make sure instructions for using the software or doing the assignment are in an obvious place and clear.
3. Provide checklist for completing assignments.

(Continued)

THEORY INTO ACTION GUIDELINES Continued

Create "trained experts" to help with computers.

Examples

1. Train student experts and rotate experts.
2. Use adult volunteers—parents, grandparents, or older siblings.

Develop systems for using the computer.

Examples

1. Make up a schedule to ensure that all students have access to the computer and no students monopolize the time.
2. Create standard ways of saving student work.

If you have more than one computer in your classroom: Plan the arrangement of the computers to fit your instructional goals.

Examples

1. For cooperative groups, arrange so students can cluster around their group's computer.
2. For different projects at different computer stations, allow for easy rotation from station to station.

Experiment with other models for using computers.

Examples

1. *Navigator Model*—4 students per computer: One student is the (mouse and keyboard) "driver," another is the "navigator." "Back-seat driver 1" manages the group's progress and "back-seat driver 2" serves as the timekeeper. The navigator attends a 10-minute to 20-minute training session in which the facilitator provides an overview of the basics of particular software. Navigators cannot touch the mouse. Driver roles are rotated.
2. *Facilitator Model*—6 students per computer: the facilitator has more experience, expertise, or training—serves as the guide or teacher.
3. *Collaborative Group Model*—7 students per computer: Each small group is responsible for creating some component of the whole group's final product. For example, one part of the group writes a report, another creates a map, and a third uses the computer to gather and graph census data.
4. Online collaboration—students work on projects with partners online using some shared virtual space such as Google Documents or Yahoo Groups.

For more ideas, see http://www.internet4classrooms.com/classroom_organization.htm#one

---

Getting Started: The First Weeks of Class

Determining rules and procedures are first steps toward having a well-managed class, but how do effective teachers gain students' cooperation in those first critical days and weeks? One study carefully analyzed the first weeks' activities of effective and ineffective elementary teachers, and found striking differences (Emmer, Evertson, & Anderson, 1980).

Effective Classroom Managers for Elementary Students

In the effective teachers' classrooms, the very first day was well organized. Name tags were ready. There was something interesting for each child to do right away. Materials were set up. The teachers had planned carefully to avoid any last-minute tasks that might take them away from their students. These teachers dealt with the children's pressing concerns first. "Where do I put my things? How do I pronounce my teacher's name? Can I whisper to my neighbor? Where is the bathroom?" The effective teachers had a workable, easily understood set of rules and taught the students the most important rules right away. They taught the rules like any other subject, with lots of explanation, examples, and practice.

Throughout the first weeks, the effective managers continued to spend quite a bit of time teaching rules and procedures. Some used guided practice to teach procedures; others used rewards to shape behavior. Most taught students to respond to a bell or some other signal to gain their attention. These teachers worked with the class as a whole on enjoyable academic activities. They did not rush to get students into small groups or to start them in readers. This whole-class work gave the teachers a better opportunity to continue monitoring all students' learning of the rules and procedures. Misbehavior was stopped quickly and firmly, but not harshly.

In the poorly managed classrooms, the first weeks were quite different. Rules were not workable; they were either too vague or very complicated. For example, one teacher made a rule that students should "be in the right place at the right time." Students were not told what this meant, so their behavior could not be guided by the rule. Neither positive nor negative behaviors had clear, consistent consequences. After students broke a rule, ineffective managers might give a vague criticism, such as "Some of my children are too noisy," or issue a warning, but not follow through with the threatened consequence.

In the poorly managed classes, procedures for accomplishing routine tasks varied from day to day and were never taught or practiced. Instead of dealing with these obvious needs, ineffective managers spent time on procedures that could have waited. For example, one teacher had the class practice for a fire drill the first day, but left unexplained other procedures that would be needed every day. Students wandered aimlessly and had to ask each other what they should be doing. Often the students talked to one another because they had nothing productive to do. Ineffective teachers frequently left the room. Many became absorbed in paperwork or in helping just one student. They had not made plans for how to deal with late-arriving students or interruptions. One ineffective manager tried to teach students to respond to a bell as a signal for attention, but later let the students ignore it. All in all, the first weeks in these classrooms were disorganized and filled with surprises for teachers and students alike.

Effective Classroom Managers for Secondary Students

What about getting started in a secondary school class? It appears that many of the differences between effective and ineffective elementary school teachers hold at the secondary level as well. Again, effective managers focus on establishing rules, procedures, and expectations on the first day of class. These standards for academic work and class behavior are clearly communicated to students and consistently enforced during the first weeks of class. Student behavior is closely monitored, and infractions of the rules are dealt with quickly. In classes with lower-ability students, work cycles are shorter;

students are not required to spend long, unbroken periods on one type of activity. Instead, during each period, they are moved smoothly through several different tasks. In general, effective teachers carefully follow each student's progress, so students cannot avoid work without facing consequences (Emmer & Evertson, 1982).

With all this close monitoring and consistent enforcement of the rules, you may wonder if effective secondary teachers have to be grim and humorless. As any experienced teacher knows, there is much more to smile about when the class is cooperative. In fact, there is another requirement for getting started, one that was evident in the class run by the "class constitution"; establishing a climate of trust and respect that creates a community for learning.

Creating a Learning Community

Nel Noddings (1992, 1995) has written about the need to create caring educational environments that encourage students take more responsibility for governing their school and classroom. As we saw in Chapter 5 when we discussed the need for social support, students are more intrinsically motivated when they feel that their teachers care about them (Grolnick, Ryan, & Deci, 1991). Historically, however, U.S. schools have emphasized regulating students' behavior through rules, not through relationships. But this is not true in every culture. For example, in the book *Learning to Teach in Two Cultures*, Shimahara and Sakai (1995) observe that the Japanese approach to classroom management emphasizes such interpersonal bonds as emotional ties, relationships, and character. Success of the Japanese system "does not depend on many rules, but on a sense of trust and interdependency between the classroom teacher and his or her students and among the students" (Shimahara & Sakai, 1995, p. 79).

One approach to developing this kind of caring and mutually trusting community is David and Roger Johnson's "Three Cs" of school and classroom management. The three Cs for safe and productive schools are cooperative community, constructive conflict resolution, and civic values (Johnson & Johnson, 1999b). Classroom management begins by establishing a learning community based on cooperative approaches such as those described in Chapter 4. At the heart of the community is the idea of positive interdependence—individuals working together to achieve mutual goals. Constructive conflict resolution is essential in the community because conflicts are inevitable and even necessary for learning. Piaget's theory of development and the research on conceptual change teaching tell us that true learning requires cognitive conflict. And individuals trying to exist in groups will have interpersonal conflict—these can lead to learning too. Table 7.2 on the next page shows how academic and interpersonal conflicts can be positive forces in a learning community. At the end of this chapter we will talk more about conflict resolution in schools.

The last C is civic values: the understandings and beliefs that hold the community together. Values are learned through direct teaching, modeling, literature, group discussions, the sharing of concerns. Some teachers have a "Concerns Box," where students can put written concerns and comments. The box is opened once a week at a class meeting and the concerns are discussed. Johnson and Johnson (1999b) give an example of a class meeting about respect. One student tells her classmates that she felt

TABLE 7.2   Academic and Interpersonal Conflict and Learning

Conflict, if handled well, can support learning. Academic conflicts can lead to critical thinking and conceptual change. Conflicts of interest are unavoidable, but can be handled so no one is the loser.

Academic Controversy	Conflicts of Interest
One person's ideas, information, theories, conclusions, and opinions are incompatible with those of another and the two seek to reach an agreement.	The actions of one person attempting to maximize benefits prevents, blocks, or interferes with another person, maximizing her or his benefits.
Controversy Procedure	*Integrative (Problem-Solving) Negotiations*
Research and prepare positions	Describe wants
Present and advocate positions	Describe feelings
Refute opposing position and refute attacks on own position	Describe reasons for wants and feelings Take other's perspective
Reverse perspectives	Invent three optional agreements that maximize joint outcomes
Synthesize and integrate best evidence and reasoning from all sides	Choose one and formalize agreement

Source: Excerpt from "The Three Cs of School and Classroom Management" by David W. Johnson and Roger Johnson, from *Beyond behaviorism: Changing the classroom management paradigm*, edited by H. Jerome Freiberg. Copyright © 1999 by H. Jerome Freiberg. Reprinted with permission of the editor.

hurt during recess the day before because no one listened when she was trying to teach them the rules to a new game. The students discussed what it means to be respectful and why respect is important. Then the students shared personal experiences of times when they felt respected versus not respected.

Maintaining a Good Learning Environment

A good start is just that, a beginning. Effective teachers build on this beginning. They maintain their management system by preventing problems and keeping students engaged in productive learning activities.

Encouraging Engagement

The format of a lesson affects student involvement. In general, as teacher supervision increases, students' engaged time also increases. For example, Frick (1990) found that elementary students working directly with a teacher were on task 97% of the time, while students working on their own were on task only 57% of the time. This does not mean that teachers should eliminate independent work for students. It simply means that this type of activity usually requires careful monitoring.

Activities with clear steps are likely to be more absorbing because one step leads naturally to the next. When students have all the materials they need to complete a task, they tend to stay involved. If their curiosity is piqued, students will be motivated to continue seeking an answer. And students tend to be more engaged if they are involved in authentic tasks, activities that have connections to real life. Also, activities are more engaging when the level of challenge is higher and when students' interests are incorporated (Emmer & Gerwels, 2006).

Of course, teachers can't supervise every student all the time or rely on curiosity to keep students motivated. Something else must keep students working on their own. In their study of elementary and secondary teachers, Evertson, Emmer, and their colleagues found that effective class managers at both levels had well-planned systems for encouraging accountability so that students managed their own work (Emmer & Evertson, 2009, 2013; Evertson & Emmer, 2009, 2013). The *Theory into Action Guidelines* should help principals and teachers plan strategies for effective classroom management.

THEORY INTO ACTION GUIDELINES
Encouraging Student Accountability

Make basic work requirements clear.
Examples
1. Specify and post the routine work requirements for headings, paper size, pen or pencil use, and neatness.
2. Establish and explain rules about late or incomplete work and absences. If a pattern of incomplete work begins to develop, deal with it early; speak with parents if necessary.
3. Make due dates reasonable, and stick to them unless the student has a very good excuse for lateness.

Communicate the specifics of assignments.
Examples
1. With younger students, have a routine procedure for giving assignments, such as writing them on the board in the same place each day. With older students, assignments may be dictated, posted, or given in a syllabus.
2. Remind students of coming assignments.
3. With complicated assignments, give students a sheet describing what to do, what resources are available, due dates, and so on. Older students should also be told about grading criteria.

4. Demonstrate how to do the assignment, do the first few questions together, or provide a sample worksheet.

Monitor work in progress.
Examples
1. When you make an assignment in class, make sure each student gets started correctly. If you check only students who raise their hands for help, you will miss those who think they know what to do but don't really understand, those who are too shy to ask for help, and those who don't plan to do the work at all.
2. Check progress periodically. In discussions, make sure everyone has a chance to respond.

Give frequent academic feedback.
Examples
1. Elementary students should get papers back the day after they are handed in.
2. Good work can be displayed in class and graded papers sent home to parents each week.
3. Students of all ages can keep records of grades, projects completed, and extra credits earned.
4. For older students, break up long-term assignments into several phases, giving feedback at each point.

Prevention Is the Best Medicine

What else can teachers do to maintain their management systems? The ideal way to manage problems, of course, is to prevent them in the first place. In a classic study, Jacob Kounin (1970) examined classroom management by comparing effective teachers, whose classes were relatively free of problems, with ineffective teachers, whose classes were continually plagued by chaos and disruption. Observing both groups in action, Kounin found that the teachers were not very different in the way they handled discipline once problems arose. The difference was that the successful managers were much better at preventing problems. Kounin concluded that effective classroom managers were especially skilled in four areas: "with-it-ness," overlapping activities, group focusing, and movement management. More recent research confirms the importance of these factors (Evertson, 1988; Larrivee, 2005).

With-it-ness.   It is important for teachers to demonstrate **with-it-ness,** communicating to students that they are aware of everything that is happening in the classroom, that they aren't missing anything. "With-it" teachers avoid becoming absorbed by distractions or interacting with only a few students because this encourages the rest of the class to wander. These teachers are always scanning the room, making eye contact with individual students, so the students know they are being monitored.

These teachers prevent minor disruptions from becoming major. They also know who instigated the problem, and they make sure the right people are dealt with. In other words, they do not make what Kounin (1970) called *timing errors* (waiting too long before intervening) or *target errors* (blaming the wrong student and letting the real perpetrators escape responsibility for their behavior). If two problems occur at the same time, effective managers deal with the more serious one first. For example, a teacher who tells two students to stop whispering but ignores even a brief shoving match at the pencil sharpener communicates to students a lack of awareness (Larrivee, 2005; Woolfolk, 2008).

Overlapping and Group Focus.   Effective teachers are good at **overlapping:** keeping track of and supervising several activities at the same time. For example, a teacher may have to check the work of an individual and at the same time keep a small group working by saying, "Right, go on," and stop an incident in another group with a quick "look" or reminder (Burden, 1995; Charles, 2011).

Maintaining a **group focus** means keeping as many students as possible involved in appropriate class activities and avoiding narrowing in on just one or two students. All students should have something to do during a lesson. For example, the teacher might ask everyone to write the answer to a question, and then call on individuals to respond while the other students compare their answers. Choral responses might be required while the teacher moves around the room to make sure everyone is participating. Some teachers have their students use small blackboards or colored cards for responding in groups. This lets the teacher check for understanding as well. For example, during a grammar lesson the teacher might say, "Everyone who thinks the answer is 'have run,' hold up the red side of your card. If you think the answer is 'has run,' hold up the green side" (Hunter, 1982). This is one way teachers can ensure that all students are involved and check that they all understand the material.

Movement Management.   **Movement management** means keeping lessons and the group moving at an appropriate (and flexible) pace, with smooth transitions and variety. The effective teacher avoids abrupt transitions, such as announcing a new activity before gaining the students' attention or starting a new activity in the middle of something else. In these situations, one-third of the class will be doing the new activity, many will be working on the old lesson, several will be asking other students what to do, some will be taking the opportunity to have a little fun, and most will be confused. Another transition problem Kounin (1970) noted is the *slowdown*, or taking too much time to start a new activity. Sometimes teachers give too many directions. Problems also arise when teachers have students work one at a time while the rest of the class waits and watches.

A teacher who successfully demonstrates with-it-ness, overlapping activities, group focus, and movement management tends to have a class filled with actively engaged students who do not escape his or her all-seeing eye. This need not be a grim classroom. It is more likely a busy place where students are actively learning and gaining a sense of self-worth rather than misbehaving in order to get attention and achieve status.

Student Social Skills as Prevention.   But what about the students? What can they do? When students lack social and emotional skills such as being able to share materials, read the intentions of others, or handle frustration, classroom management problems often follow. So all efforts to teach social and emotional self-regulation are steps toward preventing management problems. Over the short term, educators can teach and model these skills, and then give students feedback and practice using them in a variety of settings. Over the long term, teachers can help to change attitudes that value aggression over cooperation and compromise (Elias & Schwab, 2006).

Caring Relationships: Connections with School.   Students who feel connected with school are happier, more engaged in school work, more self-disciplined, and less likely to be involved in dangerous behaviors such as substance abuse, violence, and early sexual activity (Freiberg, 2006; McNeely, Nonnemaker, & Blum, 2002; Pointz, Rimm-Kaufman, Grimm, & Curby, 2009). In fact, in a synthesis of 119 studies published in either English or German conducted from 1948 to 2004, Jeffrey Cornelius-White (2007) concluded that positive, warm, encouraging relationships with teachers are related to many valuable student outcomes, including higher participation in class, greater critical thinking skills, lower drop-out rates, higher self-esteem, increased motivation, less disruptive behavior, and better attendance. When Barbara Bartholomew (2008) asked a veteran special education teacher what keeps students engaged and motivated, the teacher replied without hesitation, "Students need to know that no matter what, you will never give up on them" (p. 58).

Creating Communities of Care for Adolescents.   The transition to high school is a particularly important time to maintain caring teacher–student relationships. Students have more teachers and fewer close relationships, just at a time when emotional, social, and academic stresses are increasing. One diverse urban school with over 2,000 students confronted this problem by creating small communities of care. These were interdisciplinary teams of students and teachers who shared common interests and participated in a Freshman Focus class during the first nine weeks of school. The class helped students adjust to high school, get oriented to the building, and develop school skills like taking notes, social skills, and even skills for getting along with parents. The programs led to the development of positive teacher beliefs about students, supportive teacher–student relationships, and the promotion of academic and life skills (Ellerbrock & Kiefer, 2010).

Dealing with Discipline Problems

Every year since 1969, *Phi Delta Kappa* has published the annual Gallup Poll of the public's attitude toward public schools. From 1969 to 1999, almost every year the public identified "lack of discipline" as the number one problem facing the schools (Rose & Gallup, 1999). Since 1999, lack of funds has taken over as the top perceived problem, but lack of discipline continues to be second. Clearly, the public sees discipline as an important challenge for teachers (Bushaw & Lopez, 2011).

Being an effective manager does not mean publicly correcting every minor infraction of the rules. This kind of public attention may actually reinforce the misbehavior. Teachers who frequently correct students do not necessarily have the best-behaved classes. The key is to know what is happening and what is important so you can prevent problems.

Most students comply quickly when the teacher gives a *desist* (a "stop doing that") or redirects behavior. But some students are the targets of more than their share of desists. One study found that these disruptive students seldom complied with the first teacher request to stop. Often the disruptive students responded negatively, leading to an average of four to five cycles of teacher desists and student response before the student complied (Nelson & Roberts, 2000). Emmer and colleagues (2006) and Levin and Nolan (2000) suggest seven simple ways to stop misbehavior quickly, moving from least to most intrusive:

1. *Make eye contact* with, or move closer to, the offender. Other nonverbal signals, such as pointing to the work students are supposed to be doing, might be helpful. Make sure the student actually stops the inappropriate behavior and gets back to work. If you do not, students will learn to ignore your signals.
2. Try *verbal hints* such as "name-dropping" (simply insert the student's name into the lecture), asking the student a question, or making a humorous (not sarcastic) comment such as, "I must be hallucinating. I swear I heard someone shout out an answer, but that can't be because I haven't called on anyone yet!"
3. You might also ask students *if they are aware* of the negative effects of their actions or send an "I" message, described later in the chapter.
4. If they are not performing a class procedure correctly, *remind the students* of the procedure and have them follow it correctly. You may need to quietly collect a toy, comb, magazine, or note that is competing with the learning activities, while privately informing the students that their possessions will be returned after class.
5. In a calm, unhostile way, *ask the student to state the correct rule or procedure* and then to follow it. Glasser (1969) proposes three questions: "What are you doing? Is it against the rules? What should you be doing?"

6. Tell the student in a clear, assertive, and unhostile way to *stop the misbehavior*. (Later in the chapter we will discuss assertive messages to students in more detail.) If students "talk back," simply repeat your statement.
7. *Offer a choice.* For example, when a student continued to call out answers no matter what the teacher tried, the teacher said, "John, you have a choice. Stop calling out answers immediately and begin raising your hand to answer or move your seat to the back of the room and you and I will have a private discussion later. You decide" (Levin & Nolan, 2000, p. 177).*

Many teachers prefer the use of logical consequences, described earlier, as opposed to penalties. For example, if one student has harmed another, you can require the offending student to make an "Apology of Action," which includes a verbal apology plus somehow repairing the damage done. This helps offenders develop empathy and social perspective-taking as they think what would be an appropriate "repair" (Elias & Schwab, 2006).

If you or your teachers must impose penalties, the *Theory into Action Guidelines* taken from Weinstein and Mignano (2011) and Weinstein (2011) give ideas about how to do it. The examples are taken from the actual words of the expert teachers described in their books.

Source: Principles of classroom management: A Professional decision-making model by James Levin and James F. Nolan. Pearson Education, Inc., 2000.

THEORY INTO ACTION GUIDELINES

Penalties

Delay the discussion of the situation until you and the students involved are calmer and more objective.

Examples

1. Say calmly to a student, "Sit there and think about what happened. I'll talk to you in a few minutes," or, "I don't like what I just saw. Talk to me during your free period today."
2. Say, "I'm really angry about what just happened. Everybody take out journals; we are going to write about this." After a few minutes of writing, the class can discuss the incident.

Impose penalties privately.

Examples

1. Make arrangements with students privately. Stand firm in enforcing arrangements.
2. Resist the temptation to "remind" students in public that they are not keeping their side of the bargain.

3. Move close to a student who must be disciplined and speak so that only the student can hear.

After imposing a penalty, reestablish a positive relationship with the student immediately.

Examples

1. Send the student on an errand or ask him or her for help.
2. Compliment the student's work or give a real or symbolic "pat on the back" when the student's behavior warrants. Look hard for such an opportunity.

Set up a graded list of penalties that will fit many occasions.

Example

1. For not turning in homework: (1) receive reminder; (2) receive warning; (3) hand homework in before close of school day; (4) stay after school to finish work; (5) participate in a teacher–student–parent conference to develop an action plan.

There is a caution about penalties. Never use lower achievement status (moving to a lower reading group, giving a lower grade, giving excess homework) as a punishment for breaking class rules. These actions should be done only if the benefit of the action outweighs the possible risk of harm. As Carolyn Orange (2000) notes, "Effective, caring teachers would not use low achievement status, grades, or the like as a means of discipline. This strategy is unfair and ineffective. It only serves to alienate the student" (p. 76).

Special Problems with Secondary Students

Many secondary students never complete their work. Besides encouraging student responsibility, what else can teachers do to deal with this frustrating problem? Because students at this age have many assignments and teachers have many students, both teacher and students may lose track of what has and has not been completed. It often helps to teach students how to use a daily planner. In addition, the teacher must keep accurate records. But the most important thing is to enforce the established consequences for incomplete work. Teachers should not pass a student because they know that he or she is "bright enough" to pass. Teachers should make it clear to these students that the choice is theirs: Do the work and pass, or refuse to do the work and face the consequences.

There is also the problem of students who continually break the same rules, always forgetting materials, for example, or getting into fights, like the students described in the *Principal's Perspective* that follows. What should teachers do? Teachers should seat these students away from others who might be influenced by them and try to catch them before they break the rules. If, however, rules are broken, the teacher must be consistent in applying established consequences. Teachers should not accept promises to do better next time (Levin & Nolan, 2000). Students must be taught how to monitor their own behavior; some of the learning strategies described in Chapter 4 should be helpful. Finally, the teacher should remain friendly with the students and try to catch them in a good moment so he or she can talk to them about something other than their rule breaking. The *Principal's Perspective* tells how one administrator dealt with a few students who caused many problems.

A Principal's Perspective

When T. M. first started as the only administrator in a high school of approximately 500 students, his daily routine included a morning roundup of the students who failed to report to detention the day before. By mid-morning a line-up of new offenders was forming in the outer office, and by lunchtime it stretched out the door and down the hall. Student discipline consumed most of his time, and not only was this daily ritual wearing him out physically and emotionally, it was detracting from the instructional leadership issues he felt most passionately about. His frustration was captured in two questions: What was wrong with the kids at this school, and why couldn't these teachers handle much of their own discipline?

Recalling Ellen Langer's (1989) *Mindfulness* book, he suppressed the automatic administrative inclination to berate the faculty and dictate broad pupil control measures. Instead, he first rigorously collected and carefully analyzed data in order to more accurately understand the problem before attempting to generate a solution. He began charting which teachers referred students to the office, during what time of the day, and for what types of infractions. Wanting to know precisely how much time he was devoting to discipline, he asked his secretary to note what time each student entered and left his office. Just two weeks of data collection revealed some startling trends. Nearly half of his day was consumed by student referrals. More surprising, though, was that a small group of students was causing the most problems. Further, it seemed these students were repeatedly referred to the office by a small number of teachers. Therefore, applying expansive solutions to these very specific problems would not only be inappropriate but also would most certainly prove to be ineffective. A more focused investigation uncovered a particularly volatile mix of sophomores who simply moved from class to class through the course of a day annoying each other until they reached their breaking point at fairly predictable times. Further, he recognized that a majority of the remaining problems occurred during two exceptionally long lunch periods. By adjusting a few of the students' schedules, identifying a few others for much needed behavior intervention, and rebuilding the lunch periods, T. M. was able to reduce the time he spent on discipline by nearly 75% while markedly enhancing the overall learning environment of the school.

Sources: Langer, E. J. (1989). *Mindfulness.* Cambridge, MA: Perseus. Schmoker, M. J., & Wilson, R. B. (1993). *Total quality education.* Bloomington, IN: Phi Delta Kappa.

The defiant, hostile student can pose serious problems. If there is an outbreak, the teacher should try to get out of the situation as soon as possible; everyone loses in a public power struggle. One possibility is for the teacher to give the student a chance to save face and cool down by saying, "It's your choice to cooperate or not. You can take a minute to think about it." If the student complies, they can talk later about controlling the outbursts. If the student refuses to cooperate, the teacher can tell him or her to wait in the hall until he or she gets the class started on work, and can then step outside for a private talk. If the student refuses to leave, teachers should know that they can send another class member for help from the principal or the assistant principal. Again, follow through. If the student complies before help arrives, the teacher should not let him or her off the hook. If outbursts occur frequently, the teacher might arrange a conference with the counselor, parents, or other teachers. If the problem is an irreconcilable clash of personalities, the student should be transferred to another teacher.

It sometimes is useful to keep records of the incidents by logging the student's name, words and actions, date, time, place, and teacher's response. These records may help identify patterns and can prove helpful in meeting with administrators, parents, or special services personnel (Burden, 1995). Some teachers have students sign each entry to verify the incidents.

Violence or destruction of property is a difficult and potentially dangerous problem. For teachers, the first step is to send for help and get the names of participants and witnesses. Then get rid of any crowd that may have gathered; an audience will only make things worse. The teacher should not try to break up a fight without help. Tell teachers to make sure the school office is aware of the incident; the school should have a policy for dealing with these situations.

Programs for Classroom Management

In some situations your teachers may want to consider using a much more formal classroom management system. Two possibilities, based on behavioral principles, are group consequences and functional assessment with positive behavior supports (introduced in Chapter 4).

Group Consequences.   A teacher can base reinforcement for the class on the cumulative behavior of all members of the class, usually by adding each student's points to a class or a team total. The **good behavior game** is an example of this approach. A class is divided into two teams. Specific rules for good behavior are cooperatively developed. Each time a student breaks one of the rules, that student's team is given a mark. The team with the fewest marks at the end of the period receives a special reward or privilege (longer recess, first to lunch, and so on). If both teams earn fewer than a preestablished number of marks, both teams receive the reward. Most studies indicate that even though the game produces only small improvements in academic achievement, it can produce definite improvements in the behaviors listed in the good behavior rules.

However, caution is needed in using group approaches. The whole group should not suffer for the misbehavior or mistakes of one individual if the group has no real influence over that person (Epanchin, Townsend, & Stoddard, 1994; Jenson, Sloane, & Young, 1988). We have seen an entire class break into cheers when the teacher announced that one boy was transferring to another school. The chant "No more points! No more points!" filled the room. The "points" referred to the teacher's system of giving one point to the whole class each time anyone broke a rule. Every point meant 5 minutes of recess lost. The boy who was transferring had been responsible for many losses. He was not very popular to begin with, and the point system, though quite effective in maintaining order, had led to rejection and even greater unpopularity.

Peer pressure in the form of support and encouragement, however, can be a positive influence. **Group consequences** are recommended for situations in which students care about the approval of their peers. If the misbehavior of several students seems to be encouraged by the attention and laughter of other students, then group consequences could be helpful. Teachers might show students how to give support and constructive feedback to classmates. If a few students seem to enjoy sabotaging the system, those students may need separate arrangements.

Positive Behavior Supports: Schoolwide Programs.   Positive behavior supports (PBS), described in Chapter 4, are required under the Individuals with Disabilities Education Act for students with disabilities and those who are being considered for special education services. PBS also can be part of a schoolwide program. At the school level, the teachers and administrators

- Agree on a common approach for supporting positive behaviors and correcting problems.
- Develop a few positively stated, specific behavioral expectations and procedures for teaching these expectations to all students.
- Identify a continuum of ways (from small and simple to more complex and stronger) to acknowledge appropriate behaviors and correct behavioral errors.
- Integrate the positive behavior support procedures with the school's discipline policy.

At the classroom level, teachers are encouraged to use such preventive strategies as **precorrection,** which involves identifying the context for a student's misbehavior, clearly specifying the alternative expected behavior, modifying the situation to make the problem behavior less likely—for example, providing a cue or moving the student away from tempting distractions—and then rehearsing the expected positive behaviors in the new context and providing powerful reinforcers when the behaviors occur. There is an emphasis on keeping students engaged, providing a positive focus, consistently enforcing school/class rules, correcting disruptive behavior proactively, and planning for smooth transitions (Freiberg, 2006; www.pbis.org/schoolwide.htm).

Research on schoolwide positive behavior supports is limited, but results have been good. A study comparing middle school students in a behavioral support program with students outside the program showed that program students reported more positive reinforcement for appropriate behavior. Disciplinary referrals as well as verbal and physical aggression significantly decreased. In addition, students' perceptions of school safety improved (Metzler, Biglan, Rusby & Sprague, 2001). Students in general education may benefit from positive behavior supports as well. Studies of schoolwide PBS efforts indicate decreases in disciplinary referrals (Lewis, Sugai, & Colvin, 1998; Taylor-Green et al., 1997). In addition, Lewis & Sugai (1996) found that successful use of PBS in a general education setting benefited a student with behavioral disorders (Soodak & McCarthy, 2006).

The few pages devoted here to group consequences and PBS can offer only an introduction to these programs. If you want to allow a large-scale reward program in your school, you should probably seek more information. Remember that if they are applied inappropriately, external rewards can undermine the students' motivation to learn (Deci, 1975; Lepper & Greene, 1978). In addition, some people object to the use of rewards; see the *Point/Counterpoint* on the next page for both sides of the debate.

Student Conflicts and Confrontations

Handling conflict is difficult for most of us, and for young people, it can be even harder. Given the public's concern about violence in schools, it is surprising how

POINT/COUNTERPOINT

Should Students Be Rewarded for Learning?

School districts are being held increasingly accountable for achievement results as determined by state and federal reform legislation, and principals are searching more than ever for creative ways to increase student performance. Some elect to contract with private firms to offer lucrative incentives. Others use locally designed rewards programs to lure truant students back to school or to increase effort on standardized tests. From programs as formal as the nationally recognized Jostens Renaissance (http://www.jostens.com/educators/edu_svcs_cp_new_memeber.html) to locally organized drawings for TVs, iPads, and cars to simply exempting students from final exams, schools are offering more and more to students hoping to get better and better performance. But should they?

For years, educators and psychologists have debated whether students should be rewarded for attendance and academic accomplishments. After all, don't laws *require* compulsory attendance and proficiency testing? In the early 1990s, Paul Chance and Alfie Kohn exchanged opinions in several issues of *Phi Delta Kappan* (March 1991; November 1992; June 1993). Then, Judy Cameron and W. David Pierce (1996) published an article on reinforcement in the *Review of Educational Research* that precipitated extensive criticisms and rebuttals in the same journal from Mark Lepper, Mark Keavney, Michael Drake, Alfie Kohn, Richard Ryan, and Edward Deci. Many of the same people exchanged opinions in the November 1999 issue of *Psychological Bulletin*. What are the arguments?

POINT

Students are punished by rewards.
Alfie Kohn (1993) argues that "applied behaviorism, which amounts to saying, 'do this and you'll get that,' is essentially a technique for controlling people. In the classroom it is a way of doing things *to* children rather than working *with* them" (p. 784). He contends that rewards are ineffective because when the praise and prizes stop, the behaviors stop too. After analyzing 128 studies of

extrinsic rewards, Edward Deci, Richard Koestner, and Richard Ryan (1999) concluded that "tangible rewards tend to have a substantial effect on intrinsic motivation, with the limiting conditions we have specified. Even when tangible rewards are offered as indicators of good performance, they typically decrease intrinsic motivation for interesting activities" (pp. 658–659).

The problem with rewards does not stop here. According to Kohn, rewarding students for learning actually makes them less interested in the material.

> All of this means that getting children to think about learning as a way to receive a sticker, a gold star, or a grade—or even worse, to get money or a toy for a grade, which amounts to an extrinsic motivator for an extrinsic motivator—is likely to turn learning from an end into a means. Learning becomes something that must be gotten through in order to receive the reward. Take the depressingly pervasive program by which children receive certificates for pizzas when they have read a certain number of books. John Nicholls of the University of Illinois comments, only half in jest, that the likely consequence of this program is "a lot of fat kids who don't like to read" (p. 785).

COUNTERPOINT

Learning should be rewarding.
According to Paul Chance (1993):

> Behavioral psychologists in particular emphasize that we learn by acting on our environment. As B. F. Skinner put it: "[People] act on the world, and change it, and are changed in turn by the consequences of their actions." Skinner, unlike Kohn, understood that people learn best in a responsive environment. Teachers who praise or otherwise reward student performance provide such an environment. . . . If it is immoral to let students know they have answered questions correctly, to pat students on the back for a good effort, to show joy at a student's understanding of a concept, or to recognize the achievement of a goal by providing a gold star or a certificate—if this is immoral, then count me a sinner. (p. 788)

But don't take Skinner's or Chance's word for it. After all, Skinner wasn't a building principal. The

POINT/COUNTERPOINT   **Continued**

Jostens website offers testimonials from principals and teachers enjoying dramatic increases in student performance and school climate as a result of implementing their incentive program. "IT IS WORKING!! Our discipline referrals are down and our grades are improving," writes one educator. Another adds, "Little incentives do work!"

So, do rewards undermine interest? In their review of research, Cameron and Pierce (1994) conclude, "When tangible rewards (e.g., gold star, money) are offered contingent on performance on a task [not just on participation] or are delivered unexpectedly, intrinsic motivation is maintained" (p. 49). In a later review of research, Eisenberg, Pierce, and Cameron (1999) added that "reward procedures requiring specific high task performance convey a task's personal or social significance, increasing intrinsic motivation" (p. 677). Even psychologists such as Edward Deci and Mark Lepper,

who suggest that rewards might undermine intrinsic motivation, agree that rewards can also be used positively. When rewards provide students with information about their growing mastery of a subject or when the rewards show appreciation for a job well done, then the rewards bolster confidence and make the task more interesting to the students, especially students who lacked ability or interest in the task initially. Nothing succeeds like success. As Chance points out, if students master reading or mathematics with the support of rewards, they will not forget what they have learned when the praise stops. Would they have learned without the rewards? Some would, but some might not have. Would you continue working for a company that didn't pay you, even though you liked the work? Will freelance writer Alfie Kohn, for that matter, lose interest in writing because he gets paid fees and royalties?

little we know about conflicts among students (Johnson, Johnson, Dudley, Ward, & Magnuson, 1995; Rose & Gallup, 2001). There is some evidence that in elementary schools, conflicts most often center on disputes over resources (school supplies, computers, athletic equipment, or toys) and over preferences (which activity to do first or what game to play). Over 35 years ago, a large study of more than 8,000 junior and senior high students and 500 faculty from three major cities concluded that 90% of the conflicts among students are resolved in destructive ways or never resolved at all (DeCecco & Richards, 1974). The few studies since that time have reached similar conclusions. Avoidance, force, and threats seem to be the major strategies for dealing with conflict (Johnson et al., 1995; Johnson & Johnson, 2013).

Bullying and Cyber-Bullying

Bullying is a type of aggression characterized by systematic and repeated abuse of power intended to harm the victim (Merrell, Isava, Gueldner, & Ross, 2008). The line between good-natured exchanges and hostile teasing may seem thin, but a rule of thumb is that teasing someone who is less powerful or less popular or using any racial, ethnic, or religious slur should *not* be tolerated. Between 10% to 30% of children and youth are involved in bullying, and this seems to be the case around the world (Cook, Williams, Guerra, Kim, & Sadek, 2010; Guerra, Williams, & Sadek, 2011). Both bullies and victims are at risk for long-term academic, psychological, and behavioral problems (Swearer, Espelage, Vaillancourt, & Hymel, 2010).

Victims.   Studies from both Europe and the United States indicate that about 10% of children are chronic victims—the constant targets of physical or verbal attacks. One kind of victim tends to have low self-esteem and to feel anxious, lonely, insecure, and unhappy. These students often are prone to crying and withdrawal; in general, when attacked, they won't defend themselves. These victims may believe that they are rejected because they have flaws that they cannot change or control—no wonder they are depressed and helpless! There is a second kind of victim—highly emotional and hot-tempered students who seem to provoke aggressive reactions from their peers. Members of this group have few friends (Pellegrini, Bartini, & Brooks, 1999). Garbarino and deLara (2002) estimate that 160,000 children avoid school every day and thousands more drop out of school altogether because they are always afraid. Children who have been chronic victims through elementary and middle school are more depressed and more likely to attempt suicide as young adults (Graham, 1998; Hodges & Perry, 1999). And students who kill or injure others in schools are more often victims than bullies (Reinke & Herman, 2002a, 2002b). In the past years, we have seen tragic consequences when bullied students turned guns on their tormentors in schools in the United States and in Europe.

Bullying and Teasing.   A longitudinal study that followed a representative sample of 1st through 6th grade students for two years found that aggressive children whose teachers taught them conflict management strategies were moved away from a life path of aggression and violence (Aber, Brown, & Jones, 2003). But when teachers are silent about aggression and teasing, students may "hear" the teacher's agreement with the insult (Weinstein & Novodvorsky, 2011). Table 7.3 presents some ideas for dealing with the latest kind of bullying and teasing—cyber-bullying.

Besides following these guidelines, research has shown that having a strong sense of community in your classroom is associated with more student empathy for the victims of bullying and less "blaming the victim" for being attacked (Gini, 2008). So anything you do to develop class community based on fairness and trust will be a step toward dealing with bullying. In a study of over 2,500 students in 59 schools, Nancy Guerra and her colleagues (2011) found that providing opportunities for success, promoting achievement and self-esteem, and improving teacher–student relationships also help to prevent bullying.

Unfortunately, the results are mixed on the effectiveness of many school-wide bullying prevention programs. Another discouraging finding is that administrators prefer to adopt anti-bullying programs that they heard about from colleagues rather

TABLE 7.3   Ideas for Dealing with Cyber-Bullying

- Develop an explicit policy for acceptable in-school use of the Internet and include it in the school handbook (or your class rules). The policy should spell out what constitutes cyber-bullying and list consequences.
  - Make sure that children and young people are aware that bullying will be dealt with seriously.
  - Ensure that parents/guardians who express cyber-bullying concerns are taken seriously.
  - Explain to students that they
    - Should never share or give out personal information, PIN numbers, phone numbers, etc.
    - Should not delete messages; they do not have to read them, but they should show them to an adult they trust. Messages can be used to take action against cyber-bullies.
    - Should not open a message from someone they don't know.
    - Should *never* reply to the message.
    - Can block the sender's message if they are being bullied through e-mail or instant messaging.
    - Can forward the messages to their Internet Service Provider.
    - Should tell an adult.
    - Should show the message to the police if it contains physical threats.
    - Should speak out against cyber-bullying.
    - Should never send messages when they are angry.
    - Should never send messages they wouldn't want others to see.
- Make parents aware of the fact that all of the major Internet Service Providers offer some form of parental controls. For example, AOL has developed "AOL Guardian," which reports with whom youngsters exchange messages and what Web sites they visit; it also monitors chat rooms for children 13 and under.
  - Encourage parents to keep computers in a public room in the house.
  - Invite members of the local police department to come to school to speak with parents and students about proper Internet use.
- Make sure ethics is included in any computer instruction given at your school.

Source: Table from *Educational psychology*, 12th Edition, by Anita E. Woolfolk. Copyright © 2013 by Pearson Education, Inc. Adapted from *Middle and secondary classroom management: Lessons from research and practice*, 4th Edition, by Carol Simon Weinstein and Ingrid Novodvorsky. Copyright © 2011 by The McGraw-Hill Companies, Inc. Adapted with permission. Printed and Electronically reproduced by permission of Pearson Education, Inc., Upper Saddle River, New Jersey.

than determine if there was any scientific evidence that the programs worked—and many don't (Swearer et al., 2010).

Violence in the Schools

"Even though violence in high schools is actually decreasing, interpersonal violence among youth is a concern for parents and teachers" (Lowry, Sleet, Duncan, Powell, & Kolbe, 1995). Every day in the United States, eight children or youth under the age of twenty are killed by firearms and 186 are arrested for violent crimes (CDF, 2012). Young people ages twelve to twenty-four are the most likely victims of nonfatal violence in U.S. society, and many of these attacks happen on school property. This problem has many causes, and it is a challenge for every element of society. What can the schools do? The *Theory into Action Guidelines* on the next page have some ideas for handling potentially explosive situations.

THEORY INTO ACTION GUIDELINES

Handling Potentially Explosive Situations

Move slowly and deliberately toward the problem situation.

Examples
1. Walk slowly; then be as still as possible.
2. Establish eye-level position.

Be respectful.

Examples
1. Keep a reasonable distance.
2. Do not crowd the student. Do not get "in the student's face."
3. Speak respectfully. Use the student's name.
4. Avoid pointing or gesturing.

Be brief.

Examples
1. Avoid long-winded statements or nagging.
2. Stay with the agenda. Stay focused on the problem at hand. Do not get sidetracked.
3. Deal with less severe problems later.

Avoid power struggles.

Examples
1. Speak privately if possible.
2. Do not get drawn into "I won't, you will" arguments.
3. Don't make threats or raise your voice.

Inform the student of the expected behavior and the negative consequence as a choice or decision for the student to make. Then withdraw from the student and allow some time for the student to decide.

Examples
1. "Michael, you need to return to your desk, or I will have to send for the principal. You have a few seconds to decide." The teacher then moves away, perhaps attending to other students.
2. If Michael does not choose the appropriate behavior, deliver the negative consequences. ("You are choosing to have me call the principal.") Follow through with the consequence.

Source: Excerpt from *Educational psychology*, 12th Edition, by Anita E. Woolfolk. Copyright © 2013 by Pearson Education, Inc. Adapted from *Middle and secondary classroom management: Lessons from research and practice*, 4th Edition, by Carol Simon Weinstein and Ingrid Novodvorsky. Copyright © 2011 by The McGraw-Hill Companies, Inc. Adapted with permission. Printed and Electronically reproduced by permission of Pearson Education, Inc., Upper Saddle River, New Jersey.

Prevention.   Violence prevention should be a part of every school program. Some Chicano gang members in Chicago reported that they turned to gang activities when their teachers insulted them, called them names, humiliated them publicly, belittled their culture, ignored them in class, or blamed all negative incidents on particular students. The students reported joining gangs for security and to escape teachers who treated them badly or expected little of them because they were Latino (Padilla, 1992; Parks, 1995). We once asked a gifted educator in an urban New Jersey high school which teachers were most effective with the really tough students. He said there are two kinds: teachers who can't be intimidated or fooled and expect their students to learn, and teachers who really care about the students. When we asked, "Which kind are you?" he answered "Both!"

Besides prevention, schools can also establish mentoring programs, conflict resolution training, social skills training, more relevant curricula, and parent and community involvement programs (Padilla, 1992; Parks, 1995). One intervention that seems to be helpful is peer mediation.

Peer Mediation.   David Johnson and his colleagues provided conflict resolution training—**peer mediation**—to 227 students in 2nd through 5th grades. Students learned a five-step negotiating strategy:

1. *Jointly define the conflict.* Separate the person from the problem and the actions involved, avoid win–lose thinking, get both parties' goals clear.
2. *Exchange positions and interests.* Present a tentative proposal and make a case for it; listen to the other person's proposal and feelings; and stay flexible and cooperative.
3. *Reverse perspectives.* See the situation from the other person's point of view and reverse roles and argue for that perspective.
4. *Invent at least three agreements that allow mutual gain.* Brainstorm, focus on goals, think creatively, and make sure everyone has power to invent solutions.
5. *Reach an integrative agreement.* Make sure both sets of goals are met. If all else fails, flip a coin, take turns, or call in a third party as a mediator.

In addition to learning conflict resolution, all students in Johnson and Johnson's study were trained in mediation strategies. The role of the mediator was rotated. Every day the teacher chose two students to be the class mediators and to wear the mediator's T-shirt. Johnson and his colleagues found that students learned the conflict resolution and mediation strategies and used them successfully, both in school and at home, to handle conflicts in a more productive way. For details of the strategies, see David and Roger Johnson (1994, 2005) or David and Frank Johnson (2013).

Peer mediation has also been successful with older students and serious problems (Sanchez & Anderson, 1990). In one program, selected gang members were given mediation training, and then all members were invited to participate voluntarily in the mediation process, supervised by school counselors. Strict rules governed the process leading to written agreements signed by gang representatives. Sanchez and Anderson (1990) found that gang violence in the school was reduced to a bare minimum: "The magic of the mediation process was communication" (p. 56).

Summing It Up: Learning Environments for All Students

We have examined a number of approaches to classroom student discipline. Are some better than others? Research provides some guidance.

Research on Different Management Approaches

Emmer and Aussiker (1990) conducted a meta-analysis of three general perspectives on management: influencing students through listening and problem solving, as described by Gordon (2003); group management through class meetings and student discussion, as advocated by Glasser (1969, 1990); and control through rewards and punishments as exemplified by Canter and Canter (1997). No clear conclusions could be drawn about the impact of these approaches on student behaviors. However, some evaluations have found positive effects for Freiberg's (2012; Freiberg & Lamb, 2009) Consistency Management program and for programs that use rewards and punishments (Lewis, 2001).

In a study conducted in Australia, Ramon Lewis (2001) found that recognizing and rewarding appropriate student behaviors, talking with students about how their behavior affects others, involving students in class discipline decisions, and providing nondirective hints and description about unacceptable behaviors were associated with students taking greater responsibility for their own learning. It is interesting that these interventions represent all three of the general approaches reviewed by Emmer and Aussiker: *influence*, *group management*, and *control*. In a study of over 3,000 9th grade students in Singapore, Youyan Nie and Shun Lau (2009) found that both caring and control were positively related to student engagement, so blending control, influence, caring, and group management strategies may be necessary in order to create positive learning environments. This is not always easy. Lewis also concluded that teachers sometimes find using caring, influence, and group management difficult when students are aggressive—and most in need of these positive approaches. When teachers feel threatened, it can be difficult for them to do what students need, but that may be the most important time to act positively and combine caring with control.

Culturally Responsive Management

Research on discipline shows that African Americans and Latino Americans, especially males, are punished more often and more harshly than other students. These students lose time from learning as they spend more hours in detention or suspension (Gay, 2006; Monroe & Obidah, 2002; Skiba, Michael, Nardo, & Peterson, 2000). Why?

The notion that African American and Latino American students are punished more because they commit more serious offenses is not supported by the data. Instead, these students are punished more severely for minor offenses such as rudeness or defiance—words and actions that are interpreted by teachers as meriting severe punishment. One explanation is a lack of cultural synchronization between teachers and students. "The language, style of walking, glances, and dress of black children, particularly males, have engendered fear, apprehension, and overreaction among many teachers and school administrators" (Irvine, 1990, p. 27). African American students may be disciplined for behaviors that were never intended to be disruptive or disrespectful. Teachers do their students and themselves a service if they work at becoming bicultural—helping their students to learn how to function in both mainstream and home cultures, but also learning the meaning of their students' words and actions so they do not misinterpret and then punish their students' unintended insults (Gay, 2006).

Culturally responsive management is simply a part of the larger concept of culturally relevant teaching. Geneva Gay (2006) sums it up:

> If the classroom is a comfortable, caring, embracing, affirming, engaging, and facilitative place for students then discipline is not likely to be much of an issue. It follows then that both classroom management and school achievement can be improved for students from

different ethnic, racial, social, and linguistic backgrounds by ensuring that curriculum and instruction are culturally relevant and personally meaningful for them. (p. 364)*

We once asked a gifted African American educator in an urban New Jersey high school which teachers were most effective with the really tough students. He said there are two kinds: teachers who can't be intimidated or fooled and expect their students to learn, and teachers who really care about their students. When we asked, "Which kind are you?" he answered "Both!" He is an example of a "warm demander," a teacher who seems to be most effective with students placed at risk (Irving, 2003; Irvine & Armento, 2001).

Warm demanders are no-nonsense teachers whose classroom environments are structured and disciplined. They set the bar high for their students and then provide the academic and emotional support needed, so students can reach that high standard. These teachers know that pity or looking the other way when students don't perform is just another message to their students that they lack the ability or motivation to succeed—and warm demanders will have none of that. For example, one 1st grade teacher firmly told a student who was telling a story to "sit down" because his story had wandered off the theme he was supposed to be developing. The teacher would not allow the student to avoid the assignment by playing the fool, being a comedian, and entertaining the class (Irving & Armento, 1998). To an outside observer, the teacher may have seemed mean, but she was really committed to her students and determined to teach them effectively.

This warm demander style is consistent with the research on effective parenting styles. The early work on parental styles by Diane Baumrind (1996) found that *authoritative parents*—those who are high on warmth and high on control—have children who do well in school and get along with others. These parents set clear limits, enforce rules, and expect mature behavior. But they are warm with their children. They listen to concerns, give reasons for rules, and allow more democratic decision making. There is less strict punishment and more guidance. These parents help children think through the consequences of their actions (Hoffman, 2001).

Much of the early work on parenting styles has focused on European American middle-class families. But cultures differ in parenting styles. Research indicates that even higher control, more authoritarian parenting is linked to better grades for Asian and African American students. Parenting that is strict and directive, with clear rules and consequences, combined with high levels of warmth and emotional support, is associated with higher academic achievement and greater emotional maturity for inner-city children (Garner & Spears, 2000).

Many African American students may be more accustomed to a directive kind of management and discipline outside of school. Their families might say, "Put down that candy" or "Go to bed" whereas white parents might ask, "Can we eat candy before dinner?" or "Isn't it time for bed?" As H. Richard Milner (2006) says, "The question should not be which approach is right or wrong but which approach works with and connects with the students' prior knowledge and ways of knowing" (p. 498).

Source: "Connections between classroom management and culturally responsive teaching" by Geneva Gay, from *Handbook of classroom managment: Research, practice, and contemporary issues,* edited by Carolyn M. Evertson and Carol Simon Weinstein. Lawrence Erlbaum Associates, 2006.

Listening to Students and Teachers

Recently researchers have examined students' and teachers' perceptions about classroom management (see Woolfolk Hoy & Weinstein, 2006, for a review). Good classroom management from the students' perspective requires a fair and reasonable system of classroom rules, and procedures that protect and respect students. Teachers are expected to care for the students, their learning, and their personal lives, before the students will respect and cooperate with the teachers. Students want teachers to maintain order without being mean or punitive, and the students don't mind differential treatment as long as there is no racism, sexism, or favoritism. As they mature, students value choices and chances for responsibilities; they do not want to feel coerced or controlled.

Teachers, in contrast, seem to believe that students need to earn their respect, relationship, concern, and interest—in a word, their caring. Choices and autonomy come with successful student self-regulation and not before. And some teachers believe that being "mean" may be necessary, in the beginning at least, to establish authority: Don't smile until Christmas. Often with pressures on the teachers to raise test scores and maintain order come more directive and punitive control strategies.

The problem inherent in these contrasting views of good classroom management is a possible downward spiral of mistrust. Students withhold their cooperation until teachers "earn it" with their authentic caring. Teachers withhold caring until students "earn it" with respect for authority and cooperation. Marginalized students actually *expect* unfair treatment and behave defensively. Teachers get tough, interrogate, and punish. Students feel correct in mistrusting, and become more guarded and defiant. Teachers feel correct in mistrusting and become more controlling and punitive, and so it goes (Woolfolk Hoy & Weinstein, 2006).

This cycle is consistent with Bandura's (1997) theory of reciprocal determinism. If personal factors, behaviors, and the environment are in constant interaction, then cycles of events are progressive and self-perpetuating. For example, suppose a new student walks into class late. The student has a tattoo and several visible pierced body parts. He is actually anxious and hopes to do better at this new school, but the teacher's initial reaction to his late entry and dramatic appearance is a bit hostile. The student feels insulted and responds in kind, so the teacher begins to form expectations about him and acts more vigilant and less trusting. The student decides that this school will be just as worthless as his previous one, so why bother to try. The teacher sees the student's disengagement, invests less effort in teaching him, and the cycle goes on. A challenge for instructional leaders is to help both students and teachers avoid this downward spiral of mistrust.

Communicating with Families about Classroom Management

As we discuss throughout this book, families are important partners in education. This statement applies to classroom management as well. When parents and teachers share the same expectations and support each other, they can create a more positive classroom environment and more time for learning. The *Theory into Action Guidelines* provide ideas for principals and teachers as they work with families and the community.

THEORY INTO ACTION GUIDELINES

Working with Families

Make sure families know the expectations and rules of your class and school.

Examples

1. At a Family Fun Night, have your students do skits showing the rules—how to follow them and what breaking them "looks like" and "sounds like."
2. Make a poster for the refrigerator at home that describes, in a light way, the most important rules and expectations.
3. For older students, give families a list of due dates for the major assignments, along with tips about how to encourage quality work by pacing the effort—avoiding last-minute panic.
4. Communicate in appropriate ways—use the family's first language when possible. Tailor messages to the reading level of the home.

Make families partners in recognizing good citizenship.

Examples

1. Send positive notes home when students, especially students who have had trouble with classroom management, work well in the classroom.
2. Give ideas for ways any family, even those with few economic resources, can celebrate

accomplishment—a favorite food; the chance to choose a video to rent; a comment to a special person such as an aunt, grandparent, or minister; the chance to read to a younger sibling.

Identify talents in the community to help build a learning environment in your class.

Examples

1. Have students write letters to carpet and furniture stores asking for donations of remnants to carpet a reading corner.
2. Find family members who can build shelves or room dividers, paint, sew, laminate manipulative materials, write stories, repot plants, or network computers.
3. Contact businesses for donations of computers, printers, or other equipment.

Seek cooperation from families when behavior problems arise.

Examples

1. Talk to families over the phone or in their home. Have good records about the problem behavior.
2. Listen to family members and solve problems with them.

Summary

Classrooms are by nature multidimensional, full of simultaneous activities, fast-paced and immediate, unpredictable, public, and affected by the history of students' and teachers' actions. A classroom manager must juggle all these elements every day.

Productive classroom activity requires students' cooperation. Maintaining cooperation is different for each age group. Young students are learning how to "go to school" and need to learn the general procedures of school. Older students need to learn the specifics required for working in different subjects. Working with adolescents requires teachers to understand the power of the adolescent peer group.

The goals of effective classroom management are to make more time for learning and improve the quality of time use by keeping students actively engaged; provide access to learning for all students by making sure participation structures are clear, straightforward, and consistently signaled; and encourage student self-management. The most effective teachers set rules and establish procedures for handling predictable problems. Procedures should cover administrative tasks, student movement, housekeeping, routines for running lessons, interactions between students and teachers, and interactions among students. Consequences should be established for following and breaking the rules and procedures so that the teacher and the students know what will happen. Encouraging self-management requires extra time, but teaching students how to take responsibility for their actions is an investment well worth the effort.

For effective classroom management, it is essential to spend the first days of class teaching basic rules and procedures. Students should be occupied with organized, enjoyable activities and learn to function cooperatively in the group. Quick, firm, clear, and consistent responses to infractions of the rules characterize effective teachers. To create a positive environment and prevent problems, teachers must take individual differences into account, maintain student motivation, and reinforce positive behavior. Successful problem preventers are skilled in four areas described by Kounin: "with-it-ness," overlapping, group focusing, and movement management. When penalties have to be imposed, teachers should impose them calmly and privately.

There are several special procedures that may be helpful in maintaining positive management, including group consequences and functional assessment with behavior supports. A teacher must use these procedures with caution, emphasizing learning and not just "good" behavior.

Research on discipline shows that African Americans and Latino Americans, especially males, are punished more often and more harshly than other students. This raises the question of culturally responsive management. Both classroom management and school achievement can be improved for students from different ethnic, racial, social, and linguistic backgrounds by ensuring that curriculum and instruction are culturally relevant and personally meaningful for them.

Between 10% to 30% of children and youth are involved in bullying, and this seems to be the case around the world. Both bullies and victims are at risk for long-term academic, psychological, and behavioral problems, but aggressive children whose teachers taught them conflict management strategies can move away from a life path of aggression and violence. Cyber-bullying is a new way of attacking students outside the schools. Students need to be taught how to be safe online.

Communication between teacher and student is essential when problems arise. All interactions between people, even silence or neglect, communicate some meaning. Teachers often have to take the initiative in establishing trusting relationships with students, especially students who have had unpleasant experiences with schools. Students need guidance in resolving conflicts. Different strategies are useful, depending on whether the goal, the relationship, or both are important to those experiencing conflict. It can help to reverse roles and see the situation through the eyes of the other. In dealing with serious problems, prevention and peer mediation might be useful. No matter what the situation, the cooperation of families can help to create a positive learning environment in your classroom and school.

KEY TERMS

academic learning time (226)

classroom management (225)

culturally responsive management (254)

good behavior game (246)

group consequences (246)

group focus (240)

movement management (241)

overlapping (240)

peer mediation (253)

precorrection (247)

routines/procedures (229)

rules (229)

self-management (227)

time on-task (226)

warm demanders (255)

with-it-ness (240)

DEVELOPING YOUR PORTFOLIO

1. Reread the case at the beginning of this chapter and assume you are the principal at that school. Develop a plan for first working with this teacher and then consider a general policy on classroom management for Samuel Proctor Elementary School. Be sure to consider the following issues:
   a. How would you approach the situation? Who should be involved?
   b. Which problem behaviors should the teacher tackle first?
   c. Would giving rewards or administering punishments be useful in this situation? Why or why not?
   d. What specific suggestions would you give to this teacher?
   e. What action would you take?
   f. Should there be a schoolwide policy?
   g. Who should be involved in the development of the school policy, if needed?

2. Write a first-of-the-year newsletter for families describing your school's rules, procedures, and discipline actions. Be sure to include the following:
   a. General school rules
   b. Policy on teacher rules in the classroom
   c. Homework requirements
   d. Policies on tardiness and absences
   e. Behavior on school property
   f. Policy on suspension and expulsion
   g. Other key aspects of a good citizen policy

   Your challenge is to be clear, firm, precise, and yet humanistic and open—not an easy task.

3. Draw a floor plan of a classroom in your school, one that could be improved in its physical arrangement.
   a. Interview the teacher about his or her learning objectives and management issues.
   b. With the teacher, redesign the classroom space (furniture, workstations, storage, and so on) so that the design supports both learning and management goals.

   Your final project should include both before and after maps of the classroom, with an explicit rationale for each change.

INSTRUCTIONAL LEADER'S TOOLBOX

Readings

Emmer, E. T., & Evertson, C. M. (2013). *Classroom management for secondary teachers* (9th ed.). Boston: Allyn & Bacon.

Evertson, C. M., & Emmer, E. T. (2013*). Classroom management for elementary teachers* (9th ed.). Boston: Allyn & Bacon.

Johnson, D., & Johnson, R. (1999). The three Cs of school and classroom management. In H. J. Freiberg (Ed.), *Beyond behaviorism: Changing the classroom management paradigm* (pp. 119–144). Boston: Allyn & Bacon.

Weinstein, C. S., & Novodvorsky, I. (2011). *Middle and secondary classroom management: Lessons from research and practice* (5th ed.). New York: McGraw-Hill.

Weinstein, C. S., Romano, M. E., & Mignano, A. J. (2011). *Elementary classroom management: Lessons from research and practice* (5th ed.). New York: McGraw-Hill.

Woolfolk Hoy, A., & Weinstein, C. S. (2006). Students' and teachers' perspectives on classroom management. In C. Evertson & C. S. Weinstein (Eds.), *Handbook for classroom management: Research, practice, and contemporary issues* (pp. 181–220). Mahwah, NJ: Lawrence Erlbaum.

Video

Discipline and the law, 29 minutes. Addresses legal questions about teachers' rights to discipline children. Available from Insight Media, 2162 Broadway, New York, NY 10024.

Websites

www.stophitting.com/
Center for Effective Discipline
www.honorlevel.com
Discipline by Design
www.disciplinehelp.com/teacher/
The Master Teacher: An online resource for teachers identifying causes of misbehavior in school and needs of the child
www.kappanmagazine.org/
Phi Delta Kappan (see the September issue for the Annual PDK/Gallup Poll of the Public's Attitudes toward the Public Schools)

www.positivediscipline.com/
Positive Discipline
www.proteacher.com/030000.shtml
Proteacher Online Community, practical classroom management tips and resources
www.teachnet.com/how-to/manage/
Resources for teachers

Organizations

www.coe.uh.edu/cmcd/default.cfm
Consistency Management and Cooperative Discipline
H. Jerome Freiberg, University of Houston
College of Education
Houston, TX 77204–5872
Phone: 713-743-8663
www.clcrc.com
Roger T. Johnson and David W. Johnson
The Cooperative Learning Center, 60 Peik Hall, University of Minnesota
Minneapolis, MN 55455
Phone: 612-624-7031

Assessing Student Learning

PREVIEW: KEY POINTS

1. All teaching involves assessing and evaluating learning—that is, collecting information and making judgments about student performance.

2. There are two general types of tests: norm-referenced and criterion-referenced.

3. Criterion-referenced tests are scored using a fixed standard or minimum passing score, whereas norm-referenced tests are scored by comparing individuals with others who have taken the same test; that is, group *norms* are used to evaluate performance.

4. When norms are used, test scores are standardized as a percentile score, grade-equivalent score, or as a standard score such as a z score, T score, or stanine score. All good tests are reliable and valid.

5. There are three broad categories of standardized tests: achievement, diagnostic, and aptitude, each with a different purpose.

6. Achievement tests measure how much a student has learned in specific content areas; diagnostic tests identify specific learning problems; and aptitude tests measure abilities developed over many years and are used to predict how well a student will learn unfamiliar material in the future.

7. High-stakes, standardized testing has both positive and negative consequences; on the positive side, these tests hold teachers and students accountable, but on the negative side, they narrow the curriculum and often push out of school students who believe they are going to fail the high school graduation test.

8. Authentic assessment, portfolios, and exhibitions are alternative ways to assess and evaluate student performance in a realistic context.

9. Informal assessments, such as student journals, are ungraded (formative) assessments that gather information from multiple sources to help teachers make decisions.

10. Grades and high standards have both positive and negative consequences for students, but grades do not necessarily motivate students to learn. There is a difference between working for a grade and working to learn.

Leadership Challenge

You are the principal of Washington Middle School. April, one of your beginning 7th-grade teachers, has come to you with a question. First, she shares a computer printout with you showing the results of the fall testing, including scores on a group test of intelligence for all the 7th-grade students in her class. The printouts have been distributed to all teachers in the school by the guidance department. Then she shows you notes from two parents. They want to meet with April to see their child's scores, and especially, as one parent put it, "To find out how smart Jason really is." You look at the printouts and at the parental requests, as April asks you for advice on what to do.

1. What do the intelligence test scores tell you about these students?
2. How do you suggest that April respond to the request from the parents?
3. Do you need to talk to the guidance department about the purpose of the data?
4. Do you need a school policy on testing results?

Evaluation, Measurement, and Assessment

All teaching involves assessing and evaluating learning. At the heart of assessment is judgment, making decisions based on values. In the process of evaluation, we compare outcomes and information to some set of criteria and then make judgments. Principals and teachers must make all kinds of judgments. "Should we use a different text next year? Will Sarah do better if she repeats the first grade? Are the students ready for the proficiency testing?"

Measurement is evaluation put in quantitative terms, the numeric description of an event or characteristic. Measurement tells how much, how often, or how well a task has been accomplished by providing scores, ranks, or ratings. Instead of saying, "Sarah doesn't seem to understand addition," a teacher might say, "Sarah answered only 2 of the 15 problems correctly in her addition homework." Measurement also allows a school to compare one student's performance on one particular task either with a standard or with the performances of the other students. When we think of measurement, we often think of paper-and-pencil tests. Not all the evaluative decisions made by teachers and principals involve measurement. Some decisions are based on information that is difficult to express numerically: teacher preferences, information from parents, previous experiences, even intuition. But measurement does play a large role in many school and classroom decisions, and, properly done, it can provide unbiased data for evaluations.

Increasingly, evaluation and measurement specialists are using the term **assessment** to describe the process of gathering information about students' learning. Assessment is broader than testing and measurement. Assessment is "any of a variety of procedures used to obtain information about student performance" (Linn & Gronlund, 2000, p. 32). Assessments can be formal, such as unit tests, or informal, such as observing who emerges as a leader in a group of teachers or students. Assessments can be designed by classroom teachers or by local, state, or national agencies such as school districts or the Educational Testing Service. And today, assessments can go well beyond paper-and-pencil exercises to include observations of performances and the development of portfolios and artifacts (Popham, 2011). In this chapter, we examine formal assessments designed by groups and agencies outside the school as well as teacher-made assessment devices. Many of these assessment techniques usually involve testing and the reporting of scores, so we will start by examining two types of tests.

Formative and Summative Assessment

There are two general uses or functions for assessment: formative and summative. **Formative assessment** occurs before or during instruction. The purposes of formative assessment are to guide the teacher in planning and improving instruction and to help students improve learning. In other words, formative assessment helps form instruction and provides feedback that is "nonevaluative, supportive, timely, and specific" (Shute, 2008, p. 153). Often students are given a formative test prior to instruction, a **pretest** that helps the teacher determine what students already know. Sometimes a test is given during instruction to see what areas of weakness remain so teaching can be directed toward the specific problem areas. These formative tests are not graded, so students who tend to be very anxious about "real" tests may find this low-pressure practice in test taking especially helpful.

Summative assessment occurs at the end of instruction. Its purpose is to let the teacher and the students know the level of accomplishment attained. Summative assessment, therefore, provides a summary of accomplishment. The final exam is a classic example.

The distinction between formative and summative assessment is based on how the results are used. And any kind of assessment—traditional, performance, project, oral, portfolio, and so on—can be used for either formative or summative purposes. If the purpose of the assessment is to improve your teaching and help students guide their own learning, then the evaluation is *formative*. But if the purpose is to evaluate final achievement (and help determine a course grade), the assessment is *summative* (Nitko & Brookhart, 2011). In fact, the same assessment could be used as a formative evaluation at the beginning of the unit and as a summative evaluation at the end. Table 8.1 gives some examples of different uses of assessment.

The formative uses of assessment are really the most important in teaching. In fact, Popham believes "any teacher who uses tests dominantly to determine whether students get high or low grades should receive a solid F in classroom assessment" (2008, p. 256). Tests and all assessments should be used to help teachers make better instructional decisions.

The answers given on any type of test have no meaning by themselves; we must make some kind of comparison to interpret test results. There are two basic types of comparison: In the first, a test score is compared to the scores obtained by other people who have taken the same test, a *norm-referenced* comparison. The second type

TABLE 8.1   Using Tests to Make Instructional Decisions

The best use of assessment is to plan, guide, and target instruction. Here are some decisions that can benefit from assessment results.

Decision Category	Typical Assessment Strategy	Decision Options
What to teach in the first place?	Preassessment before instruction	Whether to provide instruction for specific objectives.
How long to keep teaching toward a particular instructional objective?	En route assessments of students' progress	Whether to continue or cease instruction for an objective either for an individual or for the whole class.
How effective was an instructional sequence?	Comparing students' posttest to pretest performances	Whether to retain, discard, or modify a given instructional sequence the next time it's used.

Source: Table from *Educational psychology*, 12th Edition, by Anita E. Woolfolk. Copyright © 2013 by Pearson Education, Inc. *Adapted from Classroom assessment: What teachers need to know*, 4th Edition, by James W. Popham. Copyright © 2005 by Pearson Education, Inc. Printed and Electronically reproduced by permission of Pearson Education, Inc., Upper Saddle River, New Jersey.

is *criterion-referenced* comparison. Here, the comparison is to a fixed standard or minimum passing score.

Norm-Referenced Tests

In **norm-referenced testing,** the people who have taken the test provide the *norms* for determining the meaning of a given individual's score. You can think of a norm as being the typical level of performance for a particular group. By comparing the individual's raw score (the actual number correct) to the norm, we can determine if the score is above, below, or around the average for that group. There are at least three types of **norm groups** (comparison groups) in education: the class or school itself, the school district, and national samples.

Norm-referenced tests cover a wide range of general objectives rather than assessing a limited number of specific objectives. Norm-referenced tests are especially useful in measuring the overall achievement of students who have come to understand complex material by different routes. Norm-referenced tests are also appropriate when only the top few candidates can be admitted to a program.

However, norm-referenced measurement has its limitations. The results of a norm-referenced test do not tell you whether students are ready to move on to more advanced material. For instance, knowing that a student is in the top 3% of the class on a test of algebraic concepts will not tell you if he or she is ready to move on to geometry; everyone else in the class may have a limited understanding of the algebraic concepts.

Norm-referenced tests also are not particularly appropriate for measuring affective and psychomotor objectives. To measure individuals' psychomotor learning, you need a clear description of standards. (Even the best gymnast in school performs certain exercises better than others and needs specific guidance about how to improve.) In the affective area, attitudes and values are personal; comparisons among individuals are not really appropriate. For example, how could we measure an "average" level of political values or opinions? Finally, norm-referenced tests tend to encourage competition and comparison of scores. Some students compete to be the best. Others, realizing that being the best is impossible, may compete to be the worst. Either goal has its casualties.

Criterion-Referenced Tests

When test scores are compared, not to those of others but to a given criterion or standard of performance, this is **criterion-referenced testing.** To decide who should be allowed to drive a car, it is important to determine just what standard of performance is appropriate for selecting safe drivers. It does not matter how your test results compare to the results of others. If your performance on the test was in the top 10%, but you consistently ran through red lights, you would not be a good candidate for receiving a license, even though your score was high.

Criterion-referenced tests measure the mastery of very specific objectives. The results of a criterion-referenced test should tell parents, teachers, and principals exactly

TABLE 8.2   Deciding on the Type of Test to Use

Norm-referenced tests may work best when you are

- Measuring general ability in certain areas, such as English, algebra, general science, or U.S. history.
- Assessing the range of abilities in a large group.
- Selecting top candidates when only a few openings are available.

Criterion-referenced tests may work best when you are

- Measuring mastery of basic skills.
- Determining if students have prerequisites to start a new unit.
- Assessing affective and psychomotor objectives.
- Providing evidence that students have met learning standards.
- Grouping students for instruction.

Source: Table from *Educational psychology*, active learning edition, 10th Edition, by Anita E. Woolfolk. Copyright © 2008 by Pearson Education, Inc. Printed and Electronically reproduced by permission of Pearson Education, Inc., Upper Saddle River, New Jersey.

what the students can and cannot do, at least under certain conditions. For example, a criterion-referenced test would be useful in measuring the ability to add three-digit numbers. A test could be designed with 20 different problems, and the standard for mastery could be set at 17 correct out of 20. (The standard is often somewhat arbitrary and may be based on such things as the teacher's experience.) If two students receive scores of 7 and 11, it does not matter that one student did better than the other because neither met the standard of 17. Both need more help with addition.

Criterion-referenced tests, however, are not appropriate for every situation. Many subjects cannot be broken down into a set of specific objectives. Moreover, although standards are important in criterion-referenced testing, they can often be arbitrary, as you have already seen. When deciding whether a student has mastered the addition of three-digit numbers comes down to the difference between 16 versus 17 correct answers, it seems difficult to justify one particular standard over another. Finally, at times it is valuable to know how the students in your school compare to other students at their grade level both locally and nationally. Table 8.2 offers a comparison of norm-referenced and criterion-referenced tests. You can see that each type of test is well suited for certain situations, but each also has its limitations.

What Do Test Scores Mean?

Millions of standardized tests are given every year. Most of these are norm-referenced standardized tests. **Standardized tests** are called *standardized* because "the same directions are used for administering them in all classrooms and standard procedures are used for scoring and interpreting them" (Carey, 1994, p. 443). Standard methods of developing items, administering the test, scoring it, and reporting the scores are all implied by the term *standardized test*.

Basic Concepts

In standardized testing, the test items and instructions have been tried out to make sure they work and then rewritten and retested as necessary. The final version of the test is administered to a **norming sample,** a large sample of subjects as similar as possible to the students who will be taking the test in school systems throughout the country. This norming sample serves as a comparison group for all students who take the test. Hence, standardized tests typically come with norms. Let's look at some of the measurements on which normative comparisons and interpretations are based.

Measurements of Central Tendency and Standard Deviation.   You have probably had a great deal of experience with means. A **mean** is simply the arithmetical average of a group of scores. The mean offers one way of measuring **central tendency,** the score that is typical or representative of the whole distribution of scores.

Two other measures of central tendency are the median and the mode. The **median** is the middle score in the distribution, the point at which half the scores are larger and half are smaller. The **mode** is the score that occurs most often. If two scores tie for the most frequent, we have a *bimodal* distribution.

The measure of central tendency gives a score that is representative of the group of scores, but it does not tell you anything about how the scores are distributed. Two groups of scores may both have a mean of 50, but be alike in no other way. One group might contain the scores 50, 45, 55, 55, 45, 50, 50; the other group might contain the scores 100, 0, 50, 90, 10, 50, 50. In both cases the mean, median, and mode are all 50, but the distributions are quite different.

The **standard deviation** is a measure of how widely the scores vary from the mean. The larger the standard deviation is, the more spread out the scores are in the distribution. The smaller the standard deviation is, the more the scores are clustered around the mean. For example, in the distribution 50, 45, 55, 55, 45, 50, 50, the standard deviation is much smaller than in the distribution 100, 0, 50, 90, 10, 50, 50. Another way of saying this is that distributions with very small standard deviations have less variability in their scores.

Knowing the mean and the standard deviation of a group of scores gives you a better picture of the meaning of an individual score. For example, suppose you received a score of 78 on a test. You would be very pleased with the score if the mean of the test were 70 and the standard deviation were 4. In this case, your score would be 2 standard deviations above the mean, a score well above average.

Consider the difference if the mean of the test had remained at 70 but the standard deviation had been 20. In the second case, your score of 78 would be less than 1 standard deviation from the mean. You would be much closer to the middle of the group, with a score above average, but not that high. Knowing the standard deviation tells you much more than simply knowing the **range** of scores. No matter how the majority scored on the tests, one or two students may do very well or very poorly and thus make the range very large.

The Normal Distribution.   Standard deviations are very useful in understanding test results. They are especially helpful if the results of the tests form a normal

FIGURE 8.1 The Normal Distribution
The normal distribution or bell-shaped curve has certain predictable characteristics. For example, 68% of the scores are clustered between 1 standard deviation below and 1 standard deviation above the mean.

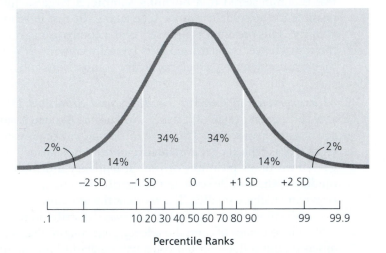

Percentile Ranks

Source: Figure from *Educational psychology*, 12th Edition, by Anita E. Woolfolk. Copyright © 2013 by Pearson Education, Inc. Printed and Electronically reproduced by permission of Pearson Education, Inc., Upper Saddle River, New Jersey.

distribution. You have encountered the **normal distribution** before. It is the bell-shaped curve, the most famous frequency distribution because it describes many naturally occurring physical and social phenomena. Many scores fall in the middle, giving the curve its bell shape. You find fewer and fewer scores as you look out toward the end points, or *tails*, of the distribution. The normal distribution has been thoroughly analyzed by statisticians. The mean of a normal distribution is also its midpoint. Half the scores are above the mean, and half are below it. In a normal distribution, the mean, median, and mode are all the same point.

Another convenient property of the normal distribution is that the percentage of scores falling within each area of the curve is known, as you can see in Figure 8.1.

A person scoring within 1 standard deviation of the mean obviously has company. Many scores pile up here. In fact, 68% of all scores are located in the area from 1 standard deviation below to 1 standard deviation above the mean. About 16% of the scores are higher than 1 standard deviation above the mean. Of this higher group, only 2% are better than 2 standard deviations above the mean. Similarly, only about 16% of the scores are less than 1 standard deviation below the mean, and of that group only about 2% are worse than 2 standard deviations below. At 2 standard deviations from the mean in either direction, the scorer has little company.

The SAT college entrance exam and the GRE test are examples of exams with normal distributions. The mean is 500 and the standard deviation is 100. If you know people who made scores in the 700s, you know they did very well. Only about 2% of the people who take the test do that well, because only 2% of the scores are better than 2 standard deviations above the mean in a normal distribution.

Types of Scores

Now you have enough background for a discussion of the different kinds of scores you may encounter in reports of results from standardized tests.

Percentile Rank Scores.   The concept of ranking is the basis for one very useful kind of score reported on standardized tests, a **percentile rank** score. In percentile ranking, each student's raw score is compared with the raw scores of the students in the norming sample. The percentile rank shows the percentage of students in the norming sample who scored at or below a particular raw score. If a student's score were the same as or better than three-quarters of the students in the norming sample, the student would score in the 75th percentile or have a percentile rank of 75. You can see that this does *not* mean that the student had a raw score of 75 correct answers or even that the student answered 75% of the questions correctly. Rather, the 75 refers to the percentage of people in the norming sample whose scores on the test were equal to or below this student's score. A percentile rank of 50 means that a student has scored as well as or better than 50% of the norming sample and has achieved an average score.

A Caution about Interpreting Percentile Scores.   Differences in percentile ranks do not mean the same thing in terms of raw score points in the middle of the scale as they do at the fringes. The graph in Figure 8.2 shows Joan's and Alice's percentile scores on the fictitious Test of Excellence in Language and Arithmetic. Both students are about average in arithmetic skills. One equaled or surpassed 50% of the norming sample, the other, 60%. However, because their scores are in the middle of the distribution, this difference in percentile ranks means a raw score difference of only a few points. Their raw scores were actually 75 and 77. In the language test, the difference in percentile ranks seems to be about the same as the difference in arithmetic because one ranked at the 90th percentile and the other at the 99th. But the difference in their raw scores on the language test is much greater. It takes a greater difference in raw score points to make a difference in percentile rank at the extreme ends of the scale. On the language test the difference in raw scores is about 10 points.

Grade-Equivalent Scores.   Generally, **grade-equivalent scores** are obtained from separate norming samples for each grade level. The average of the scores of all the 3rd graders in the norming sample defines the 3rd-grade equivalent score. Suppose the raw-score average of the 3rd-grade norming sample is 38. Any student who attains a raw score of 38 on that test will be assigned a grade-equivalent score of 3rd grade. Grade-equivalent scores are generally listed in numbers such as 2.3, 3.5, 4.6, 10.5, and so on. The whole number gives the grade. The decimals stand for tenths of a year, but they are usually interpreted as months.

Suppose a student with the grade-equivalent score of 9 is a 3rd grader. Should this student be promoted immediately? Probably not. Different forms of tests are used at

FIGURE 8.2   Percentile Ranking on a Normal Distribution Curve
Percentile scores have different meanings at different places on the scale. For example, a difference of a few raw score points near the mean might translate into a 10-point percentile difference, while it would take 6 or 7 points to make a 10-point percentile difference farther out of the scale.

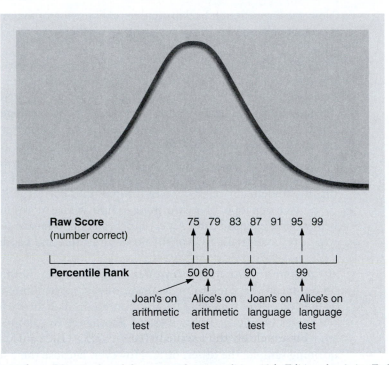

Source: Figure from *Educational psychology, active learning edition*, 10th Edition, by Anita E. Woolfolk. Copyright © 2008 by Pearson Education, Inc. Printed and Electronically reproduced by permission of Pearson Education, Inc., Upper Saddle River, New Jersey.

different grade levels, so the 3rd grader may not have had to answer items that would be given to 9th graders. The high score represents superior mastery of material at the 3rd-grade level rather than a capacity for doing 9th-grade work. Even though an average 9th grader could do as well as our 3rd grader on this particular test, the 9th grader would certainly know much more than this test covered. All the score tells us is that this 3rd grader is well above the rest of the 3rd graders, *not* that the child is actually equivalent to those in 9th grade. Also, grade-equivalent score units do not mean the same thing at every grade level. For example, a 2nd grader reading at the 1st-grade level would have more trouble in school than an 11th grader who reads at the 10th-grade level.

Because grade-equivalent scores are misleading and are so often misinterpreted, especially by parents, most educators and psychologists strongly believe they should not be used at all. In the example above, parents of the 3rd-grade student who is reading at the 9th-grade level might mistakenly think their child can do 9th-grade work; that is a misinterpretation of the score.

Standard Scores.   As you may remember, one problem with percentile ranks is the difficulty in making comparisons among ranks. A discrepancy of a certain number of raw-score points has a different meaning at different places on the scale. With standard scores, on the other hand, a difference of 10 points is the same everywhere on the scale (Hoy, 2010).

Standard scores are based on the standard deviation. A very common standard score is called the **z score.** A *z* score tells how many standard deviations above or below the average a raw score is. In the example described earlier, in which you were fortunate enough to get a 78 on a test where the mean was 70 and the standard deviation was 4, your *z* score would be +2, or 2 standard deviations above the mean. If a person were to score 64 on this test, the score would be 1.5 standard deviation units *below* the mean, and the *z* score would be −1.5. A *z* score of 0 would be no standard deviations above the mean—in other words, right on the mean.

To calculate the *z* score for a given raw score, subtract the mean from the raw score and divide the difference by the standard deviation. The formula is:

$$z = \frac{X - \overline{X}}{SD}$$

Because it is often inconvenient to use negative numbers, other standard scores have been devised to eliminate this difficulty. The ***T* score** has a mean of 50 and uses a standard deviation of 10. Thus a *T* score of 50 indicates average performance. If you multiply the *z* score by 10 (which eliminates the decimal) and add 50 (which gets rid of the negative number), you get the equivalent *T* score as the answer. The person whose *z* score was −1.5 would have a *T* score of 35.

First multiply the *z* score by 10:	−1.5 × 10 = −15
Then add 50:	−15 + 50 = 35

The scoring of the SAT or GRE test is based on a similar procedure. The mean of the scores is set at 500, and a standard deviation of 100 is used.

Before we leave this section on types of scores, we should mention one other widely used method. **Stanine scores** (the name comes from "standard nine") are standard scores. There are only nine possible scores on the stanine scale, the whole numbers 1 through 9. The mean is 5, and the standard deviation is 2. Each unit from 2 to 8 is equal to half a standard deviation.

Stanine scores provide a method of considering a student's rank because each of the nine scores includes a specific range of percentile scores in the normal distribution. For example, a stanine score of 1 is assigned to the bottom 4% of scores in a distribution. A stanine of 2 is assigned to the next 7%. Of course, some raw scores in this 7% range are better than others, but they all get a stanine score of 2.

Each stanine score represents a wide range of raw scores. This has the advantage of encouraging teachers and parents to view a student's score in more general terms instead of making fine distinctions based on a few points. Figure 8.3 compares the four types of standard scores we have considered, showing how each would fall on a normal distribution curve.

FIGURE 8.3   Four Types of Standard Scores on a Normal Distribution Curve
Using this figure you can translate one type of standard into another.

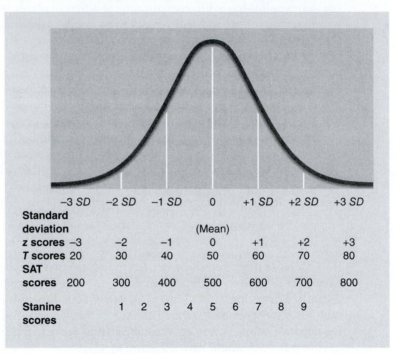

	−3 SD	−2 SD	−1 SD	0	+1 SD	+2 SD	+3 SD
Standard deviation				(Mean)			
z scores	−3	−2	−1	0	+1	+2	+3
T scores	20	30	40	50	60	70	80
SAT scores	200	300	400	500	600	700	800
Stanine scores		1 2	3	4 5 6	7	8 9	

Interpreting Test Scores

One of the most common problems with the use of tests is misinterpretation of scores. This often happens because of the belief that numbers are precise measurements of a student's ability. No test provides a perfect picture of a person's abilities; a test is only one small sample of behavior. Two factors are important in developing good tests and interpreting results: reliability and validity.

Reliability.   If you took a standardized test on Monday, then took the same test again a week later, and you received about the same score each time, you would have reason to believe the test was reliable. If 100 people took the test one day, then repeated it the following week, and the ranking of the individual scores was about the same for both tests, you would be even more certain the test was reliable. (Of course, this assumes that no one looks up answers or studies before the second test.) A reliable test gives a consistent and stable "reading" of a person's ability from one occasion to the next, assuming the person's ability remains the same. A reliable thermometer works in a similar manner, giving you a reading of 100°C each time you measure the temperature of boiling water. Measuring a test's **reliability** in this way, by giving the test on two different occasions, indicates *stability* or *test–retest reliability*. If a group of people takes two equivalent versions of a test and the scores on both tests are comparable, this indicates *alternate-form reliability*.

Reliability can also refer to the internal consistency or the precision of a test. This type of reliability, known as *split-half reliability*, is calculated by comparing performance on one half of the test questions with performance on the other half. If, for example, someone did quite well on all the odd-numbered items and not at all well on the even-numbered items, we could assume that the items were not very consistent or precise in measuring what they were intended to measure.

There are several ways to compute reliability, but all the possibilities give numbers between 0.0 and 1.0, like a correlation coefficient. Above .90 is considered very reliable; .80 to .90 is good, and below .80 is not very good reliability for standardized tests (Haladyna, 2002). The most effective way to improve reliability is to add more items to a test. Generally speaking, longer tests are more reliable than shorter ones.

True Score. All tests are imperfect estimators of the qualities or skills they are trying to measure. There are errors in every testing situation. Sometimes the errors are in the students' favor and they score higher than their ability might warrant, because, for example, they reviewed a key section just before the test. Sometimes the errors go against students; they are sick, sleepy, or focused on the wrong material in their review. But if students could be tested over and over again without becoming tired and without memorizing the answers, their good luck and bad luck would even out, and the average of the test scores would be close to a true score. In other words, we can think of a student's true score as the mean of all the scores the student would receive if the test were repeated many times.

In reality, however, students take a test only once. That means that the score each student receives is made up of the hypothetical true score plus some amount of error. How can error be reduced so that the actual score can be brought closer to a true score? As you might guess, this returns us to the question of reliability. The more reliable the test is, the less error there is in the score actually obtained. On standardized tests, test developers take this into consideration and make estimations of how much the students' scores would probably vary if they were tested repeatedly. This estimation is called the **standard error of measurement.** It represents the *standard deviation* of the distribution of scores from our hypothetical repeated testings. Thus, a reliable test can also be defined as a test with a small standard error of measurement. In their interpretation of tests, principals and teachers must also take into consideration the margin for error.

Confidence Interval. Never base an opinion of a student's ability or achievement on the exact score the student obtains. Many test companies now report scores using a **confidence interval,** or "standard error band," that encloses the student's actual score. This makes use of the standard error of measurement and allows a teacher to consider the range of scores that might include a student's true score.

Let us assume, for example, that two students in your school take a standardized achievement test in Spanish. The standard error of measurement for this test is 5. One student receives a score of 79 and the other, a score of 85. At first glance, these scores seem quite different. But when you consider the standard error bands around the scores, not just the scores alone, you see that the bands overlap. The first student's true score might be anywhere between 74 and 84 (that is, the actual score of 79 plus and minus the standard error of 5). The second student's true score might be anywhere between 80 and 90. It is crucial to keep in mind the idea of standard error bands when selecting students for special programs. No child should be rejected simply because the obtained score missed the cutoff by one or two points. The student's true score might well be above the cutoff point.

Validity.   If a test is sufficiently reliable, the next question is whether it is valid, that is, does the test measure what it is supposed to measure? To have **validity,** the decisions and inferences based on the test must be supported by evidence. This means that validity is judged in relation to a particular use or purpose, that is, in relation to the actual decision being made and the evidence for that decision (Linn & Gronlund, 2000; Oosterhof, 2009; Popham, 2011).

A test must be reliable in order to be valid. For example, if, over a few months, an intelligence test yields different results each time it is given to the same child, then by definition it is not reliable. Certainly it couldn't be a valid measure of intelligence because intelligence is assumed to be fairly stable, at least over a short period of time. However, reliability will not guarantee validity. If that intelligence test gave the same score every time for a particular child but didn't predict school achievement, speed of learning, or other characteristics associated with intelligence, then performance on the test would not be a true indicator of intelligence. The test would be reliable, but invalid.

Absence of Bias.   Reliability and validity have long been criteria for judging assessments. But over the past 25 years, educators and psychologists realized that another criterion should be added: absence of bias. **Assessment bias** "refers to qualities of an assessment instrument that offend or unfairly penalize a group of students because of the students' gender, ethnicity, socioeconomic status, religion, or other such group-defining characteristic" (Popham, 2005, p. 77). Biases are aspects of the test such as content, language, or examples that might distort the performance of a group, either for better or for worse. For example, if a reading test used passages that described boxing or football scenarios, we might expect males on average to do better than females.

Two forms of assessment bias are unfair penalization and offensiveness. The reading assessment with heavy sports content is an example of *unfair penalization;* girls may be penalized for their lack of boxing or football knowledge. *Offensiveness* occurs when a particular group might be insulted by the content of the assessment. Offended, angry students may not perform at their best.

Also, tests may not be fair because different groups have had different *opportunities to learn* the material tested. The questions asked tend to center on experiences and facts more familiar to the dominant culture than to minority group students. Consider this test item for 4th graders described by Popham (2011, p. 371):

> My uncle's *field* is computer programming

Look at the sentences on the next page. In which sentence does the word *field* mean the same as in the boxed sentence above?

A. The softball pitcher knew how to *field* her position.

B. They prepared the *field* by spraying and plowing it.

C. I know the *field* I plan to enter when I finish college.

D. The doctor used a wall chart to examine my *field* of vision.*

Items like this are on most standardized tests. But not all families describe their work as a *field* of employment. If your parents work in professional fields such as computers, medicine, law, or education, the item would make sense, but what if your parents worked at a grocery store or a car repair shop? Are these fields? Life outside of school has prepared some students, but not others, for this item.

Today most standardized tests are checked carefully for assessment bias, but teacher-made tests may have biased content. It makes sense to have teachers check their tests for bias (Popham, 2011).

Types of Standardized Tests

Several kinds of standardized tests are used in schools today. One look in the cumulative folders that include testing records for individual students over several years shows the many ways students are tested in this country. There are three broad categories of standardized tests: achievement, diagnostic, and aptitude (including interest). As an instructional leader, you will probably encounter achievement and aptitude tests most frequently.

Achievement Tests: What Has the Student Learned?

The most common standardized tests given to students are **achievement tests,** which are meant to measure how much a student has learned in specific content areas such as reading comprehension, language usage, computation, science, social studies, mathematics, and logical reasoning. There are achievement tests for both individuals (for example, the Wide-Range Achievement Test; Peabody Individual Achievement Test; KeyMath Diagnostic Tests) and groups (the California, Metropolitan, SRA, or Stanford Achievement Tests; the TerraNova; and the Iowa Tests). These tests vary in their reliability and validity. Group tests can be used for screening, to identify children who might need further testing or as a basis for grouping students according to achievement levels. Individual achievement tests are given to determine a child's academic level more precisely or to help diagnose learning problems.

Using Information from a Norm-Referenced Achievement Test.   What specific information can principals and teachers expect from achievement test results? Test publishers usually provide individual profiles for each student, showing scores on each subtest. Figure 8.4 is an example of a Student Report for a 4th grader, Sally Valenzuela, on

*Source: Excerpt from *Classroom assessment: What teachers need to know*, 6th Edition, by James W. Popham. Copyright © 2011 by Pearson Education, Inc. Printed and Electronically reproduced by permission of Pearson Education, Inc., Upper Saddle River, New Jersey.

FIGURE 8.4 A Typical Score Report

A sample test score report, with no actual test data used.

Student Report | SALLY VALENZUELA

National Comparison

STANFORD
ACHIEVEMENT TEST SERIES TENTH EDITION

with Otis-Lennon School Ability Test®, Eighth Edition

TEACHER: TILTON
SCHOOL: NEWTOWN ELEMENTARY - 215648
DISTRICT: NEWTOWN
GRADE: 04
TEST DATE: 04/03
AGE: 09 Yrs 08 Mos
STUDENT NO.: 8

About This Student's Performance:

Sally recently took the *Stanford Achievement Test*, Tenth Edition (Stanford 10). This test is one measure of this child's achievement. This report compares this child's performance to students in the same grade across the nation. Percentile Bands show ranges within which this child's true scores likely fall. For example, a student whose Percentile Band spans the 70th percentile performed as well as or better than 70% of students nationally in that subject - but not as well as 30% of students.

The chart below shows this child's performance in each subject area tested.

Lexile measure = 730L

Information on the use of Lexiles can be found at www.lexile.com. Lexiles used with permission.

Subtests and Totals	Number Possible	Number Correct	Scaled Score	National PR-S	National NCE	Grade Equivalent	AAC Range	National Grade Percentile Bands
Total Reading	114	82	639	59-5	54.8	5.4	MIDDLE	
Word Study Skills	30	25	664	76-6	64.9	7.6	HIGH	
Reading Vocabulary	30	22	627	46-5	47.9	4.5	MIDDLE	
Reading Comprehension	54	35	634	53-5	51.6	5.0	MIDDLE	
Total Mathematics	80	56	633	64-6	57.5	5.5	MIDDLE	
Mathematics Problem Solving	48	30	623	54-5	52.1	5.0	MIDDLE	
Mathematics Procedures	32	26	650	74-6	63.5	6.3	HIGH	
Language	48	28	610	39-4	44.1	3.5	MIDDLE	
Language Mechanics	24	15	617	46-5	47.9	4.3	MIDDLE	
Language Expression	24	13	603	36-4	42.5	3.5	MIDDLE	
Spelling	40	30	647	73-6	62.9	6.4	HIGH	
Science	40	30	643	69-6	60.4	6.3	MIDDLE	
Social Science	40	22	607	40-5	44.7	3.5	MIDDLE	
Listening	40	22	608	35-4	41.9	3.4	MIDDLE	
Thinking Skills	190	122	623	56-5	53.2	5.1	MIDDLE	
Basic Battery	322	218	NA	57-5	53.6	5.0	MIDDLE	
Complete Battery	402	270	NA	56-5	53.4	5.0	MIDDLE	

Otis-Lennon School Ability Test®	Number Possible	Number Correct	SAI	Age PR-S	Scaled Score	Natl Grade PR-S	National Grade Percentile Bands
Total	72	38	106	65-6	605	55-5	
Verbal	36	21	112	77-7	613	63-6	
Nonverbal	36	17	102	55-5	597	46-5	

Clusters	NP	NA	NC	Below Avg	Avg	Above Avg
Word Study Skills	30	30	25		✓	
C Structural Analysis	12	12	10		✓	
C Phonetic Analysis-Consonants	9	9	8		✓	✓
C Phonetic Analysis-Vowels	9	9	7		✓	
Reading Vocabulary	30	30	22		✓	
C Synonyms	12	12	9		✓	
P Multiple Meaning Words	9	9	5	✓		
C Context Clues	9	9	8		✓	
P Thinking Skills	18	18	13		✓	
Reading Comprehension	54	54	35		✓	
C Literary	18	18	12		✓	
C Informational	18	18	10		✓	
P Functional	18	18	13		✓	
P Initial Understanding	12	12	11		✓	
P Interpretation	20	20	12		✓	
P Critical Analysis	12	12	8		✓	
P Strategies	10	10	4		✓	
P Thinking Skills	42	42	24		✓	
Mathematics Problem Solving	48	48	30		✓	
C Number Sense & Operations	24	24	16		✓	
C Patterns/Relationships/Algebra	6	6	6			✓
C Data, Statistics & Probability	8	8	4		✓	
C Geometry & Measurement	10	10	4		✓	
C Communication & Representation	6	6	4	✓		
C Estimation	8	8	5		✓	
P Mathematical Connections	21	21	13		✓	
P Reasoning & Problem Solving	13	13	10		✓	
P Thinking Skills	40	40	26		✓	

Clusters	NP	NA	NC	Below Avg	Avg	Above Avg
Mathematics Procedures	32	32	26		✓	
C Computation w/Whole Numbers	18	18	14		✓	
C Computation with Decimals	8	8	6		✓	
C Computation with Fractions	6	6	6			✓
P Computation in Context	16	16	13		✓	
C Computation/Symbolic Notation	16	16	13		✓	
P Thinking Skills	16	16	13		✓	
Language Mechanics	24	24	15		✓	
C Capitalization	8	8	7		✓	
C Usage	8	8	3	✓		
C Punctuation	8	8	5		✓	
Language Expression	24	24	13		✓	
C Sentence Structure	8	8	4		✓	
C Prewriting	5	5	3		✓	
P Content and Organization	11	11	6		✓	
P Thinking Skills	12	12	6		✓	
Spelling	40	40	30		✓	
P Phonetic Principles	18	18	14		✓	
C Structural Principles	10	10	7		✓	
P No Mistake	7	7	7			✓
C Homophones	5	5	2		✓	
Science	40	40	30		✓	
C Life	11	11	9		✓	
C Physical	11	11	6		✓	
C Earth	11	11	10		✓	
C Nature of Science	7	7	5		✓	
P Models	14	14	11		✓	
P Constancy	13	13	10		✓	

Clusters	NP	NA	NC	Below Avg	Avg	Above Avg
Science (cont.)						
P Form & Function	13	13	9		✓	
P Thinking Skills	20	20	16		✓	
Social Science	40	40	22		✓	
C History	10	10	6		✓	
C Geography	10	10	8		✓	
C Political Science	10	10	6		✓	
C Economics	10	10	2	✓		
P App. of Knowledge/Comp.	14	14	7		✓	
P Org., Summ. & Interp. of Info.	15	15	7		✓	
P Determination of Cause/Effect	11	11	8		✓	
P Thinking Skills	20	20	11		✓	
Listening	40	40	22		✓	
C Vocabulary	10	10	3	✓		
C Comprehension	30	30	19		✓	
P Initial Understanding	8	8	6		✓	
P Interpretation	12	12	7		✓	
P Analysis	7	7	4		✓	
P Strategies	3	3	2		✓	
C Literary	10	10	7		✓	
C Informational	10	10	5		✓	
P Thinking Skills	22	22	13		✓	
Thinking Skills	190	190	122		✓	

STANFORD LEVEL/FORM: INTERMEDIATE 1/A
2002 NORMS: Spring   National

OLSAT LEVEL/FORM: E/5
2002 NORMS: Spring   National

C = Content Cluster   P = Process Cluster

Scores based on normative data copyright © 2003 by Harcourt, Inc. All rights reserved.

COPY 01

PROCESS NO. 103000255-1531251-M109-00058-1

the *Stanford Achievement Test, 10th Edition*. Note that the Student Report has three sections. The first (About This Student's Performance) is a brief narrative explanation that may include a Lexile Measure™, which is computed from the Reading Comprehension score and helps teachers identify Sally's reading level in order to select appropriate texts.

The second section (Subtests and Totals) attempts to paint a picture of the student's achievement in *Reading, Mathematics, Language, Spelling, Science, Social Studies, Listening,* and *Thinking Skills*. That section also includes total scores on the battery of tests and scores on the Otis-Lennon School Ability test—a kind of group IQ or scholastic aptitude test. Some of the subtests are further divided into more specific assessments. For example, *Reading* is broken down into "word study skills," "reading vocabulary," and "reading comprehension." Next to each subtest are several different ways of reporting Sally's score. The school decides which scores are reported, based on a list of possible reporting formats. This school chose the following types of scores:

Number Correct: Under the second column is the number of items that Sally answered correctly for that subtest (the number of items on the subtest is in the first column).

Scale Score: This basic score is used to derive all the other scores, and sometimes is called a *growth score* because it describes growth in achievement that typically occurs as students move through the grades. For example, the average score for 3rd graders might be 585, whereas the average score for 10th graders might be 714 on tests with possible scores that range from 0 to 1000 across the entire K–12 grades. Often, the difficulty of items is included in calculating scale scores. Schools are increasingly using this score because they can compare across years, classes, or schools in the district (Popham, 2005a).

National PR-S (National Percentile Rank and Stanine):   This score tells us where Sally stands in relation to students at her grade level across the country in terms of percentile rank (% with the same score or lower) and stanine.

National NCE (Normal Curve Equivalent):   This is a standard score derived from the percentile rank, with a range of 1 to 99, a mean of 50, and a standard deviation of 21.

Grade-Equivalent Score: This indicates that Sally's scale score is the same as an average student in that grade and month of school. Beware of the problems with grade-equivalent scores described earlier.

AAC (Achievement/Ability Comparison) Range: The ACC score compares Sally's achievement on each subtest to a norm group of other students who have her same ability as measured by the Otis-Lennon School Ability test. The ACC range categorizes Sally's ACC score as HIGH, MIDDLE, or LOW. You can see that Sally is in the middle on most of the subtests, so her achievement is in the middle compared to students with abilities similar to hers.

National Grade Percentile Bands: The range of national percentile scores in which Sally's true score is likely to fall. You may remember from our discussion of true scores that this range, or confidence interval, is determined by adding and subtracting the standard error of the test from Sally's actual score. Chances are high that Sally's true score is within this range. Bands that do not overlap indicate likely differences in achievement.

The bottom of Figure 8.4 (Clusters) breaks Sally's subtests down into even more specific skills. For each skill we see the number of questions possible to answer (NP), the number Sally attempted (NA), and the number she got correct (NC). The check marks beside the skills indicate if she is average, above average, or below average in each. Notice that some skills are assessed with only a few (3 to 8) questions. Remember that fewer items means less reliability.

Diagnostic Tests: What Are the Student's Strengths and Weaknesses?

If teachers want to identify specific learning problems, they may need to refer to results from the various diagnostic tests that have been developed. Most **diagnostic tests** are administered to students individually by a highly trained professional. The goal is usually to identify the specific problems a student is having. Achievement tests, both standardized and teacher made, identify weaknesses in academic content areas like mathematics, computation, or reading. Individually administered diagnostic tests identify weaknesses in learning processes. There are diagnostic tests to assess the ability to hear differences among sounds, remember spoken words or sentences, recall a sequence of symbols, separate figures from their background, express relationships, coordinate eye and hand movements, describe objects orally, blend sounds to form words, recognize details in a picture, coordinate movements, and many other abilities needed to learn, remember, and communicate learning. Elementary school students are more likely than secondary school students to take diagnostic tests. High school students are more likely to take aptitude tests.

Aptitude Tests: How Well Will the Student Do in the Future?

Both achievement and aptitude tests measure developed abilities. Achievement tests may measure abilities developed over a short period of time, such as during a week-long unit on map reading, or over a longer period of time, such as a semester. **Aptitude tests** are meant to measure abilities developed over many years and to predict how well a student will do in the future at learning unfamiliar material. These two types of tests are used for distinct purposes. Achievement tests measure final performance (and perhaps give grades), and aptitude tests predict how well people will do in particular programs like college or professional school (Anastasi, 1988).

Scholastic Aptitude.   The purpose of a scholastic aptitude test, such as the SAT (Scholastic Assessment Test) or ACT (American College Testing Program) is to predict how well a student is likely to do in college. Colleges use such scores to help decide on acceptances and rejections. The SAT may have seemed like an achievement test to you, measuring what you had learned in high school. Although the test is designed to avoid drawing too heavily on specific high school curricula, the questions are very similar to achievement test questions.

Standardized aptitude tests—such as the SAT, the School and College Ability Tests (SCAT), and the Preliminary Scholastic Assessment Test (PSAT) for younger students— seem to be reliable in predicting future achievement. Because standardized tests are less open to teacher bias, they may be even fairer predictors of future achievement than high school grades. Indeed, some psychologists believe grade inflation in high schools has made tests like the SAT even more important. Others believe that the SATs are not good predictors of success in college, particularly for women or members of cultural or ethnic minority groups. The controversy continues, with some critics demanding that colleges drop tests as criteria for admission and supporters calling for improved testing.

IQ and Scholastic Aptitude.   In Chapter 3 we discussed one of the most influential aptitude tests of all, the IQ test. The IQ test as we know it could well be called a test of scholastic aptitude. The IQ score is really a standard score with a mean of 100 and a standard deviation of 15. Thus about 68% of the general population would score between +1 and −1 standard deviations from the mean, or between about 85 and 115.

A difference of a few points between two students' IQ scores should not be viewed as important. Scores between 90 and 109 are within the average range. In fact, scores between 80 and 119 are considered within the range of low average to high average. To see the problems that may arise, consider the following conversation:

> PARENT: We came to speak with you today because we are shocked at our son's IQ score. We can't believe he has only a 99 IQ when his sister scored much higher on the same test. We know they are about the same. In fact, Sam has better marks than Lauren did in the 5th grade.
>
> PRINCIPAL: What was Lauren's score?
>
> PARENT: Well, she did much better. She scored a 103!

Clearly, brother and sister have both scored within the average range. While the standard error of measurement on the WISC-IV (Weschler Intelligence Scale for Children, 4th edition) varies slightly from one age to the next, the average standard error for the total score is around 3 points. So the bands around Sam's and Lauren's IQ scores, about 96 to 102 and 100 to 106, are overlapping. Either child could have scored 100, 101, or 102.

Discussing Test Results with Families.   At times, you and your teachers will be expected to explain or describe test results to your students' families. The *Theory into Action Guidelines* will give principals and teachers direction.

The Dangers and Possibilities of High-Stakes Testing

Principals and teachers increasingly are expected to use standardized test scores to make judgments about students, curricula, and school performance. This enhanced status of standardized testing requires teachers to be far more knowledgeable about every aspect of these tools. We begin with a basic question: Just how much testing is going on?

How Widespread Is Standardized Testing?

Test scores may affect "admission" to 1st grade, promotion from one grade to the next, high school graduation, access to special programs, placement in special education classes, teacher certification and tenure, and school funding. Because the decisions affected by test scores are so critical, many educators call this process **high-stakes testing.** The teachers we work with are frustrated that results of these high-stakes tests

THEORY INTO ACTION GUIDELINES

Family Partnerships for Using Test Results

Be ready to explain, in nontechnical terms, what each type of score on the test report means.

Examples

1. If the test is norm-referenced, know if the comparison group was national or local. Explain that the child's score shows how he or she performed *in relation to* the other students in the comparison group.
2. If the test is criterion-referenced, explain that the child's scores show how well he or she performs in specific areas.

If the test is norm-referenced, focus on the percentile scores. They are the easiest to understand.

Examples

1. Percentile scores tell what percent of students in the comparison group made the same score or lower—higher percentiles are better and 99 is as high as you can get; 50 is average.
2. Remind parents that percentile scores do not tell the "percent correct," so scores that would be bad on a classroom test (say 65% to 75% or so) are above average—even good—as percentile scores.

Avoid using grade-equivalent scores.

Examples

1. If parents want to focus on the "grade level" of their child, tell them that high grade-equivalent

scores reflect a thorough understanding of the current grade level and not the capacity to do higher grade-level work.
2. Tell parents that the same grade-equivalent score has different meanings in different subjects—reading versus mathematics, for example.

Be aware of the error in testing.

Examples

1. Encourage parents to think of the score not as a single point but as a range or band that includes the score.
2. Ignore small differences between scores.
3. Note that sometimes individual skills on criterion-referenced tests are measured with just a few (two or three) items. Compare test scores to actual class work in the same areas.

Use conference time to plan a learning goal for the child, one that families can support.

Examples

1. Have example questions, similar to those on the test, to show parents what their child can do easily and what kinds of questions he or she found difficult.
2. Be prepared to suggest an important skill to target.

---

often come too late in the year to help them plan instruction or remediation for their current students. They also are troubled by the amount of time testing takes—both to prepare for the tests and to give them. They complain that the tests cover material their curriculum does not include. Are they justified in their concerns?

Documented Problems with High-Stakes Testing. When so much rides on the results of a test, you would assume the test actually measured what had been taught. In the past, this match has been a problem. Years ago, one group of teachers in St. Louis found that fewer than 10% of the items in their curriculum overlapped in both the textbooks and the standardized tests they were using (Fiske, 1988). Recently, the overlap between what is taught and what is tested has been improving, but it still makes sense to be aware of possible mismatches.

What about time? Studies have found that in some states, 80% of the elementary schools spend about 20% of their instructional time preparing for the end-of-grade tests (Abrams & Madaus, 2003). Studies of the actual high-stakes tests in action show other troubling consequences. Testing narrows the curriculum. In fact, after examining the results of years of testing, Lisa Abrams and George Madaus (2003) concluded that wherever high-stakes tests operate, "the exam content eventually defines the curriculum" (p. 32). For example, using the *Texas Assessment of Academic Skills* has led to curriculum changes that overemphasize what is tested and neglect other areas. In addition, it seems that the test of mathematics is also a test of reading. Students with poor reading ability have trouble with the math test, especially if their first language is not English.

Another unintended consequence of the early warning testing in elementary school is to "push out" students who believe they are going to fail the high school graduation test. If they won't graduate anyway, they see no point in continuing to attend school (McNeil & Valenzuela, 2000). For example, in the 2000–2001 school year, about one-third of the English language learners dropped out of high school in New York. The main reason given was their inability to pass the required Regents Exam (Medina, 2002).

Accountability and High-Stakes Testing

One of the high-stakes uses for test results is to hold teachers, schools, and administrators **accountable** for student performance. For example, teacher bonuses might be tied to their students' achievement, or school funding might be affected by testing results. The press for accountability that accompanies the No Child Left Behind Act (NCLB) will be with us for the foreseeable future, even though some of the restrictions seem to be easing. The evidence to date, however, suggests that the NCLB goals for students are unrealistic and seem likely to produce failure and demoralization rather than success and pride. The focus on achievement for all students and the special attention on those who are performing poorly are praiseworthy, but if the AYP requirements are enforced, they will result in sanctions for many schools that are making great strides in teaching students (Linn, 2003). Like most things, accountability and high-stakes testing have their benefits, but they also have costs. Is it reasonable to hold teachers and schools accountable for student achievement?

Should Tests Be Used to Hold Teachers Accountable?   There are two possible meanings for *accountability*. The first has to do with gathering information so that we can make good educational decisions about programs, policies, and resources. The second is holding someone responsible for student learning—usually the school or the teacher (Haladyna, 2002).

The argument in favor of accountability claims the public has a right to know how their schools are doing, especially because public money is used to finance schools. Testing may help to raise expectations for the lowest-performing schools and give educators the information they need to improve the programs in their schools (Doherty, 2002). And people who make decisions about which reading programs to adopt or how to allocate resources need information about student achievement.

Will results of standardized tests really give parents information about the "quality of their children's schools" or the "qualifications of teachers"? If the test matches important objectives of the curriculum, is given to students who actually studied the curriculum for a reasonable period of time, is free of bias, fits the students' language capabilities, and was administered properly, then test results will provide some information about the effectiveness of the school. But as we have seen, studies of the actual tests in action show troubling consequences such as narrowing the curriculum and pushing some students out of school early, so high-stakes testing is a complex and controversial practice.

In sum, to be valuable, testing programs must have a number of characteristics. Of course the tests used must be reliable, valid for the purposes used, and free of bias. In addition, a testing program should:

1. *Match the content standards of the district.* This is a vital part of validity.
2. *Be part of the larger assessment plan.* No one test provides all the necessary information about student achievement. It is critical that schools avoid making pass/fail decisions based on a single test.
3. *Test complex thinking,* not just skills and factual knowledge.
4. *Provide alternate assessment strategies* for students with identifiable disabilities.
5. *Provide opportunities for retesting* when the stakes are high.
6. *Include all students* in the testing, but also provide informative reports of the results that make the students' situations clear if they have special challenges or circumstances such as disabilities.
7. *Provide appropriate remediation* when students fail.
8. Make sure all students taking the test *have adequate opportunities to learn* the material being tested.
9. *Take into account the student's language.* Students who have difficulty reading or writing in English will not perform well on tests that require English.
10. *Use test results for children, not against them.* (Haladyna, 2002)

This is important, so we repeat: Standardized achievement tests must be chosen so that the items on the test actually measure knowledge gained in the classes. Also, students must have the necessary skills to take the test. If students score low on a science test, not because they lack knowledge about science but because they have difficulty reading the questions, don't speak English, or have too little time to finish, then the test is not a valid measure of science achievement for those students.

Advantages in Taking Tests—Fair and Unfair

In this section we will consider three basic issues: Are standardized tests biased against minority students? Can students gain an advantage on admissions tests through coaching? Can they be taught test-taking skills?

Bias and Fairness in Testing.   Are tests such as the individual measures of intelligence or college admissions tests fair assessments for minority group students? This is a complex question. Research on test bias shows that most standardized tests predict school achievement equally well across all groups of students. Items that might on the surface appear to be biased against minorities are not necessarily more difficult for minorities to answer correctly (Sattler, 2001). Even though standardized aptitude and achievement tests are not biased against minorities in predicting school performance, many people believe that the tests still can be unfair. Tests may not have *procedural fairness*; that is, some groups may not have an equal opportunity to show what they know on the test. Here are a few examples:

1. The language of the test and the tester is often different from the languages of the students.
2. Answers that support middle-class values are often rewarded with more points.
3. On individually administered intelligence tests, being very verbal and talking a lot is rewarded.

The above three factors favor students who feel comfortable in that particular situation. Also, tests may not be fair because different groups have had different *opportunities to learn* the material tested. The questions asked tend to center on experiences and facts more familiar to the dominant culture than to minority group students.

Stereotype Threat.   When stereotyped individuals are in situations where a stereotype applies, they bear an extra emotional and cognitive burden. The burden is the possibility of confirming the stereotype, either in the eyes of others or in their own eyes. Thus, when girls are asked to solve complicated mathematics problems, for example, they are at risk of confirming widely held stereotypes that girls are inferior to boys in mathematics. It is not necessary that the individual even believe the stereotype. All that matters is that the person is *aware* of the stereotype and *cares about performing* well enough to disprove its unflattering implications (Aronson, Lustina, Good, Keough, Steele, & Brown, 1999). What are the results of stereotype threat? Recent research provides answers that should interest all educators.

   In the short run, the fear that you might confirm a negative stereotype can induce test anxiety and undermine performance. In a series of experiments, Joshua Aronson, Claude Steele, and their colleagues have demonstrated that when African American or Latino college students are put into situations that induce stereotype threat, their performance suffers (Aronson & Inzlicht, 2004; Aronson & Steele, 2005). For example, African American and white undergraduate subjects in an experiment at Stanford University were told that the test they were about to take would precisely measure their verbal ability. A similar group of subjects was told that the purpose of the test was to understand the psychology of verbal problem solving and not to assess individual ability. When the test was presented as diagnostic of verbal ability, the African American students solved about half as many problems as the white students. In the nonthreat situation, the two groups solved about the same number of problems. Other studies found that anxiety and distraction were the main impediments. The African American students were more likely to be thinking about the stereotypes as they tried to work.

All groups, not just minority group students, can be susceptible to stereotype threat. In another study, the subjects were white male college students who were very strong in mathematics. One group was told that the test they were taking would help experimenters determine why Asian students performed so much better than whites on that particular test. Another group just took the test. The group that faced the stereotype threat of confirming that "Asians are better in math" scored significantly lower on the test (Aronson et al., 1999).

How does stereotype threat affect test performance? One link is anxiety. Some studies have found higher levels of anxiety among African American elementary school and middle school students compared to white students. And higher anxiety is cor-related with lower scores on tests. But does stereotype threat actually cause anxiety, and does anxiety actually lead to lower scores? Jason Osborne (2001) studied a large representative national sample of white, African American, and Latino high school seniors who took achievement tests and tests of anxiety at the same time. The white students scored significantly higher, but anxiety played a role in those differences. Even after controlling for prior achievement in school, anxiety explained almost one-third of the racial differences in the scores. Anxiety and distraction appeared to be the main problems in the studies of college students, too. The African American students were more likely to be thinking about the stereotypes as they tried to work (Spencer, Steele, & Quinn, 1999).

As you saw in Chapter 5, students often develop self-defeating strategies to pro-tect their self-esteem about academics. They withdraw, claim to not care, and exert little effort; they *disidentify* or psychologically disengage from success in the domain and claim "math is for nerds" or "school is for losers." There is evidence that African Americans are more likely than whites to reject identifying with academics (Major & Schmader, 1998; Ogbu, 1997). Once students define academics as "uncool" it is unlikely they will exert the effort needed for real learning. We cannot say that all differences among scores of different groups of students are caused by stereotype threat (Sackett, Hardison, & Cullen, 2004), but the process probably plays a role.

Combating Stereotype Threat.   Stereotypes are pervasive and difficult to change. Rather than wait for changes, it may be better to acknowledge that these images exist, at least in the eyes of many, and give students ways of coping with the stereotypes. Aronson, Fried, and Good (2002) demonstrated the powerful effects of changing be-liefs about intelligence. In their study, African American and white undergraduates were asked to write letters to "at-risk" middle school students to encourage them to persist in school. Some of the undergraduates were given evidence that intelligence is *improvable* and encouraged to communicate this information to their pen pals. Others were given information about multiple intelligences, but not told that these multiple abilities can be improved. The middle school students were not real, but the process of writing persuasive letters about improving intelligence proved powerful. The African American college students, and the white students to a lesser extent, who were encour-aged to believe that intelligence can be improved had higher grade point averages and reported greater enjoyment of and engagement in school when contacted at the end of the next school quarter. Thus, believing that intelligence can be improved might inoculate students against the effects of stereotype threat when they take high-pressure tests.

Concern about cultural bias in testing has led some psychologists to try to develop **culture-fair** or **culture-neutral tests.** These efforts have not been very successful. On many of the so-called culture-fair tests, the performance of students from lower socioeconomic backgrounds and minority groups has been the same as or worse than their performance on the standard Wechsler and Binet Intelligence scales (Sattler, 2001).

Preparing Students for Testing.   Several years ago, we read about a 6th-grade class that used their statewide testing as an opportunity for problem-based learning (Ewy, with student authors, 1997). This class read a newspaper article about the upcoming test and the less than stellar performance of the 6th graders in previous years. They took on the following problem: How could they improve their own test scores on the IGAP (Illinois Goal Assessment Program)? The students talked about why the problem was important and how to solve it, generating the problem analysis chart in Table 8.3.

Then they divided into groups to do different tasks: schedule practice times, look for resources, make up questions and interview experts, and set up a tutoring program. The result? The students met or exceeded the state reading, writing, and mathematics goals. When they moved to junior high and had to take the math placement test, these students researched the test. What are cutoff points, the possible range of scores, evaluation criteria? Perhaps you can take on a similar problem in your school. Instructional leaders can use the *Theory into Action Guidelines* to give teachers suggestions for helping students take tests.

Helping Students with Disabilities Prepare for High-Stakes Tests.   Erik Carter and his colleagues (2005) tested a procedure for preparing students with learning disabilities, mild intellectual disabilities, and language impairments for the high-stakes test given in their state. The students were ages 15 to 19; over half were African American males and all had individual educational programs (see Chapter 3) to guide their education. None had passed the state-required achievement tests. Over six class periods, an instructor taught the students strategies such as filling in bubbles on answer sheets completely, sorting problems by difficulty and doing the easy ones first, using rounding to estimate answers in math, identifying exactly what the question is asking by underlining key words and phrases, and figuring out how to eliminate alternatives that have redundant information or extreme qualifiers.

The good news is that after completing the preparation program, students improved their scores significantly on the tests. But the bad news is that the increases were not large enough to bring most of the students to the passing level. The students in this study, at an average age of 16, already were discouraged. The authors recommend that preparation for testing should occur much earlier for students with disabilities. The strategies taught should be closely aligned with the specific types of problems

TABLE 8.3   Taking on "The Test": Problem-Based Learning

Students in a 6th-grade classroom produced this chart as they designed a program for improving their own test performance.

Problem Analysis Chart

Problem: How can we improve our performance on the IGAP test in such a way that we (1) keep improving each year, (2) set a good example for our school, (3) make preparing for IGAP more fun?

Our Ideas	Facts We Know	Our Questions	Our Action Plan
■ Pay attention in class ■ Hold fundraiser to get books and computer program ■ Look at actual IGAP book format ■ Practice: Use computer games ■ Get someone who knows how to coach IGAP: teacher, parent, friend, brother/sister ■ Tackle one subject at a time ■ Find out who wants to know	■ Test on reading, writing, and math ■ You get better when you practice ■ You might read questions wrong ■ Fill in circles ■ Writing is scored by time, spelling, sentence structure	■ When is IGAP? ■ How long is the test? ■ How long should we practice? ■ What should we practice (math, reading, writing)? ■ How many problems? ■ How is the test scored (math, reading, writing)? ■ How much time is given for math, reading, and writing? ■ How did I do on the last IGAP test?	■ Ask principal, teacher, tutor ■ Ask person who made test ■ Work with teacher to set up schedule ■ Look for resources for practice ■ Ask parents and principal to help

Source: From "Kids take on 'the test'," by Christine Ewy & student authors, 1997, *Educational Leadership, 54*(4), p. 77. Reprinted by permission of Christine Ewy.

THEORY INTO ACTION GUIDELINES

Becoming an Expert Test Taker

Use the night before the test effectively.

Examples

1. Study the night before the exam, ending with a final look at a summary of the key points, concepts, and relationships.
2. Get a good night's sleep. If you know you generally have trouble sleeping the night before an exam, try getting extra sleep on several previous nights.

Set the situation so you can concentrate on the test.

Examples

1. Give yourself plenty of time to eat and get to the exam room.
2. Don't sit near a friend. It may make concentration difficult. If your friend leaves early, you may be tempted to do so too.

(Continued)

THEORY INTO ACTION GUIDELINES **Continued**

Make sure you know what the test is asking.

Examples

1. Read the directions carefully. If you are unsure, ask the instructor or proctor for clarification.
2. Read each question carefully to spot tricky words, such as *not, except, all of the following but one.*
3. On an essay test, read every question first, so you know the size of the job ahead of you and can make informed decisions about how much time to spend on each question.
4. On a multiple-choice test, read every alternative, even if an early one seems right.

Use time effectively.

Examples

1. Begin working right away and move as rapidly as possible while your energy is high.
2. Do the easy questions first.
3. Don't get stuck on one question. If you are stumped, mark the question so you can return to it easily later, and go on to questions you can answer more quickly.
4. If you are unsure about a question, answer it, but mark it so you can go back if there is time.
5. On a multiple-choice test, if you know you will not have time to finish, fill in all the remaining questions with the same letter if there is no penalty for guessing.
6. If you are running out of time on an essay test, do not leave any questions blank. Briefly outline a few key points to show the instructor you "knew" the answer but needed more time.

Know when to guess on multiple-choice or true-false tests.

Examples

1. Always guess when only right answers are scored.
2. Always guess when you can eliminate some of the alternatives.

3. Don't guess if there is a penalty for guessing, unless you can confidently eliminate at least one alternative.
4. Are correct answers always longer? shorter? in the middle? more likely to be one letter? more often true than false?
5. Does the grammar give the right answer away or eliminate any alternatives?

Check your work.

Examples

1. Even if you can't stand to look at the test another minute, reread each question to make sure you answered the way you intended.
2. If you are using a machine-scored answer sheet, check occasionally to be sure the number of the question you are answering corresponds to the number of the answer on the sheet.

On essay tests, answer as directly as possible.

Examples

1. Avoid flowery introductions. Answer the question in the first sentence and then elaborate.
2. Don't save your best ideas till last. Give them early in the answer.
3. Unless the instructor requires complete sentences, consider listing points, arguments, and so on by number in your answer. It will help you organize your thoughts and concentrate on the important aspects of the answer.

Learn from the testing experience.

Examples

1. Pay attention when the teacher reviews the answers. You can learn from your mistakes, and the same question may reappear in a later test.
2. Notice if you are having trouble with a particular kind of item; adjust your study approach next time to handle this type of item better.

---

the students will encounter on the test and should be embedded in good content instruction. Finally, these students often are anxious about the negative consequences of failing—not receiving a regular diploma, no access to college or trade school. The best way to deal with this anxiety is to better equip the students with the academic skills they will need to succeed (Carter et al., 2005).

New Directions in Standardized Testing and Classroom Assessment

As traditional standardized tests became the basis for high-stakes decisions, pressure to do well led many teachers and schools to "teach to the test." What is even more troubling, say critics, is that the traditional tests assess skills that have no equivalent in the real world. Students are asked to solve problems or answer questions they will never encounter again; they are expected to do so alone, without relying on any tools or resources, and while working under extreme time limits. Real life just isn't like this. Important problems take time to solve and often require using resources, consulting other people, and integrating basic skills with creativity and high-level thinking (http://jfmueller.faculty.noctrl.edu/toolbox/index.htm).

Authentic Assessment

In response to these criticisms, the **authentic assessment** movement was born. The goal was to create standardized tests that assess complex, important, real-life outcomes. The approach is also called *direct assessment, performance assessment,* or *alternative assessment.* These terms refer to procedures that are alternatives to traditional multiple-choice standardized tests because they directly assess student performance on "real-life" tasks (Hambleton, 1996; Worthen, 1993). Some states are developing procedures to conduct authentic assessments.

It is important to be sensible about authentic assessment. Just being different from traditional standardized tests will not guarantee that the alternative tests are better. Many questions have to be answered. Assume, for example, that a new assessment requires students to complete a hands-on science project. If the student does well on one science project, does this mean the student "knows" science and would do well on other projects? One study found that students' performance on three different science tasks was quite variable: A student who did well on the absorbency experiment, for example, might have trouble with the electricity task. Thus, it was hard to generalize about a student's knowledge of science based on just the three tasks. Many more tasks would be needed to get a good sense of the student's science knowledge. Because authentic assessment is a new area, it will take time to develop high-quality alternative assessments for use by whole school districts or states. Until more is known, it may be best to focus on authentic assessment at the classroom level.

Authentic Classroom Tests

Authentic tests ask students to apply skills and abilities as they would in real life. For example, they might use fractions to enlarge or reduce recipes. If our instructional goals for students include the abilities to write, speak, listen, create, think critically, solve problems, or apply knowledge, then our tests should ask students to write, speak, listen, create, think, solve, and apply. How can this happen?

Many educators suggest we look to the arts and sports for analogies to solve this problem. If we think of the "test" as being the recital, exhibition, game, mock court trial, or other performance, then teaching to the test is just fine. All coaches, artists, and musicians gladly "teach" to these "tests" because performing well on these tests is the whole point of instruction. Authentic assessment asks students to perform. The performances may be thinking performances, physical performances, creative performances, or other forms.

It may seem odd to talk of thinking as a performance, but there are many parallels. Serious thinking is risky because real-life problems are not well defined. Often the outcomes of our thinking are public because others evaluate our ideas. Like a dancer auditioning for a Broadway show, we must cope with the consequences of being evaluated. And like a sculptor looking at a lump of clay, a student facing a difficult problem must experiment, observe, redo, imagine and test solutions, apply both basic skills and inventive techniques, make interpretations, decide how to communicate results to the intended audience, and often accept criticism and improve the solution (Eisner, 1999; Herman, 1997).

The approach is also called *direct assessment* or *alternative assessment*. These terms refer to procedures that are alternatives to traditional multiple-choice standardized tests because they directly assess student performance on "real-life" tasks (Hambleton, 1996; Popham, 2011).

Performance in Context: Portfolios and Exhibitions

The concern with authentic assessment has led to the development of several new approaches based on the goal of *performance in context*. Instead of circling answers to "factual" questions about nonexistent situations, students are required to solve real problems. Facts are used in a context where they apply; for example, the student uses grammar facts to write a persuasive letter to a software company requesting donations for the class computer center. The following is a question similar to those administered in alternative performance assessments, grades 9–12.

Description: Students are told to collect data on the temperature in two cans of soda, one wrapped in aluminum foil and the other in newspaper. Then they make predictions, record the temperatures of the soda every 5 minutes for 30 minutes, graph the trends in temperature, and describe their results and conclusions. Which material is a better insulator? The task assesses students' abilities to gather and represent data, make observations, identify trends, make predictions, draw conclusions, and relate their findings to to real life.

Content Area: Physical Science

Performance Outcomes:
- conducting experiments
- using equipment
- collecting and graphing data
- drawing conclusions based on experimental data
- applying basic principles of science to everyday problems

Students completing this "test" will use scientific knowledge to understand a real-life phenomenon—insulating liquids. In the process, they will have to think critically and write persuasively. Every year, most states release some of the items from past tests to the public. The Center for Technology in Learning of SRI International, a non-profit science research institute, also provides an online resource bank of performance-based assessments linked to the National Science Education Standards. The resource is called PALS (Performance Assessment Links in Science). Go to the site (http://pals.sri.com/) and look at the performance tasks for kindergarten through 12th grade. You can select tasks by standard and grade level. Each task comes with directions for students, a guide for administrators, and a scoring guide or rubric. Many also have examples of student work.

Portfolios and exhibitions are two approaches to assessment that require performance in context. With these approaches, it is difficult to tell where instruction stops and assessment starts because the processes are interwoven (Oosterhof, 2009; Popham, 2011).

Portfolios. For years, photographers, artists, models, and architects have had portfolios to display their skills and, often, to get jobs. A **portfolio** is a systematic collection of work, often including work in progress, revisions, student self-analyses, and reflections on what the student has learned (Popham, 2005). Written work or artistic pieces are common contents of portfolios, but students might also include graphs, diagrams, snapshots of displays, peer comments, audio- or videotapes, laboratory reports, and computer programs—anything that demonstrates learning in the area being taught and assessed (Belanoff & Dickson, 1991; Camp, 1990; Wolf, Bixby, Glenn, & Gardner, 1991).

There is a distinction between process portfolios and final or "best work" portfolios. It is similar to the difference between formative and summative evaluation. Process portfolios document learning and show progress. Best works portfolios showcase final accomplishments (Johnson & Johnson, 2002). Table 8.4 shows some examples for both individuals and groups.

Exhibitions. An **exhibition** is a performance test that has two additional features. First, it is public, so students preparing exhibitions must take the audience into account; communication and understanding are essential. Second, an exhibition often requires many hours of preparation because it is the culminating experience of a whole program of study. Thomas Guskey and Jane Bailey (2001) suggest that exhibits help students understand the qualities of good work and recognize those qualities in their own productions and performances. Students also benefit when they select examples of their work to exhibit and articulate their reasons for the selections. Having the ability to judge quality can encourage student motivation by helping students to set clear goals. The *Theory into Action Guidelines* should give principals some ideas for helping teachers use portfolios and exhibitions in their teaching.

TABLE 8.4   Process and Best Works Portfolios for Individuals and Groups

Here are a few examples of how to use portfolios in different subjects.

The Process Portfolio

Subject Area	Individual Student	Cooperative Group
Science	Documentation (running records or logs) of using the scientific method to solve a series of laboratory problems	Documentation (observation checklists) of using the scientific method to solve a series of laboratory problems
Mathematics	Documentation of mathematical reasoning through double-column mathematical problem solving (computations on the left side and running commentary explaining thought processes on the right side)	Documentation of complex problem solving and use of higher-level strategies
Language Arts	Evolution of compositions from early notes through outlines, research notes, response to others' editing, and final draft	Rubrics and procedures developed to ensure high-quality peer editing

The Best Works Portfolio

Subject Area	Individual Student	Cooperative Group
Language Arts	The best compositions in a variety of styles—expository, humor/satire, creative (poetry, drama, short story), journalistic (reporting, editorial columnist, reviewer), and advertising copy	The best dramatic production, video project, TV broadcast, newspaper, advertising display
Social Studies	The best historical research paper, opinion essay on historical issue, commentary on current event, original historical theory, review of a historical biography, account of academic controversy participated in	The best community survey, paper resulting from academic controversy, oral history compilation, multidimensional analysis of historical event, press corps interview with historical figure
Fine Arts	The best creative products such as drawings, paintings, sculptures, pottery, poems, thespian performance	The best creative products such as murals, plays written and performed, inventions thought of and built

Source: Table from EDUCATIONAL PSYCHOLOGY, 12th Edition, by Anita E. Woolfolk. Copyright © 2013 by Pearson Education, Inc. Adapted from *Meaningful assessment: A manageable and cooperative process* by David W. Johnson and Roger T. Johnson. Copyright © 2002 by David W. Johnson and Roger T. Johnson. Adapted with permission of David W. Johnson. Printed and Electronically reproduced by permission of Pearson Education, Inc., Upper Saddle River, New Jersey.

THEORY INTO ACTION GUIDELINES

Student Portfolios

Students should be involved in selecting the pieces that will make up the portfolio or exhibition.

Examples

1. During the unit or semester, ask each student to select work that fits certain criteria, such as "my most difficult problem," "my best work," "my most improved work," or "three approaches to . . . ?"
2. For their final submissions, ask students to select pieces that best show how much they have learned.

A portfolio should include information that shows student self-reflection and self-criticism.

Examples

1. Ask students to include a rationale for their selections.
2. Have each student write a "guide" to his or her portfolio, explaining how strengths and weaknesses are reflected in the work included.
3. Include self- and peer critiques, indicating specifically what is good and what might be improved.
4. Model self-criticism of your own productions.

The portfolio should reflect the students' activities in learning.

Examples

1. Include a representative selection of projects, writings, drawings, and so forth.

2. Ask students to relate the goals of learning to the contents of their portfolios.

The portfolio can serve different functions at different times of the year.

Examples

1. Early in the year, it might hold unfinished work or "problem pieces."
2. At the end of the year, it should contain only what the student is willing to make public.

Portfolios or exhibitions should show growth.

Examples

1. Ask students to make a "history" of their progress along certain dimensions and to illustrate points in their growth with specific works.
2. Ask students to include descriptions of activities outside of class that reflect the growth illustrated in the portfolio.

Teach students how to create and use portfolios and exhibitions.

Examples

1. Keep models of very well done portfolios and exhibitions as examples, but stress that each portfolio is an individual statement.
2. Examine your students' portfolios frequently, especially early in the year when they are just getting used to the idea. Give constructive feedback.

Evaluating Portfolios and Performances

Checklists, rating scales, and scoring rubrics are helpful when you assess performances, portfolios, and exhibitions because these assessments are criterion referenced, not norm referenced. In other words, the students' products and performances are compared to established public standards, not ranked in relation to other students' work (Cambourne & Turbill, 1990; Wiggins, 1991).

Scoring Rubrics. A checklist or rating scale gives specific feedback about elements of a performance. **Scoring rubrics** are rules that are used to determine the quality of a student performance. It is often helpful to have students join in the development of rating scales and scoring rubrics. When students participate, they are challenged to decide what quality work looks or sounds like in a particular area. They know in advance what is expected. As students gain practice in designing and applying scoring rubrics, their work and their learning often improve.

A Principal's Perspective

D. W. was a beginning principal at a K–6 elementary school with fourteen regular classroom teachers and approximately 300 students. Informed by the research of Doug Reeves (2000), she understood the positive correlation between the frequency of student writing and academic achievement. She knew as well that in order to be an effective instructional leader, she needed to clearly understand the academic abilities of her students and the instructional aptitudes of her faculty. Inspired by Reeves, she determined that personally evaluating student writing would be an exemplary way to do both. At a faculty meeting early in the school year, she asked all of her teachers to periodically give her writing samples from their respective classes, along with the scoring rubrics used to assess the work. She also asked that the teachers score the writing samples as they normally would, but not reveal the score to her prior to her own assessment. After reading each sample, she used the rubric to evaluate every student's writing and then compared her scores to those of the teacher. As it turned out, this practice not only helped her to gain a greater understanding of her students' abilities, but it also provided valuable insight about the teachers, generating critical talking points in individual conferences and faculty meetings regarding the frequency of writing assessments, the quality of the writing prompts, and the variations in scoring on rubrics. Additionally, participating as an external assessor of writing samples exemplified her commitment to being an instructional leader.

Reeves, D. B. (2000). *Accountability in action: A blueprint for learning organizations.* Denver, CO: Advanced Learning Press.

Performance assessment requires careful judgment on the part of teachers and clear communication to students about what is good and what needs improving. In some ways the approach is similar to the clinical method first introduced by Binet to assess intelligence: It is based on observing the student perform a variety of tasks and comparing his or her performance to a standard. Just as Binet never wanted to assign a single number to represent the child's intelligence, teachers who use authentic assessments do not try to assign one score to the student's performance. Even if rankings, ratings, and grades have to be given, these judgments are not the ultimate goals—improvement of learning is. The *Theory into Action Guidelines*, taken from Goodrich (1997), are intended for principals to help teachers develop rubrics.

Reliability, Validity, and Equity. Because judgment plays such a central role in evaluating performances, issues of reliability, validity, and equity are critical considerations. When raters are experienced and scoring rubrics are well developed and refined, however, reliability may improve (Herman & Winters, 1994; LeMahieu, Gitomer, & Eresh, 1993).

THEORY INTO ACTION GUIDELINES

Developing a Rubric

1. **Look at models:** Show students examples of good and not-so-good work. Identify the characteristics that make the good ones good and the bad ones bad.
2. **List criteria:** Use the discussion of models to begin a list of what counts in quality work.
3. **Articulate gradations of quality:** Describe the best and worst levels of quality; then fill in the middle levels based on your knowledge of common problems and the not-so-good work.
4. **Practice on models:** Have your students use the rubrics to evaluate the models that you gave them in Step 1.
5. **Use self- and peer assessment:** Give students their task. As they work, stop them occasionally for self- and peer assessment.
6. **Revise:** Always give students time to revise their work based on the feedback they get in Step 5.
7. **Use teacher assessment:** Use the same rubrics students used to access their work.

Step 1 may be necessary only when you are asking students to engage in a task with which they are unfamiliar. Steps 3 and 4 are useful but time-consuming; you can do these on your own, especially when you've been using rubrics for a while. A class experienced in rubric-based assessment can streamline the process so that it begins with listing criteria, after which the teacher writes out the gradations of quality, checks them with the students, makes revisions, then uses the rubrics for self-, peer, and teacher assessments.

Some of this improvement in reliability occurs because a rubric focuses the raters' attention on a few dimensions of the work and gives limited scoring levels to choose from. If scorers can give only a rating of 1, 2, 3, or 4, they are more likely to agree than if they could score based on a 100-point scale. So the rubrics may achieve reliability not because they capture underlying agreement among raters, but because they limit options and thus limit variability in scoring (Mabry, 1999).

In terms of validity, there is some evidence that students who are classified as "master" writers on the basis of portfolio assessment are judged less capable using standard writing assessment. Which form of assessment is the best reflection of enduring qualities? There is so little research on this question, it is hard to say (Herman & Winters, 1994). In addition, when rubrics are developed to assess specific tasks, the results of applying the rubric may not predict performance on anything except very similar tasks, so what do we actually know about students' learning more generally (Haertel, 1999; McMillan, 2004)?

Equity is an issue in all assessment, and no less so with performances and portfolios. With a public performance there could be bias effects based on a student's appearance and speech or the student's access to expensive audio, video, or graphic resources. Performance assessments have the same potential as other tests to discriminate unfairly against students who are not wealthy or who are culturally different (McDonald, 1993). And the extensive group work, peer editing, and out-of-class time devoted to portfolios means that some students may have access to more extensive networks of support and outright help. Others may have little support from home. These differences can be sources of bias and inequity.

Informal Assessments

Informal assessments are ungraded (formative) assessments that gather information from multiple sources to help teachers make decisions (Banks, 2005). Early on in the unit, assessments should be formative (provide feedback, but not count toward a grade), saving the actual graded assessments for later in the unit when all students have had the chance to learn the material (Tomlinson, 2005). Some examples of informal assessment are student observations and checklists, questioning, journals, and student self-assessment.

Journals are very flexible and widely used informal assessments. Students usually have personal or group journals that they write in on a regular basis. In their study, Michael Pressley and his colleagues (2001) found that excellent 1st-grade literacy teachers used journaling for three purposes:

1. As communication tools that allowed students to express their own thoughts and ideas.
2. As an opportunity to apply what they have learned.
3. As an outlet to encourage fluency and creative expression in language usage.

Teachers may use journals to learn about their students in order to better connect their teaching to the students' concerns and interests. But often journals focus on academic learning, usually through responses to prompts. For example, Banks (2005) describes one high school physics teacher who asked his students to respond to these three questions in their journals:

1. How can you determine the coefficient of friction if you know only the angle of the inclined plane?
2. Compare and contrast some of the similarities and the differences between magnetic, electronic, and gravitational fields.
3. If you were to describe the physical concept of sound to your best friend, what music would you use to demonstrate this concept?*

When he read the students' journals, the teacher realized that many of the students' basic assumptions about friction, acceleration, and velocity came from personal experiences and not from scientific reasoning. His approach to teaching had to change to reach the students. The teacher never would have known to make the changes without reading the journals (Banks, 2005).

There are many other kinds of informal assessments—keeping notes and observations about student performance, rating scales, and checklists. Every time teachers ask questions or watch students perform skills, the teachers are conducting informal assessments. One major message in this chapter is how important it is to match the type of assessment tools used to the target—what is being assessed.

Getting the Most from Traditional Tests

Even though there are many new ways of testing, students can still benefit from traditional tests. Both instruction and assessment are most effective when they are well

*Source: Classroom assessment: Issues and practice by Steve R, Banks. Pearson Education, Inc., 2005.

organized and planned. When you have a good plan, you are in a better position to judge the tests provided in teachers' manuals and texts and those developed by teachers.

When to Test?   Frank Dempster (1991) examined the research on reviews and tests and reached these useful conclusions for teachers:

1. Frequent testing encourages the retention of information and appears to be more effective than a comparable amount of time spent reviewing and studying the material.
2. Tests are especially effective in promoting learning if you give students a test on the material soon after they learn it, and then retest on the material later. The retestings should be spaced farther and farther apart.
3. The use of cumulative questions on tests is a key to effective learning. Cumulative questions ask students to apply information learned in previous units to solve a new problem.

Unfortunately, the curriculum in many schools is so full that there is little time for frequent tests and reviews. Dempster (1993) argues that students will learn more if we "teach them less," that is, if the curriculum includes fewer topics, but explores those topics in greater depth and allows more time for review, practice, testing, and feedback.

Judging Textbook Tests.   Most elementary and secondary school texts today come complete with supplemental materials such as teaching manuals, handout masters, and ready-made tests. Using these tests can save time, but is this good teaching practice? The answer depends on your objectives for your students, the way you taught the material, and the quality of the tests provided (Airasian, 2005; McMillan, 2004). If the textbook test matches your testing plan and the instruction you actually provided for your students, then it may be the right test to use. Table 8.5 gives key points to consider in evaluating textbook tests.

One aspect of assessment that affects every school is grading. Teachers are more directly involved with grading than parents, but everyone in a school is concerned about how grades affect students.

TABLE 8.5   Key Points to Consider in Judging Textbook Tests

1. The decision to use a textbook test must come *after* a teacher identifies the objectives that he or she taught and now wants to assess.
2. Textbook tests are designed for the typical classroom, but since few classrooms are typical, most teachers deviate somewhat from the text in order to accommodate their pupils' needs.
3. The more classroom instruction deviates from the textbook objectives and lesson plans, the less valid the textbook tests are likely to be.
4. The main consideration in judging the adequacy of a textbook test is the match between its test questions and what pupils were taught in their classes:
   - Are questions similar to the teacher's objectives and instructional emphases?
   - Do questions require pupils to perform the behaviors they were taught?
   - Do questions cover all or most of the important objectives taught?
   - Is the language level and terminology appropriate for pupils?
   - Does the number of items for each objective provide a sufficient sample of pupil performance?

Source: Excerpt adapted from *Classroom assessment: Concepts and applications,* 5th Edition, by Peter Airasian. Copyright © 2005 by The McGraw-Hill Companies, Inc. Adapted with permission.

Effects of Grades and Grading on Students

When we think of grades, we often think of competition. Highly competitive classes may be particularly hard on anxious students, students who lack self-confidence, and students who are less prepared. So, although high standards and competition do tend to be generally related to increased academic learning, it is clear that a balance must be struck between high standards and a reasonable chance to succeed.

Rick Stiggins (2007) encourages administrators to consider the assessment experience from the students' point of view. And that perspective differs radically for students who generally "win" at testing and those on a "losing streak." For students who generally do well on assessments, they experience a winning streak—continual success—and thus they are optimistic and expect to do well the next time, so they keep setting high goals and exerting effort. For these winners, school is a safe place that values their competence and gives them useful feedback so they can keep winning. The cycle continues: effort leads to success, sense of self-efficacy and engagement in school, which in turn leads to more effort and more success. For the student on a losing streak, the story is quite different. Repeated failures lead to a sense of panic and then hopelessness. Their reaction? "Why exert any effort? I just can't do this school stuff. I am confused and embarrassed—feedback is just more criticism and nothing I do seems to help." The students respond by devaluing the work or just looking for easy ways out. They are stressed at some times, bored at others, and often self-defeating. The cycle continues: avoidance and no effort lead to failure (again), disengagement, and more failure.

Effects of Failure

It may sound as though low grades and failure should be avoided in school. But the situation is not that simple.

The Value of Failing?   After reviewing many years of research on the effects of failure from several perspectives, Margaret Clifford (1990, 1991) concluded:

> It is time for educators to replace easy success with challenge. We must encourage students to reach beyond their intellectual grasp and allow them the privilege of learning from mistakes. There must be a tolerance for error-making in every classroom, and gradual success rather than continual success must become the yardstick by which learning is judged. (1990, p. 23)*

Some level of failure may be helpful for most students, especially if teachers help the students see connections between hard work and improvement. Efforts to protect students from failure and to guarantee success may be counterproductive. In fact, the more able your students are, the more challenging and important it will be to help them learn to "fail constructively." Carol Tomlinson, an expert on differentiated

*Source: "Risk taking: Theoretical, empirical and educational considerations" by Margaret M. Clifford, from *Educational Leadership*, September 1990, Volume 48(1). Association for Supervision and Curriculum Development.

instruction, puts it this way: "Students whose learning histories have caused them to believe that excellence can be achieved with minimal effort do not learn to expend effort, and yet perceive that high grades are an entitlement for them" (2005, p. 266). So maybe not failure, but accurate and critical feedback can be especially important for student who are used to easy A's (Shute, 2008).

So far, we have been talking about the effects of failing a test or perhaps a course. But what about the effect of failing an entire grade—that is, of being "held back"?

Retention in Grade.   About 10% of U.S. students ages 16–19 have been retained at least once (Wu, West, & Hughes, 2010). Retained students are more likely to be male, members of minority groups, and living in poverty (Beebe-Frankenberger, Bocian, MacMillan, & Gresham, 2004). Is retention a good idea? See the *Point/Counterpoint* to consider the question.

POINT/COUNTERPOINT

Should Students Be Held Back?

For the last 100 years, parents and educators have debated about the value of retention versus *social promotion* (passing students on to the next grade with their peers). What does the evidence say? What are the arguments?

POINT

Yes, it just makes sense.
Retention in kindergarten for children considered "not ready" for 1st grade is a common practice. Compared to students who are relatively younger (January to August birthdays), students who are relatively older (born September to November) have higher achievement in school on average (Cobley, McKenna, Baker, & Wattie, 2009). In fact, some parents hold their son or daughter back to give the child an edge over peers in each grade thereafter or because the child was born late in the year—a practice sometimes called "academic red-shirting." In the mid-1960s, 96% of 6-year-olds were enrolled in 1st grade in the United States. By 2008, the number was 84% (Barnard-Brak, 2008). The results on academic red-shirting are mixed. Some studies have found benefits for students who have been held back by their parents, but other studies have found no benefits.

With the increased emphasis on high standards and accountability, the idea of social promotion has come under fire and retention is seen as the better way. Guanglei Hong and Stephen Raudenbush (2005) summarize this and other arguments that have been made in favor of retention:

A widely endorsed argument is that, when low-achieving students are retained in a grade, the academic status of children in a classroom will become more homogeneous, easing the teacher's task of managing instructional activities (Byrnes, 1989; also see Shepard & Smith, 1988, for a review). In particular, retaining some children in kindergarten may allow the first-grade teacher to teach at a higher level, benefiting those who would be promoted under the policy. Meanwhile, children who view grade retention as a punishment may study harder to avoid being retained in the future. Some have argued that, in comparison with the social promotion policy, repeating a grade is perhaps developmentally more appropriate and may make learning more meaningful for children who are struggling (Plummer & Graziano, 1987; Shepard & Smith, 1988). If these arguments are correct, adopting a policy of grade retention will benefit those promoted and those retained, thus boosting achievement overall. (p. 206)

POINT/COUNTERPOINT   **Continued**

COUNTERPOINT

No, retention is not effective.

Retention assumes that the students just need more time and that they have the abilities necessary to catch up. But one study in California found the students retained after 2nd grade had the same average IQ score as those targeted for more intensive interventions under special education requirements. In addition, about 20% of the retained group had IQ scores in the range that would qualify as having intellectual disabilities (Beebe-Frankenberger et al., 2004), so it was probably wrong to assume that these students would benefit from the same teaching. Primary-grade students who benefit from retention tend to be more emotionally immature than their peers, but have average or above average ability (Kelly, 1999; Pierson & Connell, 1992).

After summarizing the arguments in favor of kindergarten retention, Hong and Raudenbush (2005) review the findings of almost a century of research. They note that even though there are a small number of studies that support the value of retention, the weight of the evidence indicates that it is not helpful and may even be harmful. Most research finds that grade retention is associated with poor long-term outcomes such as dropping out of school, higher arrest rates, fewer job opportunities, lower self-esteem (Jimerson, 1999; Jimerson, Anderson, & Whipple, 2002; Shepard, & Smith, 1989). Lucy Barnard-Brak (2008) studied a national sample of 986 children who had been identified as having learning disabilities and concluded, "delayed kindergarten entrance was not associated with better academic achievement for children with learning disabilities across time" (p. 50). The researchers concluded that retention "seemed to have constrained the learning potential for all but the highest-risk children" (p. 220). Another study that followed retained and promoted students for 4 years found some short-term advantages for retained students in social and behavioral skills, followed by long-term problems and vulnerabilities. The authors suggest that the "struggle-succeed-struggle" pattern may undermine academic motivation for retained students and interfere with peer relations (Wu, West, & Hughes, 2010).

Source: Excerpt from Hong & Raudenbush from "Effects of kindergarten retention policy on children's cognitive growth in reading and mathematics" by Guanglei Hong and Stephen W. Raudenbush, from *Educational Evaluation and Policy Analysis,* Autumn 2005, Volume 27(3). Sage Publications, Inc.

Beware of Either/Or: Using Research for Children.   No matter what, children who are having trouble should get help, whether they are promoted or retained. However, just covering the same material again in the same way won't solve the children's academic or social problems. As Jeannie Oakes (1999) has said, "No sensible person advocates social promotion as it is currently framed—simply passing incompetent children on to the next grade" (p. 8).* The best approach may be to promote the children along with their peers, but to give them special remediation during the summer or over the next year (Mantzicopoulos & Morrison, 1992). In addition, because the inability to focus attention and self-regulate is an important aspect of readiness to learn (Blair, 2002), help should also focus on improving these skills as well. An even better approach would be to prevent the problems before they occur by providing extra resources in the early years (McCoy & Reynolds, 1999).

**Source:* "Promotion or retention: Which one is social?" by Jeannie Oakes, from *Harvard Education Letter,* January/February 1999, Volume 15(1). Harvard Education Publishing Group.

Effects of Feedback

The results of several studies of feedback fit well with the notion of "successful" or constructive failure. These studies have concluded that it is more helpful to tell students *why* they are wrong so they can learn more appropriate strategies (Bangert-Drowns, Kulik, Kulik, & Morgan, 1991). Students often need help figuring out why their answers are incorrect. Without such feedback, they are likely to make the same mistakes again. Yet this type of feedback is rarely given. In one study, only about 8% of the teachers noticed a consistent type of error in a student's arithmetic computation and informed the student (Bloom & Bourdon, 1980).

What are the identifying characteristics of effective written feedback? With older students (late elementary through high school), written comments are most helpful when they are personalized and when they provide constructive criticism. This means the teacher should make specific comments on errors or faulty strategies, but balance this criticism with suggestions about how to improve, along with comments on the positive aspects of the work (Butler & Nisan, 1986; Elawar & Corno, 1985). Working with 6th-grade teachers, Elawar and Corno (1985) found that feedback was dramatically improved when the teachers used these four questions as a guide: "What is the key error? What is the probable reason the student made this error? How can I guide the student to avoid the error in the future? What did the student do well that could be noted?" (p. 166). Here are some examples of teachers' written comments that proved helpful (Elawar & Corno, 1985, p. 164):

> Juan, you know how to get a percent, but the computation is wrong in this instance. . . . Can you see where? (Teacher has underlined the location of errors.)

> You know how to solve the problem—the formula is correct—but you have not demonstrated that you understand how one fraction multiplied by another can give an answer that is smaller than either $\left(\frac{1}{2} \times \frac{1}{2} = \frac{1}{4}\right)$.*

These comments should help students correct errors and should recognize good work, progress, and increasing skill.

Grades and Motivation

If you are relying on grades to motivate students, you had better think again (Smith, Smith, & De Lisi, 2001). The assessments your school gives should support students' motivation to learn—not just to work for a grade. But is there really a difference between working for a grade and working to learn? The answer depends in part on how a grade is determined. Your teachers can use grades to motivate the kind of learning you intend students to achieve in your course. If they test only at a simple but detailed level of knowledge, you may force students to choose between complex learning and a good grade. But when a grade reflects meaningful learning, working for a grade and working to learn become the same thing. Finally, even though high grades may have some value as rewards or incentives for meaningful engagement in learning, low grades generally

Source: "A factorial experiment in teachers' written feedback on student homework: Changing teacher behavior a little rather than a lot" by Maria Cardelli Elawar and Lyn Corno, from *Journal of Educational Psychology*, April 1985, Volume 77(2): pp. 162–173. American Psychological Association. Reprinted with permission.

do not encourage greater efforts. Students receiving low grades are more likely to withdraw, blame others, decide that the work is "dumb," or feel responsible for the low grade but helpless to make improvements. They give up on themselves or on school (Tomlinson, 2005). Rather than give a failing grade, teachers might consider the work incomplete and give students support in revising or improving. Maintain high standards and give students a chance to reach them (Guskey, 1994; Guskey & Bailey, 2001).

Another effect on motivation occurs in high schools in the race for valedictorian. Sometimes, students and parents find clever ways to move ahead of the competition—but the strategies have little to do with learning. As Tom Guskey and Jane Bailey (2001) note, when a valedictorian wins by a 1/1,000 of decimal point, how meaningful is the learning behind the difference? Some high schools now name multiple valedictorians—as many as meet the highest standards of the school—because they believe that the educators' job is "not to *select* talent, but, rather, to *develop* talent" (Guskey & Bailey, 2001, p. 39). Principals can help teachers with grading by using the suggestions found in the *Theory into Action Guidelines*.

THEORY INTO ACTION GUIDELINES
Grading

Avoid reserving high grades and high praise for answers that simply conform to those in the textbook.

Examples
1. Give extra points for correct and creative answers.
2. Withhold your opinions until all sides of an issue have been explored.
3. Reinforce students for disagreeing in a rational, productive manner.
4. Give partial credit for partially correct answers.

Make sure each student has a good chance to be successful, especially at the beginning of a new task.

Examples
1. Pretest students to make sure they have the prerequisite abilities.
2. When appropriate, provide opportunities for students to retest to raise their grades, but make sure the retest is as difficult as the original.
3. Consider failing efforts as "incomplete" and encourage students to revise and improve.

Balance written and oral feedback.

Examples
1. Consider giving short, lively written comments with younger students and more extensive written comments with older students.

2. When the grade on a paper is lower than the student might have expected, be sure the reason for the lower grade is clear.
3. Tailor comments to the individual student's performance; avoid writing the same phrases over and over.
4. Note specific errors, possible reasons for errors, ideas for improvement, and work done well.

Make grades as meaningful as possible.

Examples
1. Tie grades to the mastery of important objectives.
2. Give ungraded assignments to encourage exploration.
3. Experiment with performances and portfolios.

Base grades on more than just one criterion.

Examples
1. Use essay questions as well as multiple-choice items on a test.
2. Grade oral reports and class participation.

Summary

All teaching involves assessing and evaluating student learning. At the heart of assessment is judgment, making decisions based on values and goals. In the process of evaluation, we measure results and compare outcomes to some set of criteria. There are two uses of assessments. Formative assessment is diagnostic and helps form instruction by determining what students do and do not know. Summative assessment determines what students have learned at the end of instruction and often is used to assign grades. Test results have no meaning by themselves; we must make some kind of comparison to interpret them. There are two basic types of comparison: in the first, a test score is compared to the scores obtained by other people who have taken the same test, a norm-referenced comparison. The second type is criterion-referenced. Here, the comparison is to a fixed standard or minimum passing score.

Increasingly, standardized tests are given to students. These tests are called standardized because they have standard methods of developing items, administering the test, scoring it, and reporting the scores. The final version of the test is administered to a large sample of subjects as similar as possible to the students who will be taking the test in school systems throughout the country. This norming sample serves as a comparison group for all students who take the test. Test scores of individuals and groups are compared to the mean (average score) and distribution in the norming sample. To make comparisons easy, the scores are also standardized using percentile scores, z scores, stanine scores, or T scores. For example, a T score of 60 for an individual means that the person has scored one standard deviation above the mean score for the normative sample. Other comparisons such as grade-equivalent scores are useful to principals and teachers as they make assessments about progress.

No test provides a perfect picture of a person's or group's ability or progress. Two critical features of any test are its reliability and validity; that is, does the test measure the results consistently, and does it measure what it is supposed to measure? At a minimum all tests should be reliable and valid. Achievement tests are designed to measure what a student has learned in a specific content area, whereas diagnostic tests measure a student's strengths and weaknesses, often to plan a course of action that will help the student learn and progress. Elementary school students are more likely than secondary school students to take diagnostic tests. High school students are more likely to take aptitude tests such as the SAT or IQ tests, which are meant to measure abilities developed over many years and to predict how well a student will perform in the future.

Today, many important decisions about students, teachers, and schools are based in part on the results of standardized tests; in fact, the No Child Left Behind Act requires each state to create content standards to measure student learning and knowledge in those areas. Because the decisions affected by test scores are so critical, many educators call this process *high-stakes testing*. But most standardized tests have been criticized as being biased against minority students. Culture-fair tests are difficult to find. There is, however, evidence that students can prepare for standardized tests and learn test-taking skills. Another criticism of traditional forms of testing is that such tests are merely samples of performance at one particular point in time; they fail to capture the student's potential for future learning. An alternative view of cognitive assessment is based on the assumption that the goal of assessment is to reveal potential for learning and to identify the psychological and educational interventions that will help the person realize this potential. Ungraded (formative) informal assessments such as journals, student observations, and self-assessments gather information from multiple sources to help teachers make decisions about student progress.

As the public and government demanded greater accountability in education and as traditional standardized tests became the basis for high-stakes decisions, pressure to do well led many teachers and schools to "teach to the test." Even more troubling, say critics, the traditional tests assess skills that have no equivalent in the real world. In response to these criticisms, the authentic assessment movement was born. The goal was to create standardized tests that assess complex, important, real-life outcomes. The approach is also called *direct assessment*, *performance assessment*, or *alternative assessment*. Similarly, more recent approaches to classroom assessment include authentic classroom tests that ask students to apply skills and abilities as they would in real life.

The concern with authentic assessment has led to the development of several approaches based on the goal of performance in context. For example, a portfolio is a purposeful collection of student work that demonstrates the student's efforts, progress, and achievements. The collection usually includes student participation in selecting contents, the criteria for judging merit, and evidence of student self-reflection. Portfolios include work in progress, revisions, student self-analyses, and reflections on what the student has learned, but the issues of reliability, validity, and equity remain important in assessment using such alternative means of testing.

High standards, a competitive class atmosphere, and a large percentage of lower grades are associated with increased absenteeism and dropout rates, especially for disadvantaged students. It may sound as though low grades and failure should be avoided in school, but the situation is not that simple. Failure can have both positive and negative effects on subsequent performance, depending on the situation and the personality of the students. For example, it is helpful to tell students *why* they are wrong so they can learn more appropriate strategies. Without such feedback, students are likely to make the same mistakes again, yet this type of feedback is rarely given. If teachers test only at a simple but detailed level of knowledge, they may force their students to choose between higher aspects of learning and a good grade; however, when a grade reflects meaningful learning, working for a grade and working to learn become the same thing. Finally, although high grades may have some value as rewards or incentives for meaningful engagement in learning, low grades generally do not encourage greater efforts. Ultimately, the task of the school is not to *identify* talent, but, rather, to *develop* it.

KEY TERMS

accountable (281)
achievement tests (275)
aptitude tests (278)
assessment (263)
assessment bias (274)

authentic assessment (288)
authentic tests (288)
central tendency (267)
confidence interval (273)
criterion-referenced testing (265)

culture-fair (culture-neutral) tests (285)
diagnostic tests (278)
exhibition (290)
formative assessment (263)

DEVELOPING YOUR PORTFOLIO

1. Based on the case at the beginning of this chapter, work with your teachers to develop a policy on sharing standardized test results with parents. Be sure that your policy is clear, precise, and can be included in a written statement to the parents of students in your school. As you draft your statement, address the following issues:
   a. School philosophy on the meaning and use of standardized test scores
   b. Brief description of the tests taken
   c. Guidance for interpreting the scores appropriately
   d. Parents' role in preparing their children for testing
   e. The role of teachers and the principal in meeting with parents about test results
   f. Any other information useful to the parents in your school

2. Analyze the state report card results for your school over the past few years (or, if there are no report card results, compile and use standardized test scores).
   a. Identify specific areas of students' strengths and weaknesses.
   b. Develop a report to your faculty that is informative but not accusatory.
   c. Then jointly devise a plan with your teachers for capitalizing on the strengths and improving the areas of weakness.

3. Investigate how four other schools are using authentic assessment. Work with a teacher to develop a supplemental authentic assessment plan for a unit of study in your curriculum.
   a. Specify the components of the assessment process, for example, portfolios, exhibitions, projects, presentations, and so on.
   b. Specify the rubrics for evaluating each component.
   c. Discuss how your plan for authentic assessment will be used in grading.

INSTRUCTIONAL LEADER'S TOOLBOX

Readings

Airasian, P. W. *Classroom assessment: Concepts and applications* (5th ed.). New York: McGraw-Hill.

Aronson, J. (2002). *Improving academic achievement: Impact of psychological factors on education.* San Diego: Academic Press.

Ewy, C., & student authors. (1997). Kids take on "the test." *Educational Leadership, 54*(4), 76–78.

Hong, G., & Raudenbush, S. W. (2005). Effects of kindergarten retention policy on children's cognitive growth in reading and mathematics. *Educational Evaluation and Policy Analysis, 27,* 205–224.

Miller, M. D., Linn, R. L., & Gronlund, N. E. (2009). *Measurement and assessment in education* (10th ed.). Boston: Pearson.

Nitko, A. J., & Brookhart, S. M. (2011). *Educational assessment of students* (6th ed.). Boston: Pearson.

Sheppard, L., Hammerness, K., Darling-Hammond, L., & Rust, F. (2005). Assessment. In L. Darling-Hammond & J. Bransford (Eds.),

Preparing teachers for a changing world: What teachers should learn and be able to do (pp. 275–326). San Francisco: Jossey-Bass.

Wu, W., West, S. G., & Hughes, J. N. (2010). Effect of grade retention in first grade on psychosocial outcomes. *Journal of Educational Psychology, 102*, 135–152.

Websites

mailer.fsu.edu/~jflake/assess.html
  Authentic Assessment
www.ericdigests.org/pre-9218/case.htm
  The Case for Authentic Assessment
www.ericdigests.org/1996-1/creating.htm
  Creating Meaningful Performance Assessments
www.ericdigests.org/1997-4/young.htm
  A Developmental Approach to Assessment of Young Children
www.ericdigests.org/1997-1/grading.html
  Grading Students
www.ericdigests.org/1998-1/development.htm
  Guidelines for the Development and Management of Performance Assessments

www.ericdigests.org/1999-4/tests.htm
  Helping Children Master the Tricks and Avoid the Traps of Standardized Tests
www.ericdigests.org/1996-1/study.htm
  Making the A: How to Study for Tests
nces.ed.gov/timss/
  Trends in International Mathematics and Science Study (TIMSS)

Organizations

www.ets.org
  Educational Testing Service
www.mcrel.org
  Mid-continent Research for Education and Learning
www.cse.ucla.edu/
  National Center for Research on Evaluation, Standards, and Student Testing
www.ncrel.org/sdrs/
  Pathways to School Improvement—Assessment
pals.sri.com/
  Performance Assessment Links in Science
www.PAREonline.net
  Practical Assessment Research and Evaluation

Assessing and Changing School Culture and Climate

PREVIEW: KEY POINTS

1. School culture and school climate are two ways to capture the feel or atmosphere of the school workplace.

2. Organizational culture is a pattern of shared orientations that binds the unit together and gives it a distinctive identity.

3. School culture can be examined at four levels: tacit assumptions, core values, shared norms, and artifacts.

4. Schools can create cultures that encourage learning and improvement among all participants.

5. Two such cultures are a culture of academic optimism and a culture of humanistic control.

6. School climate is a relatively enduring quality of the school environment that is experienced by teachers, influences their behavior, and is based on their collective perceptions of behavior.

7. School climate can be viewed using a personality metaphor and measured in terms of the openness of interactions among teachers and between teachers and the principal.

8. School climate can also be examined using a health metaphor and measured in terms of healthy interactions among students, teachers, and administrators.

9. Change is characteristic of all organizations, but change can be random or directed.

10. Schools have the potential to become learning organizations that solve their own problems.

11. An organizational development model can provide guidelines for changing school climate.

Leadership Challenge

You are the principal of an urban high school in the Northeast. About 40% of your students are minority and another 11% are newly arrived immigrants to this "ethnically rich" community. The diversity of the school and community makes your job a challenging one. You are committed to improving the school; among your goals are reducing student absenteeism, increasing the graduation rates, increasing the number of students heading to college, and, in general, making the high school a place where students *want* to be rather than *have* to be.

You are in the middle of your second year, and although the job is difficult and demands long hours, you feel like you are making progress. Most of the teachers are receptive to your initiatives. Yet, you have a nagging suspicion that things are not quite right; little things keep happening that give you pause—teachers leaving early, teachers skipping meetings, teachers not attending extracurricular activities. You decide to systematically examine the climate of your school. What you find shocks you. The teachers describe the schoolwork environment in much more negative terms than you do. They question your support of them. Morale is not high. The academic emphasis in the school is ambivalent at best. Apparently some teachers have given up on many of the poorer students. At least that is what your teachers say.

1. You are dismayed and surprised, but what do you do?
2. Where do you begin?

Think about it. Later in the chapter we will describe what principal Elbert Gibbs did in a similar situation.

The School Workplace

A collective sense of identity emerges in organizations, which gives the workplace a distinctive feel. There are many common terms used to refer to this indigenous feel of the organization: *ecology, milieu, setting, tone, field, character, atmosphere, culture,* and *climate.* All are used to refer to the internal quality of the organization as experienced by its members. *Organizational culture* and *organizational climate* are the two concepts that have captured the attention of educational researchers.

Both perspectives, climate and culture, are attempts to understand the influence of social context on organizational life. Thus, both should be useful to instructional leaders as they grapple with how social conditions in the school affect teaching and learning. Which perspective is better? You be the judge. Our position is that both frameworks are useful; the concepts are complements rather than alternatives.

Organizational Culture

There is no single accepted definition of *organizational culture.* At one level everyone agrees that culture refers to the social context of the organization and that different organizations have different cultures. The basic idea is that *groups and organizations have shared beliefs and values that make them distinctive.* But what are the critical shared elements? Some argue that they are the customs, rituals, and traditions of the organizations; others argue they are the implicit values and norms that evolve in work groups; and still others maintain they are the shared meanings that are created as members interact with each other in organizations. Indeed, organizational culture has been defined from all these perspectives. The notion of culture accentuates the need for stability, consistency, and meaning in organizational life (Schein, 1992). It's useful to think of **organizational culture** as a pattern of shared beliefs and orientations that binds the organization together and gives it a distinctive identity (Hoy & Miskel, 2008).

Levels of Culture

Culture manifests itself at different levels of abstraction. One way to begin to disentangle the concept is to examine these levels of culture. The levels range from very visible and tangible aspects that are concrete to abstract beliefs and basic assumptions that are unconscious and intangible (Schein, 1992). In between the fairly concrete artifacts and the abstract basic assumptions are informal norms and core values. The levels of analysis at which culture can be analyzed are pictured in Figure 9.1.

Culture as Tacit Assumptions.   At its most abstract level, culture is the collective manifestation of **tacit assumptions.** Such assumptions have become unconscious, basic premises about human nature, social relationships, truth, reality, and environment; they are taken for granted—and they are highly resistant to change. The pattern of basic assumptions that has developed within the organization to cope with

FIGURE 9.1 Levels of Culture

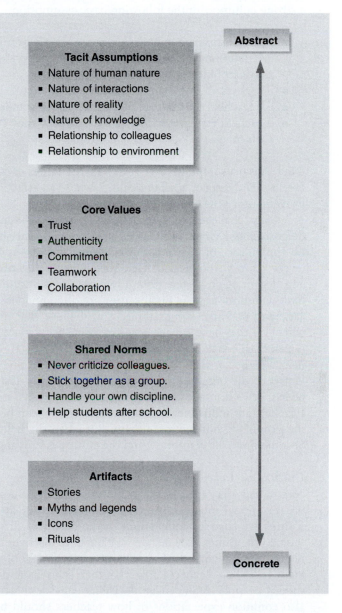

its problems of external adaptation and internal integration is its culture. When the pattern has worked well enough to be considered valid, it is taught to new members as the correct way to perceive, think, feel, and solve fundamental organizational problems.

Culture as a set of tacit assumptions defines for its members what to pay attention to, what things mean, how to react emotionally to what is going on, and what actions to take in different situations (Schein, 1992, 1999). Consider a school that has a strong culture with the following basic assumptions:

- Relationships among teachers are primarily group oriented, and shared decisions are determined through debate, which necessitates conflict and the testing and sharing of ideas.
- Teachers are highly motivated and competent.
- All teachers are evaluated by the same fair standards.
- Teachers view the school as a big family; they accept, respect, and take care of each other.

These basic assumptions give rise to shared values of cooperation, expertise, openness, fairness, and respect, a school culture where an effective program of instructional improvement is possible.

Any challenge or questioning of basic assumptions can lead to anxiety and defensiveness. Schein (1992, 1999) explains that the shared basic assumptions making up the culture of a group can be conceived of—at both the individual and group levels—as psychological defense mechanisms that protect the individual and group and permit them to function. Thus change is very difficult. Moreover, because the basic assumptions of an organization are often unconscious, distortions of information are quite possible. For example, if we believe that people will take advantage of us whenever they have a chance, we interpret events in ways that confirm that assumption. A principal's visit is perceived as an opportunity to exploit weaknesses rather than help. Further, if this belief is not only a personal one but also one that is shared and is part of the organizational culture, teachers will discuss with others how they have been taken advantage of during the principal's visits, and these beliefs are reconfirmed. If beliefs are individual and idiosyncratic, they can be corrected more easily because the group will not reinforce them. But when the beliefs are part of the culture, they become mutually reinforced and the culture is validated.

Culture as Core Values.   As groups emerge, they also develop a set of common, core values that are central to behavior; such values define, in broad terms, ideas organizational members need to embrace if they are to "fit in" and be successful. **Values** are abstract conceptions of the desirable. If we ask teachers to explain why they do the things they do, we may begin to discover the central values of the school. Shared values define the basic character of the school and give the school a distinctive identity. When teachers know what their school stands for, they know what standards should be upheld and make decisions consistent with those standards. Norms are also common expectations of how teachers should behave. Values deal with ideals and ends, whereas norms deal with the specific means to achieve those ends. In other words, values define the ends of human conduct and norms distinguish the means to accomplish those ends.

William Ouchi's (1981) book on successful Japanese corporations was one of the first analyses of organizational culture. Ouchi argued that the key to success in organizations was not so much a matter of technology as it was culture; in fact, he identified the core values of successful U.S. and Japanese organizations, which included the following: trust, commitment, cooperation, teamwork, egalitarianism, and intimacy. Notice that these are common values of the organization. There are competing values that are embodied in organizational actions such as competition, loyalty, democracy, expertise, innovation, and impersonality. Schools develop their own culture; that is, a core of common values that members embrace and that guide their behavior.

We expect, for example, that instructional leadership will be most effective in a culture that is imbued with such values as openness, authenticity, cooperation, collegiality, and innovation. On the other hand, a school culture that values competition, impersonality, correctness, and hierarchy will likely make the improvement of teaching and learning more difficult. How do shared values develop in schools? There is no easy or simple answer. Leadership can help. If a principal, for example, can convince teachers to act based on trust and collegiality and if such actions are perceived as successful, then the perceived value that trust and collegiality are "good" gradually starts a process of cognitive transformation. Over time, this transformation can lead to a common set of shared values or beliefs, but the process will proceed only if the actions continue to work well (Schein, 1992, 1999, 2004).

In strong cultures, core values are held intensely, shared widely, and guide organizational behavior; however, the content as well as the strength of culture are important. Each school has a set of core values that undergirds behavior. If improvement is to be successful, the core values must be consistent with authentic principal practices.

Culture as Shared Norms.   The next level of analysis for culture is in terms of the informal norms. **Norms** are the unwritten and informal expectations that teachers learn as they become socialized into the school. Norms are expectations, not behavior. Becoming a member of a group means learning the important informal expectations of behavior for the group. Make no mistake; norms affect behavior. The stronger the norms, the more constraining they are on behavior. Although norms are less abstract than values and tacit assumptions, they often are not obvious. It is difficult to bring to the surface the important norms of a group because members are reluctant to talk about them unless they are confident the information will not be held against them: In fact, many groups have a norm against revealing to outsiders their important unofficial expectations.

Norms are communicated to members by stories and significant events in the history of the school that vividly depict what the organization stands for. New teachers quickly learn the shared norms of the group, which are critical elements of the informal organization. Norms influence the way teachers dress, interact, respond to authority, and balance their own interests with those of the organization. In brief, norms are the informal rules that govern behavior in schools.

Although there are few, if any, universal norms for teachers, common ones exist in many schools. For example, "Handle your own discipline problems," and "Don't criticize other teachers to students," are two typical norms found in many schools. Examples of other norms that are more idiosyncratic are: "Don't rock the boat," "Innovate, try new ideas," "Support your fellow teachers even when they are wrong," "Never let students out of class before the bell rings," "Change your bulletin boards frequently," and "Don't criticize the principal in public." Norms are enforced by such informal sanctions as invitations to participate in special events (positive) and ostracism (negative). Teachers develop their own distinctive expectations for each other in their schools. Do teachers prize contentious debate or courteous restraint? Are playful and relaxed interactions appropriate, or are interactions structured and formal? Groups develop norms to answer such questions (Bolman & Deal, 2003, 2008). In brief, the shared norms of the work group define a major slice of the culture of a school.

Culture as Artifacts.   At the most basic and concrete level, the shared perspectives of which we speak are the things that members see, hear, and feel that make the organization distinctive. **Artifacts** include aspects of the physical environment (buildings, layout, classrooms, lounges, and so on) as well as the language, activities, and ceremonies that have become a routine part of organizational life. Although artifacts are easy to observe, they are sometimes difficult to decipher (Schein, 1999) because they are infused with meanings that come from that special group. For example, in one school informality may be a sign of inefficiency and fooling around, but in another school informality represents independent and efficient interaction among committed professionals.

There are many artifacts that are useful in understanding the culture of a school. Stories are narratives that become part of the school culture; they are based on true events, but often combine truth and fiction. The story of the heroic principal who supports a teacher even at risk of losing his or her job becomes retold and elaborated to embody the supportive norms that exist between the principal and teacher. Some stories are **myths;** that is, they communicate an unquestioned belief that cannot be demonstrated by the facts. Legends are stories that have become institutionalized. They have been repeated and elaborated in ways that add to the importance of the event. They capture what the organization has come to value. People who do extraordinary things that capture the essence of the culture become legends and heroes. The principal who stood by his teacher and overcame great pressure from parents becomes the focus for cohesiveness, loyalty, and commitment in a school faculty. The stories of heroes and legends provide insight into the core values of an organization.

Icons and rituals are important artifacts because they also indirectly communicate the culture of the school. Logos, mottoes, and trophies are icons that offer a glimpse of the school culture. **Rituals** are the routine ceremonies and rites that are visible examples of what is valued in the school. Beyer and Trice (1987) identify four rites that are typical of most organizations: rites of passage, degradation, enhancement, and integration. For example, the faculty lounge, coffee groups, and parties provide activities that bind the group together and make it a unique whole. Rites of enhancement are often seen in formal assemblies as the school recognizes the teacher of the year or the debate team champions. Such ceremonies reinforce appropriate behavior and signal what the school values. New teachers go through a series of rites of passage as they are assigned difficult classes, lunch duty, and after-school detention. They quickly learn to cope and discover the appropriate "way to do things around here."

Artifacts are observable and fairly concrete, but their meanings are often obscured. Only with time in the organization can one learn the meanings of the artifacts of a particular school. Stories, myths, legends, rituals, and icons typically embody the informal norms, core values, and basic assumptions of the organization. These latter elements of school culture are less obvious, but provide a fuller picture.

In summary, a school's culture can be examined at four levels: tacit assumptions, core values or beliefs, shared norms, and artifacts. Although artifacts are most concrete, they sometimes are difficult to decipher. At the other extreme, tacit assumptions are most abstract and difficult to identify. Core values or beliefs and shared norms are at the middle range of abstraction and also give meaning and understanding to the culture of the school. A thorough understanding of culture requires a comprehension of all four levels. In other words, to understand the culture of a school, one must comprehend the meanings and the shared orientations of the school: its tacit assumptions, core values or beliefs, shared norms, and artifacts.

Functions of Culture

Although there is no one best culture for all schools, strong cultures promote cohesiveness, loyalty, and commitment, which in turn reduce the propensity for members to leave the organization (Mowday, Porter, & Steers, 1982). Moreover, Robbins (1998) summarizes a number of important functions performed by the organization's culture:

1. Culture has a boundary-defining function; it creates distinctions among organizations.
2. Culture provides the organization with a sense of identity.
3. Culture facilitates the development of commitment to the group.
4. Culture enhances stability in the social system.
5. Culture is the social glue that binds the organization together; it provides the appropriate standards for behavior.
6. Culture serves to guide and shape the attitudes and behavior of organizational members.*

It is important to remember, however, that a strong culture can be either functional or dysfunctional; that is, it can promote or impede effectiveness.

Some General Propositions about School Culture

Without question, school culture is complex, symbolic, and contextual. Much of what occurs in schools can be understood and interpreted only in the unique context of the school's culture. Bolman and Deal (2003) summarize the complexities and difficulties of understanding organizational activities.

1. The most important aspect of any organizational event is not what happened but what it means. *Events are often not what they seem.*

*Source: Adapted from *Organizational behavior: Concepts, controversies, applications* by Stephen P. Robbins. Prentice Hall, 1998.

2. What an event means is often not clear because the activity must be interpreted in the context, and events have multiple meanings because people interpret them differently. *Meaning is elusive.*
3. Because events are typically ambiguous or uncertain, it is difficult to understand what happened, why it happened, and what will happen next. *Events are often puzzles: The future is problematic.*
4. The greater the ambiguity and uncertainty in events, the more difficult it is to use rational approaches to solve problems. *Rational decision making is limited as a process to solve organizational problems.*
5. When organizational members are confronted with ambiguity and uncertainty, they create symbols and stories to resolve conflict, provide understanding, and create hope. *Explanations are invented both to resolve conflict and to create positive outcomes.*
6. The importance of many organizational events rests with what the event expresses, not what it produces. *Myths, rituals, ceremonies, and sagas often give people the meanings that they seek.*

The implications of these propositions for principals are clear. The principal must be part of the culture in order to understand it. Significant events should never be accepted at face value; their meanings must be interpreted in terms of the values and norms of the school and from the points of view of different organizational members. Given the uncertainty and ambiguity of school life, rational responses to school problems are only part of the solution. The symbolic aspects of actions are often more important than the content of the action. For example, it is not so much what a principal says or does when working with teachers but how it is done and what it means. A talk with a teacher about a difficult student can be seen as a judgment of poor teaching or as an opportunity to solve a mutual problem; the meaning of the event depends on the shared norms and values of the group. Principals need to be creative in their ability to develop stories and explanations that mitigate conflict.

Although there is no one culture that is best for every school, there are some tacit assumptions that facilitate the process of improving instruction. Consider the following set of basic assumptions that Schein (1992) suggests is at the heart of a learning culture:

- Teachers and students are proactive problem solvers and learners.
- Solutions to problems derive from a pragmatic search; knowledge is found in many forms—scientific research, experience, trial and error, and clinical research in which teachers and principals work things out together.
- Teachers have good intentions and are amenable to change and improvement.
- Creativity and innovation are central to student learning.
- Both individualism and teamwork are important aspects of human interaction.
- Diversity is a resource that has the potential to enhance learning.
- Productive learning is enhanced by both challenge and support.

Schools anchored with such assumptions have created learning cultures that encourage improvement among all participants.

A Culture of Academic Optimism

One important perspective of school culture is academic optimism—shared beliefs about the potential of all students to succeed. Such optimism is a function of collective efficacy, faculty trust, and the academic emphasis of the school. These three collective properties are similar in both nature and function, and also in their potent and positive impact on student achievement; in fact, all three properties work together in a unified fashion to create a positive school culture that is called *academic optimism* (Hoy, Tarter, & Woolfolk Hoy, 2006a, 2006b; McGuigan & Hoy, 2006; Smith & Hoy, 2007). Many conceptions treat optimism as a cognitive characteristic (Peterson, 2000; Snyder et al., 2002). The current conception of academic optimism, however, includes cognitive (efficacy), affective (trust), and behavioral components (academic emphasis).

Academic optimism is a collective set of beliefs about strengths and capabilities in schools that paints a rich picture of human agency in which optimism is the overarching idea that unites efficacy and trust with academic emphasis. A school culture permeated with such beliefs has a sense of the possible.

- **Collective efficacy** is the shared belief that the faculty can make a positive difference in student learning; that is, *the faculty believes in itself.*
- **Faculty trust in students and parents** is the belief that teachers, parents, and students can cooperate to improve learning; that is, *the faculty believes in its students.*
- **Academic emphasis** is the enacted behavior of these beliefs; that is, *the faculty focuses on student success in academics.*

Thus, a school with high academic optimism defines a culture in which the faculty believes *it can* make a difference, *students can* learn, and academic performance *can be* achieved (Hoy, Tarter, & Woolfolk Hoy, 2006a, 2006b). These three aspects of collective optimism interact in a reciprocal way with each other (see Figure 9.2). For example, faculty trust in parents and students increases a sense of collective efficacy, but collective efficacy in turn reinforces the trust. Similarly, when the faculty trusts parents, teachers believe they can demand higher academic standards without fear that parents will undermine them, and emphasis on high academic standards in turn strengthens the faculty trust in parents and students. Finally, when the faculty as a whole believes it can organize and execute the actions needed to have a positive effect on student achievement, it will stress academic achievement, and academic emphasis will in turn support a strong sense of collective efficacy. In sum, all three aspects of academic optimism are in transactional relationships with each other, and they interact to create a culture of academic optimism in the school workplace.

Several factors underscore the utility of a culture of academic optimism. The term *optimism* itself suggests learning possibilities; a pessimistic school atmosphere can change. Faculty can learn to be optimistic. Academic optimism gains its name from the conviction that its composite properties all express an optimistic perspective and are malleable. Administrators and teachers have reason to be optimistic—they are empowered to make a difference. Neither the faculty nor their

FIGURE 9.2 **Reciprocal Relationships among the Three Aspects of Academic Optimism**

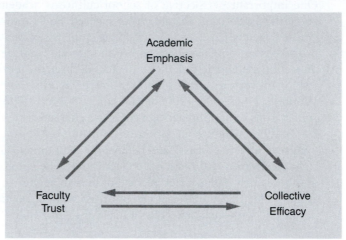

students have to be irretrievably trapped by socioeconomic factors that breed a sense of hopelessness and cynicism. The research is encouraging. Academic optimism can and does have strong positive impact on school achievement, even controlling for socioeconomic factors, previous success, and other demographic variables (Forsyth, Adams, & Hoy, 2011; Hoy, 2012; Hoy, Tarter, & Woolfolk Hoy, 2006a, 2006b; McGuigan & Hoy, 2006; Smith & Hoy, 2007).

How can leaders build a culture of academic optimism in their schools? We suspect the general way to enhance the academic optimism of a school is to improve its component parts. The one goal that virtually everyone shares for schools is academic achievement of students. The reform and accountability movements have promoted a press toward the academic achievement of all students (No Child Left Behind, 2002). The focus of schooling is clear—it is an academic one. However, a push for academic achievement in an environment where teachers do not feel efficacious is a recipe for frustration and failure. The challenge is to create school conditions in which teachers believe *they are up to the task and so are their students.* How might this be done? Principals lead a school by example. Celebrate the achievements of students and faculty, especially the academic ones. An emphasis on the honor roll, national honor societies, and extraordinary academic accomplishments of all kinds are examples of behaviors that foster academics. This may be an old list, but combined with building efficacy and trust, these activities take on new and added strength.

Collective efficacy is grounded in Bandura's social cognitive theory (Bandura, 1997); thus, we turn to his sources of efficacy for ideas about how to build collective efficacy in schools. The sources of self-efficacy are mastery experiences, vicarious experiences, social persuasion, and affective states, each of which communicates information that influences teacher perceptions about the school (Bandura, 1993, 1997; Goddard, Hoy, & Woolfolk Hoy, 2004; Hoy & Woofolk Hoy, 2011; Pajares,

1997). For example, consider a school with a poor graduation rate. A neighboring district has implemented a successful and effective program for at-risk students. The principal can orchestrate the transfer of the neighbor's success to his or her school. In so doing, the school is using a self-regulatory process informed by the vicarious learning of its teachers and, perhaps, the social persuasion of leaders. Modeling success and persuading teachers to believe in themselves and their capabilities is also a good route to improve collective efficacy and enhance academic optimism (Bandura, 1997; Forsyth, Adams, & Hoy, 2011; Goddard, Hoy, & Woolfolk Hoy, 2004; Hoy, Tarter, & Woolfolk Hoy, 2006b).

There is some research on family and community involvement in schools (cf., Epstein, 1989); however, there is little systematic research on how to build trust in students and parents in schools. Such trust can be promoted through interchanges, both formal and informal, between parents and teachers. Using vicarious learning, for example, a school can respond to a lack of trust and community participation in school activities by emulating the practices of magnet schools known for their parental cooperation and involvement. These examples demonstrate how changes in social perceptions influence what actions organizations choose to pursue. Collective perceptions about efficacy, academic emphasis, and trust shape the school's norms and can be developed through experiences that convey their value and utility.

A caveat is in order: Interventions should be supportive of all three aspects of optimism. Some ways of enhancing academic emphasis, such as more competitive grading and greater punishment for failure, may well undermine the development of trust among teachers, students, and parents. Similarly, an emphasis on developing trust could come as a result of diminishing standards and rewarding students for merely adequate work by providing only positive feedback. Constructive criticism is essential for academic growth.

The research on individual optimism suggests some ideas about encouraging a culture of optimism in schools. Peterson (2000) found that optimism is thwarted by stress; hence, decreasing stress should support optimism. Principals can lower teacher stress by increasing their agency through appropriate participation in decisions that affect their school lives (Hoy & Tarter, 2004).

Teachers learn from models because the observation of successful performance in others promotes a desire for and acquisition of their beliefs and actions. The most effective models are those who seem competent, powerful, prestigious, and similar to the observer (Pintrich & Schunk, 2002). Vicarious and observational learning are other sources of optimism. Teachers can serve as models for each other, and the way school problems are discussed should convey the possibilities for resolution rather than defeatism. Novice teachers should hear optimistic approaches to teaching from their colleagues rather than a sense of passive helplessness in teachers' lounges and school hallways (Hoy, Tarter, & Woolfolk Hoy, 2006b). Research on individual academic optimism is just beginning (Beard & Hoy, 2010; Fahy, Wu, & Hoy, 2010; Woolfolk Hoy, Hoy, & Kurtz, 2008). Individual views of academic optimism likely facilitate collective academic optimism, and hence student achievement.

In sum, a culture of academic optimism gets administrators and faculty over a wall of learned pessimism and paralyzing feelings of futility. Academic optimism creates a culture with collective beliefs and norms that view teachers as capable, students as willing, parents as supportive, and academic success as achievable. Perhaps most important, the academic optimism of a school is related to academic performance of students regardless of their socioeconomic status (Bandura, 1993; Forsyth, Adams, & Hoy, 2011; Hoy, Tarter, & Woolfolk Hoy, 2006a; McGuigan & Hoy, 2006; Smith & Hoy, 2007). You can gauge the academic optimism of your school by using the scale found on the website (www.waynekhoy.com) to measure collective efficacy. Academic optimism is an important perspective for viewing the culture of a school, but there are others (see Hoy & Miskel, 2013). We now turn to one other perspective and measure of culture.

A Culture of Control

Another way to view and measure school culture is in terms of control, especially the shared values and beliefs of the school for controlling students. Pupil control is a central and salient aspect of life in schools; in fact, most research that focuses on student control has found it to be a dominant feature of school life (Coleman, 1961; Hoy, 2001; Lunnenberg, 1983; Willower, Eidell, and Hoy, 1967). Much of what is done in school is linked to the climate of pupil control. A useful conceptual framework for viewing and studying schools was developed at the Pennsylvania State University and has spawned hundreds of studies (Hoy, 2001). The perspective aligns pupil control along a continuum ranging from humanistic to custodial schools.

The model of the **humanistic culture** is a school viewed as an educational community in which students learn through cooperation, experience, and self-control. The faculty believes that students should be self-regulated learners who take responsibility for their actions. Misbehavior is viewed in sociological and psychological terms; causes for deviant behavior are sought. The goal is for each student to be a responsible citizen of a learning community. Optimism, understanding, self-direction, and close friendly relations are hallmarks of the humanistic school.

The model for the **custodial culture** is a traditional school, with a focus on control, status, and power. Teachers believe that control is critical, teacher status is important, communication is one-way downward, and student misbehavior is a personal affront against teachers. Cynicism, strict teacher direction, mistrust, impersonality, and strong teacher control imbue the custodial school.

The control orientation of a school can be measured by aggregating individual responses on the Pupil Control Ideology (PCI) form (Hoy, 2001; Willower, Eidell, and Hoy, 1967); the higher the school PCI score, the more custodial the culture of the school. The PCI and scoring instructions can be found at www. waynekhoy.com.

The picture that emerges from the research on schools with cultures of control is consistent (Hoy, 2001). Humanistic schools have an open school climate (Hoy & Clover, 1986); greater teacher engagement and higher morale (Hoy & Appleberry, 1970); less alienated students (Hoy, 1972); students with stronger self-concepts (Diebert & Hoy, 1977); more highly motivated students (Lunnenberg, 1983), and less vandalism and fewer suspensions (Finkelstein, 1998) than custodial schools (Hoy, 2001). There are no quick fixes to changing cultures of schools, but it is clear that strong and highly motivated instructional leaders are needed.

Two conclusions are warranted from the research on organizational culture:

1. A culture of academic optimism facilitates the academic achievement of all students regardless of the socioeconomic status of parents.
2. A culture of humanistic control enhances the commitment of students to school and improves the self-concepts of students.

It is clear instructional leaders should strive to cultivate strong cultures of academic optimism and humanistic control.

Organizational Climate

Another aspect of the school context that sets the scene for effective instructional leadership is organizational climate. Teachers' performances in schools are in part determined by the climate in which they work. **Organizational climate** is a general concept that refers to teachers' perceptions of the school's work environment; it is affected by the formal organization, informal organization, and politics, all of which, including climate, affect the motivations and behavior of teachers. Simply stated, the set of internal characteristics that distinguishes one school from another and influences the behavior of its members is the organizational climate of the school. More specifically, climate is a relatively enduring quality of the school environment that is experienced by teachers, influences their behavior, and is based on their collective perceptions (Hoy & Miskel, 2005, 2013).

As we have suggested earlier, *climate* and *culture* both refer to the atmosphere of the school. Culture refers to shared *beliefs* and climate refers to basic patterns of *behavior* that exist in organizations. Admittedly, there is not a huge difference between shared assumptions, values, beliefs, and norms and shared perceptions of behavior, but the distinction is a useful one. Each provides the principal with a valuable set of conceptual capital to analyze, understand, and improve teaching and learning.

Organizational Climate: Open to Closed

Probably the best-known conceptualization and measurement of the organizational climate of a school was developed by Andrew W. Halpin and Don B. Croft (1962) in their pioneering study of elementary schools. As they visited and observed schools, they were struck by the dramatic differences they found in the "feel" of the schools. Halpin (1966) described the marked contrasts as follows:

> In one school the teachers and the principal are zestful and exude confidence in what they are doing. They find pleasure in working with each other; this pleasure is transmitted to students.... In a second school the brooding discontentment of teachers is palpable; the principal tries to hide his incompetence and his lack of direction behind a

cloak of authority…. And the psychological sickness of such a faculty spills over on the students who, in their own frustration, feed back to teachers a mood of despair. A third school is marked by neither joy nor despair, but by hollow ritual … in a strange way the show doesn't seem to be for real. (p. 131)*

These stark differences in the feel of schools led Halpin and Croft (1962) to a systematic attempt to conceptualize and measure school climate. They viewed the climate of the school in terms of its personality; that is, just as individuals have personalities, schools have organizational climates. Two general sets of social behavior were mapped: principal–teacher interactions and teacher–teacher interactions. The principal's leadership can influence teacher behavior, but so can group behavior affect the principal's behavior; hence, the leadership of the principal, the nature of the teacher group, and their mutual interaction became the key components for identifying the social climate of schools. In all, eight dimensions of teacher–teacher and teacher–principal behavior were identified as Halpin and Croft (1962) developed an instrument to measure the organizational climate of elementary schools, the Organizational Climate Description Questionnaire (**OCDQ**).

A Revised OCDQ

The original OCDQ spawned hundreds of studies in the 1960s and 1970s (Anderson, 1982). But times and conditions have changed dramatically since the first appearance of the OCDQ. Many of the items no longer measure what they were intended to measure; some of the subtests are no longer valid; the reliabilities of some of the subtests are low; and time has rendered many of the items irrelevant to contemporary school organizations (Hoy & Miskel, 2001, 2013). Consequently, it should come as no surprise that the OCDQ has been revised and updated for use in today's schools. The original OCDQ was designed for use only in elementary schools, but revised versions have been formulated and tested for elementary (Hoy & Clover, 1986), middle (Hoy & Sabo, 1998), and high schools (Hoy, Tarter, & Kottkamp, 1991). Although we will describe only the revised Organizational Climate Description Questionnaire for elementary schools (OCDQ-RE), reliable versions for use in middle and high schools are available (www.waynekhoy.com). All the climate instruments describe the behavior of principals as they interact with their teachers, and the behavior of teachers as they interact with their colleagues.

Principal Behavior.   The first element of school climate is the principal's style of interacting with teachers. Three key aspects of principal–teacher interactions set the tone for life in schools—supportive, directive, and restrictive principal behavior.

1. *Supportive* behavior reflects genuine concern for teachers. Principals respect the professional expertise of their teachers and treat them as colleagues. Assisting teachers, complimenting teachers, providing constructive criticism, and having concern for their personal welfare are examples of supportive behavior.

*Source: Theory and research in administration by Andrew Williams Halpin. Macmillan, 1966.

2. *Directive* behavior is starkly task oriented, with little attention to the personal needs of teachers. The principal's behavior is direct and controlling: Teachers are closely observed, criticized, and constrained. Communication is downward focused, with little attention to feedback from teachers. In brief, directive principal behavior is autocratic, rigid, and controlling.

3. *Restrictive* behavior is burdensome. Principals overload teachers with unnecessary work—too many committees, too much paperwork, and too much busywork. The principal hinders rather than facilitates teachers' work.

Teachers' Behavior.   The second key element of school climate is the teachers' behavior in school. Teachers do not react to the school organization as isolated individuals, but rather as members of a teacher work group; they are part of the informal organization. As they work in school, they interact with other teachers and form ideas that have important consequences for their behavior. Three important dimensions of teacher interactions are postulated to have major influence on the climate of the school: collegial, intimate, and disengaged teacher behavior.

1. *Collegial* behavior is supportive professionalism among teachers. Teachers are pleased with their school; they accept and support each other and feel a sense of accomplishment in their teaching. Above all, teachers are professionals who respect the competence and dedication of their colleagues.

2. *Intimate* behavior is close personal relations among teachers both inside and outside the school. Teachers' closest friends are often teachers in their school; they talk and confide in each other.

3. *Disengaged* behavior is a general sense of alienation and separation among teachers in the school. There is little cohesiveness among teachers. They bicker with each other and ramble when they talk in meetings. Teachers are simply going through the motions; they are not productive in group efforts or team building.

These six features are the key elements for developing school climates. But specifically, how are these dimensions of climate measured? How are the profiles determined? What do the profiles mean?

Interpreting the OCDQ-RE.   All items are simple descriptive statements of interactions in schools. Teachers are asked to describe the extent to which each item characterizes his or her school. The responses to each item are made on a four-point scale: rarely occurs, sometimes occurs, often occurs, and very frequently occurs. Sample items for each of the dimensions of the OCDQ-RE are summarized in Table 9.1 and a copy of the instrument is found in Appendix D (p. 353).

Using factor-analytic techniques and a sample of seventy elementary schools, forty-four items were identified that measured six dimensions of school climate (Hoy, Tarter, & Kottkamp, 1991). The six aspects, taken together, map a profile of the climate of each school. Scores for all subtests and schools were standardized so that the mean score was 500 and the standard deviation was 100. Then the scores are interpreted as one would SAT or GRE scores. A score of 500 is a school with average

TABLE 9.1   Sample Items for Each Dimension of the OCDQ-RE

Principal Behavior	Teacher Behavior
Supportive Behavior	*Collegial Behavior*
■ The principal uses constructive criticism.	■ Teachers help and support each other.
■ The principal compliments teachers.	■ Teachers respect the professional competence of their colleagues.
■ The principal listens to and accepts teachers' suggestions.	■ Teachers accomplish their work with vim, vigor, and pleasure.
Directive Behavior	*Intimate Behavior*
■ The principal monitors everything teachers do.	■ Teacher socialize with each other.
■ The principal rules with an iron fist.	■ Teachers' closest friends are other faculty members at this school.
■ The principal checks lesson plans.	■ Teachers have parties for each other.
Restrictive Behavior	*Disengaged Behavior*
■ Teachers are burdened with busywork.	■ Faculty meetings are useless.
■ Routine duties interfere with the job of teaching.	■ There is a minority group of teachers who always oppose the majority.
■ Teachers have too many committee requirements.	■ Teachers ramble when they talk at faculty meetings.

A copy of the entire instrument is found in Appendix D and also at www.waynekhoy.com.

openness, whereas one with a score of 600 is quite open—more than one standard deviation better than an average school. For example, the profiles of the climates for two hypothetical schools might be plotted as indicated in Figure 9.3. The school climate profiled with the gray line in the figure reflects an open school climate with a supportive, nondirective, and nonrestrictive principal and a collegial, engaged, intimate faculty committed to the teaching–learning task. The other school, indicated by the black line, represents a closed school climate with a directive, restrictive, and nonsupportive principal and suspicious (noncollegial), disengaged, and distant teachers.

Elementary school climate rests on two general factors of openness (Hoy & Clover, 1986; Hoy & Tarter, 1997b). Specifically, openness in faculty relations is characterized by teacher interactions that are meaningful and tolerant (low disengagement); friendly, close, and supportive (high intimacy); and enthusiastic, accepting, and mutually respectful (high collegial relations). Openness in principal behavior is characterized by avoiding the assignment of meaningless routines and burdensome duties to teachers (low restrictiveness); giving flexibility and freedom to teachers to act independently (low directiveness); and giving teachers respect and support in both personal and professional matters (high supportiveness). In general, this factor depicts a functional flexibility and openness in the principal's leadership behavior.

FIGURE 9.3 Contrasting School Climate Profile

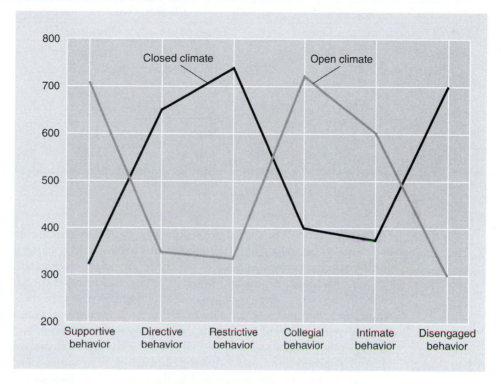

The conceptual underpinnings of the OCDQ-RE are consistent and clear. The instrument has two general factors: a measure of openness of teacher interactions and a measure of openness of teacher–principal relations. Organizational climate is a description of the perceptions of the faculty. Some may question whether a climate is open or closed just because the teachers perceive it to be. This question really cannot be answered and is probably irrelevant. Teachers' perceptions of what is "out there" motivate their behavior.

Climate Types

These two openness factors are relatively independent. That is, it is quite possible to have open faculty interactions and closed principal ones, or vice versa. Thus, theoretically, four contrasting types of school climate are possible. First, both factors can be open, producing a congruence between the principal's and teachers' behavior. Second, both factors can be closed, producing a congruence of closedness. Moreover, there are two incongruent patterns. The principal's behavior can be open with the faculty, but teachers may be closed with each other; or the principal may be closed with teachers, while the teachers are open with each other (see Figure 9.3). Table 9.2 provides a summary of the patterns of the four climate prototypes. Using this information, it is possible to sketch a behavioral picture of each climate.

TABLE 9.2   Prototypic Profiles of School Climate

Climate Dimension	Climate Type			
	Open	**Engaged**	**Disengaged**	**Closed**
Supportive	High	Low	High	Low
Directive	Low	High	Low	High
Restrictive	Low	High	Low	High
Collegial	High	High	Low	Low
Intimate	High	High	Low	Low
Disengaged	Low	Low	High	High

Open Climate.   The distinctive features of the **open climate** are the cooperation and respect that exist within the faculty and between the faculty and principal. This combination suggests a climate in which the principal listens and is open to teacher suggestions, gives genuine and frequent praise, and respects the professional competence of the faculty (high supportiveness). Principals also give their teachers freedom to perform without close scrutiny (low directiveness) and provide facilitating leadership behavior devoid of bureaucratic trivia (low restrictiveness). Similarly, teacher behavior supports open and professional interactions (high collegial relations) among the faculty. Teachers know each other well and are close personal friends (high intimacy). They cooperate and are committed to their work (low disengagement). In brief, the behavior of both the principal and the faculty is open and authentic.

Engaged Climate.   The **engaged climate** is marked, on the one hand, by ineffective attempts of the principal to control and, on the other, by high professional performance of the teachers. The principal is rigid and autocratic (high directiveness), and respects neither the professional competence nor the personal needs of the faculty (low supportiveness). Moreover, the principal hinders the teachers with burdensome activities and busywork (high restrictiveness). The teachers, however, ignore the principal's behavior and conduct themselves as professionals. They respect and support each other, are proud of their colleagues, and enjoy their work (highly collegial). Moreover, the teachers not only respect each other's competence but they like each other as people (high intimacy), and they cooperate with each other as they engage in the task at hand (high engagement). In short, the teachers are productive professionals in spite of weak principal leadership; the faculty is cohesive, committed, supportive, and open.

Disengaged Climate.   The **disengaged climate** stands in stark contrast to the engaged climate. The principal's behavior is open, concerned, and supportive. The principal listens and is open to teachers (high supportiveness), gives the faculty freedom to act on their professional knowledge (low directiveness), and relieves teachers of most of the burdens of paperwork and committee assignments (low restrictiveness).

Nonetheless, the faculty is unwilling to accept the principal. At worst, the faculty actively works to immobilize and sabotage the principal's leadership attempts; at best, the faculty simply ignores the principal. Teachers not only do not like the principal, but also neither like nor respect each other as friends (low intimacy) or as professionals (low collegial relations). The faculty is simply disengaged from the task. In sum, although the principal is supportive, concerned, flexible, facilitating, and noncontrolling (i.e., open), the faculty is divisive, intolerant, and uncommitted (i.e., closed).

Closed Climate. The **closed climate** is virtually the antithesis of the open climate. The principal and teachers simply appear to go through the motions, with the principal stressing routine trivia and unnecessary busywork (high restrictiveness) and the teachers responding minimally and exhibiting little commitment (high disengagement). The principal's ineffective leadership is further seen as controlling and rigid (high directiveness) as well as unsympathetic, unconcerned, and unresponsive (low supportiveness). These misguided tactics are accompanied not only by frustration and apathy, but also by a general suspicion and lack of respect of teachers for each other as either friends or professionals (low intimacy and noncollegial relations). Closed climates have principals who are nonsupportive, inflexible, hindering, and controlling, and a faculty that is divisive, intolerant, apathetic, and uncommitted. These four school climate types are pictured in Figure 9.4.

The OCDQ: Some Implications

A basic assumption of our analysis of instructional leadership is that a school's organizational climate is closely related to its improvement practices. The collective perceptions of teachers about their work environment influence their motivations and behaviors in the classroom. An open climate, with its authentic interpersonal relations,

FIGURE 9.4 Typology of School Climates

seems likely to produce a situation where constructive change can succeed. The closed climate, on the other hand, presents an environment of hostility, suspicion, and inauthenticity where the improvement of instruction is doomed to failure. Improving teaching and learning simply will not work in a closed climate; in fact, in such schools it seems futile to attempt to improve the teaching–learning process. If the climate of a school is closed, the first task is to change it. Such change requires a cooperative effort between the teachers and principal; in fact, the principal's leadership is a key to improving the climate. Trust and openness are necessary conditions for effective school improvement.

Research on school climates consistently supports the conclusion that the school's openness and its emotional tone are related in predictable ways. Openness is associated with less student alienation, lower student dropout rates, and more student satisfaction with schools (Finkelstein, 1998; Hoy, 1972; Mullins, 1983). Moreover, open schools are generally more effective than closed ones, and teachers are more involved in decision making (Hoy, Tarter, & Kottkamp, 1991; Hoy & Sabo, 1998). Openness and teacher commitment and teacher loyalty (Hoy, Tarter, & Kottkamp, 1991; Reiss & Hoy, 1998) are also positively associated.

Open organizational relations also have positive consequences in schools because they facilitate the process of improving instruction. No climate can guarantee effective teaching and learning because school climate in and of itself cannot make a poor program good or a weak teacher strong; however, an open school climate can provide the necessary atmosphere for reflection, cooperation, change, and improvement. There are three separate OCDQ measures for school climates, one for elementary schools (Hoy & Tarter, 1997b), another for middle schools (Hoy & Tarter, 1997a; Hoy & Tarter, 1997b), and one for high schools (Hoy, Tarter, & Kottkamp, 1991). There are no copyright restrictions for the use of any of the instruments for research or school improvement; in fact, they are all available at www.waynekhoy.com. Simply log on, download the instrument, and use it.

Open school climates likely increase faculty trust (Hoy, Smith, & Sweetland, 2002) and enhance perceptions of fairness in school (Hoy & Tarter, 2004). But schools also face a countervailing pressure to control student behavior with coercive rules. In fact, there is quite a bit of discussion today about zero tolerance for rule breaking in schools. Is such a policy a good idea? How might it affect the school climate? The *Point/Counterpoint* examines both sides of the issue.

Organizational Climate: Healthy to Unhealthy

Another framework for defining and measuring the social climate of a school is the organizational health of a school. The idea of positive health in an organization is not new, and it calls attention to factors that facilitate growth and development as well as to conditions that impede positive organizational dynamics. It is likely that the state of health of a school can tell us much about the probable success of change initiatives.

All social systems, if they are to grow and develop, must satisfy the four basic conditions of adaptation, goal attainment, integration, and latency (Parsons,

Is Zero Tolerance a Good Idea?

With the very visible violence in schools today, some districts have instituted "zero-tolerance" policies for rule breaking. One result? Two eight-year-old boys in New Jersey were suspended for making "terrorist threats." They had pointed paper guns at their classmates while playing. Do zero-tolerance policies make sense?

POINT

Zero tolerance means zero common sense.
An Internet search using keywords ["zero-tolerance" and schools] will locate a wealth of information about the policy—much of it against. For example, Oren Dorell reported this incident in the November 2, 2009 edition of *USA Today*:

> The most recent high-profile case [of zero tolerance] involved Zachary Christie, a 6-year-old who was suspended for five days on Sept. 29 after he brought a camping utensil that was part knife, fork and spoon to Downes Elementary in Newark, Del. School officials considered it a dangerous instrument and suspended the boy, adding that he couldn't return to Downes until he completed at least 45 days at an alternative school.

What does the research say? In 2006, the American Psychological Association set up a Zero Tolerance Task force to answer that question (Reynolds et al., 2008). Analyzing a decade of research, they reached the following conclusions:

- Schools are not any safer or more effective in disciplining students now than before they instituted zero tolerance.
- The higher rates of suspension caused by zero tolerance have not led to less racial bias in disciplining students.
- Zero tolerance policies can actually lead to increases in bad behavior that then lead to higher dropout rates.

In addition, zero tolerance policies can discourage students from informing teachers when the students learn that a classmate is "planning to do something dangerous." The zero tolerance rules get in the way of trusting relationships between teachers and students (Syvertsen, Flanagan, & Stout, 2009). Adolescents need both structure and support, but zero tolerance policies can create a highly structured,

rigid environment that ignores the need for support. Finally, many of the popular zero-tolerance interventions such as increased security guards, hallway monitors, and the introduction of metal detectors have no apparent effect on the incidence of school bullying (Hyman et al., 2006; NCES, 2003).

COUNTERPOINT

Zero tolerance is necessary for now.
The arguments for zero tolerance focus on school safety and the responsibilities of schools and teachers to protect the students and themselves. Of course, many of the incidents reported in the news seem like overreactions to childhood pranks or worse, overzealous application of zero tolerance to innocent mistakes or lapses of memory. But how do school officials separate the innocent from the dangerous? For example, it has been widely reported that Andy Williams (the boy who killed two classmates in Santee, California) assured his friends before the shootings that he was only joking about "pulling a Columbine."

On January 13, 2003, we read a story in *USA Today* by Gregg Toppo entitled "School Violence Hits Lower Grades: Experts Who See Violent Behavior in Younger Kids Blame Parents, Prenatal Medical Problems and an Angry Society; Educators Search for Ways to Cope." The story opened with these examples: a 2nd-grader in Indiana takes off his shoe and attacks his teacher with it, a Philadelphia kindergartner hits a pregnant teacher in the stomach, and an 8-year-old in Maryland threatens to use gasoline (he knew exactly where he would pour it) to burn down his suburban elementary school. Toppo noted, "Elementary school principals and safety experts say they're seeing more violence and aggression than ever among their youngest students, pointing to what they see as an alarming rise in assaults and threats to classmates and teachers" (p. A2). Toppo cited statistics indicating that, although the incidence of school violence has decreased overall, attacks on elementary school teachers have actually increased.

Surely we can ask adults to use good judgment in applying rules in dangerous situations, but not feeling trapped by the rules when student actions are not intended to harm and are not dangerous.

Source: Excerpt from Toppo "School violence hits lower grades" by Gregg Toppo, from *USA Today*, January 13, 2003. USA Today.

Bales, & Shils, 1953). In other words, organizations must successfully solve four basic problems:

1. The problem of acquiring sufficient resources and accommodating to their environments
2. The problem of setting and implementing goals
3. The problem of maintaining solidarity and cohesiveness within the system
4. The problem of creating and preserving the unique values of the system

Thus, organizations must be concerned with the instrumental needs of goal achievement as well as the expressive and developmental needs of its participants. Healthy organizations meet both sets of needs. All formal organizations, including schools, exhibit three distinct levels of responsibility and control over these needs—the technical, managerial, and institutional levels.

The technical level produces the basic organizational product. In schools, the technical function is the teaching–learning process. Teachers and principals are professionals who are directly responsible for student learning. Educated students are the product of schools, and the entire technical function revolves around the problems associated with effective teaching and student learning.

The managerial level mediates and controls the internal efforts of the organization. The chief managerial function is the administrative process, one that is qualitatively different from teaching. Principals are the prime administrative officers in schools. They must find ways to develop teacher loyalty and trust, motivate teacher effort, coordinate their work, and improve their instruction. The administration services the technical system in two important ways: first, it mediates between the teachers and students and parents; and second, it procures the necessary resources for effective teaching. Thus, teacher needs should be a basic concern of the administration.

The institutional level connects the organization with its environment. It is important for schools to have legitimacy and backing in the community. Principals and teachers need this support to perform their respective functions in a harmonious fashion without undue pressure and interference from individuals and groups outside the school.

This broad framework provides the integrative scheme for conceptualizing and measuring the **organizational health** of a school. Specifically, a healthy organization is one in which the technical, managerial, and institutional levels are in harmony; the organization meets its needs and successfully copes with disruptive outside forces as it directs its energies toward its mission.

Dimensions of Organizational Health

Seven specific aspects of organizational health are viewed as crucial dimensions of the interaction patterns of life in schools: institutional integrity, principal influence, consideration, initiating structure, resource support, morale, and academic emphasis.

These critical components meet both the task and social needs of the social system, and they represent each of the three levels of responsibility and control within the school.

1. **Institutional integrity** refers to the school's ability to adapt to its environment in a way that maintains the educational integrity of its programs. Teachers are protected from unreasonable community and parental demands. The school is not vulnerable to the whims of the public. Neither a few vocal parents nor select citizens' groups can affect the operation of the school when their demands are not consistent with the educational programs. The board of education and the administration are successful in enabling the school to cope with destructive outside forces.

2. **Principal influence** refers to the principal's ability to affect the decisions of superiors. Being able to persuade superiors, get additional support, and not be impeded by the hierarchy are important facets of leadership. In fact, a key to effective leadership is the ability to influence superiors while at the same time not becoming overly dependent on them.

3. **Consideration** refers to the principal's leader behavior that is friendly and open. This aspect of behavior reflects behavior indicative of respect, mutual trust, colleagueship, and support. Consideration does not denote a superficial or calculative affability; it expresses a genuine concern for teachers as colleagues and professionals.

4. **Initiating structure** refers to the principal's behavior in specifying the work relationships with teachers. The principal clearly defines the work expectations, the standards of performance, and the methods of procedure. The principal's behavior is task oriented, and the work environment is structured and achievement oriented. Like consideration, initiating structure is a major dimension of effective leadership performance.

5. **Resource support** refers to providing teachers with the basic materials they need to do an outstanding teaching job. Instructional materials and supplies are readily available. If extra or supplementary materials are needed or requested, they are quickly supplied. In brief, teachers have access to the materials they need.

6. **Morale** refers to a collective sense of friendliness, openness, and trust within the faculty. The teachers form a cohesive unit that is enthusiastic about teaching. They like each other, they like their jobs, they help each other, and they are proud of their school.

7. **Academic emphasis** refers to the extent to which the school is driven by a quest for academic excellence. High but attainable standards of academic performance are set, and an orderly, serious learning environment exists. The press for academic achievement is supported by administrators, teachers, and students alike. Teachers believe in their students, and students respond with vigor. Academic success is respected as a major accomplishment among students themselves. Good grades and scholarship earn praise and admiration from students as well as from teachers.

These seven aspects of teacher and principal patterns of interaction form the framework for defining and measuring the organizational health of schools.

The Organizational Health Inventory (OHI) is a descriptive questionnaire, not unlike the OCDQ, that measures these seven patterns of behavior. The **OHI** is administered to the professional staff of the school, and teachers are asked to describe the extent to which each item characterizes their school along a four-point scale: rarely occurs, sometimes occurs, often occurs, and very frequently occurs. The elements of the organizational health framework and sample items for each are summarized in Table 9.3.

TABLE 9.3 Dimensions and Sample Items for Each Dimension of the Organizational Health Inventory (OHI)*

Institutional Level (School)

Institutional Integrity

- Teachers are protected from unreasonable community and parental demands.
- The school is open to the whims of the public.**

Managerial Level (Administration)

Principal Influence

- The principal is able to influence the actions of his or her superiors.
- The principal is impeded by superiors.**

Consideration

- The principal is friendly and approachable.
- The principal looks out for the personal welfare of faculty members.

Initiating Structure

- The principal lets faculty members know what is expected of them.
- The principal maintains definite standards of performance.

Resource Support

- Teachers receive necessary classroom supplies.
- Supplementary materials are available for classroom use.

Technical Level (Teachers)

Morale

- There is a feeling of trust and confidence among the staff.
- Teachers in this school are cool and aloof to each other.**

Academic Emphasis

- The learning environment is orderly and serious.
- This school set high standards for academic performance.

*A copy of the entire instrument is found on the website (www.waynekhoy.com).
**These items are scored in reverse.

FIGURE 9.5 School Health Profiles

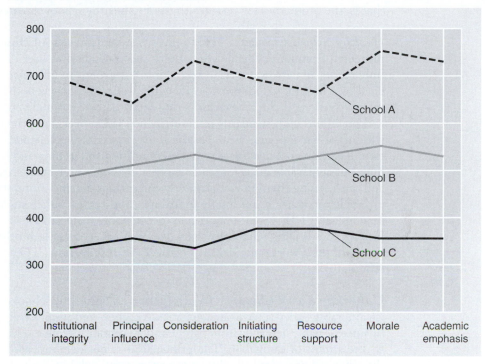

The OHI-S is a valid and the reliable instrument to measure the organizational health of secondary schools (Hoy & Feldman, 1999; Hoy, Tarter, & Kottkamp, 1991). To facilitate the interpretation of school health, school scores are standardized so the mean score is 500 and the standard deviation is 100. Then the scores are interpreted in the same way as is done with SAT or GRE scores. A school with a climate score of 500 has average health, whereas a school with a score of 610 is quite healthy, more than one standard deviation better than an average school. Profiles for three schools are graphed in Figure 9.5. School A represents a school with a healthy climate—all dimensions of health are substantially above the mean; School C, in contrast, is below the mean in all aspects of health; and School B is a typical school, about average on all dimensions.

The subtests of the OHI-S are modestly correlated with each other; that is, if a school scores high on one subtest, there is some tendency to score higher on some of the other subtests. Furthermore, factor analysis of the subtests demonstrated that one general factor explained most of the variation among the subtests, a factor we called *school health*. High schools array themselves along a continuum, with a few schools having profiles of very healthy organizations, a few having very unhealthy profiles, and most schools having somewhat mixed profiles in between the extremes. An index of health can be developed by simply adding the standard scores of the seven subtests; the higher the sum, the healthier the school dynamics.

We sketch below a behavioral picture for each of the poles of the continuum, that is, the prototypes for very healthy and unhealthy school climates.

Healthy School Climate.   Where there is a **healthy school climate,** the school is protected from unreasonable community and parental pressures. The board successfully resists all narrow efforts of vested interest groups to influence policy. The principal of a healthy school provides dynamic leadership that is both task oriented and relations oriented. Such behavior is supportive of teachers and yet provides direction and maintains high standards of performance. Moreover, the principal has influence with his or her superiors as well as the ability to exercise independent thought and action. Teachers in a healthy school are committed to teaching and learning. They set high but achievable goals for students; they maintain high standards of performance; and the learning environment is orderly and serious. Furthermore, students work hard on academic matters, are highly motivated, and respect other students who achieve academically. Classroom supplies and instructional materials are accessible if needed. Finally, in a healthy school, teachers like each other, trust each other, are enthusiastic about their work, and identify positively with the school. They are proud of their school.

Unhealthy School Climate.   When there is an unhealthy school climate, the school is vulnerable to destructive outside forces. Teachers and administrators are bombarded by unreasonable demands from parent and community groups. The school is buffeted by the whims of the public. The principal does not demonstrate leadership; that is, the principal provides little direction or structure, exhibits limited consideration and support for teachers, and has virtually no ability to influence the action of superiors. Morale of teachers is low. Teachers feel good neither about each other nor about their jobs. They act aloof, suspicious, and defensive. Finally, there is little press for academic excellence. Neither students nor teachers believe that academic matters are serious and important. Indeed, academically oriented students are ridiculed by their peers and are viewed as threats by their teachers.

The OHI: Some Implications

The OHI is a useful tool for several reasons. First, it reliably measures seven key dimensions of the organizational health of schools. Second, the conceptual underpinnings of the OHI are consistent with setting an atmosphere for improving teaching and learning. Third, a healthy school climate facilitates student achievement in schools (Hoy & Hannum, 1997; Hoy & Sabo, 1998).

Research findings using the OHI are encouraging. As one would expect, the healthier the organizational dynamics, the greater the degree of faculty trust in the principal, among colleagues, and in the organization itself. Not surprisingly, too, there is a strong correlation between the openness and health of schools; open schools are healthy schools and healthy schools are open ones (Hoy & Sabo, 1998; Hoy, Tarter, & Kottkamp, 1991). The research also strongly supports the importance of organizational health as a pivotal aspect of school life. In general, school health is positively associated with school quality, overall school effectiveness, teacher participation, effective leadership, and a strong culture (Hoy & Sabo, 1998; Hoy, Tarter, & Kottkamp, 1991). The one aspect of school health that is consistently related to student achievement regardless of socioeconomic status and irrespective of school level (elementary, middle, or secondary) is academic emphasis (Alig-Mielcarek & Hoy, 1995; Hoy & Sabo, 1998; Hoy, Tarter, & Kottkamp, 1991; Lee & Bryk, 1989).

Healthy organizational dynamics also have positive consequences because they facilitate teaching and learning. Although such an environment cannot guarantee high achievement, it does provide an atmosphere conducive to improvement of instruction. Moreover, the characteristics of healthy schools have many of the attributes stressed in the effective-school literature: an orderly and serious environment, high but attainable goals, visible rewards for academic achievement, principals who are dynamic leaders, and a cohesive unit based on mutual trust.

In sum, organizational health is another functional framework for analyzing important aspects of the character of life in schools. The OHI is a practical tool for assessing the health of a school. Like openness in school climate, healthy organizational dynamics are necessary conditions for an effective program of improvement. The principal must first have a positive climate; if it is lacking, it must be developed. Although we have described the OHI for high schools (see www.waynekhoy.com), there are also versions of the instruments for elementary and middle schools (Hoy & Tarter, 1997b).

Two additional climate measures should be mentioned briefly: the organizational climate index (OCI) and the Organizational Citizenship Behaviors (OCB). The OCI (Hoy, Smith, & Sweetland, 2002) gives a quick snapshot of school climate by focusing on only four aspects of climate—principal leadership, professionalism of teachers, school press for achievement, and vulnerability of the school to outside pressures. These four aspects of schools produce a culture of trust (Hoy et. al, 2002), which facilitates high student achievement (Forsyth, Adams, & Hoy, 2011).

The OCB taps behaviors by teachers that go beyond the formal responsibilities of the role; teachers volunteer freely to help others achieve the task at hand (DiPaola & Hoy, 2005a; DiPaola & Tschannen-Moran, 2001). Citizenship behaviors are characterized by altruism, conscientiousness, sportsmanship, courtesy, and civic virtue. Evidence suggests that schools with a strong climate of organizational citizenship are more effective and have higher levels of achievement—even controlling for socioeconomic status (DiPaola & Hoy, 2005b). Schools with good teacher citizens look for and find ways to make their schools function more efficiently and effectively. There are no copyright restrictions for use of any of the climate or culture instruments for research or school improvement; in fact, they are available at www.waynekhoy.com. Simply log on, download the instruments of your choice, copy them, and use them.

Changing School Climate

We have described several frameworks for examining school context. It should be clear that improvement of instruction is most likely in school climates that are open in interactions and healthy in organizational dynamics and where there is strong collective efficacy. Moreover, we have offered a set of instruments that enables teachers and principals to assess the organizational climate of their schools. What happens when the interactions are closed and the climates are unhealthy? Embarking immediately on a program of improvement of instruction with teachers working cooperatively with principals is difficult and usually counterproductive. Indeed, it seems futile for principals and teachers to attempt any authentic plan to improve instruction that involves cooperation, trust, and respect in such climates. At best, such attempts will be meaningless rituals, and at worst, they provide opportunities for the administration and teachers to punish and blame each other. If the school setting is inappropriate, changing *it* is the first business of the day.

Some Assumptions about Change in Schools

Before we proceed any further, we think it is useful to examine some basic assumptions about organizations and change to which we subscribe (Hoy & Tarter, 1997a):

1. *Change is a characteristic of all organizations.* Schools are in a constant state of flux. Change can be random or a resource harnessed for improvement, but it cannot be eliminated.
2. *Change has direction.* Change can be progressive, regressive, or aimless.
3. *Organizational learning is possible.* Schools can develop their own learning processes to solve their problems. Principals and teachers have the potential to learn how to solve problems together.
4. *Schools can be learning organizations.* Schools can become places where professionals can continually expand their capacity to create the results that they desire, where emergent patterns of thinking are nurtured, where collective aspiration is liberated, and where people are constantly learning how to learn. (Senge, 1990)

The process of building a healthy and open school climate can naturally transform the school into a learning organization where teacher professionals continually learn how to learn. Such organizations are functional for the improvement of teaching and student learning. We have included an actual case to illustrate one strategy for changing school climate.

A Principal's Perspective: The Case of Martin Luther King, Jr. High School

Martin Luther King, Jr. High School is on an old campus in an urban community in the Northeast on the corridor between New York City and Philadelphia. It is the only high school in Urban Park and enrolls a little over 1,200 students. Other potential students in the town are enrolled in Orthodox Jewish schools, and there is a large Catholic population that sends many of its children to St. Polycarp High School. While the school has its supporters in the town, it doesn't lack detractors. Urban Park is an ethnically rich small city of 45,000. The African American population has remained stable, comprising about a quarter of the district.

About 14% of the population is newly arrived Russians and Indians, and another 8% or so are Hispanic. A unique aspect of this urban community is its proximity to a major public university; consequently, about 20% of the students in the school are children of faculty, graduate students, and staff. By and large, however, this is a diverse working-class community that is financially pressed to support its schools.

Elbert Gibbs is a young, dynamic administrator. People who meet him are struck by his physical fitness; he jogs daily on the high school track, usually with student athletes after school. Gibbs was a former high school football player who earned athletic scholarships through college. After college, he became a successful high school teacher for several years before returning to the state university to pursue his master's degree in educational administration. He earned his principalship by dint of hard work as an assistant principal for three years in a nearby urban center. Elbert is on the fast track. In his course work at the university, Gibbs found the literature on school climate, culture, and change intriguing. He decided to do a systematic analysis of his high school.

Let's take a look at King High. First, we examine the climate profiles as described by Gibbs. In other words, the following profile is the way Gibbs and his teachers responded to the OHI and the OCDQ-RS. He sought to maintain his objectivity in filling out the forms. Gibbs also had his teachers answer the same instruments at a faculty meeting. He took pains to get a frank response from the teachers by absenting himself from the meeting and insisting that teachers provide candid responses to the anonymous questionnaires. They rather enjoyed the activity. A comparison of the climate profiles as perceived by the teachers and Gibbs is summarized below.

	Principal	Faculty
Institutional Integrity	540	420
Initiating Structure	560	555
Consideration	540	505
Principal Influence	510	465
Resources Allocation	500	445
Academic Emphasis	530	455
Morale	520	480
Overall Health	529	485
Supportive	555	490
Directive	480	540
Engaged	510	515
Frustrated	465	542
Over Openness	533	481

A Problem

Look at the *Principal's Perspective: The Case of Martin Luther King, Jr. High School* and the OCDQ-RS profiles. A quick glance at the profiles signals discrepancy. Gibbs describes a much healthier and open school climate than his teachers. Who is right?

It doesn't matter; the problem is the discrepancy in views. Gibbs see his behavior as much more positive and open than his teachers do. For example, on every dimension of health, he describes the school higher than the teachers. Similarly, on every OCDQ measure, he describes the school as more open than his teachers. Starkly, the difference between Gibbs and the faculty is that he sees an above average climate and they see one that is below average. What's happening?

Identifying and solving a problem call for different strategies. Gibbs has used climate instruments to identify the problem. That's the easy part. What to do and how to change the organization are other matters. Gibbs has to discover the root of the discrepancy: that is, why the teachers describe his behavior as more directive and less supportive than he thinks it is. There are only two aspects of school climate on which Gibbs and his faculty agree. Both judge the teachers to be slightly above average in their engagement, and both agree that the principal initiates structure and action to solve problems. But after that, there is not much agreement. Why does the faculty perceive most interactions in the school a much less positive way than Gibbs? For example, why is it that the faculty doesn't see the supportive leadership that Gibbs is trying to model? Why does the faculty describe the climate as basically unhealthy when Gibbs sees it as healthy? Does Gibbs suffer from unrealistic optimism? The principal cannot solve this problem alone because it is an interaction issue. It may be a question of misperception. But who is misperceiving?

An Organizational Development Model

What is a good strategy for developing healthy and open learning organizations? One potentially useful way to change school climate is a collaborative effort on the part of all those concerned, often called an **organizational development model.** This approach addresses both individual and organizational needs, and is a planned effort to make both the individual and the institution more productive (Hanson & Lubin, 1995). The approach is useful for principals who want to improve the climate of their school. In order to be successful, this strategy requires that administrators and teachers recognize difficulties, take responsibility for their solution, and develop and implement action plans. In the case at hand, the objective is to have teachers and the principal recognize that a challenge exists. Identifying a problem—discrepancies between the principal's and the teachers' perception of the social interactions in the workplace—was made possible by using the climate instruments described earlier in this chapter.

Before proceeding further, we outline and begin to apply the steps in an organizational development approach (Hoy & Tarter, 1997a):

1. *Identify the problem*—discrepancies in the climate profiles.
2. *Establish a problem-solving team*—usually the teachers in the school. To change climate, teachers must be involved.
3. *The team takes on the problem*—the teachers and principal come to an understanding of the difficulty. Teachers examine the data with the principal and express a willingness to resolve the troubling issues. They must understand the situation and see the need for change.

4. *Diagnose the problem*—the team diagnoses the causes of the problem.
5. *Develop an action plan*—the team develops an action plan by examining alternatives and consequences, and then selecting a course of action.
6. *Implement the action plan*—the team puts the plan into action.
7. *Evaluate*—the team assesses the consequences of the plan by collecting new data and evaluating discrepancies.

Back to Martin Luther King, Jr. High School

Principal Elbert Gibbs was startled by the school climate data. The teachers view the school in a much more negative way than he does. This discrepancy in perceptions defines the problem, which Gibbs has identified. Now, he needs to join forces with his teachers and involve them in organizational problem solving. Does this mean that he should involve all the teachers in the school? Perhaps, but especially those who want to be part of the process and have something to say should be involved. Over the long run, the goal is to routinely have all teachers participate in decision making and organizational problem solving, that is, to create a learning organization. Over the short run, however, the problem is to put together a team to begin the process.

One way to get interested teachers involved is to use an in-service workshop. Most schools have a day or two throughout the year for such activities, and Martin Luther King, Jr. High School (MLKHS) is no exception.

First, teachers need to understand the ideas of health and openness and how they are measured. In a faculty this large, the information can be presented efficiently at the workshop with accompanying PowerPoints and handouts to simplify the explanation. Our own experience is that teachers are very receptive to the climate ideas, especially because data about their school are available; the results of the OCDQ and the OHI are intriguing. An explanation of school climate and its measures can be done in a half day. That is, by the end of the morning of an in-service day, teachers should be able to interpret PowerPoint presentations of profiles of school climates.

Next, teachers are ready to look at the profile of their own school as they have described it. In this school, the teachers' score for overall health is 485 (below average) and school openness is 481 (below average). From the teachers' vantage point, this is an unhealthy school and its climate is closed. There are major discrepancies between the teachers and principal on institutional integrity (420 | 540), on principal influence (465 | 510), on resources allocation (445 | 500), on academic emphasis (455 | 530), on supportiveness (490 | 555), and on directiveness (540 | 480). These are major differences in views. What's happening here? Both the teachers and the principal need to know.

The principal must discover why the teachers viewed his behavior as less supportive and more directive than he did. Gibbs admitted to the faculty that he was puzzled by the results because he thought his relationship with the faculty was better than the teacher data suggested. Although he was perplexed, he was willing to examine his own values and choices in this open forum. This is not to say he was comfortable in doing so. Most principals are not, and he was no exception. But he felt he needed to continue what he started—an analysis of the school climate. There was no turning back. He believed that he needed to have an open mind toward his own as well as his faculty's behavior. He knew there were risks, but he wanted a platform of openness and trust to build a more effective school, one in which the improvement of instruction was a primary goal.

Actually, the problem-solving process seemed daunting. There were, after all, almost sixty professionals on the faculty, and the faculty had judged the school climate to be deficient. The thing that bothered Gibbs more than anything else was the low academic emphasis that the teachers believed existed in the school. While troubled by the teacher frustration and his reported directive leadership, the lack of academic emphasis hurt his professional pride. He wanted this school to be an important sequence in the education of all students, but minorities especially. Gibbs and the teachers need to seek explanations and avoid blaming or scapegoating. Was the problem real or imagined? Of course it was real, and the teachers recognized it.

At the next faculty meeting, Gibbs and his teachers had an open conversation about the causes of the discrepancies. With PowerPoints and charts at his disposal, Gibbs took 20 minutes to review the health profiles of MLKHS and then opened the meeting for discussion. Let's listen in:

GIBBS: I was surprised that you believe that parents are too obtrusive and there is too much community pressure. I don't just let people wander the halls, but I do want a lot of parental involvement in the school. I think it helps us to do our work.

FACULTY MEMBER: I have spent a considerable part of my adult life learning the skills of teaching. I appreciate help, but generally parents interfere; they don't help, they get in the way.

GIBBS: What do you mean? Give me an example.

FACULTY MEMBER: I have a master's in history from the university and I have taught history for fourteen years. I am interested in teaching students how to evaluate evidence, how to think. Parents want me to talk about the unique contributions of their group. Do you think the Multicultural Fair idea was our idea?

GIBBS: Well, I think multiculturalism is a good idea. After all, we have a multicultural school.

FACULTY MEMBER: We know that! But it's outside interference we resent. We think we should control those kinds of decisions, not outsiders. That's why our scores on institutional integrity differ from yours.

GIBBS: What do you think I can do? Parents have a right to come into the school.

FACULTY MEMBER: Of course they have a right to come in. But they are not here to write curriculum.

(Long period of silence.)

GIBBS: Well, well … we need to talk about this some more. I am beginning to understand why we responded to the items on institutional integrity differently. That's useful. But what really surprised me, and I don't understand, was our wholly different views of my leadership. I think of myself as being a lot more supportive and more open than you give me credit for.

(Long period of silence.)

FACULTY MEMBER: Well, we do think of you as supportive, but we get too many directives. You are always dropping in on our classes unannounced. You are always telling us what to do like we are students, not teachers. It's just too much.

GIBBS: Give me an example.

FACULTY MEMBER: We need more freedom to make the decisions that we need to make. You're an old history teacher, and I am a veteran English teacher. Why do you think you know more about teaching composition than I do?

GIBBS: I never said I did.

FACULTY MEMBER: Maybe, but you sure act like it. Here's what I mean: I am struggling in class with one of the slower students, trying to teach him the skills of writing simple sentences, and I am making progress. And you suggest that I should give the students more freedom to develop their ideas. That's not a bad idea in itself. But you just don't understand what's happening in the class. To be candid, I sometimes find your supervision obtrusive and irritating.

GIBBS: We need to talk about this later.

ANOTHER FACULTY MEMBER: I agree with Wally. You need to treat us more as colleagues and less as employees. We like you and you work hard. But so do we. You don't see us as equals. We feel like hired help.

GIBBS: I don't want to hurt your feelings, but when things go wrong, I take the heat. I am sorry you feel as you do, but I do respect you.

FACULTY MEMBER: You asked for some examples, and you got them. What are you going to do?

GIBBS: Well, I'll have to think about this. I asked for your interpretations, you have given them, but frankly, it's hard for me not to be defensive. We have some work to do.

This little exchange should give you a flavor of the kind of conversation that may occur. A close analysis of the conversation shows that the principal saw a difference in his status and he indirectly communicated it ("I'm the one accountable"). Teachers were seeking more autonomy, and some teachers felt the principal did not respect their abilities. In other parts of the dialogue, it also became obvious that teachers felt that occasionally Gibbs's observations of their performance were critical but neither insightful nor constructive. These were some of the reasons for the discrepancies between Gibbs's perception of his leadership style and the faculty's perceptions.

At this point, Gibbs needed a plan of action. Sixty professionals in a faculty meeting just was not the right format to get at the root causes of the discrepancies. Gibbs decided to ask for volunteers to work on the problems exposed by the climate analysis. Between volunteers (and all were included) and appointees, the principal put together a task force of twelve veteran teachers who were willing to work to improve the climate of the school. After the task force was appointed, Gibbs went to the superintendent and requested a modest stipend for the teachers. Gibbs argued that use of the climate measures served two important purposes. First, it got the faculty to engage in organizational problem solving, and second, it provided a useful vehicle for administrative assessment. The superintendent agreed to support Gibbs's foray into school improvement and organizational problem solving. To that end, she underwrote the cost for three Saturday morning work sessions.

What were the causes of the discrepancies? The first Saturday, the principal and teachers decided to develop a series of rival explanations for the differences in perceptions. The teachers had to be willing to take some risks in articulating their position without fear of reprisal. The teachers were divided into three groups and each developed an explanation of what was happening. The principal and his assistant were not part of any group. But nonetheless, Gibbs and his assistant also developed a tentative explanation of the data. After a couple of hours, the group as a whole reassembled and the four explanations were presented and compared. After comparing the explanations, the faculty agreed to devote the next session to trying to reconcile differences.

The next session opened with a brief recapitulation of the teachers' perspective on the climate data. The teachers saw the parents as having entirely too much access to the school; ultimately, they claimed that the parents interfered rather than helped. The faculty didn't mind parent participation in education, but they expected the principal to be a better gatekeeper. Parents were going directly to the teachers with their concerns and demands. There was agreement that Gibbs needed to serve as a buffer between community groups and the teachers. Growing out of conversations of the kind that we just witnessed, the teachers suggested that, if Gibbs were less directive, they would be less frustrated. The teachers saw themselves being drafted for too many activities. In fact, many were suspicious of his latest climate venture; they saw it as just another drain on their time that would be fruitless. A number of teachers also offered that busywork, such as written, formal lesson plans that went unreviewed, be eliminated. They suggested a committee on paperwork whose charge was to reduce paperwork wherever feasible. For his part, Gibbs still did not agree with the explanation of his faculty, but he respected the faculty's judgment and agreed that something needed to be done and he would do it.

Although Gibbs believed he had adequate support from the central administration, the teachers complained that he had little influence in getting them the things that they needed to improve their work. Making copies was always a problem; it took a long time to get class sets of materials; supplementary materials were simply not forthcoming. Gibbs saw it differently. He almost always got what he requested from the superintendent, as long as it was within reason. He believed that she respected his opinions and efforts. Gibbs was not sure the teachers understood the limited resources of the district; this was not a wealthy suburban district.

The teachers agreed that academic emphasis at MLKHS was below average. They saw little respect among students for academics. Football was king, closely followed by indifference. The teachers felt they were only being realistic in lowering their expectations of student performance. In fact, a good many teachers believed that most students simply couldn't do the work. They had difficulty getting students to do homework, and numerous classroom discipline problems. Gibbs, however, was unaware that for at least half the teachers, student homework and apathy were problems. Gibbs was probably misled by the orderly appearances of the halls and the good relations he had with students. It was not that Gibbs thought MLKHS was an academic powerhouse. Clearly, it was not. But he believed that compared to other urban high schools, his was above average.

On the measures of both directive and frustrated behavior of the principal, there were sharp discrepancies between Gibbs and the faculty. By and large, the teachers believed that his observations of their classroom teaching were intrusive and authoritarian. He didn't visit the classrooms often, but when he did, he always had many directives for improvement. The teachers resented the style if not the substance of his comments. The teachers resented the formal sign-in and sign-out required of all teachers. The teachers resented the extreme formalization in the school: forms for parking, for library materials, for audio/visual equipment, about grade distribution, and more; repetitive absentee forms, lateness forms, lunch forms, and a form for virtually anything out of the ordinary was required. Teachers believed the forms were for the most part unnecessary. Gibbs saw the forms as an essential way to monitor procedures.

If nothing else, the teachers and Gibbs were now communicating openly with each other and explaining their positions. Gibbs was interested, but he was unconvinced on many issues. The teachers, for their part, enjoyed letting Gibbs know how they felt. They believed that he was interested in them and the school and eventually would come around. At least he was open and not too defensive.

How do we develop constructive plans for reducing discrepancies and improving climate? This is the time for the teachers and the principal to work together to forge a realistic plan. There is no one best way to do this, but in the current case the principal and teachers decided to each work on the plan independently and then come back together (much in the same manner as they had framed the causes of the problem) to propose a school improvement plan.

The faculty task force met on yet another Saturday morning to discuss and formulate an improvement plan. In response to the analysis of problem causes, the principal offered the following:

1. Gibbs suggested that the teachers report all instances of parental interference to his office. Gibbs would monitor the reports and try to buffer the teachers from the parents.
2. Gibbs was genuinely concerned about the appearance of heavy-handedness in his administration, and he proposed two immediate actions. He would review

the amount of paperwork and reduce it dramatically, if possible. He respected his faculty and conceded that they should have more independence in decision making. In fact, he proposed that a leadership cabinet be formed that was composed of all the department chairs and administrators to share in decision making in the school.

3. Gibbs was still perplexed by the faculty's low student expectation; he rationalized that if it was as bad as his teachers said, the school needed some strong direct leadership. Here was his dilemma: How could he work with teachers to improve the academic climate and simultaneously remain indirect? He turned to his teachers for advice in this matter.

4. Gibbs promised that he would make himself more readily available to the faculty. He also pledged that, in the future, his criticism would be constructive and helpful. He concluded by reaffirming confidence and admiration for his faculty and pointed out the one area in which there was virtual agreement: the commitment of the teachers to the school.

5. Finally, Gibbs was concerned about the academic seriousness of the school. This was a good school in a community that supported education. He was shocked to find his teachers did not share his perception of the academic climate. He vowed to address the issue on a number of fronts. First, a series of meetings with his faculty were necessary to discover the origin of the faculty's mediocre assessment of the academic emphasis at MLKHS.

The faculty for its part came in with the following set of recommendations:

1. The teachers proposed that Gibbs become involved as a liaison between teachers and parents. They recommended that department chairs together with Gibbs and the executive committee of the PTA meet regularly to address and mollify parental concerns.

2. The teachers proposed a system of peer coaching to improve the teaching process. They also asked that they be given more input into future in-service meetings. They wanted teachers to be more directly involved, and administrators less, in improving instruction. After all, they reasoned, their job was teaching, and the principal's job was administration.

3. Because MLKHS was not a large school, the faculty asked for more informal consultation. They didn't want more meetings, just more influence and information.

4. The teachers recommended that a committee of teachers be appointed to streamline the bureaucratic procedures—and eliminate forms.

5. The teachers recommended that a schoolwide policy be established on homework and tutorials. The honor society would be approached and asked to do volunteer tutoring a few afternoons a week.

6. Finally, the faculty commended the principal for his concern and action in trying to improve the school workplace.

After the suggestions and recommendations were enumerated and discussed, Gibbs and the faculty were concerned about the number of different issues that surfaced and the time needed to confront them. Gibbs, for his part, admitted that he was unrealistically optimistic and the whole exercise provided him with a reality check. The teachers, on the other hand, were a little afraid that if they tried to do too much, nothing would be accomplished. They needed a reasonable plan that was realistic and attainable. There was, however, an inherent dilemma in their suggestions: They wanted greater involvement and more interaction but fewer meetings and less administrative work. They agreed to be idealistic and yet pragmatic. The following aspects were key elements of their eventual plan:

1. A committee of teachers would work with the principal to find ways to reduce administrative trivia and paperwork.
2. Gibbs and the teachers agreed that department chairs, the executive committee of the PTA, and Gibbs would meet regularly to address community concerns.
3. Gibbs agreed with the teachers that a system of peer coaching should be initiated.
4. Teachers agreed to combine classes on occasion so that they could serve as teaching models and coaches for each other.
5. Department chairs would work out the details. Gibbs turned over the next three professional in-service days to the teachers and department chairs; they would plan and conduct the in-service days.
6. The faculty and Gibbs agreed that a leadership cabinet composed of department chairs and elected teachers should be formed to share in the governance of the school. Gibbs agreed to consult with the faculty cabinet concerning all matters in which teachers had a personal stake and professional knowledge.
7. Gibbs suggested and the teachers agreed that the faculty would have complete independence in planning the programs for the three in-service days of professional development next year.

Clearly, this plan was not a set of step-by-step procedures to be accomplished in a rigid way. To the contrary, the plan was a set of accepted guidelines and commitments. The teachers and principal realized that their plan required increased effort. It is ironic that a major goal of the plan was to reduce unnecessary busywork, yet the cost of involvement, professional control, and autonomy meant that there was more work to do. The faculty was committed to the plan, even though they knew it meant more work—but, they believed, meaningful work.

How successful would this plan be? That is an empirical question. In six months, two activities would occur to assess its effectiveness. First, the OCDQ and OHI would be administered and scored, and then the principal and faculty would revisit the climate and changes at MLKHS.

Just to keep things in perspective, let us review what happened at MLKHS. The morning of the first day was spent explaining, discussing, and interpreting the climate frameworks, their measures, and the school profiles. In the afternoon, the teachers were confronted with the openness and health profiles of MLKHS. After some discussion of those profiles and agreement on what they meant, the principal introduced his perception of the school profile, which diverged dramatically from that of the faculty. The discrepancies led to a frank, open discussion between the principal and teachers culminating in the formation of three teacher groups to develop tentative explanations about the causes of the discrepancies in perceptions. After working in small groups for an hour or so, the teachers reconvened and shared their explanations, coming to a rough consensus about the causes of the discrepancy.

The next day was spent formulating a plan to reduce the discrepancies and improve the health and openness of the school. These two in-service days should be thought of as a beginning of a continuous program of improvement and problem solving. Even if these educators were successful in developing the school climate they all desired, periodic monitoring of the climate would be a wise course. The two goals of this process were first, that the climate of the school be improved and the stage set for effective supervision, and second, that group problem solving and organizational learning would become natural elements of school life.

Summary

Organizational culture and climate are two complementary ways to capture the feel or working atmosphere of schools. Culture is the shared set of beliefs and values that binds the organization together and gives it a distinctive identity. The culture of the school can be viewed from four vantage points—tacit assumptions, core values, shared norms, artifacts—all of which contribute to a full understanding of school culture. Schools can create cultures that encourage learning and improvement of instruction or those that discourage such outcomes. A culture of academic optimism is one that enhances the improvement of instruction and learning. Beliefs about academic optimism are social perceptions that provide school norms, which are strengthened rather than depleted through their use. Administrators are well advised to cultivate a culture of efficacy, trust, and academic emphasis to improve teaching and learning in their schools. Finally, significant events should never be accepted at face value; their meanings must be interpreted in terms of the values and norms of the school and from the points of view of different organizational members.

School climate is a relatively enduring quality of the school environment that is experienced by teachers, influences their behavior, and is based on their collective perceptions of dominant patterns of school behavior. Whereas culture is the shared beliefs and values of the school, climate refers to perceptions of the basic patterns of behavior that exist in schools. Although values and behavior should be related, they are not the same. School climate was conceptualized and measured from two perspectives: the openness and health of interpersonal relations. The OCDQ-RE is an instrument that measures the openness of interactions among teachers and administrators, whereas the OHI is an inventory that gauges the health of the interactions among students, teachers, and administrators. Both instruments give a reliable snapshot of school climate and are useful in attempts to improve the teaching–learning environment.

Organizations are in a constant state of flux. Their change can be progressive, regressive, or aimless. Schools can develop their own learning procedures to solve their problems. They can become places where teachers and principals can continually expand their capacity to create the results that they desire, where emergent patterns of thinking are nurtured, where collective aspiration is liberated, and where people are constantly learning how to learn.

We concluded this chapter with an example of how one principal used the climate frame and measures as bases for organizational change. Using an organizational development approach, he identified a climate problem, established a problem-solving team, diagnosed the potential problem causes, developed an action plan, and set the stage for effective school improvement.

KEY TERMS

academic emphasis (315)
academic optimism (315)
artifacts (312)
closed climate (325)
collective efficacy (315)
consideration (329)
custodial culture (318)
disengaged climate (324)
engaged climate (324)
faculty trust in students and parents (315)

healthy school climate (332)
humanistic culture (318)
initiating structure (329)
institutional integrity (329)
morale (329)
myths (312)
norms (311)
OCDQ (320)
OHI (330)
open climate (324)
organizational climate (319)

organizational culture (308)
organizational development model (336)
organizational health (328)
principal influence (329)
resource support (329)
rituals (312)
tacit assumptions (308)
values (310)

DEVELOPING YOUR PORTFOLIO

1. Determine the organizational climate of your school by using both the OHI and OCDQ.
   a. First you respond to each instrument.
   b. Then have the faculty of your school respond to each.
   c. Develop two profiles of the climate: yours and the faculty's.
   d. Compare the two profiles and speculate on the reasons for any differences.
   e. Develop a two-year plan of action for improving the school climate.

2. Describe the organizational culture of your school.
   a. Be sure to include a description of the norms and values for each of the following areas: innovation, stability, attention to detail, outcome orientation, people orientation, team orientation, and aggressiveness. Provide examples of the consequences of each.
   b. Also identify any other shared values that make your school distinctive and give examples.

   c. Use the questionnaires found on the website (www.waynekhoy.com) to measure collective efficacy, faculty trust, and academic emphasis, and then average the measures to gauge the academic optimism of the school.
   d. Critique your school's organizational culture; that is, discuss its strengths and weaknesses.
   e. Finally, develop a two-year plan of action for improving the school culture.

3. Over a two-year period, develop a series of in-service activities to improve the collective efficacy of the school. In particular, make sure that your activities are directed toward developing
   a. mastery experiences
   b. vicarious experiences
   c. verbal persuasion
   d. affective states

Clearly explain how your plan will address each of these sources of collective efficacy; then develop an evaluation plan to assess the effectiveness of your in-service activities.

INSTRUCTIONAL LEADER'S TOOLBOX

Readings

Bandura, A. (1997). *Self-efficacy: The exercise of control*. New York: Freeman.

Forsyth, P. B., Adams, C. M., & Hoy, W. K. (2011). *Collective trust: Why school can't improve without it*. New York: Teachers College Press.

Hoy, W. K., & Sabo, D. (1998). *Quality middle schools: Open and healthy*. Thousand Oaks, CA: Corwin.

Hoy, W. K., Tarter, C. J., & Kottkamp, R. (1991). *Open schools/healthy schools: Measuring organizational climate*. Beverly Hills, CA: Sage.

Hoy, W. K., Tarter, C. J., & Woolfolk Hoy, A. (2006). Academic optimism of schools: A force for student achievement. *American Educational Research Journal, 43*, 425–446.

McGuigan, L. & Hoy, W. K. (2006). Principal leadership: Creating a culture of academic optimism to improve achievement for all students. *Leadership and Policy in Schools, 5*, 203–229.

Schein, E. H. (2010). *Organizational culture and leadership* (4th ed.). San Francisco: Jossey-Bass.

Senge, P. M., Cambron-McCabe, N. H., Lucas, T., Kleiner, A., Dutton, J., & Smith, B. (2000). *Schools that learn*. New York: Doubleday.

Senge, P. M., Kleiner, A., Roberts, C., Rossi, R., & Smith, B. J. (1994). *The fifth discipline fieldbook*. New York: Bantam Doubleday Dell.

Websites

www.waynekhoy.com
   Climate instruments
www.infed.org/thinkers/senge.htm
   Learning organizations
www.ncrel.org/sdrs/
   Pathways to school improvement
www.tnellen.com/ted/tc/schein.html
   Organizational culture

Organizations

www.aom.pace.edu
   Academy of Management
www.teachingforchange.org/
   Teaching for Change
www.ucea.org
   University Council for Educational Administration

APPENDIX A

Conducting a Job Interview

Here is a collection of questions* to use in selecting teachers. We have grouped the questions around a number of typical topics.

Questions about why the applicant wants a position in your school system

1. Why do you want this position?
2. Why do you want to work in this district?
3. What do you know about our school/school system?

Questions about the applicant's conceptions of good teaching

1. Do you remember your favorite or best elementary or high school teacher? Tell me what there was about him/her that you admire.
2. What makes a good teacher?
3. Why would you be a good teacher? What are your strengths? Weaknesses?

Questions about the applicant's beliefs/goals/philosophy

1. What do you hope to achieve with your students?
2. If there were only one skill or concept that you could get them to learn, what would it be and why?
3. Why did you want to become a teacher?
4. What is your stance on (be familiar with the initiatives of the school or district to identify issues that might come up):
   - Inclusion?
   - Whole language versus phonics?
   - Using concrete rewards to motivate students?
   - Involving families and the community in your classroom?
   - Integrated curriculum?
5. If you were to be on an advisory committee for your college to improve the preparation of teachers, what would you suggest and why?
6. What current trends in public education please you? Displease you?

Questions about the applicant's skills/abilities

1. What is the best lesson you have taught? What made it good?
2. What has been your best experience in the classroom so far? What made it good?
3. What support do you need to make you successful?
4. Tell me about all your experiences in working with children in addition to your student teaching.
5. What has happened in your student teaching experience that you felt you were not well prepared for, and how did you handle it? What would you do differently now that you have had this experience?

Questions about the applicant's classroom management skills

1. What are the challenging aspects of classroom management for you?
2. What was your most challenging discipline problem so far and how did you handle it?
3. Here is a specific situation (interviewer describes a student who challenges your authority or refuses to follow rules or do work). What would you do?
4. How will you establish rapport with students and motivate them?

Questions about the applicant's instructional strategies

1. How do you accommodate different student abilities and learning styles in your teaching?
2. How do you make accommodations for students with special needs and challenges?
3. How would you involve families and the community in your classroom?
4. Based on what you know so far, would you prefer to work alone and be responsible for smaller numbers of students or collaborate with other teachers and be responsible for larger numbers of students?
5. What role does technology play in your teaching?

*Thanks to Dr. Harry Galinsky, former superintendent of Paramus, NJ, and Superintendent of the Year, and Dr. Michael DiPaola, former superintendent of Pitman, NJ, and Chancellor Professor, School of Education, the College of William and Mary, for their questions and suggestions.

APPENDIX B

Guidelines for Helping Beginning Teachers

- Schedule an orientation for beginning teachers.
- Develop a mentoring system for beginning teachers.
- Provide teachers with an appropriate mix of courses, students, and facilities; beginning teachers deserve good classrooms and the requisite supplies.
- If possible, provide a light load for beginning teachers. For example, keep the number of preparations for new high school teachers to two or three at most.
- Make sure that extracurricular duties are not overly demanding for beginning teachers. Protect your beginning teachers.
- Provide both social and work-related activities (e.g., team teaching, cooperative instruction, etc.) for beginning teachers. Encourage beginning teachers to interact with each other. Develop a "Rookie Roundtable," a regular meeting of beginning teachers focused on typical problems.
- Develop a newsletter that reports on the accomplishments of all teachers, but highlight those of beginning teachers.
- Avoid having the principal do formal classroom evaluation of beginning teachers, and instead have colleagues coach, monitor, provide feedback on strengths and weaknesses, and develop opportunities for practice and feedback in a nonthreatening environment.
- Plan some in-service programs specifically for beginning teachers; find out what your beginning teachers need and want, and help them get it.
- Have beginning teachers meet regularly with their mentors to identify and share problems before they become serious.
- Celebrate accomplishments. Plan and schedule events for experienced and beginning teachers such as luncheons, parties, and award recognition.
- Provide for joint planning, cooperative teaching, committee assignments, and other cooperative activities between new and experienced teachers.
- Provide opportunities for new teachers to observe master teachers at work.

Guidelines for Observing Classroom Behavior

Student–Teacher Relations

- What is the evidence of organization and clarity in teacher presentations?
- How enthusiastic is the teacher?
- How does the teacher demonstrate care, warmth, and empathy, and how does he or she nurture students?
- How does the teacher motivate students?
- What is the evidence that the teacher listens to and responds to each individual student's needs, interests, and concerns?
- How does the teacher encourage respect for other students and their views?
- How does the teacher encourage and build on student discussions?
- What is the evidence that the teacher is concerned with the social–emotional development of students?

The Teaching–Learning Process

- To what extent is the teacher concerned with understanding and applying knowledge? Analyzing, evaluating, creating?
- To what extent does the teacher use inquiry approaches?
- Which instructional methods did the students find most interesting?
- What is the evidence of student learning?
- How does the teacher use real-life examples to stimulate interest, illustrate, and integrate the concepts being taught?
- What instructional techniques are used to motivate divergent thinking?
- How does the teacher integrate different instructional activities?
- How does the teacher prevent frustration and confusion?
- To what extent is learning reinforced, and how is this being done?
- To what extent does the teacher use groups, and how are they utilized?

Classroom Management

- What student behaviors are acceptable and unacceptable in class?
- How does the teacher effectively use classroom space?
- What did you like and dislike about the physical environment of the classroom?
- How does the teacher enlist student cooperation?
- Are the rules of the classroom known and used by students?
- What activities encourage student engagement? Prevent management problems?
- How is conflict managed?
- What is the evidence that a positive learning context exists?
- What is the evidence that students are developing responsibly and managing themselves?

APPENDIX D

OCDQ-RE

DIRECTIONS: The following are statements about your school.* Please indicate the extent to which each statement characterizes your school by circling the appropriate response.

RO = Rarely Occurs   **SO = Sometimes Occurs**
O = Often Occurs   **VFO = Very Frequently Occurs**

1. The teachers accomplish their work with vim, vigor, and pleasure.	RO	SO	O	VFO
2. Teachers' closest friends are other faculty members at this school.	RO	SO	O	VFO
3. Faculty meetings are useless.	RO	SO	O	VFO
4. The principal goes out of his/her way to help teachers.	RO	SO	O	VFO
5. The principal rules with an iron fist.	RO	SO	O	VFO
6. Teachers leave immediately after school is over.	RO	SO	O	VFO
7. Teachers invite faculty members to visit them at home.	RO	SO	O	VFO
8. There is a minority group of teachers who always oppose the majority.	RO	SO	O	VFO
9. The principal uses constructive criticism.	RO	SO	O	VFO
10. The principal checks the sign-in sheet every morning.	RO	SO	O	VFO
11. Routine duties interfere with the job of teaching.	RO	SO	O	VFO
12. Most of the teachers here accept the faults of their colleagues.	RO	SO	O	VFO
13. Teachers know the family background of other faculty members.	RO	SO	O	VFO
14. Teachers exert group pressure on nonconforming faculty members.	RO	SO	O	VFO
15. The principal explains his/her reasons for criticism to teachers.	RO	SO	O	VFO
16. The principal listens to and accepts teachers' suggestions.	RO	SO	O	VFO
17. The principal schedules the work for the teachers.	RO	SO	O	VFO
18. Teachers have too many committee requirements.	RO	SO	O	VFO
19. Teachers help and support each other.	RO	SO	O	VFO
20. Teachers have fun socializing together during school time.	RO	SO	O	VFO
21. Teachers ramble when they talk at faculty meetings.	RO	SO	O	VFO
22. The principal looks out for the personal welfare of teachers.	RO	SO	O	VFO
23. The principal treats teachers as equals.	RO	SO	O	VFO
24. The principal corrects teachers' mistakes.	RO	SO	O	VFO
25. Administrative paperwork is burdensome at this school.	RO	SO	O	VFO
26. Teachers are proud of their school.	RO	SO	O	VFO
27. Teachers have parties for each other.	RO	SO	O	VFO

28. The principal compliments teachers.	RO	SO	O	VFO
29. The principal is easy to understand.	RO	SO	O	VFO
30. The principal closely checks classroom (teacher) activities.	RO	SO	O	VFO
31. Clerical support reduces teachers' paperwork.	RO	SO	O	VFO
32. New teachers are readily accepted by colleagues.	RO	SO	O	VFO
33. Teachers socialize with each other on a regular basis.	RO	SO	O	VFO
34. The principal supervises teachers closely.	RO	SO	O	VFO
35. The principal checks lesson plans.	RO	SO	O	VFO
36. Teachers are burdened with busy work.	RO	SO	O	VFO
37. Teachers socialize together in small, select groups.	RO	SO	O	VFO
38. Teachers provide strong social support for colleagues.	RO	SO	O	VFO
39. The principal is autocratic.	RO	SO	O	VFO
40. Teachers respect the professional competence of their colleagues.	RO	SO	O	VFO
41. The principal monitors everything teachers do.	RO	SO	O	VFO
42. The principal goes out of his/her way to show appreciation to teachers.	RO	SO	O	VFO

*OCDQ instruments for all levels are available at www.waynekhoy.com?

Administering the OCDQ-RE Instrument

The OCDQ-RE is best administered as part of a faculty meeting. It is important to guarantee the anonymity of the teacher respondent; teachers are not asked to sign the questionnaire and no identifying code is placed on the form. Most teachers do not object to responding to the instrument, which takes less than ten minutes to complete. It is probably advisable to have someone other than an administrator collect the data. It is important to create a nonthreatening atmosphere where teachers can give candid responses. All of the health and climate instruments follow the same pattern of administration.

REFERENCES

Aber, J. L., Brown, J. L., & Jones, S. M. (2003). Developmental trajectories toward violence in middle childhood: Course, demographic differences, and response to school-based intervention. *Developmental Psychology, 39,* 324–348.

Abrams, I. M., & Madaus, G. F. (2003). The lessons of high stakes testing. *Educational Leadership, 61*(32), 31–35.

Abrevaya, S. (2010, March 15). *Press releases: Obama Administration's education reform plan emphasizes flexibility, resources and accountability for results.* Available online at http://www2.ed.gov/news/pressreleases/2010/03/03152010.html

Ackerman, B. P., & Brown, E. D. (2006). Income poverty, poverty co-factors, and the adjustment of children in elementary school. In R. V. Kail (Ed.), *Advances in child development and behavior* (Vol. 34, pp. 91–129). New York: Elsevier.

Ackerman, B. P., Brown, E. D., & Izard, C. E. (2004). The relations between contextual risk, earned income, and the school adjustment of children from economically disadvantaged families. *Developmental Psychology, 40,* 204–216.

Airasian, P. W. (2005). *Classroom assessment: Concepts and applications* (5th ed.). New York: McGraw-Hill.

Airasian, P. W., & Walsh, M. E. (1997). Constructivist cautions. *Phi Delta Kappan, 78,* 444–449.

Albanese, M. A., & Mitchell, S. A. (1993). Problem-based learning: A review of literature on its outcomes and implementation issues. *Academic Medicine, 68,* 52–81.

Alberto, P. A., & Troutman, A. C. (2006). *Applied behavior analysis for teachers: Influencing student performance* (7th ed.). Saddle River, NJ: Prentice-Hall/Merrill.

Alberto, P. A., & Troutman, A. C. (2009). *Applied behavior analysis for teachers* (8th ed.). Boston: Pearson.

Alderman, M. K. (2004). *Motivation for achievement: Possibilities for teaching and learning.* Mahwah, NJ: Erlbaum.

Alexander, P. A., & Murphy, P. K. (1998). The research base for APA's learner-centered psychological principles. In N. Lambert & B. McCombs (Eds.), *How students learn: Reforming schools through learner-centered education.* Washington, DC: American Psychological Association.

Alig-Mielcarek, J., & Hoy, W. K. (2005). Instructional leadership: Its nature, meaning, and influence. In W. K. Hoy & C. M. (Eds.), *Educational leadership and reform* (pp. 29–54). Greenwich, CT: Information Age.

Allington, R. L., & McGill-Frazen, A. (2003). The impact of summer setback on the reading achievement gap. *Phi Delta Kappan, 85*(1), 68–75.

Allport, G. (1954). *The nature of prejudice.* Cambridge, MA: Addison-Wesley.

Anastasi, A. (1988). *Psychological testing* (6th ed.). New York: Macmillan.

Anderman, E. M., & Anderman, L. H. (2010). *Motivating children and adolescents in schools.* Columbus, OH: Merrill/Prentice Hall.

Anderman, E. M., & Maehr, M. L. (1994). Motivation and schooling in the middle grades. *Review of Educational Research, 64,* 287–310.

Anderman, E. M., & Patrick, H. (2012). Achievement goal theory, conceptualization of ability/intelligence, and classroom climate. In S. L. Christenson, A. L. Reschly, & C. Wylie (Eds.), *The handbook of research on student engagement* (pp. 173–192). New York: Springer Science.

Anderman, L. H. (2004). Student motivation across subject-area domains. *Journal of Educational Research, 97*(6), 283–285.

Anderson, C. S. (1982). The search for school climate: A review of the research. *Review of Educational Research, 52,* 368–420.

Anderson, C. W., Holland, J. D., & Palincsar, A. S. (1997). Canonical and sociocultural approaches to research and reform in science education: The story of Juan and his group. *Elementary School Journal, 97,* 359–384.

Anderson, J. R. (1995). *Cognitive psychology and its implications* (4th ed.). New York: Freeman.

Anderson, J. R., Reder, L. M., & Simon, H. A. (1995). *Applications and misapplication of cognitive psychology to mathematics education.* (Unpublished manuscript). Available online at http://www.psy.cmu.edu/~mm4b/misapplied.html

Anderson, J. R., Reder, L. M., & Simon, H. A. (1996). Situated learning and education. *Educational Researcher, 25,* 5–11.

Anderson, L. M. (1989a). Learners and learning. In M. Reynolds (Ed.), *Knowledge base for beginning teachers* (pp. 85–100). New York: Pergamon.

Anderson, L. M. (1989b). Classroom instruction. In M. Reynolds (Ed.), *Knowledge base for beginning teachers* (pp. 101–116). New York: Pergamon.

Anderson, L. W., & Krathwohl, D. R. (Eds.). (2001). *A taxonomy for learning, teaching, and assessing: A revision of Bloom's taxonomy of educational objectives.* New York: Addison, Wesley, Longman.

Anderson, L. W., & Sosniak, L. A. (Eds.). (1994). *Bloom's Taxonomy: A forty-year retrospective.* Ninety-third yearbook for the National Society for the Study of Education: Part II. Chicago: University of Chicago Press.

Angier, N., & Chang, K. (2005, January 24). Gray matter and the sexes: Still a scientific gray area. *New York Times,* A11.

Anthony, A. B. (2011). Innovation in educational organizations: Implications for research and administrative practice. In M. DiPaola & P. Forsyth (Eds.), *Leading research in educational administration: A festschrift for Wayne K. Hoy* (pp. 163–182). Greenwich, CT: Information Age.

Antonenko, P., Paas, F., Grabner, R., & van Gog, T. (2010). Using electroencephalography to measure cognitive load. *Educational Psychology Review, 22,* 425–438.

Anyon, J. (1980). Social class and the hidden curriculum of work. *Journal of Education, 162,* 67–92.

Ardila, A., Rosselli, M., Matute, E., & Inozemtseva, O. (2011). Gender differences in cognitive development. *Developmental Psychology, 47,* 984–990.

Arends, R. I. (2004). *Learning to teach* (6th ed.). New York: McGraw-Hill.

Arends, R. I., & Kilcher, A. (2010). *Teaching for student learning: Becoming an accomplished teacher.* New York: Routledge.

Armbruster, B. B., & Anderson, T. H. (1981). Research synthesis on study skills. *Educational Leadership, 39,* 154–156.

Aronson, E. (2000a). Building empathy, compassion and achievement in the jigsaw classroom. In J. Aronson & D. Cordova, *Improving education: Classic and contemporary lessons from psychology.* Mahwah, NJ: Erlbaum.

Aronson, E. (2000b). *Nobody left to hate: Teaching compassion after Columbine.* New York: Worth.

Aronson, E., & Patnoe, S. (1997). *Cooperation in the classroom: The Jigsaw method.* New York: Longman.

Aronson, J. (2002). *Improving academic achievement: Impact of psychological factors on education.* San Diego: Academic Press.

Aronson, J., Fried, C., & Good, C. (2002). Reducing the effects of stereotype threat on African American college students by shaping theories of intelligence. *Journal of Experimental Social Psychology, 38,* 113–125.

Aronson, J., & Inzlicht, M. (2004). The ups and downs of attributional ambiguity: Stereotype vulnerability and the academic self-knowledge of African American college students. *Psychological Science, 15,* 829–836.

Aronson, J., Lustina, M. J., Good, C., Keough, K., Steele, C. M., & Brown, J. (1999). When white men can't do math: Necessary and sufficient factors in stereotype threat. *Journal of Experimental Social Psychology, 35,* 29–46.

Aronson, J., & Steele, C. M. (2005). Stereotypes and the fragility of human competence, motivation, and self-concept. In C. Dweck & E. Elliot (Eds.), *Handbook of competence and motivation.* New York: Guilford.

Ashcraft, M. H., & Radvansky, G. A. (2010). *Cognition* (5th ed.). Upper Saddle River, NJ: Prentice-Hall/Pearson.

Association for the Gifted. (2001). *Diversity and developing gifts and talents: A national action plan.* Arlington, VA: Author.

Association for Supervision and Curriculum Development. (2008, September). ASCD Positions. Available online at http://www.ascd.org/news-media/ASCD-Policy-Positions/ASCD-Positions.aspx#educatingstudents

Au, K. H. (1980). Participation structures in a reading lesson with Hawaiian children: Analysis of a culturally appropriate instructional event. *Anthropology and Education Quarterly, 11,* 91–115.

Avramidis, E., Bayliss, P., & Burden, R. (2000). Student teachers' attitudes toward the inclusion of children with special education needs in the ordinary school. *Teaching & Teacher Education, 16,* 277–293.

Baddeley, A. L. (2006). Working memory: An overview. In S. J. Pickering (Ed.), *Working memory and education.* New York: Elsevier.

Baddeley, A. L. (2007). *Working memory, thought, and action.* New York: Oxford University Press.

Baddeley, A. L., Hitch, G. J., & Allen, R. J. (2009). Working memory and binding in sentence recall. *Journal of Memory and Language, 61,* 438–456.

Bailey, S. M. (1993). The current status of gender equity research in American schools. *Educational Psychologist, 28,* 321–339.

Ball, D. L., Lubienski, S. T., & Mewborn, D. S. (2001). Research on teaching mathematics: The unsolved problem of teachers' mathematical knowledge. In V. Richardson (Ed.), *Handbook of research on teaching* (4th ed., pp. 433–456). Washington, DC: American Educational Research Association.

Bandura, A. (1993). Perceived self-efficacy in cognitive development and functioning. *Educational Psychologist, 28,* 117–148.

Bandura, A. (1997). *Self-efficacy: The exercise of control.* New York: Freeman.

Bangert-Drowns, R. L., Kulik, C. C., Kulik, J. A., & Morgan, M. (1991). The instructional effect of feedback in test-like events. *Review of Educational Research, 61,* 213–238.

Banks, J. A. (1997). *Teaching strategies for ethnic studies* (6th ed.). Boston: Allyn & Bacon.

Banks, J. A. (2002). *An introduction to multicultural education* (3rd ed.). Boston: Allyn & Bacon.

Banks, S. R. (2005). *Classroom assessment: Issues and practice.* Boston: Allyn & Bacon.

Barnard-Brak, L. (2008). Academic red-shirting among children with learning disabilities. *Learning Disabilities: A Contemporary Journal, 6,* 43–54.

Barnhill, G. P. (2005). Functional behavioral assessment in schools. *Intervention in School & Clinic, 40,* 131–143.

Baron, R. A. (1998). *Psychology* (4th ed.). Boston: Allyn & Bacon.

Bartholomew, B. (2008). Sustaining the fire. *Educational Leadership, 65*(6), 55–60.

Basow, S. A., & Rubin, L. R. (1999). Gender influences on adolescent development. In N. G. Johnson, M. C. Roberts, & J. Worell (Eds.), *Beyond appearance: A new look at adolescent girls* (pp. 25–52). Washington, DC: American Psychological Association.

Battistich, V., Solomon, D., & Delucci, K. (1993). Interaction processes and student outcomes in cooperative groups. *The Elementary School Journal, 94,* 19–32.

Bauer, S. (2007, January 25). More public schools dividing boys, girls. *Houston Chronicle.*

Baumeister, R. F., & Leary, M. R. (1995). The need to belong: Desire for interpersonal attachments as a fundamental human motivation. *Psychological Bulletin, 117,* 497–529.

Baumert, J., Kunter, M., Blum, W., Brunner, M., Voss, T., Jordan, A., Klusmann, U., Krauss, S., Neubrand, M., & Tsai, Y.-M. (2010). Teachers' mathematical knowledge, cognitive activation in the classroom, and student progress. *American Educational Research Journal, 47*(1), 133–180.

Baumrind, D. (1996). The discipline controversy revisited. *Family Relations, 45,* 405–414.

Bear, G. G. (with Cavalier, A. R., & Manning, M. A.). (2005). *Developing self-discipline and preventing and correcting misbehavior.* Boston: Pearson/Allyn & Bacon.

Beard, K. S., & Hoy, W. K. (2010). The nature, meaning, and measure of teacher flow: A test of rival hypotheses. *Educational Administration Quarterly, 46,* 426–458.

Beebe-Frankenberger, M., Bocian, K. L., MacMillan, D. L., & Gresham, F. M. (2004). Sorting second grade students with academic deficiencies: Characteristics differentiating those retained in grade from those promoted to third grade. *Journal of Educational Psychology, 96,* 204–215.

Beghetto, R. A. (2008). Prospective teachers' beliefs about imaginative thinking in K–12 schooling. *Thinking Skills and Creativity, 3,* 134–142.

Belanoff, P., & Dickson, M. (1991). *Portfolios: Process and product.* Portsmouth, NH: Heinemann, Boynton/Cook.

Bennett, C. I. (1999). *Comprehensive multicultural education: Theory and practice* (4th ed.). Boston: Allyn & Bacon.

Berg, C. A., & Clough, M. (1991). Hunter lesson design: The wrong one for science teaching. *Educational Leadership, 48*(4), 73–78.

Bergin, D. (1999). Influences on classroom interest. *Educational Psychologist, 34,* 87–98.

Berk, L. E. (2005). *Infants, children, and adolescents* (5th ed.). Boston: Allyn & Bacon.

Berliner, D. C. (1987). But do they understand? In V. Richardson-Koehler (Ed.), *Educators' handbook:*

A research perspective (pp. 259–293). New York: Longman.

Berliner, D. C. (1988). Simple views of effective teaching and a simple theory of classroom instruction. In D. Berliner & B. Rosenshine (Eds.), *Talks to teachers* (pp. 93–110). New York: Random House.

Berliner, D. C. (2005). Our impoverished view of educational reform. *The Teachers College Record, 108,* 949–995.

Berlyne, D. (1966). Curiosity and exploration. *Science, 153,* 25–33.

Berry, R. Q., III. (2005). Voices of success: Descriptive portraits of two successful African American male middle school mathematics students. *Journal of African American Studies, 8*(4), 46–62.

Berthold, K., & Renkl, A. (2009). Instructional aids to support a conceptual understanding of multiple representations. *Journal of Educational Psychology, 101,* 70–87.

Beyer, J. M., & Trice, H. M. (1987). How an organization's rites reveal its culture. *Organizational Dynamics, 15,* 4–24.

Bialystok, E. (2001). *Bilingualism in development: Language, literacy, and cognition.* New York: Cambridge University Press.

Bialystok, E., Majumder, S., & Martin, M. M. (2003). Developing phonological awareness: Is there a bilingual advantage? *Applied Linguistics, 24,* 27–44.

Blair, C. (2002). School readiness: Integrating cognition and emotion in a neurobiological conceptualization of children's functioning at school entry. *American Psychologist, 57,* 111–127.

Blair, C. (2006). How similar are fluid cognition and general intelligence? A developmental neuroscience perspective on fluid cognition as an aspect of human cognition. Main article with commentaries. *Behavioral & Brain Sciences, 29,* 109–160.

Bleeker, M. M., & Jacobs, J. E. (2004). Achievement in math and science: Do mothers' beliefs matter twelve years later? *Journal of Educational Psychology, 96*(1), 97–109.

Bloom, B. S., Engelhart, M. D., Frost, E. J., Hill, W. H., & Krathwohl, D. R. (1956). *Taxonomy of educational objectives. Handbook I: Cognitive domain.* New York: David McKay.

Bloom, R., & Bourdon, L. (1980). Types and frequencies of teachers' written instructional feedback. *Journal of Educational Research, 74,* 13–15.

Blumenfeld, P. C., Puro, P., & Mergendoller, J. R. (1992). Translating motivation into thoughtfulness. In H. Marshall (Ed.), *Redefining student learning: Roots of educational change* (pp. 207–240). Norwood, NJ: Ablex.

Bodine, R., & Crawford, D. (1999). *Developing emotional intelligence: Behavior management and conflict resolution in schools.* Champaign, IL: Research Press.

Bolman, L. G., & Deal, T. E. (2003). *Reframing organizations: Artistry, choice, and leadership* (3rd ed.). San Francisco: Jossey-Bass.

Bolman, L. G., & Deal, T. E. (2008). *Reframing organizations: Artistry, choice, and leadership* (4th ed.). San Francisco: Jossey Bass.

Bong, M. (2009). Age-related differences in achievement goal differentiation. *Journal of Educational Psychology, 101,* 879–896.

Borich, G. D. (2011). *Effective teaching methods: Research-based practice* (7th ed.). Columbus, OH: Pearson.

Borko, H., & Livingston, C. (1989). Cognition and improvisation: Differences in mathematics instruction by expert and novice teachers. *American Educational Research Journal, 26,* 473–498.

Borko, H., & Putnam, R. (1996). Learning to teach. In D. Berliner & R. Calfee (Eds.), *Handbook of educational psychology* (pp. 673–708). New York: Macmillan.

Borman, G. D., & Overman, L. T. (2004). Academic resilience in mathematics among poor and minority students. *The Elementary School Journal, 104,* 177–195.

Borwein, J. M. (2005). The experimental mathematician: The pleasure of discovery and the role of proof. *International Journal of Computers for Mathematical Learning, 10,* 75–108.

Boyd, D., Goldhaber, D., Lankford, H., & Wyckoff, J., (2008). The effect of certification and preparation on teacher quality. *The Future of Children, 17*(1), 45.

Brannon, L. (2002). *Gender: Psychological perspectives* (3rd ed.). Boston: Allyn & Bacon.

Bransford, J. D., Brown, A. L., & Cocking, R. R. (2002). *How people learn: Brain, mind, experience, and school.* Washington, DC: National Academy Press.

Bransford, J., Derry, S., Berliner, D., & Hammerness, K. (2005). Theories of learning and their roles in teaching. In L. Darling-Hammond (Ed.), *Preparing teachers for a changing world: What teachers should learn and be able to do* (pp. 40–87). San Francisco: Jossey-Bass.

Bredderman, T. (1983). Effects of activity-based elementary science on student outcomes: A qualitative synthesis. *Review of Educational Research, 53,* 499–518.

Brice, A. E., & Brice, R. G. (2009). *Language development: Monolingual and bilingual acquisitions.* Boston: Allyn & Bacon.

Bronfenbrenner, U., McClelland, P., Wethington, E., Moen, P., & Ceci, S. (1996). *The state of Americans: This generation and the next.* New York: Free Press.

Brophy, J. E. (1983). Conceptualizing student motivation to learn. *Educational Psychologist, 18,* 200–215.

Brophy, J. E. (1985). Teacher-student interaction. In J. Dusek (Ed.), *Teacher expectancies.* Hillsdale, NJ: Erlbaum.

Brophy, J. E. (1988). On motivating students. In D. Berliner & B. Rosenshine (Eds.), *Talks to teachers* (pp. 201–245). New York: Random House.

Brophy, J. E. (1997). Effective teaching. In H. Walberg & G. Heartel (Eds.), *Psychology and educational practice* (pp. 212–232). Berkeley, CA: McCutchan.

Brophy, J. E. (2003). An interview with Jere Brophy by B. Gaedke & M. Shaughnessy. *Educational Psychology Review, 15,* 199–211.

Brophy, J. E. (2008). Developing students' appreciation for what is taught in school. *Educational Psychologist, 43,* 132–141.

Brophy, J. E., & Good, T. (1986). Teacher behavior and student achievement. In M. Wittrock (Ed.), *Handbook of research on teaching* (3rd ed., pp. 328–375). New York: Macmillan.

Brophy, J. E., & Kher, N. (1986). Teacher socialization as a mechanism for developing student motivation to learn. In R. Feldman (Ed.), *Social psychology applied to education* (pp. 256–288). New York: Cambridge University Press.

Brown, A. L. (1992). Design experiments: Theoretical and methodological challenges in creating complex interventions in classroom settings. *Journal of the Learning Sciences, 2,* 141–178.

Brown, A. L., & Campione, J. C. (1996). Psychological theory and the design of innovative learning environments: On procedures, principles, and

systems. In L. Schauble & R. Glaser (Eds.), *Innovations in learning: New environments for education* (pp. 289–325). Mahwah, NJ: Erlbaum.

Bruer, J. T. (1999). In search of brain-based education. *Phi Delta Kappan, 80,* 648–657.

Bruner, J. S. (1966). *Toward a theory of instruction.* New York: Norton.

Bruning, R. H., Schraw, G. J., & Norby, M. M. (2011). *Cognitive psychology and instruction* (5th ed.). Boston: Pearson.

Burden, P. R. (1995). *Classroom management and discipline: Methods to facilitate cooperation and instruction.* White Plains, NY: Longman.

Burke-Spero, R. (1999). *Toward a model of civitas through an ethic of care: A qualitative study of preservice teachers' perceptions about learning to teach diverse populations.* (Doctoral dissertation, The Ohio State University, 1999). Dissertation Abstracts International, 60, 11A, 3967.

Burke-Spero, R., & Woolfolk Hoy, A. (2002). *The need for thick description: A qualitative investigation of developing teacher efficacy.* Unpublished manuscript, University of Miami.

Bushaw, W. J., & Lopez, S. J. (2011). Betting on teachers: The 43rd annual Phi Delta Kappa/Gallup Poll of the Public's Attitudes Toward the Public Schools. *Phi Delta Kappan, 93*(1), 8–26.

Buss, D. M. (1995). Psychological sex differences: Origin through sexual selection. *American Psychologist, 50,* 164–168.

Butler, R., & Neuman, O. (1995). Effects of task and ego achievement goals on help-seeking behaviors and attitudes. *Journal of Educational Psychology, 87,* 261–271.

Butler, R., & Nisan, M. (1986). Effects of no feedback, task-related comments, and grades on intrinsic motivation and performance. *Journal of Educational Psychology, 78,* 210–224.

Butzin, S. M. (2007). NCLB: Fix it, don't nix it. *Phi Delta Kappan, 88*(10), 768–769.

Byrnes, D. A. (1989). Attitudes of students, parents, and educators toward repeating a grade. In L. A. Shepard & M. L. Smith (Eds.), *Flunking grades: Research and policies on retention* (pp. 108–131). Philadelphia, PA: Falmer.

Calderhead, J. (1996). Teacher: Beliefs and knowledge. In D. Berliner & R. Calfee (Eds.), *Handbook of educational psychology* (pp. 709–725). New York: Macmillan.

Callahan, C. M., Tomlinson, C. A., & Plucker, J. (1997). *Project START using a multiple intelligences model in identifying and promoting talent in high-risk students.* Storrs, CT: National Research Center for Gifted and Talented. University of Connecticut Technical Report.

Cambourne, B., & Turbill, J. (1990). Assessment in whole-language classrooms: Theory into practice. *Elementary School Journal, 90,* 337–349.

Cameron, J., & Pierce, W. D. (1994). Reinforcement, reward, and intrinsic motivation: A meta-analysis. *Review of Educational Research, 64,* 363–423.

Cameron, J., & Pierce, W. D. (1996). The debate about rewards and intrinsic motivation: Protests and accusations do not alter the results. *Review of Educational Research, 66,* 39–52.

Camp, R. (1990, Spring). Thinking together about portfolios. *The Quarterly of the National Writing Project, 27,* 8–14.

Cangelosi, J. S. (1990). *Designing tests for evaluating student achievement.* New York: Longman.

Canter, L. (1988). Let the educator beware: A response to Curwin and Mendler. *Educational Leadership, 46*(2), 71–73.

Canter, L. (1989). Assertive discipline—More than names on the board and marbles in a jar. *Phi Delta Kappan, 71*(1), 41–56.

Canter, L., & Canter, M. (1997). *Lee Canter's assertive discipline: Positive behavior management for today's classrooms.* Santa Monica, CA: Lee Canter & Associates.

Cantrell, S. C., Almasi, J. F., Carter, J. S., Rintamaa, M., & Madden, A. (2010). The impact of a strategy-based intervention on the comprehension and strategy use of struggling adolescent readers. *Journal of Educational Psychology, 102,* 257–280.

Capa, Y. (2005). *Novice teachers' sense of efficacy.* (Doctoral dissertation, The Ohio State University, Columbus, OH).

Caprara, G. V., Barbaranelli, C., Borgogni, L., & Steca, P. (2003). Efficacy beliefs as determinants of teachers' job satisfaction. *Journal of Educational Psychology, 95,* 821–832.

Carey, L. M. (1994). *Measuring and evaluating school learning* (2nd ed.). Boston: Allyn & Bacon.

Carter, E. W., Wehby, J., Hughes, C., Johnson, S. M., Plank, D. R., Barton-Arwood, S. M., & Lunsford, L. B. (2005). Preparing adolescents with high-incidence disabilities for high-stakes testing with strategy instruction. *Preventing School Failure, 49*(2), 55–62.

Castle, S., Deniz, C. B., & Tortora, M. (2005). Flexible grouping and student learning in a high-needs school. *Education & Urban Society, 37,* 139–150.

Cattell, R. B. (1987). *Intelligence: Its structure, growth, and action.* New York: Elsevier.

Cazden, C. (2001). *Classroom discourse: The language of teaching and learning* (2nd ed.). Portsmouth, NH: Heinemann.

Centers for Disease Control. (2010). *Community report from the autism and developmental disabilities monitoring (ADDM) network.* Atlanta, GA: Author. Available online at http://www.cdc.gov/ncbddd/autism/

Centers for Disease Control. (2012). *Data and statistics: Prevalence.* Available online at http://www.cdc.gov/ncbddd/autism/data.html

Chance, P. (1993). Sticking up for rewards. *Phi Delta Kappan, 74,* 787–790.

Chang, I.-H., Chin, J. M., & Hsu, C.-M. (2008). Teachers' perceptions of the dimensions and implementation of technology leadership of principals in Taiwanese elementary schools. *Educational Technology & Society, 11*(4), 229–245.

Chang, L., Mak, M. C. K., Li, T., Wu, B. P., Chen, B. B., & Lu, H. J. (2011). Cultural adaptations to environmental variability: An evolutionary account of East–West differences. *Educational Psychology Review, 23,* 99–129.

Charles, C. M. (2002a). *Essential elements of effective discipline.* Boston: Allyn & Bacon.

Charles, C. M. (2002b). *Building classroom discipline* (7th ed.). Boston: Allyn & Bacon.

Charles, C. M. (2011). *Building classroom discipline* (10th ed.). Boston, MA: Allyn & Bacon.

Cheeseman Day, J., & Newburger, E. C. (2002). *The big payoff: Educational attainment and synthetic estimates of work-life earnings.* Washington, DC: U.S. Bureau of the Census. Available online at http://usgovinfo.about.com/od/moneymatters/a/edandearnings.htm

Chen, J. A., & Pajares, F. (2010). Implicit theories of ability of Grade 6 science students: Relation to epistemological beliefs and academic motivation and achievement in science. *Contemporary Educational Psychology, 35,* 75–87.

Children's Defense Fund. (2007). *Each day in America [Electronic Version]. Children's Defense Fund.*

Available online at http://www.childrensdefense.org/site/PageServer?pagename=research_national_data_each_day

Children's Defense Fund. (2010). *The state of America's children: 2010*. Washington, DC: Author. Available online at http://www.childrensdefense.org/child-research-data-publications/data/state-of-americas-children-2010-report.html

Children's Defense Fund. (2012). *Each day in America*. Available online at http://www.childrensdefense.org/child-research-data-publications/each-day-in-america.html

Chorzempa, B. F., & Graham, S. (2006). Primary grade teachers' use of within-class ability grouping in reading. *Journal of Educational Psychology, 98*, 529–541.

Christensen, C. M., & Horn, M. B. (2008). How do we transform our schools? Use technologies that compete against nothing. *Education Next, 8*(3), 12–19.

Christensen, C. M., Horn, M. B., & Johnson, C. W. (2008). *Disrupting class: How disruptive innovation will change the way the world learns*. New York: McGraw-Hill.

Clark, C. M., & Yinger, R. (1988). Teacher planning. In D. Berliner & B. Rosenshine (Eds.), *Talks to teachers* (pp. 342–365). New York: Random House.

Clarke, J. H., & Agne, R. M. (1997). *Interdisciplinary high school teaching*. Boston: Allyn & Bacon.

Clarke, J. H., & Agne, R. M. (1997). *Curriculum development; Interdisciplinary high school teaching*. Boston, MA: Allyn & Bacon.

Clifford, M. M. (1990). Students need challenge, not easy success. *Educational Leadership, 48*(1), 22–26.

Clifford, M. M. (1991). Risk taking: Empirical and educational considerations. *Educational Psychologist, 26*, 263–298.

Cobley, S., McKenna, J., Baker, J., & Wattie, N. (2009). How pervasive are relative age effects in secondary school education? *Journal of Educational Psychology, 101*, 520–528.

Coffield, F., Moseley, D., Hall, E., & Ecclestone, K. (2004). *Learning styles and pedagogy in post-16 learning: A systematic and critical review*. Trowbridge, Wiltshire, England: The Learning and Skills Research Centre.

Cohen, A. B. (2009). Many forms of culture. *American Psychologist, 64*, 194–204.

Cohen, A. B. (2010). Just how many different forms of culture are there? *American Psychologist, 65*, 59–61.

Cohen, E. G. (1986). *Designing groupwork: Strategies for the heterogeneous classroom*. New York: Teachers College Press.

Coladarci, T. (1992). Teachers' sense of efficacy and commitment to teaching. *Journal of Experimental Education, 60*, 323–337.

Colangelo, N., Assouline, S. G. & Gross, M. U. M. (2004). *A nation deceived: How schools hold back America's brightest children (Vols. 1& 2)*. The Connie Belin & Jacqueline N. Blank International Center for Gifted Education and Talent Development, College of Education, The University of Iowa, Ames, Iowa. Available online at http://www.accelerationinstitute.org/Nation_Deceived/Get_Report.aspx

Cole, M. (1985). The zone of proximal development: Where culture and cognition create each other. In J. V. Wertsch (Ed.), *Culture, communication, and cognition: Vygotskian perspectives* (pp. 146–161). Cambridge: Cambridge University Press.

Coleman, J. S. (1961). *The adolescent society*. New York: Free Press.

Coleman, J. S. (1966). *Equality of educational opportunity*. Washington, DC: U.S. Government Printing Office.

Collins, A., Brown, J. S., & Holum, A. (1991). Cognitive apprenticeship: Making thinking visible. *American Educator, 15*(3), 38–39.

Collins, A., Brown, J. S., & Newman, S. E. (1989). Cognitive apprenticeship: Teaching the crafts of reading, writing, and mathematics. In L. B. Resnick (Ed.), *Knowing, learning, and instruction: Essays in honor of Robert Glaser* (pp. 453–494). Hillsdale, NJ: Erlbaum.

Collins, A., & Halverson, R. (2009). *Rethinking education in the age of technology: The digital revolution and schooling in America*. New York: Teachers College Press.

Comadena, M. E., Hunt, S. K., & Simonds, C. J. (2007). The effects of teacher clarity, nonverbal immediacy, and caring on student motivation, affective and cognitive learning. *Communication Research Reports, 24*, 241–248.

Comer, J. P., Haynes, N. M., & Joyner, E. T. (1996). The school development program. In J. P. Comer, N. M. Haynes, E. T. Joyner, & M. Ben-Avie (Eds.), *Rallying the whole village: The*

Comer process for reforming education (pp. 1–26). New York: Teachers College Press.

Committee on Increasing High School Students' Engagement and Motivation to Learn (2004). *Engaging schools: Fostering high school students' motivation to learn.* Washington, DC: The National Academies Press.

Connell, R. W. (1996). Teaching the boys: New research on masculinity and gender strategies. *Teachers College Record, 98*, 206–235.

Cooper, H. M. (2004). Special Issue: Homework. *Theory Into Practice, 43*(3).

Cooper, H. M., Robinson, J. C., & Patall, E. A. (2006). Does homework improve academic achievement? A synthesis of research, 1987–2003. *Review of Educational Research, 76*, 1–62.

Cooper, H. M., & Valentine, J. C. (Eds.). (2001). Special Issue: Homework. *Educational Psychologist, 36*(3), Summer.

Cooper, H. M., Valentine, J. C., Nye, B., & Kindsay, J. J. (1999). Relationships between five after-school activities and academic achievement. *Journal of Educational Psychology, 91*, 369–378.

Cordova, D. I., & Lepper, M. R. (1996). Intrinsic motivation and the process of learning: Beneficial effects of contextualization, personalization, and choice. *Journal of Educational Psychology, 88*, 715–730.

Cornelius-White, J. (2007). Learner-centered teacher–student relationships are effective: A meta-analysis. *Review of Educational Research, 77*, 113–143.

Corno, L. (2000). Looking at homework differently. *Elementary School Journal, 100*, 529–548.

Corno, L. (2008). On teaching adaptively. *Educational Psychologist, 43*, 161–173.

Corno, L., & Snow, R. E. (1986). Adapting teaching to individual differences in learners. In M. Wittrock (Ed.), *Handbook of research on teaching* (3rd ed., pp. 605–629). New York: Macmillan.

Corpus, J. H., McClintic-Gilbert, M. S., & Hayenga, A. O. (2009). Within-year changes in children's intrinsic and extrinsic motivational orientations: Contextual predictors and academic outcomes. *Contemporary Educational Psychology, 34*, 154–166.

Council of Chief State School Officers. (2008). *Educational leadership policy standards: ISLLC 2008.* Washington, DC: CCSSO.

Covey, S. R. (2004). *The 7 habits of highly effective people: Powerful lessons in personal change.* New York: Free Press.

Covington, M. V. (1992). *Making the grade: A self-worth perspective on motivation and school reform.* New York: Holt, Rinehart, & Winston.

Covington, M. V., & Mueller, K. J. (2001). Intrinsic versus extrinsic motivation: An approach/avoidance reformulation. *Educational Psychology Review, 13*, 157–176.

Covington, M. V., & Omelich, C. L. (1987). "I knew it cold before the exam": A test of the anxiety-blockage hypothesis. *Journal of Educational Psychology, 79*, 393–400.

Cowley, G., & Underwood, A. (1998, June 15). Memory. *Newsweek*, 48–54.

Craik, F. I. M., & Lockhart, R. S. (1972). Levels of processing: A framework for memory research. *Journal of Verbal Learning & Verbal Behavior, 11*, 671–684.

Crawford, J. (1996). *Best evidence: Research foundations of the bilingual education act.* Washington, DC: National Clearinghouse for Bilingual Education.

Creese, A. (2009). Building on young people's linguistic and cultural continuity: Complementary schools in the United Kingdom. *Theory Into Practice, 48*, 267–273.

Cremin, L. (1961). *The transformation of the school: Progressivism in American education, 1876–1957.* New York: Vintage.

Crone, D. A., & Horner, R. H. (2003). *Building positive behavior support systems in schools: Functional behavioral assessment.* New York: Guilford.

Crosnoe, R., Morrison, F., Burchinal, M., Pianta, R., Keating, D., Friedman, S. L., & Clarke-Stewart, K. A. (2010). Instruction, teacher–student relations, and math achievement trajectories in elementary school. *Journal of Educational Psychology, 102*, 407–417.

Cuban, L., Kirkpatrick, H., & Peck, C. (2001). High access and low use of technologies in high school classrooms: Explaining an apparent paradox. *American Educational Research Journal, 38*(4), 813–834.

Daley, T. C., Whaley, S. E., Sigman, M. D., Espinosa, M. P., & Neumann, C. (2003). IQ on the rise: The Flynn Effect in rural Kenyan children. *Psychological Science, 14*(3), 215–219.

Darling-Hammond, L., & Youngs, P. (2002). Defining "highly qualified teachers": What does "scientifically-based research" actually tell us? *Educational Researcher, 31*(9), 13–25.

Darnon, C., Dompnier, B., Gillieron, O., & Butera, F. (2010). The interplay of mastery and performance goals in social comparison: A multiple-goal perspective. *Journal of Educational Psychology, 102,* 212–222.

Davidson, J. (2003). A new role in facilitating school reform: The case of the educational technologist. *Teachers College Record, 105*(5), 729–252.

Davis, G. A., Rimm, S. B., & Siegle, D. (2011). *Education of the gifted and talented* (6th ed.). Boston: Pearson.

Davis, R. B., Maher, C. A., & Noddings, N. (Eds.). (1990). *Constructivist views on the teaching and learning of mathematics.* Monograph 4 of the National Council of Teachers of Mathematics, Reston, VA.

Deaux, K. (1993). Commentary: Sorry, wrong number: A reply to Gentile's call. *Psychological Science, 4,* 125–126.

DeCecco, J., & Richards, A. (1974). *Growing pains: Uses of school conflicts.* New York: Aberdeen.

Deci, E. L. (1975). *Intrinsic motivation.* New York: Plenum.

Deci, E. L., Koestner, R., & Ryan, R. M. (1999). A meta-analytic review of experiments examining the effects of extrinsic rewards on internal motivation. *Psychological Bulletin, 125,* 627–668.

Deci, E. L., & Ryan, R. M. (1985). *Intrinsic motivation and self-determination in human behavior.* New York: Plenum.

Deci, E. L., & Ryan, R. M. (Eds.). (2002). *Handbook of self-determination research.* Rochester, NY: University of Rochester Press.

Deci, E. L., Vallerand, R. J., Pelletier, L. G., & Ryan, R. M. (1991). Motivation and education: The self-determination perspective. *Educational Psychologist, 26,* 325–346.

De Corte, E., Greer, B., & Verschaffel, L. (1996). Mathematics teaching and learning. In D. Berliner & R. Calfee (Eds.), *Handbook of educational psychology* (pp. 491–549). New York: Macmillan.

Delpit, L. (1995). *Other people's children: Cultural conflict in the classroom.* New York: The New Press.

Delpit, L. (2003). Educators as "seed people": Growing a new future. *Educational Researcher, 7*(32), 14–21.

Dempster, F. N. (1991). Synthesis of research on reviews and tests. *Educational Leadership, 48*(7), 71–76.

Dempster, F. N. (1993). Exposing our students to less should help them learn more. *Phi Delta Kappan, 74,* 432–437.

Dettmers, S., Trautwein, U., Lüdtke, O., Kunter, M., & Baumert, J. (2010). Homework works if homework quality is high: Using multilevel modeling to predict the development of achievement in mathematics. *Journal of Educational Psychology, 102,* 467–482.

Deutsch, M. (1949). An experimental study of the effects of cooperation and competition upon group processes. *Human Relations, 2,* 199–231.

Dewan, S. (2010, January 10). Southern schools mark two minorities. *New York Times,* p. A19+.

Dewey, J. (1910). *How we think.* Boston: D.C. Heath.

Dewey, J. (1913). *Interest and effort in education.* Cambridge, MA: Houghton Mifflin.

Dexter, S. (2008). Leadership for IT in schools. In J. Voogt & G. Knezek (Eds.), *International handbook of information technology in primary and secondary education* (pp. 543–554). New York: Springer Science+Business Media, LLC.

DeZolt, D. M., & Hull, S. H. (2001). Classroom and school climate. In J. Worrell (Ed.), *Encyclopedia of women and gender* (p. 265). San Diego: Academic Press.

Diebert, J. P., & Hoy, W. K. (1977). Custodial high schools and self-actualization of students. *Educational Research Quarterly, 2,* 24–31.

Dillon, S. (2011, August 8). Overriding a key education law: Waivers offered to sidestep a 100 percent proficiency rule. *New York Times,* A11.

Dingfelder, S. F. (2005). Closing the gap for Latino patients. *Monitor on Psychology, 36*(1), 58–61.

DiPaola, M., & Hoy, W. K. (2005a). Organizational properties that foster organizational citizenship. *Journal of School Leadership, 15,* 391–410.

DiPaola, M., & Hoy, W. K. (2005b). Organizational citizenship of faculty and student achievement. *The High School Journal, 88*(3), 35–44.

DiPaola, M., & Hoy, W. K. (2008). *Principals improving instruction: Supervision, evaluation, and professional development.* Boston: Allyn and Bacon.

DiPaola, M. F., & Tschannen-Moran, M. (2001, September). Organizational citizenship behavior in schools and its relationship to school climate. *Journal of School Leadership, 11,* 424–447.

Doherty, K. M. (2002, July 12). Assessment. *Education Week on the Web.* Available online at

http://edweek.org/context/topics/issuespage
.cfm?id=41

Dole, J. A., Duffy, G. G., Roehler, L. R., & Pearson, P. D. (1991). Moving from the old to the new: Research on reading comprehension instruction. *Review of Educational Research, 61,* 239–264.

Dolezal, S. E., Welsh, L. M., Pressley, M., & Vincent, M. (2003). How do nine third-grade teachers motivate their students? *Elementary School Journal, 103,* 239–267.

Doll, B., Zucker, S., & Brehm, K. (2005). *Resilient classrooms: Creating healthy environments for learning.* New York: Guilford.

Dorell, O. (2009, November 9). Schools' zero-tolerance policies tested. *USA Today.* Available online at http://www.usatoday.com/news/nation/2009-11-01-zero-tolerance_N.htm

Dotterer, A. M., McHale, S. M., & Crouter, A. C. (2009). The development and correlates of academic interests from childhood through adolescence. *Journal of Educational Psychology, 101,* 509–519.

Doyle, W. (1986). Classroom organization and management. In M. C. Wittrock (Ed.), *Handbook of research on teaching* (3rd ed., pp. 392–431). New York: Macmillan.

Doyle, W. (2006). Ecological approaches to classroom management. In C. Evertson & C. Weinstein (Eds.), *Handbook of classroom management: Research, practice, and contemporary issues* (pp. 97–126). Mahwah, NJ: Erlbaum.

Driscoll, M. P. (2005). *Psychology of learning for instruction* (3rd ed.). Boston: Allyn & Bacon.

Dubarry, M., & Alves de Lima, D. (2003). *Notes on Generation 1.5.* De Anza College, Cupertino, CA. Available online at http://faculty.deanza.edu/alvesdelimadiana/stories/storyReader$438

Dunn, K., & Dunn, R. (1978). *Teaching students through their individual learning styles.* Reston, VA: National Council of Principals.

Dunn, K., & Dunn, R. (1987). Dispelling outmoded beliefs about student learning. *Educational Leadership, 44*(6), 55–63.

Dunn, R., Dunn, K., & Price, G. E. (1989). *Learning Style Inventory (LSI): An inventory for identification of how individuals in grades 3 through 12 prefer to learn.* Lawrence, KS: Price Systems.

Dunn, R., & Griggs, S. A. (Eds.). (2003). *Synthesis of the Dunn and Dunn learning-style model research:*

Who, what, when, where, and so what? New York: St. John's University's Center for the Study of Learning and Teaching Styles.

Dweck, C. S. (2000). *Self-theories: Their role in motivation, personality, and development.* Philadelphia: Routledge Press.

Dweck, C. S. (2002). The development of ability conceptions. In A. Wigfield & J. Eccles (Eds.), *The development of achievement motivation.* San Diego: Academic Press.

Dweck, C. S., & Bempechat, J. (1983). Children's theories on intelligence: Consequences for learning. In S. Paris, G. Olson, & W. Stevenson (Eds.), *Learning and motivation in the classroom* (pp. 239–256). Hillsdale, NJ: Erlbaum.

Ebmeier, H. (2003). How supervision influences teacher efficacy and commitment: An investigation of a path model. *Journal of Curriculum & Supervision, 18,* 110–141.

Eccles, J. (2009). Who am I and what am I going to do with my life? Personal and collective identities as motivators of action. *Educational Psychologist, 44,* 78–89.

Eccles, J., & Wigfield, A. (1985). Teacher expectations and student motivation. In J. Dusek (Ed.), *Teacher expectancies* (pp. 185–226). Hillsdale, NJ: Erlbaum.

Echevarria, J., & Graves, A. (2011). *Sheltered content instruction: Teaching English learners with diverse abilities* (4th ed.). Columbus, OH: Pearson.

Echevarria, M. (2003). Anomalies as a catalyst for middle school students' knowledge construction and scientific reasoning during science inquiry. *Journal of Educational Psychology, 95,* 357–374.

Eisenberg, R., Pierce, W. D., & Cameron, J. (1999). Effects of rewards on intrinsic motivation—Negative, neutral, and positive: Comment on Deci, Koestner, and Ryan (1999). *Psychological Bulletin, 125,* 677–691.

Eisner, E. W. (1999). The uses and limits of performance assessments. *Phi Delta Kappan, 80,* 658–660.

Elawar, M. C., & Corno, L. (1985). A factorial experiment in teachers' written feedback on student homework: Changing teacher behavior a little rather than a lot. *Journal of Educational Psychology, 77,* 162–173.

Elias, M. J., & Schwab, Y. (2006). From compliance to responsibility: Social and emotional learning and classroom management. In C. Evertson & C. S. Weinstein (Eds.), *Handbook for classroom management: Research, practice, and contemporary issues.* Mahwah, NJ: Erlbaum.

Ellerbrock, C. R., & Kiefer, S. M. (2010). Creating a ninth-grade community of care. *The Journal of Educational Research, 103,* 393–406.

Else-Quest, N. M., Hyde, J. S., & Linn, M. C. (2010). Cross-national patterns of gender differences in mathematics: A meta-analysis. *Psychological Bulletin,136,* 103–127.

Emmer, E. T., & Aussiker, A. (1990). School and classroom discipline programs: How well do they work? In O. Moles (Ed.), *Student discipline strategies: Research and practice* (pp. 105–142). Albany, NY: SUNY Press.

Emmer, E. T., & Evertson, C. M. (1982). Effective classroom management at the beginning of the school year in junior high school classes. *Journal of Educational Psychology, 74,* 485–498.

Emmer, E. T., & Evertson, C. M. (2013). *Classroom management for middle and high school teachers* (9th ed.). Boston, MA: Allyn & Bacon.

Emmer, E. T., Evertson, C. M., & Anderson, L. M. (1980). Effective classroom management at the beginning of the school year. *Elementary School Journal, 80,* 219–231.

Emmer, E. T., Evertson, C. M., & Worsham, M. (2006). *Classroom management for middle and high school teachers* (7th ed.). Boston: Allyn & Bacon.

Emmer, E. T., & Gerwels, M. C. (2006). Classroom management in middle school and high school classrooms. In C. Evertson & C. S. Weinstein (Eds.), *Handbook for classroom management: Research, practice, and contemporary issues.* Mahwah, NJ: Erlbaum.

Emmer, E. T., & Stough, L. M. (2001). Classroom management: A critical part of educational psychology with implications for teacher education. *Educational Psychologist, 36,* 103–112.

Epanchin, B. C., Townsend, B., & Stoddard, K. (1994). *Constructive classroom management: Strategies for creating positive learning environments.* Pacific Grove, CA: Brooks/Cole.

Epstein, J. L. (1989). Family structure and student motivation. In R. E. Ames & C. Ames (Eds.), *Research on motivation in education: Volume 3: Goals and cognitions* (pp. 259–295). New York: Academic Press.

Evans, G. W. (2004). The environment of childhood poverty. *American Psychologist, 59,* 77–92.

Evensen, D. H., Salisbury-Glennon, J. D., & Glenn, J. (2001). A qualitative study of six medical students in a problem-based curriculum: Toward a situated model of self-regulation. *Journal of Educational Psychology, 93,* 659–676.

Evertson, C. M. (1988). Managing classrooms: A framework for teachers. In D. Berliner & B. Rosenshine (Eds.), *Talks to teachers* (pp. 54–74). New York: Random House.

Evertson, C. M., & Emmer, E. T. (2009). *Classroom management for elementary school teachers* (8th ed.). Boston, MA: Allyn & Bacon.

Evertson, C. M., & Emmer, E. T. (2013). *Classroom management for elementary school teachers* (9th ed.). Boston, MA: Allyn & Bacon.

Evertson, C. M., Emmer, E. T., & Worsham, M. E. (2006). *Classroom management for elementary teachers* (7th ed.). Boston: Allyn & Bacon.

Ewy, C., & student authors. (1997). Kids take on "the test." *Educational Leadership, 54*(4), 76–78.

Fabiano, G. A., Pelham, W. E., Coles, E. K., Gnagy, E. M., Chronis-Tuscano, A., & O'Connor, B. C. (2009). A meta-analysis of behavioral treatments for attention-deficit/hyperactivity disorder. *Clinical Psychology Review, 29,* 129–140.

Fahy, P. F., Wu, H. C., & Hoy, W. K. (2010). Individual academic optimism of teachers: A new concept and its measure. In W. K. Hoy & M. DiPaola (Eds.), *Analyzing school contexts: Influences of principals and teachers in the service of students* (pp. 209–227). Greenwich, CT: Information Age.

Fast, L. A., Lewis, J. L., Bryant, M. J., Bocian, K. A., Cardullo, R. A., Rettig, M., & Hammond, K. A. (2010). Does math self-efficacy mediate the effect of the perceived classroom environment on standardized math test performance? *Journal of Educational Psychology, 102,* 729–740.

Fennema, E., & Peterson, P. (1988). Effective teaching for boys and girls: The same or different? In D. Berliner & B. Rosenshine (Eds.), *Talks to teachers* (pp. 111–127). New York: Random House.

Fenstermacher, G. D., & Richardson, V. (2005). On making determinations of quality in teaching. *Teachers College Record, 107,* 186–213.

Ferguson, D. L., Ferguson, P. M., & Bogdan, R. C. (1987). If mainstreaming is the answer, what is the question? In V. Richardson-Koehler (Ed.), *Educators' handbook: A research perspective* (pp. 394–419). New York: Longman.

Ferrer, E., & McArdle, J. J. (2004). An experimental analysis of dynamic hypotheses about cognitive abilities and achievement from childhood to early adulthood. *Developmental Psychology, 40,* 935–952.

Ferretti, R. P., Lewis, W. E., & Andrews-Weckerly, S. (2009). Do goals affect the structure of students' argumentative writing strategies? *Journal of Educational Psychology, 101,* 577–589.

A Field Trip to the Sea [Computer software] (1999). Hazelton, PA: Sunburst Software.

Fillmore, L.W., & Snow, C. (2000). *What teachers need to know about language.* Available online at http://citeseerx.ist.psu.edu/viewdoc/download?doi=10.1.1.92.9117&rep=rep1&type=pdf

Finkel, D., Reynolds, C. A., McArdle, J. J., Gatz, M., & Pedersen, N. L. (2003). Latent growth curve analyses of accelerating decline in cognitive abilities in adulthood. *Developmental Psychology, 39,* 535–550.

Finkelstein, R. (1998). *The effects of organizational health and pupil control ideology on the achievement and alienation of high school students.* (Unpublished doctoral dissertation, St. Johns University, Queens, NY).

Fiske, E. B. (1988, April 10). America's test mania. *New York Times* (Education Life Section), pp. 16–20.

Fives, H. R., Hamman, D., & Olivarez, A. (2005, April). *Does burnout begin with student teaching? Analyzing efficacy, burnout, and support during the student-teaching semester.* Paper presented at the Annual Meeting of the American Educational Research Association, Montreal, CA.

Flammer, A. (1995). Developmental analysis of control beliefs. In A. Bandura (Ed.), *Self-efficacy in changing societies* (pp. 69–113). New York: Cambridge University Press.

Flanagan, L., & Jacobsen, M. (2003). Technology leadership for the twenty-first century principal. *Journal of Educational Administration, 41*(2), 124–142.

Flavell, J. H., Green, F. L., & Flavell, E. R. (1995). Young children's knowledge about thinking. *Monographs of the Society for Research in Child Development, 60*(1) (Serial No. 243).

Ford, D. Y. (2000). *Infusing multicultural content into the curriculum for gifted students.* (ERIC EC Digest #E601). Arlington, VA: ERIC Clearinghouse on Disabilities and Gifted Education.

Forsyth, P. B., Adams, C., & Hoy, W. K. (2011). *Collective trust: Why schools can't improve without it.* New York: TC Press.

Foster, W. (1981, August). *Social and emotional development in gifted individuals.* Paper presented at the Fourth World Conference on Gifted and Talented, Montreal.

Fox, E., & Riconscente, M. (2008). Metacognition and self-regulation in James, Piaget, and Vygotsky. *Educational Psychology Review, 20,* 373–389.

Francis, D. J., Lesaux, N., & August, D. (2006). Language of instruction. In D. August & T. Shanahan (Eds.), *Developing literacy in second language learners: Report of the national literacy panel on language-minority children and youth* (pp. 365–413). Mahwah, NJ: Erlbaum.

Franklin, J. (2007). Achieving with autism: Dispelling common misconceptions is essential for success. *Education Update, 49*(7), 1–9.

Fredricks, J. A., Blumenfeld, P. C., & Paris, A. H. (2004). School engagement: Potential of the concept, state of the evidence. *Review of Educational Research, 74,* 59–109.

Freiberg, H.J. (Ed.). (1999). *Beyond behaviorism: Changing the classroom management.* Boston: Allyn & Bacon.

Freiberg, H. J., (2012). Classroom management and student achievement. In J. Hattie and E. Anderman (Eds.). *International Handbook of Student Achievement.* New York: Routledge.

Freiberg, H. J., & Driscoll, A. (2005). *Universal teaching strategies* (4th ed.). Boston: Allyn & Bacon.

Freiberg, H. J., & Lamb, S. M. (2009). Dimensions of person-centered classroom management. *Theory Into Practice, 48,* 99–105.

Freiberg, J. (2006). Research-based programs for preventing and solving discipline problems. In C. Evertson & C. S. Weinstein (Eds.), *Handbook for classroom management: Research, practice, and contemporary issues.* Mahwah, NJ: Erlbaum.

Freisen, J. (2010, March 10). The hanging face of Canada: Booming minority populations by 2031. *The Globe and Mail: National.*

Frenzel, A. C., Goetz, T., Lüdtke, O., Pekrun, R., & Sutton, R. E. (2009). Emotional transmission in the classroom: Exploring the relationship between teacher and student enjoyment. *Journal of Educational Psychology, 101,* 705–716.

Frick, T. W. (1990). Analysis of patterns in time: A method of recording and quantifying temporal relations in education. *American Educational Research Journal, 27*, 180–204.

Friedman-Weieneth, J. L., Harvey, E. A., Youngswirth, S. D., & Goldstein, L. H. (2007). The relation between 3-year-old-children's skills and their hyperactivity, inattention, and aggression. *Journal of Educational Psychology, 99*, 671–681.

Friend, M. (2008). *Special education: Contemporary perspectives for school professionals* (7th ed.). Boston: Allyn & Bacon.

Friend, M. (2011). *Special education: Contemporary perspectives for school professionals* (3rd ed.). Boston: Allyn & Bacon/Pearson.

Friend, M., & Bursuck, W. D. (2006). *Including students with special needs: A practical guide for classroom teachers* (4th ed.). Boston: Allyn & Bacon.

Fuchs, L. S., Fuchs, D., Hamlett, C. L., & Karns, K. (1998). High-achieving students' interactions and performance on complex mathematical tasks as a function of homogeneous and heterogeneous pairings. *American Educational Research Journal, 35*, 227–268.

Furrer, C., & Skinner, E. (2003). Sense of relatedness as a factor in children's academic engagement and performance. *Journal of Educational Psychology, 95*(11), 148–161.

Gagné, E. D. (1985). *The cognitive psychology of school learning.* Boston: Little, Brown.

Gagné, E. D., Yekovich, C. W., & Yekovich, F. R. (1993). *The cognitive psychology of school learning* (2nd ed.). New York: HarperCollins.

Galambos, S. J., & Goldin-Meadow, S. (1990). The effects of learning two languages on metalinguistic development. *Cognition, 34*, 1–56.

Gallagher, M. (2001, June 11). *More on zero-tolerance schools.* Available online at http://www.newsmax.com/archives/articles/2001/6/11/123253.shtml

Galton, M., Hargreaves, L., & Pell, T. (2009). Group work and whole-class teaching with 11–14-year-olds compared. *Cambridge Journal of Education, 39*, 119–140.

Gamoran, A., & Mare, R. D. (1989). Secondary school detracking and educational inequity: Compensation, reinforcement, or neutrality? *American Journal of Education, 106*(3), 385–415.

Garbarino, J., & deLara, E. (2002). *And words can hurt forever: How to protect adolescents from bullying, harassment, and emotional violence.* New York: Free Press.

Garcia, E. (2002). *Student cultural diversity: Understanding the meaning and meeting the challenge.* Boston: Houghton Mifflin.

Garcia, E. E. (1992). "Hispanic" children: Theoretical, empirical, and related policy issues. *Educational Psychology Review, 4*, 69–94.

Garcia, S. B., & Tyler, B-J. (2010). Meeting the needs of English language learners with learning disabilities in the general curriculum. *Theory Into Practice, 49*, 113–120.

Gardner, H. (1983). *Frames of mind: The theory of multiple intelligences.* New York: Basic Books.

Gardner, H. (1991). *The unschooled mind: How children think and how schools should teach.* New York: Basic Books.

Gardner, H. (1993). *Multiple intelligences: The theory in practice.* New York: Basic Books.

Gardner, H. (1998). Reflections on multiple intelligences: Myths and messages. In A. Woolfolk (Ed.), *Readings in educational psychology* (2nd ed., pp. 61–67). Boston: Allyn & Bacon.

Gardner, H. (2003, April 21). *Multiple intelligence after twenty years.* Paper presented at the American Educational Research Association, Chicago.

Gardner, H. (2009). Birth and the spreading of a meme. In J-Q Chen, S. Moran, & H. Gardner (Eds.), *Multiple intelligences around the world* (pp. 3–16). San Francisco: Wiley.

Garmon, A., Nystrand, M., Berends, M., & LePore, P. C. (1995). An organizational analysis of the effects of ability grouping. *American Educational Research Journal, 32*, 687–715.

Garner, P. W., & Spears, F. M. (2000). Emotion regulation in low-income preschool children. *Social Development, 9*, 246–264.

Garnets, L. (2002). Sexual orientations in perspective. *Cultural Diversity & Ethnic Minority Psychology, 8*, 115–129.

Gay, G. (2000). *Culturally responsive teaching: Theory, research, and practice.* New York: Teachers College Press.

Gay, G. (2006). Connections between classroom management and culturally responsive teaching. In C. Evertson & C. S. Weinstein (Eds.), *Handbook for classroom management: Research, practice, and contemporary issues.* Mahwah, NJ: Erlbaum.

Geary, D. C. (1995). Sexual selection and sex differences in spatial cognition. *Learning and Individual Differences, 7*, 289–303.

Geary, D. C. (1999). Evolution and developmental sex differences. *Current Directions in Psychological Science, 8,* 115–120.

Geary, D. C. (2006). Development of mathematical understanding. In D. Kuhn & R. S. Siegler (Eds.), *Handbook of child psychology* (Vol. 2, Cognition, Perception, and Language, pp. 777–810). New York: Wiley.

George, P. S. (2005). A rationale for differentiated instruction in the regular classroom. *Theory Into Practice, 44,* 185–193.

Gergen, K. J. (1997). Constructing constructivism: Pedagogical potentials. *Issues in Education: Contributions from Educational Psychology, 3,* 195–202.

Gershoff, E. T., Aber, J. L., Raver, C. C., & Lennon, M. C. (2007). Income is not enough: Incorporating material hardship into models of income associations with parenting and child development. *Child Development, 78,* 70–95.

Gersten, R. (1996a). The language-minority students in transition: Contemporary instructional research. *The Elementary School Journal, 96,* 217–220.

Gersten, R. (1996b). Literacy instruction for language-minority students: The transition years. *The Elementary School Journal, 96,* 217–220.

Gersten, R. (Ed.). (2006). Scientific research on instruction of English Language Learners: The beginnings. *The Elementary School Journal* (special issue).

Gerwe, M., Stollhoff, K., Mossakowski, J., Kuehle, H-J., Goertz, U., Schaefer, C., ... Heger, S. (2009). Tolerability and effects of OROS® MPH (Concerta®) on functioning, severity of disease and quality of life in children and adolescents with ADHD: Results from a prospective, noninterventional trial. *Attention Deficit Hyperactive Disorder, 1,* 175–186.

Gess-Newsome, J. (2012). Pedagogical content knowledge. In J. Hattie & E. Anderman (Eds.), *International handbook of student achievement.* New York: Routledge.

Gillies, R. (2003). The behaviors, interactions, and perceptions of junior high school students during small-group learning. *Journal of Educational Psychology, 96,* 15–22.

Gillies, R. (2004). The effects of cooperative learning on junior high school students during small group learning. *Learning and Instruction, 14,* 197–213.

Gillies, R. M., & Boyle, M. (2011). Teachers' reflections of cooperative learning (CL): A two-year follow-up. *Teaching Education, 22,* 63–78.

Gini, G. (2008). Italian elementary and middle school students' blaming the victim of bullying and perception of school moral atmosphere. *The Elementary School Journal, 108,* 335–354.

Glasser, W. (1969). *Schools without failure.* New York: Harper & Row.

Glasser, W. (1990). *The quality school: Managing students without coercion.* New York: Harper & Row.

Glickman, C. D. (2002). *Leadership for learning: How to help teachers succeed.* Alexandria, VA: Association for Supervision and Curriculum Development.

Gluck, M. A., Mercado, E., & Myers, C. E. (2008). *Learning and memory: From brain to behavior.* New York: Worth.

Goddard, R. D., Sweetland, S. R., & Hoy, W. K. (2000). Academic emphasis of urban elementary schools and student achievement: A multi-level analysis. *Educational Administration Quarterly, 36,* 683–702.

Goddard, R. G., Hoy, W. K., & Woolfolk Hoy, A. (2004). Collective efficacy: Theoretical development, empirical evidence, and future directions. *Educational Researcher, 33,* 3–13.

Godden, D. R., & Baddeley, A. D. (1975). Context dependent memory in two natural environments: On land and underwater. *British Journal of Psychology, 66,* 325–331.

Goetz, T., Cronjaeger, H., Frenzel, A. C., Ludtke, O., & Hall, N. (2010). Academic self-concept and emotion relations: Domain specificity and age effects. *Contemporary Educational Psychology, 35,* 44–58.

Goetz, T., Frenzel, A. C., Hall, N. C., & Pekrun, R. (2008). Antecedents of academic emotions: Testing the internal/external frame of reference model for academic enjoyment. *Contemporary Educational Psychology, 33,* 9–33.

Gonzalez, A. L. (2010, June). *Hispanics in the US: A new generation.* BBC News: US and Canada. Available online at http://www.bbc.co.uk/news/10209099

Gonzalez, V., Brusca-Vega, R., & Yawkey, T. (1997). *Assessment and instruction of culturally diverse students with or at-risk of learning problems: From research to practice.* Boston: Allyn & Bacon.

Good, T. L., & Brophy, J. E. (2003). *Looking in classrooms* (9th ed.). New York: Allyn & Bacon/ Longman.

Good, T. L., & Brophy, J. E. (2008). *Looking in classrooms* (10th ed.). Boston: Allyn & Bacon.

Goodenow, C. (1993). Classroom belonging among early adolescents: Relationships to motivation and achievement. *Journal of Early Adolescence, 13,* 21–43.

Goodrich, H. (1997). Understanding rubrics. *Educational Leadership, 54*(4), 14–17.

Gordon, J. A. (1998). Caring through control: Reaching urban African American youth. *Journal for a Just and Caring Education, 4*, 418–440.

Gordon, T. (2003). Teacher Effectiveness Training: The program proven to help teachers bring out the best in students of all ages. New York: Random House.

Graham, S. (1994). Motivation in African Americans. *Review of Educational Research, 64*, 55–117.

Graham, S. (1995). Narrative versus meta-analytic reviews of race differences in motivation. *Review of Educational Research, 65*, 509–514.

Graham, S. (1996). How causal beliefs influence the academic and social motivation of African-American children. In G. G. Brannigan (Ed.), *The enlightened educator: Research adventures in the schools* (pp. 111–126). New York: McGraw-Hill.

Graham, S. (1998). Self-blame and peer victimization in middle school: An attributional analysis. *Developmental Psychology, 34*, 587–599.

Graham, S., & Harris, K. R. (1994). The effects of whole language on children's writing: A review of literature. *Educational Psychologist, 29*, 187–192.

Graham, S., & Weiner, B. (1996). Theories and principles of motivation. In D. Berliner & R. Calfee (Eds.), *Handbook of educational psychology* (pp. 63–84). New York: Macmillan.

Gredler, M. E. (2005). *Learning and instruction: Theory and practice.* Columbus, OH: Merrill/Prentice-Hall.

Gredler, M. E. (2009). Hiding in plain sight: The stages of mastery/self-regulation in Vygotsky's cultural-historical theory. *Educational Psychologist, 44*, 1–19.

Greeno, J. G., Collins, A. M., & Resnick, L. B. (1996). Cognition and learning. In D. Berliner & R. Calfee (Eds.), *Handbook of educational psychology* (pp. 15–46). New York: Macmillan.

Gregorc, A. F. (1982). *Gregorc style delineator: Development, technical, and administrative manual.* Maynard, MA: Gabriel Systems.

Grigorenko, E. L., Jarvin, L., Diffley III, R., Goodyear, J., Shanahan, E. J., & Sternberg, R. J. (2009). Are SSATs and GPA enough? A theory-based approach to predicting academic success in secondary school. *Journal of Educational Psychology, 101*, 964–981.

Grigorenko, E. L., & Sternberg, R. J. (2001). Analytical, creative, and practical intelligence as predictors of self-reported adaptive functioning: A case study in Russia. *Intelligence, 29*, 57–73.

Grolnick, W. S., Gurland, S. T., Jacob, K. F., & Decourcey, W. (2002). The development of self-determination in middle childhood and adolescence. In A. Wigfield & J. Eccles (Eds.), *Development of achievement motivation* (pp. 147–171). New York: Academic Press.

Grolnick, W. S., Ryan, R. M., & Deci, E. L. (1991). Inner resources for school achievement: Motivational mediators of children's perceptions of their parents. *Journal of Educational Psychology, 83*, 508–517.

Gronlund, N. E. (2004). *Writing instructional objectives for teaching and assessment* (7th ed.). Columbus: OH: Prentice Hall/Merrill.

Gronlund, N. E. (2006). *Assessment of student achievement* (8th ed.). Boston: Allyn & Bacon.

Gronlund, N. E., & Brookhart, S. M. (2009). *Gronlund's writing instructional objectives* (8th ed.). Upper Saddle River, NJ: Pearson.

Grossman, H., & Grossman, S. H. (1994). *Gender issues in education.* Boston: Allyn & Bacon.

Guerra, N. G., Williams, K. R., & Sadek, S. (2011). Understanding bullying and victimization during childhood and adolescence: A mixed methods study. *Child Development, 82*, 295–310.

Guilford, J. P. (1988). Some changes in the Structure-of-Intellect model. *Educational and Psychological Measurement, 48*, 1–4.

Guilfoyle, C. (2006). NCLB: Is there life beyond testing? *Educational Leadership, 64*(3), 8–13.

Gurian, M. (2006). *The wonder of boys: What parents, mentors, and educators can do to shape boys into exceptional men.* London: Penguin.

Gurian, M., & Henley, P. (2001). *Boys and girls learn differently: A guide for teachers and parents.* San Francisco: Jossey-Bass.

Gurian, M., & Stevens, K. (2005). *The minds of boys: Saving our sons from falling behind in school and life.* San Francisco: Jossey-Bass.

Gurian, M., & Stevens, K. (2011). *Boys and girls learn differently: A guide for teachers and parents.* San Francisco: Jossey-Bass.

Gurian, M., Stevens, K., & Daniels, P. (2009). *Successful single-sex classrooms: A practical guide to teaching boys and girls separately.* San Francisco: Jossey-Bass.

Gurian, M., Stevens, K., & King, K. (2008). *Strategies for teaching boys and girls: Secondary level.* San Francisco: Jossey-Bass.

Gurian, M., Stevens, K., & King, K. (2008). *Strategies for teaching boys and girls: Elementary level.* San Francisco: Jossey-Bass.

Guskey, T. R. (1994). Making the grade: What benefits students? *Educational Leadership, 52*(2), 14–21.

Guskey, T. R., & Bailey, J. M. (2001). *Developing grading and reporting systems for student learning.* Thousand Oaks, CA: Corwin.

Guthrie, J. T., & Alao, S. (1997). Designing contexts to increase motivations of reading. *Educational Psychologist, 32,* 95–105.

Gutman, L. M., Sameroff, A., & Cole, R. (2003). Academic growth curve trajectories from 1st grade to 12th grade: Effects of multiple social risk factors and preschool child factors. *Developmental Psychology, 39,* 777–790.

Haertel, E. H. (1999). Performance assessment and educational reform. *Phi Delta Kappan, 80,* 662–666.

Haladyna, T. H. (2002). *Essentials of standardized achievement testing: Validity and accountability.* Boston: Allyn & Bacon.

Hallahan, D. P., & Kauffman, J. M. (2006). *Exceptional learners* (10th ed.). Boston: Allyn & Bacon.

Hallahan, D. P., Lloyd, J. W., Kauffman, J. M., Weiss, M. P., & Martinez, E. A. (2005). *Learning disabilities: Foundations, characteristics, and effective teaching.* Boston: Allyn & Bacon.

Halpern, D. F. (2000). *Sex differences in cognitive abilities.* Mahwah, NJ: Erlbaum.

Halpern, D. F., Benbow, C. P., Geary, D. C., Gur, R. C., Hyde, J. S., & Gernsbacher, M. A. (2007). The science of sex differences in science and mathematics. *Psychological Science in the Public Interest, 8,* 1–51.

Halpin, A. W. (1966). *Theory and research in administration.* New York: Macmillan.

Halpin, A. W., & Croft, D. B. (1962). *The organization climate of schools.* Contract #SAE 543–8639. U.S. Office of Education, Research Project.

Hamann, D. L., Baker, D. S., McAllister, P. A., & Bauer, W. I. (2000). Factors affecting university music students' perceptions of lesson quality and teaching effectiveness. *Journal of Research in Music Education, 48,* 102–113.

Hambleton, R. K. (1996). Advances in assessment models, methods, and practices. In D. C. Berliner & R. C. Calfee (Eds.), *Handbook of educational psychology* (pp. 899–925). New York: Macmillan.

Hamers, J. F., & Blanc, M. H. A. (2000). *Bilinguality and bilingualism* (2nd ed.). Cambridge, England: Cambridge University Press.

Hamman, D., Berthelot, J., Saia, J., & Crowley, E. (2000). Teachers' coaching of learning and its relation to students' strategic learning. *Journal of Educational Psychology, 92,* 342–348.

Hamre, B. K., & Pianta, R. C. (2001). Early teacher–child relationships and the trajectory of children's school outcomes through eighth grade. *Child Development, 72,* 625–638.

Hansen, R. A. (1977). Anxiety. In S. Ball (Ed.), *Motivation in education.* New York: Academic Press.

Hanson, P. G., & Lubin, B. (1995). *Answers to questions most frequently asked about organizational development.* Thousand Oaks, CA: Sage.

Hardman, M. L., Drew, C. J., & Egan, M. W. (2005). *Human exceptionality: Society, school, and family* (8th ed.). Boston: Allyn & Bacon.

Harklau, L., Losey, K. M., & Siegal, M. (Eds.) (1999). *Generation 1.5 meet college composition: Issues in the teaching of writing to U.S.-educated learners of ESL.* Mahwah, NJ: Erlbaum Associates.

Harp, S. F., & Mayer, R. E. (1998). How seductive details do their damage: A theory of cognitive interest in science learning. *Journal of Educational Psychology, 90,* 414–434.

Harris, K. R., Alexander, P., & Graham, S. (2008). Michael Pressley's contributions to the history and future of strategies research. *Educational Psychologist, 43,* 86–96.

Harris, K. R., & Graham, S. (1996). Memo to constructivists: Skills count too. *Educational Leadership, 53*(5), 26–29.

Harris, P. L. (2006). Social cognition. In D. Kuhn & R. Siegler (Eds.), *Handbook of child psychology* (6th ed., Vol. 2). New York: Wiley.

Hattie, J. (2008). *Visible learning: A synthesis of over 800 meta-analyses relating to achievement.* New York: Routledge.

Hattie, J., & Timperley, H. (2007). The power of feedback. *Review of Educational Research, 77,* 81–112.

Hawkins, J., Spielvogel, B., & Panush, E. M. (1996). National study tour of district technology integration (Summary report). Available online at http://cct.edc.org/admin/publications/report/natstudy_dti96.pdf

Henderson, M. (1996). *Helping your students get the most from homework* [brochure]. Chicago: National Parent-Teacher Association.

Herman, J. (1997). Assessing new assessments: How do they measure up? *Theory into Practice, 36,* 197–204.

Herman, J., & Winters, L. (1994). Portfolio research: A slim collection. *Educational Leadership, 52*(2), 48–55.

Hess, F. M., & Petrilli, M. J. (2004). The politics of No Child Left Behind: Will the coalition hold? *Boston University Journal of Education, 185*(3), 13–25.

Hess, F. M., & Rotherham, A. J. (2007). NCLB and the competitiveness agenda: Happy collaboration or a collision course? *Phi Delta Kappan, 88,* 344–352.

Hickey, D. T. (2003). Engaged participation vs. marginal non-participation: A stridently sociocultural model of achievement motivation. *The Elementary School Journal, 103*(4), 401–429.

Hidi, S., & Renninger, K. A. (2006). The four-phase model of interest development. *Educational Psychologist, 41,* 111–127.

Hill, C., Corbett, C., & St. Rose, A. (2010). Why so few? Women in science, technology, engineering, and mathematics. Washington, DC: American Association of University Women. Available online at http://www.aauw.org/learn/research/whysofew.cfm

Hill, H. C., Rowan, B., & Ball, D. L. (2005). Effects of teachers' mathematics knowledge for teaching on student achievement. *American Educational Research Journal, 42,* 371–406.

Hill, K. T., & Wigfield, A. (1984). Test anxiety: A major educational problem and what can be done about it. *The Elementary School Journal, 85,* 105–126.

Hill, W. F. (2002). *Learning: A survey of psychological interpretations* (7th ed.). Boston: Allyn & Bacon.

Hiroto, D. S., & Seligmen, M. E. P. (1975). Generality of learned helplessness in man. *Journal of Personality and Social Psychology, 31,* 311–327.

Hirvikoski, T., et al. (2011). Reduced ADHD symptoms in adults with ADHD after structured skills training group: Results from a randomized controlled trial. *Behavioural Research and Therapy, 49,* 175–185.

Hmelo-Silver, C. E. (2004). Problem-based learning: What and how do students learn? *Educational Psychology Review, 16,* 235–266.

Hmelo-Silver, C. E., Ravit, G. D., & Chinn, C. A. (2007). Scaffolding and achievement in problem-based and inquiry learning: A response to Kirschner, Sweller, and Clark (2006). *Educational Psychologist, 42,* 99–107.

Hodges, E. V. E., & Perry, D. G. (1999). Personal and interpersonal antecedents and consequences of victimization by peers. *Journal of Personality and Social Psychology, 76,* 677–685.

Hoeffler, T. N., & Leutner, D. (2011). The role of spatial ability in learning from instructional animations—Evidence for an ability-as-compensator hypothesis. *Computers in Human Behavior, 27,* 209–216.

Hofferth, S. L., & Sandberg, J. F. (2000). *Changes in American children's time, 1981–1997.* Ann Arbor, MI: University of Michigan Population Studies Center.

Hoffman, M. L. (2001). A comprehensive theory of prosocial moral development. In A. Bohart & D. Stipek & (Eds.), *Constructive and destructive behavior* (pp. 61–86). Washington, DC: American Psychological Association.

Hogan, T., Rabinowitz, M., & Craven, J. A. III. (2003). Representation in teaching: Inferences from research of expert and novice teachers. *Educational Psychologist, 38,* 235–247.

Hong, G., & Raudenbush, S. W. (2005). Effects of kindergarten retention policy on children's cognitive growth in reading and mathematics. *Educational Evaluation and Policy Analysis, 27,* 205–224.

Horn, J. L. (1998). A basis for research on age differences in cognitive capabilities. In J. J. McArdle & R. W. Woodcock (Eds.), *Human cognitive theories in theory and practice* (pp. 57–87). Mahwah, NJ: Erlbaum.

Hoy, W. K. (1972). Dimensions of student alienation and characteristics of public high schools. *Interchange, 3,* 38–51.

Hoy, W. K. (2001). The pupil control studies: A historical, theoretical, and empirical analysis. *Journal of Educational Administration, 39,* 424–441.

Hoy, W. K. (2002). Faculty trust: A key to student achievement. *Journal of School Public Relations, 23*(2), 88–103.

Hoy, W. K. (2010). *Quantitative research in education: A primer.* Los Angeles: Sage.

Hoy, W. K. (2012). School characteristics that make a difference for the achievement of all students: A 40-year academic odyssey. *Journal of Educational Administration, 50,* 76–97.

Hoy, W. K., & Appleberry, J. B. (1970). Teacher-principal relationships in 'humanistic' and 'custodial' elementary schools. *Journal of Experimental Education, 39,* 27–31.

Hoy, W. K., & Clover, S. I. R. (1986). Elementary school climate: A revision of the OCDQ. *Educational Administration Quarterly, 22,* 93–110.

Hoy, W. K., & Feldman, J. (1999). Organizational health profiles for high schools. In J. Freiberg (Ed.), *School climate: Measuring, sustaining, and improving* (pp. 84–103). Philadelphia: Falmer Press.

Hoy, W. K., & Hannum, J. (1997). Middle school climate: An empirical assessment of organizational health and student achievement. *Educational Administration Quarterly, 33*, 290–311.

Hoy, W. K., & Miskel, C. G. (2001). *Educational administration: Theory, research, and practice* (6th ed.). New York: McGraw-Hill.

Hoy, W. K., & Miskel, C. G. (2005). *Educational administration: Theory, research, and practice* (7th ed.). New York: McGraw-Hill.

Hoy, W. K., & Miskel, C. G. (2008). *Educational administration: Theory, research, and practice* (8th ed.). New York: McGraw-Hill.

Hoy, W. K., & Miskel, C. G. (2013). *Educational administration: Theory, research, and practice* (9th ed.). New York: McGraw Hill.

Hoy, W. K., & Sabo, D. J. (1998). *Quality middle schools: Open and healthy.* Thousand Oaks, CA: Corwin Press.

Hoy, W. K., & Smith, P. A. (2007). Influence: A key to successful leadership. *The International Journal of Educational Management, 21*, 158–167.

Hoy, W. K., Smith, P. A., & Sweetland, S. R. (2002). The development of the organizational climate index for high schools: Its measure and relationship to faculty trust. *High School Journal, 86*(2), 38–49.

Hoy, W. K., & Tarter, C. J. (1997a). *The road to open and healthy schools: A handbook for change, secondary edition.* Thousand Oaks, CA: Corwin Press.

Hoy, W. K., & Tarter, C. J. (1997b). *The road to open and healthy schools: A handbook for change, elementary edition.* Thousand Oaks, CA: Corwin Press.

Hoy, W. K., & Tarter, C. J. (2004). Organizational justice in schools: No justice without trust. *International Journal of Educational Management, 18*, 250–259.

Hoy, W. K., Tarter, C. J., & Kottkamp, R. (1991). *Open schools/healthy schools: Measuring organizational climate.* Beverly Hills, CA: Sage.

Hoy, W. K., Tarter, C. J., & Woolfolk Hoy, A. (2006a). Academic optimism of schools. In W. K. Hoy & C. Miskel (Eds.), *Contemporary issues in educational policy and school outcomes* (pp. 135–156). Greenwich, CT: Information Age.

Hoy, W. K., Tarter, C. J., & Woolfolk Hoy, A. (2006b). Academic optimism of schools: A force for student achievement. *American Educational Research Journal, 43*, 425–446.

Hoy, W. K., & Tschannen-Moran, M. (2003). The conceptualization and measurement of faculty trust in schools. In W. K. Hoy & C. Miskel (Eds.), *Studies in leading and organizing schools* (pp. 181–207). Greenwich, CT: Information Age.

Hoy, W. K., & Woolfolk, A. E. (1990). Organizational socialization of student teachers. *American Educational Research Journal, 27*, 279–300.

Hoy, W. K., & Woolfolk, A. E. (1993). Teachers' sense of efficacy and the organizational health of schools. *The Elementary School Journal, 93*, 355–372.

Hoy, W. K., & Woolfolk Hoy, A. (2011, Summer). *An organizational model for school achievement.* Paper presented at the annual convention of European Association for Research on Learning and Instruction (EARLI). University of Exeter, United Kingdom.

Hudley, C., & Novak, A. (2007). Environmental influences, the developing brain, and aggressive behavior. *Theory Into Practice, 46*, 121–129.

Hulleman, C. S., Godes, O., Hendricks, B. L., & Harackiewicz, J. M. (2010). Enhancing interest and performance with a utility value intervention. *Journal of Educational Psychology, 102*, 880–895.

Hung, D. W. L. (1999). Activity, apprenticeship, and epistemological appropriation: Implications from the writings of Michael Polanyi. *Educational Psychologist, 34*, 193–205.

Hunt, E. (2000). Let's hear it for crystallized intelligence. *Learning and Instruction, 12*, 123–129.

Hunter, M. (1982). *Mastery teaching.* El Segundo, CA: TIP Publications.

Hutchinson, N. L. (2009). *Inclusion of exceptional learners in Canadian classrooms: A practical handbook for teachers* (3rd ed.). Toronto, Canada: Prentice Hall.

Hyde, J. S. (2005). The gender similarities hypothesis. *American Psychologist, 60*, 581–592.

Hyman, I., Kay, B., Tabori, A., Weber, M., Mahon, M., & Cohen, I. (2006). Bullying: Theory, research and interventions about student victimization. In C. Evertson & C. S. Weinstein (Eds.), *Handbook for classroom management: Research, practice, and contemporary issues.* Mahwah, NJ: Erlbaum.

Idol, L. (2006). Toward inclusion of special education students in general education: A program evaluation of eight schools. *Remedial and Special Education, 27*, 77–94.

International Society for Technology in Education. (2009). National Educational Technology Standards for Administrators (NETS-A). Available online from http://www.iste.org/standards/nets-for-administrators.aspx

Irvine, J. J. (1990). *Black students and school failure: Policies, practices, and prescriptions.* New York: Praeger.

Irvine, J. J. (2003). *Educating teachers for diversity: Seeing with a cultural eye.* New York: Teachers College Press.

Irvine, J. J., & Armento, B. J. (2001). *Culturally responsive teaching: Lesson planning for elementary and middle grades.* New York: McGraw-Hill.

Irvine, J. J., & Fraser, J. W. (1998, May). Warm demanders. *Education Week.* Available online at http://www.edweek.org/ew/ewstory.cfm?slug=35irvine.h17&keywords=Irvine

Irving, O., & Martin, J. (1982). Withitness: The confusing variable. *American Educational Research Journal, 19,* 313–319.

Jackson, A., & Davis, G. (2000). *Turning points 2000: Educating adolescents in the 21st century.* New York: Teachers College Press.

Jagacinski, C. M., & Nicholls, J. G. (1987). Competence and affect in task involvement and ego involvement: The impact of social comparison information. *Journal of Educational Psychology, 76,* 107–114.

Jang, H., Reeve, J., & Deci, E. L. (2010). Engaging students in learning activities: It is not autonomy support or structure but autonomy support and structure. *Journal of Educational Psychology, 102,* 588–600.

Jang, H., Reeve, J., Ryan, R. M., & Kim, A. (2009). Can self-determination theory explain what underlies the productive, satisfying learning experiences of collectivistically oriented Korean students? *Journal of Educational Psychology, 101,* 644–661.

Jarrold, C., Tam, H., Baddeley, A. D., & Harvey, C. E. (2011). How does processing affect storage in working memory tasks? Evidence for both domain-general and domain-specific effects. *Journal of Experimental Psychology: Learning, Memory, and Cognition, 37,* 688–705.

Jennings, J., & Rentner, D. S. (2006). Ten big effects of the No Child Left Behind Act on public schools. *Phi Delta Kappan, 88*(2), 110–113.

Jensen, E. (2009). *Teaching with poverty in mind: What being poor does to kids' brains and what schools can do about it.* Alexandria, VA: Association for Supervision and Curriculum Development.

Jenson, W. R., Sloane, H. N., & Young, K. R. (1988). *Applied behavior analysis in education: A structured teaching approach.* Englewood Cliffs, NJ: Prentice-Hall.

Jerome, E. M., Hamre, B. K., & Pianta, R. C. (2009). Teacher–child relationships from kindergarten to sixth grade: Early childhood predictors of teacher-perceived conflict and closeness. *Social Development, 18*(4), 915–945.

Jimenez, R. (2000). Literacy and identity development of Latina/o students who are successful English readers: Opportunities and obstacles. *American Educational Research Journal, 37,* 971–1000.

Jimerson, S. R. (1999). On the failure of failure: Examining the association between early grade retention and education and employment outcomes during late adolescence. *Journal of School Psychology, 37,* 243–272.

Jimerson, S. R., Anderson, G. E., & Whipple, A. D. (2002). Winning the battle and losing the war: Examining the relation between grade retention and dropping out of high school. *Psychology in the Schools, 39,* 441–457.

Johnson, D. W., & Johnson, F. P. (2013). *Joining together: Group theory and group skills* (11th ed.). Boston: Pearson.

Johnson, D. W., & Johnson, R. (1994). *Learning together and alone: Cooperation, competition, and individualization* (4th ed.). Boston: Allyn & Bacon.

Johnson, D. W., & Johnson, R. (1999a). *Learning together and alone: Cooperation, competition, and individualization* (5th ed.). Boston: Allyn & Bacon.

Johnson, D. W., & Johnson, R. (1999b). The three Cs of school and classroom management. In H. J. Freiberg (Ed.), *Beyond behaviorism: Changing the classroom management paradigm* (pp. 119–144). Boston: Allyn & Bacon.

Johnson, D. W., & Johnson, R. (2002). *Meaningful assessment: A manageable and cooperative process.* Boston: Allyn & Bacon.

Johnson, D. W., & Johnson, R. (Eds.). (2005). Peace education. *Theory into Practice, 44* (special issue).

Johnson, D. W., & Johnson, R. T. (2009a). An educational psychology success story: Social interdependence theory and cooperative learning. *Educational Researcher, 38,* 365–379.

Johnson, D. W., & Johnson, R. T. (2009b). Energizing learning: The instructional power of conflict. *Educational Researcher, 38,* 37–51.

Johnson, D. W., Johnson, R., Dudley, B., Ward, M., & Magnuson, D. (1995). The impact of peer mediation training on the management of school and home conflicts. *American Educational Research Journal, 32,* 829–844.

Johnson, L., Smith, R., Levine, A., & Haywood, K. (2010). *2010 Horizon Report: K–12 Edition.* Austin, TX: The New Media Consortium.

Jones, E. D., & Southern, W. T. (1991). Conclusions about acceleration: Echoes of a debate. In W. Southern & E. Jones (Eds.) *The academic acceleration of gifted children* (pp. 223–228). New York: Teachers College Press.

Kagan, S. (1994). *Cooperative learning*. San Juan Capistrano, CA: Kagan Cooperative Learning.

Kanaya, T., Scullin, M. H. & Ceci, S. J. (2003). The Flynn effect and U.S. policies: The impact of rising IQ scores on American society via mental retardation diagnoses. *American Psychologist, 58,* 1–13.

Kanazawa, S. (2010). Evolutionary psychology and intelligence research. *American Psychologist, 65*(4), 279–289.

Kaplan, A., & Maehr, M. L. (2007). The contributions and prospects of goal orientation theory. *Educational Psychology Review, 19*, 141–184.

Karweit, N. (1989). Time and learning: A review. In R. E. Slavin (Ed.), *School and classroom organization* (pp. 69–95). Hillsdale, NJ: Erlbaum.

Kazdin, A. E. (2001). *Behavior modification in applied settings* (6th ed.). Belmont, CA: Wadsworth.

Keefe, J. W. (1982). Assessing student learning styles: An overview. In *Student learning styles and brain behavior*. Reston, VA: National Association of Secondary School Principals.

Keefe, J. W., & Monk, J. S. (1986). *Learning style profile: Examiner's manual*. Reston, VA: National Association of Secondary School Principals.

Keller, M., Neumann, K., & Fischer, H. E. (2012). Teacher enthusiasm and student learning. In J. Hattie & E. Anderman (Eds.), *International handbook of student achievement*. New York: Routledge.

Kelly, K. (1999). Retention vs. social promotion: Schools search for alternatives. *Harvard Education Letter, 15*(1), 1–3.

Kemp, C., & Carter, M. (2006). The contribution of academic skills to the successful inclusion of children with disabilities. *Journal of Developmental and Physical Disabilities, 18*, 123–146.

Kennedy, M. M. (2011). Attribution error and the quest for teacher quality. *Educational Researcher, 39*, 591–598.

Keyser, V., & Barling, J. (1981). Determinants of children's self-efficacy beliefs in an academic environment. *Cognitive Therapy & Research, 5*, 29–40.

Kindsvatter, R., Wilen, W., & Ishler, M. (1988). *Dynamics of effective teaching*. New York: Longman.

King, A. (1990). Enhancing peer interaction and learning in the classroom through reciprocal questioning. *American Educational Research Journal, 27*, 664–687.

King, A. (2002). Structuring peer interactions to promote high-level cognitive processing. *Theory into Practice, 41*, 31–39.

Kirschner, P. A., Sweller, J., & Clark, R. E. (2006). Why minimal guidance during instruction does not work: An analysis of the failure of constructivist, discovery, problem-based experiential and inquiry-based teaching. *Educational Psychologist, 41*(2), 75–86.

Kirst, M. (1991a). Interview on assessment issues with Lorrie Shepard. *Educational Researcher, 20*(2), 21–23.

Kirst, M. (1991b). Interview on assessment issues with James Popham. *Educational Researcher, 20*(2), 24–27.

Knapp, M. S., & Woolverton, S. (2003). Social class and schooling. In J. A. Banks & C. A. Banks (Eds.), *Handbook of research on multicultural education*. San Francisco, CA: Jossey-Bass.

Koeppen, K. E. (1998). The experiences of a secondary social studies student teacher: Seeking security by planning for self. *Teaching & Teacher Education, 14*, 401–411.

Kohn, A. (1991). Caring kids: The role of the schools. *Phi Delta Kappan, 72*(7), 496–506.

Kohn, A. (1993). Rewards versus learning: A response to Paul Chance. *Phi Delta Kappan, 74*, 784–785.

Kohn, A. (2002). How not to teach values. In L. Abbeduto (Ed.), *Taking sides: Clashing on controversial issues in educational psychology* (pp. 138–153). Guilford, CT: McGraw-Hill/Duskin.

Kohn, A. (2006). *The homework myth: Why our kids get too much of a bad thing*. Cambridge, MA: Da Capo Press.

Kolb, D. (1985). *Learning Styles Inventory* (Rev. ed.). London: McBer.

Kornhaber, M., Fierros, E., & Veenema, S. (2004). *Multiple intelligences: Best ideas for research and practice*. Boston: Allyn & Bacon.

Kounin, J. S. (1970). *Discipline and group management in classrooms*. New York: Holt, Rinehart & Winston.

Kratchovil, C. J. (2009). Current pharmacotherapy for ADHD. 2nd International Congress on ADHD. From Childhood to Adult Disease. May 21–24,

2009, Vienna, Austria. *Attention Deficit and Hyperactivity Disorders, 1*: 61.

Krathwohl, D. R., Bloom, B. S., & Masia, B. B. (1964). *Taxonomy of educational objectives. Handbook II: Affective domain.* New York: David McKay.

Kratzig, G. P., & Arbuthnott, K. D. (2006). Perceptual learning style and learning proficiency: A test of the hypothesis. *Journal of Educational Psychology, 98*, 238–246.

Kreitzer, A. E., & Madaus, G. F. (1994). Empirical investigations of the hierarchical structure of the taxonomy. In L. W. Anderson & L. A. Sosniak (Eds.), *Bloom's taxonomy: A forty-year retrospective. Ninety-third yearbook for the National Society for the Study of Education: Part II* (pp. 64–81). Chicago: University of Chicago Press.

Kronholz, J. (2011). Challenging the gifted: Nuclear chemistry and Sartre draw the best and brightest to Reno. *Education Next, 11*(2), 1–8. Available online at http://educationnext.org/challenging-the-gifted/

Labaree, D. F. (1997). *How to succeed in schools without really trying: The credentials race in American education.* New Haven, CT: Yale University Press.

Lachter, J., Forster, K. I., & Ruthruff, K. I. (2004). Forty-five years after Broadbent (1958): Still no identification without attention. *Psychological Review, 111*, 880–913.

Ladson-Billings, G. (1990). Like lightning in a bottle: Attempting to capture the pedagogical excellence of successful teachers of black students. *Qualitative Studies in Education, 3*, 335–344.

Ladson-Billings, G. (1992). Culturally relevant teaching: The key to making multicultural education work. In C. A. Grant (Ed.), *Research and multicultural education* (pp. 106–121). London: Falmer Press.

Ladson-Billings, G. (1994). *The dream keepers.* San Francisco: Jossey-Bass.

Ladson-Billings, G. (1995). But that is just good teaching! The case for culturally relevant pedagogy. *Theory into Practice, 34*, 161–165.

Landrum, T. J., & Kauffman, J. M. (2006). Behavioral approaches to classroom management. In C. M. Evertson & C. S. Weinstein (Eds.), *Handbook of classroom management: Research, practice, and contemporary issues.* Mahwah, NJ: Erlbaum.

Lane, K., Falk, K., & Wehby, J. (2006). Classroom management in special education classrooms and resource rooms. In C. M. Evertson & C. S. Weinstein (Eds.), *Handbook of classroom management: Research, practice, and contemporary issues.* Mahwah, NJ: Erlbaum.

Langer, E. J. (1989). *Mindfulness.* Cambridge, MA: Perseus.

Language Development and Hypermedia Group. (1992). "Open" software design: A case study. *Educational Technology, 32*, 43–55.

Larrivee, B. (1985). *Effective teaching behaviors for successful mainstreaming.* New York: Longman.

Larrivee, B. (2005). *Authentic classroom management: Creating a learning community and building reflective practice.* Boston: Allyn & Bacon.

Lashley, T. J., II, Matczynski, T. J., & Rowley, J. B. (2002). *Instructional models: Strategies for teaching in a diverse society* (2nd ed.). Belmont, CA: Wadsworth/Thomson Learning.

Lave, J., & Wenger, E. (1991). *Situated learning: Legitimate peripheral participation.* Cambridge, MA: Cambridge University Press.

Lee, J., & Shute, V. J. (2010). Personal and social-contextual factors in K–12 academic performance: An integrative perspective on student learning. *Educational Psychologist, 45*, 185–202.

Lee, R. M. (2005). Resilience against discrimination: Ethnic identity and other group orientation as protective factors for Korean Americans. *Journal of Counseling Psychology, 52*, 36–44.

Lee, V., & Bryk, A. S. (1989). A multilevel model of social distribution of high school achievement. *Sociology of Education, 62*, 172–192.

Leinhardt, G. (2001). Instructional explanations: A commonplace for teaching and location for contrasts. In V. Richardson (Ed.), *Handbook of research on teaching* (4th ed., pp. 333–357). Washington, DC: American Educational Research Association.

Lelyveld, N. (1999). "Parachute" Children: Landing Can Be Rough. Young Asians In The States For An Education Are Often Kidnap Targets. *Philadelphia Inquirer.* Available at http://articles.philly.com/1999-01-20/living/25490387_1_parachute-children-parachute-children-kidnapping-cases

LeMahieu, P., Gitomer, D. H., & Eresh, J. T. (1993). *Portfolios in large-scale assessment: Difficult but not impossible.* (Unpublished manuscript, University of Delaware).

Lemelson, R. (2003). Obsessive-compulsive disorder in Bali. *Transcultural Psychiatry, 40*, 377–408.

Lepper, M. R. (1988). Motivational considerations in the study of instruction. *Cognition & Instruction, 5,* 289–309.

Lepper, M. R., & Greene, D. (1978). *The hidden costs of rewards: New perspectives on the psychology of human motivation.* Hillsdale, NJ: Erlbaum.

Lessow-Hurley, J. (2005). *The foundations of dual language development.* Boston: Allyn & Bacon.

Levin, J. R., & Nolan, J. F. (2000). *Principles of classroom management: A professional decision-making model.* Boston: Allyn & Bacon.

Lewis, A. C. (2007). How well has NCLB worked? How do we get the revisions we want? *Phi Delta Kappan, 88*(5), 353–358.

Lewis, R. (2001). Classroom discipline and student responsibility: The students' view. *Teaching & Teacher Education, 17,* 307–319.

Lewis, T. J., & Sugai, G. (1996). Functional assessment of problem behavior: A pilot investigation of the comparative and interactive effects of teacher and peer social attention on students in general education settings. *School Psychology Quarterly, 11,* 1–19.

Lewis, T. J., Sugai, G., & Colvin, G. (1998). Reducing problem behavior through a school-wide system of effective behavioral support: Investigation of a school-wide social skills training program and contextual interventions. *School Psychology Review, 27,* 446–459.

Liben, L. S., & Signorella, M. L. (1993). Gender-schematic processing in children: The role of initial interpretations of stimuli. *Developmental Psychology, 29,* 141–149.

Lindberg, S. M., Hyde, J. S., Peterson, J. L., & Linn, M. C. (2010). New trends in gender and mathematics performance: A meta-analysis. *Psychological Bulletin, 136,* 1123–1135.

Linn, R. L. (2003). Accountability: Responsibility and reasonable expectations. *Educational Researcher, 32*(7), 3–13.

Linn, R. L., & Gronlund, N. E. (2000). *Measurement and assessment in education* (8th ed.). Columbus, OH: Merrill.

Locke, E. A., & Latham, G. P. (1990). *A theory of goal setting and task performance.* Englewood Cliffs, NJ: Prentice-Hall.

Locke, E. A., & Latham, G. P. (2002). Building a practically useful theory of goal setting and task motivation: A 35-year odyssey. *American Psychologist, 57,* 705–717.

Lowenstein, G. (1994). The psychology of curiosity: A review and reinterpretation. *Psychological Bulletin, 117,* 75–98.

Lowry, R., Sleet, D., Duncan, C., Powell, K., & Kolbe, L. (1995). Adolescents at risk for violence. *Educational Psychology Review, 7,* 7–40.

Lucas, S. R., & Berends, M. (2002). Sociodemographic diversity, correlated achievement, and de facto tracking. *Sociology of Education, 75,* 328–348.

Luckner, A. E., & Pianta, R. C. (2011). Teacher student interactions in fifth grade classrooms: Relations with children's peer behavior. *Journal of Applied Developmental Psychology, 32,* 257–266. doi:10.1016/j.appdev.2011.02.010.

Lunnenberg, F. C. (1983). Pupil control ideology and self-concept as a learner. *Educational Research Quarterly, 8,* 33–39.

Lyon, G. R., Shaywitz, S. E., & Shaywitz, B. A. (2003). A definition of dyslexia. *Annals of Dyslexia, 53,* 1–14.

Ma, X. (2012). The relation of teacher characteristics to student achievement. In J. Hattie & E. Anderman (Eds.), *International handbook of student achievement.* New York: Routledge.

Maag, J. W., & Kemp, S. E. (2003). Behavioral intent of power and affiliation: Implications for functional analysis. *Remedial & Special Education, 24,* 57–64.

Mabry, L. (1999). Writing to the rubrics: Lingering effects of traditional standardized testing on direct writing assessment. *Phi Delta Kappan, 80,* 673–679.

Madsen, K. (2003). The effect of accuracy of instruction, teacher delivery, and student attentiveness on musicians' evaluation of teacher effectiveness. *Journal of Research in Music Education, 51,* 38–51.

Magnusson, S. J., & Palincsar, A. S. (1995). The learning environment as a site of science reform. *Theory into Practice, 34,* 43–50.

Major, B., & Schmader, T. (1998). Coping with stigma through psychological disengagement. In J. Swim & C. Stangor (Eds.), *Stigma: The target's perspective* (pp. 219–241). New York: Academic Press.

Manning, M. L., & Baruth, L. G. (1996). *Multicultural education of children and adolescents* (2nd ed.). Boston: Allyn & Bacon.

Mantzicopoulos, P., & Morrison, D. (1992). Kindergarten retention: Academic and behavioral outcomes through the end of second grade. *American Educational Research Journal, 29,* 182–198.

Marsh, H. W., Walker, R., & Debus, R. (1991). Subject-specific components of academic self-concept and self-efficacy. *Contemporary Educational Psychology, 16*, 331–345.

Marshall, H. H. (Ed.). (1992). *Redefining student learning: Roots of educational change*. Norwood, NJ: Ablex.

Martin, C. L., & Little, J. K. (1990). The relation of gender understanding to children's sex-typed preferences and gender stereotypes. *Child Development, 61*, 1427–1439.

Martin, J. (2006). Social cultural perspectives in educational psychology. In P. A. Alexander & P. H. Winne (Eds.), *Handbook of educational psychology* (2nd ed., pp. 595–614). Mahwah, NJ: Erlbaum.

Marzano, R. J. (2003). *What works in schools: Translating research into action*. Alexandria, VA: Association of Supervision and Curriculum Development.

Marzano, R. J., & Marzano, J. S. (2003, September). The key to classroom management. *Educational Leadership, 61*(1), 6–13.

Maslow, A. H. (1968). *Toward a psychology of being* (2nd ed.). New York: Van Nostrand.

Maslow, A. H. (1970). *Motivation and personality* (2nd ed.). New York: Harper & Row.

Mason, D. A., & Good, T. L. (1993). Effects of two-group and whole-class teaching on regrouped elementary students' mathematics achievement. *American Educational Research Journal, 30*, 328–360.

Matsumara, L. C., Slater, S. C., & Crosson, A. (2008). Classroom climate, rigorous instruction and curriculum, and students' interactions in urban middle schools. *The Elementary School Journal, 108*, 293–312.

Mayer, R. E. (2004). Should there be a three-strikes rule against discovery learning? A case for guided methods of instruction. *American Psychologist, 59*, 14–19.

Mayer, R. E. (2011). *Applying the science of learning*. Boston: Pearson.

Mayer, R. E., & Massa, L. J. (2003). Three facets of visual and verbal learners: Cognitive ability, cognitive style, and learning preference. *Journal of Educational Psychology, 95*, 833–846.

McCaslin, M., & Good, T. L. (1998). Moving beyond management as sheer compliance: Helping students to develop goal coordination strategies. *Educational Horizons, 76*, 169–176.

McCaslin, M., & Hickey, D. T. (2001). Self-regulated learning and academic achievement: A Vygotskian view. In B. Zimmerman & D. Schunk (Eds.), *Self-regulated learning and academic achievement: Theoretical perspectives* (2nd ed., pp. 227–252). Mahwah, NJ: Erlbaum.

McClelland, D. C. (1985). *Human motivation*. Glenview, IL: Scott, Foresman.

McClelland, D. C., Atkinson, J. W., Clark, R. W., & Lowell, E. L. (1953). *The achievement motive*. New York: Appleton-Century-Crofts.

McClelland, D. C., & Pilon, D. (1983). Sources of adult motives in patterns of parent behavior in early childhood. *Journal of Personality & Social Psychology, 44*, 564–574.

McCoach, D. B., Kehle, T. J., Bray, M. L., & Siegle, D. (2001). Best practices in the identification of gifted students with learning disabilities. *Psychology in the Schools, 38*, 403–411.

McCoy, A. R., & Reynolds, A. J. (1999). Grade retention and school performance: An extended investigation. *Journal of School Psychology, 37*, 273–298.

McCutcheon, G., & Milner, H. R. (2002). A contemporary study of teacher planning in a high school. *Teachers & Teaching: Theory and Practice, 8*, 81–94.

McDonald, J. P. (1993). Three pictures of an exhibition: Warm, cool, and hard. *Phi Delta Kappan, 6*, 480–485.

McGuigan, L., & Hoy, W. K. (2006). Principal leadership: Creating a culture of academic optimism to improve achievement for all students. *Leadership & Policy in Schools, 5*, 203–229.

McLoyd, V. C. (1998). Economic disadvantage and child development. *American Psychologist, 53*, 185–204.

McMillan, J. H. (2004). *Classroom assessment: Principles and practice for effective instruction* (3rd ed.). Boston: Allyn & Bacon.

McNabb, M. L., Hawkes, M., & Rouk, U. (1999). *Critical issues in evaluating the effectiveness of technology*. U.S. Department of Education National Conference on Educational Technology.

McNabb, M. L., Valdez, G., Nowakowski, J., & Hawkes, M. (1999). *Technology connections for school improvement: Planners' handbook* (p. 153). U.S. Department of Education and North Central Regional Educational Laboratory.

McNeely, C. A., Nonnemaker, J. M., & Blum, R. W. (2002). Promoting school connectedness: Evidence from the National Longitudinal Study of Adolescent Health. *Journal of School Health, 72*(4), 138–146.

McNeil, L. M., & Valenzuela, A. (2000). *The harmful impact of the TAAS system of testing in Texas: Beneath the accountability rhetoric.* Cambridge, MA: Harvard University Civil Rights Project. Retrieved from www.law.harvard.edu/groups/civilrights/testing.html

Means, B. (1994). *Technology and education reform: The reality behind the promise.* San Francisco, CA: Jossey-Bass.

Mears, T. (1998, April 12). Saying 'Si' to Spanish. *Boston Globe.*

Medina, J. (2002, June 23). Groups say Regents Exam English tests push immigrants to drop out. *New York Times,* p. A28.

Medley, D. M. (1979). The effectiveness of teachers. In P. Peterson & H. Walberg (Eds.), *Research on teaching: Concepts, findings, and implications* (pp. 11–27). Berkeley, CA: McCutchan.

Meece, J. L., & Kurtz-Costes, B. (2001). Introduction: The schooling of ethnic minority children and youth. *Educational Psychologist, 36,* 1–7.

Meijer, A. M., & van den Wittenboer, G. L. H. (2004). The joint contribution of sleep, intelligence and motivation to school performance. *Personality & Individual Differences, 37,* 95–106.

Mendell, P. R. (1971). Retrieval and representation in long-term memory. *Psychonomic Science, 23,* 295–296.

Merrell, K. W., Isava, D. M., Gueldner, B. A., & Ross, S. W. (2008). How effective are school bullying intervention programs? A meta-analysis of intervention research. *School Psychology Quarterly, 23,* 26–42.

Metzler, C. W., Biglan, A., Rusby, J. C., & Sprague, J. R. (2001). Evaluation of a comprehensive behavior management program to improve schoolwide positive behavior support. *Education & Treatment of Children, 24*(4), 448–470.

Miller, E. (1994). Peer mediation catches on, but some adults don't. *Harvard Education Letter, 10*(3), 8.

Miller, G. A. (1956). The magical number seven, plus or minus two: Some limits on our capacity for processing information. *Psychological Review, 63,* 81–97.

Miller, G. A., Galanter, E., & Pribram, K. H. (1960). *Plans and the structure of behavior.* New York: Holt, Rinehart & Winston.

Miller, P. H. (2002). *Theories of developmental psychology* (4th ed.). New York: Worth.

Milner, H. R. (2006). Classroom management in urban classrooms. In C. Evertson & C. Weinstein (Ed.), *Handbook of classroom management: Research, practice, and contemporary issues* (pp. 491–522). Mahwah, NJ: Erlbaum.

Mitchell, M. (1993). Situational interest: Its multifaceted structure in the secondary school mathematics classroom. *Journal of Educational Psychology, 85,* 424–436.

Moll, L. C., Amanti, C., Neff, D., & Gonzalez, N. (1992). Funds of knowledge: Using a qualitative approach to connect homes and classrooms. *Theory into Practice, 31,* 132–141.

Moller, A. C., Deci, E. L., & Ryan, R. M. (2006). Choice and ego-depletion: The moderating role of autonomy. *Personality and Social Psychology Bulletin, 32*(8), 1024–1036.

Monroe, C. R., & Obidah, J. E. (2002, April). *The impact of cultural synchronization on a teacher's perceptions of disruption: A case study of an African American middle school classroom.* Paper presented at the American Educational Research Association, New Orleans.

Montrul, S. (2010). Dominant language transfer in adult second language learners and heritage speakers. *Second Language Research, 26,* 293–327.

Moore, K. A., Redd, Z., Burkhauser, M., Mbwana, K., & Collins, A. (2009). *Children in poverty: Trends, consequences, and policy options.* Washington, DC: Child Trends, #2009-11.

Morine-Dershimer, G. (2006). Instructional planning. In J. Cooper (Ed.), *Classroom teaching skills* (7th ed., pp. 20–54). Boston: Houghton-Mifflin.

Morrow, L. M., & Weinstein, C. (1986). Encouraging voluntary reading: The impact of a literature program on children's use of library centers. *Reading Research Quarterly, 21,* 330–346.

Moshman, D. (1997). Pluralist rational constructivism. *Issues in Education: Contributions from Educational Psychology, 3,* 229–234.

Mowday, R. T., Porter, L. W., & Steers, R. M. (1982). *Employee-organizational linkages: The psychology of commitment, absenteeism, and turnover.* New York: Academic Press.

Mullins, T. (1983). *Relationships among teachers' perceptions of principal's style, teachers' loyalty to the principal, and teachers' zone of acceptance.* Unpublished doctoral dissertation, Rutgers University, New Brunswick, NJ.

Mullis, I. V. S., Martin, M. O., Gonzalez, E., & Kennedy, A. M. (2003). *PIRLS 2001 International report: IEA's study of reading literacy achievement in primary schools.* Chestnut Hill, MA: Boston College. Available online at http://timss.bc.edu/pirls2001i/PIRLS2001_Pubs_IR.html

Murayama, K., & Elliot, A. J. (2009). The joint influence of personal achievement goals and classroom goal structures on achievement-relevant outcomes. *Journal of Educational Psychology, 101,* 432–447.

Murdock, S. G., O'Neill, R. E., & Cunningham, E. (2005). A comparison of results and acceptability of functional behavioral assessment procedures with a group of middle school students with emotional/behavioral disorders (E/BD). *Journal of Behavioral Education, 14,* 5–18.

Murphy, P. K., & Alexander, P. A. (2000). A motivated exploration of motivation terminology. *Contemporary Educational Psychology, 25,* 3–53.

Myers, D. G. (2005). *Exploring psychology* (6th ed. in modules). New York: Worth.

Myers, D. G. (2008). *Exploring psychology* (7th ed.). New York: Worth.

National Alliance of Black School Educators. (2002). *Addressing over-representations of African American students in special education: The prereferral intervention process.* Arlington, VA: Council for Exceptional Education.

National Center for Educational Statistics. (2003). *Indicators of school crime and safety 2002.* Available online at http://nces.ed.gov/pubs2003/school-crime/6.asp?nav=1

National Poverty Center. (2011). *Poverty in the United States: Frequently asked questions.* The University of Michigan, Gerald R. Ford School of Public Policy, Ann Arbor, MI. Available online at http://npc.umich.edu/poverty/

National Research Council, Institute of Medicine. (2004). *Engaging schools: Fostering high school students' motivation to learn.* Washington, DC: The National Academies Press.

Naveh-Benjamin, M. (1991). A comparison of training programs intended for different types of test-anxious students: Further support for an information-processing model. *Journal of Educational Psychology, 83,* 134–139.

Naveh-Benjamin, M., McKeachie, W. J., & Lin, Y. (1987). Two types of test-anxious students: Support for an information processing model. *Journal of Educational Psychology, 79,* 131–136.

Needles, M., & Knapp, M. (1994). Teaching writing to children who are underserved. *Journal of Educational Psychology, 86,* 339–349.

Nelson, J. R., & Roberts, M. L. (2000). Ongoing reciprocal teacher-student interactions involving disruptive behaviors in general education classrooms. *Journal of Emotional and Behavioral Disorders, 4,* 147–161.

Nelson, T. O. (1996). Consciousness and metacognition. *American Psychologist, 51,* 102–116.

Nicholls, J. G., & Miller, A. (1984). Conceptions of ability and achievement motivation. In R. Ames & C. Ames (Eds.), *Research on motivation in education. Volume 1: Student Motivation* (pp. 39–73). New York: Academic Press.

Nie, Y., & Lau, S. (2009). Complementary roles of care and behavioral control in classroom management: The self-determination theory perspective. *Contemporary Educational Psychology, 34,* 185–194.

Nitko, A. J., & Brookhart, S. M. (2011). *Educational assessment of students* (6th ed.). Boston: Pearson.

No Child Left Behind Act of 2001. (2002). Pub. L. No. 107–110, 115 Stat. 1925.

Noddings, N. (1990). Constructivism in mathematics education. In R. Davis, C. Maher, & N. Noddings (Eds.), *Constructivist views on the teaching and learning of mathematics* (pp. 7–18). Monograph 4 of the National Council of Teachers of Mathematics, Reston, VA.

Noddings, N. (1992). *The challenge to care in schools: An alternative approach to education.* New York: Teachers College Press.

Noddings, N. (1995). Teaching themes of care. *Phi Delta Kappan, 76,* 675–679.

Noguera, P. (2005). The racial achievement gap: How can we assume an equity of outcomes. In L. Johnson, M. E. Finn, & R. Lewis (Eds.), *Urban education with an attitude.* Albany, NY: SUNY Press.

Norbert, F. (2005). Research findings on early first language attrition: Implications for the discussion of critical periods in language acquisition. *Language Learning, 55*(3), 491–531.

Nungester, R. J., & Duchastel, P. C. (1982). Testing versus review: Effects on retention. *Journal of Educational Psychology, 74,* 18–22.

Nylund, D. (2000). *Treating Huckleberry Finn: A new narrative approach to working with kids diagnosed ADD/HDD.* San Francisco: Jossey-Bass.

Oakes, J. (1999). Promotion or retention: Which one is social? *Harvard Education Letter, 15*(1), 8.

Oakes, J., & Wells, A. S. (1998). Detracking for high student achievement. *Educational Leadership, 55*(6), 38–41.

O'Donnell, A. M., & O'Kelly, J. (1994). Learning from peers: Beyond the rhetoric of positive results. *Educational Psychology Review, 6,* 321–350.

Ogbu, J. U. (1997). Understanding the school performance of urban blacks: Some essential background knowledge. In H. Walberg, O. Reyes, & R. P. Weissberg (Eds.), *Children and youth: Interdisciplinary perspectives* (pp. 190–240). Norwood, NJ: Ablex.

Ogbu, J. U. (1999). Beyond language: Ebonics, Proper English, and identity in a Black-American speech community. *American Educational Research Journal, 36,* 147–184.

Okagaki, L. (2001). Triarchic model of minority children's school achievement. *Educational Psychologist, 36,* 9–20.

Okagaki, L. (2006). Ethnicity, learning. In P. Alexander & P. Winne (Eds.), *Handbook of educational psychology* (2nd ed., pp. 615–634). Mahwah, NJ: Erlbaum.

Ong, W., Allison, J., & Haladyna, T. M. (2000). Student achievement of third graders in comparable single-age and multiage classrooms. *Journal of Research in Childhood Education, 14,* 205–215.

Oosterhof, A. (2009). *Developing and using classroom assessments* (4th ed.). Columbus, OH: Pearson/Merrill.

Orange, C. (2000). *25 biggest mistakes teachers make and how to avoid them.* Thousand Oaks, CA: Corwin.

Orange, C. (2005). *44 smart strategies for avoiding classroom mistakes.* Thousand Oaks, CA: Corwin.

Ortony, A., Clore, G. L., & Collins, A. (1988). *The cognitive structure of emotions.* Cambridge: Cambridge University Press.

Osborne, J. W. (2001). Testing stereotype threat: Does anxiety explain race and sex differences in achievement? *Contemporary Educational Psychology, 26,* 291–310.

Ouchi, W. (1981). *Theory Z.* Reading, MA: Addison-Wesley.

Padilla, F. M. (1992). *The gang as an American enterprise.* New Brunswick, NJ: Rutgers University Press.

Pai, Y., & Adler, S. A. (2001). *Cultural foundations of education* (3rd ed.). Upper Saddle River, NJ: Merrill.

Pajares, F. (1997). Current directions in self-efficacy research. In M. L. Maehr & P. R. Pintrich (Eds.), *Advances in motivation and achievement* (Vol. 10, pp. 1–49). Greenwich, CT: JAI Press.

Palincsar, A. S. (1998). Social constructivist perspectives on teaching and learning. In J. T. Spence, J. M. Darley, & D. J. Foss (Eds.), *Annual Review of Psychology* (pp. 345–375). Palo Alto, CA: Annual Reviews.

Palincsar, A. S., Magnusson, S. J., Marano, N., Ford, D., & Brown, N. (1998). Designing a community of practice: Principles and practices of the GIsML community. *Teaching & Teacher Education, 14,* 5–19.

Paris, S. G., Byrnes, J. P., & Paris, A. H. (2001). Constructing theories, identities, and actions of self-regulated learners. In B. J. Zimmerman & D. H. Schunk (Eds.), *Self-regulated learning and academic achievement: Theoretical perspectives* (2nd ed., pp. 253–287). Mahwah, NJ: Erlbaum.

Paris, S. G., & Cunningham, A. E. (1996). Children becoming students. In D. Berliner & R. Calfee (Eds.), *Handbook of educational psychology* (pp. 117–146). New York: Macmillan.

Parks, C. P. (1995). Gang behavior in the schools: Myth or reality? *Educational Psychology Review, 7,* 41–68.

Parsons, T., Bales, R. F., & Shils, E. A. (1953). *Working papers in the theory of action.* New York: Free Press.

Partnership for 21st Century Skills. (2004). *A framework for 21st century learning.* Available online at http://www.p21.org/

Pashler, H. (2006). How we learn. *APS Observer, 19*(3), 22–24.

Pashler, H., McDaniel, M., Rohrer, D., & Bjork, R. (2009). Learning styles: Concepts and evidence. *Psychological Science in the Public Interest, 9,* 105–119.

Pate, P. E., McGinnis, K., & Homestead, E. (1995). Creating coherence through curriculum integration. In M. Harmin, *Inspiring active learning: A handbook for teachers* (pp. 62–70). Alexandria, VA: Association for Supervision and Curriculum Development.

Paulman, R. G., & Kennelly, K. J. (1984). Test anxiety and ineffective test taking: Different names, same construct? *Journal of Educational Psychology*, *76*, 279–288.

Pea, R. (1987). Cognitive technologies for mathematics education. In A. H. Schoenfeld (Ed.), *Cognitive science and mathematics education* (pp. 89–122). Hilldale, NJ: Erlbaum.

Pekrun, R., Goetz, T., Daniels, L. M., Stupinisky, R. H., & Perry, R. P. (2010). Boredom in achievement settings: Exploring control–value antecedents and performance outcomes of a neglected emotion. *Journal of Educational Psychology*, *102*, 531–549.

Pekrun, R., Goetz, T., Titz, W., & Perry, R. P. (2002). Academic emotions in students' self-regulated learning and achievement. A program of qualitative and quantitative research. *Educational Psychologist*, *37*, 91–105.

Pellegrini, A. D., Bartini, M., & Brooks, F. (1999). School bullies, victims, and aggressive victims: Factors relating to group affiliation and victimization in early adolescence. *Journal of Educational Psychology*, *91*, 216–224.

Peregoy, S. F., &. Boyle, O. F. (2009). *Reading, writing, and learning in ESL: A resource book for teaching K–12 English learners* (5th ed.). Boston: Allyn & Bacon/Pearson.

Perry, N. E., & Collie, R. J. (2011, April). *School climate and social and emotional learning: Predictors of early career teacher well-being and efficacy*. Paper presented at the annual meeting of the American Educational Research Association, New Orleans, LA.

Peterson, C. (2000). The future of optimism. *American Psychologist*, *55*, 44–55.

Phillips, D. (1997). How, why, what, when, and where: Perspectives on constructivism and education. *Issues in Education: Contributions from Educational Psychology*, *3*, 151–194.

Piaget, J. (1971). *Biology and knowledge*. Edinburgh, UK: Edinburgh Press.

Piaget, J. (1985). *The equilibrium of cognitive structures: The central problem of intellectual development* (T. Brown & K. L. Thampy, Trans.). Chicago: University of Chicago Press.

Pianta, R. C., Belsky, J., Vandergrift, N., Houts, R., & Morrison, F. J. (2008). Classroom effects on children's achievement trajectories in elementary school. *American Educational Research Journal*, *45*, 365–397.

Pianta, R. C., Howes, C., Burchinal, M., Bryant, D. M., Clifford, R. M., Early, D. M., & Barbarin, O. (2005). Features of pre-kindergarten programs, classrooms, and teachers: Do they predict observed classroom quality and child–teacher interactions? *Applied Developmental Science*, *9*(3), 144–159.

Picciano, A. G. (2006). *Educational leadership and planning for technology* (4th ed.). Saddle River, NJ: Pearson Education.

Pierson, L. H., & Connell, J. P. (1992). Effect of grade retention on self-system processes, school engagement, and academic performance. *Journal of Educational Psychology*, *84*, 300–307.

Pintrich, P. R. (2003). A motivational science perspective on the role of student motivation in learning and teaching. *Journal of Educational Psychology*, *95*, 667–686.

Pintrich, P. R., Marx, R. W., & Boyle, R. A. (1993). Beyond cold conceptual change: The role of motivational beliefs and classroom contextual factors in the process of conceptual change. *Review of Educational Research*, *63*, 167–199.

Pintrich, P. R., & Schunk, D. H. (2002). *Motivation in education: Theory, research, and applications* (2nd ed.). Columbus, OH: Merrill.

Pintrich, P. R., & Zusho, A. (2002). The development of academic self-regulation: The role of cognitive and motivational factors. In A. Wigfield & J. Eccles (Eds.), *Development of achievement motivation* (pp. 249–284). San Diego: Academic Press.

Plummer, D. L., & Graziano, W. G. (1987). Impact of grade retention on the social development of elementary school children. *Developmental Psychology*, *23*, 267–275.

Polk, J. A. (2006). Traits of effective teachers. *Arts Education Policy Review*, *107*(4), 23–29.

Ponitz, C. C., Rimm-Kaufman, S. E., Grimm, K. J., & Curby, T. W. (2009). Kindergarten classroom quality, behavioral engagement, and reading achievement. *School Psychology Review*, *38*, 102–120.

Popham, W. J. (2005). *Classroom assessment: What teachers need to know* (4th ed.). Boston: Allyn & Bacon.

Popham, W. J. (2008). *Classroom assessment: What teachers need to know* (5th ed.). Boston: Allyn & Bacon.

Popham, W. J. (2011). *Classroom assessment: What teachers need to know* (6th ed.). Boston: Allyn & Bacon.

Prawat, R. S. (1996). Constructivism, modern and postmodern. *Issues in Education: Contributions from Educational Psychology*, *3*, 215–226.

Pressley, M., Allington, R., Wharton-McDonald, R., Block, C., & Morrow, L. (2001). *Learning to read: Lessons from exemplary first-grade teachers.* New York: Guilford.

Proctor, C. P., August, D., Carlo, M. S., & Snow, C. (2006). The intriguing role of Spanish language vocabulary knowledge in predicting English reading comprehension. *Journal of Educational Psychology, 98,* 159–169.

Project Tomorrow. (2010). *The new 3 E's of education: Enabled, engaged, empowered. How today's students are leveraging emerging technologies for learning.* Irvine, CA: Project Tomorrow. Available online at http://www.tomorrow.org/about/team.html

Puncochar, J., & Fox, P. W. (2004). Confidence in individual and group decision-making: When "Two Heads" are worse than one. *Journal of Educational Psychology, 96,* 582–591.

Quinn, D. M. (2003). Legal issues in educational technology: implications for school leaders. *Educational Administration Quarterly, 39*(2), 187–207.

Rachlin, H. (1991). *Introduction to modern behaviorism* (3rd ed.). New York: Freeman.

Raffini, J. P. (1996). *150 ways to increase intrinsic motivation in the classroom.* Boston: Allyn & Bacon.

Raudenbush, S., Rowen, B., & Cheong, Y. (1992). Contextual effects on the self-perceived efficacy of high school teachers. *Sociology of Education, 65,* 150–167.

Reeve, J. (1996). *Motivating others: Nurturing inner motivational resources.* Boston: Allyn & Bacon.

Reeve, J. (2009). Why teachers adopt a controlling motivating style toward students and how they can become more autonomy supportive. *Educational Psychologist, 44,* 159–175.

Reeve, J., Deci, E. L., & Ryan, R. M. (2004). *Self-determination theory: A dialectical framework for understanding the sociocultural influences on motivation and learning: Big theories revisited* (Vol. 4, pp. 31–59). Greenwich, CT: Information Age.

Reeves, D. B. (2000). *Accountability in action: A blueprint for learning organizations.* Denver, CO: Advanced Learning Press.

Refugee Council USA. (2011). *History of the U.S. refugee resettlement program.* Washington, DC: Author. Available online at http://www.rcusa.org/index.php?page=history

Reid, J. M., & Byrd, P. (1998). *Grammar in the composition classroom.* New York: Heinle & Heinle.

Reinke, W. M., & Herman, K. C. (2002a). A research agenda for school violence prevention. *American Psychologist, 57,* 796–797.

Reinke, W. M., & Herman, K. C. (2002b). Creating school environments that deter antisocial behaviors in youth. *Psychology in the Schools, 39,* 549–560.

Reis, S. M., & Renzulli, J. S. (2004). Current research on the social and emotional development of gifted and talented students: Good news and future possibilities. *Psychology in the Schools, 41,* 119–130.

Reisberg, D., & Heuer, F. (1992). Remembering the details of emotional events. In E. Winograd & U. Neisser (Eds.), *Affect and accuracy in recall: Studies of "flashbulb" memories* (pp. 162–190). Cambridge, England: Cambridge University Press.

Reiss, F., & Hoy, W. K. (1998). Faculty loyalty: An important but neglected concept in the study of schools. *Journal of School Leadership, 8,* 4–21.

Renninger, K. A., Hidi, S., & Krapp, A. (Eds.). (1992). *The role of interest in learning and development.* Hillsdale, NJ: Erlbaum.

Renzulli, J. S., & Reis, S. M. (1991). The schoolwide enrichment model: A comprehensive plan for the development of creative productivity. In N. Colangelo & G. Davis (Eds.), *Handbook of gifted education* (pp. 111–141). Boston: Allyn & Bacon.

Renzulli, J. S., & Reis, S. M. (2003). The schoolwide enrichment model: Developing creative and productive giftedness. In N. Colangelo, & G. A. Davis, (Eds.), *Handbook of gifted education* (pp. 184–203). Boston: Allyn & Bacon.

Reynolds, C. R., Skiba, R., Graham, S., Sheras, P., Conoley, J. C., & Garcia-Vazquez, E. (2008). Are zero tolerance policies effective in school: An evidentiary review and recommendations. *American Psychologist, 63,* 852–862.

Ricciardelli, L. A. (1992). Bilingualism and cognitive development: Relation to threshold theory. *Journal of Psycholinguistic Research, 21,* 301–316.

Richardson, T. M., & Benbow, C. P. (1990). Long-term effects of acceleration on the social-emotional adjustment of mathematically precocious youths. *Journal of Educational Psychology, 82,* 464–470.

Richell, R., Deakin, J., & Anderson, I. (2005). Effect of acute tryptophan depletion on the response to controllable and uncontrollable noise stress. *Biological Psychiatry, 57,* 295–300.

Rivkin, S. G., Hanushek, E. A., & Kain, J. F. (2001). *Teachers, schools, and academic achievement.* Amherst, MA: Amherst College.

Robbins, S. B., Lauver, K., Davis, H. L., Davis, D., Langley, R., & Carlstrom, A. (2004). Psychosocial and study skill factors predict college outcomes? A meta-analysis. *Psychological Bulletin, 130,* 261–288.

Robbins, S. P. (1998). *Organizational behavior: Concepts, controversies, applications.* Upper Saddle River, NJ: Prentice Hall.

Roberge, M. M. (2002). California's Generation 1.5 Immigrants: What experiences, characterisitcs, and needs do they bring to our English classes? *The CATESOL Journal, 14*(1), 107–129.

Robinson, A., & Clinkenbeard, P. R. (1998). Giftedness: An exceptionality examined. In J. T. Spence, J. M. Darley, & D. J. Foss (Eds.), *Annual Review of Psychology* (pp. 117–139). Palo Alto, CA: Annual Reviews.

Rogers, C. R., & Freiberg, H. J. (1994). *Freedom to learn* (3rd ed.). Columbus, OH: Merrill.

Rogoff, B. (1998). Cognition as a collaborative process. In W. Damon (Series Editor) & D. Kuhn & R. S. Siegler (Volume Eds.), *Handbook of child psychology: Volume 2* (5th ed., pp. 679–744). New York: Wiley.

Rogoff, B., Turkanis, C. G., & Bartlett, L. (2001). *Learning together: Children and adults in a school community.* New York: Oxford.

Rose, L. C., & Gallup, A. M. (1999). The 31st annual Phi Delta Kappa/Gallup Poll of the public's attitude toward the public schools. *Phi Delta Kappan, 81*(1), 41–58.

Rose, L. C., & Gallup, A. M. (2001). The 33rd annual Phi Delta Kappa/Gallup Poll of the public's attitude toward the public schools. *Phi Delta Kappan, 83*(1), 41–58.

Rosenberg, M. S., Westling, D. L., & McLeskey, J. (2011). *Special education for today's teachers: An introduction.* Boston: Allyn & Bacon/Pearson.

Rosenshine, B. (1988). Explicit teaching. In D. Berliner & B. Rosenshine (Eds.), *Talks to teachers* (pp. 75–92). New York: Random House.

Rosenshine, B., & Furst, N. (1973). The use of direct observation to study teaching. In R. Travers (Ed.), *Second handbook of research on teaching.* Chicago: Rand McNally.

Rosenshine, B., & Stevens, R. (1986). Teaching functions. In M. Wittrock (Ed.), *Handbook of research on teaching* (3rd ed., pp. 376–391). New York: Macmillan.

Roskos, K., & Neuman, S. B. (1998). Play as an opportunity for literacy. In O. N. Saracho & B. Spodek (Eds.), *Multiple perspectives on play in early childhood education* (pp. 100–115). Albany, NY: State University of New York Press.

Ross, J. A., Cousins, J. B., & Gadalla, T. (1996). Within teacher predictors of teacher efficacy. *Teaching & Teacher Education, 12,* 385–400.

Rubin, B. (Ed.). (2006). Detracking and heterogeneous grouping. *Theory into Practice, 45*(1) (special issue).

Ruble, D. N., Martin, C. L., & Berenbaum, S. A. (2006). Gender development. In *Handbook of child psychology* (Vol. 3, pp. 858–932). Hoboken, NJ: John Wiley & Sons.

Rueda, R., & Moll, L. C. (1994). A sociocultural perspective on motivation. In F. O'Neil Jr. & M. Drillings (Eds.), *Motivation: Theory and research* (pp. 117–137). Hillsdale, NJ: Erlbaum.

Ruopp, F., & Driscoll, M. (1990, January/February). Access to algebra. *Harvard Education Letter, 6*(A), 4–5.

Ryan, R. M., & Deci, E. L. (1996). When paradigms clash: Comments on Cameron and Pierce's claim that rewards do not undermine intrinsic motivation. *Review of Educational Research, 66,* 33–38.

Sackett, P. R., Hardison, C. M., & Cullen, M. J. (2004). On interpreting stereotype threat as accounting for African American–White differences on cognitive tests. *American Psychologist, 59*(1), 7–13.

Sadker, D., & Sadker, D. (2000). *Teachers, schools, and society* (5th ed.). New York: McGraw-Hill.

Sadker, M., Sadker, D., & Klein, S. (1991). The issue of gender in elementary and secondary education. *Review of Research in Education, 17,* 269–334.

Sanchez, F., & Anderson, M. L. (1990, May). Gang mediation: A process that works. *Principal,* 54–56.

Sanders, W. L., & Rivers, J. C. (1996). *Cumulative and residual effects of teachers on student academic achievement.* Knoxville: University of Tennessee Value-Added Research and Assessment Center.

Sattler, J. (2001). *Assessment of children* (4th ed. rev.). San Diego: Jerome M. Sattler.

Savage, T. V. (1999). *Teaching self-control through management and discipline.* Boston: Allyn & Bacon.

Savin-Williams, R. C. (2006). Who's gay? Does it matter? *Current Directions in Psychological Science, 15*(1), 40–44.

Sawyer, R. K. (2006). *Explaining creativity: The science of human motivation*. New York: Oxford University Press.

Scardamalia, M., & Bereiter, C. (1996). Adaptation and understanding: A case for new cultures of schooling. In S. Vosniado, E. De Corte, R. Glasse, & H. Mandl (Eds.), *International perspectives on the design of technology-supported learning environments* (pp. 149–163). Hillsdale, NJ: Erlbaum.

Schein, E. H. (1992). *Organizational culture and leadership* (2nd ed.). San Francisco: Jossey-Bass.

Schein, E. H. (1999). *The corporate culture*. San Francisco: Jossey-Bass.

Schein, E. H. (2004). *Organizational culture and leadership* (3rd ed.). San Francisco: Wiley.

Schiefele, U. (1991). Interest, learning, and motivation. *Educational Psychologist, 26*, 299–324.

Schmoker, M. J., & Wilson, R. B. (1993). *Total quality education*. Bloomington, IN: Phi Delta Kappa.

Schneider, W., & Bjorklund, D. F. (1992). Expertise, aptitude, and strategic remembering. *Child Development, 63*, 416–473.

Schon, D. (1983). *The reflective practitioner*. New York: Basic Books.

Schraw, G. (2006). Knowledge: Structures and processes. In P. A. Alexander & P. H. Winne (Eds.), *Handbook of educational psychology* (2nd ed., pp. 825–847). Mahwah, NJ: Erlbaum.

Schraw, G., & Lehman, S. (2001). Situational interest: A review of the literature and directions for future research. *Educational Psychology Review, 13*, 23–52.

Schunk, D. H. (2012). *Learning theories: An educational perspective* (6th ed.). Boston: Allyn & Bacon/Pearson.

Schunk, D. H., Pintrich, P. R., & Meece, J. L. (2008). *Motivation in education: Theory, research, and applications* (3rd ed.). Columbus, OH: Merrill.

Seligman, M. E. P. (1975). *Helplessness: On depression, development, and death*. San Francisco: Freeman.

Senge, P. M. (1990). *The fifth discipline: The art and practice of the learning organization*. New York: Doubleday.

Senge, P. M., Cambron-McCabe, N. H., Lucas, T., Kleiner, A., Dutton, J., & Smith, B. (2000). *Schools that learn*. New York: Doubleday.

Senge, P. M., Kleiner, A., Roberts, C., Rossi, R., & Smith, B. J. (1994). *The fifth discipline fieldbook*. New York: Bantam Doubleday Dell.

Serpell, R. (1993). Interface between sociocultural and psychological aspects of cognition. In E. Forman, N. Minick, & C. A. Stone (Eds.), *Contexts for learning: Sociocultural dynamics in children's development* (pp. 357–368). New York: Oxford University Press.

Shanker, A. (1995, May 15). Restoring the connection between behavior and consequences. In *Vital speeches of the day*. Washington, DC: America Federation of Teachers.

Shavelson, R. J. (1987). Planning. In M. Dunkin (Ed.), *The international encyclopedia of teaching and teacher education* (pp. 483–486). New York: Pergamon Press.

Sheets, R. H. (2005). *Diversity pedagogy: Examining the role of culture in the teaching-learning process*. Boston: Allyn & Bacon.

Shepard, L. A., & Smith, M. L. (1988). Escalating academic demand in kindergarten: Counterproductive policies. *Elementary School Journal, 89*(2), 135–145.

Shepard, L. A., & Smith, M. L. (1989). Academic and emotional effects of kindergarten retention. In L. Shepard & M. Smith (Eds.), *Flunking grades: Research and policies on retention* (pp. 79–107). Philadelphia: Falmer Press.

Shih, S. S. (2008). The relation of self-determination and achievement goals to Taiwanese eighth graders' behavioral and emotional engagement in schoolwork. *The Elementary School Journal, 108*, 313–334.

Shimahara, N. K., & Sakai, A. (1995). *Learning to teach in two cultures*. New York: Garland.

Shipley, J., & Wescott, M. C. (2000). *Systems check: School improvement resource guide*. Seminole, FL: Jim Shipley & Associates.

Shonkoff, J. P. (2006). A promising opportunity for developmental and behavioral pediatrics at the interface of neuroscience, psychology, and social policy: Remarks on receiving the 2005 C. Anderson Aldrich Award. *Pediatrics, 118*, 2187–2191.

Shuell, T. J. (1996). Teaching and learning in a classroom context. In D. Berliner & R. Calfee (Eds.), *Handbook of educational psychology* (pp. 726–764). New York: Macmillan.

Shulman, L. S. (1987). Knowledge and teaching: Foundations of the new reform. *Harvard Educational Review, 19*(2), 4–14.

Shute, V. J. (2008). Focus on formative feedback. *Review of Educational Research, 78*, 153–189.

Sirin, S. R. (2005). Socioeconomic status and academic achievement: A meta-analytic review of research. *Review of Educational Research, 75,* 417–453.

Skiba, R. J., Michael, R. S., Nardo, A. C., & Peterson, R. (2000). *The color of discipline: Sources of racial and gender disproportionality in school punishment* (Report #SRS1). Bloomington, IN: Indiana Education Policy Center.

Skinner, B. F. (1950). Are theories of learning necessary? *Psychological Review, 57,* 193–216.

Slavin, R. E. (1987). Ability grouping and student achievement in elementary schools: A best-evidence synthesis. *Review of Educational Research, 57,* 293–336.

Slavin, R. E. (1995). *Cooperative learning* (2nd ed.). Boston: Allyn & Bacon.

Slavin, R. E., & Fashola, O. S. (1998). *Show me the evidence: Proven and promising programs for America's schools.* Thousand Oaks, CA: Corwin.

Slavin, R. E., Karweit, N. L., & Madden, N. A. (1989). *Effective programs for students at risk.* Boston: Allyn & Bacon.

Smith, D. D., & Tyler, N. C. (2010). *Introduction to special education: Making a difference* (7th ed.). Columbus, OH: Merrill.

Smith, J. K., Smith, L. F., & DeLisi, R. (2001). *Natural classroom assessment.* Thousand Oaks, CA: Corwin.

Smith, P. A., & Hoy, W. K. (2007). Academic optimism and student achievement in urban elementary schools. *Journal of Educational Administration, 45,* 550–568.

Smith, S. M., Glenberg, A., & Bjork, R. A. (1978). Environmental context and human memory. *Memory and Cognition, 6,* 342–353.

Snyder, C. R., Shorey, H. S., Cheavens, J., Pulvers, K. M., Adams, V. H., III, & Wiklund, C. (2002). Hope and academic success in college. *Journal of Educational Psychology, 94,* 820–826.

Soar, R. S., & Soar, R. M. (1979). Emotional climate and management. In P. Peterson & H. Walberg (Eds.), *Research on teaching: Concepts, findings and implications* (pp. 97–119). Berkeley, CA: McCutchan.

Solomon, D., Battistich, V., Watson, M., Schaps, E., & Lewis, C. (2000). A six-district study of educational change: Direct and mediated effects of the Child Development Project. *Social Psychology of Education, 4,* 3–51.

Solomon, D., Watson, M. S., & Battistich, V. A. (2001). Teaching and schooling effects on moral/prosocial development. In V. Richardson (Ed.), *Handbook of research on teaching* (4th ed., pp. 566–603). Washington, DC: American Educational Research Association.

Soodak, L. C., & McCarthy, M. R. (2006). Classroom management in inclusive settings. In C. M. Evertson & C. S. Weinstein (Eds.), *Handbook of classroom management: Research, practice, and contemporary issues* (pp. 461–490). Mahwah, NJ: Erlbaum.

Spearman, C. (1927). *The abilities of man: Their nature and measurement.* New York: Macmillan.

Spelling, M. (2007, January). *Building on results: A blueprint for strengthening the No Child Left Behind Act.* Washington, DC: U.S. Department of Education. Available online at: www.ed.gov/policy/elsec/leg/nclb/buildingonresults.html

Spencer, S. J., Steele, C. M., & Quinn, D. M. (1999). Stereotype threat and women's math performance. *Journal of Experimental Social Psychology, 35,* 4–28.

Spiro, R. J., Feltovich, P. J., Jacobson, M. L., & Coulson, R. L. (1991). Cognitive flexibility, constructivism, and hypertext: Random access instruction for advanced knowledge acquisition in ill-structured domains. *Educational Technology, 31*(5), 24–33.

Stage, S. A., Jackson, H. G., Erickson, M. J., Moscovitz, K. K., Bush, J. W., Violette, H. D., Ogier-Thurman, S., Olson, E., Bain, N., Jesse, W., & Pious, C. (2008). A validity study of functionally-based behavioral consultation with students with emotional/behavioral disabilities. *School Psychology Quarterly, 23,* 327–353.

Stemler, S. E., Sternberg, R. J., Grigorenko, E. L., Jarvin, L., & Sharpes, K. (2009). Using the theory of successful intelligence as a framework for developing assessments in AP physics. *Contemporary Educational Psychology, 34,* 195–209.

Stepien, W., & Gallagher, S. (1993). Problem-based learning: As authentic as it gets. *Educational Leadership, 50*(7), 25–28.

Sternberg, R. J. (1985). *Beyond IQ: A triarchic theory of human intelligence.* New York: Cambridge University Press.

Sternberg, R. J. (1997). *Successful intelligence.* New York: Plume.

Sternberg, R. J. (2000). *Handbook of human intelligence.* New York: Cambridge University Press.

Sternberg, R. J. (2001). Beyond g: The theory of successful intelligence. In R. J. Sternberg & E. L. Grigorenko (Eds.), *The general factor of intelligence: How general is it?* (pp. 447–479). Mahwah, NJ: Erlbaum.

Sternberg, R. J. (2004). Culture and intelligence. *American Psychologist, 59,* 325–338.

Sternberg, R. J., & Sternberg, K. (2012). *Cognitive psychology* (6th ed.). Belmont, CA: Wadsworth.

Stevenson, H. W., & Stigler, J. (1992). *The learning gap.* New York: Summit Books.

Stiggins, R. (2007). Assessment through the students' eyes. *Educational Leadership, 64*(8), 22–26.

Stipek, D. J. (2002). *Motivation to learn* (4th ed.). Boston: Allyn & Bacon.

Stipek, D. (2006). Relationships matter. *Educational Leadership, 64*(1), 46–49.

Stormont, M., Stebbins, M. S., & Holliday, G. (2001). Characteristics and educational support needs of underrepresented gifted adolescents. *Psychology in the Schools, 38,* 413–423.

Stumpf, H. (1995). Gender differences on tests of cognitive abilities: Experimental design issues and empirical results. *Learning & Individual Differences, 7,* 275–288.

Suzuki, B. H. (1983). The education of Asian and Pacific Americans: An introductory overview. In D. Nakanishi & M. Hirano-Nakanishi (Eds.), *The education of Asian and Pacific Americans: Historical perspectives and prescriptions for the future* (pp. 1–14). Phoenix: Oryx Press.

Svoboda, J. S. (2001). *Review of Boys and Girls Learn Differently. The Men's Resource Network.* Available online at www.themenscenter.com/reviews/Svoboda/boysandgirls.htm

Swanson, H. L. (1990). The influence of metacognitive knowledge and aptitude on problem solving. *Journal of Educational Psychology, 82,* 306–314.

Swanson, H. L. (2001). Research on interventions for adolescents with learning disabilities: A meta-analysis of outcomes related to higher-order processing. *The Elementary School Journal, 101,* 332–348.

Swartz, B., Wasserman, E., & Robbins, S. (2002). *Psychology of learning and behavior* (5th ed.). New York: Norton.

Swearer, S. M., Espelage, D. L., Vaillancourt, T., & Hymel, S. (2010). What can be done about school bullying? Linking research to educational practice. *Educational Researcher, 39,* 38–47.

Sweller, J., Kirschner, P. A., & Clark, R. E. (2007). Why minimally guided teaching techniques do not work: A reply to commentaries. *Educational Psychologist, 42,* 115–121.

Syvertsen, A. K., Flanagan, C. A., & Stout, M. D. (2009). Code of silence: Students' perceptions of school climate and willingness to intervene in a peer's dangerous plan. *Journal of Educational Psychology, 101,* 219–232.

Taylor, E. (1998). Clinical foundation of hyperactivity research. *Behavioural Brain Research, 94,* 11–24.

Taylor-Green, S., Brown, D., Nelson, L., Longton, J., Gassman, T., Cohen, J., Swartz, J., Horner, R. H., Sugai, G., & Hall, S. (1997). School-wide behavioral support: Starting the year off right. *Journal of Behavioral Education, 7,* 99–112.

TenBrink, T. D. (2006). Assessment. In J. Cooper (Ed.), *Classroom teaching skills* (8th ed., pp. 55–78). Boston: Houghton Mifflin.

Tharp, R. G. (1989). Psychocultural variables and constants: Effects on teaching and learning in schools. *American Psychologist, 44,* 349–359.

Thome, J., & Reddy, D. P. (2009). The current status of research into attention deficit hyperactivity disorder: Proceedings of the 2nd International Congress on ADHD: From childhood to adult disease. *Attention Deficit Hyperactive Disorder, 1,* 165–174.

Thompson, G. (1991). *Teaching through themes.* New York: Scholastic.

Thompson, G. (2008). Beneath the apathy. *Educational Leadership, 65*(6), 50–54.

Tomlinson, C. A. (2003). *Fulfilling the promise of the differentiated classroom.* Alexandria, VA: Association for Supervision and Curriculum Development.

Tomlinson, C. A. (2005a). Grading and differentiation: Paradox or good practice? *Theory Into Practice, 44,* 262–269.

Tomlinson, C. A. (2005b, Summer). Differentiating instruction. *Theory Into Practice, 44*(3).

Tomlinson-Keasey, C. (1990). Developing our intellectual resources for the 21st century: Educating the gifted. *Journal of Educational Psychology, 82,* 399–403.

Toppo, G. (2003, January 13). School violence hits lower grades: Experts who see violent behavior in younger kids blame parents, prenatal medical problems and an angry society; educators search for ways to cope. *USA Today.* Available online at http://www.usatoday.com/educate/college/education/articles/20030119.htm

Torrance, E. P. (1986). Teaching creative and gifted learners. In M. Wittrock (Ed.), *Handbook of research on teaching* (3rd ed., pp. 630–647). New York: Macmillan.

Toth, E., Klahr, D., & Chen, Z. (2000). Bridging research and practice: A cognitively based classroom intervention for teaching experimentation to elementary school children. *Cognition & Instruction, 18,* 423–459.

Trautwein, U. (2007). The homework–achievement relation reconsidered: Differentiating homework time, homework frequency, and homework effort. *Learning and Instruction, 17,* 372–388.

Trautwein, U., & Koller, O. (2003). The relationship between homework and achievement—Still much of a mystery. *Educational Psychology Review, 15,* 115–145.

Trautwein, U., & Lüdtke, O. (2007). Students' self-reported effort and time on homework in six school subjects: Between-students differences and within-student variation. *Journal of Educational Psychology, 99,* 232–234.

Trebaticka, J., Paduchova, Z., Suba, J. et al. (2009). Markers of oxidative stress in ADHD and their modulation by Polyhenolic extract, Pycnogenal. From Childhood to Adult Disease. May 21–24, 2009, Vienna, Austria. *Attention Deficit and Hyperactivity Disorders, 1:* 33.

Tschannen-Moran, M., & Woolfolk Hoy, A. (2001). Collaborative learning: A memorable model. *Teacher Educator, 37,* 148–165.

Tschannen-Moran, M., & Woolfolk Hoy, A. (2007). The differential antecedents of self-efficacy beliefs of novice and experienced teachers. *Teaching and Teacher Education, 23,* 944–956.

Tschannen-Moran, M., Woolfolk Hoy, A., & Hoy, W. K. (1998). Teacher efficacy: Its meaning and measure. *Review of Educational Research, 68,* 202–248.

Umbreit, J. (1995). Functional analysis of disruptive behavior in an inclusive classroom. *Journal of Early Intervention, 20*(1), 18–29.

Urdan, T. C., & Maehr, M. L. (1995). Beyond a two-goal theory of motivation and achievement: A case for social goals. *Review of Educational Research, 65,* 213–243.

U.S. Bureau of the Census. (2010a). *State and country quick facts.* Available online at http://quickfacts.census.gov/qfd/states/00000.html

U.S. Bureau of the Census. (2010b). *Hispanic population of the United States: Projections.* Available online at http://www.census.gov/population/www/socdemo/hispanic/hispanic_pop_presetation.html

U.S. Citizenship and Immigration Services. (2011). *Home page.* Available online at http://www.uscis.gov/portal/site/uscis

U.S. Department of Education. (2009, November). *Race to the Top Program: Executive summary.* Washington, DC: U.S. Department of Education. Available online at http://www2.ed.gov/programs/racetothetop/executive-summary.pdf

U.S. Department of Education. (2010, March). *ESEA Blueprint for Reform.* Washington, DC: USDE, Office of Planning, Evaluation and Policy Development. http://www2.ed.gov/programs/racetothetop/index.html

Usher, E. L., & Pajares, F. (2009). Sources of self-efficacy in mathematics: A validation study. *Contemporary Educational Psychology, 34,* 89–101.

Uttal, D. H., Hand, L. L., & Newcombe, N. S. (2009, April). *Malleability of spatial cognition: Results of a meta-analysis.* Paper presented at the biennial meeting of the Society for Research in Child Development, Denver, CO.

Valentine, J. C., DuBois, D. L., & Cooper, H. (2004). The relations between self-beliefs and academic achievement: A systematic review. *Educational Psychologist, 39,* 111–133.

van de Pol, J., Volman, M., & Beishuizen, J. (2010). Scaffolding in teacher–student interaction: A decade of research. *Educational Psychology Review, 22,* 271–296.

van der Mass, H. L. J., Dolan, C. V., Grasman, R. P. P. P., Wicherts, J. M., Huizenga, H. M., & Raijmakers, M. E. J. (2006). A dynamic model of general intelligence: The positive manifold of intelligence by mutualism. *Psychological Review, 113,* 842–861.

van Gog, T., Pass, F., & Sweller, J. (2010). Cognitive load theory: Advances in research on worked examples, animations, and cognitive load measurement. *Educational Psychology Review, 22,* 375–378.

Vasquez, J. A. (1990). Teaching to the distinctive traits of minority students. *The Clearing House, 63,* 299–304.

Vaughn, S., Mathes, P., Linan-Thompson, S., Cirino, P., Carlson, C., Pollard-Durodola, S., et al. (2006). Effectiveness of English intervention for first-grade English language learners at risk for reading problems. *The Elementary School Journal, 107,* 153–180.

Vitto, J. M. (2003). *Relationship-driven management: Strategies that promote student motivation.* Thousand Oaks, CA: Corwin.

Vogt, M. E., Echevarria, J, & Short, D. J. (2010). *The SIOP® Model for teaching English-language arts to English learners.* Boston: Pearson.

von Glaserfeld, E. (1995). A constructivist approach to teaching. In L. Steffe & J. Gale (Eds.), *Constructivism in education* (p. 5). Hillsdale, NJ: Erlbaum.

Vroom, V. (1964). *Work and motivation.* New York: Wiley.

Vygotsky, L. S. (1978). *Mind in society: The development of higher mental process.* Cambridge, MA: Harvard University Press.

Vygotsky, L. S. (1997). *Educational psychology* (R. Silverman, Trans.). Boca Raton, FL: St. Lucie.

Wade, S. E., Schraw, G., Buxton, W. M., & Hayes, M. T. (1993). Seduction of the strategic reader: Effects of interest on strategies and recall. *Reading Research Quarterly, 28,* 3–24.

Walberg, H. J. (1990). Productive teaching and instruction: Assessing the knowledge base. *Phi Delta Kappan, 72,* 470–478.

Wang, M. C., Haertel, G. D., & Walberg, H. J. (1993). Toward a knowledge base for school learning. *Review of Educational Research, 63,* 249–294.

Wang, M. C., Haertel, G. D., & Walberg, H. J. (1997). Learning influences. In H. Walberg & G. Haertel (Eds.), *Psychology and educational practice* (pp. 199–211). Berkeley, CA: McCutchan.

Waterhouse, L. (2006). Multiple intelligences, the Mozart effect, and emotional intelligence: A critical review. *Educational Psychologist, 41,* 207–225.

Wayne, A. J., & Youngs, P. (2003). Teacher characteristics and student achievement gains: A review. *Review of Educational Research, 73,* 89–122.

Webb, N. (1985). Verbal interaction and learning in peer-directed groups. *Theory into Practice, 24,* 32–39.

Webb, N., Farivar, S. H., & Mastergeorge, A. M. (2002). Productive helping in cooperative groups. *Theory into Practice, 41,* 13–20.

Webb, N., & Palincsar, A. (1996). Group processes in the classroom. In D. C. Berliner & R. C. Calfee (Eds.), *Handbook of educational psychology* (pp. 841–876). New York: Macmillan.

Wechsler, P. (2010, November 12). *ADHD diagnoses soar in 4 years.* Columbus Dispatch, Columbus, OH.

Available online at http://www.dispatch.com/content/stories/national_world/2010/11/12/adhd-diagnoses-soar-in-4-years.html.

Wenger, E. (1998) *Communities of practice: learning, meaning, and identity.* New York: Cambridge University Press.

Weiner, B. (1986). *An attributional theory of motivation and emotion.* New York: Springer.

Weiner, B. (1992). *Human motivation: Metaphors, theories, and research.* Newbury Park, CA: Sage.

Weiner, B. (1994). Ability versus effort revisited: The moral determinants of achievement evaluation and achievement as a moral system. *Educational Psychologist, 29,* 163–172.

Weiner, B. (2000). Interpersonal and intrapersonal theories of motivation from an attributional perspective. *Educational Psychology Review, 12,* 1–14.

Weiner, B. (2010). The development of an attribution-based theory of motivation: A history of ideas. *Educational Psychologist, 45,* 28–36.

Weiner, B., & Graham, S. (1989). Understanding the motivational role of affect: Life span research from an attributional perspective. *Cognition & Emotion, 4,* 401–419.

Weiner, B., Russell, D., & Lerman, D. (1978). Affective consequences of causal ascriptions. In J. H. Harvey, W. J. Ickes, & R. F. Kidd (Eds.), *New directions in attribution research* (Vol. 2). Hillsdale, NJ: Erlbaum.

Weinert, F. E., & Helmke, A. (1995). Learning from wise mother nature or big brother instructor: The wrong choice as seen from an educational perspective. *Educational Psychologist, 30,* 135–143.

Weinstein, C. S. (1999). Reflections on best practices and promising programs: Beyond assertive classroom discipline. In H. J. Freiberg (Ed.), *Beyond behaviorism: Changing the classroom management paradigm* (pp. 147–163). Boston: Allyn & Bacon.

Weinstein, C. S., & Novodvorsky, I. (2011). *Middle and secondary classroom management: Lessons from research and practice* (5th ed.). New York: McGraw-Hill.

Weinstein, C. S., Romano, M. E., & Mignano, A. J. (2011). *Elementary classroom management: Lessons from research and practice* (5th ed.). New York: McGraw-Hill.

Wentzel, K. R. (1999). Social-motivational processes and interpersonal relations: Implications for understanding motivation in school. *Journal of Educational Psychology, 91,* 76–97.

Wigfield, A., & Eccles, J. (1989). Test anxiety in elementary and secondary school students. *Educational Psychologist, 24,* 159–183.

Wigfield, A., & Eccles, J. (2002). The development of competence beliefs, expectancies for success, and achievement values from childhood through adolescence. In A. Wigfield & J. Eccles (Eds.), *Development of achievement motivation* (pp. 91–120). San Diego: Academic Press.

Wiggins, G. (1991). Standards, not standardization: Evoking quality student work. *Educational Leadership, 48*(5), pp. 18–25.

Wiggins, G. (1993). Assessment, authenticity, context, and validity. *Phi Delta Kappan, 75,* 200–214.

Willcutt, E. G., Pennington, B. F., Boada, R., Ogline, J. S., Tunick, R. A., Chabildas, N. A., and Olson, R. K. (2001). A comparison of the cognitive deficits in reading disability and attention-deficit/hyperactivity disorder. *Journal of Abnormal Psychology, 110,* 157–172.

Willingham, W. W., & Cole, N. S. (1997). *Gender and fair assessment.* Mahwah, NJ: Erlbaum.

Willoughby, T., Porter, L., Belsito, L., & Yearsley, T. (1999). Use of elaboration strategies by grades two, four, and six. *The Elementary School Journal, 99,* 221–231.

Willower, D. J., Eidell, T. L., & Hoy, W. K. (1967). *The school and pupil control ideology.* University Park, PA: Penn State Press, Monograph No. 24.

Wilson, M. (2001). The case for sensorimotor coding in working memory. *Psychonomic Bulletin and Review, 8,* 44–57.

Windschitl, M. (2002). Framing constructivism in practice as the negotiation of dilemmas: An analysis of the conceptual, pedagogical, cultural, and political challenges facing teachers. *Review of Educational Research, 72*(2), 131–175.

Winerip, M. (2005, June 29). Test scores are up. So why isn't everybody cheering? *New York Times.*

Wingate, N. (1986). Sexism in the classroom. *Equity & Excellence, 22,* 105–110.

Winner, E. (2000). The origins and ends of giftedness. *American Psychologist, 55,* 159–169.

Wintergerst, A. C., DeCapua, A., & Itzen, R. C. (2001). The construct validity of one learning styles instrument. *System, 29,* 385–403.

Wittrock, M. (Ed.). (1986). *Handbook of research on teaching* (3rd ed.). New York: Macmillan.

Wolf, D., Bixby, J., Glenn, J., III, & Gardner, H. (1991). To use their minds well: New forms of student assessment. *Review of Research in Education, 17,* 31–74.

Wolters, C. A., Yu, S. L., & Pintrich, P. R. (1996). The relation between goal orientation and students' motivational beliefs and self-regulated learning. *Learning & Individual Differences, 8,* 211–238.

Woolfolk, A. E. (2008). *Active learning edition: Educational psychology* (10th ed.). Boston: Allyn & Bacon.

Woolfolk, A. E., & Hoy, W. K. (1990). Prospective teachers' sense of efficacy and beliefs about control. *Journal of Educational Psychology, 82,* 81–91.

Woolfolk, A. E., & Perry, N. E. (2012). *Child development.* Boston: Allyn & Bacon/Pearson.

Woolfolk, A. E., Perry, N., & Winne, P. (2006). *Educational psychology: Third Canadian edition* (3rd ed.). Toronto, CA: Pearson.

Woolfolk, A. E., Rosoff, B., & Hoy, W. K. (1990). Teachers' sense of efficacy and their beliefs about managing students. *Teaching & Teacher Education, 6,* 137–148.

Woolfolk Hoy, A. E., & Burke-Spero, R. (2005). Changes in teacher efficacy during the early years of teaching: A comparison of four measures. *Teaching & Teacher Education, 21,* 343–356.

Woolfolk Hoy, A., Hoy, W. K., & Davis, H. (2009). Teachers' self-efficacy beliefs. In K. Wentzel & A. Wigfield (Eds.). *Handbook of motivation in school.* Mahwah, NJ: Erlbaum.

Woolfolk Hoy, A. W., Hoy, W. K., & Kurtz, N. M. (2008). Teacher's academic optimism: The development and test of a new construct. *Teaching and Teacher Education, 24,* 821–832.

Woolfolk Hoy, A., & Murphy, P. K. (2001). Teaching educational psychology to the implicit mind. In R. Sternberg & B. Torff (Eds.), *Understanding and teaching the implicit mind* (pp. 145–185). Mahwah, NJ: Erlbaum.

Woolfolk Hoy, A. E., & Tschannen-Moran, M. (1999). Implications of cognitive approaches to peer learning for teacher education. In A. O'Donnell & A. King (Eds.), *Cognitive perspectives on peer learning* (pp. 257–284). Mahwah, NJ: Erlbaum.

Woolfolk Hoy, A. E., & Weinstein, C. S. (2006). Students' and teachers' perspectives about classroom management. In C. Evertson & C. S. Weinstein (Eds.), *Handbook for classroom management: Research, practice, and contemporary issues* (pp. 181–219). Mahwah, NJ: Erlbaum.

Worthen, B. R. (1993). Critical issues that will determine the future of alternative assessment. *Phi Delta Kappan, 74*, 444–457.

Wu, W., West, S. G., & Hughes, J. N. (2010). Effect of grade retention in first grade on psychosocial outcomes. *Journal of Educational Psychology, 102*, 135–152.

Yang, L., Shuai, L., Du, Q., et al. (2009). Atomoxetine and executive functioning in Chinese ADHD children. From Childhood to Adult Disease. May 21–24, 2009, Vienna, Austria. *Attention Deficit and Hyperactivity Disorders, 1*, 135.

Yarhouse, M. A. (2001). Sexual identity development: The influence of valuative frameworks on identity synthesis. *Psychotherapy, 38*(3), 331–341.

Yerkes, R. M., & Dodson, J. D. (1908). The relation of strength of stimulus to rapidity of habit formation. *Journal of Comparative Neurology, 18*, 459–482.

Young, A. J. (1997). I think, therefore I'm motivated: The relations among cognitive strategy use, motivational orientation, and classroom perceptions over time. *Learning & Individual Differences, 9*, 249–283.

Zeidner, M. (1995). Adaptive coping with test situations. *Educational Psychologist, 30*, 123–134.

Zimmerman, B. J. (1995). Self-efficacy and educational development. In A. Bandura (Ed.), *Self-efficacy in changing societies* (pp. 202–231). New York: Cambridge University Press.

Zucker, A. (2008). *Transforming schools with technology.* Cambridge, MA: Harvard Education Press.

NAME INDEX

SUBJECT INDEX

Note: Page numbers followed by "f" or "t" refer to figures or tables respectively. Words in **bold** refer to key terms.